Women
in
Ireland

Women
in
Ireland

An Annotated Bibliography

Compiled by
Anna Brady

Bibliographies and Indexes in Women's Studies, Number 6

Greenwood Press
New York • Westport, Connecticut • London

Library of Congress Cataloging-in-Publication Data

Brady, Anna.
  Women in Ireland.

  (Bibliographies and indexes in women's studies, ISSN
0742-6941 ; no. 6)
  Includes indexes.
  1. Women—Ireland—History—Bibliography. 2. Women—
Northern Ireland—History—Bibliography. I. Title.
II. Series.
  Z7964.I73B7 1988   016.3054'09415   87-25043
  [HQ1600.3]
  ISBN 0-313-24486-3 (lib. bdg. : alk. paper)

British Library Cataloguing in Publication Data is available

Library of Congress Catalog Card Number: 87-25043
ISBN: 0-313-24486-3
ISSN: 0742-6941

First published in 1988

Greenwood Press, Inc.
88 Post Road West, Westport, Connecticut 06881

Printed in the United States of America

The paper used in this book complies with the
Permanent Paper Standard issued by the National
Information Standards Organization (Z39.48-1984).

10 9 8 7 6 5 4 3 2 1

This work is dedicated to women in general,
Irish women in particular, and my family —
most especially my sister Mary, and brother,
Pat, for their support during its compilation.

Contents

Preface

Research on this bibliography began in 1980 with a small
grant from the Research Foundation, City University of New
York, a two week research leave, and a great deal of
enthusiasm - the first two of which were rapidly depleted.
The enthusiasm lasted a little longer! I will admit that I
was more familiar with the usefulness of bibliographies than
with what was involved in their compilation and the
time-consuming nature of such an endeavor. Since most of the
relevant literature in this instance is only, or more
readily, available in Ireland, research was mostly confined
to a few weeks each summer. Given the range of subject
matter, encompassing not only works dealing directly with
women and their familial roles but the whole array of human
enterprise in which women have participated, or at least
where their presence has been acknowledged and reflected upon
(politics, history, religion, economic life, the arts...),
I found that problems of inclusion were constant and final
decisions in some cases less than purely logical. Materials
relating to Northern Ireland are probably underrepresented
since I did not have the opportunity to visit major libraries
there. In general, many materials pertaining directly to
England but also applying to Northern Ireland were not
included. A similar problem arises in connection with the
period from the Union to 1921. Many publications covering
that period deal with Great Britain as a whole and thus
include Ireland but in most cases these were excluded lest
the primary focus of the bibliography be submerged.

        This listing then is neither exhaustive, definitive, nor
fully comprehensive. New publications are appearing with
increasing rapidity; many identified works could not be
located in Ireland or the United States; some located in
Ireland could not be examined due to time constraints and
were either totally unavailable in the United States or
unavailable on interlibrary loan; others had incomplete
citations. For some tangential areas only a selection of
materials was included to prevent the expansion of the work
to unwieldy proportions.

        Despite these limitations, I hope that this bibliography

will provide a useful beginning resource and facilitate research about Irish women, which in time may improve their opportunities for full participation in Irish society.

Acknowledgments

Throughout the course of this project many individuals
and institutions provided direct and indirect assistance,
support and encouragement. I am grateful to all of them and
want specifically to thank the following:

The Research Foundation, City University of New York for
the financial support which launched and continued to support
this effort and especially to Brenda Newman, liaison from the
Foundation, and Mike Prasad, Grants Officer, Queens College;
also, Matt Simon, Chief Librarian at Queens College, for
additional financial support.

Izabella Taler, Ruth Hollander, and the staff of the
Inter-Library Loan Department at Queens College for their
cheerful processing of my voluminous requests and research
assistance with incomplete citations; staff of all the
libraries consulted in person and by mail including, though
not limited to, the following: Deirdre Hamill, Trinity
College, Dublin; Valerie McKernan, University College,
Dublin; Judith Burke, Queens University of Belfast; and
Lindsay Mitchell, National Institute for Higher Education,
Limerick; also, Yolanda Bell, Research Officer, Equal
Opportunities Commission for Northern Ireland, for sharing
with me bibliographical information on the Commission's
publications; staff in the National, Trinity and University
College, Dublin and Cork libraries; New York University,
Columbia and Fordham (Lincoln Center) Universities, and the
New York Public Library.

Scholars in the fields of Women's/Irish Studies who
scanned my manuscript and offered suggestions, advice,
citations or simple encouragement, including Clara Cullen,
University College Dublin; Mary Cullen, Maymooth; Margaret
McCurtain, University College, Dublin; Catherine McKenna,
Queens College, City University of New York; Michael Shannon,
Lehman College, City University of New York; Ailbhe Smyth,
University College, Dublin; Jean Tansey, Women's Studies
Unit, the Irish Foundation for Human Development.

Mary Tomaselli, who conscientiously prepared the
detailed subject indexes which accompany this bibliography;
Paul Hannon, research assistant; Rosemary Segreti, research
assistant, editorial assistant and typist without whose word

processing skills, the process of classification — not to mention reclassification — would have been interminable. I am particularly grateful to Rosemary for staying with this project despite having graduated and taken on full time employment in the interim.

Lastly I should like to thank the many individuals who shared information or bibliographies; Marilyn Brownstein, Humanities Editor, Greenwood Press for editorial advice, and last but not least my family and friends who helped me see this project through.

Introduction

The past several years have witnessed a tremendous outpouring
of literature in the area of women's studies, including some
excellent bibliographies which enable students and scholars
to identify appropriate sources for use in their research and
thus advance the cause of scholarship. However, quite a few
gaps still exist - both in bibliography and scholarship - and
some areas are almost totally neglected. One such area is
<u>Women in Ireland</u>. The need for such a tool was brought home
to me by a reference question from a student at Queen's
College. No really adequate guide to the literature exists
though recently we have had some useful bibliographies of
Irish materials. (See WORKS CONSULTED.) Also, some of the
relevant periodical literature appears in other than Irish
journals. My aim is to fill this gap by providing an
annotated, classified listing which will provide access to
the relevant literature in one source. The purpose is
twofold: (1) to provide quick and convenient access in a
single source to what has been published and (2) to stimulate
additional research in the area by indicating what gaps exist
in the literature. I also think that such a listing should
facilitate comparative studies designed to differentiate that
which is intrinsic in women's biology and temperament from
that which is culturally conditioned. In this connection
studies of women worldwide under variant social arrangements,
with variant political, ethical and social philosophies, or
undergoing social change become especially helpful. Ireland,
at once "underdeveloped" and "developed," English-speaking
and yet culturally unique, religiously conservative in a
secular ambience, offers an interesting focus for such
studies.

<u>Selection Criteria</u>:
        In general the criterion was to include only women of
Irish ancestry whose lives were spent primarily in Ireland,
or those of whatever ancestry or place of residence whose
achievement or recognition was related to Irish affairs or to
intimate connection with well-known Irish figures. Thus the
inclusion of Mary Lavin or Kitty O'Shea poses no real

conceptual problems. It becomes much less clear with a Peg
Woffington. In the final analysis, my selections, though not
totally arbitrary, were definitely subjective.

Subject Matters and Disciplines:
     All aspects of women's lives and activities - as
mothers, wives, citizens, office holders, artists, employees,
itinerants, students, religious devotees or founders of
religious orders, revolutionaries, etc. - are considered
relevant. The objective is to provide a comprehensive survey
of materials; to include scientific and factual accounts as
well as popular, inaccurate, romanticized, impressionistic,
or biased material. The aim is to serve the interested
reader, the student doing a research paper and the serious
researcher. Items are included on the basis of their
pertinence to women whether describing these or their
activities either as individuals or groups even if not
limited to female subjects, or personal accounts of women's
concerns or interests such as journals or diaries.
     The material listed under any specific category
indicates only items in that area both identified and
examined (except where otherwise noted).

Time Period and Selection of Materials:
     The time period covered ranges from the early Celtic to
the present. All materials actually examined are included
(some recent important publications not personally reviewed
are identified by an asterisk). Only English-language entries
- comprising the bulk of the bibliography - are annotated
though some clarification or note on contents is supplied in
the case of selected non-English language entries. In the
case of multiple biographies of a single subject only one
book-length study is annotated though reviews of such
biographies are indicated where identified. The kinds of
publications included are secondary sources, including books,
separate chapters in books, articles, pamphlets, memoirs,
travel accounts, correspondence, and other types of material
judged to be pertinent. Fiction and poetry are excluded.
Literary criticism is excluded except in those cases where
the depiction of femininity is the subject of the study.
However, biographies of female authors are included (despite
the inclusion of literary criticism). Novelized biographies
and historical novels or other fictional treatments are
included. Newspaper items are excluded, except where
reprinted in a periodical or other publication.

Arrangement of the Bibliography:
     Arrangement is by major, single or collective subject
categories, plus general sections where appropriate, each one
preceded by scope notes which describe the contents of that
particular section, and indicate what other sections may be
pertinent. (Because any one item may fall into several
categories readers are advised to check the subject index and
also to check related categories and scope notes.) The table
of contents indicates these subject categories. Some
categories may be subdivided (e.g. Arts is divided into
Performing Arts and Fine Arts). Items are listed
alphabetically by author within these categories or by the
title if the author is unknown. If the topic of an item does

not clearly fall into one of the major subject categories it
is located in the General section. Because one item may
relate to several subject categories, there are cross
references in the subject index.

Entries:
        Entries are numbered consecutively and provide a
complete citation with publication information. The author's
name is given in full, if known; otherwise initials are used.
Real names are also provided if a pseudonym was used where
identified. Only Arabic numbered pages are indicated.
Illustrations, tables, graphs, plates, portraits,
bibliographies are noted. Most entries are annotated.
(Exceptions: dissertations, masters theses, non-English
language materials, pamphlets, multiple book-length
biographies; recent publications not personally examined are
identified by an asterisk.) Periodical titles are
abbreviated; consult Periodical Abbreviations for full
titles.

Form of entry for a book:
    Cardoza, Nancy. _Lucky Eyes and a High Heart: the Life of
    Maud Gonne_. New York: Bobbs Merrill Company, 1978. 468pp.

Form of entry for a periodical article:
    McKenna, Edward E. "Age, Region and Marriage in Post-
    Famine Ireland: an Empirical Examination." _Econ Hist R_
    31 (1978): 238-256. tables. bibl.

Form of entry for a chapter in a book:
    Porter, Mary Cornelia and Corey B. Venning. "Catholicism
    and Women's Role in Italy and Ireland." In _Women in the
    World: A Comparative Study_, eds. Lynne Iglitzin and Ruth
    Ross, pp. 315-400. Santa Barbara, California: Clio
    Books, 1976. bibl.

The annotations are descriptive rather than evaluative. Their
purpose is to provide a summary or description of the
contents of the works compiled. Thus, they aim to identify
the various topics or individuals treated in a work, dates of
research, methodology, hypotheses, conclusions, and other
information judged to be relevant. They are of varying length
depending on the publication itself - size, content,
interest, value, etc. - and are based on an examination of
the publication (exceptions noted above). A list of major
works consulted in the search for bibliographic entries is
included.

Indexes:
        An author index lists all the authors of items in the
bibliography. A subject index will serve the purpose of
cross-reference and also will provide more detailed access to
items that contain information on several topics or persons.
The indexes cite entry number rather than page number for
locating an item.

        The overall purpose of the work is best expressed in
Meri Knaster's words from the preface to her excellent
bibliography _Women in Spanish America: An Annotated_

<u>Bibliography from Pre-Conquest to Contemporary Times</u> (Boston,
Mass.: G. K. Hall, 1970), which was an inspiration and, in
some ways, a model for this book: "to facilitate access to a
topic which for years has been neglected by some; by others
gives attention in a limited, minor, and unsatisfactory way,
fraught with a biased perspective and written mostly from
male viewpoint." The history of women in Ireland has just
begun to be written. The purpose of this bibliography is to
facilitate such research.

Periodical Abbreviations

Acad	Academy
Acad Chr Art J	Academy of Christian Art Journal
Acct Ire	Accounting, Ireland
Acorn	Acorn
Admin	Administration
Adult Ed	Adult Education
Agenor	Agenor
Alex Col Mag	Alexandra College Magazine
All The Year R	All The Year Round
Allied Ir Bank R	Allied Irish Bank Review
Am Hist R	American Historical Review
Am J Ed	American Journal of Education
Am J Sociol	American Journal of Sociology
Am Pol Sci R	American Political Science Review
Am Scholar	American Scholar
Am Sociol R	American Sociological Review
America	America
An Bealoideas	An Bealoideas
An Forus Taluntais	An Forus Taluntais
An Gael	An Gael
Analectica Bollandiana	Analectica Bollandiana
Ang Sax R	Anglo-Saxon Review
Annales	Annales: Economies, Societies, Civilisations
Aontas R	Aontas Review
Archaeo Cambr	Archaeologia Cambrensis (Cardiff)
Architect R	Architectural Review
Arch Gen Psych	Archives of General Psychiatry
Argosy	Argosy
Art J	Art Journal (London)
Arts Ire	Arts in Ireland
Atlan Mon	Atlantic Monthly
Belf Hist & Phil Soc	Belfast Natural History and Philosophy Society: Proceedings and Reports
Belgra	Belgravia
Bell	The Bell
Bentley	Bentley's Miscellany
Bet Bus	Better Business

Bibelet	Bibelet
Blackw	Blackwood's Magazine
Bon Ton	Bon Ton Magazine or Microscope of Fashion and Folly
Bonaventura	Bonaventura
Book News	Book News
Book W	Book World
Booklist	Booklist
Bookman	The Bookman
Books & Bookm	Books & Bookmen
Books Ire	Books Ireland
Breifore	Breifore
Brit J Addict	British Journal of Addiction
Brit J Criminol	British Journal of Criminology
Brit J Ed Psychol	British Journal of Educational Psychology
Brit J Prev Soc Med	British Journal of Preventive and Social Medicine
Brit J Psych	British Journal of Psychiatry
Brit J Soc Clin Psychol	British Journal of Social and Clinical Psychology
Brit Q R	British Quarterly Review
Brit Psychol Soc Bull	Bulletin of the British Psychological Society
Bus & Fin	Business and Finance
Butler Soc J	Butler Society Journal
CARA	CARA
Can Forum	Canadian Forum
Can J Ir Stud	Canadian Journal of Irish Studies
Can Lit	Canadian Literature
Capital & Class	Capital and Class
Capu An	Capuchin Annual
Carleton News	Carleton Newsletter
Carloviana	Carloviana
Case	Case
Cath Bull	Catholic Bulletin
Cath Hist R	Catholic Historical Review
Cath U Bull	Catholic University Bulletin
Cath W	Catholic World
Celt	The Celt
Cent	Century
Cent Mag	Century Magazine
Chamber	Chamber's Journal
Chaut	Chautaquan
Child Devel	Child Development
Choice	Choice
Chr Cent	Christian Century
Chr Obs	Christian Observer
Chr Sci Monit	Christian Science Monitor
Chr Rex	Christus Rex
Church & State	Church and State
Citizen	Citizen
Civ Serv R	Civil Service Review
Class Strug	Class Struggle
Clio	Clio
Clon Hist & Arch Soc	Clonnel Historical and Archaeological Society Journal
Colburn	Colburn's New World Magazine
Commentary	Commentary

Commonweal	Commonweal
Comp Stud Soc & Hist	Comparative Studies in Society and History
Conc Poetry	Concerning Poetry
Connoisseur	Connoisseur
Contemp Crises	Contemporary Crises
Contemp Lit	Contemporary Literature
Contemp R	Contemporary R
Convergence	Convergence
Co Louth Arch J	County Louth Archaeological Journal
Coop Ire	Coop Ireland: The Irish Co-operative Journal
Core	Core
Cork U Rec	Cork University Record
Cornhill Mag	Cornhill Magazine
Crane Bag	The Crane Bag
Crit Q	Critical Quarterly
Critic	Critic: A Catholic Review of Books and Arts
Cross	The Cross
Cross Curr	Cross Currents
Ctry Life	Country Life
Curr Anthrop	Current Anthropology
Daily News	Daily News (London)
Dalhousie R	Dalhousie Review
Demography	Demography
Dept Agric & Fish J	Ireland (Eire) Department of Agriculture and Fisheries Journal
Doct & Life	Doctrine and Life
Donahue	Donahue's Magazine
Donegal An	Donegal's Annual
Down & O'Connor	Down and O'Connor Historical Society Journal
Dublin Build	Dublin Builder
Dublin Hist Rec	Dublin Historical Record
Dublin J Med Sci	Dublin Journal of Medical Science
Dublin Mag	Dublin Magazine
Dublin Met Mag	Dublin Metropolitan Magazine
Dublin R	Dublin Review
Dublin U Law J	Dublin University Law Journal
Dublin U Mag	Dublin University Magazine
Dubliner	The Dubliner
Duffy Hibern Mag	Duffy's Hibernia Magazine
Easter Wk	Easter Week
Ecl Mag	Eclectic Magazine
Ecl Mus	Eclectic Museum
Econ Hist R	Economic History Review
Econ Soc R	Economic and Social Review
Economist	The Economist
Ed Matters	Educational Matters
Ed Theatre J	Educational Theatre Journal
Edinburgh R	Edinburgh Review
18th Cent Li	Eighteenth Century Life
18th Cent Stud	Eighteenth Century Studies
Eigse	Eigse
Eire	Eire
Eire Ire	Eire/Ireland
Eirigh	Eirigh
Ekistics	Ekistics
Eng Hist R	English Historical Review

Eng R	English Review
Engwoman	Englishwoman
Environ	The Environment
Environ & Plan	Environment and Planning
Eriu	Eriu
Ethnology	Ethnology
Etud Celt	Etudes Celtiques
Etud Irland	Etudes Irlandaises
Eugenics Q	Eugenics Quarterly
Eugenics R	Eugenics Review
Eur Ind Rel R	European Industrial Relations Review
Eur Mag	European Magazine
Ever R	Evergreen Review
Fam Plan	Family Planning
Farm & Food	Farm and Food
Feilscribhinn Torna	Feilscribhinn Torna
Femin R	Feminist Review
Flor State U Stud	Florida State University Studies
Folk Inst J	Folklore Institute Journal
Folklore	Folklore
Fortn R	Fortnightly Review
Fraser	Fraser's Magazine
Furrow	The Furrow
G K 's Wkly	G K's Weekly
Gael	The Gael
Galaway Re	Galaway Reader
Galaway Arch Soc J	Galway Archealogical Society Journal
Gen Mag & Hist Chro	The General Magazine and Historical Chronicle
Gent Mag	Gentleman's Magazine
Geo J	Geographical Journal
Geography	Geography
Hague J	The Hague Journal
Harper	Harper's Magazine
Harper's Baz	Harper's Bazaar
Harv Theo R	Harvard Theological Review
Heresies	Heresies: A Feminist Publication on Art and Politics
Hermathena	Hermathena
Hermes	Hermes
Hew Humanist	Hew Humanist
Hibernia	Hibernia
Hist	History
Hist Today	History Today
Histoire	Histoire
Hon Ulsterm	Honest Ulsterman
Hum Beh	Human Behavior
Hum Ev	Human Events
Hum Hered	Human Heredity
ISIS Int Bull	ISIS International Bulletin
Ill Lond News	Illustrated London News
Image	Image
Inc Law Soc Gaz	Gazette of the Incorporated Law Society of Ireland.
Ind & Comm Tra	Industrial and Commercial Training
Ind Rel R & Rep	Industrial Relations Review and Reports
Ind & Comm	Industry and Commerce
Inde Shavian	Independent Shavian

India J Eng Stud	Indian Journal of English Studies
Int Cnl Soc Dem Wom	International Council of Social Democratic Women: Bulletin
Int J Nurs Stud	International Journal of Nursing Studies
Int J Offend Ther	International Journal of Offender Therapy and Comparative Criminology
Int Labour R	International Labour Review
Int Q	International Quarterly
Int R Com Devel	International Review of Community Development
Int R Ed	International Review of Education
Int Socia	International Socialism
Integrated Ed	Integrated Education
Intercom	Intercom
Ir Ancest	Irish Ancestor
Ir Book Lov	Irish Book Lover
Ir Bookl	Irish Booklore
Ir Bookm	Irish Bookman
Ir Build	Irish Builder
Ir Bus	Irish Business
Ir Eccl Rec	Irish Ecclesiastical Record
Ir Eco Soc Hist	Irish Economic and Social History
Ir Farm Mon	Irish Farmer's Monthly
Ir Geneal	Irish Genealogist
Ir Geo	Irish Geography
Ir Hist Stud	Irish Historical Studies
Ir J Bus & Admin Res	Irish Journal of Business & Administration Research
Ir J Med Sci	Irish Journal of Medical Science
Ir J Psychol	Irish Journal of Psychology
Ir Jur	Irish Jurist
Ir Law Times	Irish Law Times
Ir Law Times & Sol J	Irish Law Times and Solicitor's Journal
Ir Lib Bull	Irish Library Bulletin
Ir Lit Supp	Irish Literary Supplement
Ir Med J	Irish Medical Journal (continues as Journal of the Irish Medical Association)
Ir Mon	Irish Monthly
Ir Natur J	Irish Naturalists' Journal
Ir Nurs News	Irish Nursing News
Ir Q R	Irish Quarterly Review
Ir R	Irish Review
Ir Rosary	Irish Rosary
Ir Soc	Irish Society
Ir Socia R	Irish Socialist Review
Ir Sword	Irish Sword
Ir Theo Q	Irish Theological Quarterly
Ir U R	Irish University Review
Ir Writ	Irish Writing
Ire Welcomes	Ireland of the Welcomes
Ire Today	Ireland Today
J Am Folk	Journal of American Folklore
J Aust U Lang & Lit	Journal of the Australian Universities Language and Literature Association

J Biol Sci	Journal of Biological Science
J Biosoc Sci	Journal of Biosocial Science
J Butler Soc	Journal of the Butler Society
J Co Kild Arch Soc	Journal of the Kildare Archaeological Society
J Comp Fam Stud	Journal of Comparative Family Studies
J Comp Leg	Journal of Comparative Legislation
J Cork Hist Arch Soc	Journal of the Cork Historical and Archaeological Society
J Crim	Journal of Criminology
J Crim Law	Journal of Criminal Law
J Div	Journal of Divorce
J Eco & Soc Geo	Journal of Economic and Social Geography
J Fam Law	Journal of Family Law
J Ir Lit	Journal of Irish Literature
J Ir Med Assoc	Journal of the Irish Medical Association (previous title : Irish Medical Journal)
J Ir Stud	Journal of Irish Studies
J Marr & Fam	Journal of Marriage and the Family
J Ment Defic Res	Journal of Mental Deficiency Research
J Mod Lit	Journal of Modern Literature
J Occ Psychol	Journal of Occupational Psychology
J Pers	Journal of Personality
J Roy Anthr Inst	Journal of the Royal Anthropological Institute
J Roy Soc Antiq	Journal of the Royal Society of Antiquaries
J Stud Alcohol	Quarterly Journal of Studies of Alcohol
J Urb Hist	Journal of Urban History
J Youth & Adol	Journal of Youth and Adolescence
James Joyce Q	James Joyce Quarterly
John O'London's	John O'London's
Kilk Mag	Kilkenny Magazine
Kilk Arch Soc J	Kilkenny South-East of Ireland Archaeological Society Journal
Kirkus R	Kirkus Review
Krimin	Kriminalistik
Labour Mon	Labour Monthly
Ladies Home J	Ladies Home Journal
Lancet	The Lancet (London)
Landmark	Landmark (London)
Law J	Law Journal (London)
Leis Hour	Leisure Hour
Lib R	Library Review
Liberty	Liberty
Life	Life
Liguorian	Liguorian
Lippinc	Lippincott's Magazine
Listener	Listener
Lit Anec 19th Cent	Literary Anecdotes of the 19th Century
Lit Half Yrly	Literary Half Yearly
Lit W	Literary World
Lit & Psychol	Literature and Psychology
Liv Age	Living Age

Local Pop Stud	Local Population Studies
Lond Merc R	London Mercury Review
Lond Q	London Quarterly
Longm	Longman's Magazine
L'Osservatore Romano	L'Osservatore Romano
Lughnasa	Lughnasa
MLA	Modern Language Association of America Publications
MacMil	MacMillan's Magazine
Mademoiselle	Mademoiselle
Mag Art	Magazine of Art
Magill Mag	Magill Magazine
Man	Man (London)
Market News	Marketing News
Marx Persp	Marxist Perspectives
Med Gynaec	Medical Gynaecology
Metron	Metron
Mgt	Management
Midwest Q	Midwest Quarterly
Mod Drama	Modern Drama
Mod Fict Stud	Modern Fiction Studies
Mod Philo	Modern Philosophy
Mod Stud	Modernist Studies
Monat	Monat (Berlin)
Month	Month (London)
Ms	Ms
N Y	New York
N Y Her Trib Bk	New York Herald Tribune Books
N Y Times Bk R	New York Times Book Review
N Y Times Mag	New York Times Magazine
Nassau R	The Nassau Review
Nat & Eng R	National and English Review
Nat R	National Review
Nation	Nation
New Com	New Community
New Ire R	New Ireland Review
New Mon Mag	New Monthly Magazine
New Repub	New Republic
New Soc	New Society
New Statesm	New Statesman
Newsweek	Newsweek
19th Cent	Nineteenth Century
19th Cent & After	Nineteenth Century and After
No Amer R	North American Review
No Ire	Northern Ireland
No Ire L Q	Northern Ireland Legal Quarterly
No Munst Antiq J	North Munster Antiquarian Journal
Notes & Quer	Notes and Queries
Novel	Novel
Now & Then	Now and Then
O Bair	O Bair
Observer	Observer
Occult R	Occult Review
Old Kilk R	Old Kilkenny Review
Once A Week	Once A Week
Ossory Arch Soc J	Ossory Archaeological Society Journal
Outlook	Outlook
PMLA	PMLA

Papers Bibl Soc Am	Papers of the Bibliographical Society of America
Papers Lang & Lit	Papers on Language and Literature: a Journal for Scholars and Critics of Language & Literature
Partisan R	Partisan Review
Past & Pres	Past and Present
Peace News	Peace News
Peritia	Peritia
Phys Cult	Physical Culture
Pop	Population
Pop & Devel R	Population and Development Review
Pop Index	Population Index
Pop Stud	Population Studies
Post Work	The Postal Worker
Prim Man	Primitive Man
Progressive	Progressive
Psychiatr Clin	Psychiatria Clinica
Psychol Med	Psychological Medicine
Psychol Today	Psychology Today
Pub Affairs	Public Affairs
Pub Health Rept	Public Health Reports
Publ Wkly	Publisher's Weekly
Quarterly R	Quarterly Review
Queen Q	Queen's Quarterly
Quest	Quest
Ramparts Mag	Ramparts Magazine
Reality	Reality
Relate	Relate (NSSC)
R Eng Stud	Review of English Studies
R Pol	Review of Politics
R Celt	Revue Celtique
Riocht Na Midhe	Riocht Na Midhe
Round Tab	Round Table (United Kingdom)
Roy Hist & Arch Assoc J	Royal Historical and Archaeological Association of Ireland Journal
Roy Ir Acad Proc	Royal Irish Academy Proceedings
Roy Soc Antiq Ire J	Royal Society of Antiquaries of Ireland Journal
Saothar	Saothar
St.Steph Stu Pub	St. Stephen's Student Publications (University College, Dublin)
Sat R	Saturday Review
Sat R Lit	Saturday Review of Literature
Scene	Scene
Scott Gael Stud	Scottish Gaelic Studies
Scriblerian	Scriblerian
Seanchas Aramhacha	Seanchas Aramhacha
Seanchas Duthalla	Seanchas Duthalla
Seirbhis Phoibli	Seirbhis Phoibli
Senior Sch Stud	Senior Scholastic Studies
Sewanee R	Sewanee Review
Sex Transm Dis	Sexually Transmitted Diseases
Shaw R	The Shaw Review
Shaw Soc Bull	Shaw Society Bulletin
Shenandoah	Shenandoah
Show	Show (New York)
Sign	The Sign
Soc & Eco Admin	Social and Economic Administration
Soc Biol	Social Biology

Soc Compass	Social Compass
Soc Forces	Social Forces
Soc Order	Social Order
Soc Stud	Social Studies: Irish Journal of Sociology
Sociol Rur	Sociologia Ruralis
So Folk Q	Southern Folklore Quarterly
So Hum R	Southern Humanities Review
So R	Southern Review
Spare Rib	Spare Rib
Spectator	Spectator
Speculum	Speculum
Springf Rep	Springfield Republican
Stat & Soc Inq Soc J	Statistical and Social Inquiry Society of Ireland Journal
Stat Surv Ir Sis	Statistical Survey of Irish Sisters
Status	Status
Stony Thurs Bk	Stony Thursday Book
Stud Celt	Studia Celtica
Stud Hibern	Studia Hibernica
Studies	Studies
Supp Doct & Life	Supplement to Doctrine and Life
Tablet	Tablet
Technology	Technology
Tech Ire	Technology Ireland
*Temp Bar	Temple Bar
Tenn Stud Lit	Tennessee Studies in Literature
Teoiric	Teoiric
Tex Stud Lit & Lang	Texas Studies in Literature and Language
Th Wk Ire	This Week in Ireland
Theatre Arts	Theatre Arts
Theo Stud	Theological Studies
Threshold	Threshold
Time	Time
Time & Tide	Time and Tide
Times Lit Supp	Times Literary Supplement
Trade Un Info	Trade Union Information (I.C.T.U.)
Trans Hist Soc	Transactions of the Historic Society of Lancashire and Chesire
Trib Mag	Tribune Magazine
Tuarascial	Tuarascial
20th Cent	Twentieth Century
20th Cent Lit	Twentieth Century Literature
U Dayton R	University of Dayton Review
U Mich Pap Wom Stud	University of Michigan Papers in Women's Studies
U S News	U.S. News and World Reports
U Windsor R	University of Windsor Review (Ontario)
Ulster Folk	Ulster Folklife
Ulster J Archae	Ulster Journal of Archaeology
Ulster Med J	Ulster Medical Journal
Union Wage	Union Wage
Unita R	Unitarian Review
Univ Mag	University Magazine
Univ R	University Review
Urb Anthrop	Urban Anthropology
Urb Life	Urban Life

Urb R	Urban Review
Vict Stud	Victorian Studies
Vogue	Vogue
WICCA	WICCA
W Ir Nurs	World of Irish Nursing
Wake News	A Wake Newslitter: Studies in James Joyce's Finegan's Wake
Waterf Arch Soc J	Waterford and Southeast of Ireland Architectural Society Journal
Wkly Bk R	Weekly Book Review
Westm R	Westminster Review
Wil Lib Bull	Wilson Library Bulletin
Wolfe Tone An	Wolfe Tone Annual
Woman Ch	Woman's Choice
Woman Stud Int Forum	Woman's Studies International Forum
Women	Women: a Journal of Liberation
Women & Lit	Women and Literature
Women View	Women's View
Word	Word
Yale R	Yale Review
Yale U Lib Gaz	Yale University Library Gazette
ZCP	ZCP

Works Consulted

A major source for periodical material was Hayes'
Articles in Irish Periodicals 1940-1967. In addition, mostly
complete runs through 1985 of selected, general indexes in
the Social Sciences and Humanities, both manual and online,
were searched systematically for relevant materials. These
include: _Abstracts in Anthropology_, _Abstracts of English
Studies_, _Accountants Index_, _Annual Bibliography of British
and Irish History_, _Anthropological Literature_, _Arts and
Humanities Citation Index_, _British Humanities Index_, _Business
Periodicals Index_, _Catholic Periodical Index_, _Crime and
Delinquency Abstracts_, _Combined Retrospective Index to
Journals in History_, _Combined Retrospective Index to Journals
in Sociology_, _Combined Retrospective Index to Journals in
Political Science_, _Dissertation Abstracts_, _Education Index_,
Economic Abstracts, _ERIC_, _Historical Abstracts_, _Humanities
Index_, _Index to Religious Periodicals_, _Index to theses
accepted for higher degrees by the Universities of Great
Britain and Ireland_, _International Bibliography of the Social
Sciences_ (Anthropology, Economics, Political Science,
Sociology), _International Bibliography of Crime and
Delinquency_, _International Index_, _Inventory of Marriage and
Family Literature_, _International Political Science Abstracts_,
Masters Abstracts, _MLA Bibliography_, Nineteenth Century
Readers Guide, _P.A.I.S._, _Population Index_, _Poole's Index to
Periodical Literature_, _Psychological Abstracts_, _Readers Guide
to Periodical Literature_, _Social Science Citation Index_,
Social Science Index, _Sociological Abstracts_, _The Year's Work
in English Studies_, _Women's Studies Abstracts_. (Owing to the
large volume of literary material no effort was made to
search all entries for individual Irish authors for articles
dealing with the portrayal of women in their work except if
this was explicitly identified as a category in the
particular index consulted.)

Other sources were the bibliographies included with
articles or books listed in the body of this work and in some
cases, local library files. Irish journals not indexed in
above but listed in _Articles in Irish Periodicals_ were
scanned selectively, where appropriate, for post 1967

citations. Other fruitful sources were the annual
bibliographies included in journals such as Irish Historical
Studies.
     The major sources for identification of relevant
monographs were the card catalogs of the National, Trinity
and University College, Dublin, libraries; Columbia
University and the New York Public Library supplemented by
the British Museum Catalog and the National Union Catalog;
the annual listings in the Irish Publishing Record for the
years covered and the books noted as received in the
quarterly issues of Books Ireland as well as the reviews in
that and other sources, and numerous bibliographies the most
pertinent of which are listed below:

A.A.A.S. Seminar on Women in Development, Mexico, 1975. Women
and World Development: With an Annotated Bibliography.
[Edited by Irene Tinker, Michele J. Bramsen, Mayra Buvinic.]
New York: Prarger, 1976. 382pp.

American Library Association. American Library Association
Index to General Literature. 2nd ed. Ann Arbor, Michigan:
American Library Association, 1970.

Anglo-Irish Literature: A Review of Research. ed. by Richard
J. Finneran. New York: Modern Language Association, 1976.
576pp.

Bilboul, Rogel R. ed. Retrospective Index to Theses of Great
Britain and Ireland, 1716-1950. Santa Barbara, Ca. and
Oxford: Clio Press, 1975.

Brown, Stephen J.M. ed. A Guide to Books on Ireland. Part I.
Prose Literature, Poetry, Music and Plays. New York: ,
1970. First edition published in Dublin, 1912.

Civin, Laraine. Iris Murdoch: A Bibliography. Johannesburg:
University of the Witwatersrand Department of Bibliography,
Librarianship and Typography, 1968. 23pp.

Committee of National and University Libraries (CONUL). List
of Higher Degree Theses Deposited in the University Libraries
of the Republic of Ireland. Cork: University Collge, Cork,
1975-.

Conroy, Roisin. Equal Pay: a Bibliography. Dublin: Irish
Transport and General Workers Union, 1978. 56pp.

Conroy, Roisin. "Images of the Irish Woman: Bibliography."
Crane Bag 4 (1) (1980): 73-80.

Dictionary of Irish Literature. Robert Hogan ed.-in-chief;
Westport, Conn.: Greenwood Press, 1979. 815pp.

Driver, Edwin D. World Population Policy: An Annotated
Bibliography. Lex, Mass.: D.C. Heath & Co., 1971. 1279pp.

Doyle, Paul A. "Mary Lavin: A Checklist." Papers of the
Bibliographical Society of America 63 (Fourth Quarter 1969):
317-321.

Eager, Alan R. A Guide to Irish Bibliographic Materials.
London: The Library Association, 1964. 392pp.

Eager, Alan. A Guide to Irish Bibliographical Material: A
Bibliography of Irish Bibliographies and Sources of
Information. 2nd ed. Westport, Conn.: Greenwood Press, 1980.
502pp.

Educational Studies Association of Ireland. Register of
Theses on Educational Topics in Universities in Ireland.
Galway: Officina Typographica, 1980. 87pp.

Fairbanks, Carol. More Women in Literature. Criticism of the
Seventies. Metuchen, New Jersey: The Scarecrow Press, Inc.,
1979. 457pp.

Frey, Linda, Marsha Frey and Joanne Schneider. (eds.) Women
in Western European History: A Select Chronological,
Geographical and Topical Bibliography. Westport, Conn.:
Greenwood Press, 1982. 2 vols.

Hayes, Richard J. Sources for the History of Irish
Civilisation: Articles in Irish Periodicals, 1940-1967.
Boston: G.K. Hall, 1970. 9 vols.

Henderson, Lucille K. "Shaw and Women: A Bibliographical
Checklist." Shaw R 17 (1) (Jan. 1974): 60-66.

History of the Family and Kinship: A Select International
Bibliography. Millwood, New York: Kraus International, 1980.
410pp.

Holloway, Penny. [comp.] Feminism and Women's Studies: A
Bibliography of Material held in the Ulster Polytechnic
Library. 2nd ed. Belfast: Ulster Polytechnic, 1982. 117pp.

Johnston, Edith Mary. Irish History: A Selected Bibliography.
Revised ed. London: Historical Association, 1972. 76pp.

Kersnowski, Frank L. and others. A Bibliography of Modern
Irish and Anglo-Irish Literature. San Antonio, Texas: Trinity
Uniniversity Press, 1976. 157pp.

Krichmar, Albert. The Women's Movement in the Seventies: An
International English-language Bibliography. Metuchen, New
Jersey: Scarecrow Press, 1977. 875pp.

Lunday, G. Albert. Sociology Dissertations in American
Universities 1893-1966. Commerce: East Texas State
University, 1969. 277pp.

"Mary Lavin: A Bibliography." Ir U R 9 (2) (Autumn 1979):
294-295.

McKenna, Brian. Irish Literature 1800-1875: A Guide to Information Sources. Detroit, Michigan: Gale Research Co., 1978. 388pp.

Mikhail, E.H. Dissertations on Anglo-Irish Drama; a Bibliography of Studies 1870-1970. Totowa, New Jersey: Rowman and Littlefield, 1973. 73pp.

Mikhail, E.H. Lady Gregory: An Annotated Bibliography of Criticism. Troy, New York: Whilson Publishing Co., 1982. 258pp.

Murray, Fiona. Women's Studies: A Bibliography. Dublin: College of Industrial Relations, the Library, 1984. [14] leaves.

[Myers] Fairbanks, Carol. Women in Literature: Criticism of the Seventies. Metuchen, New Jersey: The Scarecrow Press, 1976. 256pp.

O Donoghue, David J. The Poets of Ireland: A Biographical and Bibliographical Dictionary of Irish Writers of English Verse. Dublin: Hodges, Figgis & Co. Ltd., 1912. 504pp.

O Higgins, Paul. A Bibliography of Periodical Literature Relating to Irish Law. Belfast: Northern Ireland Legal Quarterly, 1966. 401pp.

Parker, Franklin. Women's Education - A World View. Westport, Conn.: Greenwood Press, 1979. 2 vols.

Population Index Bibliography, 1935-1968. Princeton: Office of Population Research, Princeton University; Boston, Mass.: G.K. Hall, 1971.

Queen's University, Belfast. Institute of Irish Studies. Theses on subjects relating to Ireland presented for higher degrees 1950-1967. Belfast: Queen's University, Institute of Irish Studies, 1968. 28 leaves.

Rolston, William. et al. A Social Science Bibliography of Northern Ireland 1945-1983. Belfast: Queens University, 1983. 270pp.

Rosenberg, Marie Barovic. Women and Society: A Critical Review of the Literature with a Selected, Annotated, Bibliography. Beverly Hills, London: Sage Pubs., 1975. 354pp.

Schwartz, Narda Lacey. Articles on Women Writers: A Bibliography. ABC -CLIO, 1977. 236pp.

Sellery, J'Nan. "Elizabeth Bowen: A Checklist." NYPL Bull 74 (Apr. 1970): 219-274.

Shannon, Michael. Modern Ireland: A Bibliography for Research, Planning and Development. London: The Library Association, 1981. 733pp.

Stineman, Esther. Women's Studies: A Recommended Core
Bibliography. Littleton, Colorado: Libraries Unlimited, 1979.
670pp.

Tansey, Jean and Cliona Kernan. Register of Completed and
Current Work Relating to Women's Studies in Ireland. Dublin:
Women's Studies Unit, the Irish Foundation for Human
Development, 1985.

Tominaga, Thomas T. and Wilma Schneidermeyer. Irish Murdoch
and Muriel Spark: A Bibliography. Metuchen, New Jersey:
Scarecrow Press, 1976. 237pp.

Unesco. Bibliographic Guide to Studies on the Status of
Women: Development and Population Trends. London: Bowker,
1983. 284pp.

Women and Literature: An Annotated Bibliography. 3rd ed.
Cambridge, Mass.: Women and Literature Collective, 1976.
212pp.

Women
in
Ireland

Biography and Autobiography

      This includes full length books and articles about women
as a group and as individuals arranged under major subject
headings e.g. LITERATURE, the ARTS, RELIGION, etc. Collective
biographies are arranged alphabetically by compiler at the
beginning of this section and also at the beginning of each
division and sub-division. Thus accounts dealing with women
of many periods or groups will be found under BIOGRAPHY and
AUTOBIOGRAPHY - GENERAL while those covering groups of women
in specific fields will be arranged in the GENERAL section
under that area e.g. BIOGRAPHY and AUTOBIOGRAPHY - LITERATURE
- GENERAL, BIOGRAPHY and AUTOBIOGRAPHY - THE ARTS -
PERFORMING ARTS - GENERAL, etc. Biographies of individuals
will be found in alphabetical order under the area with which
they are associated - e.g. biographies of nuns and saints
under BIOGRAPHY and AUTOBIOGRAPHY - RELIGION - MARY
AIKENHEAD, CATHERINE MC AULEY, etc.; of novelists under
BIOGRAPHY and AUTOBIOGRAPHY - LITERATURE - MARIA EDGEWORTH,
MARY LAVIN, etc. Multiple biographies of the same individual
are arranged alphabetically by author. Where an individual
was distinguished in more than one area her biography/
biographies will be found under the field with which she is
primarily identified with cross references to other areas.
(e.g. Senator Margaret Pearse is thought of primarily in the
Nationalist context and so located in the category HISTORY,
POLITICS AND REVOLUTIONARY MOVEMENTS though she was also an
educator.) One should also consult relevant sections of the
other major subject divisions including BIOGRAPHY and
AUTOBIOGRAPHY - GENERAL as well as the GENERAL biographical
section; also DISSERTATIONS AND THESES should be checked for
additional biographical or contextual information on specific
individuals; (e.g. the scanty biographical material on the
artist Sarah Purser in the FINE ARTS section (individual)
might be supplemented by a check of the general biographical
sections of FINE ARTS and the GENERAL biography section. In
the absence of a full length biography in this case the most
detailed source will probably be the dissertation listed. On
he other hand, material on a well known figure such as Nano
Nagle will be found in general biographical sources, in

collective biographies of religious figures, in biographical
and other sources dealing with education, in dissertations
and theses dealing with either the Presentation Sisters or
the history of education, in addition to the many individual
biographies of this subject.) Biographies of women known
mainly because of their association with major male figures
will be found under the area with which he is primarily
identified e.g. Nora Joyce or Esther Van Homrigh ("Vanessa")
under BIOGRAPHY and AUTOBIOGRAPHY - LITERATURE - NORA JOYCE,
ESTHER VAN HOMRIGH. However women who had careers in their
own right are listed under that area e.g. Eileen O Casey will
be found under PERFORMING ARTS rather than LITERATURE despite
being primarily identified as the wife of the playwright,
Sean O Casey. In the case of multiple biographies of a single
individual only one full length study is annotated. While the
intent of this listing is descriptive rather than evaluative
it may be noted that biographies in general tend to be overly
partisan or overly critical. Annotations will only note
extreme examples of these tendencies.

     The attempt here is to list works dealing primarily with
women in Ireland. Some general sources covering both Irish
men and women are noted where there is a reasonable
representation of females. For additional sources of Irish
biography, one should consult the recent excellent works by
Eagar[1] and Shannon[2]. No attempt has been made to include the
standard general biographical sources though these do
frequently include major Irish figures and should be
consulted accordingly.

GENERAL

1   Berkery, Rita. <u>Behind The Scenes</u>. Bognor Regis, W.
Sussex: New Horizon. n.d. 45pp.

     Extremely brief profiles of Kitty O'Shea, Maria
     Edgeworth, Constance Markievicz, Sarah Curran, Sinead
     Flanagan (Mrs. E. de Valera).

2   Blackburne, E. Owens. <u>Illustrious Irishwomen: Being
Memoirs of Some of the Most Noted Irishwomen from the
Earliest Times to the Present Century</u>. London: Tinsley Bros.,
1877. 2 vols.

     Brief sketches of mainly historical figures (with the
     exception of the mythological Queens Macha and Meave).

1. Eager, Alan R. <u>A Guide to Irish Bibliographical Material:
A Bibliography of Irish Bibliographies and Sources of
Information</u>. 2nd ed. Westport, Connecticutt: Greenwood, 1980.
560pp.

2. Shannon, Michael Owen. <u>Modern Ireland: A Bibliography on
Politics, Planning, Research, and Development</u>. Westport,
Connecticut: Greenwood Press, 1981. 733pp.

Criteria for inclusion not specified — many are Irish by descent rather than birth. Sources are, for the most part, not indicated. For most subjects includes birth and death dates — many tentative.

3   Boylan, Clare. "It's Terrific at the Top." Image (Sept. 1982): 43-44. portrs.

Success stories of writer/journalist Maeve Binchy and executive Margaret Downes.

4   Boylan, Henry. A Dictionary of Irish Biography. New York: Barnes and Noble, 1978. 385pp. bibl.

Excludes living persons. Definition of "Irish" includes all those born in Ireland or those who "though born abroad had an Irish parent, or were of Irish descent, lived and worked in Ireland or made a considerable contribution to Irish affairs." Entries are brief: the aim is to include the important facts and events of the subject's career in chronological order, "including where possible a sentence or quotation to give the flavour of the man." Women are included.

5   Concannon, Helena. Daughters of Banba. Dublin: M.H.Gill and Son, Ltd., 1922. 275pp. refs.

Described as an attempt to "supplement the knowledge of Ireland's history contained in the ordinary text-books by bringing into greater relief the figures of some of her women." This popular account covers the period from the earliest days to the end of the 18th century.

6   Coxhead, Elizabeth. Daughters of Erin: Five Women of the Irish Renaissance. London: Secker and Warburg, 1965. 236pp. il. portrs. refs.

Brief profiles of five women contemporaries (Maud Gonne MacBride, Constance Markievicz — political figures; Sarah Purser — artist; and the actresses Sara Allgood and Maire O'Neill.) Based on letters to/from Yeats, Synge and the personal recollections of many surviving friends of the women profiled.

7   Crone, John S. A Concise Dictionary of Irish Biography. Dublin: The Talbot Press, 1928. 270pp. refs.

Includes notable Irish men and women in every sphere of activity with very brief annotations. Alphabetically arranged.

8   Dunsany, [Lord]. "Some Writers Whom I Have Known." Ir Writ No.20-21 (Nov. 1952): 78-82.

Brief mention of Dr. Edith Somerville, Violet Martin (Martin Ross), Mrs. Hamilton, Katherine Tynan, Anne Crone and Mary Lavin.

9   Eccles, C[harlotte] O'Conor. "Some Irishwomen in London." Donahue 54 (1905): 183-193. portrs.

Brief biographical sketches of some eminent Irishwomen living in London. Those included are Alice Stopford Green, historian; Misses Geraldine and Anna Griffin, active in the Irish Literary Society of London and the Gaelic League; Miss May Crommelis, popular novelist and her sister, Caroline (Mrs. Barton Shaw), an interior decorator; Dr. Sophie Bryant, educator, the first woman to attend London University; Mrs. Humphreys, the "doyenne of women journalists in London," also known as "Madge of Truth"; Miss Elizabeth Magill, animal painter.

10   An Exhibition of Portraits of Great Irish Men and Women. Ulster Museum, Belfast June 24 - July 24th 1965. (Pub. no. 173) [Belfast: Ulster Museum, 1965] 94pp. refs.

Catalog of the exhibit includes brief biographical accounts of the subjects and full descriptions of the portraits. Seventeen well known Irish women from all walks of life represented.

11   Fox, Richard Michael. Rebel Irishwomen. Dublin: Talbot Press, 1935. 204pp. portrs.

Short chapters on Maud Gonne MacBride, Constance de Markievicz, Eva Gore Booth, Mary McSwiney, Grace Plunkett, Nora Connolly O'Brien, Helena Molony, Hanna Sheehy Skeffington, Maeve Cavanagh MacDowell, Dora Maguire, Charlotte Despard, Mother Jones.

12   Gerard, Frances A. Some Fair Hibernians being a supplementary volume to Some Celebrated Irish Beauties of the Last Century. London: Ward and Downey, 1897. 279pp. il. plates. portrs. refs.

Brief biographical sketches of Dorothea Jordan, Lady Anne and Lady Gertrude Fitzpatrick, Mary Birmingham and Anne Birmingham, Sarah Curran, Melesina Chenevix Trench, Marguerite Power (Lady Blessington), Sydney Owenson (Lady Morgan), Olivia Owenson (Lady Clarke), Caroline Elizabeth Sheridan (Mrs. Norton, later Lady Stirling Maxwell of Keir), Elizabeth O'Neill (Lady Wrixon Becher), Marie Delores Gilbert (Lola Montez).

13   Gerard, Frances A. Some Celebrated Irish Beauties of the Last Century. London: Ward and Downey, 1895. 299pp. il. portrs. refs.

Chapters on Mary Molesworth, Countess of Belvedere;
Eleanor Ambrose, the "dangerous papist;" the Gunnings;
Maria, Countess of Coventry; Elizabeth, Duchess of
Hamilton and Argyll; Mrs. Travis and the other two
daughters (the other Gunning sisters); Gunilda Gunning (a
niece of the famous beauties, Maria and Elizabeth
Gunning); Peg Woffington; Dorothea Monroe; the three Miss
Montgomerys; Elizabeth LaTouche, Countess of
Lanesborough; Anne Luttrell, Duchess of Cumberland; the
Coghlans of Ardo; Miss Farren, Countess of Derby.
Biographical sketches vary in length and are based on
secondary sources.

14   Hamilton, Catherine Jane. Notable Irishwomen. Dublin:
Sealy, Bryers & Walker, 1904? 202pp. plates.

Brief biographical sketches and some portraits of mid
18th - end of 19th century women include: the beautiful
Gunnings; Elizabeth Farren (The Countess of Cork and
Orrery), Mary Leadbeater, The Ladies of Llangollen, Maria
Edgeworth, Lady Morgan, Mrs. Tighe, Elizabeth O'Neill
(Lady Becher), Mrs. S.C.Hall, Lady Dufferin, Catherine
Hayes, Lady Wilde, Julia Kavanagh.

15   Hickey, D.J. and J.E.Doherty. A Dictionary of Irish
History Since 1800. Toyowa, N.J.: Barnes and Noble, 1980.
615pp.

Includes biographical sketches for the period since 1800.

16   Holloway, Joseph. Joseph Holloway's Abbey Theatre:
Impressions of a Dublin Playgoer. A Selection from his
Unpublished Journals. Edited by Robert Hogan and Michael J.
O'Neill. Carbondale: Southern Illinois Univerity Press, 1967.
296pp.

Selections from the diary of the eccentric architect and
theatre-lover. Critical commentary on actresses -
including most of the Abbey players, playwrights, and
political figures, notably Lady Gregory, Maud Gonne, The
Allgood sisters, Maire nic Shiubhlaigh, Countess
Markievicz, etc.

17   If You Can Talk, You Can Write. Dublin: Kilbarrack
Women's Writing Group With Women's Community Press, 1983.
63pp.

Papers from a women's writing group which developed out
of an adult basic English class. Includes short stories,
poems and articles recording the everyday lives of the
authors.

18   Ireland: A Cultural Encyclopedia. New York: Facts on
File, 1983. 256pp.

Includes brief biographical sketches of some literary figures.

19   MacCraith, L.M. The Romance of Irish Heroines. London: Longman's Green and Co., 1913. 174pp. il.

A popular and romantic account of fourteen notable Irish females ranging from the mythological to the historical. Includes Queens Macha and Maeve, St. Brigid, Queens Gormlaith and Gormflaith, Princess Dervogilla, Margaret O'Carrol, Margaret, Eleanor, Elizabeth and Cathelyn Fitzgerald, Grainne O'Malley, Nuala O'Donell, Honora de Burgh.

20   Missing Pieces: Women in Irish History 1: Since the Famine. Dublin: Irish Feminist Information Pubs. With Women's Community Press, 1983. 64pp. portrs.

21   More Missing Pieces. Dublin: Attic Press, 1985. 64pp.

A co-operative biographical reference work profiling over one hundred women some well known, other less so, "who have made a contribution to Irish life and culture over the last century." The six women authors (compilers) undertook this as a project begun and completed on a "Women in Community Publishing Course" commissioned by ANCO for unemployed women.

22   Ponsonby, Arthur Augustus. Scottish and Irish Diaries from the Sixteenth to the Nineteenth Century. London: Methuen and Co. Ltd., 1927. 192pp.

Part 2, Irish Diaries, includes very brief excerpts from the diaries of Countess of Warwick and Lady Arabella Denny with comment and explications by the editor. The introduction has brief notes on other "minor" diaries not included in this collection.

23   Ryan, Richard. A Biographical Dictionary of the Worthies of Ireland from the Earliest Period to the Present Time. London: John Warren, 1821. 2 vols.

Includes biographical sketches of varying length but with no indication of selection criteria. Notices are somewhat effusive. Indexes are included in each volume. Some women are listed.

24   Share, Bernard. Irish Lives: Biographies of Fifty Famous Irish Men and Women. Dublin: Allen Figgis and Co. Ltd., 1971. 420pp. il. table. portrs.

The scope of this biographical dictionary ranges from the middle of the 10th century to the beginning of the 20th

century. Classified arrangement includes the categories:
patriots and politicians; scholars and teachers; writers;
artists and musicians; scientists and businessmen; the
Irish abroad. Five women are included: Grainne Ni
Mhaille, Constance de Markievicz, Margaret Woffington,
Sarah Purser, Augusta Gregory.

25   Thom's Irish Who's Who. A Biographical Book of Reference
of Prominent Men and Women in Irish Life at Home and Abroad.
Dublin: Alexander Thom and Co. Ltd., 1923. 266pp.

     The first edition of the Directory "contains life
     sketches of upwards of 2500 Irish men and women, who are
     conspicuous in the Nation's history, and includes leaders
     of thought and action in all fields of enlightment and
     civilization" (Introduction). Of the less than 100 women
     included, most seem to have been selected on the basis of
     their titles rather than personal accomplishments. Dates
     of birth are not given for these.

26   Tynan, Katherine. Memories. London: Eveleigh Nash and
Grayson Ltd., 1924. 432pp.

     Twenty-six prose portraits of the artistic, literary,
     political and religious personalities of the day many of
     whom were her personal friends. The women profiled
     include Ellen O'Leary, a minor poet and ardent patriot,
     sister of the Fenian, John O'Leary; Rose Kavanagh,
     editor, poet and nationalist; the poets Dora Sigerson
     (later Mrs. Clement Shorter) and Jane Barlow; the
     novelist Rosa Mulholland (Lady Gilbert).

27   Wallace, Martin. One Hundred Irish Lives. Totowa: Barnes
and Noble, 1983. 184pp. il.

     Brief biographical sketches, some with illustrations and
     suggestions for additional reading. Includes Grace
     O'Malley, Peg Woffington, Maria Edgeworth, Sarah Purser,
     Lady Gregory, Maud Gonne McBride, Constance Markievicz,
     Somerville and Ross.

28   Webb. Alfred. A Compendium of Irish Biography Comprising
Sketches of Distinguished Irishmen....Dublin: M.H.Gilland
Son, 1878. 598pp.

     Still useful for period covered. Includes "all deceased
     Irishmen and Irishwomen from earliest times to the date
     of publication who have been distinguished by their deeds
     or remarkable for their qualities;" those not born in
     Ireland who nevertheless took a prominent part in the
     affairs of the country or wrote important works
     respecting it. Eminent persons born abroad are excluded
     as are those born in Ireland of non-native parents unless
     they spent a considerable portion of their lives in

Ireland, were educated there or were in some way
distinguished in connection with its annals. Entries are
generally comprehensive.

LITERATURE

    This section lists biographical and some bibliographical
material on women in their capacity as writers of novels,
plays, poetry, short stories, essays, memoirs, letters, and
travel accounts. Collective biographies whether on women in
literature generally or in the sub-fields of prose, poetry or
drama are arranged alphabetically by compiler under GENERAL.
The remainder of this section is arranged alphabetically by
individual writer and includes full length and shorter
biographical references. Multiple entries for the same artist
are arranged alphabetically. The works included are primarily
biographical though in many cases there is an overlap of
biographical and critical material. An effort has been made
to exclude purely literary studies especially in the case of
well known individuals like Lady Gregory, Maria Edgeworth or
Iris Murdoch. The concern is primarily the personal lives of
these women and their subject matter as it relates to their
lives. Works concerned with the depiction of women in
literature will be found in the section immediately following
this. Literary merit has not been a criterion for inclusion.
Some of the women listed herein are relatively minor figures
who for various reasons - themselves of sociological interest
- received biographical notice. Many of considerable literary
merit are excluded because no relevant material could be
identified or remains to be written. In common with men,
women in Ireland who have achieved distinction have done so
primarily in the field of literature. However, unlike men,
this was one of the few fields open to them and thus
attracted many who might more profitably have followed other
vocations. Thus a relatively smaller percentage of female
than male authors could be considered major literary figures.
Besides while a few women writers received in their own
lifetimes what could only be regarded as excessive attention
relative to their literary merits, minor figures generally
received less recognition than equally minor male figures, a
situation that is beginning to change as a result of feminist
ideology and the current literary marketplace. There are
still, however, no general nor specialized collective
biographies which deal solely with Irish women writers. It is
therefore necessary to consult general Irish (and Anglo-
Irish) literary biographical sources only a few of which are
listed here. Other relevant sources are general and
specialized (Prose, Poetry, Drama, Short Story) literary
biographical dictionaries and encyclopedias, similar
biographical sources focusing exclusively on women, and
general biographies.

General

29   A Biographical Dictionary of Irish Writers. Ed. by Anne
M. Brady and Brian Cleeve. New York: St, Martin's Press,
1985. 387pp.

> A new edition of the earlier Dictionary of Irish Writers,
> completely revised and considerably enlarged. Endeavors
> to include present day writers - frequently the only
> source of information on important, modern women authors
> who have not yet attained the attention they deserve.

30   Finneran, Richard J. (ed.) Anglo-Irish Literature: A
Review of Research. New York: Modern Language Assoc., 1976.
596pp.

> Includes detailed biographical essays on Maria Edgeworth
> and Lady Gregory with briefer discussion of Somerville
> and Ross and Lady Morgan. The chapter on the Modern Drama
> includes biographical information on some modern women
> playwrights.

31   "Gossip." Ir Book Lov 1 (1) (1910): 147.

> Brief mention of a dinner given by the Corinthian Club,
> Dublin to "Irishwomen of Letters." Responding to the
> toast were Mrs. Stopford Green, Mrs. Power O'Donoghue,
> Dr. Annie Paterson and Mrs. Katherine C. Thurston.

32   Hamilton, Catherine. Women Writers: Their Work and Ways.
London: Ward, Lock, Bowden & Co., 1892. 280pp. il. portrs.

> Chapters on Maria Edgeworth (pp.158-174) and Lady Morgan
> (Sydney Owenson) (pp.207-226) with brief biographical
> sketch and short discussion of major works.

33   Herigan, Robert. "Contemporary Women Poets in Ireland."
Conc Poetry 18 (1&2) (1985): 103-113. refs.

> Brief note on poetry of Eilean Ni Chuilleanain, Eavan
> Boland, Medbh McGuckian.

34   Hogan, Robert. (Ed.) Dictionary of Irish Literature.
Westport, Conn.: Greenwood Press, 1979. 815pp. bibl.

> Biographical and critical essays on approximately 500
> major Irish authors who wrote mainly in the English
> language including bibliographies of their significant
> work. About 60 of those profiled are women.

35   "Irish Literary Society." Ir Book Lov 2 (May 1911): 165.

> Report of a lecture given by Mr. Hugh Law on April 1st,

1911 on "Some Irish Women Poets." Notes the apparent
absence of these before the 19th century and discusses
three who contributed patriotic verse to The Nation.
Subsequent discussion referred to Irish female poets in
the early Celtic period.

36   O'Donoghue, D.J. The Poets of Ireland: A Biographical
and Bibliographical Dictionary of Irish Writers of English
Verse. Dublin: Hodges Figgis and Co., Ltd, 1912. 504pp.

Endeavors to include only Anglo-Irish writers with a
"genuine poetical gift".

37   O'Toole, L.M. "The Woman Writers of the Nation." In
Thomas Davis and Young Ireland, ed. by M.J. MacManus,
pp.119-122. Dublin: Stationery Office, 1945.

Identification and biographical note on five women who
contributed to "The Nation": Speranza (Lady Wilde), Mary
(Ellen Mary Patrick Downing), Eva (Mary Anne Kelly),
Thomasine (Olivia Knight), and Finola (Elizabeth
Willoughby Treacy).

38   Read, Charles A. The Cabinet of Irish Literature.
Selections from the works of the chief poets, orators, and
prose writers of Ireland. With biographical sketches and
literary notices. London: Blakie and Son, 1879. 4 vols.
portrs. plates.

Include brief biographical sketches of over 60 Irish
women of literature. Includes creative prose writers,
poets and non-fiction writers of varying ability, mostly
minor. The biographical sketches vary in length and
completeness of data - some include birth and death dates
- and provide a bibliography of their more important
works with some selections. In general the annotations
tend to be rather fulsome.

39   Wilson, Mona. These Three Muses. New York: Kennikat
Press, 1924. 235pp. il. front.

Includes brief chapters on the authors Sydney Owenson,
Lady Morgan and Frances Sheridan.

40   Z. (O). "From a Modern Irish Portrait Gallery VI: An
Adelphi Group." New Ire R 111 (Mar. 1895): 24-32.

Critical account of the activities of the Irish Literary
Society, London. Emily H. Hickey, Elsa d'Esterre Keeling,
Sophie Bryant, Katherine Tynan and Charlotte O'Conor
Eccles are among those discussed.

Sarah Atkinson (1823-1893)

41   Atkinson, Sarah. _Essays_. [2nd ed.] Dublin: M.H. Gill
and Son, 1896. 533pp. bibl. refs.

A eulogistic memoir of Sarah Gaynor Atkinson by Rosa
Mulholland Gilbert prefaces this collection of essays by
the former. Notes briefly her family background, her
personal qualities, her social work with workhouse girls
and various hospitals, and her writings. The collection
includes an essay on Saint Brigid, Abbess of Kildare
(pp.27-79) and the Lady Dervorgilla (pp.367-379).
(Review: _Ir Eccl Rec_ 3rd Ser. 16 (Apr. 1895): 384.)

42   Belloc, Bessie R. "My Acquaintance With Ireland and
Mrs. Atkinson." _Ir Mon_ 2 3 (Jan. 1895): 22-25.

Tribute to Mrs. Sarah Atkinson, a personal friend and to
Irish Catholicism. The author attributes her conversion
to Catholicism to these combined influences.

43   Russell, Matthew (S.J.) "In Memory of a Noble
Irishwoman." _Ir Mon_ 21 (Sept. 1893): 464-469.

44   - - - "Mrs. Sarah Atkinson. A Few Notes In
Remembrance." _Ir Mon_ 21 (Nov. 1893): 601-611.

45   - - - "A Few More Notes on Mrs. Atkinson." _Ir Mon_ 22
(Apr. 1894): 179-189.

The editor of the _Irish Monthly_ pays tribute to Mrs.
Sarah Atkinson one of the two most important benefactors
of his magazine and discusses her literary contributions,
her historical studies, acclaimed biographies, and her
charitable works. Includes tributes from the poets
Katherine Tynan Hinkson and Mrs. John T. Gilbert (the
former Rosa Mulholland).

46   Woodnutt, K. (mrs.) "Sarah Atkinson as a Social
Worker." _Dublin Hist Rec_ 21 (4) (Sept. 1967): 132-138.
(Paper read to the Old Dublin Society.)

Biographical sketch of Sarah Gaynor, later Mrs. Atkinson
born in Athlone 1823. When she was 15 her family moved to
Dublin. At 25 she married George Atkinson with whom she
travelled extensively. After the sudden death of her four
year old son she became involved in social work. With
Mrs. Woodlock founded St. Joseph's Industrial Institute
for vocational education and was also involved with the
Children's Hospital at Temple St. and The Hospice for the
Dying.

Jane Barlow (1857-1917)

47   Hinkson, Katherine Tynan. "Miss Jane Barlow." <u>Cath W</u>
69 (Apr. 1899): 101-105. portr.

Brief profile of the shy, retiring poet by her better
known literary friend with excerpts from her
correspondence.

48   Kiely, Benedict. "Yesterday Is Forever." <u>Ir Bookm</u> 1
(9) (Apr.-May 1947): 11-26.

Mainly literary criticism but some biographical material
on the poet and novelist, Jane Barlow.

49   "Miss Jane Barlow." <u>Book News</u> 13 (Aug. 1895): 156.
portr.

Brief note on appearance and publications.

50   "Obituary." [Jane Barlow.] <u>Ir Book Lov</u> 8 (11-12)
(June-July 1917): 141-142.

Brief note on her life and achievement. Fame said to
rest on her short stories of Irish peasant life. Includes
a bibliography of her works.

Beatrice Behan

51   Behan, Beatrice, Des Hickey and Gus Smith. <u>My Life With
Brendan</u>. London: Frewin, 1973. 252pp. il. frontis. portrs.

An episodic account of their marriage by the wife of
playwright Brendan Behan. Consists mostly of a series of
drinking debacles in France, Sweden, Germany and the
United States, an account of his attempts to combat his
alcoholism and his death from this in 1964.

Kathleen Behan (1889-   )

52   Behan, [Kathleen]. <u>Mother of All the Behans: The Story
of Kathleen Behan as Told to Brian Behan</u>. London: Hutchinson,
1984. 138pp. portrs. plates.

Tape recorded by another of her sons, Brendan Behan's
mother reminisces about Easter 1916, her marriages, life
in Dublin tenements, and her children.

Maeve Binchy (1940-   )

53   O'Callaghan, Tanis. "Profile: Tanis O'Callaghan Talks
to Maeve Binchy About Her Life, Her Work and Her New Book."
Image (Aug. 1978): 38-41. portr.

Helen Selina Sheridan Blackwood (1807-1867)

54   Dufferin and Clandeboye, Helen Selina (Sheridan)
Blackwood. Fourth Baroness of...Songs, Poems and Verses by
Helen, Lady Dufferin (Countess of Gifford). Edited with a
memoir and some account of the Sheridan family, by her son
the Marquess of Dufferin and Ava. [2nd Ed.] London: John
Murray, 1894. 429pp. geneal. tables. portr. front.

     Brief biographical sketch of Helen Sheridan,
     granddaughter of Richard Brinsley Butler Sheridan and an
     extended discussion of the Sheridan family introduces
     this anthology of Lady Dufferin's poetry.

55   H., (J.) "The Countess of Dufferin, C.I." Leis Hour 37
      (1888): 798-802. portr.

     Biographical note on the ancestry of Lady Dufferin,
     daughter of A.R. Hamilton, of Killyleagh Castle, County
     Down whose husband, Frederick Temple Blackwood was born
     heir to the Irish barony of Dufferin and succeeded to the
     title in 1841. Lady Dufferin accompanied her husband
     (then an Earl) when he went to Canada as Governor General
     and later to Russia, Constantinople and Egypt. Finally in
     India, as the Governor's wife she founded and was the
     first president of an Association to bring medical
     knowledge and medical relief to the women of India.
     Details on the work of the Association included.

Countess of Blessington (1789?-1849)
(Marguerite Power)

56   Blessington, Marguerite Power Farmer Gardiner. Journal
of Correspondence and Conversation Between Lord Byron and
the Countess of Blessington. Cincinnati: Lorenzo Stratton,
1851. 242pp.

     In 1823 the Countess of Blessington with her husband and
     the Count d'Orsay spent several weeks in Genoa where they
     met Byron and exchanged correspondence. Lady Blessington
     kept a journal of these meetings in which she recorded
     her impressions of Byron, and the topics of their
     conversations including womanly beauty, marriage, love,
     etc.

57   Blessington, Marguerite Power Farmer Gardiner. A Journal
of Conversations of Lord Byron with the Countess of
Blessington. New ed. reviewed and annotated to which is
prefixed a contemporary sketch of Lady Blessington by her
sister and a memoir of her by the editor of this edition.
London: Richard Bentley, 1893. 376pp. il. portrs.

    This later edition of the Journal omits the life of Byron
    and adds two brief biographical sketches of Marguerite
    Power, later Lady Blessington, one by her sister and the
    other by the editor.

58   [Blessington, Marguerite Power, Countess of] "Lady
Blessington." Ir Q R 2 (Dec. 1852): 773-817.

    Autobiography of Marguerite Power, later Lady
    Blessington, includes a list of her works.

59   Blessington (Power) Farmer Gardiner. "The Landor-
Blessington Papers." Lit Anec 19th Cent 1 (1895): 165-234.
refs.

    Includes an autobiographical sketch written by Walter
    Savage Landor for Lady Blessington; an excerpt from her
    diary after her first meeting with Landor in 1827 in
    which she gives a physical description of him and her
    evaluation of his personality, some prose and verse
    written by both for each other and hitherto unpublished
    correspondence between them. Also includes an account by
    Landor of the beginning of their friendship.

60   Clermont-Tonnerre, Elizabeth (de Gramont) duchesse de.
Le Comte d'Orsay et Lady Blessington. Paris: Hachette, 1955.
139pp. portr.

61   "Countess of Blessington." Liv Age 4 (37) (Jan.25,
1845): 227-228.

    Mild disparagment of her literary efforts.

62   Didier, Eugene L. "Lady Blessington." Chaut 17 (5) (Aug.
1893): 605-611. portrs.

    Biographical sketch.

63   Fraser, A.M. "Marguerite Power, Countess of
Blessington." With Portrait and Poem Entitled To Lady
Blessington by Lord Byron. Clon Hist & Arch Soc 1 (3)
(1954-1955): 45; 1 (4) (1955-1956): 53-60. portr.

    Biographical sketch.

64   Fyvie, John. "The Most Gorgeous Lady Blessington." Ang
Sax R 10 (Sept. 1901): 6-23. (Front of this issue has a
portrait of Lady Blessington by Sir Thomas Lawrence.)

    A brief biographical sketch of Marguerite Power, later
    the Countess of Blessington which relies heavily on
    Madden for the main events of her life (See item# 68).
    Unlike Madden, raises the question of the "missing" years
    and her whereabouts during that time, presents various
    opinions on the "tone" of the salon she ran at Gore House
    and alludes to the hint of scandal surrounding her
    sharing Gore House with the Count d'Orsay. A generally
    positive evaluation of her character and behavior while
    admitting that other biographers present a different
    judgement.

65   "Gallery of Literary Characters No. XXXIV - Countess of
Blessington." Fraser 7 (34) (Mar. 1833): 267. portr.

    Brief note on her Conversations with Lord Byron.

66   "Interesting Paper Read to Clonnel Society." Clon Hist &
Arch Soc 1 (3) (1934-1935): 45.

    News item on the paper read by Mrs. Fraser, on Marguerite
    Power, Countess of Blessington. (See item #63.) Notes an
    exhibit of two of her portraits.

67   "Lady Blessington." Ir Q R 11 (Dec. 1852): 773-817.

    Biographical sketch.

68   Madden, R.R. The Literary Life and Correspondence of
the Countess of Blessington. New York: Harper and Row,
1855. 2 vols.

    The first part of this definitive study has a brief
    account of Lady Blessington's early years covering her
    ancestry, her brief unhappy marriage, the death of her
    husband and the marriage to Lord Blessington which is
    based mainly on a memoir by Miss Power - the Countess'
    niece - and details supplied by the Countess herself. A
    period of approximately nine years is left unaccounted
    for. The remainder of the biography is based on Madden's
    close friendship with the Countess for many years and her
    travel books and correspondence - much of which is
    included and connected by a thread of biographical
    illustration. Details on the Blessington's salon in
    London, their Continental tour with the Count d'Orsay,
    death of the Earl of Blessington, return to England of
    the Lady Blessington and the Count d'Orsay now married to
    the daughter of Blessington by a previous marriage; their
    salon at Gore House. Debt forced the auction of the house
    and d'Orsay and the Countess fled to Paris. Discusses her
    literary career and income from this.

(Review: Ir U R 2 (1) (1855): 31.)
(Review: Dublin U Mag 45 (Mar. 1855): 333-353.)
(Review: Sat R 81 (1855): 332-353.)

69   Molloy, James Fitzgerald. Lady Blessington. London: The Grolier Society. [190-?] 445pp. il. portrs.

70   Molloy, James Fitzgerald. The Most Gorgeous Lady Blessington. London: Downey & Co., 1896. 2 vols. front.

(Review: Sat R 81 (1896): 332-333.)

71   "Obituary - Countess of Blessinton." Gent Mag 32 (Aug. 1849): 202-203.

72   Sadlier, Michael. Blessington - d'Orsay. A Masquerade. London: Constable and Co. Ltd., 1933. 411pp. plates. tables. geneal. portrs. bibl.

73   Sadlier, Michael. The Strange Life of Lady Blessington. Boston: Little, Brown and Co., 1933. 370pp. geneal. portrs.

   Tells of unhappy early life of Sally Power sold into marriage at the age of 15 to a drunken brute, afterwards lived with a protector for a period before becoming the wife of Lord Mountjoy and becoming Lady Blessington. Ostracized by the "ladies" of society her house was a salon at which everyone who was anyone in arts, politics, etc. attended.

74   Stoddard, Richard Henry. Personal Recollections of Lamb, Hazlitt and Others. New York: Scribner, Armstrong and Co., 1875. 322pp. portrs.

   Includes a chapter on Lady Blessington (pp.283-317) with brief excerpts of the author's correspondence with her and his comments on her social circle.

Mrs. Francis Blundell (nee M.E. Sweetman)
pseud. M.E. Francis (1855-1930)

75   Blundell, Margaret. M.E. Francis: An Irish Novelist's Own Story. Dublin: Catholic Truth Society, Inc., 1935. 32pp.

   Brief biographical sketch of the novelist Mary (Mollie) Sweetman by her daughter and based mainly on Things of A Child: Memoirs of M.E. Francis (pseud. of Mary Sweetman). Includes excerpts from her correspondence and her novels. At 14 she was taken by her family to study music,

painting and languages in Brussels where she met her
husband. They moved to England. After his premature death
four years later she devoted herself to literature and
piety.

76   S., (G.M.) "M.E. Francis." Ir Mon 58 (1930): 229-239.

Biographical sketch of the author, Mary Sweetman, based
mainly on her autobiographical Things of A Child.
Severely depressed after her husband's untimely death
she, at the editor's request, began a successful literary
career writing for The Nation. Her industry, charity,
resignation and piety extolled.

                  Elizabeth Bowen (1899-1973)

77   Beck, Martha A. "Vassar Student Talks About Elizabeth
Bowen." Mademoiselle 51 (July 1960): 6, 88. il.

A report by a Vassar student on a senior writing seminar
in which she studied with visiting writer, Elizabeth
Bowen - "one of the nicest things that ever happened to
me."

78   "Books." Time 27 (March 2, 1936): 79. il.

Very brief biographical sketch of Elizabeth Bowen and a
review of her novel The House of Paris.

79   Bowen, Elizabeth. Bowen's Court. London: Longmans,
Green and Co., 1942. 341pp. il. map. geneal.

A family history of the Bowens in Ireland beginning with
Henry Bowen, the III, the builder of Bowen's Court, the
family home which later "has made all the succeeding
Bowens." The final chapter presents glimpses of her
parents, her childhood, her education by a series of
governesses, her father's illness, her life in England
with her mother, and the political climate in Ireland at
the time of the 'Troubles.'
(Review: Bell 4 (5) (Aug. 1942): 368-371.)
(Review: Studies 31 (Sept. 1942): 396-397.)
(Review: Dublin Mag New Ser. 17 (4) (Oct.-Dec.1942):46-68.)
(Review: Ir Mon 70 (1942): 391-393.)
(Review: Ir Lit Supp 3 (2) (Fall 1984): 5.)
(Review: Ir Hist Stud 3 (12) (1943): 416-417.)

80   [Bowen, Elizabeth.] "Miss Bowen on Miss Bowen." N Y
Times Bk R (Mar. 6, 1949): 33. portr.

Brief comments on her childhood and adolescence; her work
habits, favorite authors and her evaluation of her own
work.

81   Bowen, Elizabeth. "On Writing The Heat of the Day." Now
& Then 79 (Autumn 1949): 11.

    Brief note on what she tried to accomplish in this novel.

82   Bowen, Elizabeth. Pictures and Conversations. New York:
Alfred A. Knopf, 1975. 193pp.

    The foreward by Elizabeth Bowen's literary executor
    discusses the Anglo-Irish author's character and
    personality and her literary achievement. This is
    followed by a semi-autobiographical section in which
    Elizabeth Bowen discusses her origins, places and their
    influence, and people; the relationship between living
    and writing. Much of this section illuminates her life in
    England with her mother, their many homes, her various
    schools, etc. The balance of the book is comprised of a
    long article of literary criticism on Proust's character
    Bergotte, a Nativity Play, and "Notes on Writing a Novel"
    by Elizabeth Bowen.
  (Review: Atlan Mon 235 (Mar. 1975): 133.)
  (Review: Commonweal 102 (July 18, 1975): 282.)
  (Review: New Repub 172 (Feb. 8, 1975): 30.)

83   Bowen, Elizabeth. Seven Winters: Memoirs of a Dublin
Childhood and Afterthoughts: Pieces on Writing. New York:
Alfred A. Knopf, 1962. 273pp.

    This brief "fragment of autobiography" evokes the
    atmosphere of the author's childhood in Dublin up to the
    age of seven; describes her nursery, governesses, walks,
    shops, The Horse Show, Stephen's Green, dancing classes,
    children's parties. The remainder of the book includes
    essays on writing, prefaces, reviews and the text of some
    radio broadcasts.
  (Review: Show 2 (Aug. 1962): 95.)

84   Bowen, Elizabeth. "Through A Glass Lightly." Times Lit
Supp 63 (Feb. 20, 1964): 146.

    Includes biographical remarks but mainly a critical
    review of The Little Girls.

85   Byran, Mary. "Ten Years After: A Tribute To Elizabeth
Bowen." Ir Lit Supp 2 (1) (1983): 30-31. portr.

    Brief note on her literary achievement and her self
    identification as an Irish artist.

86   Cecel, David [Lord]. "Chronicler of the Heart: The
British Writer Elizabeth Bowen." Vogue (Nov.1, 1953):
118-119. portr.

    A profile of Elizabeth Bowen with comments on her
    background, character and complex personality.

87   Davenport, Gary T. "Elizabeth Bowen and the Big House."
So Hum R 8 (1) (1974): 27-34. refs.

Discussion of Elizabeth Bowen's Anglo-Irish aristocratic
background and the thematic importance of this culture in
her literary work.

88   "Elizabeth Bowen, C.B.E." Now & Then 77 (Autumn 1948):
12-13.

News item on the appearance of Miss Bowen in the last
Honours List and of the further addition to her stature
by the appearance of the first two volumes of her works
in the Uniform Edition e.g. The Last September and The
Death of the Heart. Includes brief reviews of these and
notice of a new novel - The Heat of the Day - described
as her best.

89   Glendinning, Victoria. Elizabeth Bowen. New York: Knopf,
1978. 331pp. il. portrs. bibl.

A biography and critical study. Explores in detail her
Ascendancy background, her unsettled childhood and
interrupted schooling, her marriage, her literary career
and achievement, her sojourn in America and her
friendships.
(Review: Ir Univ R 8 (1) (Spring 1978): 119-120.)
(Review: New Repub 11 (Mar. 1978): 38.)

90   "Hypnotic Days at Montefort." Sat R 38 (Jan. 15, 1955):
16. il.

A brief biographical sketch of the novelist and a review
of her A World of Love.

91   Kenney, Edwin J. (Jr.) Elizabeth Bowen. Lewisberg,
Pennsylvania: Bucknell University Press, 1975. 107pp. bibl.

A brief study based primarily on interviews with the
subject and her writings explores the nature of Elizabeth
Bowen's literary sensibility as this was affected by her
life situation - an only child and Anglo-Irish. Includes
a biographical sketch of the main events of her life.

92   Lond Merc R 39 (Dec. 1938): 112a.

A drawing of Elizabeth Bowen, the novelist.

93   "Love for a Traitor." Sat R 32 (Feb. 19, 1949): 9.
portr.

Review of The Heat of the Day by Elizabeth Bowen and a
brief biographical sketch.

94   [McLiammoir, Michael.] [pseud. The Bellman.] "Meet
Elizabeth Bowen." Bell 4 (6) (Sept. 1942): 420-426.

    Profile of Elizabeth Bowen notes her aristocratic quality
    and includes excerpts from his conversation with her in
    which she comments on her love for Cork, her early
    attachment to painting, reluctance to being identified as
    a writer, her working methods, her "Irishness".

95   Monaghan, Charles. "Portrait of a Woman Reading." Book W
2 (Nov. 10, 1968): 6. portr.

    Interview with the author, Elizabeth Bowen, in which she
    comments on her Irish background, her education in
    England, the 1st World War, her reading as a teenager and
    during the decades of the 20's - 30's and her favorite
    authors.

96   Stokes, Edward. "Elizabeth Bowen. Pre-assumptions or
Moral Angle?" J Aust U Lang & Lit No. 11 (Sept. 1959): 35-47.
refs.

    Stokes accuses Miss Bowen of pre-assumptions in her work
    despite her own philosophy that the novelist should avoid
    these - whether national, social, or sexual. He
    identifies two main pre-assumptions in her work: one of
    which is that men are rather more likely than not to be
    unreliable, unfaithful, and undependable.

97   "Tips." Publ Wkly 185 (5) (Feb. 3, 1964): 81.

    Elizabeth Bowen talks about her lifestyle; her theories
    on short story writing; plans for a new edition of
    Bowen's Court and her experiences as a writer-in-
    residence at Vassar College and the University of
    Wisconsin.

98   Why Do I Write? An Exchange of Views Between Elizabeth
Bowen, Graham Greene and V.S. Pritchett. With a preface by
V.S. Pritchett. London: Percival Marshall, 1948. 58pp.

    A triangular correspondence between these authors on the
    role of the artist in society.

                    Sybil le Brocquy (1892-1973)

99   Sybil le Brocquy 1892-1973. Compiled by Andrew
Carpenter. Dublin: Dolmen Press, 1976. 32pp. plates. front.
portrs.

    A brief tribute to Sybil le Brocquy best known for her
    writings on Swift's friend, Esther Van Homrigh on the
    occasion of the restoration of the Rutland Memorial

fountain in Merrion Square in 1975 partly financed by a
memorial fund in her honor. Notes her manifold
involvements with various political and literary
organizations.

Charlotte Brooke (1740-1793)

100   Alspach, Russell K. "Charlotte Brooke: A Forerunner of
the Celtic Renaissance." Gen Mag & Hist Chro VXL (1938): 178-
183.

A brief biographical account of Charlotte Brooke and
mention of her importance in the history of Irish
literature. Alspach notes that when she published her
volume of verse translations dealing with both the
language and legends of native Ireland there was little
cultural interest in such matters - thus Brooke
anticipated by 100 years the Gaelic Revival.

101   Breatnach, R.A. "Two Eighteenth-Century Irish Scholars:
J.C. Walker and Charlotte Brooke." Stud Hibern No. 5 (1965):
88-97. (A Radio Eireann Thomas Davis lecture originally
broadcast in a series entitled "Pioneers of Irish
Scholarship."

Walker, a member of the newly founded Royal Irish
Academy, set himself the task of providing an historical
account of the development of Irish poetry and music; his
close friend and collaborator, Charlotte Brooke was
concerned with fostering contemporary literary
appreciation of vernacular Irish poetry. Their respective
contributions - his Historical Memoirs of the Irish Bards
and her Reliques of Irish Poetry critically evaluated;
while both are seen as breaking new literary ground, her
achievement is considered the first work of Irish
literary scholarship.

Brigid Brophy

102   Dock, Leslie. "An Interview With Brigid Brophy."
Contemp Lit 17 (Spring 1976): 151-170.

A brief biographical sketch of the Anglo-Irish novelist,
playwright, critic and essayist, Brigid Brophy followed
by a transcript of an interview with her in July 1975.
Brophy comments briefly on her work, influences, her
social attitudes, freudianism, feminism, journalism and
authors' rights.

Frances Browne (1816-1879)

103   Bonner, Patrick. "The Blind Poetess." Donegal An 14 (1)
(1981): 66.

Biographical note.

104   "The Blind Girl of Donegal." <u>Ir Book Lov</u> 8 (5-6) (Dec. 1916-Jan. 1917): 49-51.

A brief biographical sketch of the blind poet, Frances Browne, based mainly on her autobiographical essay in her first book of published verse <u>The Star of Atteghei</u>, 1844.

105   Russell, Matthew (Rev.) "Our Poets: 29 - Frances Browne." <u>Ir Mon</u> 24 (May 1896): 262-268.

Brief biographical account which includes excerpts from her poetry.

Selina Bunbury (1802-1882)

106   "Selina Bunbury." <u>Ir Book Lov</u> 7 (6) (Jan. 1916): 105-107.

A brief account of the ancestry and career of the voluminous writer and traveller, Selina Bunbury, with evaluative comments on her work, mainly historical fiction and travel books.

107   "Selina Bunbury." <u>Ir Mon</u> 44 (July 1916): 475-476.

Biographical details.

Frances Calvert (1767-1859)

108   Blake, Mrs. Warrenne. <u>An Irish Beauty of the Regency</u>. Compiled from "My Souvenirs," the unpublished journals of the Honorable Mrs. Calvert (1789-1822). London: John Lane, 1911. 428pp. il. geneal. front. refs.

Excerpts from the diary of Frances Pery, later Mrs. Calvert, who was born in Dublin in 1767 but spent most of her life in England. Consists mainly of social gossip, superficial politics and comments on her Continental trip in 1817 when she visited France, Germany, Belgium and Holland.

109   "Forthcoming Works: <u>An Irish Beauty of the Regency</u> (Mrs. Nicholson Calvert) by Warrenne Blake." <u>Ir Book Lov</u> 2 (Feb. 1911): 108.

News item on forthcoming work based on the unpublished journals of the Honorable Mrs. Frances Calvert, daughter of Lord Pery, Speaker of the Irish House of Commons.

Ethna Carbery (1866-1902)

110   Colby, Elbridge. "Ethna Carbery: A Woman Who Loved
Ireland." Cath U Bull 20 (1914): 533-540.

   Effusive tribute to the poet Anna Johnston MacManus
   (Ethna Carbery) comments briefly on her themes,
   especially patriotism, and includes excerpts from her
   work.

111   Concannon, Helena. "The Ethna Carbery Country." Cath
Bull 18 (2) (1928): 876-880. portrs.

   Identification of places in Counties Donegal and Antrim
   that figure in the poetry of Anna Johnston MacManus.

112   Eaton, Charlotte. "Ethna Carbery - Poet of the Celts."
With a Memoir by Seamus MacManus. Cath W 121 (Apr.-Sept.
1925): 321-333.

   A brief preface by Eaton introduces this effusive tribute
   to the poet "Ethna Carbery" (Anna Johnston) by her
   husband Seamus MacManus. Her personal qualities and her
   political sympathies stressed. Her role in founding the
   literary magazine The Shan Van Vocht viewed as the
   opening voice of the Irish Revival and her poetic
   achievement, characterized as "designedly national,"
   discussed.

113   Nic Shuibhne, Maire. "Women Pioneers." Wolfe Tone An
(1945): 21-23.

   (See Nic Shuibhne, Maire #291.)

114   Tynan, Katherine. "Ethna Carbery: An Irish Singer."
Cath W 109 (Apr.-Sept. 1919): 477-486.

   Brief memoir of the author's friendship with Anna
   Johnston. She is described as a Catholic Nationalist who
   played a major role in the Irish Revival through the
   literary magazine The Shan Van Vocht which she and her
   friend, Alice Milligan founded and edited. Excerpts from
   her poems and her husband's poem on her death included.

Juanita Casey (1925-   )

115   "An Interview with Juanita Casey Conducted by Gordon
Henderson." J Ir Lit 1 (3) (Sept. 1972): 42-54.

   Juanita Casey, short story writer, poetess and novelist
   talks about her background and childhood - born in
   England of an Irish tinker (traveler) mother who died at

her birth and an English Romany father who abandoned her
after a year. Her early life was divided between private
boarding schools and the circus. Married three times she
has three children, the youngest still living with her in
Ireland. She wrote mainly for her 3rd husband, an Irish
journalist. She comments on her present situation, her
work, treatment of tinkers in Ireland, etc.

Frances Alexander Cecil (1818-1895)

116   Cecil, Frances Alexander. Poems. Ed. with a preface by
William Alexander. London: MacMillan and Co., 1896. 463pp.
portr.

Preface includes a biographical and critical sketch of
the author by her husband. Notes her involvement in the
Oxford Movement and tract writing with comment on her
religious formation and influences. Effusive tribute to
her charity and sanctity.

117   "Some Irish Centenaries." Ir Book Lov 10 (1818): 35-36.

Biographical sketch of Frances Alexander Cecil described
as the most popular hymn writer of the last century with
some account of her work and a list of her publications.

Veronica Cleeve

118   Cleeve, Veronica. A Woman's Story. Dublin: Capel, 1982.
206pp.

Autobiography by the wife of the novelist Brian Cleeve
details their bohemian existence in wartime Dublin and
later in London which included smuggling operations,
their subsequent travels in France, Italy, Switzerland
and the West Indies and her husband's religious
conversion.

Mary Colum (1887-1957)

119   Colum, Mary. Life and The Dream. Garden City, New York:
Doubleday and Co. Inc., 1947. 466pp.

Memoirs of the writer and literary critic, Mary Colum
describe her convent school background, her student years
in prewar Dublin, the personalities of the literary,
artistic and political circles of the Irish Revival, the
New York literary and social circles in which she and her
husband moved after 1914, and their reactions to Ireland
on their return after the Treaty.

(Review: <u>Ir Writ</u> No. 3 (Nov. 1947): 92-93.)
(Review: <u>Ir Book Lov</u> 30 (May 1948): 118.)
(Review: <u>Dublin Mag</u> New Ser. 23 (2) (June 1948): 62-63.)

120   Rimo, Patricia A. "Mollie Colum and Her Circle." <u>Ir Lit Supp</u> (Fall 1983): 26-27. portr.

    Brief biographical sketch of the one time well-known and
    highly regarded author, now primarily remembered as the
    wife of the poet and playwright, Padraic Colum. Her
    literary achievement is evaluated from a feminist
    perspective as that of a strong, independent,
    professional woman operating in the male bastion of
    criticism whose best work consists of her articles, her
    book of comparative criticism and her autobiography.

Geraldine Dorothy Cummins (1890-1969)

121   Arbuthnot, Felicity. "A Lunch With Bernard Shaw." <u>Books Ire</u> 82 (Spr. 1984): 69.

    A biographical sketch of the psychic Geraldine Dorothy
    Cummins born in 1890 in County Cork who also was well
    known as an author, playwright and suffragette.

Polly Devlin (1944-   )

122   Devlin, Polly. <u>All of Us There</u>. London: Weidenfeld and
Nicolson, 1983. 200pp.

    Memoir of growing up in a large Catholic family of seven
    children in Ardboe, County Tyrone in the 1950's.

Ellen Downing (1828-1869)

123   Markham, Thomas. <u>Ellen Mary Downing: "Mary of the Nation</u>." Dublin: Catholic Truth Society. [n.d.] 28pp.

    Brief biographical sketch of the minor poet, Ellen Mary
    Downing who wrote patriotic verse for <u>The Nation</u> and
    later the <u>United Irishman</u>. She later briefly became a
    religious (Sister Mary Alphonsus) in the North
    Presentation Convent, Cork, but had to leave for health
    reasons.

124   [Russell, Matthew.] "Ellen Downing - 'Mary' of the
Nation." <u>Ir Mon</u> 6 (1878): 459-465, 506-512.

125   - - - "The Late Ellen Downing of Cork - 'Mary' of the
Nation." <u>Ir Mon</u> 6 (1878): 573-580, 621-630, 661-667.

Biographical sketch by the Editor of the <u>Irish Monthly</u>
with lengthy excerpts from her poems and correspondence.

126   Russell, Matthew. "More About 'Mary of the Nation."<u>Ir</u>
<u>Mon</u> 36 (1908): 69-82.

A biographical sketch highlighting the spiritual life of
Ellen Downing written by a Redemptorist, Rev. J. Masnier,
C.SS.R. and originally published in the <u>Irish Rosary</u> of
1900 here reproduced with introductory commentary by the
editor.

127   "Unpublished Relics of Ellen Downing 'Mary of the
Nation.'" <u>Ir Mon</u> 12 (1884): 315-320, 425-432, 534-540.

Miss Ellen Downing of Cork was Mary of the 'Nation' and
later Sister Mary Alphonsus of the third order of St.
Dominick. The 'relics' include prose and verse excerpts
from a manuscript collection presented to Sir Gavin Duffy
(founder of <u>The Nation</u>) by the poet in 1849 and
subsequently donated by him to the editor of the <u>Irish</u>
<u>Monthly</u>.

Biddy Early (1799-1874)

128   MacMahon, Bryan. "The Strange Story of Biddy Early."
<u>CARA</u> 3 (3) (July-Sept. 1970): 29-31. il.

Brief biographical sketch of Biddy Early, the "wise
woman" with an excerpt from the <u>Limerick Chronicle</u> of
July 29, 1869 reporting her marriage to her fourth
husband, a young man whereas she was over 80 years of
age. Recounts other legends of her prophetic powers,
cures, etc.

129   Ryan, Meda. <u>Biddy Early. The Wise Woman of Clare</u>.
Dublin and Cork: The Mercier Press, 1978. 11pp. refs.

A brief anecdotal account of an old, four times widowed
woman in County Clare in the 19th century who was
renowned either as a witch or a person of God because she
possessed unusual gifts. She was reputed to be able to
effect "cures," foresee the future, etc. and was widely
consulted.

130   Schmitz, Nancy. "An Irish Wise Woman - Fact and Legend.
Folklore Institute." <u>Haque J</u> 14 (3) (1977): 169-179. refs.

A critical examination of the various accounts of the
life and activities of Biddy Early, a "wise" woman in
18th century Ireland. While the actual facts about her
existence cannot be proved the legends provide a
composite picture of a "bean feasa" (wise woman), one who
is credited with having contact with the fairies and

having magical powers of insight, fore-knowledge and
healing. Her particular sphere was to counteract the
results of spells cast by evil-wishers and of fairy
mischief; she emerges in the Irish tradition as a
generally benevolent figure.

Maria Edgeworth (1768?-1849)

131   Butler, Harriet. "Letters of Harriet Butler." Butler
Soc J 1 (8) (1978): 648-655. refs.

Letters written by Maria Edgeworth's half sister in 1826
to her family while she travelled on the Continent with
Maria with identification of individuals named in these.

132   Butler, Maria and Christina Colvin. "A Revised Date of
Birth for Maria Edgeworth." Notes & Quer 216 (Sept. 1971):
339-340.

Offers evidence from Maria Edgeworth's letters and
contemporary records to indicate that her date of birth
was probably January 1, 1768 not 1767 as previously
generally accepted.

133   Butler, Marilyn. Maria Edgeworth: A Literary Biography.
Oxford: Clarendon Press, 1972. 531pp. il. bibl.

More than a strictly literary account, this definitive
biography of the 19th century Anglo-Irish novelist
explores the social background from which she emerged,
her father's influence, their ideas on education, their
experience of Irish politics and how her literary
creation documents the social history of her era. Butler
views Edgeworth's development of the techniques of
documentation as her major innovation.
 (Review: Ir Hist Stud 18 (1972-73): 444.)
 (Review: Eng Hist R 89 (1974): 199.)

134   Butler, Ruth F. "Maria Edgeworth and Sir Walter Scott:
Unpublished Letters 1 1823." R Eng Stud 9 (Feb. 1958): 23-40.
refs.

A selection of letters from the family papers of the
Edgeworth family some of which are included in previous
collections (Zimmern. Hare. Barry. Clarke.) mostly
written after Maria's visit to Scotland in 1823 and her
meeting and stay with Sir Walter Scott. Eleven letters in
all are included nine of which were written by Maria
Edgeworth; recipients, dates and interest of this
correspondence briefly discussed by Butler.

135   Clarke, Isabel C. Maria Edgeworth: Her Family and
Friends. London, etc.: Hutchinson and Co. [1949?] 208pp. il.
portrs. bibl.

Based on previously published biographies, various
editions of the Edgeworth correspondence and memoirs of
various members of the family, this informal biography
concentrates on the details of the personal life and the
many relatives and friends of Maria Edgeworth. Her
portrait of Maria stresses her filial and family
devotion, her simplicity, warmth and generosity untouched
by fame while enjoying her encounters with the
celebrities of her epoch, and a warm friendship with Sir
Walter Scott.
(Review: Studies 39 (Sept. 1950): 346-347.)

136   Colvin, Christina. "Maria Edgeworth." Times Lit Supp
(Sept. 29, 1972): 1157.

Letter to the editor states that Maria Edgeworth's hair
was not dark but light brown.

137   Edgeworth, Frances Anne (Mrs.) A Memoir of Maria
Edgeworth, With a Selection from Her Letters, by the late
Maria Edgeworth. Ed. by her children. London: J.Masters &
Son, 1867. 3 vols.

This earliest written (publication was delayed) biography
of Maria Edgeworth with a selection of her letters from
1776 (written to her mother Mrs. Honora Edgeworth from
school in Derby) through 1849, the year of her death.

138   Edgeworth, Maria. Letters of Maria Edgeworth and Anna
Letitia Barbauld. Selected from The Lushington Papers, and
edited by Walter Sidney Scott. Illustrations by Letitia
Sandford. London: The Golden Cockerel Press, 1953. 86pp. il.

Letters to her friend Sarah Carr, later Mrs. Lushington,
from Maria Edgeworth written between 1818-1836. Includes
brief biographical sketches and explanatory notes by the
editor.

139   Edgeworth, Maria. Maria Edgeworth: Chosen Letters. With
an introduction by F.V. Barry. Boston and New York: Houghton
Meflin, Co., 1931. 468pp. front.

Most of the letters in this selection come from the text
of the Memoir of Maria Edgeworth compiled by the fourth
Mrs. Edgeworth and edited by her children in 1867. Also
includes some letters published for the first time. The
recipients include her aunt, Mrs. Ruxton, her cousins,
brothers and sisters. In her introduction Ms Barry
comments on Maria's literary achievement and the literary
and social context in which she wrote. The letters are
grouped by period and indexed.

140   Edgeworth, Maria. Maria Edgeworth in France and
Switzerland. Selections from the Family Letters. Ed. by

Christina Colvin. Oxford: Clarendon Press, 1979. 309pp. il.
portrs. bibl.

The texts of the surviving letters written by the
Edgeworth family group from France and Switzerland on two
separate visits, the first in 1802/03, the second in
1820. Editor indicates that some of these letters were
previously published in the Memoir of Maria Edgeworth
where they were sometimes altered; some of these are now
missing but others are included: less than half of the
collection here reproduced has been previously published.
The introduction identifies the members of the social/
literary/scientific/political circles in which they moved
in France and Switzerland, gives brief biographical
profiles of the travellers and of their family
correspondents. Letters are arranged chronologically.
There are personal, place and subject indexes.

141   Flanagan, Thomas. "Maria Edgeworth: the Crisis of the
'Protestant Nation.'" In his The Irish Novelists. pp.53-106.
New York: Columbia University Press, 1959.

Mainly a literary analysis of Maria Edgeworth's key theme
in four of her major novels, viz the fate of the Anglo-
Irish, the landlord class, in Ireland but includes
biographical material on Maria and Edgeworthstown in the
troubled years of the Agitation and Tithe wars and The
Great Famine of 1846.
(Review: Studies 50 (1961): 99-103.)
(Review: Cath Hist R 46 (1961): 480.).

142   "A Glimpse of Maria Edgeworth." Argosy 62 (July-Dec.
1896): 283-284.

Anecdotes about the author by an acquaintance.

143   Grey, Rowland. "Heavy Fathers." Fortn R LXXXVI (July
1909): 80-89.

Brief comment on Mr. Edgeworth's pernicious influence on
his daughter, Maria's, literary production.

144   Grey, Rowland. "Maria Edgeworth and Etienne Dumont."
Dublin R 145 (1909): 239-265.

Letters of Maria Edgeworth to her Swiss friend, Etienne
Dumont, bequeathed by him to a member of his family, with
editorial comment by Grey. Grey claims these letters
reveal the real Maria Edgeworth for the first time and
show a romantic interest on her part in the recipient.

145   Hall, Mrs. S.C. "Edgeworthstown, Memories of Maria
Edgeworth." Art J 11 (1849); 225-229.

Eulogistic account of the character of Maria Edgeworth,
details her daily life at Edgeworthstown, notes her
acquaintances and friends who included all the 'notables'
of her time and conveys the author's deep sense of loss
at her passing.

146   Hare, Augustus. (Editor) The Life and Letters of Maria
Edgeworth. Boston, New York: Houghton Miflin, 1895. 2 vols.
portr.

The most complete collection of Maria Edgeworth's letters
and the first such collection to be published. The
letters are arranged chronologically and their context
explicated by the editor who, in his own words, has
written such a "thread of biography as might unite the
links of the chain."
(Review: Lond Q R New Ser. 24 (1895): 15-30.)
(Review: Acad 46 (1181) (Dec. 22, 1894): 525-526.)
(Review: Sat R 79 (Mar. 2, 1895): 288-289.)
(Review: Leis Hour 44 (1895): 286-300.)
(Review: Nation 60 (1546): (Feb. 14, 1895): 129-130.)

147   Hayward, A[braham]. "Maria Edgeworth: Her Life and
Writings." In his Biographical and Critical Essays 2nd ed.
vol.1 pp. 130-146. London: Longmans, Green & Co., 1873.
(Originally published in The Edinburgh Review for October
1867.

A reprint of his review of the then unpublished A Memoir
of Maria Edgeworth, With a Selection from Her Letters
(1867). Hayward briefly outlines the main events of
Richard Lovell Edgeworth and Maria's lives, his influence
on her literary career and includes excerpts from the
Edgeworth family correspondence.

148   Hill, Constance. Maria Edgeworth and Her Circle in the
Days of Buonaparte and Bourbon. John Lane: The Bodley Head,
1974. 301pp. plates.

A detailed account of Maria Edgeworth's travels in
France, England and Geneva in the years 1800-1820 and the
social and artistic society in which she moved. Draws
heavily on the correspondence with her family throughout
this period and personal comments of her contemporaries.
The political background - notably French-British
relations - briefly sketched.

149   Hone, J.M. "Maria Edgeworth and the Moores of Moore
Hall." New Statesm 13 (Apr. 1937): 553-554.

Brief note on the friendship of the Protestant Anglo-
Irish novelist, Maria Edgeworth and the Catholic Moores
of Moore Hall, grandparents of the novelist, George
Moore. Includes excerpts from Maria's letters to Mrs.
Moore with explanatory comment by Hone.

150   Howitt, William. "Visit to Edgeworthstown - Miss
Edgeworth." Ecl Mag 14 (May 1848): 57-61.

    Brief note on the author's visit to Edgeworthstown in
    County Longford in 1845 and his conversation with Maria
    Edgeworth.

151   Hurst, Michael. Maria Edgeworth and the Public Scene.
Florida: University of Miami Press, 1969. 206pp. plates.
bibl.

  (Review: Amer Hist R 75 (4/7) (1970): 1725-1726.)
  (Review: Cath Hist R 59 (1973-74): 474.)
  (Review: Eng Hist R 86 (1971): 862.)
  (Review: Hist 55 (1970): 289.)

152   Inglis-Jones, E. The Great Maria: A Portrait of Maria
Edgeworth. London: Faber and Faber, 1959. 265pp. plates.

  (Review: Studies 50 (1961): 98.)

153   Lawless, Emily. Maria Edgeworth. [English Men of
Letters Series.] London: MacMillan and Co. Ltd., 1904. 219pp.

  (Review: Atlan Mon 96 (1905): 423-424.)
  (Review: Int Q 10 (Dec. 1904): 190-195.)

154   Longford, Christine. "Maria Edgeworth and Her Circle."
Ir Writ No. 6 (1948): 70-75.

    Comment on real life counterparts of the characters in
    Castle Rackent and brief mention of the people who
    comprised Maria Edgeworth's social circle in Ireland.

155   MacCarvill, Mary. "Maria Edgeworth: Her Letters, Life
and Times." Capu An (1933): 215-219. portrs.

    A discussion of the Chosen Letters of Maria Edgeworth
    (See item #139). Notes that despite Maria's lack of
    popularity with her own class in Ireland she was highly
    regarded in England and on the Continent both as a
    literary figure and an educator. Concedes her importance
    in the development of the realistic tradition in the
    English novel but records her apparent indifference to
    the major events of her day in Ireland whereas her
    letters manifest knowledge of, and interest in, English
    and continental affairs.

156   "Maria Edgeworth." Dublin U Mag 33 (June 1849):
795-796.

    Obituary.

157   "Maria Edgeworth." Temp Bar 105 (1895): 317-351. refs.

   Brief sketch based mainly on the then unpublished Memoir
   by Mrs. Edgeworth and Memoirs by Richard Lovell Edgeworth
   begun by himself and concluded by Maria.

158   Maria Edgeworth Letters from England 1813-1844. Ed. by
Christina Colvin. Oxford: Clarendon Press, 1971. 649pp.

   Includes observations on the British, social and
   intellectual scene during the course of seven visits by
   the author during period indicated with helpful
   annotations by the editor.
   (Review: Ir Hist Stud 18 (71) (Mar. 1973): 444-445.)

159   Maxse, Mary. "Books New and Old: Maria Edgeworth." Nat
& Eng R 118 (May 1942): 483-488.

   Discussion of the influence of Maria Edgeworth's father
   on her life and work, her familial role, her travels and
   her personal qualities.

160   "Miss Edgeworth." Cornhill Mag 46 (1882): 404-426; 526-
545.

   Biographical sketch of Maria and her father with some
   discussion of her work.

161   "Miss Edgeworth at Edgeworthstown." (From Mr. and Mrs.
S.C. Hall's Ireland) Ecl Mus 1 (Feb. 1843): 162-165.

   Description of the house and lifestyle of the family at
   Edgeworthstown, Maria Edgeworth's residence in County
   Longford.

162   Murray, Patrick. Maria Edgeworth: A Study of the
Novelist. Cork: The Mercier Press, 1971. 94pp. bibl.

163   Newby, P.H. Maria Edgeworth. Denver: Alan Swallow.
[1950] 98pp.

164   "Obituary: Miss Edgeworth." Gent Mag 32 (July 1849):
99-100.

165   "Obituary Notice on Maria Edgeworth." Roy Ir Acad Proc
Ser. 1 IV (1847-1850): 495.

166   Oliver, Grace A. A Study of Maria Edgeworth. Boston: A.
Williams and Co., 1882. 567pp. il. portr.

   (Review: Atlan Mon 51 (1883): 413-416.)

(Review: <u>Lit W</u> 13 (Dec. 30, 1882): 486-487.)
(Review: <u>Nation</u> 36 (928) (Apr. 12, 1883): 322-324.)
(Review: <u>Unita R</u> 19 (1) (Jan. 1883): 82-86.)
(Review: <u>Unita R</u> 19 (4) (Apr. 1883): 333-345.)

167   Repplier, Agnes. "Three Famous Old Maids." <u>Lippinc</u> 47
(Mar. 1981): 390-394.

    Comment on the apparently well rounded and contented
    lives of Jane Austen, Maria Edgeworth and Jessica Mitford
    despite their spinsterhood.

168   Ritchie, Anne Isabella (Thackeray). <u>A Book of Sybils</u>.
London: Smith, Elder & Co., 1883. 229pp.

    Has a chapter on Maria Edgeworth based mainly on Mrs.
    Edgeworth's memoirs (pp. 51-148) reprinted from <u>Cornhill
    Magazine</u>.

169   Romilly, Samuel H. "The Lost Letters of Maria
Edgeworth." <u>Quarterly R</u> 268 (1937): 103-117.

    A supplement to the <u>Romilly-Edgeworth Letters, 1813-1818</u>,
    ed. by Samuel Henry Romilly published in 1936 (See #170).
    This artcle includes excerpts from Maria Edgeworth's side
    of that correspondence with notes and comments by the
    compiler.

170   <u>Romilly-Edgeworth Letters, 1813-1818</u>. With an
Introduction and Notes by Samuel Henry Romilly. London: John
Murray, 1936. il. portrs.

    Includes letters written by Anne Romilly to Maria
    Edgeworth, during the period 1812-1817 and one reply by
    Maria. Also has four letters written by Richard Lovell
    Edgeworth. Contextual notes by the editor, grandson of
    Anne Romilly.

171   Saintsbury, George. "Maria Edgeworth." <u>MacMil</u> 72 (July
1895): 161-170.

    Biographical sketch with critical comment on her work and
    evaluation of her overall achievement.

172   Slade, Bertha C. "Maria Edgeworth." <u>Yale U Lib Gaz</u> XIV
(1940): 59-61.

    Brief note on the author's difficulties in obtaining
    first editions of Maria Edgeworth's early works,
    bibliographical notes on some of these and a description
    of a visit to the empty mansion which was once the
    Edgeworth family home.

173   Zimmern, Helen. <u>Maria Edgeworth</u>. London: W.H.Allen & Co., 1883. 219pp.

   The first published biography based on the then unpublished memoir by her step-mother and on some of her private correspondence.
(Review: <u>Sat R</u> 57 (Apr. 26, 1884): 554-555.)

Alice Furlong (1875-1946)

174   Little, Arthur (S.J.) "Lest We Forget: Alice Furlong." <u>Ir Mon</u> 75 (1947): 137-143.

   Brief tribute to the poet, Alice Furlong for whom it is claimed a mastery of pure lyric song unequalled at her death by any other Irish poet after Yeats.

175   O'Brennan, Kathleen. "Alice Furlong - Some Memories." <u>Ir Book Lov</u> 30 (5) (May 1948): 105-106.

   Reprint of an article in the Irish Press of October 29, 1946 comments briefly on her family background and poetic achievement.

176   Russell, Matthew. "Poets I Have Known: Alice Furlong." <u>Ir Mon</u> 36 (1908): 389-398.

   Brief biographical sketch and excerpts from contemporary critical comment.

Eva Gore-Booth (1870-1926)

177   Gore-Booth, Eva. <u>Poems of Eva Gore-Booth</u>. Complete edition with the <u>Inner Life of a Child</u> and <u>Letters</u>, and a biographical introduction by Esther Roper. London: Longman's Green and Co., 1929. 654pp. portrs.

   The brief biographical sketch by her friend and colleague profiles Eva Gore-Booth, sister of the better known, Countess Markievicz. Describes her personality, her poetic achievement, her work with Esther Roper for the political and economic enfranchisement of women in Manchester and the role of this effort in the general Women's Franchise Movement, her efforts to free Irish political prisoners and her involvement in the Peace Movement.
(Review: <u>Ir Book Lov</u> 18 (Nov.-Dec. 1930): 182.)

Queen Gormlay

178   Scott, Charles (Rev.). "The Great Sorrow of a Celtic Queen." <u>Dublin U Mag</u> LXXXII (1873): 475-477.

Note on lyrics (with text) composed by Queen Gormlay,
wife of Niall Glundubh (BlackKnee), King of Ireland, who
died in the battle of Ath-Cliath (Dublin) in A.D. 919
fighting against the Danish invaders. The lyrics were
discovered in the Dean of Lismore's compilation of Gaelic
poetry.

Dame Isabella Augusta Gregory (1852-1932)

179   Adams, Hazard. _Lady Gregory_. Lewisburg: Bucknell
University Press, 1973. 106pp. bibl.

The introductory chapter deals briefly with Lady
Gregory's life and her varied activities as author,
director and translator while the remainder of the book
concentrates on her achievement as a dramatist.
(Review: _Choice_ 2 (Apr. 1974): 254.)

180   Ayling, Ronald. "Charwomen of the Abbey." _Shaw R_ IV
(Sept. 1961): 7-15.

Comments on the unjustified bad press Lady Gregory has
received at the hands of Oliver St.John Gogarty and Denis
Johnston and her omission from St. John Ervine's
biography of George Bernard Shaw despite her close
friendship with the latter. Ayling welcomes the
appreciate assessment of her achievement as portrayed by
Elizabeth Coxhead.

181   Coxhead, Elizabeth. _Lady Gregory: A Literary Portrait_.
New York: Harcourt, Brace & World, Inc., 1961. 241pp. il.
bibl.

More than the title indicates this "literary portrait"
also includes material on Lady Gregory's personal life,
her friendships with Yeats, Synge, Shaw and O'Casey and
her contributions as co-founder and director of the Abbey
Theatre. The emphasis however is on a discussion of Lady
Gregory's own literary talents.
(Review: _Kilk Mag_ No.4 (Summer 1961): 49-50.)
(Review: _Stud Hibern_ No.2 (1962): 249-253.)
(Review: _Studies_ 51 (Autumn 1962): 438-440.)

182   Coxhead, Elizabeth. _J.M. Synge and Lady Gregory_.
London: Longman's Green & Co., 1962. 35pp. portr. bibl.

Brief resume of Lady Gregory's many activities - writing
folklore, play-writing, running the house and estate at
Coole, playing hostess and providing "santuary" to
literary figures, notably Yeats; her struggle to have the
Lane pictures restored to Ireland and her part in
creating the Abbey Theatre. Includes a critical
evaluation of her dramatic writing.
(Review: _Acorn_ No.1 (Winter 1961): 89.)

183   Dalmasso, Michele. _Lady Gregory et le Renaissance
Irlandaise_. Aix-en-Provence; Marseilles: Publications, Univ.
de Province; 1982. il. 688pp.

   Includes biographical material.

184   Fallon, Gabriel. "Sitting at the Play: The Journals of
Lady Gregory." _Ir Mon_ LXXV (Feb. 1947): 76-82.

   Excerpts from the abridged edition of _The Journals_.

185   Fitzgerald, Mary. "Sean O'Casey and Lady Gregory: the
Record of a Friendship." In _Sean O'Casey Centenary Essays_,
ed. by David Krause and Robert G. Lowery, pp. 67-99. Totowa,
New Jersey: Barnes and Noble. (c.1980) 257pp. refs.

   Describes their seven year friendship as "one of the most
   crucial relationships of his professional life and one of
   the happiest of hers." Based on the Krause edition of the
   Letters of Sean O'Casey not available prior to 1975 and
   Lady Gregory's own journals, with some excerpts.

186   Gregory, Anne. _Me and Nu: Childhood at Coole_. Gerrards
Cross, Buckinghamshire: Colin Smythe, 1970. 128pp. il.

   Anne Gregory, grand-daughter of Lady Gregory, recollects
   her and her sister, Catherine's childhood at Coole, Lady
   Gregory's estate in Galway. Includes anecdotes regarding
   Shaw, William Butler and Jack Yeats, O'Casey, Augustus
   John, Mrs. Pope Hennessy and Dr. Gogarty - all frequent
   visitors at Coole and the children's perceptions of them.
   But mainly a nostalgic evocation of their affection for
   Lady Gregory herself.
(Review: _Hermathena_ 111 (1971): 100.)

187   [Gregory, Augusta Isabella, Lady.] _Coole_. Completed
from the manuscript and edited by Colin Smythe. Dublin:
Dolmen Press, 1971. 105pp. il.

   Lady Gregory's account of the house at Coole describes
   the library, the woods, the gardens, the drawing room and
   breakfast room, their contents, the personal significance
   to her of all that Coole represented, and most cherished,
   the letters of the many writers, artists and patriots who
   were her friends and visitors at Coole.

188   Gregory, Augusta [Lady]. _Lady Gregory's Journals_.Ed. by
Daniel J. Murphy. Gerrards Cross, Colin Smythe, 1978. 707pp.
il. bibl. refs.

   The entire record of the diary covering the period
   October 10, 1916 - February 24, 1925 deals with her
   attempts to recover for Dublin the pictures bequeathed by
   her nephew, Hugh Lane, the early days of the Abbey
   Theatre and its problems, Coole Park and her struggle to

keep it, her opinions on The Terror and The Civil War, her plays, her relations with all the great literary figures of this period, especially her long friendship with Yeats, her affection for her family especially her grandchildren.
(Review: Hermathena 126 (Summer 1979): 86.)
(Review: Hon Ulsterm No. 61 (Jan.-Feb. 1979): 77-78.)
(Review: Studies 69 (1980): 102-103.)
(Review: Times Lit Supp No. 4004 (Dec. 14, 1979): 133.)

189   Gregory, Augusta Lady. Lady Gregory's Journals 1916-1930. Ed. by Lennox Robinson. New York: The Macmillan Company, 1947. 342pp.

An abridged early edition of The Journals with notes and comments by the editor arranged thematically.
(Review: Ir Bookm 2 (1) (1947): 71-74.)
(Review: Ir Mon 75 (1947): 76-82.)

190   [Gregory, Augusta Isabella, Lady.] "The Lady Gregory Letters to G.B. Shaw." Ed. by Daniel J. Murphy. Mod Drama 10 (Feb. 1968): 331-345. refs.

An annotated selection of fourteen letters written between 1911-1923 include discussion of the Abbey staging of Shaw's The Shewing-Up of Blanco Posnet; The Playboy riots in America and Lady Gregory's ongoing fight with the National Gallery of England to force them to return the pictures collected by her nephew, Sir Hugh Lane.

191   [Gregory, Augusta Isabella, Lady.] "The Lady Gregory Letters to Sean O'Casey." Ed. by A.C. Edwards. Mod Drama 8 (May 1965): 95-111.

A selection of letters, 23 in all, written by Lady Gregory to Sean O'Casey with an introduction and editorial notes on the content. Covers Lady Gregory's early recognition and encouragement of O'Casey, the rejection of the Silver Tassie by the Abbey and the subsequent break in their friendship.

192   [Gregory, Augusta Isabella, Lady.] "Letters from Gregory: a Record of her Friendship with T.J. Kiernan." Ed. by Daniel Joseph Murphy. NYPL Bull 71 (Dec. 1967): 621-661; 72 (Jan. 1968): 19-63; 72 (Feb. 1968): 123-131.

A three part article gives a brief biographical sketch of the correspondents, a note on the circumstances in which they met and the text of eighty letters written by Lady Gregory in the period 1924-1928. Lady Gregory originally consulted Dr. Kiernan for help with her taxes; later as Official Secretary in the Irish High Commissioner's Office in London he supported her fight to have the Hugh Lane pictures restored to Ireland and she became involved in his efforts to further Irish interests in London. Parts II and III add additional letters bringing the

correspondence up to May 9, 1932 about two weeks before
her death.

193   Gregory, Augusta (Lady.) Our Irish Theatre: A Chapter
of Autobiography. New York: Oxford University Press, 1972.
[1913] 279pp. il.

     Deals with her role in the Irish dramatic movement and
     the founding of the Abbey Threatre. Combines her personal
     reminiscence, correspondence and notes written at the
     time of the events described, descriptions of people and
     discussion of principles.
    (Review: Ir Book Lov 5 (1973): 125.)
    (Review: Hermathena 115 (1973): 121.)

194   Gregory, Augusta (Lady). Seventy Years: Being the
Autobiography of Lady Gregory. Ed. and with a foreward by
Colin Smythe. Gerrards Cross, Buckinghamshire: Colin Smythe,
1974. 583pp. il.

     This lengthy autobiography discovered forty years after
     the author's death, records her childhood in Ireland, her
     marriage, her life in Egypt and England, her friendships,
     the death of her husband, her return to Ireland, her
     literary and dramatic career, her directorship of The
     Abbey Theatre, The Boer War and the Irish uprising of
     1916.
    (Review: Nation 222 (16) (Apr. 24, 1976): 504-505.)
    (Review: Times Lit Supp No. 3869 (May 7, 1976): 547.)
    (Review: Ed Theatre J 29 (May 1977): 271-273.)

195   Howarth, Herbert. The Irish Writers. New York: Hill and
Wang, 1959. 318pp.

     Chapter three (pp.83-129) presents a brief biographical
     sketch of Lady Gregory.
    (Review: Cath Hist R 46 (1961): 489.)
    (Review: 20th Cent 165 (1959): 524.)

196   Von Klenze, Hilda. Lady Gregory's Leben und Werke.
Bochum-Langendreer: H. Poppinghaus, 1940. New York: Johnson
Reprint, 1966. 92pp.

197   Kohfeldt, Mary Lou. Lady Gregory: The Woman Behind The
Irish Renaissance. New York: Antheneum, 1985. 366pp.

     First full length American biography of Lady Gregory.
    (Review: Choice 22 (May 1985): 1333.)
    (Review: America 152 (May 11, 1985): 397.)
    (Review: Booklist 81 (Nov. 1984): 333.)
    (Review: Book W 6 (Feb. 10, 1985): 15.)

198   Kopper, Edward A. Jr. Lady Isabella Persse Gregory.
Boston: Twayne Pub., 1976. 160pp. portr. bibl. refs.

(Review: <u>Ed Theatre J</u> 29 (May 1977): 271-273.)
(Review: <u>Choice</u> 14 (Apr. 1977): 201.)

199   "Lady Gregory, The Abbey, Yeats, Moore, Synge." <u>Times
Lit Supp</u> 69 (July 16, 1970): 761-762. portrs.

   Review article includes a brief biographical sketch of
   Lady Gregory and comments on her literary achievement.

200   Leslie, Sir Shane. "Ireland's Boadicea." <u>Nat R</u> 11 (20)
(Nov. 18, 1961): 344-345.

   A review of Elizabeth Coxhead's biography of Lady Gregory
   and text of two unpublished letters written by Lady
   Gregory in 1924 and 1926 to the author's mother, Lady
   Leslie, aunt of Sir Winston Churchill. Lady Gregory wrote
   of her efforts to restore the Lane art collection to
   Ireland.

201   McHugh, Roger. "Sean O'Casey and Lady Gregory." <u>James
Joyce Q</u> 8 (Fall 1970): 119-123. refs.

   A brief comment on the reasons for the unusal friendship
   of Lady Gregory and Sean O'Casey who might have been
   expected to be separated by the barriers of class and
   belief.

202   Malone, Andrew E. (pseud.) "Lady Gregory: 1852-1932."
<u>Dublin Mag</u> VIII (1) (Jan. 1933): 37-47.

   A dramatic and literary appraisal of Lady Gregory's
   achievement includes a brief biographical sketch
   detailing her development from a Unionist upbringing to
   friendship with a Fenian leader, a supporter of the
   Gaelic League, translator and publisher of Irish folklore
   and founder of a theatre and drama for Ireland.

203   Mikhail, E.H. (Ed.) <u>Lady Gregory: Interviews and
Recollections</u>. London: MacMillan and Co., 1977. 113pp. refs.

   Includes excerpts relevant to Lady Gregory from
   autobiographical and other books by George Moore, W.B.
   Yeats, Maire Nic Shiubhlaigh, William G. Fay, Joseph
   Holloway, Walter Starkie, Wilfrid S. Blunt, Maurice
   Brown, Sean O'Casey, Hallie Flanagan; articles by Signe
   Toksuig and John Quinn; and excerpts from some of lady
   Gregory's own writings and pertinent articles and reviews
   in the American press during the Abbey Players U.S. tour
   in 1911-12. Includes notes on the contributors and
   contextual information.
 (Review: <u>Choice</u> 15 (Sept. 1978): 869-870.)
 (Review: <u>Times Lit Supp</u> (Jan. 20, 1978): 57.)
 (Review: <u>Booklist</u> 74 (May 1, 1978): 1404.)

204   Murphy, Daniel Joseph. "Yeats and Lady Gregory: A
Unique Dramatic Collaboration." Mod Drama VII (1964):
322-328. refs.

    Discusses the contributions of Lady Gregory to many of
    Yeats' plays and the central role he and the Abbey
    Theatre played in her life.

205   O'Casey, Sean. Inishfallen Fare Thee Well. New York:
The MacMillan Co., 1949. 396pp.

    Pages 163-199 present a vivid and affectionate if
    somewhat idealized sketch of Lady Gregory and some
    details on O'Casey's first visit to Coole. He delineates
    her courage in fighting for the freedom of the theatre
    against priest, peasant and politician, her stoicism
    under personal loss, her understanding of literature, her
    grace, warmth and humanity and her encouragement of other
    writers even at the expense of her own literary efforts.
    (Review: Ir Writ No. 8 (July 1949): 88-89.)
    (Review: Ir Book Lov 31 (June 1949): 44.)
    (Review: Ir Mon 77 (Mar. 1949): 119-123.)

206   "Personal Paragraphs from Periodicals." Ir Book Lov XII
(809): Mar.-Apr. 1921): 119-120.

    Quotation from The Bookman by C.E. Lawrence regarding
    Lady Gregory's work for the Irish Theatre.

207   Quinn, John. "Lady Gregory and the Abbey Theatre."
Outlook (Dec. 16, 1911): 916-919. [Reprinted in Lady Gregory:
Interviews and Recollections.]

    Recounts a visit to Ireland and to Lady Gregory's house
    at Coole; comments on her collaboration with Yeats, her
    work at the Abbey and her support of other Irish artists
    many of whom he met at Coole.

208   Robinson, Lennox. "Lady Gregory." Ire Today 1 (2)
(1936): 49-51.

    Brief profile and tribute to Lady Gregory and her work on
    behalf of the Abbey Theatre.

209   Saddlemyer, Ann and Colin Smythe. Lady Gregory, Fifty
Years After. Gerrards Cross, Buckinghamshire: Colin Smythe,
1983.

    Conceived to mark the fiftieth anniversary of Lady
    Gregory's death, includes essays on various aspects of
    her life and work.

210   Theatre Business: The Correspondence of the First Abbey

<u>Abbey Theatre Directors: William Butler Yeats, Lady Gregory</u>
<u>and J.M. Synge</u>. Selected and edited by Ann Saddlemyer.
University Park: Pennsylvania State University Press, 1982.
330pp. il.

    The letters to and from Synge are the controlling pattern
    for this collection. Includes contextual notes,
    bibliography, chronology and location.

211   Toksuig, Signe. "A Visit to Lady Gregory." <u>No Amer R</u>
CCVIV (Aug. 1921): 190-200. [Reprinted in <u>Lady Gregory:</u>
<u>Interviews and Recollections</u>.]

    Describes a visit to Lady Gregory's residence at Coole
    and characterizes Lady Gregory as a straightforward,
    practical warm personality with a passion to preserve and
    develop the arts in Ireland.

Constantia Grierson (1706-1733)

212   Dix, E.R. Mc C. "Mrs. Constantia Grierson." <u>Ir Book Lov</u>
11 (Apr. 1911): 136-137.

    Query regarding origins and maiden name of the poet
    Constantia Grierson.

213   MacArthur, William. "Mrs. Constantia Grierson." <u>Ir Book</u>
<u>Lov</u> 11 (Apr. 1911): 161-162.

    Response to above query. Other responses on pp. 179-180.

Florence Hackett (1884-1963)

214   Delehanty, James. "The Cruelist Month: In Memoriam
Florence Hackett 1884-1963." <u>Kilk Mag</u> 10 (Aut./Winter
1963/64): 35-53.

    A brief tribute and biographical account of Florence
    Hackett, short story writer. Most of the article deals
    with critical reaction to her only novel, <u>With Benefit of</u>
    <u>Clergy</u>, published in 1924 on her 40th birthday.

Elizabeth Hamilton (1906-   )

215   Hamilton, Elizabeth. <u>An Irish Childhood</u>. Illustrated by
Norah McGuiness. London: Chatto and Windus, 1963. 212pp. il.

    Recollections of seven years in Ireland by a member of
    the Ascendancy class, when the author was between four
    and eleven years of age. Offers somewhat romanticized
    glimpses of the activities and lifestyle of the class and
    period in County Wicklow around the turn of the century.

Dorothea Herbert (1770-1789)

216   Herbert, Dorothea. _Retrospections of Dorothea Herbert,_
_1770-1789_. London: Gerald Howe, 1929. 215pp. il.

These recollections by the daughter of a country
clergyman, the Rev. Nicholas Herbert of Carrick-on-Suir
and his wife, a child of the first Lord Desart, vividly
portrays the social background and manners of the day in
rural Ireland.
(Review: _Dublin Mag_ New Ser. 4 (Oct.-Dec.1929): 56-57.)
(Review: _Ir Book Lov_ 17 (Nov.-Dec. 1929): 140.)

Emily Hickey (1845-1924)

217   Dinnis, Enid. _Emily Hickey: Poet, Essayist - Pilgrim. A_
Memoir. London: Harding & Mole, Ltd., 1927. 127pp. portr.

A brief eulogistic tribute to the minor poet Emily Hickey
daughter of a Protestant rector precedes a selection from
her verse. Recounts her entry into London literary life
with the success of some early poems, her championship of
Browning, and her co-founding with Dr. Furnival of the
Browning Society. In 1901, converted to Catholicism, her
subsequent literary efforts were of a religious nature.
(Review: _Ir Mon_ 55 (1927): 559.)

218   Russell, Matthew. "Poets I Have Known: Emily Hickey."
Ir Mon 31 (1903): 192-202.

Tribute with excerpts from her correpondence with Robert
Browning and her own verses.

Emily Hughes

219   MacManus, Francis. "Tribute to Emily Hughes." _Ir Mon_
(1944): 409-411.

The author pays tribute to the style of the essayist
Emily Hughes commenting on her freshness, humor, tart
phrasing, feminine wit and apt observation.

Mary Ann Hutton (1862-1953)

220   "Irish Literary Society." _Ir Book Lov_ 2 (Apr. 1911):
147-148.

News item on a lecture by Mrs. Hutton on "Irish Mediaeval
Translations from the Classics" delivered to the society
on February 18, 1911. She published an English verse
rendition of the "Tain" in 1907.

221   O H[egarty] P.S. "Obituary: Mrs. Mary Ann Hutton."
Dublin Mag New Ser. XXVIII (4) (Oct.-Nov. 1953): 45.

    Note on death at age 91 of a "scholar, a patriotic Irish
    woman" and author of an English verse rendition of the
    Tain in 1907.

Esther Johnson (1681-1728)

222   le Brocquy, Sybil (Ed.) Stella's Birth-days. Poems by
Jonathan Swift. Dublin: Dolmen Editions, 1967. 40pp. portr.
refs.

    Includes a brief biographical note on the life of
    "Stella," Esther Johnson - characterized by Swift as his
    "truest," most virtuous and valuable friend" - poems he
    wrote for her, a poem by Stella to Dr. Swift for his
    birthday, and her poem on "Jealousy" - regarded as
    autobiographical and related to her rival for Swift's
    affection, Esther Van Homrigh.
  (Review: Dublin Mag 6 (3,4) (Aut. Winter 1967): 81-84.)

223   le Brocquy, Sybil. Swift's Most Valuable Friend.
Dublin: The Dolmen Press, 1968. 128pp. refs.

    Less a biography than a series of speculations based on
    Swift's writings and secondary sources regarding the
    relationship of Jonathan Swift and Esther Johnson, the
    "Stella" of Swift's Journals. Le Brocquy reviews the
    evidence regarding Stella's illegitimacy and apparently
    accepts this as conclusive; considers the question of why
    Swift and Stella never married and accepts that the boy
    for whom Stella made some provision in her will was the
    illegitimate offspring of Swift and Esther Van Homrigh
    (Vanessa). Presents brief outline of the known facts of
    Stella's life and includes excerpts from Swift's account
    of her, written after her death.
  (Review: Scriblerian 1 (2) (Spring 1969): 26.)

224   C.M.P.G.N.S.T.N.S. "New and Curious Anecdotes of the
Late Dean Swift and His Favorite Stella." Gent Mag 27 (Nov.
1757): 487-491.

    Asserts that Stella was the illegitimate daughter of Sir
    William Temple and his housekeeper, Esther Johnson. Being
    thus related to him, Swift could not live with her as her
    husband although they had married before he knew of her
    parentage. The exact relationship of Swift to Temple not
    specified but he is apparently considered to be Temple's
    son.

225   Davis, Herbert. Stella: A Gentlewoman of the Eighteenth
Century. New York: The MacMillan Co., 1942. 103pp.

A series of lectures discussing Swift's attitude to women
and his description of the gentlewoman of his day based
mainly on his Journal to Stella and other writings.
Swift's use of satire, comedy and sentiment in this
portrayal analyzed.

226   Delany, Patrick. Observations Upon Lord Orrery's
Remarks on the Life and Writings of Jonathan Swift,
containing several anecdotes relating to the character and
conduct of that great Genius, and the most deservedly
celebrated Stella. London: Reeve, 1754. 310pp.

In a series of letters to Orrery collected here Delany
agrees with Lord Orrery that Swift and Stella were
married but disagrees with the latter's explanation as to
why the marriage was concealed.

227   Ehrenpresis, Irwin. "Patterm of Swift's Women." PMLA 70
(Sept. 1955): 706-716. refs.

Asserts that Swift's attitude to women originated in the
inadequacy of his own lonely, fatherless childhood.
Ehrenpresis sees in Swift's parental relationships with
Jane Waring (Varina), Esther Johnson (Stella) and Esther
Van Homrigh (Vanessa) - all first born, fatherless girls,
in bad health and all much younger than Swift - a
compensatory pattern linked to his own posthumous birth,
his early lack of an immediate family and his constant
struggle against illness.

228   Ehrenpresis, Irwin. "Swift and Stella." Times Lit Supp
(Jan. 8, 1954): 25.

Brief note on financial trasactions of Swift and Esther
Johnson (Stella) involving collusive and coincidental
property transfers, particularly the purchase, sale and
resale of Talbot's Castle, Trim, County Meath.

229   Gold, Maxwell B. Swift's Marriage to Stella, Together
With Unprinted and Misprinted Letters. New York: Russell and
Russell, 1937. 189pp. bibl.

Reviews the evidence offered by various biographers both
for and against the alleged marriage of Swift and Stella.
Introduces what are claimed to be new pieces of evidence,
mainly the transcripts of Mrs. Whiteway's letters to
Orrery. Gold advances the argument that Swift and Stella
were married about 1716 and that Swift offered to
acknowledge the matter publicly, however a pathological
unfitness for the married state prevented Swift from
living with Stella as her husband.

230   Gregory, Alyce. "Stella, Vanessa and Swift." 19th Cent
113 (June 1933): 755-764.

Speculative article, interspersed with brief extracts
from his correspondence, on the relationship of Swift
with two women in his life - Vanessa Van Homrigh and
Esther Johnson.

231   Hardy, Evelyn. The Conjured Spirit Swift: A Study of
the Relationship of Swift, Stella and Vanessa. London:
Hogarth Press, 1949. 266pp. il. portrs. bibl.

A well researched and fascinating study based on Swift's
entire opus and his correspondence strives at a
sympathetic presentation and understanding based on the
available evidence of the relationships of Swift and the
two women who loved him: Esther Johnson (Stella) and
Esther Van Homrigh (Vanessa). Hardy, unlike other
biographers of Swift strives to be non-partisan rather
than "pro" either Stella or Vanessa. Portraits of both
women and Swift are included.

232   Hearsey, Marguerite. "New Light on the Evidence for
Swift's Marriage." PMLA 42 (1927): 157-161. refs.

The new evidence concerns the date when Bishop Berkeley
went abroad which, it is asserted, was the Fall of 1716
(not 1715 as previously accepted). Thus it is
theoretically possible that he had been informed of
Swift's marriage that year by Bishop Clogher who
supposedly performed the ceremony.

233   Jackson, Robert Wyse. "Stella: Her Relationship With
Jonathan Swift." In North Munster Studies. Essays in
Commemoration of Monsignor Michael Maloney. Ed. by Etienne
Rynne, pp. 375-394. Limerick: The Thomond Archaelogical
Society, 1967. il. maps. portrs.

More speculation about whether or not Swift and Stella
were ever married. Agrees substantially with Maxwell
Gold's conclusions (Swift's Marriage to Stella, 1937
#229).

234   Lane-Poole, Stanley. "The Alleged Marriage of Swift and
Stella." Fortn R 93 (87) (Feb. 1910): 319-332.

Comments on the "new" evidence offered by Dr. Bernard in
The Bell edition of The Prose Works of Jonathan Swift
e.g. a letter from Dr. Evans, Bishop of Meath to
Archbishop Wake in 1723 which mentions the marriage of
Jonathan Swift and Estella Johnson. Lane-Poole reviews
all the other "evidence" pro and con and concludes that
no such marriage ever took place.

235   Lawlor, H.J. "The Graces of Swift and Stella." Eng Hist
R 33 (1918): 89-93. refs.

Discusses the various theories as to the exact burial
place of Jonathan Swift and Estella Johnson (Stella) in
light of the documentary evidence in the register of St.
Patrick's Cathedral, Dublin and a letter written by Dr.
Houston in whose presence Swift's coffin was exhumed in
1835. Concludes that the legend that Swift was buried in
Stella's coffin has no foundation.

236   Leslie, A. Von W. Was Swift Married to Stella? A
Discussion. Halle: M.Neimeyer, 1895. 55pp. refs. [Reprinted
for the author from the September issue of the Anglia.]

A review of the evidence pro and con on the subject of
Jonathan Swift's alleged marriage to Esther Johnson,
concludes that no such marriage ever occured.

237   Tyne, James L. "Swift and Stella: The Love Poems." Tenn
Stud Lit 19 (1974): 35-47. refs.

An analysis of the eleven poems written by Swift to
Esther Johnson, his "Stella" and his special relationship
with her.

238   Wilde, Jane Francesca [Lady]. Notes on Men, Women and
Books. First Series. London: Ward and Downey, 1891. 352pp.

Has a chapter on "Stella and Vanessa" (pp. 85-111)
(Esther Johnson and Esther Van Homrigh) and their
relationship with Jonathan Swift and a chapter on Lady
Blessington (pp. 127-170).

239   Woods, Margaret. "Swift, Stella and Vanessa." 19th Cent
& After LXXIV (July-Dec. 1913): 1230-1247.

A discussion of the relationship of Swift and Stella and
of Swift and Vanessa. Argues against the idea that Swift
married Stella in 1716 because he did not break with
Vanessa until 1722. Woods argues further that while Swift
only loved Stella he did have more of an emotional
entanglement with Vanessa than is presented in "Cadenus
and Vanessa."

Jennifer Johnston (1930-   )

240   Campbell, Stella. "Life Style: Jennifer Johnston."
Image 4 (3) (Mar. 1979): 7-9. portr.

Interview.

241   "Q. & A. with Jennifer Johnston." Ir Lit Supp 3 (2)
(Fall 1984): 25-27. portr.

Interview with the author in Montreal during her
September 1983 visit to Canada and the United States
where she comments on her writing, World War I, Northern
Ireland and the role of the writer in society.

Nora Barnacle Joyce (1886-1951)

242   Meyers, Jeffrey. Married to Genius. New York: Barnes
and Noble, 1977. 214pp. bibl.

A biographical work which claims to consider "relation
between emotional and artistic commitment in the
marriages of nine modern writers" (Introduction) has
chapters on Shaw and Joyce. Meyers concludes that Joyce's
marriage to Nora Barnacle complemented and completed him
and represented the marriage of mind and body, of art and
life. Shaw's marriage is judged to have stabilized his
emotional behavior and disciplined his intellectual
energy.

243   O Laoi, Padraic. Nora Barnacle Joyce. Galway: Kennys,
1982. 115pp. il. fronts.

First full length biography of the Galway born, Nora
Barnacle, whom Joyce met in 1904 and who was his devoted
partner during the next thirty-six years. Details on her
family background, elementary education, employment and
romantic involvement prior to meeting Joyce, their
elopment and the subsequent development of their
relationship during the years of struggle and the later
ones of success and fame.

244   Power, Arthur. "On the Presentation of Ulyssess to
Nora." Dublin Mag 9 (Summer 1972): 10-13. il.

Brief comment on Nora's reaction to receiving the first
printed copy of "Ulysses" from her husband, James Joyce
on February 2nd, 1922. Power, who was present on this
occasion records his own initial response to this work -
which possibly colors his perception of Nora's
indifference to this masterpiece at that time.

245   Reynolds, M.T. "Joyce and Nora: the Indispensable
Counter-Sign." Sewanee R 72 (Jan. 1964): 29-64. refs.

A discussion of the correspondence between James Joyce
and his wife Nora during the periods when they were
briefly separated in 1909 - she remaining in Trieste
while he visited Dublin. Thirty-five of the letters
written by Joyce have survived - none of Nora's have.

Julia Kavanagh (1824-1877)

246   C.J. [i.e.James Coleman?] "Julia Kavanagh, Biographer,
Writer and Novelist." <u>Waterf Arch Soc J</u> X (1907): 158.

Very brief biographical note on Julia Kavanagh born in
Thurles, the only daughter of Dr. Morgan Kavanagh. She
spent most of her life abroad and died at Nice in 1877.
Author of <u>Women of Christianity</u>, <u>French Women of the 18th
Century</u>, <u>A Winter in Two Sicilies</u> and several novels.

Rose Kavanagh (1860?-1891)

247   O [Kennedy], R [ichard]. (Rev.) "Uncle Remus." <u>Ir Mon</u>
XIX (July 1891): 363-366.

Tribute to Rose Kavanagh after her death by a personal
friend. 'Uncle Remus' was the name she used in her
children's corner in the <u>Irish Fireside</u>, later
incorporated into the <u>Weekly Freeman</u>.

248   Russell, Matthew. Rev. (S.J.) <u>Rose Kavanagh and Her
Verses</u>. Dublin: M.H.Gill & Son, Ltd., 1909. 70pp.

Effusive tribute to the minor poet, Rose Kavanagh
includes a brief biographical sketch, excerpts from some
contemporary reviews of her poetry and elegies by her
friends including Mrs. Tynan Hinkson upon her death.
(Review: <u>Ir Mon</u> 37 (1909): 475-476.)

249   Russell, Matthew. (Rev.) "Rose Kavanagh: Some Scraps
from Her Life and Letters." <u>Ir Mon</u> XIX (Oct.-Nov. 1891):
512-521; 601-607.

Biographical sketch of Rose Kavanagh born in Tyrone in
1860 who died after prolonged illness in 1890. Her
contributions to Irish literature as essayist, short-
story writer and editor of the children's section of a
local newspaper noted. Includes excerpts from her letters
to Russell, then editor of <u>The Irish Monthly</u> and brief
excerpts from her friends' comments on her character.

Mary Anne Kelly (c1826-1910)

250   Dillon, P.J. "Eva of the Nation." <u>Capu An</u> (1933):
261-266. portrs.

Brief biographical sketch of the minor poet, Mary Anne
Kelly (Eva) who with Lady Wilde (Speranza) and Ellen Mary
Downing (Mary) contributed patriotic verses to the
<u>Nation</u>. Includes her reminiscences of various young
Irelanders and her part in the successful escape attempt
to America of John Blake Dillon.

251   "Irish Literary Celebrities 5: Mary Izod O'Doherty."
Nation (Dec. 8, 1888): 3.

Treats of the poetry Kelly contributed to The Nation
1846-1848.

252   McCarthy, Justin. "'Eva of the Nation': Biographical
Sketch." In Poems by Eva of the Nation [pseud for Kelly],
pp.xi-xxi. Dublin: Gill, 1909.

LaTouche Family

253   John Ruskin and Rose LaTouche; Her Unpublished Diaries
of 1861 and 1867. Introduced and edited by Van Akin Burd.
Oxford: Clarendon Press, 1979. 192pp. plates. front. portrs.

Includes the transcript of the two surviving fragments of
the diaries of Rose LaTouche, the young Irish girl whom
John Ruskin had met in 1858 when she was yet a child and
whom he later came to love and hoped to marry. She died
in 1875. The long introduction by Burd places the diaries
and the personages involved in context and highlights the
tragic events culminating in Rose's early death.
(Review: Ir U R 11 (1) (Sept. 1981): 98-99.)

254   The Letters of a Noble Woman (Mrs. LaTouche of
Harristown), Ed. by Margaret Ferrier Young. London: George
Allen and Sons, 1908. 252pp. plates. portrs.

Brief memoir of the English born, Maria (Polly) (Desart)
Price daughter of Catherine, Countess of Desart and her
second husband, Lieutenant Rose Lambert Price who married
Mr. John LaTouche. Cultivated, Mrs. LaTouche had little
in common with her hard-riding husband and his circle.
She met Ruskin in 1858 and they became friends - later he
bacame involved with her daughter, Rose. Mrs. LaTouche
founded the Kilcullen Dorcas Society for charitable work
and helped the victims of the Famine. Includes her
correspondence with Ruskin and some of his to her and
other non-family letters (mostly to intimate friends on
ordinary, everyday events).

255   Young, M.F. "The LaTouche Family of Harristown, County
Kildare." J Co Kild Arch Soc 7 (1912-1914): 33-40. il.

Traces the genealogy of the Irish branch of this Huguenot
family who settled in Ireland after helping William of
Orange gain the British throne.

Mary Lavin (1912-   )

256   Bowen, Zack. Mary Lavin. Lewisberg: Bucknell University
Press, 1975. 77pp. bibl.

Mainly a thematic and stylistic analysis but contains
some biographical information based on interviews with
the author and her husband.
(Review: Choice 12 (Nov. 1975): 1160.)

257   Caswell, Robert W. "Mary Lavin: Breaking a Pathway."
Dublin Mag 6 (2) (1967): 32-44. refs.

Brief discussion of her work and her literary connection
with Seamus O'Sullivan, editor of The Dublin Magazine
(later her husband) and Lord Dunsany.

258   Dunleavy, T.E. "The Making of Mary Lavin's A Memory."
Eire Ire 12 (3) (1977): 90-99. refs.

A discussion of Mary Lavin's method of creating a work of
fiction based on discussion with the author and a close
examination of her manuscripts at various stages in their
composition.

259   Harmon, Maurice. "The Landscape of Mary Lavin." Ire
Welcomes 18 (6) (1970): 34-57. portr.

Biographical notes on the novelist Mary Lavin and comment
on her use of the rural landscape of Bective, County
Meath in her work.

260   Kelly, A.A. Mary Lavin: A Study of Her Short Stories.
New York: Barnes and Noble, 1980. 200pp. bibl. refs.

Includes a brief biographical introduction.
(Review: Ir U R 11 (2) (Autumn 1981): 240.

261   "Mary Lavin." Wil Lib Bull 20 (3) (Nov. 1945): 188.
portr.

Brief biographical sketch.

262   Murphy, Catherine. "Mary Lavin: An Interview." Ir U R 9
(2) (Autumn 1979): 207-224.

Comments on her approach to writing and on the short
story as an art form.

263   Peterson, Richard F. Mary Lavin Boston: Twayne Pubs.,
1978. 171pp. portrs. bibl. [Twayne's English Author's Series]

This predominantly literary study includes in chapter one
a biographical account of the novelist born in 1912 in
Massachusetts (U.S.A.) who came to Ireland in 1921.
Educated in Dublin she taught there for a period. Her
literary career began after she had raised her children
and was interrupted for several years by her husband's

untimely death. She remarried in 1969. Peterson examines
her fiction chronologically and sees Vera Traske as her
most autobiographical character.
(Review: Choice 15 (Feb. 1979): 1666.)

264   Weeks, Edward. "The Peripatetic Reviewer." (The
Atlantic Bookshelf) Atlan Mon (Aug. 1959): 78-79. portr.

   Biographical and critical notes on Mary Lavin.

265   "Writer at Work: An Interview With Mary Lavin." St.
Steph Stu Pub Series 2. No. 12 (1967): 19-22. portr.

   The American/Irish author comments on how she began to
   write, her choice of the short story format, getting
   published, autobiographical elements in her fiction and
   her identification with world literature.

Emily Lawless (1845-1913)

266   Brewer, Betty Webb. "She Was Part of It: Emily Lawless
(1845-1913)." Eire Ire 18 (4) (1983): 119-131. refs.

   An examination of the causes of the relative neglect
   accorded to Emily Lawless, identifies as one contributing
   factor the general low esteem in which her primary genre,
   the novel, was held by students of the Irish Renaissance.
   Also, her Unionist sympathies set her apart from what was
   considered the "real" Ireland. Includes a critical
   evaluation of her fiction, historical novels and other
   prose works.

267   Fenton, Seamus. The Honorable Emily Lawless: An
Inspirational Poetess and Novelist. (Lecture delivered
November 1944 to the Women's Social and Progressive League,
Dublin.) n.d. 9pp.

   Biographical details interspersed with excerpts from her
   prose and poetry and explication of contextual allusions.

268   "Irish Literary Society." Ir Book Lov 7 (Feb./Mar.
1916): 129-130.

   News item on an evening honoring the poet, Emily Lawless,
   held by the Irish Literary Society.

269   Lawless, Emily. The Poems of Emily Lawless. Edited with
an Introduction by Padriac Fallon. Dublin: Dolmen Press,
1965. 52pp.

   The introduction to this selection from three books of
   her poems has a brief biographical account of the poet.

270   "Obituary (of the Honorable Emily Lawless.)" Ir Book
Lov 5 (Dec. 1913): 84-85.

Includes a brief biographical sketch and a note on her
achievement as novelist, poet and biographer.

271   Sichel, Edith. "Emily Lawless." 19th Cent & After 76
(July 1914): 80-100.

Tribute to Emily Lawless following her death in October
1913. Described as "an Irishwoman first and all the rest
afterwards" - the rest being: novelist, historian,
naturalist, science-lover, thinker. A brief biographical
sketch describes her ancestry, her childhood in the West
of Ireland on her father's estate, her love of reading
and horsemanship, her literary career and her many
friends and admirers among the intellectuals and
political figures of her period, her political views and
opinion on Women's Suffrage.

Mary Leadbeater (1758-1826)

272   "Ballitore in 'XCVIII. From the Unpublished Memoirs of
the Late Mary Leadbeater." Citizen 2 (1840): 418-430.

Includes a biographical sketch (pp.418-419). Refers
readers to her letters to George Crabbe (Life and Works
of Crabbe, vol.1, pp.228-234) for insight into her
personality.

273   Gandy, Clara I. "The Condition and Character of the
Irish Peasantry as Seen in the Annals and Cottage Dialogues
of Mary Leadbeater." Women & Lit 3 (Spring 1975): 28-38.
refs.

Brief biographical background on Mary Leadbeater and her
sympathetic concern and endeavor on behalf of the Irish
peasantry in the first decades of the 19th century.
Description of the politcial and economic background
against which she wrote her Annals of Ballitore and
Cottage Dialogues Among the Irish Peasantry in which, it
is claimed, she presented accurate and convincing
sketches of the peasantry of her day.

274   Goodbody, Olive C. "Letters of Mary and Sarah
Shackleton, 1767 to 1775." J Co Kild Arch Soc 14 (4) (1969):
415-439.

A selection of 19 letters out of 55 written at this
period mostly by Mary Shackleton, later Leadbeater and
her sister, Sarah when they were children. Note and
introduction by Goodbody who finds the main interest of
the letters, "the picture given of an apparently
uninhibited childhood."

275   <u>The Leadbeater Papers. The Annals of Ballitore by Mary</u>
<u>Leadbeater with a memoir of the author; letters from Edmund</u>
<u>Burke heretofore unpublished; and the correspondence of Mrs.</u>
<u>Richard Trench and Rev. George Crabbe with Mary Leadbeater</u>.
London: Bell and Daldy, 1862. 2 vols.

> Includes a memoir of Mary Shackleton Leadbeater, her
> journals, <u>The Annals of Ballitore</u>, and a portion of her
> extensive correspondence.
> (Review: <u>Dublin U Mag</u> 60 (Aug. 1862): 236-246.)

276   Young, Margaret Ferrier. "Ballitore and its
Institutions." <u>J Co Kild Arch Soc</u> 8 (1916): 167-179. portr.

> Correspondence between the author, Mary Leadbeater and
> her neighbors, the Keatinges of Narraghmore after these
> had moved from Kildare during the period 1811-1813.
> Includes contextual notes by Young.

Margaret Leeson (Peg Plunket (? - 1797)

277   Leeson, Margaret. <u>Memoirs. Written by Herself</u>. Dublin:
[Priv. Printing] 1795. 2 vols.

> Autobiography of the courtesan Peg Leeson details her
> seduction, affairs and lifestyle.

278   Leeson, Francis. "Peg Plunket, Lady of Pleasure." <u>Ir</u>
<u>Ancest</u> 3 (1) (1971): 1-4.

> An undocumented account, based apparently on her own
> memoirs of the life of the courtesan, Peg Plunket born
> around the period 1727-1736. Seduced at an early age an
> rejected by both her lover and her family, she became the
> mistress of a wealthy wine merchant with aristocratic
> connections. Abandoned by him she had a series of lovers
> then set up a professional establishment with a female
> partner. Eventually deciding to "reform" she ran out of
> money and was jailed for debt; released she wrote her
> memoirs to improve her financial situation.

Ladies of Llangollen
Eleanor Butler (1739-1829)
Sarah Ponsonby (1755-1831)

279   Armytage, Mrs. "Fragmentary Recollections of Lady
Eleanor Butler and Miss Ponsonby, The Ladies of Llangollen
With extracts from their diary and a series of letters
addressed to them from 1760 to 1820 by men and women of
note." <u>Belgra</u> 72 (June 1890): 136-155; (July 1890): 248-264.

> Comment on and excerpts from the diary of 1788-1790 kept
> by Lady Eleanor Butler after her withdrawal to Plas
> Newydd, Wales with her companion, Miss Ponsonby with some

biographical information on the 'Ladies' and some
excerpts from observations by some of their distinguished
visitors.

280   Bell, Eva Mary. The Hamwood Papers of the Ladies of
Llangollen and Caroline Hamilton. London: MacMillan and Co.,
1930. 417pp. front. portrs.

Includes excerpts from the existing journals of Lady
Eleanor Butler, the journal of Caroline Hamilton, the
diary of Lucy Goddard, a friend of Sarah Ponsonby an
Elizabeth Fownes, with portions of their correspondence.
Edited with biographical information on the "Ladies",
Eleanor Butler and Sarah Ponsonby by Eva Bell, formerly
Hamilton.

281   Gordon, Mary. Chase of the Wild Goose. The Story of
Lady Eleanor Butler and Miss Sarah Ponsonby Known as the
Ladies of Llangollen. London: Hogarth Press, 1936. 279pp.
plates. portrs.

282   Gore, John. "The Ladies of Llangollen." Lond Merc R XVI
(91) (1927): 19-23.

Author argues that the "Ladies of Llangollen," e.g. Lady
Eleanor Butler and Miss Sarah Ponsonby were, in fact, not
the unconventional pioneers of women's enfranchisement as
has been claimed, but were slavish observers of the
polite conventions of their day. His argument is based on
a letter written by these ladies to his great-great-
grandmother (quoted).

283   Hicklin, John. The "Ladies of Llangollen" As Sketched
By Many Hands With Notices of Other Objects of Interest In
"That Sweetest of Vales." Chester: Thomas Catherall. [n.d.]
66pp.

An account of the singular friendship of Lady Eleanor
Butler and Miss Ponsonby whose unusual mode of life
induced many literary figures to visit them. Includes
excerpts from the correpondence of many of these with
their impressions and their account of the history and
situation of the two recluses. Details of the auction of
their house and its contents.

284   Jones, Sara Pugh. "Plas Newydd and the Ladies of
Llangollen." Butler Soc J 1 (7) (1977): 530-537. portrs.

285   Mavor, Elizabeth. The Ladies of Llangollen: A Study in
Romantic Friendship. London: M. Joseph, [1971]. 238pp. il.
portrs. refs.

The definitive biography of Lady Eleanor Butler and Sarah
Ponsonby based on their journals and voluminous

correspondence to and from the "Ladies." Their daily life
together in Wales minutely described – their
pecuniary difficulties, their fame and their numerous
distinguished visitors. Mavor places her subjects in the
context of their age, one in which a romantic interest in
a return to nature was prevalent and in which "romantic
friendship" among literary women was common.
(Review: Books & Bookm 19 (July 1974): 112.)
(Review: New Statesm 81 (Feb.12, 1971): 215-216.)
(Review: Economist 238 (Feb. 13, 1971): 53-54.)

286   Yorke, (John) General. Plas Newydd: As It Was And As It
Is. With a catalogue of its contents. Llangollen [Wales]:
H.Jones, 1888. 4pp. il. portr.

Brief gossipy account of the "Ladies" after their arrival
in Llangollen. Describes their cottage, their dress,
their formal and informal requirements of visitors, the
statesmen and nobles who came, decorations worn by them,
the grounds of the cottage and a poem written for them by
W.Wordsworth. Contains a full description of the contents
of their cottage.

Nell McCafferty

287   Kerrigan, G. "The Essential Nell." Magill Mag 8 (4)
(Dec. 1984): 21-22. portr.

Note on varied career of journalist Nell McCafferty
formally with the Irish Times who now free lances upon
publication of a collection of her work The Best of Nell.

Florence Mary McDowell

288   McDowell, Florence Mary. Other Days Around Me. Belfast:
Blackstaff Press, 1972. [c.1966] 172pp. il.

The author recaptures her memoirs of her Victorian Ulster
childhood on a County Antrim farm before the turn of tbe
century. One of five children of a North Derry farmer and
his wife, daughter of the owner of the local linen mill,
orphaned young, she was reared by an aunt and became a
National school teacher.

Alice Milligan (1866-1953)

289   MacDonagh, Thomas. "The Best Living Irish Poet." Ir R 4
(Sept.-Nov. 1914): 287-293.

Brief tribute to the poet, novelist and dramatist, Alice
Milligan "Ulster protestant, Gaelic leaguer,
Fenian,friend of all Ireland..." by a personal friend
with excerpts from her Nationalist verse.

290   Milligan, Alice. Poems. Selected and Edited with an
Introduction by Henry Mangan. Dublin: Gill, 1954. 195pp.
front.

    Introduction includes a biographical account of the poet
    with details on her education, her work for the Gaelic
    League, her joint editorship, with Anna Johnston, of The
    Northern Patriot and later The Shan Van Vocht and her
    patriotic verse. Includes excerpts from reviews of her
    work and a note on the arrangement of the poems.

291   Nic Shuibhne, Maire. "Women Pioneers." Wolfe Tone An
(1944-45): 21-23.

    Note on founding of and contributions to The Shan Van
    Vocht by Eithne Carbery (Anna Johnston) and Alice
    Milligan with excerpt from a poem by the former.

292   "Obituaries. Alice Milligan." Ir Book Lov 32 (1952-
1957): 63-64.

    Tribute to the poetess, Alice Milligan. Information on
    her parents, education and her activities as an organizer
    for the Gaelic League and founder with her friend Anna
    Johnston (Eithne Carbery) of the journal The Shan Van
    Vocht which was influential in the early Republican
    movement and which published among other things, their
    poetry.

293   O H[egarty.], P.S. "Obituary: Alice L. Milligan."
Dublin Mag New Series 28 (4) (Oct.-Dec. 1953): 45.

    Her contribution to the Irish Revival including the
    foundation and editorship of the monthly national journal
    The Shan Van Vocht of Belfast, her work for the Gaelic
    League and her achievement as prose-writer, dramatist and
    primarily poet, briefly noted.

                    Susan L. Mitchell (1866-1926)

294   "Cupid and Psyche." [Cartoon by Grace Gifford of George
Moore and Susan L. Mitchell.] Ir R 4 (Sept.-Nov. 1914):
facing 281.

295   Kain, Richard M. Susan Mitchell. Lewisberg: Bucknell
University Press, 1972. 103pp. bibl.

    Mainly a literary analysis of the work of the poet,
    journalist and satirist Susan Mitchell described as "an
    amused observer and minor participant in the Irish
    Literary Revival." In addition to her poetic achievement
    she also was an editorial assistant to George William
    Russell [A.E.] in his work on the Irish Homestead and the
    Irish Statesman and she contributed almost 200 items to

these publications including book and drama reviews,
topical essays, etc. Includes a brief biographical and
character sketch.
(Review: Ir Bookm 2 (2) (1976): 314-315.)

Lady Morgan (Sydney Owenson) (1776-1859)

296   Atkinson, Colin B. and Jo Atkinson. "Sydney Owenson,
Lady Morgan: Irish Patriot and First Professional Woman
Writer." Eire Ire 15 (2) (1980): 60-90. refs.

An analysis of the career of Sydney Owenson, Lady Morgan
seen as the epitome of the woman writer of the early 19th
century who at once helped to articulate and raise the
consciousness of both men and women on the Woman question
and at the same time was able to profit professionally
from the new opportunities available to achieve fame and
financial independence through her work.

297   B[utler], [H.] "Lady Morgan in Kilkenny." Butler Soc J
1 (7) (1977): 537-564.

Excerpts from Memoirs.

298   Corrigan, Beatrice. "Three Englishwoman in Italy."
Queen Q 79 (1972): 147-158. refs.

The title is a misnomer: the three women in question are
Lady Mary Montagu (English), Mrs. Hester Lynch T. Piozzi
(Welsh) and Lady Morgan (Irish). All visited Italy and
published their observations of Italian life and customs.
Lady Morgan's was the first commissioned travel account
of that country and Corrigan describes her as "the ideal
recorder of a society in transition" because of her
personality and background.

299   Davies, William W. "Lady Morgan and Lisburn." Edited by
Francis Joseph Bigger. With note by John Salmon. Ulster J
Archae Ser. 2 II (July 1896): 265-267; III (Oct. 1896): 61.
portr.

Asserts that Lady Morgan was older than her husband at
the time of their marriage and that they were not married
in church.

300   Fitzpatrick, William John. The Friends, Foes and
Adventures of Lady Morgan. Dublin: W.B. Kelly, 1859. 144pp.

A reprint of the biography first published in the Irish
Quarterly Review of July 1859 and later expanded. (See
#301.)

301   [Fitzpatrick, William John] "Lady Morgan." Ir Q R 9
(July 1859): 380-512. bibl. refs. [Reprinted as The Friends,
Foes and Adventures of Lady Morgan.]

302   Fitzpatrick, William John. (J.P.) Lady Morgan: Her
Career, Literary and Personal, With a Glimpse of Her Friends,
and a Word to her Calminators. London: Charles J. Skeet,
1860. 308pp. refs.

    An expanded version of the same author's previous
    biography of Lady Morgan: Friends, Foes and Adventures of
    Lady Morgan (See #300.) details her early career, the
    career of her actor/father, her early writing, critical
    reception of her work, the controversy which later came
    to surround this because of the attacks of the well known
    Tory critic, Croker, her lionization by fashionable, Whig
    elements in British society, her marriage, her travels.
    More a social than a literary biography written from a
    very partisan viewpoint.
  (Review: Dublin U Mag 56 (Sept. 1860): 277-287.)
  (Review: Ir Mon 16 (1888): 629.)
  (Review: Colburn 119 (1860): 354-357.)

303   Flanagan, Thomas. "Sentimental Patriotism: The Wild
Irish Girl." In his The Irish Novelists, pp.109-124. New
York: Columbia University Press, 1959):

    Mainly literary analysis but includes a brief
    biographical sketch of the novelist, Sydney Owenson, Lady
    Morgan whose most successful "fiction" according to
    Flanagan was the legend of herself, Sydney Owenson, "The
    Wild Irish Girl" from Connaught. Includes an evaluation
    of her literary and political significance.
  (Review: Cath Hist R 46 (1961): 480.)
  (Review: Studies 50 (1961): 99-103.

304   "Gallery of Literary Characters No. LX - Lady Morgan."
Fraser 11 (65) (May 1835): 529. portr.

    Unflattering comment on Lady Morgan.

305   Godwin, (George). "Chairs of Some Celebrities." Ir
Build 20 (456) (Dec. 15, 1878): 358.

    Note on chairs belonging to Lady Morgan and other
    celebrities which came into the possession of Mrs. S.C.
    Hall.

306   "Gossip." Ir Book Lov 2 (May 1911): 157-158.

    Note that the late Sir Charles Dilke, owner of The
    Athenaeum has bequeathed to the Royal Irish Academy
    various portraits of Lady Morgan and other objects of her
    property. Her biographer, Hepworth Dixon, was editor of
    The Anthenaeum.

307   Hall, J.C., F.S.A. and Mrs. S.C. Hall. "Memories of the Authors of the Age. Sydney, Lady Morgan." Ecl Mag 2 (Oct. 1865): 424-431.

Mainly a biographical sketch based on Lady Morgan's published Memoirs but includes some personal reminiscences.

308   "Lady Morgan: A Biographical Article Dealing With Her Books." Ir Q R 9 (July 1859): 380-512. refs.

Includes excerpts from her autobiography.

309   Lambe, Athill (M.D.) "O'Connell, Lady Morgan, Zozimus."Ir Bookm 1 (3) (Oct. 1946): 63-64.

Author recalls as a student hearing about Lady Morgan, a contemporary of Daniel O'Connell's, described as an authoress, a great conversationalist and one of Dublin's "characters."

310   [MacDonagh, Michael.] "Lexture on Lady Morgan to the Irish Literary Society on May 9th, 1925." Ir Book Lov 15 (July 1925): 39.

A news item on the paper presented by The Times journalist Michael MacDonagh on "Lady Morgan Makin' Tay," in which he commented on the salon of Lady Morgan in Kildare Street, her work, her travels and literary skirmishes with John Wilson Croker and other reviewers. The author of the contemporary ballad from which his title is derived, has not been identified.

311   MacDonagh, Michael. "The Wild Irish Girl." Ir Eccl Rec 5th Ser. 38 (Sept. 1926): 272-285.

Brief biographical sketch of the author, Lady Morgan based partly on reminiscences and partly on the previously published biography by W.J. Fitzpatrick, with some comment on her literary achievement - the first of the "national novelists" of Ireland.

312   Moraud, Marcel Ian. Lady Morgan, 1775-1859, une Irlandaise Liberale en France sous la Restauration; sa vie et ses Ecrits de 1775 a 1816, ses Sejours a Paris de 1816 a 1830, le role qu'elle a y Joue, ses Tableaux de la France, Polemiques qu'ils ont Soulevies. Paris: M.Dider, 1954. 204pp. bibl. (Etudes de Literature Etranjere et Comparee [no.] 25.)

313   Morgan, Lady [Sydney Owenson.] "The Life and Writings of Lady Morgan." New Mon Mag 10 (1818): 139-143. portr.

314   Morgan, Sydney (Owenson) Lady. Lady Morgan's Memoirs:
Autobiography, Diaries and Correspondence. 2 vols. 2nd ed.
London: W.H. Allen and Co., 1863. fronts.

    Begun by Lady Morgan herself, the Memoirs were completed
    by Miss Jewsbury and edited by her literary executor, W.
    Hepworth Dixon.. Based largely on copious correspondence
    to and from its subject and her diaries and written in
    the third person.
  (Review: Cornhill Mag 7 (1863): 132-135.)
  (Review: Liv Age 76 (Jan. 17, 1863): 108-117.)
  (Review: Liv Age 76 (Feb. 7, 1863): 262-267.)
  (Review: Westm R 79 (Apr. 1863): 248-265.)

315   Morgan, Sydney (Owenson) Lady. Passages From My
Autobiography London: Richard Bentley, 1859. 339pp. portr.

    Portions of her diary covering the period from August
    1818 to April 1819 and selected correspondence mainly to
    her sister, Lady Clarke; also letters to her husband and
    Caroline Lamb. Mainly comments on her work and its
    reception, gossip about friends and acquaintences, her
    social life in London, and her travels in France and
    Geneva.
  (Review: Brit Q R 29 (1859); 507-531.)
  (Review: Fraser 67 (Feb. 1863): 172-191.)

316   "The Mss in the Wilson Croker Collection." Ir Book Lov
3 (10) (May 1912): 160-164.

    Discussion of Croker's vindicative criticism of Lady
    Morgan's work and the possibility that he was a rejected
    suitor.

317   Paston, George. Little Memoirs of the Nineteenth
Century. London: Grant Richards, 1902. 376pp. portrs.

    Sketches of minor celebrities of the 19th century chosen
    to illustrate the literary and artistic life of the first
    half of the century. Includes a chapter on Lady Morgan
    (pp. 95-155.)

318   "The Queen of Irish Society." All The Year 3rd Ser. 74
(May 5, 1894): 420-426.

    Biographical sketch of Sydney Owenson, Lady Morgan.

319   Redding, Cyrus. "Lady Morgan." New Mon Mag 116 (1859):
206-216.

    Mainly a consideration of her literary achievements but
    with some biographical information. Includes excerpts
    from her correspondence and writings.

320   Sanborn, Kate A. "Lady Morgan." Lippinc 22 (Oct. 1878):
466-474.

Brief, anecdotal biographical sketch with some comment on
her literary works.

321   Stevenson, Lionel. The Wild Irish Girl: The Life of
Sydney Owenson, Lady Morgan (1776-1859). London: Chapman and
Hall, [c.1936.] 330pp. bibl.

A detailed analysis of the social and literary career of
Lady Morgan, described as the first professional woman
author, based on primary and secondary sources, diaries
and correspondence of contemporaries and Lady Morgan's
own autobiographical and other writings. Describes her
parentage, the ups and downs of her actor father's
theatrical career, her education, her work as a
governess, her first literary efforts, her social success
in both Dublin and London after the publication of The
Wild Irish Girl; later publications and their reception,
her marriage, travels to France and Italy, her friends
and acquaintances and her literary reputation.
(Review: Studies 25 (Dec. 1936): 680-681.)

322   "Sydney, Lady Morgan." Liv Age 61 3rd Ser. (June 18,
1859): 759-761.

Obituary notice and effusive tribute.

323   "Sydney Owenson, Lady Morgan." Temp Bar 97 (1893): 341-
362.

Brief biographical sketch.

324   "A Wild Irish Girl." Temp Bar 58 (1880): 204-212.

Brief biographical sketch.

325   Whitfield, J.H. "Mr Eustace and Lady Morgan in Italy."
In Italian Studies. Presented to E.R. Vincent on his
retirement from the Chair of Italian at Cambridge ed. by
Charles Peter Brand, pp. 166-189. Cambridge: W. Heffer and
Sons, Ltd., 1962. il. portrs. refs.

Compares the treatment of Italy by both these Irish
writers. Mr. Eustace, an Irish Catholic clergyman
travelled there in 1802; Lady Morgan, the popular
novelist, in 1819/1820. Whitfield considers that their
concern with religion, politics and literature sets them
apart from other travel writers of the period but he
considers Lady Morgan a writer of much greater brillance
and an observer of much greater acumen than Eustace.

Rosa Mulholland (Lady Gilbert) (1841-1921)

326   [Obituary of Rosa Mulholland, Lady Gilbert.] Ir Book
Lov 13 (Aug.-Sept. 1921): 21-22.

Note on her career and accomplishment as poet, biographer
and primarily novelist. Includes a partial bibliography
of her fiction.

327   O'Neill, George. (S.J.) "The Poetry of Rosa Mulholland,
Lady Gilbert." Ir Mon 49 (Oct. 1921): 397-405.

Discusses the influence of Rosa Mulholland's Catholic
religion and the Irish landscape in her work with some
excerpts from her poems.

Iris Murdoch (1919-   )

328   Barrows, John. "Living Writers: Iris Murdoch." John
O'Londons 4 (4) (May 1961): 498. portr.

Mainly literary criticism but some biographical details
on the Anglo-Irish author.

329   Bryden, Ronald. "Talking to Iris Murdoch." Listener 79
(Apr. 4, 1968): 433-434. portr.

Report of a radio interview in which the novelist
discusses themes, structure, character and patterns in
her work and the influence of other writers.

330   Colby, Vineta. "Biographical Sketch [Iris Murdoch]."
Wil Lib Bull 33 (1958): 268. portr.

Brief descriptive biography of the author, born in Dublin
in 1919 and educated in England obtaining her B.A. from
Oxford in 1942. She then worked for two years as
Assistant Principal in the British Treasury, later as
Administrative Officer with UNRRA. In 1947 she returned
to academia with a research studentship at Cambridge and
the following year as a fellow and tutor in philosophy at
Oxford. Includes a discussion of her work.

331   Heyd, Ruth. "An Interview With Iris Murdoch." U Windsor
R 1 (1965): 138-143. refs.

Discussion of the author's concepts of freedom. She now
considers Satre's definition too narrow and no longer
subscribes to Existentialist doctrines on this point and
some others; discusses the nature of love, illusion/
reality, death as these are reflected in her work. Heyd
feels that Murdoch practices in her personal life some of
the policies that mark her fictional heroes/heroines e.g.

involvement, self-abnegation, gentleness, concern for others.

332   Kermode, Frank. "House of Fiction: Interviews With Seven English Novelists." Partisan R 30 (Spring 1963): 61-82.

Includes an interview with Iris Murdoch in which she discusses her distinction between "crystalline" and "journalistic" modes of fiction and her own writing.

333   Nettell, Stephanie. "An Exclusive Interview." Books & Bookm 11 (Sept. 1966): 14-15, 66. portr. bibl.

Report of an interview with Iris Murdoch includes comments on the novelist's function and techniques, her working methods, authors she admires, etc. Includes a list of her works in print.

334   "Philosophy and Literature. Dialogue With Iris Murdoch." In Men of Ideas: Some Creators of Contemporary Philosophy, pp. 263-284. London: British Broadcasting Corporation, 1978. bibl. portrs.

A conversation in which the British Broadcasting Corporation interviewer Magee discusses with the novelist, Iris Murdoch, who was for fifteen years a tutor in philosophy at Oxford, (1) the distinction between philosophy and literature, (2) philosophical ideas about literature and (3) philosophy in literature.

335   Rose, W.K. "An Interview With Iris Murdoch." Shenandoah 19 (Winter 1968): 3-22. (Also appeared in London Mag 8 (June 1968): 59-73.) portr.

Informal comment by the novelist on the novel of commitment; the artist's social responsibility; her nationality, nature of Irish writing, her career, philosophy, politics, her novels, and working methods.

                    Dervla Murphy (1931-   )

336   Addis, Jeremy. "The Uses of Snowballs: Books Ireland Talks to Dervla Murphy." Books Ire no. 12 (Apr. 1977): 64-65. portr.

In this interview the author, Dervla Murphy who has six books to her credit discusses her most recent one Where The Indus In Young, diary entries recorded during a winter spent in Balistan, a remote Himalayan province, and her plans for a book about Northern Ireland.

337   Murphy, Dervla. Wheels Within Wheels. [London]: John Murray, [1979]. 236pp. il. portrs.

In her autobiography, Dervla Murphy one of Ireland's
modern authors, describes her middle-class background and
childhood in Lismore Ireland; her family, her education -
which ended at 14 due to her invalid mother's
deteriorating condition. From then until she was 30 she
was chiefly responsible for her mother's care. The
emotional toll of these years graphically portrayed. Free
to travel after the death of her parents, she wrote the
first of her travel epics, an account of her bicycle trip
to India.
(Review: Books & Bookm 25 (Oct. 1979): 58.)
(Review: Economist 273 (Oct. 27, 1979): 123.)
(Review: Kirkus R 48 (Feb. 1, 1980): 195.)
(Review: Publ Wkly 217 (Feb. 15, 1980): 98.)
(Review: Blackw 327 (Feb. 1980): 152-153.)

338   "Profile: Dervla Murphy." Image 5 (2) (Feb. 1980): 3-4.
portr.

Katherine Murphy (1840-1885)

339   Russell, Matthew. "Our Poets No. 14: Katherine Murphy
('Brigid') Ir Mon 13 (1885): 433-440.

Short biographical sketch of the minor poet who
contributed verse to The Nation and other periodicals
under various signatures, the best known of which was
"Brigid" of the Nation. Born in County Cork both of her
parents died before her mid-twenties. Includes lengthy
excerpts from her poetry.

Ni Shuilleabhain Eibhlis (1911-   )

340   Ni Shuilleabhain Eibhlis. Letters from the Great
Blasket. Dublin and Cork: Mercier Press, 1978. 87pp. il.

Letters written to her friend in London from 1931 deal
with her love of the island, its people and its ways and
her anxiety over its decline. Eventually she and her
husband and child moved to the mainland. Her father-
in-law (Tomas O Criomhthain) was the author of An t
Oileanach (The Islandman) which originally focused
attention on the island.

Edna O' Brien (1930-)

341   Cronin, Bart. "Talking With Edna O'Brien." CARA 3(4)
(Oct.- Dec. 1970): 24-27. portr.

The novelist, Edna O'Brien, comments on her writing,
authors she admires, things she enjoys most in life,
living in Ireland.

342   Dunn, Nell. <u>Talking to Women</u>. St. Philips: Bristol,
1965. 233pp. portrs.

    Includes an interview with Edna O'Brien (pp.69-107) in
    which she comments on the conflicts involved in being a
    mother and a writer and the nature of love.

343   Eckley, Grace. <u>Edna O'Brien</u>. Lewisberg: Bucknell
University Press, 1974. 88pp. bibl.

    Mainly a literary study but includes a brief biographical
    sketch.

344   Heycock, David. "Edna O'Brien Talks to David Heycock
About Her New Novel A Pagan Place." <u>Listener</u> 83 (2145) (May
7, 1970): 616-617.

    An interview with Edna O'Brien in which she discusses her
    new novel and her childhood yearnings and experiences,
    what she read and the importance of the Church in her
    literary formation.

345   McCulloch, Joseph. <u>Under Bow Bells: Dialogues With
Joseph McCulloch</u>. London: Sheldon Press, 1974. 200pp.

    Includes an interview with Edna O'Brien (chapter 1).

346   Merrill, Charles. "Edna O'Brien Super Star." <u>Arts Ire</u> 3
(2) (June 1975): 14-17.

    Edna O'Brien comments on her attitudes toward her
    upbringing in Ireland, critical reception of her play,
    "The Gathering" - (both negative) and offers her opinion
    of critics, Irish and American (unflattering).

347   O'Brien, Edna. "Three Loves of Childhood: Irish
Thoughts." <u>Listener</u> (June 3, 1976): 701-702. portr.

    An extended version of a BBC 2 interview with Edna
    O'Brien conducted by Ludovic Kennedy on the occasion of
    publication of her book, <u>Mother Ireland</u>. She talks about
    her childhood and life in Ireland and her writing.

348   O'Brien, Edna. "Night Thoughts on Love." <u>Listener</u>
(June 3, 1976): 701-702. portr.

    Comments by O'Brien on the power of love and the pain of
    its loss.

Kate O'Brien (1897-1974)

349   Jordan, John. "Kate O'Brien: Towards an Appreciation."
Stony Thurs Bk 3 (Summer 1976): 1-3. portr.

Brief note on her literary career.

350   Mercier, Vivian. "Kate O'Brien." Ir Writ 1 (1946):
86-100.

A mostly biographical sketch of the author details her
education at Laurel Hill, Convent, County Limerick and
later at University College Dublin; her career as a
translator, teacher, free lance journalist visiting the
United States and Spain for short intervals; her
short-lived marriage; her first attempt at drama in 1926
and her subsequent novels, one of which The Anteroom is
proclaimed a masterpiece. Includes discussion of her
literary achievement.

351   Mulkerns, Val. "Kate O'Brien: A Memoir." Stony Thurs Bk
7 (1979): 19-23.

A special issue includes a biographical sketch, memoir of
a meeting, and literary appraisals of her work.

352   O'Brien, Kate. "Two Letters From Kate O'Brien to Mary
Hanley." Stony Thurs Bk 5 (1978): 6-8.

Editor's note explains that Mary Hanley was president of
the Yeats Kiltartan Society and a close friend of the
writer, Kate O'Brien, who writes to her of her peaceful
stay in Avila.

353   O'Brien, Kate. "U.C.D. as I Forget It." Univ R 111 (2)
(1962): 6-11.

Brief reminiscences by the multi-faceted Kate O'Brien
(novelist, critic, playwright, journalist, travel writer)
of her student days at University College, Dublin and
some of her teachers including Douglas Hyde and Austin
Clarke.

Kate Cruise O'Brien (1948-   )

354   Greacen, Lavinia. "The Catherine Wheel." Books Ire
No.24 (June 1978): 97. portr.

Brief biographical note on Kate Cruise O'Brien and
commentary on her writing, described by her as largely
autobiographical prior to the publication of her first
collection of short stories - The Gift House and Other
Stories.

355   O'Callaghan, Tanis. "Profile: Kate Cruise O'Brien."
Image 3 (7) (June 1978): 51-52. portr.

The author discusses her work, her parents' failed
marriage, her father (Conor Cruise O'Brien) and
maternity.

Ellen O'Leary (1831-1889)

356   [Tulloch, Miss.] "Some Recollections of Ellen O'Leary."
Ir Mon 39 (1911): 456-462.

Reprint of a tribute to the patriotic poet Ellen O'Leary,
sister of John O'Leary, the Fenian (originally published
in St. Joseph's Sheaf). Notes her patriotism, often
expressed in poetry; her piety, charity. Includes
excerpts from her poetry and an introduction by Matthew
Russell, editor of the Irish Monthly.

Nora Tynan O'Mahony (1865- ?)

357   Russell, Matthew. "Poets I Have Known: Nora Tynan
'Mahony." Ir Mon 36 (1908): 511-520.

A tribute to Nora Tynan O'Mahony, younger sister of
Katherine Tynan Hinkson with excerpts from her poetry.

Fanny Parnell (1849-1882)

358   Blunt, Hugh F. "Fanny Parnell - Poet and Patriot." Cath
W CXLII (1936): 182-190.

Eulogy of Fanny Parnell, described as the "Poet Laureate
of the Fenian Movement." The brief biographical sketch
discusses her ancestry, education, her patriotic verse
for the Irish People, a newspaper run by the Fenian
Society and her activities on behalf of the Land League.
Includes excerpts from her poetry.

359   Pilkington, Laetitia. Memoirs. With an introduction by
Iris Barry. London: Routledge and Sons, Ltd., [1748] [1754].
Reprinted 1928. 487pp. il. portrs.

Laetitia Pilkington and her husband were frequent guests
at Dean Swift's parsonage in the years 1730-1737.
Sometime later her husband instituted divorce proceedings
against her. Her self-serving, rather rambling memoirs
detail her version of the break up of her marriage and
her subsequent efforts to pursue a literary career in
London or otherwise support herself. Her memoirs when
published had a success de scandal owing to her divorce.
Today they remain important not only for the information
on Swift's later years, but because, as Barry states in

the introduction, they evoke "the behavior and the cant, the day to day sentiments and reactions of her time." (Review: <u>Sat R Lit</u> 4 (Mar. 31, 1928): 715-716.) (Review: <u>N Y Times Bk R</u> (June 1928): 9.)

360   Woolf, Virginia. "The Lives of the Obscure: Laetitia Pilkington." In her <u>The Common Reader</u>. pp. 160-167. London: L & V Woolf, 1925.

Brief, gently ironic comment on the life of the clergyman's daughter, the adventuress, Laetitia Pilkington, as recounted in her Memoirs.

Katherine Frances Purdon (? -1920)

361   Mitchell, Susan L. "Katherine Frances Purdon." <u>Ir Book Lov</u> 12 (Jan.-Feb. 1921): 79-80.

Obituary notice for the relatively obscure short story writer viewed as an interpreter of "rural Ireland." Her main achievement was in the area of children's literature.

Amanda McKittrick Ros (1860-1939)

362   Loudan, Jack. <u>O Rare Amanda: The Life of Amanda McKittrick Ros</u>. London: Chatto and Windus, 1954. 200pp. plates. portrs. bibl.

A biographical and literary study based mainly on her correspondence, of Amanda McKittrick Ros who has been described as "the world's worst novelist!" Of farming stock she trained as a teacher but after her first marriage turned to novel-writing. The critics were generally unfavorable and she carried on a running battle with these; also with lawyers after she had legal problems involving her management of a lime kiln. (Review: <u>Ir Writ</u> No. 30 (March 1955): 65-66.)

Peig Sayers (1873-1958)

363   O Gaoithin, Micheal. <u>Beata Pheig Sayers</u>. Foilsiuchain Naisiunta Teoranta. Baile ata Cliat. [1970] 151pp. portr.

Life story of Peig Sayers told by her son.

364   O Maonaigh, Tomas. <u>Peig: Eolas agus Leirmheas ar a Sceal</u>. Baile ata Cliat: Helicon, 1977. 40pp.

365   O Suilleabhain, Sean. "Peig Sayers." <u>Eire</u> 5 (1) (1970): 86-91.

Brief account of the erection of a memorial at the grave
of Peig Sayers at Dunquin, County Kerry - the first
monument to a story teller in Ireland. A brief
biographical sketch of Peig Sayers recounts her role in
preserving the folk history of the Blasket Islands and
discusses the various folklore collectors who recorded
her tales.

366   Sayers, Peig. _Mactnam Seana Mna. Peig Sayers do ceap_.
Maire Ni Cinneide do cuir in eagar. Baile Ata Cliat: Oifig
anz Solatair. 1939. 269pp.

 (Review: _Ir Mon_ 68 (1940): 50.)

367   Sayers, Peig. _Machnamh Seanmhna. Maire Ni Cinneide a
Chuir in eagar_. Eagran nua Eagar ag Padraig ua Maoleoin.
Baile Ata Cliat: Oifig an z Solathair. 1980. 142pp. (New
edition of above.) portr.

368   Sayers, Peig. _Peig: a Sceal Fein. Maire Ni Cinneide do
cuir in eagar_. Baile Ata Cliat: Cloluct na Talboidig,
1936.251pp. portr.

 (Review: _Dublin Mag_ New Ser. 12 (1) (Jan.-Mar. 1937):
        93-94.)

369   Sayers, Peig. _Peig: The Autobiography of Peig Sayers
ofthe Great Blasket Island_. [Translated into English by
Bryan MacMahon.] Dublin: Talbot Press, 1973. 212pp. il.
front.

    An autobiography of an old Irish woman dictated to her
    poet son, this book recounts the life of the author from
    her childhood in Kerry to her married life on the Great
    Blasket Island. Her story reveals much about the life of
    the ordinary people of the time - their stoicism and
    resilience in the face of poverty, death, evictions,
    emigration and other hardships and their simple
    pleasures. Also gives glimpses of how the old life style
    is being superseded.
 (Review: _Studies_ 63 (1974): 193-196.)

370   Sayers, Peig. _An Old Woman's Reflections_. Translated
from the Irish by Seamus Ennis and Introduced by W.R.
Rogers.London: Oxford University Press, 1962. 131pp.

    Story of Peig Sayers "the Queen of Gaelic story-tellers."
    She was born in the parish of Dunquin in Kerry and
    married into a neighbor island, the Great Blasket where
    she spent most of her life. Students and scholars of the
    Irish language came from far and wide to visit her -
    described as "a natural orator." Her reflections are a
    collection of her fireside stories most of them tales of
    her friends and neighbors on the Great Blasket.
    [Introduction.]

(Review: <u>Ulster Folk</u> 10 (1964): 98-99.)
(Review: <u>Kilk Mag</u> No. 8 (Aut.-Win. 1962): 67-69.)
(Review: <u>Studies</u> 69 (1979): 226-227.)

Elizabeth Shackleton

371   <u>Memoirs and Letters of Richard And Elizabeth
Shackleton, Late of Ballitore, Ireland</u>. Compiled by their
daughter Mary Leadbeater. London: Harvey and Darton, 1822.
221pp.

372   <u>Memoirs and letters of Richard and Elizabeth
Shackleton, late of Ballitore, Ireland</u>. Compiled by their
daughter, Mary Leadbeater. A new edition containing many
valuable letters never before published. London: Charles
Gilpin, 1849. 272pp.

    Includes a biographical sketch and some letters of Mary
    Leadbeater's grandfather, Abraham Shackleton; memoirs of
    Richard Shackleton, her schoolteacher father and his
    letters to his family; memoir of Mrs. Elizabeth
    Shackleton (the second wife of Richard Shackleton) and a
    few of her letters to her husband - arranged
    chronologically with explanatory comments and anecdotes
    of the compiler. The second edition includes additional
    letters and omits others.

Charlotte Shaw

373   Du Cann, C.G.L. <u>The Loves of George Bernard Shaw</u>.
London: Arthur Barker Ltd., 1963. 288pp. portrs.

    Chapter nine discusses Shaw's "unconsummated" marriage
    with Charlotte Payne-Townshend and has a brief account of
    her childhood and adolescence.

374   Dunbar, Janet. <u>Mrs. G.B.S. A Portrait</u>. New York: Harper
and Row, 1963. 303pp. il. portrs.

    A biography of Charlotte Payne-Townshend, the Anglo-Irish
    heiress who became the wife of George Bernard Shaw
    despite mutual opposition to marriage as an institution.
    Details on her family background and lifestyle before
    marriage to Shaw, their friendship with the Webbs and
    their life together when she hosted and managed their
    various residences and acted as her husband's secretary.
(Review: <u>Can Forum</u> 43 (Sept. 1963): 138.)
(Review: <u>N Y Times Bk R</u> (June 16, 1963): 1.)
(Review: <u>Harper</u> 226 (June 1963): 104.)
(Review: <u>New Statesm</u> (June 28, 1963): 979.)
(Review: <u>Sat R Lit</u> (June 8, 1963): 33.)

Lucinda Shaw

375   Shaw, George Bernard. "My Mother and Her Relatives." In
his Sixteen Self Sketches, pp. 23-37. New York: Dodd, Mead
and Company, 1949. il. portrs.

A brief impressionistic personality sketch of Mrs. Shaw
vividly evokes the shock which marrying an impoverished
drunk had on the genteel Lucinda Elizabeth Gurley. Cut
off by her family she withdrew into stoicism with music
her only passion. The children George Bernard and Lucy
were left to fend for themselves.

Frances Sheridan (1724-1766)

376   LeFanu, Alicia. Memoirs of the Life and Writings of
Mrs. Frances Sheridan, Mother of the late right Honorable,
Richard Brinsley Sheridan with remarks upon a late life of
the Right Honorable R.B. Sheridan...also criticisms and
selections from the works of Mrs. Sheridan by her
grand-daughter, Alicia LeFanu. London: G. & W.R. Whittaker,
1824. 435pp. portrs. fronts.

Born in Dublin the daughter of an Anglo-Irish clergyman,
Rev. Chamberlaine, Frances had early been attracted to
writing but was mainly involved with her family from her
marriage in 1747 until 1761 when she had success with her
novel The Memoirs of Miss Sidney Bidulph and the
following year, her play The Discovery. The family were
then living at Windsor and later moved to France. This
informal memoir includes comments and anecdotes on her
family life, friends, working habits, and travels with
excerpts from her work.

377   Pim, Sheila. "Sheridan's Father and Mother: A Romance
of the Dublin Stage." Chamber Ser.8 (1939): 653-657.

Account of the Smock Alley Theatre riot involving in
court action the manager Thomas Sheridan which occasioned
his introduction to a sympathiser, Frances Chamberlaine
who later became his wife (and a well known novelist and
playwright.)

Dora Sigerson Shorter (1866-1918)

378   [Clarke, John.] Remembered, a Daughter of Erin, Dora
Sigerson Shorter, Died 6th January 1918, Gifted and
Patriotic. By 'Benmore' [i.e. John Clarke] Antrim: Glenarm
Co., 1918. 8pp.

Eulogistic tribute to the poet Dora Sigerson Shorter
stresses her patriotic contributions to the Irish/Ireland
movement with excerpts from some of her poems.

379   "Editor's Gossip." Ir Book Lov 9 (Apr.-May 1918): 104.

Note on K. Tynan's article on Frances Ledwidge in the
English Review of February 1918 and her memoir on Dora
Sigerson Shorter in The Bookman. Includes excerpts from
both.

380   Hyde, Douglas. "Dora Sigerson Shorter." Studies 7 (25)
(Mar. 1918): 139-144. bibl.

Brief memoir of the Dublin born poet who lived most of
her life in London while maintaining a strong Irish
involvement in her work. Hyde identifies the main
currents in her work and evaluates her achievement.

381   Lawlor, Bridget F. "Dora Sigerson Shorter: An
Appreciation." Ir Mon 48 (1920): 100-106.

Effusive tribute to Dora Sigerson Shorter with excerpts
from some of her poems and comments on their themes -
sadness, exile, patriotism.

382   O'Brien, Deirdre. "Dora Sigerson Shorter." Ir Mon 56
(1928): 403-408.

Brief tribute to Dora Sigerson with excerpts from some of
her poems. Speaks of how grievously the Rebellion of
Easter 1916 affected the poet then living in London.

383   Shorter, Dora Sigerson. The Sad Years. With a Tribute
by Katherine Tynan. New York: George H. Doran Co., 1918.
106pp. front. (portr.)

Katherine Tynan's introduction to this collection of
poems by Dora Sigerson [Shorter] offers glimpses of their
shared lives in Dublin and their literary and political
activities before their respective marriages caused their
paths to diverge.

384   Tynan, Katherine. "Dora Sigerson (Shorter):A Memory."
Bookman LIII (317) (Feb. 1918): 154.

Tribute and short memoir of her girlhood friend, the poet
Dora Sigerson (Shorter) by the better known literary
figure Katherine Tynan (Hinkson).

Annie M.P.Smithson (1883-1948)

385   Smithson, Annie M.P. Myself and Others: An
Autobiography. Dublin: Talbot Press, 1944. 293pp.

This informal autobiography by the popular author of
Dublin Protestant descent describes her childhood, her

removal to England upon her mother's second marriage,
their return to Ireland and a poverty-stricken existence
due to her mother's improvidence, her nursing career in
Scotland and later in Ireland, her unhappy love affair
with a married doctor, her conversion to Catholicism and
her activities as a member of Cumann na mBan during the
1916 Rebellion and later with the anti-Treaty faction in
the Civil War.
(Review: Ir Mon 73 (1945): 180.)
(Review: Dublin Hist Rec 7 (1) (Dec. 1944-Feb.1945): 39-40.)

Edith Somerville (1858-1949)
Viola Martin (Martin Ross) (1862-1915)

386   Barlow, J.E.M. "A Memory of Martin Ross." Ctry Life 39
(Jan.29 1916): 136. portrs.

Brief tribute to the author Viola Martin , the "Martin
Ross" of the literary partnership of Somerville and Ross,
by a personal friend.

387   Coghill, Patrick (Sir). "Somerville and Ross."
Hermathena 79 (1952): 47-60.

Brief discussion of the lives and backgrounds of the
literary cousins Edith Somerville and Violet Martin and
their working methods by Edith Somerville's nephew.

388   Collis, Maurice. Somerville and Ross. London: Faber and
Faber, 1968. 286pp. il.

A biography based on 102 volumes of diaries, 6000 letters
and a collection of other manuscripts relating to the
personal life of the literary cousins Edith Somerville
and Violet Martin, best known for their collaboration on
Some Experiences of an Irish RM.
(Review: Dublin Mag 7 (2,3 &4) (Aut.-Winter 1968): 94-96.)
(Review: Hist Today 18 (1968): 589.)

389   Cronin, John. Somerville and Ross. Lewisberg,
Pennsylvania: Bucknell University Press, 1972. 111pp. bibl.

Brief biographical background and details on the literary
collaboration of the cousins with critical evaluation of
their achievements.

390   Cummins, Geraldine. Dr.E.OE. Somerville: A Biography.
London: Andrew Dakers Limited, 1952. 271pp. portr.(front.)
bibl.

A somewhat rambling, anecdotal biography by a close
friend of the longer lived member of the literary
partnership of Somerville and Ross: E.OE. Somerville.
Relies mainly on the autobiographical material in Irish

Memoirs, Wheel-tracks and the travel books of Somerville and Ross. The major part of the book is concerned with Edith's life and activities after the death of her cousin.
(Review: Ir Book Lov 32 (July 1953): 43.)
(Review: Dublin Mag New Ser. 27(3) (July-Sept.1952): 54-56.)
(Review: Ir Writ No. 19 (June 1952): 53-54.)

391   "Dr. Edith Somerville." [Obituary] Ill Lond News (Oct. 15, 1949): 568. portr.

Note of the death in County Cork on October 8, 1949 aged 91 years of the artist and author.

392   Fehlmann, Guy. Somerville et Ross: Temoins de l'Irlande d'hier. Publicationes de la Faculte des Lettres et Sciences Humaines de l'Universite de Caen, 1970. 516pp. bibl.

(Review: Ir U R 3 (1) (Sept. 1973): 111-113.)

393   Lewis, Gifford. Somerville and Ross: The World of the Irish. R.M. Harmondsworth: Viking (Penguin), 1985. 215pp. il. portrs.

A compilation of biographical essays including photographs.
(Review: Books Ire (Dec. 1985): 89.)

394   MacCarthy, B.G. "E.O.E. Somerville and Martin Ross." Studies 24 (June 1945): 183-194.

Mainly a literary discussion of the cousins' authorship techniques, subject matter and The Real Charlotte considered as their major work. Includes some biographical information.

395   Powell, Violet. The Irish Cousins: The Books and Background of Somerville and Ross. London: Heinemann, 1970. 214pp. portr.

Brief biographical background but mainly a discussion of their literary contribution and their collaboration. Includes a list of their works.
(Review: Lond Mag 9 (Mar. 1970): 112-115.)

396   Power, Ann. "The Big House of Somerville and Ross." Dubliner 3 (1) (Spring 1964): 43-53.

Mainly a literary analysis but has biographical material including a discussion of their "apartness," in both the literary and cultural sense, from their contemporaries in the Irish Revival by virtue of their Unionist sympathies and subject matter (the Anglo-Irish of the Big House).

397   Robinson, Hilary. <u>Somerville and Ross: A Critical</u>
<u>Appreciation</u>. New York: St. Martins Press, 1980. 217pp. bibl.

Chapter one contains a brief biographical sketch.
(Review: <u>Books Ire</u> No.45 (July-Aug. 1980): 143.)
(Review: <u>Ir U R</u> 10 (2) (Aut.1980):296-297.)
(Review: <u>Choice</u> 18 (Nov. 1980): 398.)

398   <u>Somerville and Ross: A Symposium</u>. Belfast: Queen's
University, 1969. 37pp. bibl.

Papers delivered at a weekend school at Queen's College,
Belfast in 1968 by Sir P. Coghill (Edith's nephew and
Martin's cousin) include a brief biographical sketch of
the authors and Hilary Mitchell examines to what extent
being women and being Anglo-Irish influenced their
literary development.

399   Somerville, Edith. "Two of a Trade." <u>Ir Writ</u> 1 (1)
(1946): 79-85.

Comments by Edith Somerville on the nature of her
literary collaboration with Martin Ross.

400   Somerville, Edith OE and Martin Ross. <u>Irish Memories</u>.
New York: Longman's Green and Co., 1918. 339pp. il. front.
bibl.

Mainly written by Miss Somerville, except for the sketch
of the Martins of Ross, County Galway, written by Violet
Martin, this is a combination of biography,
autobiography, family history, and anecdotes regarding
the cousin authors, E.O. Somerville and Martin Ross
[Violet Martin] and their literary collaboration.
(Review: <u>Ir Book Lov</u> 9 (Apr.-May 1918): 107-109.)
(Review: <u>Nat R</u> 71 (1918): 349-359.)

Mary Tighe (1772-1810)

401   Dix, Ernest R. McC. "The First Edition of Mrs. Tighe's
Psyche." <u>Ir Book Lov</u> 3 (1912): 141-143.

Refutes theory that this was first printed at her home at
Rosanna.

402   <u>Keats and Mary Tighe: The Poems of Mary Tighe With</u>
<u>Parallel Passages From the Works of John Keats</u>. Ed. by Earle
Vonard Weller. New York: The Century Co., 1928. 333pp. il.
portr.

Includes a memoir of Mary Tighe: brief note on her
ancestry, education, marriage, the publication of her
major work, "Psyche," and her death of consumption.

403   O'C.S. [O'Casaide, Seamus.] "Printing at Rosanna." Ir
Book Lov 8 (1916): 17.

   Excerpt from a biographical sketch in Bolster's Quarterly
   Magazine (August 1828) states that Tighe's well-known
   poem Psyche was printed first at Rosanna, her home. For
   refutation see Dix (#401).

404   Weller, Earle Vonard. "Keats and Mary Tighe." MLA 42
(3) (Sept. 1927): 963-985. refs.

   A brief biographical sketch of Mary Tighe and a
   discussion of her influence on Keats, especially through
   her poem "Psyche."

Melesina Trench (1768-1827)

405   Trench, Melesina. Journal Kept During a Visit to
Germany in 1799, 1800. Ed. by The Dean of Westminster [i.e.
Richard Chenevix Trench, afterwards Archbishop of Dublin.]
n.p. 1861. 97pp. refs.

   (See following entry.)

406   Trench, Melesina. The Remains of the Late Mrs. Richard
Trench Being Selections From Her Journals, Letters and Other
Papers. Edited by her son, the Dean of Westminster. London:
Parker, Son & Bourn, 1862. 528pp. portr.

   A selection from the surviving documents covering the
   period 1768-1827 include a brief autobiographical sketch
   of the author, Melesina Trench, grand-daughter of the
   Bishop of Waterford with excerpts from her journals
   covering visits to Germany (previously published but with
   a few additional entries), Austria, France and England,
   and her correspondence interspersed. Contextual notes by
   her son and editor.

Katherine Tynan (Hinkson) (1861-1931)

407   C. (J.S) "Sgeala o Chathair na g Ceo: on the death of
Katherine Tynan." Ir Book Lov 19 (Mar.-Apr.1931): 35.

   Brief tribute to the poet comments on her prodigious
   output in verse, fiction, travel, biography,
   autobiography and journalism.

408   Fallon, Ann Connerton. Katherine Tynan. Boston: Twayne,
1979. 191pp. bibl.

   A biographical and critical study of the poet/novelist/
   short story writer, journalist, Katherine Tynan whose
   life spanned the period of the Irish Literary Revival of

which she was an important member. Fallon acknowledges
her subject's achievement as a good minor poet but
stresses that her primary significance is being one of
the few women of her time and generation who supported
themselves by writing.
(Review: Choice 17 (July 1980): 670.)

409   "Gossip." Ir Book Lov 4 (Nov. 1912): 66-67.

Note on Katherine Tynan's writing of her memoirs.
(Excerpt from notice in "Public Opinion.")

410   "Mrs. Tynan Hinkson." Dublin Mag 6 (6) (Jan. 1924):
485.

Portrait.

411   Hinkson, Pamela. "The Friendship of Yeats and Katherine
Tynan." Fortn R 180 (174) (Oct. 1953): 253-264; (Nov. 1953):
323-336.

An account of the relationship of the author's mother,
Katherine Tynan Hinkson with the poet, William B. Yeats,
with excerpts from Yeats' letters to Tynan.

412   Maguire, C.E. "Incense and the Breath of Spice."
Bookman LXXII (June 1931): 375-380.

A review of The Collected Poems of Katherine Tynan
includes a brief biographical sketch of the poet,
examines influences on her work and evaluates her
literary achievement. Includes excerpts from her poetry.

413   O'Mahony, Nora Tynan. "Katherine Tynan's Girlhood." Ir
Mon 59 (1931): 358-363.

Brief memoir of the poet, Katherine Tynan (Mrs. Hinkson)
by her sister recalls their home in Dublin and their
guests at Katherine's 'at homes' which included Yeats,
George Russell (A.E.), the Sigersons, Ethna Carbery.

414   Rose, Marilyn Gaddis. Katherine Tynan. Lewisburg and
London: Bucknell and Assoc. University Press. (c.1974). 97pp.
bibl.

This first full length critical study of the minor but
immensely popular and prolific writer, Katherine Tynan,
later Mrs. Hinkson, clarifies and evaluates her basic
themes and techniques as products of her own life and
time (1861-1931). In 1885 she published her first book of
poetry. Her later writings from 1887 onwards included
novels, autobiography, journalism, reviews, etc. She
returned to Ireland in 1911 with her husband and three
children. After her husband's death in 1919 she was

forced to support herself and her family by her writing
and her output was immense.
(Review: Lib R 100 (Feb.15, 1975): 394.)
(Review: Booklist 71 (May 15, 1975): 935.)
(Review: Choice 12 (Dec. 1975): 1311.)

415   Russell, Matthew. "Poets I Have Known: Katherine
Tynan." Ir Mon 31 (1903): 250-267.

416   Tynan, [Hinkson] Katherine. Twenty-Five Years:
Reminiscences. London: Smith, Elder and Company, 1913. 355pp.
portr. (front.)

    This, the first volume of the memoirs, covers the first
    30 years of her life. She dwells lovingly on her carefree
    childhood, indulgent father and her schooldays. The bulk
    of the book deals with her social/literary life after the
    publication of her first volume of poetry gave her entree
    into artistic/literary circles both in Dublin and later
    in London and her numerous friends among these.
    (Review: Ir Book Lov 5 (Dec. 1913): 86.)
    (Review: Ir Mon 42 (July 1914): 357-365.)

417   Tynan, [Hinkson] Katherine. The Middle Years. London:
Constable and Company, 1916. 415pp.

    A continuation of the author's memoirs, this volume
    covers the years 1891 to approximately 1907. Comments on
    the aftermath of Parnell's death, excerpts from the
    correspondence of Francis Thompson and William Butler
    Yeats, a description of her life in England after her
    marriage. Throughout new and old friends - many of the
    foremost literary or political personalities of the day -
    are introduced.
    (Review: Ir Book Lov 8 (Feb.-Mar. 1917): 85-86.)

418   Tynan, [Hinkson] Katherine. The Years of the Shadow.
Boston and New York: Houghton Miflin Co., 1919. 343pp.

    The continuation of Katherine Tynan's memoirs touch on
    her return to Ireland, new and old friends, her visit to
    Rome for the annual meeting of the International Congress
    of women, the great strike of 1913, Volunteer Activity,
    and the outbreak of war. Though she was in Mayo during
    the 1916 uprising in Dublin she includes several first
    hand accounts of witnesses and describes her own later
    visit to the battle torn city and the aftermath of the
    rebellion. Includes details on her daily life, work and
    topical events.
    (Review: Ir Book Lov 11 (1919): 11.)

419   Walsh, Michael. "Katherine Tynan's Poetic Harvesting."
Ir Mon 58 (1930): 627-631.

    Brief tribute to the poet including excerpts from her

poetry and comment on her themes: religion, exile,
motherhood.

Esther Van Homrigh (1690-1723)

420   le Brocquy, Sybil. Cadenus: A Reassessment In the Light
of New Evidence of the Relationships Between Swift, Stella
and Vanessa. Dublin: The Dolman Press, 1962. 160pp. il. bibl.

     The title of this work is something of a misnomer for it
     mainly examines the relationship of Esther Van Homrigh
     and Jonathan Swift. The new "evidence" offered is the
     Petition of the Van Homrigh family to the House of Lords
     to enable them to dispose of their Irish estate - a
     petition supported by Swift. Le Brocquy speculates that
     Swift was bethrothed to Esther, that they lived together
     for a period and that she bore him a son; that the break
     between them which caused her to cut him out of her will
     was a consequence of her contacting Stella - Swift's
     other intimate friend - to make provision for this child
     after her death. Highly speculative.

421   le Brocquy, Sybil. A View on Vanessa. A Correspondence
With Interludes for the Stage. Dublin: Dolmen Press, 1967.
80pp.

     A dramatic rendering of the relationship of Jonathan
     Swift and Esther Van Homrigh based on some of their
     actual correspondence linked by imaginary interludes.
     (Review: Dublin Mag 6 (3,4) (Aut.-Win. 1967): 81-84.)

422   [Van Homrigh, Esther.] Vanessa and Her Correspondence
With Jonathan Swift. With an introduction by A. Martin
Freeman. London: Selwyn and Blount, 1921. 216pp. portr.

     The first separate publication of what is preserved of
     the correspondence between the famous Irish writer,
     Jonathan Swift and Esther Van Homrigh. A few letters and
     passages are published for the first time. In the
     introduction the editor, relying mainly on Swift's
     Journal to Stella details the context of their friendship
     and analyzes the letters in terms of this. Part II
     contains other relevant documents - the text of the
     largely biographical poem "Cadenus and Vanessa" written
     by Swift for Vanessa; her "Refus", Swift's answer to
     this, and her will.
     (Review: Ir Book Lov 12 (1921): 136.)

423   Yost, George Jr. "Well-filled Silences: The Case of
Swift and Vanessa." Flor State U Stud 11 (1953): 25-55. refs.

     A discussion of the existing correspondence between
     Jonathan Swift and Esther Van Homrigh and what they
     indicate of the nature of the relationship between them
     in terms of the letters themselves; the early

biographical evidence, and the published poem Cadenus and
Vanessa. Yost judges that Swift throughout tried to
impress upon Vanessa the impossibility of passionate
requital of her love but was not averse to her
friendship.

Helen Waddell (1889-1965)

424   Blackett, Monica. The Mask of the Maker: A Portrait of
Helen Waddell. London: Constable, 1973. 256pp. portr.

A biography of the medieval scholar, Helen Waddell also
known for her translations, interpretations and novels.
Based mainly on the author's personal recollection of
their thirty-year friendship, conversations with Helen's
sister, Meg and letters to Meg from Helen. Helen
Waddell's reputation was established with The Wandering
Scholars (1927) for which she received a medal from the
Royal Society of Literature and was later made a fellow,
while her novel, Peter Abelard, was both a popular and
scholarly success. She was elected to the Irish Academy
of Letters in 1932.
(Review: Economist 247 (Apr. 21, 1973): 113-114.)
(Review: New Statesm 85 (May 4, 1973): 662.)

Lady Wilde ("Speranza") (1826-1896)

425   Bremont, Anna (Contesse de). Oscar Wilde and and His
Mother. London: Everett and Co., 1911. 199pp. front. portr.

Bremont, who knew both Oscar Wilde and his mother,
reminisces about "Speranza's" "at homes"; her charm and
personality and her suffering during the scandal which
destroyed Wilde.
(Review: Ir Book Lov 2 (1911): 178.)

426   Lambert, Eric. Mad With Much Heart: A Life of the
Parents of Oscar Wilde. London: Frederick Muller, Ltd., 1967.
165pp. il. portrs.

No sources are noted for this somewhat muck-raking
account of the personal lives of Oscar Wilde's parents. A
particularly unflattering portrait of Jane Francesca
Wilde - Speranza - is presented. Characterized as an
Amazon in physical appearance, a poseur, hypocrite and a
"complete stranger to common sense" she is held
responsible for urging her son, Oscar, into a role which
brought about his ruination.

427   "Living Irish Literary Celebrities 2: Lady Wilde."
Nation (Nov. 10, 1888): 4-5.

428   O'Connor, Ulick. "The Wildes of Merrion Square." Ire
Welcomes 25 (6) (Nov.-Dec.1976): 33-37.

Brief note on the parents of Oscar Wilde.

429   [O'Donoghue, David J.] "The O'Donoghue Papers." Ir Book
Lov 12 (1925): 126-128.

Memoir of Lady Wilde's salon, and her connection with the
Irish Literary Society.

430   Sherard, Robert Harborough. The Life of Oscar Wilde.
New York: Dodd, Mead and Co., 1928. 470pp. il. bibl.

Includes a brief, generally unfavorable, account of Lady
Wilde's family background, literary and nationalistic
aspirations and achievements, her relationships with her
family and her lifestyle. Includes the text of her
Nationalist tract "Jacta Alea Est."

431   White, Terence de Vere. The Parents of Oscar Wilde.
London: Hodder and Stoughton., 1967. 303pp. il. tables.
geneal. portrs. refs.

A generally sympathetic account of "Speranza", Jane
Francesca Wilde discusses her patriotic contributions to
The Nation, her other literary efforts, her background,
her marriage to Dr. William Wilde and her "salon" in
Dublin and later in London, her intense loyalty to her
husband during the scandal which involved him and Mary
Travers, a one time patient, and her poverty in the years
following her husband's death. White notes her "divine
impracticality" and her snobbery but also her tolerance,
kindness, pride in and devotion to her family.
(Review: Dublin Mag 6 (3,4) (Aut.-Win. 1967): 86-89.)

432   Wyndham, Horace. Speranza: A Biography of Lady Wilde.
New York: Philosophical Library, 1951. 247pp. il. plates.

(Review: Spectator 186 (Apr. 27, 1951): 562.)
(Review: Theatre Arts 36 (Feb. 1952): 24.)
(Review: Times Lit Supp (Apr. 27, 1951): 259.)

Catherine Wilmot (1773?-1824)
Martha Wilmot (1775-1873)

433   [Wilmot, Catherine.] An Irish Peer on the Continent.
(1801-1803) Being a narrative of the tour of Stephen, 2nd
Earl Mount Cashell through France, Italy etc. as related by
Catherine Wilmot. Ed. by Thomas U. Sadlier. London: Williams
and Nougate, 1924. 227pp. il. portrs. refs.

Catherine Wilmot, daughter of a retired Army captain,
later a landowner and Customs official, travelled with

Stephen Moore [Mount Cashell] and his wife on their
continental tour of France, Italy and Germany in the
period following the French Revolution. Catherine kept a
diary of these travels written in the form of letters.
The introduction includes a biographical sketch of her
and her fellow travellers. A well educated, witty and
observant woman around thirty at the time of the tour,
her letters include vivid characterizations of notables
she encountered.
(Review: Ir Book Lov 12 (Dec. 1920): 62.)

434   [Wilmot, Catherine.] More Letters from Martha Wilmot:
Vienna 1819 to 1829. Ed. with an introduction and notes by
the Marchioness of Londonderry and Montgomery Hyde. London:
MacMillan, 1935. 339pp. il. portr. refs.

"Relating her experiences in the brilliant cosmopolitan
society of Vienna as the wife of the Rev. William
Bradford, Chaplain to the British Embassy during a period
when Austria was the political and social centre of
Europe and including a journal of a tour in Italy and the
Tyrol, and extracts from the diary of her eldest daughter
Catherine for 1829." (Editor) The majority of the letters
are addressed to her mother and her unmarried sister
Alicia.

435   Wilmot, Martha and Catherine. The Russian Journals of
Martha and Catherine Wilmot...as Guests of Princess
Daschkaw...1803-1808. Ed. with an introduction and notes by
the Marchioness of Londonderry and H.M. Hyde. London:
MacMillan, 1934. 423pp. portr. plates.

The introduction gives a brief biographical sketch of the
sisters and details the circumstances of Martha Wilmot's
(afterwards Martha Bradford) five year visit to Russia as
the guest of Princess Daschkaw, one time director of the
Academy of Arts and Sciences in St. Petersburg, where her
sister later joined her. The journals are arranged
chronologically and cover their travels, their
impressions of Russian life and the various personalities
with whom they came into contact which included most of
the Court entourage, political celebrities of the day and
members of rich merchant classes.
(Review: Eng Hist R 51 (1936): 183.)
(Review: Ir Book Lov 22 (Nov.-Dec. 1934): 138-140.)

Frances Wynne (1866-1893)

436   Hinkson, Katherine Tynan. "Frances Wynne." Longm 23
(Nov. 1893): 66-67.

Tribute to the deceased minor poet with some excerpts
from her poetry by her friend and sometime critic.

George Yeats

437   Bradford, Curtis B. "George Yeats: Poet's Wife."
Sewanee R 77 (1969): 385-404.

     Bradford records conversations he had with W.B.Yeats'
     wife. Topics covered include her activities as Yeats'
     wife — secretary, business manager, gardener, cook, etc.,
     her relationship with the poet, her feelings about Maud
     and Iseult Gonne, Yeats' friends.

Ella Young (1865-1951)

438   Lyman, W.W. "Ella Young: A Memoir." Eire Ire 8 (3)
(1973): 65-69.

     Personal reminescences by a friend characterizes Ella
     Young as theosophist, nationalist and writer of
     children's stories. Comments on her life style,
     appearance and friends.

439   Young, Ella. Flowering Dusk. Things Remembered
Accurately and Inaccurately. New York: Longman's Green and
Co., 1945. 356pp. il. portrs.

     Not an actual autobiography but a series of sketches
     recording events, moods, impressions and personalities of
     the poet and Celtic scholar's childhood and life in
     Ireland up to 1925 and her subsequent life in America.
     Dublin in the period of the National Revival is
     nostalgically and impressionistically evoked with
     somewhat more detail on the 1916 Easter rebellion and its
     aftermath.

THE ARTS

     This section includes the subdivisions PERFORMING ARTS
and FINE ARTS and considers women noted for their achievement
on stage or related areas whether as actresses, directors,
dancers or musicians or offstage as painters, designers or
other artists. Crafts such as embroidery, lacemaking, etc.
though examples of considerable artistry are considered under
EMPLOYMENT. Collective biographies for the PERFORMING ARTS
and FINE ARTS are listed under the GENERAL sub-divisions of
those categories; works about individual actresses or
painters are arranged in one alphabetical sequence in the
appropriate category with multiple entries for the same
performer arranged alphabetically by author.
     No consideration of the Irish stage can ignore the role
of the Abbey theatre and Lady Gregory's contribution as
assistant director in the early period. For material on Lady
Gregory see BIOGRAPHY and AUTOBIOGRAPHY — LITERATURE — LADY
GREGORY.

PERFORMING ARTS

General

440   Fyvie, John. <u>Comedy Queens of the Georgian Era</u>. London:
Constable & Co., 1906. 445pp. plates.

A series of biographical sketches of some of the most
prominent comedy actresses on the English stage in the
Georgian period. Includes Margaret Woffington (Peg),
George Anne Bellamy, Eizabeth Farren, Countess of Derby,
Dora (Dorothy) Jordan.

441   MacLiammoir, Michael. "Some Talented Women." <u>Bell</u> 8 (2)
May 1944): 117-127.

Brief profiles of the playwright, Mary Manning and the
actresses Meriel Moore, Sara Allgood, Ria Mooney and Jean
Forbes-Robertson. (Excerpts from the author's memoirs
then unpublished.)

George Ann Bellamy (1731-1788)

442   [Bellamy, George Ann] <u>An Apology for the Life of George
Ann Bellamy Late of Covent Garden Theatre</u>. Written by
herself. 2nd ed. Dublin: Moncriffe, Burnet, Jenkin, 1785. 2
vols.

The actress' own account of her life written as a series
of letters. Born illegitimately in 1733 (1731? 1727?) she
was educated in France from whence she returned to
England and was for a period under the protection of her
father Lord Tyrawley. She became acquainted with various
actors/ actresses and later went on the stage achieving
much success and patronage. Her private life was somewhat
chaotic and living extravagantly she was frequently in
poor financial circumstances.

443   [Bellamy, George Anne]. <u>Memoirs of George Anne Bellamy
Including All Her Intrigues with Genuine Anecdotes of All Her
Public and Private Connections</u>. By a Gentleman of Covent-
Garden Theatre. London: Printed for J.Walker and J.Debrett,
1785. 204pp.

Believed to have been written by the actress herself.

444   "George Ann Bellamy: an Irish Actress." Part 1. <u>Dublin
U Mag</u> 64 (Oct. 1864): 447-459; Part 2. 64 (Nov. 1864):
559-566.

Biographical sketch.

445   Hartmann, Cyril Hughes. <u>Enchanting Bellamy</u>. London:
William Heinemann, 1956. 339pp. il. portrs. bibl.

(Review: <u>Hist</u> 42 (1957): 159.)

446   "Our Old Actors: 'Peg' Woffington and George Anne
Bellamy." <u>Temp Bar</u> 52 (1878): 316-331.

   Biographical sketch.

                    Harriet Berlioz (1800-   )

447   Rynne, Etienne. "Harriet Smithson, the Ennis-born Wife
of Hector Berlioz." <u>No Munst Antiq J</u> 12 (1969): 81-84.

   Biographical account of the actress Harriet Smithson who
   achieved great acclaim on the French stage and was
   married to the composer Berlioz in 1833 despite his
   family's opposition.

                    Ina Boyle (1892-1967)

448   Maconchy, Elizabeth. <u>Ina Boyle: An Appreciation With a
Select List of Her Music</u>. Dublin: Dolmen Press for Trinity
College Library, 1974. 16pp. front.

   Short tribute to Ina Boyle characterizes her as a strong
   and interesting character with an original creative mind.
   Brief note on her musical career and her other interests.

                    Elizabeth Farren (1759-1829)

449   Broadbent, R.J. "Elizabeth Farren, Countess of Derby."
<u>Trans Hist Soc</u> LXI (n.s.XXV) (1910): 83-96. portrs.

   A brief biographical sketch.

450   "An Irish Actress - Elizabeth Farren: With
Contemporaneous Notices." <u>Dublin U Mag</u> LXV (Jan.-Feb. 1865):
68-77, 202-209.

   Brief biographical account of Elizabeth Farren, later
   wife of the 12th Earl of Derby. Her Irish surgeon father,
   a heavy drinker left the family heavily in debt at his
   death and they took up residence with the mother's family
   in Liverpool. At 15, Elizabeth began her theatrical
   career which she continued successfully until her
   marriage when she retired from the stage. Includes brief
   accounts of some of her contemporaries.

451   The Testimony of Truth to Exalted Merit; or a
Biographical Sketch of the Right Honourable, The Countess of
Derby; In Refutation of a False and Scandalous Libel. 2nd ed.
London: G. Cawthorn, 1797. 37pp. front. portr. (A reply to
the memoirs of the present Countess of Derby by Petronious
Arbiter.)

Mrs. Fitzhenry (d.1790)

452   "An Irish Actress of the Last Century: Mrs. Fitzhenry."
Dublin U Mag LXII (Sept. 1863): 324-334.

    Brief biographical sketch of Mary Flanagan born in Dublin
    who after the death of her husband, had a successful
    theatrical career in London and Dublin which she
    continued despite her second marriage. Excerpts from
    contemporary reviews and anecdotes on theatre history.

Fionnuala Flanagan

453   McCafferty, Nell. "Fionnuala Flanagan: An Age of
Uncertainty." Image 7 (Aug. 1982): 16-17. portr.

    Brief profile of the actress.

Bernadette Greevy

454   Pine, Richard. "A Touch of Class." Magill Mag 2 (6)
1979): 83-84. il.

    Brief sketch of Bernadette Greevy described as one of
    world's finest contraltos.

Catherine Hayes (1825-1861)

455   Hayes, Catherine. Memoir of Miss Catherine Hayes. "The
Swan of Erin." by a Contributor to the Dublin University
Magazine. London: Cramer and Co., 1851. 40pp. portr.

    Brief effusive account of the career of the opera singer
    Catherine Hayes with details on her appearances in
    Dublin, London, Milan, Venice and Genoa. Includes
    excerpts from contemporary reviews.

456   "Our Portrait Gallery No. LXI: Catherine Hayes." Dublin
U Mag 36 (Nov. 1850): 584-595.

    Note on the musical training and accomplishments of the
    vocalist with excerpts from contemporary reviews.

Dorothy Jordan (1761-1816)

457   Aspinall, A. (ed.) Mrs. Jordan and her Family Being the
Unpublished Correspondence of Mrs. Jordan and the Duke of
Clarence, later William IV. London: Arthur Barker, Ltd.,
1951. 295pp. portrs.

    A selection of letters, mainly from the correspondence of
    Mrs. Jordan and the Duke, exchanged during the period
    1808-1811; also includes other letters for subsequent
    years (1812-1814). Arranged chronologically with
    introduction and notes, including a brief biographical
    sketch of Mrs. Jordan.

458   Boaden, James. The Life of Mrs. Jordan; Including
Private Correspondence and Numerous Anecdotes of her
Contemporaries. London: Edward Bull, Frontis Facsim, 1831. 2
vols.

459   Fothergill, Brian. Mrs. Jordan. Portrait of an Actress.
Dublin: Faber, 1965. 334pp. portrs.

 (Review: Times Lit Supp (Dec. 2, 1965):1100.)
 (Review: Listener (Dec. 2, 1965): 922.)

460   The Great Illegitimates! Public and Private Life of
that Celebrated Actress Miss Bland, otherwise Mrs. Ford or
Mrs. Jordan; Late Mistress of H.R.H. the Duke of Clarence;
now King William IV. founder of the Fitzclarence
family...London: J.Duncombe. [n.d.] 266pp. portrs.

461   Jerrold, Clare. The Story of Dorothy Jordan. London:
Eveleigh Nash, 1914. 429pp. il. portrs.

462   Grinsted, T.P. "Gallery of Theatrical Portraits IV -
Mrs. Jordan." Bentley 41 (1857): 408-418.

    Details on theatrical career of Dorothea Bland later
    known as Mrs. Jordan. Brief mention of her 20 year
    liaison with the Duke of Clarence (later William IV). She
    died in St. Cloud in 1816.

463   Higgins, P. "Query Concerning Dorothy Jordan, nee
Bland, Actress. Answered by William H. Grattan Flood." Waterf
Arch Soc J   10 (1907): 160,258.

    A response to a request for confirmation of the actress'
    birthdate in 1762 can not verify this but supplies some
    data on her early career which it is claimed, has been
    reported incorrectly in earlier biographies.

464   "Obituary; with Anecdotes of Remarkable Persons." Gent
Mag 86 (July 1816): 93-94.

Obituary for the actress, Dorothy Jordan.
465   Sergeant Philip W. <u>Mrs. Jordan: Child of Nature</u>.
London: Hutchinson & Co., 1913. 356pp. il. front.

Probably the definitive biography of the famous actress
and mistress of the Duke of Clarence based on previous
accounts, both biographical and autobiographical,
contemporary reviews/commentaries and memoirs. Seduced by
Daly, the manager of the Smock Allen Theatre in Dublin
where she was an aspiring actress, she fled to London and
achieved much success on the stage there. From 1789-1811
she was the mistress of the Duke of Clarence but then,
discarded by him, she returned to the stage in 1813. Her
final years were spent in France, in debt: a mental and
physical wreck.

466   [Text of Mr. Ford's letter to Mrs. Jordan clearing her
of accusations that she behaved improperly towards her
children in regard to pecuniary matters at the break up of
their relationship.] <u>The Bon Ton Magazine or Microscope of
Fashion and Folly</u> (Oct. 1791): 319.

467   Williamson, Usher A.F. "An Unknown Miniature of Mrs.
Jordan." <u>Ir Ancest</u> 11 (1) (1970): 1-2. portr.

A short biographical sketch of the actress with a
reproduction of a miniature of her attributed to
Frederick Buck of Cork, presumably painted in 1780 or
1781 while she was in Cork with Richard Daly's company,
now in possession of the author.

Lady Longford (1900-1980)

468   Fitzgerald, Marion. "Lady of the Theatre." <u>Word</u> (Dec.
1969): 17-19. il. portrs.

Interview with Lady Longford, then Chair of the Board of
the Gate Theatre, Dublin who comments on the theatre and
her present activities.

Anna McGoldrick

469   "Anna Mc Goldrick." <u>Word</u> (July 1973): 15. portr.

Brief biographical note on the Irish popular singer,
winner of the British Variety Club Award in 1969.

Siobhan McKenna (1923-1986)

470   Kelly, Rhondda. "Siobhan McKenna." <u>Scene</u> 1 (2) (July
967): 33-39. portrs.

Excerpts from an interview with the actress Siobhan McKenna, in which she comments on her career, roles, her education, the Abbey Theatre, likes and dislikes.

471   O'Connor, Ulick. "Siobhan McKenna." Image 4 (1) (Sept. 1979): 57-59. portr.

Interview with the actress.

Ria Mooney (1904-1973)

472   Mooney, Ria. "Playing Rosie Redmond." J Ir Lit 6 (2) (May 1977): 21-27. il. (excerpted from her unpublished autobiography Players and the Painted Stage ed. by Val Mulkerrns)

The Irish actress, Ria Mooney, reminisces about her creation of the role of Rosie Redmond, the prostitute, in O'Casey's famous play "The Plough and the Stars." She was O'Casey's own choice for the part and he was very pleased with her performance. At later performances there were audience demonstrations and Yeats denounced the disrupters.

Maire Nic Shiublhaigh (Mary Walker)

473   Nic Shiublhaigh, Maire. The Splendid Years. Dublin: James Duffy and Co. Ltd., 1955. 207pp. il.

Brief personal account of the Irish Theatre movement in Dublin at the turn of the century by one of its leading actresses. Details on the original Irish Theatre Society, the early years of the Abbey, the artistic and political ferment in Dublin in the years prior to the 1916 Rising. Final chapter treats the author's experience as a member of an Irish Volunteer garrison during the Easter rebellion.

Eileen O'Casey

474   O'Casey, Eileen. Eileen. Edited with an introduction by J.C. Trewin. London: MacMillan, 1976. 224pp. portrs.

In her autobiography the widow of the playwright Sean O'Casey describes her poverty-striken, lonely, unhappy childhood in Dublin and later in London; her education, first at an orphanage and later at a convent boarding school; her theatrical career and romances in London and New York; her marriage to Sean O'Casey and subsequent retirement from the stage. The routine of her married life, the children, the constant moves, the chronic shortage of money, her occasional boredom, the lack of social life and withal the deep affection and happiness

of these years described. Later she records the painful
loss of her son and husband, her travels and ultimate
return to Dublin.
(Review: <u>Publ Wkly</u> 211 (Jan. 10, 1977): 60.)
(Review: <u>Contemp R</u> 230 (Feb. 1977): 109-110.)

Mary O'Hara

475   O'Toole, Patsy. "Mary O'Hara Sings Again." <u>Word</u> (June
1976): 8-11. il. portrs.

Brief profile of the songstress and harpist Mary O'Hara
who had already established a reputation as an
interpreter of Irish and Scottish songs before her entry
into the strict Benedictine Monastery. Now she has
extended her repertoire to include Elizabethan, French
and medieval Manx songs.

Geraldine O'Grady

476   Williams, Gabrielle. "Lifestyle: Geraldine O'Grady."
<u>Image</u> 5 (7) (June 1980): 58-59. portr.

Profile of the leading violinist of Radio Telefis Eireann
Symphony Orchestra.

Elizabeth O'Neill (1791-1872)

477   <u>A Descriptive Portrait of Miss O'Neill in a Critique on
Her Exhibition of the Characters of Mrs. Haller and Jane
Shore</u>. London: E. Williams, 1815. 108pp. (Shakspeareana:
Miscellaneous Essays. v. 1 [No.15])

A review of the performance of Elizabeth O'Neill,
afterwards Lady Becher, in the plays, <u>The Stranger</u> and
<u>Jane Shore</u> pays effusive tribute to her appearance and
her acting talent. Includes most of the texts of the
plays.

478   "The Drama." <u>Lond Mag</u> (Feb. 1820): 162-165.

Brief note on appearance and acting ability of Miss
O'Neill (Lady Becher).

479   Grinsted, T.P. "Gallery of Theatrical Portraits VI -
Miss O'Neill." <u>Bentley</u> 41 (1857): 642-652.

Brief biographical account interspersed with theatrical
anecdotes and details on the various parts played by the
actress and her reception. She quit the stage in 1819 to
marry William Becher.

480   Jones, Charles Inigo. <u>Memoirs of Miss O'Neill;</u>
<u>Containing Her Public Character, Private Life and Dramatic</u>
<u>Progress, From Her Entrance Upon the Stage; with a Full</u>
<u>Criticism of Her Different Characters, Appropriate Selections</u>
<u>From Then, and Some Account of the Plays She Has Preferred</u>
<u>for Her Representations</u>. London: D.Cox, 1816. 100pp. portr.

    Brief biograpgical sketch with reviews of her major
    performances and excerpts from the plays in which she
    performed, with a testimonial to her exemplary private
    life.

481   "Our Old Actors: Maccready and Miss O'Neill." <u>Temp Bar</u>
54 (1878): 239-255.

    Brief discussion of the acting ability of Miss Elizabeth
    O'Neill.

482   Stocqueler, J.H. "Miss O Neill." <u>Belgra</u> IX 2nd ser.
(XIX 1st ser.) (Dec. 1872): 238-243.

    Obituary of the actress by an ardent fan who saw her in
    every character she played.

Maureen Potter

483   Bannister, Ivy. "The World of Maureen Potter." <u>Image</u> 4
(12) (Dec. 1979): 4-7. portr.

    Interview with the comedienne.

484   Nicassno, Susan. "Just Make Them Laugh, That's All."
<u>Ire Welcomes</u> 26 (6) (1974): 36-39. il. portr.

    Brief report of an interview with the comedienne, Maureen
    Potter, includes some biographical information and
    comment on her attitude to her work.

485   Rushe, Desmond. "Ireland's Comedienne." <u>Word</u>
(Aug.1970): 14-17. portrs.

    Interview with Maureen Potter who comments on comics, her
    career, childhood and school days, religion, social and
    political issues and her other interests.

Margaret Burke Sheridan

486   McLiammoir, Michael. [pseud. The Bellman] "Meet
Margaret Burke Sheridan." Bell 5 (2) (Nov. 1942): 111-118.

An interview with the Irish opera singer who achieved
success on the Italian stage. Comments on her education
and training, her friends and compeers, operas created by
her, and the qualities needed to be an international
artist.

Lucy Shaw (-1920)

487   Farmer, Henry George. Bernard Shaw's Sister and Her
Friends: A New Angle on George Bernard Shaw. London: Brill,
1959. 274pp. il. portrs. refs.

A somewhat partisan biography of George Bernard Shaw's
sister based on her correspondence with her friend Janey
Drysdale, her nurse, Shaw's secretaries and other
acquaintances and personal recollections by her cousin
and others. Details her career as a performer in light
opera, her marriage and divorce, her early death from
tuberculosis and Shaw's financial support during her
illness.
(Review: Anglo-Irish Literature: A Review of Research. Ed.
      by Richard J. Finnerman. p.174. New York: Modern
      Language, 1976. 596pp.)

488   Kelley, Nora. "A Sketch of the Real Lucy Shaw." Inde
Shavian 8 (1974): 12.

A brief biographical sketch of G.B. Shaw's sister Lucy,
an opera singer, and her relationship with her famous
brother.

489   Sime, Georgina and Frank Nicholson. Brave Spirits.
Plymouth: Latimer, Trend and Co. Ltd., n.d. 165pp.

Includes a brief character sketch of Lucy Shaw (pp.149-
154), a singer in light opera and sister of George
Bernard Shaw.

Margaret Woffington (1717-1760)

490   Cook, Dutton. "Margaret Woffington." Once a Week 9
(211) (July 11, 1863): 61-67.

Brief biographical note with discussion of theatrical
roles.

491   Daly, Augustin. Woffington: A Tribute to the Actress
and the Woman. New York: Benjamin Blom, 1972. 2nd ed. 172pp.
il. portrs. refs. (Reprint of work originally published in
1888.)

The most reliable early full length account of the actress' life and work written by her manager.
(Review: Sat R 65 (June 2, 1888): 671-672.)

492   Dobson, Austin. "Peg Woffington." Mag Art 8 (1885): 256-259. portrs.

Comment on her theatrical career and brief biographical sketch.

493   Dunbar, Janet. Peg Woffington and Her World. London: Heinemann, 1968. 245pp. il. bibl.

A serious, well-documented biography of the actress, Margaret (Peg) Woffington, which contains a wealth of theatrical history for both Dublin and London. Avoiding the sensationalism of most previous accounts, Dunbar stresses her subject's professional dedication to her craft which, with her great beauty, made her one of the most successful actresses of her day. Includes details of her poverty stricken background and her various affairs including that with the actor, David Garrick.
(Review: Economist 229 (Dec. 28, 1968): 31.)
(Review: Times Lit Supp (Sept. 19, 1968): 1054.)
(Review: Chr Sci Monit (Sept. 26, 1968): 13.)

494   "An Irish Actress - Margaret Woffington." Dublin U Mag 64 (Aug. 1864): 180-197.

A fairly objective biographical sketch includes excerpts from contemporary reviews, accounts of contemporaries and description of the theatrical scene in London and Dublin.

495   Lawrence, W.J. "Peg Woffington's Last Appearance." Dublin Mag 11 (Nov.1924): 237-239. portr.

Argues that the actor Tate Wilkinson in his memoirs incorrectly dates Peg Woffington's sudden illness on stage as May 15, 1757. Date should read May 3, 1757. Also mention of the portrait of her by Arthur Pond which shows her in her illness.

496   Lawrence, W.J. "Peg Woffington's Recantation and its Sequel." Dublin Mag 14 (3) (July/Sept.1939): 25-33.

An account of a trip taken by the actress, Peg Woffington, in the company of her manager, Thomas Sheridan to County Cavan to "convert" to the church of Ireland so she might claim her legacy left to her by Owen Swiney, former manager of the Queens Theatre, London. The problems subsequently encountered by Peg when trying to claim her legacy, detailed.

497   Lucey, Janet C. _Lovely Peggy: The Life and Times of Margaret Woffington_. London: Hurst and Blackett, 1952. 268pp. il. portrs. bibl.

   (Review: _Dublin Mag_ New Ser. 27 (4) (Oct.-Dec. 1952): 63.)

498   [Macklin, Charles.] "Mackliniana; or Anecdotes of the Late Mr. Charles Macklin, Comedian." _European Mag_ (May 1980): 354-355.

   Anecdotes on Garrick's relationship with Peg Woffington.

499   McAsey, C.C. "Peg Woffington." _Dublin Hist Rec_ 23 (1) (1869): 23-35. refs. (Read to the Old Dublin Society March 9th 1959)

   A judicious attempt to sort fact from fiction in the accounts of the life of the popular actress Peg Woffington.

500   Molloy, James Fitzgerald. _The Life and Adventures of Peg Woffington with pictures of the period in which she lived_. London: Hurst and Blackett, 1884. 2 vols.

501   "Our Old Actors: 'Peg' Woffington and George Anne Bellamy." _Temp Bar_ 52 (1878): 316-331.

   Brief biographical sketch of Peg Woffington and George Anne Bellamy with comments on their acting abilities and their rivalry.

502   "Peg Woffington." _New Mon Mag_ 52 (1838): 383-387.

   Biographical sketch.

503   Stewart, Ian. "A Belle Among the Beaux: Peg Woffington's Return to Dublin." _Ctry Life_ 148 (3832) (Oct. 1 1970): 804-806. il. portr.

Anne Yeats

504   Rose, Marilyn Gaddis. "A Visit With Anne Yeats." _Mod Drama_ VII (1964): 299-307.

   Anne Yeats comments briefly on her work as stage designer at the Abbey Theatre, her reasons for leaving, her father's work habits, their family life, her mother's reaction to Maud Gonne and the production of Yeats' plays.

FINE ARTS

General

505   Robinson, Lennox. "Here Were Ladies: Gregory, Leslie, Purser." Bell 7 (1) (Oct. 1943): 34-38.

Brief tributes to Lady Gregory and Sarah Purser.

506   Walker, Dorothy. "Portrait of the Artist as a Young Woman." Crane Bag 4 (1) (1980): 106-111. il.

Brief biographical and critical mention of 20th century women artists in Ireland, particularly Evie Hone and Maimie Jellett.

Deborah Brown

507   Crookshank, Anne. "Deborah Brown." Arts Ire 6 (4) (1973): 38-49. il.

A brief biographical sketch of the modern Belfast born artist Deborah Brown comments briefly on her education, her painting career, the evolution of her style and prizes awarded to her.

Lady Butler (1877-1933)

508   Butler, Rhona. Lady Butler: "Portrait and Memories." Butler Soc J 6 (1976): 439-442. il. portr.

Biographical sketch by her daughter-in-law of the English born military painter who came to live in Ireland upon her marriage to Major (later General) William Butler.

Mildred Anne Butler (1858-1941)

509   "Mildred Anne Butler 1858-1941." [Christie's London Exhibit] Connoisseur 208 (835) (Sept. 1981): 10-11.

Notice of an exhibit by the artist Mildred Anne Butler and brief biographical note.

Sybil Connolly (1921-   )

510   O'Callaghan, Tanis. "Profile: Tanis O'Callaghan Talks to Sybil Connolly." Image 3 (12) (Nov. 1978): 27-30. portr.

Comment on the designer's house-cum-workspace and her comments on publicity, fashion and designers, her career in America and some of her famous clients.

Eileen Grey (1879-1976)

511   Grehan, Ida. "Pioneer from Enniscorthy." CARA 9 (2)
(Apr.-June 1976): 11-13. il. portrs.

Profile of Eileen Grey, a pioneer in design whose
furniture, lamps, carpets and houses designed in the
twenties and thirties and then considered too radical,
are now "le dernier cri." Honoured by a fellowship from
the Royal Institute of Irish Architects she had her first
London exhibit in 1973 and was even before that a
commercial success. Lives in France but considers her
roots to be in Ireland.

Evie Hone (1894-1955)

512   Curran, C.P. "Evie Home: Stained Glass Worker." Studies
XLIV (44) (1955): 129-140.

Brief biographical sketch of the artist with information
on her education and career and a catalog of her work in
stained glass.

513   "Evie at Eton." Time 59 (26) (June 30, 1952): 66.

Brief biographical sketch comments on the Eton window,
considered her major achievement, her working habits and
future plans.

514   Frost, Stella. (ed.) Evie Hone. Dublin: Browne and
Nolan, 1958. 63pp. il. portr.

Collection of biographical and critical sketches.

515   Frost, Stella (ed.) A Tribute to Evie Hone and Maimie
Jellett. Dublin: Browne and Nolan, 1957. 77pp. il.

Short articles by friends, pupils, fellow-artists,
critics and art-lovers (some reprints) on the artists,
Hone and Jellett.
(Review: Studies 46 (1957): 377-378.)

516   "Miss Evie Hone." Architect R 117 (700) (Apr. 1955):
211. il.

Obituary notice of Miss Evie Hone, stained glass artist
with a reproduction of her "most brilliant work " - viz.
the New East Window in Eton College Chapel.

517   Pollen, Patrick. "Thoughts on the Art and Life of Evie
Hone." Univ R 1 (8) (Spring 1956): 38-42. plates.

    Mainly a consideration of Evie Hone's roots, artistic
    qualities and context.

518   Walker, Dorothy. "Portrait of the Artist as a Young
Woman." J Ir Stud 6 (2) (May 1977): 39-44. il.

    (See #506.)

            Maimie Jellett (1897-1944)

519   Arnold, Bruce. Maimie Jellett 1897-1944. [a catalogue]
Dublin: The Neptune Gallery. n.d. [c1976] 64pp.

    Catalog of an exhibit of paintings by the modern Irish
    artist is prefaced by a brief biographical sketch which
    details her Dublin childhood, her artistic education
    under Orpen, Sickert and Andre Lhote, initial negative
    reaction to her exhibited work, her early death at the
    age of 46. Includes a brief critical evaluation of her
    artistic achievement.

520   Arnold, Bruce. "The Quiet Revolution of Maimie
Jellett." Image 7 (June 1982): 61-63. portr.

    Brief biographical sketch with comment on her artistic
    achievement.

521   Bowen, Elizabeth. "Maimie Jellett." Bell 9 (3) (Dec.
944): 250-256.

    Brief tribute to the artist by her friend, the novelist,
    recalls their similar childhoods, Ms Jellett's education
    in Dublin, London and Paris, her concept of art and the
    role of the artist, her evaluation of her own work and
    the three major revolutions in her ideas and style under
    the respective influences of Sickert, Lhote and Gleizes.

522   Jellett, Maimie. The Artist's Vision: Lectures and
Essays on Art With an Introduction by Albert Gleizes.
Dundalk: Dundalgan Press, 1958. 120pp. il.

    Foreward includes a brief biographical sketch of Maimie
    Jellett with an account of her artistic development. Also
    included is a tribute to Jellett from Albert Gleizes, one
    of her teachers.

523   Maimie Jellett, 1897-1944. Dublin: The Neptune Gallery.
[n.d.] 90pp.

Catalog of an exhibit of the author's work includes a
brief biographical account. Describes the artist as
Ireland's first and best Cubist painter.

524   Walker, Dorothy. "Portrait of the Artist as a Young
Woman." J Ir Stud 6 (2) (May 1977): 39-44. il.

(See #506.)

525   White, James. "The Art of Maimie Jellett." Studies 128
(June 1945): 192-193. il.

Very brief note on her artistic training and style with
some biographical information.

Anne Madden (1932-   )

526   "An Artist in Her Setting." Image 7 (July 1982): 66-71.
il. portr.

Feature on home of artists Anne Madden and Louis le
Brocquy with a brief note on Anne Madden.

527   "The Stone's in the Midst of All." Interview with Anne
Madden [by] Richard Kearney. Crane Bag 4 (1) (1980): 112-119.
il.

The artist-wife of Louis de Brocquy comments on feminine
versus masculine painting, the meaning of artistic
expression, her reconciliation of the exigencies of
maternity and creativity, sharing a studio with her
husband, Irish motifs/vision in her work.

Sarah Purser (1848-1943)

528   O'Grady, John. "Sarah Purser 1848-1943." Capu An 44
(1977): 89-104. il. refs.

Brief biographical sketch of the well known Irish artist
Sarah Purser highlights her major achievements both as
artist and art patron.

Nano Reid

529   Curran, Elizabeth. "The Art of Nano Reid." Bell 3 (2)
(Oct. 1941): 128-131. il.

Note on professional career of artist educated at the
Dublin School of Art under Keating before she left for
Paris and then London. Her subject matter, working

methods and exhibits are briefly noted.

Estella Solomons (1882-   )

530   Fallon, Brian. "Estella Solomons, Painter" In
Retrospect: the Work of Seamus O'Sullivan 1879-1958 and
Estella F. Solomons 1882-1968. ed. by Lian Miller, pp.32-45.
Dublin: Dolmen eds., 1973. il. portr.

    Mainly a critical evaluation but includes some
    biographical data on the minor painter Estella Solomons
    whose reputation today is seen to rest primarily on her
    portraiture of the Dublin literati and intelligentsia of
    her day.
    (Review: Ir U R 3 (1973): 114.)

531   The Portraits of Patriots. With a biographical sketch
of the artisit by Hilary Pyle. Dublin: Figgis, 1966. 39pp.
plates.

    A biographical sketch of the artist, Estella Solomons
    with discussion of the portraits of her most notable
    sitters.

532   Pyle, Hilary. "The Portraits of Estella Solomons."
Dublin Mag 3 (3) (1964): 16-20. portrs.

    Includes biographical detail on her education, training
    and professional career. While she produced many
    landscape paintings, her portraits are considered her
    major achievement. Her sitters included members of her
    distinguished family, her friends - among whom were many
    of the main participants in the Irish Literary
    Renaissance and the 1916 rebellion - and other eminent
    personages.

Margaret Stokes (1832-1900)

533   "In Memoriam: Miss Margaret Stokes." J Co Kild Arch Soc
3 (1899/1902): 201-205. portr. refs.

    A brief tribute to Miss Stokes describes her historical
    work on ancient Irish art. Includes a list of her
    publications which included descriptions and drawings of
    the sculptured high crosses of Ireland.

Mary Swanzy (1882-   )

534   Mary Swanzy. Retrosepective Exhibition of Paintings
June 6-29, 1968 at the Municipal Gallery of Modern Art,
Parnell Square Dublin. [Dublin: Municipal Gallery, 1968.]
47pp.

Introduction has a brief biographical note on the artist.

Frances Wynne (1866-1893)

535   Wynne, Frances. <u>Eastward of All</u>. Dublin: M.H.Gill and
Son, 1945. 194pp. il.

   Autobiography by the painter wherein she reminisces about
   her Protestant Unionist background, her art education in
   Paris and London, her marriage, the ups and downs in her
   life and her eventual conversion to Catholicism.

RELIGION AND EDUCATION

   This section considers women primarily in their capacity
as founders or members of religious communities who were also
in many cases pioneers of female Catholic education. It is
also concerned with saints whether canonically anointed or in
popular tradition. The primary emphasis is on the lives and
achievements of individual women rather than on the orders to
which they belonged, or places or practices associated with
the cult of a particular saint, though there is, obviously,
great overlap. Also included here are works on major
philanthropists who would appear to have been motivated
primarily by religious impulses; lay women with major
involvement with religious groups or practices; the role of
women in the religious formation of their children and the
influence of major religious figures on the development of an
Irish ideal of womanhood. Collective works are arranged
alphabetically by author in the GENERAL section followed by
an alphabetical listing of individual religious figures.
Multiple entries for the same individual are arranged
alphabetically by author.
   The role of women in the Church, religious vocations,
convent life, role of religious communities in society at
large and their relationships with other social groups, and
religious beliefs and practices will be found in the section
on RELIGION. The section on EDUCATION should be consulted for
additional information on non Catholic educators and their
work in the development of Irish female education. For the
influence of religious beliefs on family planning see HUMAN
SEXUALITY, REPRODUCTION AND HEALTH; on intermarriage or
divorce see MARRIAGE AND THE FAMILY; for feminist critiques
of religion and religious critiques of feminism see
PERSPECTIVES ON WOMEN'S LIBERATION.
   While many of the biographies of nuns included share a
general tendency toward undue adulation, many of the full
length studies appear to be well researched and generally
reliable. The same can not be said for the "Lives" of the
saints which are for the most part based on legend and
involve in many cases simply a listing of miracles and/or
practices of extreme self denial attributed to their
subjects, or ideal depictions of female character.

General

536   Concannon, Helena. "The Holy Women of the Gael." Ir Mon
XLV (Feb. 1917): 83-93. refs.

    A discussion of the legends surrounding St. Brigid, St.
    Ita and other female Irish saints and their
    characteristic virtues. Their role in the formation of
    the Gaelic ideal of womanhood - chaste, loyal,
    hospitable, charitable, homemakers, thrifty - briefly
    noted.

537   Concannon, Helena. "The Mothers of the Saints of Erin."
Ir Mon 44 (1916): 345-557. notes.

    Legends surrounding St. Comghall of Bangor and Brija, his
    mother; Eithne, the Princess of Tirconaill, the mother of
    Columcille; Cara, the Mother of Brendan, the Voyager;
    Darerca, Mother of Ciaran; the Mother of Columban; Cumne,
    Mother of Mochua of Balla; Coimgell, Mother of St. Senan.

538   Dease, Alice. Good Women of Erin. London: R & T
Washborne, Ltd. n.d. 119pp. il.

    Legends regarding noble women who became converts to
    Christianity in the era of Saint Patrick: Lafinda,
    Darlughacha, Franchea, Sister Dara, Sister Blart,
    Princess Dympna, St. Gobnata, Princesses Eithne and
    Fedelin - daughters of King Leary, chief ruler of Erin,
    St. Modwenna, St. Ita, Rathnata, St. Colman's sister and
    Abbess Attracta.

539   "Legends of the Celtic Saints." Univ Mag LXVI (Oct.
1865): 388-406.

    Brief account of miracles associated with St. Bridget,
    her follower Daria and St. Edna's sister Fanchea, and the
    hermit, Enora.

540   Mould, Daphne D.C. Pochin. The Irish Saints. Dublin:
Clonmore and Reynolds Ltd., 1964. 316pp. bibl.

    Critical short biographies of the principal Irish saints
    from the time of St. Patrick to that of St. Laurence
    O'Toole based on original documents and secondary
    scholarly works. Women saints include Brigit (Brigid),
    Gobnet, Damhnat, Attracht (Attracta), Liadhain (Lalia-a
    composite), Monenna.

541   O'Gorman, John (Rev.) Three Irish Nuns. Kingston,
Ontario: Catholic Truth Society of Canada, 1929. 29pp. (A
lecture delivered in St. Mary's Cathedral, Kingston, on St.
Patrick's Night, 1929, by Rev. John J. O'Gorman.)

Brief overview of the careers of Nano Nagle, foundress of the Irish Sisters of Charity; Catherine McAuley, the foundress of the Presentation Order and Mary Aikenhead, foundress of the Sisters of Mercy.

542   O'Hanlon, John. Lives of the Irish Saints, compiled from calendars, martyrologies and various sources. Dublin: 1875-1903. 10 vols.

Listed chronologically by festivals with an extensive, introductory bibliographical essay detailing authorities consulted, original manuscripts, secondary sources and locations.

Mary Aikenhead (1787-1858)

543   A[tkinson], S[arah]. Mary Aikenhead: Her Life, Her Work, and Her Friends. Giving a history of the foundation of the congregation of the Irish Sisters of Charity. Dublin: M.H.Gill and Son.,1879. 512pp. portrs. refs.

The author has utilized the Annals of the Sisters of Charity, original documents and letters and personal accounts to produce this highly detailed history of the Order. The social context - Ireland in the Penal Days - is presented along with an account of the Foundress' Mary Aikenhead's birth, parentage, childhood and adolescence; the social circle in which the family moved, her vocation to the religious life and her realization of her goal of devoting her life to the care of the poor. The first convent of the Sisters of Charity was on the North Side of Dublin where they undertook also the running of an orphange. Later their work extended to visiting the sick in their homes, education - with the help of the Christian Bros. - in schools for the poor, visiting the gaols and later the hospitals. Eventually they were able to realize the Foundress' dream and open up a hospital run by the Sisters themselves. Daily life and activities, visitors, friends, trials and expansion of the Order both in Ireland and overseas minutely described.
(Review: Hibernia 1 (June 1882): 93-94.)
(Review: Ir Mon VII (Aug. 1879): 422-431.)
(Review: Ir Eccl Rec 4th Ser. XXX (Dec. 1911): 662.)
(Review: Ir Mon X (1882): 53-54))

544   Aikenhead, family of; Query Concerning the Foregoing Family from which sprang Sister Mary Aikenhead, Founder of the Sisters of Charity. Clon Hist & Arch Soc J 5th ser. XVIII (1912): 54.

545   Aikenhead, (Mother Mary). "Extract From the Decree... Concerning The Beatification and Canonization of... Mary Aikenhead." Capu An (1958): 120-121. portr.

The Sacred Congregation of Rites approved the Commission
of the Introduction of the cause of the Servant of God
Mary Aikenhead, Foundress of the Institute of the Sisters
of Charity in Ireland on the 20th of March 1921.

546   Aikenhead, Mary A. Letters. Dublin: M.H.Gill and Son,
1914. 570pp. portr. [Preface by P.M. MacSweeney]

    A chronological arrangement by recipient of Mother Mary
    Aikenhead's correspondence covering the years 1831-1854.
    Recipients include her religious colleagues Mother Mary
    de Chartal, Sister Mary Peter O'Byrne, Mother Francis
    Magdalen, Mother Mary Ignatius, Mother Mary Agnes, Mother
    Magdalen Regis, Mother Mary Elizabeth, Mother Mary
    Justinian, Mother Mary Baptist.
    (Review: Ir Eccl Rec 5th Ser. 3 (Mar. 1914): 323-327.)
    (Review: Ir Mon XLII (Apr. 1914): 118-201.)

547   Belloc, Bessie Raymer Parkes. Historic Nuns. Edinburgh,
London: Sands & Co., 1911. 223pp.

    Biographies of Mrs. Aikenhead, foundress of the Irish
    Sisters of Charity and Mrs. McAuley, foundress of the
    Sisters of Mercy selected and condensed from the
    biography of the former by Mrs. Atkinson (See #543) and
    Leaves from the Annals of the Sisters of Mercy by Mother
    Austin Carroll. (See #665)

548   de Buitleir, Eiblin. "Mary Aikenhead: Foundress of the
Congregation of the Irish Sisters of Charity." Ir Mon 53
(1925): 147-150; 188-192.

    A summary of the main features of Mary Aikenhead: Her
    Life, Her Work, and Her Friends. (See #543)

549   Carey, F.P. Ireland's Valient Woman. Stories of Graces
and Favours Attributed to the Intercession of Mother Mary
Aikenhead. Dublin: Irish Messenger Office, 1935. 28pp.

550   Curtayne, Alice. The Servant of God: Mother Mary
Aikenhead: Foundress of the Irish Sisters of Charity
1787-1858. Dublin: The Anthonian Press, 1935. 53pp. il.
portr.

551   Degnan, Sister M. Bertrand. Mercy Unto Thousands.
Dublin: Browne and Nolan, 1958. 394pp. il. map. front. bibl.

    A biography of Mother Mary Aikenhead.
    (Review: Studies XLIX (1960): 225-228.)
    (Review: Ir Eccl Rec Ser. 2 XCII (4) (Oct. 1959): 262-263.)

552   Gallagher, Frank. "The Gay Soul of Mary Aikenhead, A Strange Story of an Heroic Life." Capu An (1958): 141-151. il.

553   Hallack, Cecily. The Servant of God: Mother Mary Aikenhead, Foundress of the Irish Sisters of Charity, 1785-1858. A Sketch of Her Life. Dublin: Anthonian Press, 1937. 40pp. il. plates.

554   Hallack, Cecily. A Wise Woman. The Spirit of Mother Mary Aikenhead, Foundress of the Irish Sisters of Charity. Dublin: Anthonian Press. 1943. 36pp. portr.

    Eulogistic tribute to Mother Aikenhead stresses her courage, strong-mindedness, statesmanship, foresight, insight, kindness and prudence.

555   Hilary (Rev. Father) (O.F.M. Cap.) "Mother Mary Aikenhead. The Charity Of Christ Presents Us." Ir Eccl Rec 5th ser. XC (July 1958): 28-37.

    Brief overview of the life of Mother Mary Aikenhead and work of the Congregation in Dublin, Cork and Australia.

556   Mageean, Robert.(C.SS.R.) Holiness of Mother Mary Aikenhead: Did She Practice Heroic Virtue? Dublin: The Anthonian Press, 1958. 19pp.

    Devotional pamphlet discusses the nature of heroic virtue and the life of Mary Aikenhead. Author concludes that she lived "in active conformity with God's will" and thus her cause (for Beatification) warrants promotion with the Congregation of Rites who alone can make a determination.

557   Nethercott, Maria. The Story of Mary Aikenhead, Foundress of the Irish Sisters of Charity. London: Burns and Oates, 1897. 196pp.

    Abbreviated summary of the definitive biography by Sarah Atkinson. (See #543.)
  (Review: Ir Mon 25 (1897): 500.)

558   O'Carroll, Michael (Rev.) "The Personality of Mary Aikenhead." Capu An (1958): 122-131. il.

    Brief biographical note includes an overview of her achievement and notes her spiritual qualities.

559   O'Dea, Father Colga. Our Lady's Handmaid: The Story of Mary Aikenhead's Devotion to the Mother of God. Dublin: Clonmore and Reynolds, 1961. 64pp.

Mainly excerpts from the letters and spiritual sayings of Mary Aikenhead illustrative of her sanctity and deep devotion to Our lady.

560   Purcell, Mary. "Reading Between the Lines of Mary Aikenhead's Letters." Capu An (1958): 132-140.

Comment on content, context and recipients of letters mostly written by Mary Aikenhead between her 41st and 71st year when she was a chronic invalid. Includes excerpts.

Mother Arsenius (1828?-1931)

561   Gildea, Denis. Mother Arsenius of Foxford. Dublin, London: Burns, Oates and Washbourne, 1936. 198pp. plates. portr.

A detailed biography of a Sister of Charity who combined personal holiness with skills as a teacher, administrator and businesswoman. Agnes Morrogh Bernard had an indulged childhood as the daughter of a rich Kerry landlord. She joined the Irish Sisters of Charity in 1854 and taught for many years before being assigned administrative responsibilities, at Ballaghaderreen County Mayo and at Foxford, where she established a woolen industry to combat pervasive unemployment.
(Review: Ir Mon 64 (1936): 704-705.)

562   Ryan, John (Rev.) "A Centenary and a Golden Jubilee: Mother Morrogh Bernard and the Providence Woolen Mills. [Foxford] 1842-1892." Studies 31 (1942): 229-236.

Brief note on career and achievements of Mother Arsenius.

Margaret Aylward (1810-1889)

563   Gibbons, Margaret. The Life of Margaret Aylward, Foundress of the Sisters of the Holy Faith. London: Sands and Co., 1928. 426pp. il. front.

Detailed account, based mainly on her correspondence and convent records, of the career of Margaret Aylward who after initial efforts to pursue a religious career with the Irish Sisters of Charity and later, the Ursulines, established a secular society, the Association of the Ladies of Charity in Dublin in 1851 and later in 1856, St. Brigid's Orphanage Association which later developed into the religious community of the Sisters of the Holy Faith dedicated to Catholic Education.
(Review: Studies XVII (Dec. 1928): 718.)
(Review: Cath Bull 19 (1929): 95-96.)

(Review: Ir Mon 57 (1929): 559.)
(Review: Ir Book Lov XVII (Mar. Apr. 1929): 48.)

564   Gibbons, Margaret. "Margaret Aylward, Foundress of the
Sisters of the Holy Faith (1810-1889)." Ir Mon 54-56
(1926-1928): 138 ff.

    Serialized biography of Margaret Aylward later published
    in a monograph. (See #563)

565   Gibbons, Margaret. A Prisoner of the Poor: Margaret
Aylward, Foundress of the Holy Faith Sisters. Dublin: Irish
Messenger Office. [1967] 28pp.

    A much abbreviated edition of the same author's biography
    of Margaret Aylward, published in 1928.

Mother Frances Mary Teresa Ball (1794-1861)

566   Coleridge, Henry James (S.J.) The Life of Mother
Frances Mary Teresa Ball, Foundress in Ireland of the
Institute of the Blessed Virgin Mary. Dublin, London:
M.H.Gill and Son, Burns & Oates, 1881. 368pp. il. portrs.

    Valuable early biography of Frances Ball based on the
    archives of the order and her own correspondence.
    Includes an introductory chapter on the Rev. Daniel
    Murray, Archbishop of Dublin, 1809-1852 and his role in
    this and other foundations.
(Review: Ir Mon 9 (Jan. 1881): 55.)
(Review: Ir Eccl Rec 3rd Ser. 2 (May 1881): 314-315.)

567   Hutch, William. Mrs. Ball: Foundress of the Institute
of The Blessed Virgin Mary in Ireland and the British
Colonies. A Biography. Dublin: Duffy, 1879. 590pp. refs.

(Review: Ir Mon 7 (July 1879): 391.)
(Review: Ir Eccl Rec 3rd. Ser. 2 (May 1881): 314-315.)

568   A Loreto Sister. Joyful Mother of Children: Mother
Frances Mary Teresa Ball. Dublin: M.H.Gill & Son. Ltd., 1961.
347pp. portr. plates. bibl.

    A detailed account of the life of Frances Ball based on
    previously published biographies and unpublished
    manuscripts, memoirs and correspondence in the archives
    of Loreto convents in Ireland. Describes her affluent
    childhood, her education at St. Mary's convent in York,
    her family's initial opposition to her decision to
    become a religious, her noviceship and profession at the
    Yorke convent, her return to Ireland to head the branch
    of the Loreto order established at Rathfarmham, Dublin
    and to direct the first boarding school for Catholic

girls; also a free day school for the children of the
Catholic poor. The subsequent expansion of the Loreto
order in Ireland and abroad and Mother Ball's
administrative talents minutely detailed.
(Review: Stud Hibern No. 3 (1963): 221-222.)

569   Margaret Mary, Mother. Call to Happiness: Life of
Mother Francis Mary Teresa Ball, Foundress of the Irish
Branch of the Institute of the Blessed Virgin Mary Popularly
Known as "Loreto". Dublin: Catholic Truth Society, 1963.
37pp. portr.

Mother Mary Genevieve Beale (1822-1878)

570   Life of Mother Mary Genevieve Beale, Foundress of The
Sisters of St. Louis in Ireland. Dublin: Office of the Irish
Messenger, 1935. 27pp. portr.

Brief biographical sketch of Priscilla Beale born in
London of Protestant parents. At age 23 she came to
Ireland and was converted to Catholicism. Later as a
novice she went to Paris and entered the convent of the
Dames of St. Louis at Juilly. Invited by the Bishop of
Clogher to set up a foundation of the St. Louis Order in
Monaghan she returned to Ireland and the sisters taught
in the local school, visited the sick, etc. Subsequent
expansion of the order briefly noted.

571   Pauline, Sister Mary. God Wills It: Centenary Story of
The Sisters of St. Louis. Dublin: Browne and Nolan, 1959.
320pp.

Written for the Centenary Celebrations of the St. Louis
order in Ireland by a young Sister of that order this
book includes a biography of Mother Genevieve Beale,
foundress of the First St. Louis convent in Ireland and
an account of the origins and history of the
congregation.
(Review: Studies 49 (Summer 1960) 225-228.)
(Review: Stud Hibern No.1 (1961): 239-240.)

Sister Clare Boylan (-1876)

572   Life Sketch of Sister Clare Boylan, Superioress of the
Sisters of Charity in Drogheda. Dublin: M.H.Gill and Son.,
1877.

This short biographical account details Sister Boylan's
entry into the order of the Sisters of Charity who then
had no Irish Foundation. She became a postulant at Amiens
and later at Paris. After her profession she was sent to
Smyrna where she taught English in the School and

assisted in the Orphanage. She was recalled to work among
the Irish poor in London and later Liverpool. Finally in
1872 she was placed as Superior over the convent of her
Order in Drogheda.
(Review: Ir Mon 5 (1877): 474.)

                    Saint Brigid (453-523)

573   Atkinson, Sarah. "St. Brigid" In Ireland's Spiritual
Shamrock: Being Lives of St. Patrick, St. Brigid and St.
Columba. London: Catholic Truth Society, 1895. 48pp.
[Reprinted from the Irish Monthly Vol. XVI.]

     Brief popular account of the Saint differs from most
     other versions in according Brigid noble birth on both
     parents side. Recounts characteristics and illustrative
     legends of the Saint, her missionary travels and her
     monastic settlement at Kildare.

574   Barrett, Rosa M. "St. Brigid, or St. Mary of the Gael."
Occult R 35 (1921): 333-340. il.

     Asserts that it was through St. Brigid, the first
     prominent woman worker in the Irish church, that the
     whole status of women was elevated and the military was
     abolished. A brief sketch of the life - admits that most
     existing accounts are legendary, recounts one version of
     these. Also brief note of her miracles, shrines - the
     various lifes of the Saint.

575   Bethu Brigte. Ed. by Donncha O h Aodha. Dublin:
Institute for Advanced Studies, 1978. 91pp. refs.

     The text of the earliest surviving life of Saint Brigid
     written largely in Irish (7th century) with an English
     translation, summary and critical commentary. This
     account compared with the "Life" by Cogitosus (also 7th
     century). The Latin "Life" most closely related to this
     text dates from mid-9th century.
(Review: Eigse 17 (4) (1979): 565-570.)

576   de Blacam, Aodhsamdrach. The Saints of Ireland: the
Life Stories of St. Brigid and Columcille. Milwaukee: the
Bruce Publishing Company, 1942. 218pp. il. maps. front. refs.

     Most of Book One devoted to Saint Brigid: the Mary of the
     Gael (pp.14-66). Chief source would appear to be the
     "Life" by Cogitosus.

577   Bowen, E.G. "The Cult of St. Brigit." Stud Celt 8-9
(1973-74): 33-47. maps. refs.

Discusses the cult of St. Brigit; fertility and other rites associated with her feast day, the major symbolism connected with the Saint, and the geographical distribution of the cult in the Celtic lands - e.g. all of Atlantic Britain and parts of Brittany - as exemplified by the churches and chapels bearing her name.

578   Cambier, l'Abbe G. Histoire de Sainte Brigide de Kildare: Vierge et Thaumaturge. 2nd ed. Lodelinsart: Imprimerie Cambier - Bouquiaux, 1901. 64pp.

579   Certani (Giacomo): LaSantita Prodigiosa, Vita di S. Brigida. Ibernese. Venetia, [1677] 16+568pp.

580   Colgan, John. Triadis Thaumaturgae, seu Divorum Patricii, Columbae et Brigidae, Trium Veteris et Maioris Scotiae, seu Hiberniae Sanctorum Insulae, Communium Patronorum acta, a Variis... Authoribus Scripta, ac Studio J. Colgani... Collecta... Illustrata... aucta; Complectitur. Tomas Secundus Sacrarum Ejusdem Insulae Antiquitatum. Lovanii: Apud Genestenium, 1647. 742pp.

581   Connolly, Sean. "Verbal Usage in Vita Peima Brigitae and Bethu Brigte." Peritia 1 (1982): 268-272. refs.

   A detailed examination of some semantic and syntactic features of verbal usage in two 'Lives' of Saint Brigid.

582   Cowell, George Young (Rev.). "St. Brigid and the Cathedral Church of Kildare." J Co Kild Arch Soc 2 (1896-1899): 236-251. il. refs.

   Brief biographical sketch of the Saint with an account of the foundation of the monastery at Kildare which later had affiliated with it many other monasteries both female and male. Author traces references to the monastery and the successive attacks on it by invaders in the historical record.

583   Curtayne, Alice. "The Rediscovery of Saint Brigid." Ir Mon 63 (1935): 412-420.

   Note on revival of cult of St. Brigid with the first National Pilgrimage to her birthplace, Faughert in July 1934.

584   Curtayne, Alice. Saint Brigid the Mary of Ireland. Dublin: Anthonian Press, 1933. 31pp. il.

585   Curtayne, Alice. Saint Brigid of Ireland. Dublin: Browne and Nolan, 1933. 162pp.

A popular biography which the author admits is not a
critical life. The limitations of the work from the point
of view of scholarly research are noted.
(Review: Ir Book Lov 21 (1933): 141.)
(Review: Ir Mon LXVII (Aug. 1939): 577-586.)
(Review: Studies 45 (1956): 128.)

586   Cusack, Mary Frances. The Lives of Saint Columba and
Saint Brigit. London: Burns and Oates; Dublin: M.H.Gill and
Son, 1877. 256pp. notes.

(Also formed part of The Trias Thaumaturga by the same
author. See #587)
(Review: Ir Mon v.6 (1878): 529-530.)

587   Cusack, Mary Frances. The Trias Thaumaturga or Three
Wonder-Working Saints of Ireland: St. Patrick, St. Bridget,
and St. Columba. London: J.G. Murdoch. (n.d.) 959pp. il.

588   Donnelly, Maureen. Patrick, Brigid and Colmcille.
Bangor: Donard Pub., 1977. 31pp. il.

Brief version of the life of Saint Brigid written for
school children. (pp. 14-19)

589   Esposito, Mario. "On the Latin Life of St. Brigid of
Kildare." Roy Ir Acad Proc Section C. 30 (Sept. 1912):
307-326. plates. refs.

The author presents the notes he assembled from having
collated thoroughly two manuscripts, one at London, the
other at Oxford both based on the most ancient Latin
document dealing with St. Brigid of Kildare e.g. the life
by Cogitosus. Author points out that a host of other
manuscripts of this Vita exist in many continental
libraries and hopes that some scholar might collate all
of these so that this Vita might be re-edited.

590   Fitzgerald, Walter (Lord). "The Erection of a Church to
St. Brigid at Kildare in A.D. 868." J Co Kild Arch Soc 4
(1903-1905): 65.

Note on the erection of a church in honor of St. Brigid
by Queen Flanna, wife of the monarch of Ireland.

591   Fitzgerald, Walter (Lord). "The Patron Saint of Kill."
J Co Kild Arch Soc 8 (1915-1917): 222-223. refs.

Note on St. Brigid's church at Kill, County Kildare and
St. Brigid's well in the adjoining townland of Hartwell
Lower.

592   "Fragments from the Early Irish Church." Ir Eccl Rec 5
(Jan. 1869): 224-229. refs.

Includes an excerpt from the Leabhar Breac (Speckled
Book) in the Royal Irish Academy consisting of a very
ancient sermon in praise of St. Brigid written partly in
Latin and partly in Irish with a translation of the Irish
portion.

593   Hayden, Tadhg. St. Brigid and Kildare Cathedral: Their
Backgrounds, Pagan and Christian, Irish and European: A
Summary of a Lecture. Kildare: [The author], 1979. 12pp.

Brief overview of Celtic society described as ordered and
heirarchical where Christianity and Paganism overlapped
at the period when the Kildare foundation was
established.

594   Irvine, Christopher. (Rev.) St. Brigid and Her Times
According to the Account of the Honorable Algernon Herbert.
Dublin: Hodges, 1903. 101pp.

An account of druidism in the British Isles argues that
St. Brigid was not an historical figure but simply a
personification of the Druidical mythical goddess, vestal
keeper of the sacred fire whom the hagiologists located
in the Christian tradition and endowed with a specific
biography.

595   King, Robert (Rev.) The Saintly Triad or the Lives of
St. Patrick, St. Columkille and St. Bridget... Taken from the
Ancient Irish Records Published by Father Colgan and Other
Eminent Men. Dublin: The Booksellers, 1844. 223pp. portrs.

Brief account of the life of Saint Bridget (pp. 168-188.)

596   Knowles, J.A. St. Brigid, Patroness of Ireland. New
York, etc.: Benziger Bros., 1907. 292pp. il. front. (portr.)
refs.

 (Review: Ir Mon 35 (1907): 409.)

597   Knowles, Joseph. St. Brigid: Patroness of Ireland.
Dublin: Browne and Nolan, 1929. 220pp. portr.

598   Leatham, Diana. The Story of Saint Brigid of Ireland.
London: Faith Press, 1955. 66pp. il. bibl.

 (Review: Ir Book Lov 32 (July 1956): 119.)

599   Lynch, Maud. St. Brigid of Ireland. Dublin: M.H.Gill &
Son, Ltd., 1940. 24pp. il.

600   Mac Aodha. An T Athar Padraig. <u>Naom Brigid</u>. Gaillim: O
Gormain, 1937. 32pp.

601   McCarroll, James (Rev.) <u>St. Brigid Patroness of the
Irish Race: The Story of the Homecoming Of Her Relic</u>. Dublin:
Printed at the Sign of the Three Candles, 1930. 12pp.

602   McClintock, H. "The Mantle of Saint Brigid at Bruges."
<u>Co Louth Arch J</u> 12 (3) (1951): 119-122. il.

    A critical discussion of the piece of fabric in the
    Treasury of the Cathedral at Bruges, Belgium supposed to
    be a relic of St. Brigid. McClintock considers it
    plausible that this was in fact brought there by Princess
    Gunhild of England, a sister of King Harold, after the
    death of her brother and husband at the Battle of
    Hastings and speculates on how it came to be in their
    possession. Age of fabric can not be conclusively
    established - considered to be at least as early as 1050.

603   McCone, Kim. "Brigit in the Seventh Century: A Saint
With Three Lives?" <u>Peritia</u> 1 (1982): 107-145. refs.

    Reviews evidence from three seventh century 'Lives' of
    St. Bridget, each with a more or less determinable
    regional and political bias, to suggest that the struggle
    between Armagh and Kildare for ecclesiastical supremacy
    may not have been resolved by mutual consent until the
    eight century.

604   Mc Crait, Micheal. <u>Beitil z Brigid</u>. Cille-dara, Baile
Atha Cliath. Comhlucht na Firinne Catoilice i nEirinn. 1919.
12pp.

605   Mc Gahan, L. "St. Brigid's Birthplace." <u>Ir Mon</u> 17
(1889): 372-379.

    Description of Faughard Churchyard located between
    Dundark and Newry where the ruined church is supposed to
    be the site of the house in which St. Brigid was born.
    Author describes the "station" celebrating the memory of
    the Saint which is observed by frequent pilgrims and
    recounts some of the legends associated with the Saint.

606   McKeown, L. (Rev.) "St. Brigid in Antrim and Down."
<u>Down & O'Connor</u> 6 (1934): 58-59.

    Note on various shrines and places of worship dedicated
    to St. Brigid and some legends attached to these.

607   Mac Suibhne, Peader and Patrick McCormack. <u>Saint Brigid
and the Shrines of Kildare</u>. Naas: Leinster Leader, 1972.
67pp. il.

Brief account of the history and legends of Kildare with
a biographical sketch of St. Brigid based on earlier
accounts and the published researches of modern scholars.

608   Maire. (pseud.) "Saint Brigid." Cath Bull 5 (2) (Feb.
1915): 156-157.

Brief article on devotion to St. Brigid among the
Scottish Catholics.

609   Maire. (pseud.) "The School of Kildare." Cath Bull 6
(8) (Aug. 1916): 452-454. refs.

Very brief note on the position of women in ancient
Ireland, St. Brigid and the monastery she founded at
Kildare.

610   Mould, D.D.C. Pochin. Saint Brigid. Dublin: Clonmore
and Reynolds, 1964. 75pp. refs.

One of the few critical accounts of the life of Ireland's
patron saint stresses the very little that can be
factually established about her life - e.g. that she was
born in the mid-5th century of a slave woman called
Broicsech by her pagan master Dubtoch (Dubtach); that she
made a public vow of virginity and settled with other
like minded young women in Kildare and devoted her life
to doing good. She died around 524. Mould contrasts the
enormity of her reputation with the paucity of factual
information - most of the other "lives" are dismissed as
simply legends. The sources for many of the legends, the
spread of the liturgical and popular cult of the Saint
and the role of political factors critically discussed.
(Review: J Co Kild Arch Soc 14 (2) (1966-1967): 276-278.)

611   Murray, Laurence P.C.C. "Devotion to St. Brigid in
South -East Ulster." Cath Bull 11 (5) (May 1921): 295-300.
refs.

Author reviews the evidence of the strong devotion to St.
Brigid three or four centuries ago in the territory of
her birthplace in southeast Ulster. Details of the
ceremonies marking her feast day provided.

612   Nolan, Patrick. (O.S.B.M.A.) "Notes on the Foreign
Cultures of St. Brigid of Ireland." Cath Bull 8 (2) (Feb.
1918): 83-86. refs.

Author decries the fact that to date there has not been a
worthy biography of St. Brigid and discusses devotion to
St. Brigid on the Continent - mainly in Germany and
Alsace- Lorraine.

613   Norris, Sylvester. The Guide of Faith. Menston: Scholar
Press, 1974. [Reprint:1621] 216pp.

    Includes a chapter on the life of Saint Brigid
    (pp.107-140).

614   O'Brien, M.A. "The Old Irish Life of St. Brigit." Ir
Hist Stud 1 (2,4) (Sept. 1938-39): 121-134; 343-353. refs.

    Part 1 is a literal translation of the manuscript in the
    Bodleian Library, Oxford - a Life of St. Brigit written
    in Irish with numerous Latin phrases. Part 2 comprises a
    critical study of the "Life" with notes on the text and
    dating of the manuscript. The "Life" is not a biography
    in any real sense but brief paragraphs on various aspects
    or incidents in the life of the Saint.

615   O Domhnaill, Maghnus, Ed. Beata Bridghde Ar Lr. Baile
ata Cliat, Oifig an t Solatair, 1940. 72pp.

    (Review: Eigse 2 (1940): 291-293.)

616   O'Flanagan, M. "The Mary of the Gael." Cath Bull 7 (1)
(Jan. 1917): 77-79.

    In this brief article the author discusses the deep
    popular devotion to St. Bridget manifested in Cologne,
    Germany and decries the Irish apathy that results in her
    not having official church recognition as a Saint.

617   O h Aodha, Donncha. Bethu Brigte. Dublin: Institute
for Advanced Studies, 1978. 91pp.

    (See #575.)

618   O h Aodha, Donncha. "The Early Lives of Saint Brigit."
J Co Kild Arch Soc XV (4) (1974-75): 397-405. refs.

    Bibliographical essay comparing and contrasting the two
    earliest accounts of the life of St. Brigid.

619   Paterson, T.G.F. "Brigid's Crosses in County Armagh."
Ulster J Archae 8 (1945): 43-48. il. plates. refs. (Also in
Co Louth Arch J 2 (1) (1945): 15-20.)

    Discusses the traditional custom - now falling into decay
    - of making crosses on the Eve of the St. Brigid's
    festival. Details exact procedure, materials used,
    patterns, etc. Also lists places, shrines associated with
    the Saint's memory in Armagh.

620   Redemptorist Father (A) and Micheal ua Flainn. <u>Saint Brigid (Irish-English)</u>. New And Revised Edition. Dublin: Catholic Truth Society, 1914. 62pp.

(Review: <u>Ir Mon</u> 40 (1912): 172.)

621   Robinson, John L. (Archdeacon) "St. Brigid and Glastonbury." <u>Roy Soc Antiq Ire J</u> LXXXIII Part I (1953): 97-99. refs.

   Legend of the visit by St. Brigid to the monastery of Glastonbury in the West of England with a discussion of its historical validity.

622   Ronan, Myles V. (Rev.) "Early Irish Foundations of St. Patrick, St. Brigid and St. Coluimchille." <u>Acad Chr Art J</u> 1 (1937): 36-38. plates.

   Summary of papers read before the Academy includes a note on St. Brigid's "Teach Mor" or oratory.

623   Ryan, John. <u>Saint Brigid of Cill Dara</u>. Dublin: Irish Meesenger Office, 1978. 31pp.

624   Schmid, Toni. "Le Culte en Suede de Ste. Brigide l' Irlandaise." <u>Analectica Bollandiana</u> 61 (1943):108-115.refs.

625   Seyler, Clarence A. "Seinhenyd, Ystumilwynarth and Ynysgynwraid: Some Placenames and Folklore in Wales." <u>Archaeo Cambr</u> 101 Part 1 (1950): 23-37. il.

   The village of Skenfrith in Wales was formerly known as St. Brigid's Cloak; a church dedicated to St. Brigid honors a piece of cloth as the "mantle" of St. Brigid. Seyler explores source of linkage between St. Brigid and a mantle in Welsh and Irish legend, folklore and other legends associated with the Saint.

626   Sharkey, P.A. (Rev.) <u>The Lily of Erin; Saint Brigid</u>. New York: Published by the author, 1921. 158pp. il. refs.

(Review: <u>Cath Bull</u> 12 (May 1922): 322.)

627   Sharpe, Richard. "Vitae S. Brigidae: the Oldest Texts." <u>Peritia</u> 1 (1982): 81-106.

   Analysis of various 'Lives' in terms of their utility in clarifying the general development of Hiberno - Latin hagiography in the Middle Ages. Also their unique value as literary texts explored.

628   Sherlock, William. _Some Account of St. Brigid, and of the See of Kildare, With its Bishop, and the Cathedral, Now Restored_. Dublin: Hodges, Figgis and Co., 1896. 52pp. il.

629   Stokes, Whitley. (Ed.) _Three Middle-Irish Homilies on the Lives of Saints Patrick, Brigit and Columba_. Calcutta, 1877. 140pp. refs.

   Hitherto unprinted transcription from the lithographic facsimile of the Lebar Breac, a manuscript of the 5th century, preserved in the library of the Royal Irish Academy. The homily on Saint Brigid "furnishes a good example of the way in which heathen mythological legends become annexed to historical Christian saints."

630   Stubbs, (F.W.) "The Birthplace and Life of St. Brigit of Kildare." _J Co Kild Arch Soc_ 3 (July 1899-1902): 216-228. il. refs.

   Reviews the various editions of the ancient lives of the Saint: Colgan in his _Trias Thaumaturga_ lists six. Four of these are mainly records of miracles attributed to her, legends of a later date or amplification of traditions devoid of any sequence. Presents main outlines of her biography assembled from Dr. Whitley Stokes version taken from the Book of Lismore - which corresponds with Colgan's "3rd Life" - and the "Life" by Cogitosus.

631   Tatlock, J.S.P. "Greater Irish Saints in Lawman and in England." _Mod Philo_ 43 (Aug. 1945): 72-76. refs.

   A discussion of the British epic poet, Lawman's knowledge of Ireland as revealed by passages in his work showing acquaintance with its saints, especially the three contemporaries of ancient Christian Ireland e.g. Columba, Brendan and Brigid.

632   _Triadis Thaumaturgae, seu Divorum Patricii, Columbar et Brigidae, trium Veteris et Maioris Scotiae, seu Hiberniae Sanctorum Insulae, Communium Patronorum Acta, a Variis... Authoribus Scripta, ac studio. J. Colgani...Collecta... Illustrata...aucta; Complecilur Tomas Securdus Sacrarum Ejusden Unsulae Antiquitalum_. pp[22+] 742. Louani, Apud Coenestenium, 1647.

633   Walsh, James J. "St. Bridget: Pioneer Feminine Educator." In his _These Splendid Sisters_, pp. 23-41. Freeport, New York: Books for Libraries, [1927], [1970].

634   Wilkie, James. _Saint Bridget: The Greatest Woman of the Celtic Church_. London: T.N.Foulis, 1913. 53pp. refs.

Mainly a retelling of some of the legends associated wit
St. Bridget with a discussion of her appeal in Scotland.
Explains the tremendous veneration for her in the Celtic
world as a combination of the repute of the historical
Brigid and the prestige of a preChristian goddess of the
same name.

Mother Dominic O'Brien Butler

635   M.R. "Two Irish Nuns." Ir Mon 11 (1883): 479-484.

(See Mother Bridget Carroll #637.)

Anne Jane Carlile (1775-1864)

636   Barron, Thomas J. "Anne Jane Carlile." Breifne 2 (6)
1963): 234-237. refs.

The wife of a Presbyterian Minister, after whose death
and the subsequent deaths of three of her seven children,
became an activist in the cause of temperance and made
frequent visits to Scotland and England to advocate
formation of temperance societies.

Mother Bridget Carroll

637   R[ussell], M[atthew]. "Two Irish Nuns." Ir Mon 11
(Sept. 1883): 479-484.

Tribute to Mother Bridget Carroll of the Presentation
Order at George's Hill, Superior of that convent for 30
years who died the previous January. Also includes the
text of "In Memoriam" composed in honor of Mother Dominic
O'Brien Butler of the Dominican Convent, Sion Hill, who
died on February 20, 1883.

Sister Consilio

638   O'Callaghan, Tanis. "Profile: Sister Consilio." Image
(3) (Feb. 1978): 35. portr.

Interview with a religious famous for her alcohol
treatment centre, Cuan Mhuire in Athy.

Margaret Anna Cusack (Sister Mary Frances) (1829-1899)

639   Cusack, Sister Mary Frances. The Nun of Kenmare. An
Autobiography. Boston: Tickner and Co., 1889. 556pp. portr.

Impassioned "apologia pro vita sua" in which the author
dwells on her problems with the Roman Catholic heirarchy
in Ireland and the United States.

640   Eager, Irene Ffrench. Margaret Anna Cusack: A
Biography. Dublin: Arlen House, The Women's Press, 1979.
250pp.

This is the second edition of this life. The first
edition had the title <u>The Nun of Kenmare</u> (See # 641.)
The reissue has the sub-title "One Woman's Campaign for
Women's Rights" and has an introduction by Dr. Margaret
MacCurtain, O.P.
(Review: <u>Studies</u> 70 (1981): 117.)

641   Eager, Irene Ffrench. <u>The Nun of Kenmare</u>. Cork: Mercier
Press, 1970. 248pp. refs.

Sympathetic biography of Margaret Anna Cusack, the
controversial "Nun of Kenmare" described as Ireland's
first suffragette of the 19th century and an ardent
campaigner for Home Rule. Born in Coolock of Protestant
ancestry, she became briefly a member of an Anglican
sisterhood. In 1858 she became a Roman Catholic. She
spent 20 years as a member of the Poor Clare Order before
leaving this to form a new order and eventually leave the
Catholic Church. A prolific author, notably of religious
works, she also wrote on womens issues.

642   "Query." <u>Ir Book Lov</u> 6 (8) (Mar. 1915): 133-134.

Query from L.Grogan as to who was the "Nun of Kenmare"
and what she wrote. Reply by E.J. Byard saying she was
Sister Mary Frances [Cusack] and giving a list of her
works.

643   Schulenberg, Charlotte. "One Woman's Campaign for
Women's Rights." <u>Women View</u> 2 (Summer 1980): 19-21. il.

Brief summary of the life of Margaret Anna Cusack, <u>The
Nun of Kenmare</u>, based on the book by Irene F. Eager. (See
#641.)

Miriam Daly (1928-1980)

644   Gribbon, Harry and Joseph Leckey. "Miriam Daly 1928-
1980." <u>Ir Eco & Soc Hist</u> 7 (1980): 5-6.

Two brief separate tributes to Miriam Daly, former
lecturer in economic history at Queen's University,
Belfast.

Mrs. Deane

645   O'Brien, Mrs. William. "Mrs. Deane of Ballaghderreen."
Ir Mon 65 (1937): 475-485.

   Biographical sketch of Anne Duff, later Mrs. Deane,
   described as the most actively charitable woman in her
   neighborhood and the head of the best managed business
   house in the West of Ireland.

Arabella Denny (1707-1792)

646   Butler, Beatrice Bayley. "Lady Arabella Denny,
1707-1792." Dublin U Rec 9 (1) (Dec. 1946-Feb.1947): 1-20.
refs.

   A profile, based mainly on her diary and correspondence,
   of the Anglo-Irish philanthropist, Lady Arabella Denny
   details her work on behalf of the orphaned poor of the
   Dublin Foundling Hospital and other charitable efforts
   including the Magdalen Asylum which she founded in 1767.
   A member of the Royal Dublin Society she is credited with
   introducing carpet weaving and silkworms to Ireland.

Polly Devlin

647   Devlin, Polly. "Get Thee to a Nunnery." New Statesm 71
(Mar. 11, 1966): 334.

   Author comments on her convent school days in Ireland.

Mother Emmanuel (1831-1902)

(See Mother Mary Baptist Russell #688.)

Mother Mary Xaveria Fallon (1832-1888)

648   Tynan, Katherine. A Nun, Her Friends and Her Order:
Being a Sketch of the Life of Mother Mary Xaveria Fallon.
London: Kegan Paul, 1891. [2nd ed.] 277pp. portr.

   A biographical sketch of Jane Fallon (1832-1888)
   "sometime Superior-General of the Institute of the
   Blessed Virgin in Ireland and its dependencies,"
   describes her early years in France, her return to
   Ireland in 1848, her education with the Loreto nuns at
   Rathfarnham where she returned as a novice, and her
   subsequent religious career as she advanced to positions
   of increasing responsibility within the Order: Mistress
   of Schools in the Galway branch, Mistress of Novices at
   Rathfarnham and later Superior General. Her teaching
   innovations - the employment of specialized lay teachers

for special subjects, introduction of written and oral
examinations - are highlighted. The appendix includes
extracts from her correspondence.
(Review: Ir Mon 19 (1891): 379-380.)

Sister Mary Francis of the Blessed Sacrament (1823-1876)

649   Cusack, Mary Frances. In Memoriam of Mary O'Hagan:
Abbess and Foundress of the Convent of Poor Clares. Kenmare.
London: Burns and Co., 1876. 407pp.

Brief popular memoir of Mary O'Hagan, the foundress of
the Poor Clares by the member of that order who later
received much notoriety as the Nun of Kenmare. Based on
the account in the Annals of the Poor Clares in the
Kenmare convent.

650   Russell, Matthew. "A Sweet and Sacred Memory." Ir Mon
37 (Dec. 1909): 661-665.

Obituary for Hon. Mrs. O'Hagan (Sister Mary Francis of
the Blessed Sacrament who after her husband's death,
entered the Franciscan College of Perpetual Adoration at
Drumshambo. Her works of charity and her sanctity
stressed.

Sister de Fena

651   Fenning, Hugh (Rev.) "Dominican Nuns of Meath 1671-
1713." Riocht na Midhe 111 (3) (1965): 201-203.

(See Mother Bridget Nugent #682.)

Nella Hughes (1865-1927)

652   Gearon, (Rev.) P.J. Nella Hughes: an Irish Soul After
God's Own Heart. Dublin: Carmelite Church (St. Anthony's
Annals), 1927. 48pp. portr.

Brief account of the pious self denying life of the Cork
born Nella Hughes and her service to others.

Mother Mary John

653   Gilbert, Rosa Mulholland. "A Servant of the Dying." Ir
Mon 27 (1899): 252-254.

Tribute to Miss Anna Gaynor (later Mother Mary John)
foundress and first Superior of the Hospice for the
Dying, formerly Superioress of St. Vincent's Hospital,
Stephens Green, sister of Sarah Atkinson.

Sister Joseph Agnes of Jesus and Mary

654   Joseph Agnes of Jesus and Mary, Sister; an Irish
Carmelite 1890-1929. Dublin: Irish Messenger, 1941. 20pp.
portr.

   Brief sketch of the childhood, education and spiritual
   life of a woman who was professed as a Carmelite at age
   29. Includes some of her spiritual writings.

Maud Joynt (1870?-1940)

655   K[noh], E[leanor]. "Maud Joynt." Eigse 11 (1940):
226-229.

   Biographical note.

656   Scarlett, M.E. "An Irish Scholar - Maud Joynt." Alex
Col Mag 94 (Dec. 1940): 1-7.

   Details on education and professional career of the
   Alexandra College lecturer, translator and Gaelic
   scholar, a major contributor to the Royal Irish Academy's
   Irish Dictionary.

Mother Kevin (1875-1957)

657   Louis, Sister M. Missionary Mother: Memoirs of Mother
Kevin. Dublin: Catholic Truth Society, 1959. 20pp. portr.
[Later reissued in 1968 under the title "The Unconventional
Nun: Mother Kevin, First Superior General of The Franciscan
Missionary Sisters for Africa and Foundress of the Little
Sisters of St. Francis.]

   Brief tribute to Teresa Kearney born in Arklow, County
   Wicklow, Ireland describes her education, her entry to
   the community of the Franciscan Sisters at St. Mary's
   Abbey, Mill Hill, London; her work there among Irish
   immigrants and her subsequent missionary career in Uganda
   where she founded a community of African girls - The
   Little Sisters of St. Francis.

Catherine McAuley (1778-1841)

658   Barry, K.M. Catherine McAuley and the Sisters of Mercy.
A Sketch. Dublin: Fallon and Son, 1894. 108pp. portr.

   Brief biographical sketch and tribute to the foundress of
   the Irish Sisters of Mercy, Catherine McAuley. Includes
   some previously unpublished letters.

659   Belloc, Bessie Raymer Parkes. Historic Nuns. Edinburgh,
London: Sands & Co., 1911. 223pp.

(See Mrs. Aikenhead #547.)

660   Carroll, Mary Teresa Austin (Mother). Life of Catherine
McAuley, Foundress and First Superior of the Institute of
Religious Sisters of Mercy. St. Louis, Mo.: The Vincentian
Press, 1866. 508pp. portr.

   The first full length biography of the foundress of the
   Sisters of Mercy based upon documentary and narrative
   sources, including her letters and other writings.
   Describes in great detail her early life, her charitable
   activities among the poor, her perserverence in the
   Catholic faith despite opposition, her foundation of the
   home for indigent women which eventually became the Order
   of the Sisters of Mercy. The dress, rule and work of the
   Order and its expansion at home and overseas minutely
   detailed.

661   Catherine McAuley 1778-1978: Bi-Centenary Souvenir
Book. Ed. by Sister M. Angela Bolster. Dublin: Irish
Messenger Office, 1978. 39pp.

   A diary of the nine day period September 23rd to October
   1st, 1978 during which the Sisters of Mercy in Ireland
   and England paid tribute to their Foundress on the
   Bi-Centenary of her birth.

662   The Children's Friend. A Life of Mother Mary Catherine
McAuley for Children. By one of her daughters. Dublin: Office
of the Irish Messenger, 1953. 16pp.

663   "The First Sister of Mercy." Month 4 (1866): 111-127.

   Summary of the biography of Mother Catherine McAuley
   written by "A Sister of Mercy."

664   [Gaffney, Dean.] "La Rigola e Le Costituzioni delle
Religiose Nominate Sorelle della Misericordia." Roma: (The
Order of Mercy and its Foundress) Dublin R XXII (XLIII)
(1846): 1-25.

   A memoir of Catherine McAuley, foundress of the Sisters
   of Mercy, by her friend and spiritual director. Provides
   the first detailed account of this foundation.

665   Leaves from the Annals of the Sisters of Mercy. [Volume
1 Ireland.] By a Member of the Order of Mercy. New York:
Catholic Publications Society, 1881. 519pp.

   Biographical sketch of the Foundress of the Sisters of
   Mercy in Ireland, Mother Catherine McAuley, other sisters
   and a detailed account of the spread of this order in
   Ireland.
(Review: Ir Mon 2 (1883): 520.)

666   Mahoney, F. "Woman For Our Times: Catherine McAuley 1778-1978." Cross Curr 28 (Winter 1978/79): 468-470.

A brief tribute to Catherine McAuley marking her 200th anniversary. Stresses her role as an innovator in the society of her time by showing how women could provide leadership in the fields of health care and education.

667   Savage, Roland Burke. Catherine McAuley. The First Sister of Mercy. Dublin: M.H.Gill & Son,Ltd, 1949. 434pp. maps. plates. portr.

A biography of Catherine McAuley based on her correspondence describes her as a leader in the field of education and social welfare. Recounts her childhood in Dublin, her early involvement in social work activities, mainly the education of the poor and her dream of founding a school for these and also a shelter for homeless young women. She journeyed to France to study the educational system there and back in Dublin abandoned her idea of a lay community and despite much resistance, some clerical, founded a religious order - the Sisters of Mercy. The work of the Sisters during the cholera epidemic in Dublin and the subsequent growth and spread of the Order described.
(Review: Ir Mon 78 (1950): 143-145.)
(Review: Studies 39 (1950): 102-104.)

Teresa McMahon

668   Centenary Souvenir Roscrea 1842-1942. [Brigidine Order, Roscrea...] 61pp. il. portrs.

A miscellaneous collection of articles includes a retrospective overview of the Roscrea Branch of the Brigidine Order founded in 1823. Profile of Teresa McMahon, first Superior and other sisters.

Mother Mary Martin (1892-1975)

669   Medical Missionary Of Mary. Mother Mary Martin 1892-1975, Foundress. Drogheda: Medical Missionaries of Mary. [n.d.] 16pp. il. portr.

Account of the burial service; excerpts from telegrams and letters of condolence on the death of Mother Mary Martin.

Mary Teresa Mulally

670   Savage, Roland Burke. A Valiant Woman: The Story of George's Hill (1766-1940). With a preface and two maps by Rev. T. Corcoran. S.J. Dublin: M.H.Gill, 1940. 312pp. bibl.

A biography of Mary Teresa Mulally, the foundress of the Presentation Order based on the archives of the convent at George's Hill including her private papers, correspondence and business documents. Mary Mulally's achievement as the pioneer of free primary education for poor Catholic girls in Dublin despite the restriction of the Penal Laws stressed. Her achievement is all the more impressive since her family lacked influence or money and she had no special education. The second half of the book details the subsequent history of the order she founded.
(Review: Ir Mon 69 (Feb. 1941): 97-105.)
(Review: Studies 30 (1941): 294-296.)

Ethel Mulvany

671   Grahame, J.A.K. "Miss Ethel Mulvany, F.R. Econ.S. (obituary)." Ir Geo 8 (1975): 132-133.

Tribute to Miss Ethel Mulvany, teacher at the Rathmines Technical Institute in Dublin (then called the High School of Commerce), President of the Geographical Society of Ireland for three years, book and film reviewer, who died January 1975.

Nano Nagle (1728-1784)

672   Coppinger, William (Bp. of Cloyne and Ross). The Life of Miss Nano Nagle. Cork: James Haly, 1794. 31pp.

The earliest 'life', actually, the text of a sermon preached by Bishop Cloyne, a personal friend, on the annivererary of her death. Dr. Cloyne had close family ties with her Ursuline foundation and was intimate with the earliest phase of her work. [Reprinted in the Religious Reportes, August/September 1814 and in the Life by Walsh.]
(Review: Dublin R XV (1843): 363-386.)

673   Forrestal, Desmond. "Nano Nagle." Reality 39 (12) (Dec. 1975): 8-10. il. portr.

Profile of the foundress of the Presentation Order whose life is being researched by Forrestal for a possible film. He describes her as "the first modern Irishwoman and possibly the greatest."

674   Hutch, William. Nano Nagle: Her Life, Her Friends, Her Labour and Their Fruits. Dublin: McGlashan and Gill, 1875. 520pp. refs.

(Review: Ir Mon 3 (1875): 419.)

675   McGee, J.C. "Nano Nagle: Foundress of the Presentation Order." Cath W 18 (107) (Feb. 1874): 658-667.

676   Murphy, Dominick (Rev.) Memoirs of Miss Nano Nagle and of the Ursuline and Presentation Orders in Ireland. Cork: Roche, 1845. 110pp.

   An expansion of a brief biographical notice of Nano Nagle which appeared in The Dublin Review of the same year.

677   Murphy, J.N. "Honora Nagle and Presentation Nuns." Am J Ed 26 (1876): 705-720. refs.

   (See Religion - Presentation Order #1117.)

678   Mc Donnell, Basil. The Nagles of Ballygriffin, And Nano Nagle. (Reprinted from the Irish Genealogist 3 (2) July 1957.) 7pp.

   Traces the lineage of the Ballygriffin branch of the Nagel family. Details on Nano's paternal grandfather, her father, uncles, brothers and sisters.

679   Russell, Matthew (Rev.) "Nano Nagle and the Centenary of the Presentation Order." Ir Mon 5 (Nov.1877): 713-718.

680   Walsh, T.J. Nano Nagle and the Presentation Sisters. Dublin: M.H. Gill & Son, Ltd., 1959. 427pp. il. maps. charts. portrs. bibl.

   A scholarly, detailed study based on original documents - the annals of the Ursuline and Presentation Convents in Ireland and overseas, diocesan archives, public records, correspondence and earlier biographies of Nano Nagle, founder of the Presentation Order. The historical background of 18th century Ireland and the Penal days succinctly drawn. Walsh describes Nano Nagle's family background - well-off, Catholic, landlord class and her education in France, her return to Ireland to organize schools for the poor, her efforts to introduce the Ursuline order to Ireland and her later foundation of a new order - the Presentation Sisters - to cater exclusively for the poorer sections of society. The remainder of the book details the evolution and spread of the Presentation Order, in Ireland and overseas, The Ursulines in Ireland, the struggle for Catholic education at all levels, the system of state education and the role of nuns as educators.
   (Review: Studies 49 (1960): 225-228.)
   (Review: Stud Hibern No.1 (1961): 237-239.)
   (Review: Ir Eccl Rec Ser.5. 93 (5) (May 1960): 338.

681   Walsh, T.J. "Nano Nagle: Undaunted Daughter of Desires: A Study in Sanctity." Capu An (1976): 322-330. il. refs.

Text of an address delivered at a convention of her order
at Cork, October 25, 1975, the bi-centenary of the
foundation of the Irish Presentation Sisters.

Mother Bridget Nugent

682   Fenning, Hugh (Rev.) "Dominican Nuns of Meath 1671-
1713." Riocht na Midhe 111 (3) (1965): 201-203.

An account of two sisters, Mother Bridget Nugent and
Sister de Fena who were professed Dominican nuns from at
least as early as 1671 and were members of a religious
community in or near Drogheda. Based on archives of the
Dominican Order at the Roman convent of Santa Sabina.

Edel Quinn (1907-1944)

683   Duff, Frank. Edel Quinn. Dublin: Catholic Truth Society
of Ireland, 1958. 24pp.

A brief biographical sketch.

684   I Knew Edel Quinn. By an Irish Carthusian Nun. Dublin:
Catholic Truth Society, 1969. 35pp.

Brief tribute to Edel Quinn, by a personal friend.
Comments on her warm personality, her spiritual life, her
self-denial and obedience, her dedication to the Legion
of Mary.

685   Suenens, Leon-Joseph.(Bishop) A Heroine of the
Apostolate (1907-1944): Edel Quinn, Envoy of the Legion of
Mary to Africa. Preface by His Eminence, Archbishop Riberi.
Dublin: Fallon, 1954. 275pp. maps. plates. portrs.

A biography of Edel Quinn describes her comfortable
middleclass background, her work as a secretary in
Dublin, her membership of the secular organization
devoted to Catholic action, the Legion of Mary. Despite
severe illness she expanded her involvement with the
Legion and was sent as an envoy to Central Africa. The
major portion of the book devoted to her activities there
as a lay missionary. Her sanctity, dedication and
perserverence despite severe health problems stressed.
(Review: Ir Eccl Rec 5th Ser. LXXXI (June 1954): 475.)

Cecile O'Rahilly (-1980)

686   "In Memoriam Cecile O'Rahilly." Etud Irland No. 5 n.s.
(Dec. 1980): 337-339. portr.

Tribute by her nephew to the Gaelic scholar with a reproduction of her obituary notice in the _Irish Times_. (Professor in the School of Celtic Studies in the Dublin Institute.)

Mother Mary Baptist Russell (1829-1898)

687   Russell, Matthew. _The Life of Mother Mary Baptist Russell, Sister of Mercy_. New York: The Apostleship of Prayer, 1901. 187pp. il. portrs.

This eulogistic biography of Mother Russell written by her brother details her childhood in Killowen, Ireland, her convent life in the Kinsale Convent of the Sisters of Mercy and her work as Superior of the first mission established by that Order in San Francisco. Based largely on correspondence to and from Mother Russell, memoirs of the convent (_Leaves from the Annals of the Sisters of Mercy_) and personal reminiscences of the author and contemporaries of Mother Russell.

688   Russell, Matthew (S.J.) _The Three Sisters of Lord Russell of Killowen and their Convent Life_. New York, etc.: Longman's Green and Co., 1912. 302pp. il. portrs. fronts.

The first part of this volume is a slightly revised edition of the author's earlier biography of one of the sisters, Mother Mary Baptist Russell (See above.) Here he includes also a biographical sketch of Elizabeth Russell (Sister Mary Aquin) (1827-1876) and her work in establishing the convent of the Sisters of Mercy in Newry and later a branch at Rostrevor; and Sarah Russell (Mother Emmanuel) (1831-1902) Superior of the convent of the Sisters of Mercy at Newry.

Saint Damhnat

689   O'Daly, B. (Rev.) "St. Damhnat." _Co Louth Arch J_ XI (1948): 243-251. il.

An effort to bring together the known facts, admittedly meagre, concerning St. Damhnat and a refutation of the assertation by John Colgan, historian and hagiographer, that Damhnat and Dympna were the same person. The only facts regarding Damhnat that are established concern her status as virgin, the date of her feast (June 13th) and the long standing tradition of veneration of her in the diocese of Clogher.

Saint Dympna

690   Kuyl, Petrus D. _Gheel Vermaerd Door der Eerdinst der Heilige Dimphna Geschiden Oudscheidskundige beschryving der_

Kerken Gestichten en Kapellen dier oude Vryheid. Antwerpen:
J.E. Buschmann, 1863. 396+pp. il. maps. plates.

691   O'Hanlon, [Very Rev. Canon] John. The Life of St.
Dympna, Virgin, Martyr, and Patroness of Gheel; with some
notices of St. Gerebern, priest, martyr and patron of
Sonsbeck. Dublin: J. Duffy, 1863. 232pp. front. refs.

     Popular account retells legends of the high-born Irish
     Dympna's flight, on the advice of her confessor Geribern,
     from the impious marriage proposal of her own father. Her
     father pursued them to Gheel where he killed them both.
     Includes accounts of miracles attributed to the Saint and
     details on spread of her cult.
  (Review: Dublin Build 5 (95) (Dec.1, 1863): 194.)

692   Routledge, J.M. (Rev.) St. Dympna. Dublin: Catholic
Truth Society, 1926. 16pp.

     Biographical account based on the Acta Sanctorum
     published in 1643 and a biography by Canon O'Hanlon
     written around 1876. The daughter of noble parents St.
     Dympna consecrated herself to God in opposition to her
     pagan father's wishes and escaped to Flanders where he
     pursued and killed her. Devotion to her is widespread in
     Belgium, France, Germany and Italy and many miracles are
     attributed to her.

693   "Shrine of St. Dympna." Duffy Hibern Mag 4 (20) (Aug.
1863): 144-153.

     An account of the legend of the Saint and the shrine in
     her honour at Gheel, Belgium where the mentally ill are
     taken by their relatives and housed with local families
     after being processed in an infirmary.

                         Saint Gobnet

694   Harris, Dorothy C. "Saint Gobnet, Abbess of
Ballyvourney." J Roy Soc Antiq 7th Series. 68 (1938):
272-277. map. plates.

     Notes previous historical references and gives a detailed
     description with present location of various relics
     belonging to St. Gobnet including an oak statue from the
     13th century.

695   O h Ealuighthe, D. "St. Gobnet of Ballyvourney." J Cork
Hist Arch Soc (Jan.-June 1952): 43-61. refs.

     Brief account of the special saint of Ballyvourney,
     County Cork: St. Gobnet linked by tradition with Abban a
     monk who lived in the 6th century. Legend claims that she
     had to build her church where she found nine white deer

grazing together and after many travels she found these
at Ballyvourney. Her charity and sanctity were famous —
later a convent of nuns grew up around her. Includes a
critical discussion of sources of the historical Gobnet,
her cult in the district, the subsequent history of the
site, other regions of the country where shrines exist in
her honour and legends associated with the Saint.

696   O'Kelly, Michael J. "St. Gobnet's House. Ballyvourney,
County Cork." J Cork Hist Arch Soc (Jan.-June 1952): 18-40.
il. refs.

Reports the results of an archaeological excavation of
the site known locally as St. Gobnet's "house" in 1951.
Description of the "finds" — described as disappointing
not only in quantity but also of little use as indicators
of date. The excavation produced no evidence which would
confirm or controvert the belief that St. Gobnet lived
there in the 6th and 7th century. Other structures in the
vicinity however have been dated to the latter part of
the 7th century and so O'Kelly feels that there is every
indication that the neighborhood was one of importance in
the early Christian period.

Saint Ita

697   Ni Riain, Ide. Saint Ita. Dublin, London: Clonmore &
Reynolds, Burns & Oats, 1964. 135pp. il.

Based on Plummer's Vita Sanctae Ytae which he edited from
a manuscript in the Bodleian Library, itself based on a
more ancient text supposedly one of the few such Lives
with any claim to be a contemporary record. Other sources
include Lives of Saint Brendan and others of her famous
foster sons. Mostly legendary material and miracles
attributed to this 6th century princess who supposedly
founded a monastery in Munster.

Saint Monenna

698   Esposito, Mario. "Conchubrani Vita Sanctae Monennae."
Roy Ir Acad Proc 28 (1910): 202-247. refs.

The principal authority for the life of St. Monenna is
the Vita Sanctae Monennae compiled by an Irishman named
Conchubranus. This work is extant in one manuscript only,
the Codex Cotton Cleopatra, A, ii preserved in the
Library of the British Museum. Esposito here presents the
definitive edition of this manuscript — an earlier
edition printed by the Bollardists in 1721 is, according
to Esposito very defective. Esposito states that other
accounts which he notes in the Appendix seem to have
confused several saints of the same name — of Monenna's
authentic history, little is known.

699   Esposito, Mario. "The Sources of Conchubranus' Life of St. Monenna." Eng Hist R 35 (Jan. 1920): 71-78. refs.

A critical analysis of the Life of St. Monenna compiled by Conchubranus. Dating, sources and authenticity of the life considered.

700   "The Life of Saint Monenna by Conchubramus. ed. Ulster Society for Medieval Latin Studies." Seanchas Ardmhacha 9 (2) (1979): 250-272; 10 (1,2) (1980-81): 117-141, 426-454. refs.

New edition of text of Life based on the Latin text by Conchubramus with translation but without commentary except for some provisional identification of names and reflections on some problems raised.

Mother Mary Stanislaus (1849-1897)

701   Hogan, Katherine. "Mother Stanislaus." Ir Mon 36 (1908): 400-404.

Tribute to the daughter of Denis Florence MacCarthy, the Dominican nun and poet, from one of her pupils.

702   Russell, Matthew. "Denis Florence MacCarthy's Daughter." Ir Mon 25 (Nov. 1897): 561-574.

703   - - - "Poets I Have Known: Mary Stanislaus MacCarthy. O.S.D." Ir Mon 36 (1908): 301-320.

704   - - - "Sister Mary Stanislaus MacCarthy O.S.D. R.I.P." Ir Mon 25 (1897): 495-496.

Excerpts from poems by Sister Mary Stanislaus of Sion Hill with some contextual and biographical notes and an obituary notice by the editor of the Irish Monthly. Educated at St. Mary's Convent, Sion Hill she became a religious there in 1867 and spent almost thirty years as a Dominican nun. Includes also excerpts from poems written by her father, Denis Florence MacCarthy.

Sister Stanislaus

705   "Sister Stanislaus." Word (June 1976): 7. portr.

Brief profile of the first nun to be appointed Chair of an Irish Government Commission set up two years previously "to indicate and co-ordinate pilot schemes to combat poverty."

Ellen Woodlock (1811-1884)

706   Russell, Matthew. "Mrs. Ellen Woodlock, An Admirable
Irishwoman of the Last Century." Ir Mon 36 (1908): 171-176.

   Excerpt from the obituary written by Sarah Atkinson in
   the Weekly Register, notes Mrs. Woodlock's activities on
   behalf of the Reformatory and Industrial Schools Movement
   in England and Ireland and her efforts to help workhouse
   inmates' hospitalized children, etc. Includes other
   tributes by Dr. Thomas More Madden and Mr.Thomas
   Woodlock.

HISTORY, POLITICS AND REVOLUTIONARY MOVEMENTS

      This section considers women who have been involved in
political affairs defined to include both constitutional
politics and revolutionary activities or who were personally
connected with male political figures or were well known
public figures in their own right. Again the focus is on the
individual women, their lives or political careers insofar as
these affect or were affected by their political involvement.
Works dealing with the role of women in politics (suffrage
activity, voting behavior, political party membership or
office-holding, political party platforms with respect to
women), or women's contribution to the national struggle and
the effects of this on the feminist cause will be found in
the sections on POLITICS, REVOLUTIONARY MOVEMENTS and
PERSPECTIVES ON WOMEN'S LIBERATION, respectively. Ideological
positions on women's political role including feminist and
anti-feminist arguments will be found in the section
PERSPECTIVES ON WOMEN'S LIBERATION. Material on women who
were politically involved but primarily literary figures will
be found under BIOGRAPHY AND AUTOBIOGRAPHY - LITERATURE.
Works dealing with legendary political women (e.g. Queen
Maeb) will be found under LITERATURE, FOLKLORE and MYTHOLOGY
- DEPICTION OF WOMEN.

General

707   "Events of Easter Week." Cath Bull VII (Feb. 1917):
125- 130. il.

   Short biographical notices of women associated with the
   1916 Rising with photographs of nine of these.

708   Kennedy, Geraldine. "Ireland's Women TD's." Word (Jan.
1975): 19-22. portrs.

   Brief report on the contribution made by Ireland's four
   female Parliamentarians, their views on their
   achievements, and the causes and consequences of
   imbalance between male and female legislators.

709   O'Kelly, Seamus G. Sweethearts of the Irish Rebels.
Dublin: AlBooks, 1968. 107pp.

Profiles of Matilda Witherington (Mrs. Wolfe Tone), Mary
Anne McCracken (who loved Thomas Russell), Miss Swete and
Sarah Neville (first and second wives of Henry Sheares),
Maria Steele (beloved of John Sheares), Lady Lucy
Fitzgerald (beloved of Bartholomew Teeling), Lady Pamela
Fitzgerald (wife of Lord Edward), Jane Patton (Mrs.
Thomas Addis Emmet), Jane Verner (Mrs. John Mitchell),
Annie Hutton (beloved of Thomas Davis), Ellen O'Leary
(beloved of Edward Duffy), Mary Jane Irwin (third wife of
O'Donovan Rossa), Anne Bryson (wife of Samuel Neilson),
Mary Taaffe (Mrs. Luke Teeling).

710   O Saothrai, Seamas. Mna Calma '98. Ata Cliath Clo
Grianreime. 1966. 62pp. il. bibl.

Dr. Thekla Beere

711   O'Rourke, Frances. "Dr. Thekla Beere - A Profile."
Admin 23 (1) (Spring 1975): 19-30. il.

Brief biographical sketch of Dr. Beere, former Secretary
of the Department of Transport and Power, the first woman
secretary in the Irish civil service and Chair of the
Commission on the Status of Women in Ireland with
comments by her colleagues.

Louie Bennett (1870-1956)

712   Fox, Richard Michael. Louie Bennett: Her Life and
Times. Dublin: Talbot Press, 1958. 123pp. plates. (including
portrs.)

Brief popular style biography of Louie Bennett. Details
her early interest in woman's suffrage, the international
peace movement and her life's work, the revival and
consolidation of a women's trade union in Ireland.

Olga Pyne Clarke (1915-   )

*713 Clarke, Olga Pyne. She Came of Decent People. London:
Pelham Books, 1985. 190pp. il. portrs.

Helena Concannon (1878-1952)

714   Macken, Mary M. "Musings and Memories: Helena
Concannon, M.A. D. Litt." Studies 42 (Feb. 27, 1952): 90-97.

The author recalls her student days in Dublin, Germany
and Paris and offers biographical details on her fellow
student, Helena Walsh, later Mrs. Concannon. Notes the
latter's scholarly historical works and linguistic
attainment and her political career as a member of the
Dail and Senate.

Lady Louisa Connolly (1743-1821)

715   Boylan, Lena. "Lady Louisa Connolly's Chip Hat
Factory." J Co Kilk Arch Soc 15 (1975): 468-472.

Speculation on origin of hat factory in Celbridge seen as
an outgrowth of efforts by Louisa Connolly to educate and
train the youth of the area.

716   Fittzgerald, Brian. Lady Louisa Connolly. 1743-1821: An
Anglo-Irish Biography. London: New York: Staples Press, 1950.
196pp. il. front. refs.

The English born Lady Louisa Lennox came to live in
Ireland in 1751 under the guardianship of her sister,
Emily, later Duchess of Leinster. At 15 she married
Thomas Connolly, a neighboring landlord and thereafter
lived mainly in Ireland. Both she and her husband were
fully involved in the social and political life of
Ireland and were very concerned with the well being of
their tenants.

Margaret E. Cousins (1878-1954)

717   Denson, Alan. (comp.) James H. Cousins (1873-1956) and
Margaret E. Cousins (1878-1954): a Bio-Bibliographical
Survey. Family reminiscences and an autobiographical note by
William D. Cousins. Kendal: Alan Denson. 1967.   350pp.

Contains biographical tables; a biographical sketch of
Margaret Cousins by Denson who comments briefly on her
work for women's suffrage in Ireland and England and her
activities on behalf of other progressive social,
political and economic reforms mainly in India.
Bibliography includes books, periodicals, articles and
pamphlets written, or edited by the Cousins and writings
about them.
(Review: Dublin Mag 7 (2,3 &4) (Aut.-Win. 1968): 105.)

718   P.P.L. "James Cousins and Margaret Cousins: An
Appreciation." Dublin Mag 31 (2) (Apr.-June 1956): 29-32.

Biographical details on James Cousins and his wife,
Margaret (formerly Margaret Elizabeth Gillespie) and
their work on behalf of the Women's Suffrage Movement in
Ireland and later in India.

Sarah Curran (1782-1808)

719   Curran, Sarah. The Voice of Sarah Curran. Unpublished
Letters together with the full story of her life told for the
first time by Major General H.T. MacMullen. Dublin: Greene's
Library, 1955. 76pp. il. plates.

    Short biographical sketch of Sarah Curran. Details on her
    early oppressive home life, her meeting and friendship
    with Robert Emmet, her knowledge of his plans for an
    uprising, his capture and execution. Turned out of her
    father's home she was befriended by the Penrose family
    and subsequently married Captain Sturgeon. Includes
    letters from Sarah to the Penrose sisters; her two
    surviving letters to Robert and one of his to her.

720   Morton, J.B. "The End of the Story." G.K.'s Wkly (Aug.
5, 1934): 72-73.

    Brief account of Sarah Curran's life after the execution
    of her fiance Robert Emmet. She died in 1808 at the age
    of 26.

721   Sirr, Harry. Sarah Curran's And Robert Emmet's Letters.
Plaistow And Dublin: Whitwell Press and Hodges, Figgis and
Co. Ltd., 1910. 16pp.

    A clarification by the grandson of Major Sirr as to the
    fate of the correspondence between Robert Emmet and Sarah
    Curran. This was destroyed by Major Sirr to spare the
    feelings of the parties concerned except for two letters
    from Sarah to Robert and one from him to her by which her
    identity was discovered. These were retained by the Home
    Office.
    (Review: Ir Book Lov 2 (1) (Aug.1910): 10-11.)

Sydney Gifford Czira (1889-1974)

722   Czira, Sydney Gifford. The Years Flew By. Dublin:
Gifford and Craven, 1974. 108pp. il. portrs.

    Memoirs of the journalist Sydney Gifford, pseud. John
    Brennan. She recalls briefly her Dublin childhood but is
    mainly concerned with anecdotal descriptions of the
    groups and individuals with Nationalist sympathies/
    activities in the years prior to the 1916 uprising. Two
    of her sisters were widows of key figures in the
    rebellion (Thomas McDonagh, Joseph Plunkett). She also
    describes her propaganda work for Ireland in America
    where she came in 1914 and the various factions on the
    Irish American scene.

Anne Devlin (1778-1851)

723   Debroey, Steven. Anne Devlin. Germany: Louvain
Davidsfonds. n.d. [1961] 256pp.

724   Devlin, Anne. The Anne Devlin Jail Journal. Faithfully
written down by Luke Cullen. Ed. by John J. Finnegan. Cork:
The Mercier Press, 1968. 128pp. refs.

    Recounts the story of Anne Devlin, the County Wicklow
    girl who was Robert Emmet's housekeeper and her arrest
    and imprisonment after the failure of the attempted
    insurrection of 1803. Her own role in the preparation for
    the Rising as messenger and confident of the leaders and
    the revolutionary activities of her cousins are detailed.
    Finally released in 1806 she was broken in health. There
    is little information on her remaining years. She married
    and had two children and after the death of her husband
    apparently lived in poverty and obscurity until her death
    in 1851.

725   Finegan, John (ed.) The Prison Journal of Anne Devlin.
1968

  (Review: No Munst Antiq J 11 (1968): 94.)

Bernadette Devlin (1947-)

726   Ardill, Jill. "The Girl Who Stays Out in the Cold."
This Wk Ire (Nov. 14, 1969): 6-7. il.

    A brief article discussing Bernadette Devlin's political
    future in the aftermath of her participation in the Derry
    riots of August and six months after her entry into
    Parliament.

727   Breslin, Sean. "Ulster's Bernadette." Reality 31 (7)
(July 1969): 12-15. portrs.

    Comment on the election of Bernadette Devlin as MP for
    Mid Ulster. Presents a brief biographical sketch focusing
    on the evolution of the young Queen's College psychology
    student into a political activist. Brief consideration of
    her political philosophy and her major strength e.g. her
    youth and her idealism which have captured the
    imagination of Northern Ireland.

728   Buckley, William F. Jr. "On the Left, Bernadette
Devlin." Nat R 22 (Aug. 11, 1970): 856-857.

    Profiles of Bernadette Devlin and Ian Paisley and a
    consideraton of the religious sectarianism in Northern
    Ireland.

729   Buckman, P. "Ireland's Niggers: With Interview With
Bernadette Devlin." <u>Ramparts Mag</u> 8 (July 1969): 19-22. il.

    Brief background and analysis by Bernadette Devlin of the
    causes of social unrest in Northern Ireland and the
    evolution of the Civil Rights Movement.

730   Chamberlain, John. "Bernadette Devlin and the 'Stupid'
Capitalists." <u>Hum Ev</u> 3 (1971): 11. portr.

    Comment on Bernadette Devlin's changing rhetoric and
    tactics on her fund raising American tour and her
    intended audiences.

731   Chisholm, Ann. "A Year of Bernadette." <u>New Statesm</u> 79
(204) (Apr. 24, 1970): 574-576. portr.

    Considers the public image of Bernadette Devlin at the
    end of her first year in the House of Commons, the
    general failure of the media to either understand or
    depict her realistically and the broader implications of
    the communications breakdown for English/Irish relations.

732   Davidson, Sara. "Bernadette Devlin: An Irish
Revolutionary in Irish America." <u>Harper</u> 240 (Jan. 1970):
78-87. Discussion 240 (Mar. 1970): 6+. il.

    A chronological account of Bernadette Devlin's U.S. tour.
    Details on her goals, her sponsors, her personality and
    the make-up of her audiences.

733   Devlin, Bernadette. <u>The Price of My Soul</u>. New York:
Alfred A Knopf, 1969. 224pp.

    A combination of personal biography, chronology of the
    Civil Rights Movement in Northern Ireland and an attempt
    at a historical analysis of the present "troubles". The
    author making no claim to objectivity traces the process
    by which she became involved in radical politics and the
    developments in the protest movement in Ulster during
    1968-69 which led to her election as MP.
  (Review: <u>Commonweal</u> 91 (Nov.28, 1969): 281-282.)
  (Review: <u>Am Pol Sci R</u> 66 (1972): 636.)
  (Review: <u>R Pol</u> 32 (1970): 271.)

734   Devlin, Polly. "Bernadette Devlin. M.P.P." <u>Vogue</u> 154
(Aug. 1, 1969): 125+. il.

    Brief biographical sketch of Ms Devlin — at 22 the
    youngest woman ever to sit in the British House ofCommons
    — and a short account of the political struggle in
    Northern Ireland which brought her to that position.

735   Dozier, Thomas. "Sure and It's Miss Devlin For a Seat
in Parliament." Life 66 (May 2, 1969): 58A-58B. il.

    News item on Bernadette Devlin's maiden speech in the
    House of Commons includes a brief biographical sketch.

736   Dreifus, Claudia. "St Joan of the Bogside: An Interview
With Bernadette Devlin." Ever R 15 (July 1971): 25+. il.

    Brief account of Bernadette Devlin's first trip to
    America in 1969 and excerpts from an interview with her
    during her second visit a year and a half later.
    Bernadette comments among other things on Irish
    Americans, the British Parliament, Women's liberation and
    the Catholic Church in Ireland.

737   Gannon, T.M. "Bernadette On Fifth Avenue." America 121
(Sept. 6, 1969): 137-139.

    An account of an Irish-American demonstration of August
    23rd organized by the National Association for Irish
    Justice. Main speaker was Bernadette Devlin in the U.S.
    on a fund-raising mission who spoke about the problems in
    Northern Ireland.

738   Target, G.W. Bernadette: The Story of Bernadette
Devlin. London, Sydney, Auckland, Toronto: Hodder and
Staughton, 1975. 384pp. il. portrs.

    A sympathetic biographical account of the youthful
    political activist which attempts to clarify the
    political situation in Northern Ireland through an
    examination of her role in the Civil Rights Movement
    there.
 (Review: Studies 65 (1976): 73-75.)

        Countess Elizabeth Mary Margaret (Burke) Plunkett
                 Fingall (-1944)

739   Fingall, Elizabeth Mary Margaret (Burke) Plunkett,
Countess. Seventy Years Young. Memoirs of Elizabeth, Countess
of Fingall Told to Pamela Hinkson. New York: E.P. Dutton and
Co. Inc., 1939. 441pp. il. portrs.

    Mostly a nostalgic evocation of Ascendancy Ireland
    describes Elizabeth Burke's childhood in Connemara, her
    marriage to Fingall Plunkett, social life at Dublin
    Castle during the vice-royalties of Spencer, Londonderry,
    Wyndham, Dudley and in London where she was a frequent
    visitor, her numerous friends and acquaintances in
    aristocratic and political circles, she and her husband's
    support of his cousin, Horace Plunkett's co-operative
    movement, their restoration of the ancestral home,
    Killeen, World War I, the 1916 Rebellion and the

"troubles" during which many of the homes of the landlord
    class were destroyed (Killeen was spared.)
 (Review: N Y Times Bk R (Feb. 19, 1939): 12.)
 (Review: Sat R Lit 19 (Mar. 18, 1939): 12.)
 (Review: Springf Repub (Mar. 1, 1939): 8.)
 (Review: Ir Book Lov 30 (Jan. 1948): 78-79.)
 (Review: N Y Her Trib Books (Feb. 12, 1939):12.)

                    Emily Fitzgerald (1731-1814)
                       Duchess of Leinster

740   Correspondence of Emily, Duchess of Leinster:
1731-1814. Ed. by Brian Fitzgerald. Dublin: Irish MSS
Commission, 1949. 3 vols.

    Includes her letters to her first and second husbands:
    James Fitzgerald, first Duke of Leinster and William
    Ogilvie respectively and their replies; letters by two
    members of the families of Fitzgerald and Lennox and by
    friends and persons of the Duchess' household. Includes
    some 1770 letters comprising a "vivid impression of the
    social life of the 18th century in all its aspects"
    (introduction). The letters are arranged by writer rather
    than chronologically except for those written by Lady
    Emily which are arranged chronologically. Each volume has
    a biographical sketch of authors of letters included in
    that volume. Includes letters written by her sisters,
    Lady Louisa Connolly, Caroline Fox (Lady Holland) and
    Lady Sarah Napier, and by her son Lord Edward Fitzgerald.

741   Fitzgerald, Brian. Emily, Duchess of Leinster
1731-1814: A Study of Her Life and Times. London, New York:
Staples Press, 1948. 295pp. il. front. refs.

    Detailed account of the family, friends and lifestyle of
    the mother of Lord Edward Fitzgerald within the context
    of historical events in both Ireland and England during
    her lifetime. Relies heavily on her correspondence with
    her first and second husbands, Lord Kildare, and William
    Ogilvie, respectively and her children, notably Edward.
 (Review: Studies 58 (Sept. 1949): 360-362.)
 (Review: Dublin Mag New Ser. 24 (3) (July-Sept.1949)
        :70-71.)
 (Review: Ir Eccl Rec 5th Ser. 72 (Oct. 1949): 368-369.)

                  Katherine Fitzgerald (1464-1604)
                     The Countess of Desmond

742   Eagle, Judith. "'What a Frisky Old Girl.' The Old
Countess of Desmond." Ctry Life 164 (4227) (July 13, 1978):
98-99. il.

    Brief biographical sketch of Katherine Fitzgerald, the
    Old Countess of Desmond whose claim to fame rests on her
    supposed extreme longevity and the legend of her journey

on foot at an advanced age to petition the monarch in a
dispute over her property rights. Reproductions of some
of the paintings titled "The Old Countess of Desmond" and
their authenticity discussed.

743   Sainthill, Richard. The Old Countess of Desmond: An
Inquiry, Did She Ever Seek Redress at the Court of Queen
Elizabeth, As Recorded in the Journal of Robert Sydney, Earl
of Leicester? And Did She Ever Sit For Her Portrait? [From
the Proceedings of the Royal Irish Academy, vil. 7] Dublin:
University Press, 1861. 76pp. geneal. bibl. refs.

744   Sainthill, Richard. The Old Countess of Desmond: An
Inquiry (concluded) When Was She Married? Dublin: University
Press, 1863. 106pp. plate. chart. bibl. refs.

   Sainthill answers both these questions in the negative:
   he refutes the idea that The Old Countess was dipossessed
   of her jointure lands or that she sought redress by a
   personal appearance at the English Court: he also refutes
   the claim that the painting at Muckross is an original
   portrait of her and he claims that she never sat for her
   portrait. He identifies her as Katherine Fitzgerald, wife
   of Thomas who became 12th Earl of Desmond in 1529. Book 2
   claims that she was at least 140 yeasr old at the time of
   her death.

Lady Lucy Fitzgerald (1771-   )

745   Fitzgerald, Brian. "Lord Edward's Sister." Dublin Mag
22 (3) (1947): 35-41.

   Biographical note on youngest daughter of the first Duke
   and Duchess of Leinster and her sympathy with the
   revolutionary politics of her favorite brother, Lord
   Edward and their mutual friend, Arthur O'Connor.

Pamela Fitzgerald

746   Campbell, Gerald Fitzgerald. Edward and Pamela
Fitzgerald: Some Account of their Lives. London: Edward
Arnold, 1904. 256pp. portrs.

   A partial biography based mainly on letters, many of
   which are reproduced, written by members of Lord Edward's
   family including his mother, the Duchess of Leinster, his
   aunts, Lady Sarah Napier and Lady Louisa Connolly, his
   sisters, Lucy, Sophia and Charlotte, and his wife Pamela.
   Also includes some excerpts from his sister, Lucy's
   journal. The historical context is briefly sketched and
   the family attitudes toward Edward's fervent nationalism
   and subsequent execution for his role in the aborted
   rebellion of 1798, illuminated.

Mary Furlong (1868-1898)

747   "In Memory of Mary Furlong." Ir Mon 26 (1898): 609-611.

Obituary notice for a nurse at St. Stephens Hospital who
died as a result of ministering to victims of a typhus
outbreak in Roscommon in 1898.

Alice Stopford Green (1847-1929)

748   de Blacam, Aodh. "A Memory of Alice Stopford Green." Ir
Bookm 1 (8) (Mar. 1947): 64-73.

Brief evaluative comments on the historical writings of
Alice Stopford Green, the first to write social history
in Ireland. Some of her work seen as of permanent value;
overall she is characterized as Ireland's best historian.

749   McDowell, Robert B. Alice Stopford Green: A Passionate
Historian. Dublin: A. Figgis, 1967. 116pp. portrs. refs.

A sympathetic biography of the historian Alice Stopford
Green based on primary sources details her Calvinist
upbringing, her early life in Ireland, migration to
England upon her father's death, her marriage to the
well-known historian John Richard Green who trained her
in historical writing. A supporter of liberal causes and
Irish Nationalism she wrote on early Irish history and
was much concerned with contemporary events in Ireland,
including Home Rule and the Gaelic revival. She returned
to Ireland in 1918 and was a supporter of the 1921 treaty
and one of the first Irish female Senators.
(Review: Times Lit Supp (Dec. 28, 1967): 1262.)

Elizabeth Gunning (1734-1790)

750   Bleackley, Horace. The Beautiful Duchess, Being an
Account of the Life and Time of Elizabeth Gunning, Duchess of
Hamilton and Argyl. London: Archibald Constable, 1907. 362pp.
front. portrs.

Popular account based largely on newspaper items of the
life of one of the celebrated beauties who after her
removal to London with her mother and sister married the
Duke of Hamilton and moved to Scotland where she founded
a charity school. Later the family live in London and
visited Ireland. After her husband's death she remarried
and became Duchess of Argyl.

751   Bowen, [Essex.] Captain. A Statement of Facts in Answer
to Mrs. Gunning's Letter, Addressed to His Grace The Duke of
Argll. Dublin: Printed for W. Wilson, etc. 1791. 42pp.

Miss Gunning presumably forged a letter from the Duke of
Marlborough to her father, concerning the intentions of
his son, the Marquis of Blandford with regard to her.
Captain Bowen and his wife were named in the affair and
Captain Bowen presents here his version of the matter.

752   Gunning, Susannah. <u>A Letter from Mrs. Gunning Addressed
to His Grace The Duke of Argyll</u>. 3rd ed. London: The Author,
1791. 143pp.

A letter by Elizabeth Gunning's mother to the man her
daughter later married explaining her daughter's apparent
duplicity as a conspiracy to blacken her in his eyes and
protesting her innocence.

Mrs. Haughey

753   Kelly, Rhondda. "Mrs. Haughey at Home." <u>Scene</u> 1 (1)
(June 1969): 62-69. il. portrs.

The wife of Irish Cabinet Minister, Charles Haughey,
comments on politics, her home life as daughter of the
former Taoiseach, Sean Lemass, her meeting and friendship
with her husband, their children, her life style,
husband's tastes, work; famous people she has met, etc.

Anna Maria (Annie) Hutton (1825-1853)

754   [Anna Maria Hutton.] <u>The Love Story of Thomas Davis
Told in the Letters of Annie Hutton</u>. Edited with an
introduction by Joseph Hone. Shannon: Irish University Press,
1971. (c.1945). 19pp.

A reprint of seven letters written by Annie Hutton,
fiancee of the poet/patriot, Thomas Davis. Six of these
were written during their short engagement, July-August
1845, which ended with Davis' death. The seventh was
written six months later to his sister Charlotte. The
editor in the introduction supplies a brief sketch of the
family background and circumstances of both Annie Hutton
and Thomas Davis and gives a brief account of Annie's
life after the death of Davis until her death in 1853.

Nan Joyce

*755   Joyce, Nan. <u>Traveller: The Autobiography of Nan Joyce</u>.
Gill and MacMillan, 1985.

Mary Kenny

756   O'Callaghan, Tanis. "The Women Who Lead A Double Life:
Tanis O'Callaghan Talks to Mary Kenny About Her New Book."
Image 3 (6) (1978): 3-5. portr.

Mainly discussion of her book, Woman Two, but includes
some comments by Mary Kenny, the one time radical
feminist, on her experience of motherhood, men, etc.

Kitty Kiernan (-1945)

757   Collins, Michael and Kitty Kiernan. In Great Haste: the
Letters of Michael Collins and Kitty Kiernan. Ed. by Leon
O'Brien. Dublin: Gill and MacMillan, 1983. 229pp. bibl.

Brief biographical account of Kitty Kiernan accompanies
this collection of some 241 letters exchanged between her
and her fiance, Michael Collins from 1919 until his
assassination in 1922.

Lady Sarah Lennox (1745-1826)

758   Curtis, Edith Roekler. Lady Sarah Lennox: An
Irrepressible Stuart. 1745-1826. London: W.H. Allen, 1946.
278pp. refs.

Another of the famous Lennox beauties, Sarah was wooed
briefly by King George III. Later unhappily married to
Lord Bunbury she had numerous affairs which led finally
to her divorce and social ostracism. In 1781 she
remarried Colonel George Napier, had a large family and
regained respectability. Includes some account of the
political scene in Ireland particularly the role of her
nephew, Lord Edward Fitzgerald in the aborted rebellion
of 1798.
(Review: Sat R 29 (April 13, 1946): 79-80.)
(Review: Wkly Bk R (Mar. 10, 1946): 4.)

759   The Life and Letters of Lady Sarah Lennox, 1745-1826.
Ed. by the Countess of Ilchester and Lord Stavordale. London:
John Murray, 1901. 2 vols. portrs.

The majority of the letters were written by Lady Sarah to
her friend Lady Susan Fox Strangways, later Lady O'Brien
during the period 1761-1768 and 1775-1817. Includes a
brief biography of Lady Sarah with contextual notes by
the editor, and the Memoirs of Lord Holland and Henry
Napier which have brief biographical sketches of Lady
Sarah.

June Levine

760   Levine, June. <u>Sisters: The Personal Story of an Irish Feminist</u>. Dublin: Ward River Press, 1982. 306pp.

Autobiography of the free lance journalist and feminist details her marriage, breakdown, divorce and involvement in the Women's Liberation Movement. Also a detailed account of the political debates and the personalities in the movement in Ireland.

Kathleen Lynn (1874-1955)

761   Smyth, Hazel P. "Kathleen Lynn, M.D. F.R.C.S.J. (1874-1955)." <u>Dublin Hist Rec</u> 30 (2) (Mar. 1977): 51-56.

Brief biographical sketch of Dr. Lynn, daughter of a Church of Ireland rector details her education, medical practice and political activities. Her role in the Irish Citizen Army in the 1913 lockout and later in the Easter Rebellion and her subsequent imprisonment and her heroic efforts to combat the flu epidemic in later years highlighted.

Maud Gonne MacBride (1866-1953)

762   Balliett, Conrad A. "The Lives and Lies of Maud Gonne." <u>Eire Ire</u> 14 (3) (1979): 17-44. refs.

Balliett essays "a critical commentary and an update" of previous biographies of Maud Gonne including her auto-biography <u>A Servant of the Queen</u> using primary sources including interviews, letters and newspaper accounts not used by these. Points on which he claims to offer new information include date and place of Maud's birth, her father's political opinions, her importance in the Nationalist struggle, the date of her daughter's birth, and the reasons for her marriage and subsequent separation from John McBride and her physical relationship with William B. Yeats.

763   Bradford, Curtis B. "Yeats and Maud Gonne." <u>Tex Stud Lit & Lang</u> 111 (1962): 452-474. refs.

An examination of William Butler Yeats' relationship with Maud Gonne and the effect of his love for her on his life and art. Bradford argues that if Yeats "had not known her he might not have thrust himself into the world of action; if his courtship had succeeded, his poetry would have been less concerned with themes such as mask and face, the self and the anti-self, the Unity of Being."

764   Cardoza, Nancy. Lucky Eyes and a High Heart: The Life
of Maud Gonne. New York: The Bobbs-Merrill Company, 1978.
468pp.

This definitive biography paints a vivid portrait of the
famous Anglo-Irish woman who progressed from society
belle to champion the cause of anarchists, homeless
tenants, prisoners and revolutionaries. Actress, artist,
mystic, orator, as well as radical social and political
reformer she counted among her friends all the important
figures of the period in literary, political and artistic
cliques both in France and Ireland. Cardozo's account
goes beyond Maud Gonne McBride's own autobiography and
the earlier biography by Levenson to chart the
connections between Maud's political activities in
France, Russia, Ireland, England, and America; clarifies
the nature of her relationships with Millevoye and Yeats
and her unhappy marriage with Major McBride.
(Review: Books Ire No. 32 (Apr. 1979): 60.)

765   Levenson, Samuel. Maud Gonne. New York: Readers' Digest
Press, 1976. 436pp. il. bibl.

766   Lupton, Mary Jane. "What I Don't Know About Maude
Gonne." Women 1 (Spring 1970): 33-35. refs.

Brief note based on the biography of Maud Gonne by Anne
Marreco. (See #779.)

767   [MacBride, Maud Gonne.] Im Dienste Einer Konigin: Eime
Frau Kampft fur Irland. ["A Servant of the Queen."] Einzig
Berechtigte Ubertragung von Ruth Weiland. Bremen: Schumemann,
1939. 372pp. map.

768   MacBride, Maud Gonne. A Servant of the Queen. Dublin:
Standard House, [1938] [1950]. 319pp.

An informal autobiography details the author's happy
childhood in Ireland, England, France, Switzerland and
Italy and the turning point in her life: e.g. the
evictions she witnessed in 1885 which transformed her
into an ardent nationalist. Despite initial resistance on
account of her Ascendancy background (her father was
Assistant Adjutant General of the British Army) she was
eventually accepted by the various Nationalist groups.
She graphically describes her work with the evicted in
Donegal and Mayo, her work with the Land League, her
lectures and journalistic activities in France, her work
for political prisoners in England and her fund-raising
tours in the U.S., while, also, conveying the atmosphere
of the early years of the Irish Literary movement.
(Review: Dublin Mag New Ser. 14 (Oct.-Dec. 1939): 92-93.)
(Review: Studies 39 (June 1950): 225-226.)
(Review: Ir Eccl Rec 5th Ser. 74 (Nov. 1950): 468-469.)
(Review: Ir Mon 78 (1950): 446-447.)

769   MacLiammoir, Michael. "Michael MacLiammoir Recalls Maud
Gonne MacBride. An Interview Conducted by Conrad A.
Balliett." J Ir Stud 6 (2) (May 1977): 39-44. il.

   MacLiammoir reminisces about his first and subsequent
   meetings with Maud Gonne MacBride, the impression she
   made on him and his overall opinion as to her character
   and personality.

770   MacManus, Francis. "The Delicate High Head: A Portrait
of a Great Lady." Capu An (1960): 127-132. il.

   An enthusiastic portrait of Maud Gonne as she was when
   the author first saw her in 1926. He speaks of her
   repose, serenity and luminous spirit and equates her with
   the image of the Countess Cathleen.

771   Ni Eireamhaoin Eibhlin. Two Great Irishwomen - Maud
Gonne MacBride, Constance Markievicz. Dublin: Fallon, 1971.
78pp. plates.

   This brief study written for children of top primary and
   post primary age levels, details the main events in the
   public lives of the Irish activists, Maud Gonne MacBride
   and The Countess Markievicz and endeavors to evaluate the
   contribution of each to the movement for Irish
   independence.

772   Pomeranz, Victory. "Maud Gonne and M. Millevoye." James
Joyce Q 11 (1974): 169.

   A passage in Ulysses refers to Millevoye as licentious.
   Pomeranz explicates this by reference to a passage in
   William Butler Yeats' Memoirs in which Yeats wrote that
   Maud Gonne was Lucien Millevoye's mistress and had two
   children by him.

773   Stock, A.G. "The World of Maud Gonne." India J Eng Stud
1 (1965): 56-79. refs.

   A brief biographical sketch of Maud Gonne contrasting the
   portrait Yeats draws of her in his poetry with her own
   self portrait presented in her book A Servant of the
   Queen. Her single-minded commitment to the struggle for
   Irish freedom is evident in both views.

                    Mary Ann McCracken (1770-1866)

774   Historical Notes of Old Belfast and its Vicinity. A
Selection from the MSS collected by William Pinkerton...
Biography of Mary Ann McCracken, now first printed. Edited
with notes, by Robert M.Young. Belfast: Marcus Ward, 1896.
287pp. maps. plates. portrs.

Biographical sketch of Mary Ann McCracken written by her
grand niece, Anna McClery (pp. 175-197.)

775   McNeill, Mary. The Life and Times of Mary Ann McCracken
1770-1866. A Belfast Panorama. Dublin: Allen Figgis and Co.,
Ltd., 1960. 328pp. il. maps. geneal. portrs. refs.

A scholarly biography based mainly on the correspondence
of Mary McCracken and her circle and other contemporary
sources documents the multi-faceted career of the subject
who is known primarily as the devoted sister of the most
famous Northern leader in the Irish rebellion of 1798 -
Henry Joy McCracken. In addition to the active role she
played in that movement, she was associated with the
renaissance of Irish harp music, with her sister she
established a successful muslin business, did charitable
work on behalf of the women and girls in, among others,
the Belfast Poor House and was Honorary Secretary of the
Ladies Committee of the Belfast Charitable Society; was a
friend and collaborator of the historian Dr. R.R. Madden.
The historical, social and intellectual background is
skillfully portrayed.
(Review: Stud Hibern No.1 (1961): 247-248.)
(Review: Studies 50 (1961): 111.)
(Review: Threshold 5 (1) (Spring-Summer 1961): 58-64.)

Countess Markievicz (1868-1927)

776   Graves, C. Desmond. "Constance Markievicz and the
Woman's Struggle." Labour Mon 50 (2) (Feb. 1968): 82-85.

Capsule overview of the life of Constance Gore Booth,
later Countess Markievicz, described as a socialist,
feminist and nationalist revolutionary. Emphasis on
vindication of the right of women to serve in the highest
military and political offices.

777   MacDowell, Bairbre. "Countess Markievicz." Clio 1,
Trinity term, (1965): 19-22.

Brief biographical note on Countess Markievicz and a
critical assessment of her political contribution. The
author concludes that the course of her life was directed
more by chance and circumstances than by any deep
conviction but her assets were useful during the disorder
and romanticism of a revolution.

778   Markievicz, Constance. Prison Letters of Countess
Markievicz: Also Poems and Articles Relating to Easter Week
by Eva Gore-Booth and a biographical sketch by Esther Roper.
Ed. by Esther Roper. New York: Kraus Reprint Co., 1970
[1934]. 315pp. il. (Preface by the late President E. de
Valera.)

Includes Constance Markievicz letters from prison and some from the period after her release. Also includes her sister Eva's poems to Constance in prison, her account of a visit to Dublin after Easter Week to see Constance, her short account of the Rebellion and of Roger Casement's death, also, a few other papers relating to the period. The biographical sketch by Esther Roper includes the text of the 1916 Proclamation, the proceedings of the trial of Constance Markievicz and her own account of Easter Week.
(Review: Ir Book Lov 23 (Jan.-Feb.1935): 19.)
(Review: Cath Bull 24 (Sept. 1934): 756-759.)

779   Marreco, Anne. The Rebel Countess; the Life and Times of Constance Markievicz. Philadelphia: Chilton Books, 1967. 330pp. bibl.

Sympathetic biography details Constance Gore-Booth's Anglo-Irish aristocratic background, her marriage to a Polish nobleman, her involvement with the Sinn Fein movement and her role in the Easter rebellion of 1916. Accounts of other women prominent on the political scene, notably Maud Gonne, Helena Malony, Mary McSwiney, etc. and the activities of women's organizations such as Cumann na mBan, Inghinidhe na h Eireann are also included as is a genealogy of the Gore-Booth family.

780   Mitchell (David.) Women on the Warpath; The Story of the Women of the First World War. London: Cape, 1966. 400pp. plates.

Includes a brief, somewhat critical, biography of Countess Markievicz (pp. 349-365).

781   "O.: At the Countess's Obsequies (Extracts from a Letter Written to an Irishman in Berlin by a Dublin Friend)." Cath Bull 18 (Feb. 1928): 156-158.

Account of the funeral of the Countess Markievicz and the crowds of people who were there to pay their respects who had been on line from the previous day.

782   O Faolain, Sean. Countess Markievicz. London: Sphere Books Ltd., [1934]. 220pp.

A somewhat critical early biography by a younger contemporary with a new introduction by the author. Based on the published records of the period and oral testimony.
(Review: Ir Book Lov 22 (Nov.-Dec. 1934): 138.)

783   O'Mahony, T.P. "The Joan of Erin." Word (Apr. 1968): 16-19. il. portrs.

Brief biographical sketch of Constance Markievicz.

784   Ui Thallamhain, Caitlin Bean. <u>Ros Fiain Lios an Dail</u>.
Baile Ata Cliat. Connradh na Gaeilze, 1967. 86pp.

    Life of Countess Markievicz in Gaelic.

785   VanVoris, Jacqueline. <u>Constance de Markievicz: In The
Cause of Ireland</u>. Amherst: University of Mass. Press, 1967.
384pp.

    Biography of Constance de Markievicz viewed as always a
    "second-in-command," "an instrumental but not a
    determining figure in Irish politics" but "who was bound
    into the rebellion by connections with art, literature,
    theatre, labor, suffrage and youth movement" thus one of
    the best representatives of the whole course of
    rebellion." [Preface] Covers much the same material as
    the Marreco biography with perhaps less detail.
    (Review: <u>Studies</u> 57 (Autumn 1968): 321-324.)
    (Review: <u>Univ R</u> 5 (1968): 255-257.)
    (Review: <u>Nation</u> 206 (Jan. 1968): 20-21.)
    (Review: <u>Dublin Mag</u> 7 (2,3 &4) (Aut. Win. 1968): 114-115.)

Charlotte Grace O'Brien (1845-1909)

786   <u>Charlotte Grace O'Brien</u>. Selections from her Writings
and Correpondence with a Memoir by Stephen Gwynn. Dublin:
Maunsell and Co., 1909. 232pp. il. front. portrs.

    A memorial volume prepared by her nephew, includes a
    biographical sketch of the subject and selections from
    her poetry and prose, of mainly biographical interest.
    Details on her family life, political opinions and
    activities on behalf of the Irish emigrants in the Famine
    years.
    (Review: <u>Ir Book Lov</u> 1 (1910): 89.)
    (Review: <u>Ir Mon</u> 37 (1909): 703-704.)

787   Joyce, Mannix. "Charlotte Grace O'Brien." <u>Capu An</u>
(1874): 324-340. portr. refs.

    Biographical sketch.

788   Keogh, M.C. "Charlotte Grace O'Brien." <u>Ir Mon</u> 38 (May
1910): 241-245.

    Brief biographical note recounts her efforts to publicize
    the appalling conditions on the emigrant ships and to
    improve accomodation facilities for emigrant girls both
    in the ships themselves and on land, in Ireland and the
    United States.

Nora Connolly O'Brien (? - 1981)

789   O'Brien, Nora Connolly. We Shall Rise Again. London: Mosquito Press, 1981. 117pp. il. plates.

> Daughter of James Connolly, Nora O'Brien discusses the Easter Rising of 1916 and her father's role in it, her own 65 years of activity in the Republican cause, as a propagandist in the United States after the Rising, as Acting Paymaster General in Ireland in 1923, as Senator in the Dail, as a prisoner, as a socialist. Gives her views on socialism, women in the National struggle and the ongoing struggle in Ireland.

Sophie O'Brien

790   O'Brien, Sophie. Golden Memories: More Love Letters, Prison Letters and Others. Ed. with a foreward and introduction by Sophie O'Brien. Dublin: M.H.Gill and Son, Ltd., 1929. 238pp.

> A companion volume to Golden Memories: The Love Letters and the Prison Letters of William O'Brien, edited with a personal appreciation by his widow, Sophie O'Brien, consists mainly of her letters to her future husband, her mother's letters to him and her letters to her mother (1888-1890).
> (Review: Ir Mon 58 (Sept. 1930): 480.)

Margaret O'Connor (? -1451)

791   Green, Alice Stopford. "A Great Irish Lady" In The Old Irish World, pp. 100-129. Dublin: M.H.Gill and Son, Ltd., 1912. 197pp.

> Brief account of Margaret, daughter of O'Carroll, Lord of Ely, wife of Calvagh O'Connor Fahy, lord of Offaly, described as the most illustrious woman of the 15th century in Ireland, a patron of commerce, learning and religion with details on the historical context.
> (Review: Ir Mon XL (July 1912): 405.)
> (Review: Ir Eccl Rec 4th Ser. 32 (Nov. 1912): 557-558.)
> (Review: Ir Book Lov 3 (July 1912): 211-212.)
> (Review: Ir R 2 (Nov. 1912): 502-504.)

Rose O'Dogherty (1588-1660)

792   Casway, Jerrold. "Rose O'Dogherty: A Gaelic Woman." Seanchas Ardmhadha 10 (1980-81): 42-62. il. refs.

> Biographical account of the granddaughter of Shane O'Neill, her political and economic place in Gaelic aristocratic society, her marriage and subsequent exile with the "Wild Geese" in the Low Countries; her second

marriage to Owen Roe O'Neill and her role as his
political intermediary, lobbyist and purchasing agent in
the exiled Irish communities ongoing political and
military machinations against Britain.

Siobhan and Nuala O'Donnell

793   Concannan, Helena. "The Woman of the Piercing Wail.
(The Lady Nuala O'Donnell)." Ir Eccl Rec 5th Ser. XVI (Sept.
1920): 216-240. refs.

Account of the daughters, Siobhan and Nuala, of Sir Hugh
O'Donnell and Ineen Dubh. The eldest, Siobhan born around
1569 died in 1590 leaving two sons. Nuala was married to
her cousin Niall Garbh who later deserted to the English
slaying her brother.

794   Walsh, Paul (Rev.). "Hugh Roe O'Donnell's Sisters." Ir
Eccl Rec 5th Ser. XIX (Jan.-June 1922): 358-364. refs.

Walsh makes some corrections and additions to Concannon's
account of the two sisters Siobhan (or Joan) and Nuala,
daughters of Hugh, son of Manus O'Donnell, sisters to
Hugh Roe O'Donnell.

Grainnua Uaile (Grace O'Malley) (c.1530-1603)

795   Chambers, Anne. "Granuaile 'a Most Famous
Sea-Captain.'" Etud Irland No. 6 (Dec. 1981): 101-107.

Brief overview of role played by Grace O'Malley in the
maritime and political affairs of 16th century Ireland.

796   Chambers, Anne. Granuaile: The Life and Times of Grace
O'Malley. c.1530-1603. Dublin: Wolfhound Pr., 1979. 213pp.
il. maps. portrs. refs.

The first attempt at a scholarly biography this account
of the legendary Irish figure, Grace O'Malley daughter of
a powerful Gaelic chieftain in the west of Ireland who
became a leader and warrior in her own right, is based
primarily on English State papers. Grace crested the
social and political upheavals of a stormy period marked
by inter-Irish and Irish-British warfare, through her
skill in war, seamanship and leadership ability. She
attained mythic importance in Irish literature as a
symbol of Irish Nationalism.
(Review: Books Ire No. 42 (Apr. 1980): 77.)

797   "Grainne O'Mailley, the She Pirate." Dublin U Mag 55
(Apr. 1860): 387.

An early biographical sketch which is partly based on an
autobiographical description written by herself in 1593
in London and addressed to the Privy Council.

798   Mac Dermott, Commander A. "Grainne O'Malley, the Sea
Queen of Connacht." Ir Geneal 1 (7) (April 1940): 211-219.
geaneal. table.

   Brief popular account. Includes a list of her descendants
   by her first and second husbands with notes on the
   pedigree.

799   Maguire, Conor. "Grace O'Malley: The Queen of the
West." Studies 32 (1943): 225-230.

   Brief undocumented account of legends surrounding the
   life and exploits of Grainne Ni Maille anglisized
   incorrectly according to Maguire, as Grace O'Malley.

800   Power, Arthur. "Some Facts About Grainnua Uaile."
Galaway Re 3 (5) (1951): 99-109.

   Brief biographical sketch of Grace O'Malley based to some
   extent on English State Papers.

801   Schwind, Mona L. "'Nurse to All Rebellions': Grace
O'Malley and Sixteenth Century Connacht." Eire Ire 13 (1)
(1978): 40-61. refs.

   An analysis of the fate of 16th century Connacht and one
   of of its ruling clans, the O'Malleys viewed as "both an
   episode in Anglo-Irish relations of the Tudor period and
   a micro-cosmic case history of the clash between the
   antique and modern worlds these two islands represented."

Catherine O'Mullane

802   O'Connell, Basil. Catherine O'Mullane, Mrs. O'Connell,
Mother of Daniel O'Connell, The Liberator. [Reprinted from
the Irish Genealogist 2 (10).]

   Brief note tracing the pedigree of Catherine O'Mullane,
   daughter of John O'Mullane of Brittas, the mother of
   Daniel O'Connell famous for his role in securing Catholic
   Emancipation for Ireland.

Mary Lenihan O'Rourke

803   Savage, Tom. "Lifestyle: Mary Lenihan O'Rourke." Image
5 (9) (Sept. 1980): 9-11. portr.

Profile of a female politician on the National Executive of Fianna Fail.

Rose O'Toole (-1597?)

804   MacCarthy, B.C. "The Riddle of Rose O'Toole." Feilscribhinn Torna (1947): 171-182. refs.

Speculation on possible motivation of Rose O'Toole, wife of Fiach Mac Hugh O Bryne, in informing her husband that her stepson, Turlough had arranged to betray him to the English. Context of 16th century Irish resistance to English rule, intrigues and alliances briefly indicated and Rose's role in these.

The Parnell Sisters

Anna Parnell (1852-1911)
Fanny Parnell (1849-1882)
Emily Monroe Dickinson (Parnell) (? - 1918)

805   Blunt, Hugh F. "Fanny Parnell - Poet and Patriot." Cath W CXLII (1936): 182-190.

(See Biography - Literature #358.)

806   Dickinson, Emily Monroe. A Patriot's Mistake, Being Personal Recollections of the Parnell Family. By a Daughter of the House. Dublin: Hodges, Figgs & Co. Ltd.; London: Simpkin, Marshall & Co. Ltd., 1905. 243pp. plates. fronts. portrs.

This uneventful, rather gossipy autobiography by Charles Stewart Parnell's sister Emily details the family background, her upbringing and London "season", her disavowal by her father because of her secret engagement to the man she subsequently married. After his death in 1885 she lived at Avondale, until the sale of the house. Later in Dublin she remarried. She died in 1918 in the workhouse.

807   Hughes, Marie. "The Parnell Sisters." Dublin Hist Rec XXI (1) (Mar. 1966): 14-27. refs.

Based on previous accounts: Emily Parnell's autobiography, A Patriot's Mistake, a biography by Charles Stewart Parnell and Katherine Tynan's Memoirs, supplies some biographical material on the sisters of the patriot - especially Anna and Fanny. Details on Fanny's work for the Ladies Land League in America, including her literary efforts and Anna's involvement with the Land League in Ireland and her subsequent estrangment from her brother, Charles.

808   Moody, T.W. "Anna Parnell and the Land League."
Hermathena 117 (Summer 1974): 5-17. refs.

     Biographical sketch and physical description of Anna
     Parnell with particular note of her activities on behalf
     of the Ladies Land League and the historical context
     occasioned by the discovery of her unpublished manuscript
     treatise on the Land League titled The Tale of a Great
     Sham.

809   Wyse-Power, Senator. "My Recollections of Anna
Parnell." Dublin Met Mag (1935): 15-17+. il. portr.

     Describes Anna Parnell's work for the Ladies Land League
     (1881-2) which took over from the Men's League when the
     male leaders were arrested.

                    Saidie Patterson (1906-   )

810   Bleakley, David. Saidie Patterson: Irish Peacemaker.
Belfast: Blackstaff Press. [c.1980] 118pp. il.

     A fulsome, non-scholarly account of the career of Saidie
     Patterson from her early years as a mill worker in
     Belfast in the 1920's. Provides an overview of her
     activity in the organization of trade unions in the
     textile industry which led to her emergence as the only
     full time woman officer in the transport union; her
     subsequent political career first as treasurer and later
     Chair of the Labour Party and her activities on behalf of
     Moral Rearmament and Women Together, an organization
     working to unite Catholics and Protestants in Northern
     Ireland.
     (Review: Books Ire No. 47 (Oct. 1980): 190-191.)

                Senator Margaret Pearse (1878-1968)

811   Barra, Eamon de. "A Valiant Woman." Capu An (1969):
53-56. portr.

     Brief memoir of Senator Margaret Pearse, sister of the
     heroes of the 1916 Rebellion, Patrick and Willie. A
     former teacher at St.Edna's, the school established by
     Patrick, she presented the house and grounds to the
     Nation as a memorial to her brothers.

812   Ryan, Desmond. "Margaret Pearse." Capu An (1933):
91-97. portr.

     Biographical sketch. (Reprinted in Capuchin Annual of
     1942, pp. 312-318.)

813   deValera, Eamon. "Margaret Pearse. Panegyric April
26th, 1932." Capu An (1942): 336.

Senator Mary Robinson

814   "Senator Mary Robinson." Word (June 1975): 22. portr.

Profile of Ireland's best known woman politician educated at Trinity and Harvard Law School, who in addition to her Senatorial responsibilities still practices as a barrister on the Dublin circuit and also lectures in European Law at Dublin University.

Catherine Rose

815   Graecen, Lavina. "Fighting the Good Fight." Image 3 (9) (Aug. 1978): 44-45.

Interview with Catherine Rose, feminist book publisher (Arlen House) and her evolution from author to publisher.

Margaret Russell

816   Concannon, Helena. "Valiant Irish Mothers." Ir Rosary 3 (1944): 298-307.

Brief note on Margaret Russell, based mainly on biographies of her son, Lord Russell of Killowen and three of her daughters who entered the convent (See "Three Sisters of Lord Russell" #688.)

Hanna Sheehy-Skeffington (1877-1946)

817   Levenson, Leah. Hanna Sheehy-Skeffington, Irish Feminist. Syracuse: Syracuse University Press, 1986. 227pp.

First full length biography of the feminist, pacifist, nationalist and socialist who won a first class honours MA despite the exclusion of women from Royal University lectures at that period. She married the pacifist and feminist Francis Sheehy-Skeffington and despite ill health pursued actively myriad causes, all her life. After her husband's murder in 1916 she toured the United States to publicize British brutality in trying to enforce conscription in Ireland.

Betty Sinclair (1910-1981)

818   Morrissey, Hazel. "Betty Sinclair: A Woman's Fight for Socialism: 1910-1981." Saothar 9 (1983): 121-131. portr. refs.

Brief overview of career of the trade union activist who became a full time organizer for the Communist Party, Ireland.

Elizabeth Smith (1797-1885)

819   Smith, Elizabeth. The Irish Diaries of Elizabeth Smith 1840-1850: A Selection. Ed. by David Thomson and Moyra McGusty. Oxford: Clarendon Press, 1980. 326pp. map.

Born in Scotland, Elizabeth Smith lived with her husband, Colonel John Smith on his estate at Balliboys, County Wicklow from 1830. She commenced her journal in 1840 which includes much social data on living and working conditions, domestic arrangements and social attitudes of both the tenant and landlord classes of the period and the Smiths' efforts to improve conditions on their estate.
(Review: Ir Hist Stud 22 (87) (Mar. 1981): 285-287.)
(Review: Ir Eco Soc Hist 8 (1981): 134.)

Rosemary Smith

820   "Rosemary Smith." Word (Dec. 1973): 7. portr.

Brief biographical note on the 36 year old Irish rally driver who began driving in competitions in 1959 and has since won 32 of the 38 international rallies in which she competed.

Annie M.P. Smithson (1873-1948)

821   Kearns, Linda. In Times of Peril: Leaves from the Diary of Nurse L. Kearns From Easter Week, 1916 to Mountjoy, 1921. Edited by Annie M.P.Smithson. Dublin: Talbot Press, 1922. 61pp.

Brief description by the popular author of her activities as red cross nurse and dispatch rider during the Easter Rebellion, 1916 and continued Republican activities culminating in her arrest in 1920, her courtmartial, sentence to 10 years imprisonment, her jail term in Walton, Liverpool and later in Mountjoy and her escape.

Betty Williams
Mairead Corrigan

822   Deutsch, Richard. Mairead Corrigan. Betty Williams. Translated from the French by Jack Bernard. Woodbury, New York: Barron's, 1977. 204pp. il. maps.

A journalistic account of the Peace Movement in Northern Ireland from its beginnings in August 1976 to October 1977 when the 1976 Nobel Peace Prize was awarded to Mairead Corrigan and Betty Williams, original founders of the Movement. Includes a brief sketch of the political background of the violence in Northern Ireland and biographical profiles of the leaders of the Peace

Movement - Mairead Corrigan, Betty Williams and Ciaran
McKeown.

823   Servan-Schreiber, Claude. "Can Two Women Stop The
Killing in Ireland?" Ms 5 (6) (Dec. 1976): 62-65. il.

Interviews with Betty Williams and Mairead Corrigan, the
primary organizers of peace marches by women, both
Catholic and Protestant. They comment on the initial
impetus for the "peace movement" and the factors
responsible for its widespread support. Opposing
statement from Maire Drumm, vice-president of Sinn Fein.
She states that she also wants peace but it must be peace
with justice and claims that the Peace Movement people
are looking for peace at any price.

Literature, Folklore and Mythology

DEPICTION OF WOMEN

   This section contains works which examine how women are
portrayed in prose, poetry and drama whether written for
stage screen or television and regardless of whether the
authors of these literary works are male or female. Literary
critiques of individual women characters are excluded except
these are viewed as representative "types". Works dealing
with the relationship of male authors with the women in their
lives are included insofar as the real life women are judged
to have been partial models for, or otherwise conditioned or
affected, the author's created female characters. Purely
biographical accounts of women in the lives of male literary
figures will be found under BIOGRAPHY AND AUTOBIOGRAPHY —
LITERATURE as will biographies of female authors. Also
included here are depiction of women in folklore and
mythology including descriptions of attributes, artifacts and
locations associated with these. Discussion of territorial
and other goddesses are included here rather than in the
section on RELIGION because of their role in shaping the
literary imagination and conceptions of female character,
real or ideal. Possibly mythological female characters
primarily identified as saints will be found in the section
on BIOGRAPHY AND AUTOBIOGRAPHY — RELIGION as will studies
dealing with the contribution of religious figures to the
Irish ideal of womanhood. Biographical material on women
identified as witches can be found under WITCHCRAFT.

824   Adams, Elsie. "Feminism and Female Stereotypes in
Shaw." Shaw R XVII (i) (Jan. 1974): 17-22. refs.

   Asserts that Shaw while departing from the 19th century
   stereotypes of the demure, fragile, "womanly" woman,
   nonetheless more often than not creates women characters
   who belong to types long familiar in western literature:
   e.g. the temptress, goddess, mother, or the "emancipated"
   woman.

825   Antiquaries (pseud.) "Exclusion of Women." Ulster J
Archae Series 1. 5 (1857): 345.

   Note regarding the island of Inniscathy, an episcopal see
   founded by St. Senan in the 5th century where according
   to legend the monks of the Abbey never permitted a woman
   to enter the island.

826   Armstrong, E.C.R. "Sheela-na-gig discovered by Major H.
Trevelyan." Roy Soc Antiq Ire J Ser.6 1 (1911): 385-387; 2
(1912): 69.

   Photo and description of Sheela-na-gig that Major
   Trevelyan discovered on Lustymore Island.

827   Atkinson, Colin B. and Jo Atkinson. "Maria Edgeworth,
Belinda and Women's Rights." Eire/Ire 19 (4) (Winter 1984):
94-118. refs.

   Argues that Belinda's "moral" is that women should be
   educated not for equality of rights but for their duties
   - e.g. their roles as partners to their husbands and
   teachers of their children. Maria Edgeworth's political
   stance is characterized as paternalistic.

*828   Bannister, Ivy. The Shavian Woman. 1984.

829   Barnicoat, Constance. "Counterfeit Presentation of
Women." Fortn R 85 (Mar. 1906): 516-527.

   Critique of the women characters in Shaw's plays seen as
   representing several types: hard as nails, colossally
   selfish, useless, lacking in all womanly restraint or in
   common sense - more caricatures than characters. Candida
   seen as the most attractive but her practicality seen as
   having its limitations. Shaw is also accused of rendering
   his contemptable types of women without any sympathy.

830   Barron, T.J. "The Black Pig and the Cailleach
Geargain." Ulster Folk 4 (1958): 75-76. refs.

   Brief account of the legend of the Cailleach Geargain.
   Author speculates on the connection of the monster of the
   legend with primitive notions of the Earth Mother.

831   Beebe, M. "James Joyce: Barnacle Goose and Lapwig."
PMLA 71 (June 1956): 302-320. refs.

   Beebe questions whether James Joyce's common law union
   with Nora Barnacle caused him to reject his own theory of
   the artist's necessary alienation from life and whether
   Joyce then presented this theory satirically in his
   treatment of Stephen Dedalus in Ulysses.

832   Benstock, Bernard. "The Mother-Madonna-Matriach in Sean
O'Casey." So R 6 (1970): 603-623.

A discussion of Sean O'Casey's treatment of mother
figures in his drama and autobiographies. Benstock argues
that while four such figures are larger-than-life e.g.
Juno, Bessie Burgess (in Juno and the Paycock; The Plough
and the Stars) Susan Casside (O'Casey's mother in the
autobiography) and Lady Gregory (in Irishfallen)- there
exist countering these venerated women a galaxy of lesser
lights torn between holding on to the best that is in
life and a destructive pettiness and self-interest.

833   Benstock, Bernard. Paycocks and Others: Sean O'Casey's
World. Dublin, New York: Gill and Macmillan, Barnes and
Noble, 1976. 318pp. bibl.

An analysis of mother characters in O'Casey's plays and
the possible relation of aspects of these with his own
beloved mother and his dear friend Lady Gregory. While
not all of his mother characters are presented as heroic,
Benstock concludes they are treated with a delicate
sympathy.

834   Bergin, Osborn and R.I. Best. "Tochmarc Etaine." Eriu
12 Part 2 (1938): 137-196. refs.

Translation and explication of the complete "wooing of
Etain," the principal tale of the mythological cycle
which is concerned with Midir, king of the elfmounds of
Bri Leith, with commentary on various versions.

835   Blesch, Edwin J. (Jr.) "A Species Hardly a Degree Above
a Monkey: Jonathan Swift's Concept of Woman." Nassau R
(1977): 74-84. refs.

Disagrees with other critics that Swift's late deplorable
poems about women suggest his deteriorating mental
condition. Blesch argues that these poems written between
1723 and 1731 are not radically different in their
attitudes toward the female sex than many of his earlier
creations; that from his earliest work, Swift revealed a
deep psychological fear and hatred of women and their
bodies.

836   Block, Tony. "Shaw's Women." Mod Drama 11 (2) (1959):
133-138.

A discussion of Shaw's women characters and their
genesis. Block argues that these are modeled on actual
women of Shaw's acquaintance; the women in his own family
and the "Ibsen Woman" - all very strong personalities.
However their speech is Shaw's own. The only character
based on real life is Violet in Man and Superman and she,
while a strong character, is ideologically opposite to
all his other women characters.

837   Borkat, Roberta Sarfatt. "The Case of Custom." U Dayton
R 10 (3) (1974): 47-57.

Discusses the narrow role allocated to women in the 17th
and 18th centuries and the three qualities - beauty,
chastity and obedience - prescribed for them. Literary
heroines embody this restricitve ideal and even some of
the most perceptive satirists, men who knew and admired
women of intelligence and strong character could not seem
to detach themselves from traditional expectations even
when they wished to propose a new ideal. Work of Lillo,
Swift and Pope analyzed in terms of their female
heroines.

838   Bourden, Patricia. "No Answer From Limbo: an Aspect of
Female Portraiture." Crane Bag 4 (1) (1980): 95-100.

Consideration of the depiction of women by certain Irish
novelists. Works of Brian Moore, John Broderick, Desmond
Hogan discussed.

839   Bowen, Charles. "Great Bladdered Medb; Mythology and
Invention in the Tain Bo Cuailnge." Eire Ire 10 (4) (Winter
1975): 14-34. refs.

An examination of the relative roles of myth and
invention in the character of Queen Medb in the Tain Bo
Cuailnge. Various prototypes in the pagan mythological
tradition in Ireland are identified with their salient
characteristics and functions: the goddess of fertility/
sovereignty and the war goddess. Bowen examines the
portrayal of Medb in terms of these prototypes.

840   Bowen, Zack R. "Goldenhair: Joyce's Archetypal Female."
Lit & Psychol 17 (1967): 219-228. refs.

Discusses Joyce's Chamber Music in terms of the
appearance therein of the prototypes of the figures
expressive of the many faceted dominant female principle
in Portrait, Exiles, Ulysses and Finnegans Wake. This
composite woman, virgin and temptress, creator and
destroyer, prisoner and jailer, a source of fulfillment
and a source of denial, is for Bowen, most clearly
embodied in the figure of the girl on the beach in
Portrait but reappears throughout Joyce's work.

841   Breathnach, R.A. "The Lady and the King: A Theme of
Irish Literature." Studies 42 (Autumn 1953): 321-336.

A general overview of the allegorical representation of
Ireland in Gaelic literature, portrayed as a poor old
woman (the Shan Van Vocht) or a young maiden (in
Aislings) and the principle of kinship.

842   "A Bunch of Blue Ribbons: Conversation With Mrs. Sean [O] Casey and Brenna Katz on the Women in O'Casey's Plays." Arts Ire No.1 (1972): 13-23. portrs.

The Assistant Editor of The Arts in Ireland talks with Eileen O'Casey about the women in O'Casey's life who are the prototypes for many of his female characters, notably his mother, Lady Gregory and Eileen herself.

843   Carpenter, Andrew. "Synge and Women." Etud Irland 4 (2979): 89-106. refs.

Comments on the crucial role played by women in Synge's life and the development in his portrayal of them in his plays - from the cardboard Celliniani of the Etude Morbide through the earthy extravagance of the brash Pegeen of the Playboy to the stately dignity of Deirdre seen again from afar but now seen with knowledge and maturity - which parallels the progression of his life and talent.

844   Chessman, Harriet S. "Women and Language in the Fiction of Elizabeth Bowen." 20th Cent Lit 29 (1) (Spring 1983): 69-85. refs.

Argues that women, in Bowen's vision are inherently outsiders to discourse, unless they turn traitor and defect to the other side. Her female characters are further seen as representing her own impulse toward a breaking of narrative form, while her containment of them as a narrator and as an author, prevents the attempt to embody this impulse.

845   Clibborn, Edward. "On the Use of the Distaff and Spindle Considered as the Insignia of Unmarried Women." Roy Ir Acad Proc Series 1 7 (1857-1861): 164-165.

Author argues that as unmarried women in the middle ages were considered spinsters and as married women, or wives were considered weavers the instrument used by spinners e.g. the distaff, the spindle and the harrow, might with propriety be assigned as insignia to the unmarried but not to the married whose proper insignia should connect them with the loom or its production, rather than with spinning.

846   Clibborn, Edward. "On Sheela na gigs." Roy Ir Acad Proc II (1844): 565-575. refs.

Discussion of the figures known as 'Sheela na gigs' speculates on their probable function as charms to avert the evil eye and comments on their similarity to other figures used elsewhere for this purpose. The influence of Gnosticism on early Irish Christianity briefly traced. Details and locations on five examples of Sheela na gigs in Ireland.

847   Concannon, Helena. "The Women of the Irish Sagas." Ir
Mon 45 (Oct. Nov. 1917): 619-631, 686-698. refs.

Discussion of the depiction of women and love in ancient
Irish poetry.

848   Crane, Gladys. "Shaw's Misalliance: the Comic Journey
from Rebellious Daughter to Conventional Womanhood." Ed
Theatre J 25 (Dec. 1973): 480-489. refs.

A discussion of Hypatia Tarleton in Shaw's play,
Misalliance viewed as Shaw's most complete development of
the rebellious daughter theme and also, incorporating his
ideas about middle-class life, marriage, respectability
and women's role in general. Crane sees Hypatia as going
beyond the usual parental rejection to totally reverse
the standards of middle class society by rejecting
conventional standards for women. However, she is
revealed as self deceived in her pose as a liberated
woman and ultimately reveals her essentially conventional
attitudes. Her character is contrasted with that of Lina
whose ideas are as unconventional as her behavior.

849   Crane, Gladys. "Shaw and Women's Lib." Shaw R 17 (1)
(Jan. 1974): 23-31. refs.

Crane argues that Shaw created women characters who were
real people. Discusses the characteristics his heroines
share in common with the modern liberated woman: both
seek greater independence socially, economically and
psychologically.

850   Dalton, G.F. "The Tradition of Blood Sacrifice to the
Goddess Eire." Studies 63 (1974): 343-354. refs.

Traces the continuity in the cult of Eire or Eriu, the
earth goddess of pre-Christian Ireland and how the belief
in her fertilization through blood sacrifice later became
conjoined with Nationalism and the giving or taking of
life for Ireland.

851   Dalton, G.F. "The Loathy Lady: A Suggested
Interpretation." Folklore 2 (1971): 124-131.

The theme of the hideous hag who is transformed into a
beautiful young woman is considered by the Chaucerian
scholar, Maynadier, to be of Irish origin. Dalton
considers several versions of this event in Irish
mythology and concludes that the theme originated in
pre-Christian dramatic performance.

852   Denman, C. George. "Carleton's Characterization of
Women." Carleton News 1 (1970): 10-11. il. refs.

Describes typical female types in Carleton's fiction -
peasant maidens pure and virtuous; wise and clever older
women who can manipulate any situation - and speculates
on his relationship with the actual women in his life.

853   Donahue, Charles. "The Valkyries and the Irish War-
Goddesses." PMLA LVI (1) (1941): 1-12. refs.

Notes that similarities have been documented in previous
research between the Germanic Valkyries and the Irish War
Goddesses and argues that these result from an
interchange of ideas between the Celts and Germanic
peoples on the Continent.

854   Dunlea, Rev. John. "A New Sheela-na-gig (at Swords,
County Dublin)." Roy Soc Antiq Ire J Ser.7 15 (1945): 114.

855   Dunn, James H. "Sile-na-gCioch." Eire 12 (1) (1977):
68-85. refs.

Reviews various theoretical explanations of the Sile na
gCioch figures (Sheela-na-gig) after the Gaelic name
above. Offers an interpretation of these as apotropaic
devices whose power to terrorize and protect derives from
the woman's image as she is portrayed in old Irish
literature. The conquest of the woman by Christianity has
resulted in a degeneration of the female image from
powerful to a bestial image - from Eriu to Sile.

856   Eggers, Tilly. "Darling Milly Bloom." James Joyce Q 12
(Summer 1975): 386-395. refs.

Discusses how most critics have ignored the character of
Milly, Bloom's daughter and suggest that biographical
information about Lucia (Joyce's own daughter) and
Joyce's attempt to reconcile the spiritual and physical,
especially in relation to women justify that more
critical attention be focused on Milly.

857   Fabian Feminist: Bernard Shaw and Woman. Ed. by Rodelle
Weintraub. Pennsylvania State University Press, 1977. 274pp.
bibl. refs.

A collection of articles most of which have been
previously published in The Shaw Review attempt to trace
literary, mythic, political and economic influences on
Shaw's delineation of women, discuss his treatment of sex
roles, liberated women in the plays and the influence of
Shaw's feminism. A selection of Shaw's speeches and
articles on feminist issues also previously published
elsewhere is included.

858   Fernando, Lloyd. "New Women" in the Late Victorian
Novel. University Park: Pennsylvania State University Press,
1977. 168pp. refs.

    Chapter 4 (pp. 84-106) entitled "Moore: Realism, Art, and
    the Subjection of Women", considers Moore's contribution
    to the issue of women's liberation. He is seen as
    offering a carefully discriminated account of the
    relevance of feminist issues to women at different levels
    of society. However also present on occasion in his work
    "is a note of patronizing sympathy;" and Fernando
    suggests, "one suspects that his demonstration of actual
    limitations to which women were subject was inspired by a
    conviction of women's decided inferiority."

859   Fitzgerald, Lord Walter. "Sheela-na-Gig in the
FitzEustace Castle of Blackhall." Co Kild Arch Soc J   II
(1896-99): 330.

860   Flacker, Herbert V. "Ninteenth Century Sources for the
Deirdre Legend." Eire Ire 4 (4) (1969): 56-63. refs.

    Discussion of manuscript versions of both the early and
    late form of the legend, the latter being the one most
    used by writers of the Irish Renaissance. Pseudo-
    historical sources and oral tradition discussed.

861   Ford, Jane M. "Why is Milly in Mullingar?" James Joyce
Q 14 (Summer 1977): 436-449. refs.

    Speculates on father-daughter incest theme in Ulysses.

862   Gilbert, Elliot L. "In the Flesh. Esther Waters and the
Passion for Yes." Novel 12 (Fall 1978): 48-65. refs.

    According to Gilbert, Moore defines new terms of heroism
    within the centext of the naturalistic novel - acceptance
    of the body. Thus Esther Waters is a woman whose freedom
    is not the freedom to affirm the destiny already implicit
    in her; the freedom to choose to be who she is without
    the necessity of calling that choice a defeat.

863   Gill, Stephen M. "Shaw, The Suffragist." Lit Half Yrly
14 (2) (1973): 153-156. refs.

    Discusses Shaw's position on the status of women,
    references to the suffragettes in his plays and his
    writings on behalf of their struggle for the franchise.

864   Gilmartin, Andrina. "Mrs. Shaw's Many Mothers." Shaw R
8 (Sept. 1965): 93-103. refs.

    A discussion of the mother characters in the plays of
    G.B. Shaw.

865   Gleeson, Dermot F. "Sheela na Gig in County Clare." Roy
Soc Antiq Ire J Ser.7 12 (1943): 24.

866   Gleeson, Dermot F. "Sheela na gig at Ballyportray
Castle, County Clare." No Munst Antiq J II (1940-41): 174.

867   Gleeson, Dermot F. "Sheela-na-gig at Burgesbeg, County
Tipperary." Roy Soc Antiq Ire J Ser. 7 9 (1939): 47-48.

868   Graves, James. "Letter About a Carved Stone Effigy on
the Rock of Cashel." Ir Build 12 (264): (Dec. 15, 1870): 303.

869   Grosskurth, Phyllis. "A Woman Is a Woman Is a Woman."
Can Lit No. 72 (Spring 1977): 77-80.

       General comments on the treatment of women in Brian
       Moore's novels. Grosskurth finds these least effective
       when Moore attempts to portray his version of the
       contemporary woman's search for identity. The heroines in
       The Doctor's Wife and I Am Mary Dunne find
       self-realization only by merging with a man - a view of
       women's options apparently shared by their creator.

870   Guest, Edith M. "A Sheela-na-gig at Clonmacnoise." Roy
Soc Antiq Ire J Ser. 7 9 (1939): 48.

871   Guest, Edith M. "Ballyvourney and its Sheela-na-gigs."
Folklore 48 (1937): 374-384. il. refs.

       Discussion of the female fertility figures called
       Sheela-na-gigs (Sheila of the Breasts) and their
       significance. Pagan origins of the cult of Saint Gobnet
       and the linkage with fertility rites detailed.
       Description and location of other Sheela-na-gigs; the
       legends surrounding them and methods of dating these
       discussed.

872   Guest, Edith M. "The Dating of Sheela-na-gigs." Roy Soc
Antiq Ire J 67 (1937): 176-180. refs.

       Evidence from ornamentation, motives etc. for the late
       date of many Sheela-na-gigs but Guest cautions that this
       does not rule out the early origin and practice of the
       related fertility cult nor the probability of earlier
       symbols.

873   Guest, Edith M. "Irish Sheela-na-gigs in 1935." Roy Soc
Antiq Ire J 66 Part I (1936): 107-129. maps. plates.

       Listing with descriptive annotation of Irish
       "Sheela-na-gigs" as known in 1935. Term "Sheela-na-gig"

used to denote a female figure so displaying or calling
attention to anatomical features as to suggest that it is
a symbol of a fertility cult.

874   Gwynn, Lucius. "Cinaed ua Hartacain's Poem on Brugh na
Boinne." _Eriu_ 7 (1914): 210-238. refs.

Translation with summary and explication of the first
part of the saga of the "Wooing of Etain," missing from
Leabhar na hUidhre, based on a poetical version of the
opening tale preserved in the Book of Leinster, which was
composed by the fmous poet and scholar, Cinaed ua
hArtacain who died in 987.

875   Gwynn, Lucius.   "The Two Versions of Tochmarc Etain."
ZCP 9 (1927): 353-356. refs.

Versions identified are those in Leabhar na hUidre and
Leabhar Buidhe Leacain (of the first tale) and of the
second in the British Museum MS. Egerton 88 (16th
century). Both have been printed by Windisch in the first
volume of his _Irische Texte_. These are compared for
language, style, and sources.

876   Hamlin, Ann and Claire Foley. "A Woman's Graveyard at
Carrickmore, County Tyrone and the Separate Burial of Women."
Ulster J Archae XLVI (1983): 41-45.

Discussion of practice of separate burial places for
various categories - including women - with details on
one such location. Local traditions associated with the
area and explanations for practice discussed.

877   Harnett, P.J. "Sheela na Gig at Abbeylara, County
Longford." _Roy Soc Antiq Ire J_ LXXXIV (1954): 181.

878   Harnett, P.J. "Sheela na Gig at Malahide 'Abbey',
County Dublin." _Roy Soc Antiq Ire J_ LXXXIV (1954): 179.
plate.

879   Harris, Wendell V. "Molly's 'Yes': the Transvaluation
of Sex in Modern Fiction." _Tex Stud Lit & Lang_ 10 (1968):
107-118. refs.

A study of sex in modern fiction traces "the evolution
from the insistence that sexual satisfaction is important
for happiness to the use of the successful sexual act as
a symbol of fulfillment and thence to the confusion of
this symbolic representation with complete fulfillment of
the human personality." Work of Joyce among examples
discussed.

880   Helbig, Althea K. "Women in Ireland: Three Heroic
Figures." U Mich Pap Wom Stud 1 (2) (June 1974): 73-88. refs.

Examines the characteristics of the "hero" and examples
of female heroes in the Irish oral tradition. In the
earliest Irish tales, the most notable are the Ulster
cycle: in these Maeve, Emer and Deirdre are seen as
heroic types. These are contrasting types — Maeve
represents the formidable warrior woman and ruler similar
to the male fighting type of hero. Emer is the
self-assured wife who ultimately sacrifices herself for
her people; Deirdre, beautiful and courageous, figures as
an independent thinker and leader. Brief summaries of
main events in their lives and their achievements.

881   Henke, Suzette. "James Joyce and Women The Matrimonial
Muse." In Work in Progress: Joyce Centenary Essays, ed.
Richard F. Peterson; ed. and intro. Alan M. Cohen; ed. Edmund
L. Epstein, pp.117-131. Carbondale: Southern Illinois
University Press, 1983.

Discussion of varying interpretations of Joyce's view of
women. For Henke, Joyce came to terms with the adolescent
misogyny exhibited by Stephen Dedalus, his fictional
persona, through his relationship with Nora Barnacle and
goes beyond prevalent stereotypes of male prowess/female
passivity to advocate a more enlightened ideal of
andogynous behavior for both sexes.

882   Henke, Suzette. "Feminist Perspectives on James Joyce."
Can J Ir Stud 6 (1) (June 1980): 14-21. refs.

The virgin/whore dichotomy which traditional critics
claim Joyce's fictional women consistently reflect is
challenged by feminist analyses.

883   Henke, Suzette and Elaine Unkeles eds. Women in Joyce.
Illinois: University Press, 1982. 216pp.

(See #981.)

884   Hennessy, W.M. "The Ancient Irish Goddess of War." R
Celt 1 (1870): 32-55. il. (Appendix by C. Lottner, pp. 55-
57.)

Discussion of characteristics and different personalities
of the Irish war queens, e.g. Neman who afflicted her
victims with madness; Morrigu who incited to deeds of
valor and Macha who revelled amidst the bodies of the
slain, as described in the Irish mythological literature.
Lottner points out the common elements between these and
the Scandanavian/Germanic Valkyrias which are not simply
coincidental but a result of long-standing cultural
exchange in the pre-historic period.

885   Herring, Phillip W. "The Bedsteadfastness of Molly
Bloom." Mod Fict Stud 15 (Spring 1969): 49-61. refs.

    Relates the character of Molly Bloom in Ulyssess to the
    ambiguous relationship Joyce had with his own wife, Nora,
    and his profound preoccupation with marital infidelity.

886   Hoffman, C.G. and A.C. Hoffman. "Re-echoes of the Jazz
Age: Archetypal Women in the Novels of 1922." J Mod Lit 7
(1979); 62-86. refs.

    Discusses the portrayal of women in archetypal roles of
    love goddess or mother image in representative novels of
    1922. Argues that it is as true for women novelists and
    the younger writers despite the post-war social and
    political changes in the actual status of women. Works
    discussed include Joyce's Portrait and Ulysses.

887   Hopkins, Gerald. "Elizabeth Bowen." Landmark 16 (1934):
409-412. portr.

    Tribute to Ms. Bowen's style, her lucidity, limpidness,
    and conciseness. Special tribute to her portrayal of male
    characters especially in To The North. Hopkins claims
    that "in no woman's novel since Miss Austen's Emma has a
    man been so clearly understood, so mercilessly appraised,
    so completely exposed, yet so tolerantly felt. He might
    have been cheaply caricatured; he is, in fact, fully and
    fairly handled."

888   Hull, Vernan. "Aided Meidbe: The Violent Death of
Medb." Speculum 13 (1) (1938): 52-61. refs.

    Critical discussion of the texts of variant manuscript
    versions of the tale here published for the first time
    with English translation. Locations of manuscripts given.

889   Huneker, James. "Bernard Shaw and Women." Harper's Baz
39 (June 1905): 535-538.

    Comment on the disagreeable character of Shaw's women
    characters and how this is at variance with English
    literary tradition which idealizes these.

890   Hunt, John. "An Unrecorded Sheela-na-gig from County
Limerick." Roy Soc Antiq Ire J Ser.7 XVII (1947): 158-159.

891   Hynes, Samuel. "All the Wild Witches: the Woman in
Yeats' Poems." Sewanee R 85 (Fall 1977): 565-582. refs.

    Comments on Yeats' feelings about women, the women in his
    life, their dramatization in his poetry and the
    development of his poetic genius from the early
    conventional stereotyped expressions of sexual attitudes

to greater complexity of understanding and appreciation
of the central importance for creativity of sexual
energy.

892   Kiberd, Declan. Men and Feminism in Modern Literature.
New York: St. Martin's Press, 1985. 250pp.

Includes chapters on Yeats and Joyce (chapter five and
seven) in a perceptive analysis of the portrayal of
androgynous characters in modern literature.

*893   Kline, Gloria.   The Last Courtly Lover: Yeats and the
Idea of Woman. UMI Research, 1983. (Studies in Modern
Literature 6) 199pp. il. bibl.

894   Kopper, Edward A. (Jr.) "Lady Gregory and Finnegans
Wake." Wake News IX (6) (Dec. 1972): 103-107.

Discusses the satirical treatment of Lady Gregory's work
and her personality in Joyce's fiction, especially in
Finnegan's Wake where, according to Kopper, her
characteristics are distributed over many of the women
characters, and the events of her life treated in
serio-comic fashion.

895   Krappe, A. Haggerty. "La Cailleach Bheara: Notes de
Mythologie Gaelique." Etud Celt No.1 (1936): 292-302. refs.

Purvoyance, attributes and legends associated with the
female giant, the Hag of Beare, goddess of fertility and
death, subject of a poem by an anonymous poet of the
middle ages in Ireland, discussed and Gaelic elements in
myth isolated.

896   Lawlor, H.C. [M.R.I.A.] "Two Typical Irish 'Sheela-
na-gigs.'" Man 31 (4-6) (Jan. 1931): 5-6. il. refs.

Brief note and illustration of two examples of the
fertility figures known as Sheela-na-gigs.

897   Lawlor, H.C. "Grotesque Carvings Improperly Called
Sheela-na-gigs." Ir Natur J I (9) (Jan. 1927): 182-185. il.

Disputes some of the assertions made by Stokes regarding
imputed sex and origin of Sheela-na-gigs with specific
discussion of those on White Island.

898   Leask, Harold G. "Sheela-na-gig, Bunratty Castle,
County Clare." Roy Soc Antiq Ire J Ser. 7 VI (1936): 313.

899   Legends of the Cloister or, Convents and Monasteries in
the Olden Time. Dublin: J. Duffy, [18-?]. 150pp.

Includes a legend of the convent of Kildare, or the
Knight of St. John and the Fair Aileen (pp.112-128).
Treats of the ill-fated love of Redmond de Burgh, related
to the noble de Burghs, Earls of Ulster and Aileen
Fitzgerald, the orphan heiress of the near Kinsman of the
great Earl of Kildare, chief of the Geraldines.

*900   Llywelyn, Morgan. Grania: She-King of the Irish Seas.
New York: Crown, 1986. 437pp.

901   Loomis, R. "Morgain La Fee and the Celtic Goddesses."
Speculum 20 (April 1945): 183-203. refs.

An account of the genesis and evolution of the fairy
Morgain from the reign of Caligula to the 20th century.
The part played by Irish legends of Macha and the
Morrigan in the composite legend of Morgain noted.

902   Lorichs, Sonja. The Unwomanly Woman in Bernard Shaw's
Drama and Her Social And Political Background. Uppsala:
Uppsala University, 1973. 196pp. plates. (Acta Universitatis
Upsaliensis: Studia Anglistica Upsaliensia 15)

Author argues that Shaw was a propagandist for equality
between men and women in most of his major plays as well
as some of the minor ones. His female characters were
designed to depict the actual situation of women in
Victorian society - the society that he wished to reform.

903   Love, John. "An Ancient Ivory Carving of Sheela-na-gig,
Found Near Annagh, County Tipperary." Roy Hist & Arch Assoc J
Ser. 4 III (1874): 241.

904   Lowry, Thomas. C.F. "G.B.S. and the Fair Sex." Ladies
Home J LXXXI (Jan. 1974): 128+. il.

Comments on strong women in Shaw's family, his high
opinion of women in general and presents excerpts from
Shaw's written work presenting his views on morals,
marriage and women's character and status.

905   Lynch, John. "O'Casey Kept Best Character Roles for
Women." Women's View 2 (1980): 22-24. il.

Discussion of women in the works of the Irish dramatist,
Sean O'Casey.

906   Lyons, Patrick. "Sheela-na-gig at Kilacomma, County
Waterford." Roy Soc Antiq Ire J Ser. 7 VII (1937): 127-128.

*907   Lysaught, Patricia. The Banshee: The Irish
Supernatural Death Messenger. Dublin: Glendale Press, 1986.

908   Lysaught, Patricia. "An Bhean Chaointe: the
Supernatural Woman in Irish Folklore." Eire Ire 14 (4)
(1979): 7-29. refs.

Identity and various characteristics of this "solitary
female spirit that attends certain families and cries or
keens at night when a certain member of that family is
about to die" are explored. Includes a list of the
families the Banshee follows - old Irish names for the
most part.

909   Lysaught, Patricia. "Irish Banshee Traditions." An
Bealoideas 42-44 (1974-1976): 88-119. refs.

A survey of Irish banshee traditions based on manuscript
materials in the Archives of the Department of Irish
Folklore at University College, Dublin, illustrating
prominent aspects of the banshee legends and beliefs:
e.g. tradition associated with a supernatural woman
believed to manifest herself in connection with death.
The Bhean Si means literally "fairy woman" - anglicised
as the "banshee."

910   MacCana, Proinsias. "Women in Irish Mythology." Crane
Bag 4 (1) (1980): 7-11. il.

Notes the significance of women in early Irish literature
and tradition, a significance not lost on the ancient
kings and heroes of Ireland whose power or success could
not be validated without the co-operation and approval of
the ancient goddesses. The archetypal goddess figure
behind all the feminine portrayals in Irish myth traced.

911   MacCana, Proinsias. "Aspects of the theme of King and
Goddess in Irish Literature." Etud Celt 7 Part 1   (1955/6):
76-114. refs.

A discussion of the "goddess of sovereignty" in Irish
literature with particular reference to Mor Muman.
Legends surrounding Mor Incorporate the familiar themes:
the madness or frenzy of Mor, her marriages to kings
whose reign is thus authenticated; her changes of form
(from an old hag to a beautiful young woman) libation and
coition. Author concludes that in the Mor Muman of Irish
literary and oral tradition we find preserved yet another
representation of the territorial goddess.

912   MacCana, Proinsias. "Aspects of the theme of King and
Goddess in Irish Literature." Etud Celt 7 (2) (1955/6):
356-413. refs.

The second part of an article on this topic with studies
of several tales dealing with various Goddesses in Irish
prose and verse. Various recurring themes in these tales
such as the frenzy element where the heroine is deranged

and flies off to the wilderness where she remains until
the encounter and sexual intercourse with her destined
husband restore her to her senses, analyzed.

913   MacCana, Proinsias. "Aspects of the theme of King and
Goddess in Irish Literature." <u>Etud Celt</u> 8 (1) (1958): 59-65.
refs.

The conclusion of a series of articles by the author
tracing the origin of the theme of King and Goddess in
Irish literature and historical connections. The basis of
the myth seen as the idea that it was only through union
with the territorial goddess of Ireland or her provinces
that legal title to the kinship might be won.

914   McCarthy, Desmond. "What Is Sauce For The Goose." <u>New
Statesm</u> 27 (Apr. 15, 1944): 255-256.

Review of George Bernard Shaw's <u>The Philanderer</u> in which
the author discusses Shaw's two types of women (1) the
acquisitive possessive type whom the man who wants to
call his soul his own or has an aim in life must resist
at all costs and (2) Grace Tranfield who possesses
herself a "masculine" sense of independence and purpose.
These seen as recurring 'types' in Shaw's drama.

915   McCarthy, Patrick A. "The Jeweleyed Harlots of His
Imagination: Prostitution and Artistic Vision in Joyce." <u>Eire
Ire</u> 17 (4) (Winter 1982): 91-109. refs.

An analysis of Joyce's recurring use of prostitutes in
his work as (1) illustrations of larger thematic patterns
and (2) as an aspect of the fallen world.

916   McCauley, Janie Caves. "Kipling on Women: A New Source
For Shaw." <u>Shaw R</u> 17 (1) (Jan. 1974): 40-44. refs.

A discussion of Kipling's views on the role of woman in
the universe seen as closely paralleled in Shaw: e.g. the
predatory woman driven by the desire to nurture and
protect her young; her deadly effect on the artist man,
her unconsciousness of her destructive role in the
male/female relationship.

917   McCurtain, Margaret. "Towards an Appraisal of the
Religious Image of Women." <u>Crane Bag</u> 4 (1) (1980): 26-30.
refs.

A brief, impressionistic survey of the portrayal of women
in the early Christian Church and in post-famine Irish
Catholicism. The strength, fertility and psychological
freedom of these in the myths concerning the early Celtic
saints seen to deteriorate gradually and the image of
woman as helper is denigrated to that of temptress as

Irish Christianity became preoccupied with male chastity. In post-famine Ireland, Mary the Mother of Sorrows became the female model. These elements are seen as fused in the work of the novelist, Mary Lavin, to produce an image of woman which is most representative of the middle years of the 20th century in Ireland.

918   McKay, J.G. "Comh-abartachor Eador Cas-shiubhal-an-t-sleighe Agus An Chailleach Bheara." Scott Gael Stud 3 (1) (Sept. 1929): 10-51. refs. (Bibl. of versions of the legend.)

Comparison of the Scottish and Irish versions of the legend dealing with a duel between a witch and a hard-headed man of a sceptical turn of mind who may or may not have been himself a wizard. The man was victorious in most or all of the events in their complicated duel. Basis of legend seen as involving a struggle of a mortal man with a priestess of an ancient Celtic or pre-Celtic deer-goddess.

919   McSweeney, Kerry. "Brian Moore: Past and Present." Crit Q 18 (Summer 1976): 53-66.

Considers Brian Moore's work as a whole in terms of his central thematic oppositions: past versus present, parental love versus sexual love, the old world versus the new.

920   Malcomson, R. [...The Brank or "scold's bridle" devised for the Punishment or Restraint of Voluble Females...] Roy Soc Antiq Ire J 5 (Part 2) (1865): 293-294.

Brief note on an ancient instrument of torture used to punish "loquacious ladies." Several specimens of the brank have been found in England but this is the only Irish example.

921   Manganiello, Dominic. "That Forty Bonnets Woman." Wake News 14 (1977): 13.

Asserts that a mysterious woman character in Finnegan's Wake was based on a real woman personally known by Joyce, e.g. Mrs. Healy wife of Tommy Healy, Joyce's wife's uncle whose nickname was Forty Bonnets.

922 Marcus, Jane Connor. "Salome: the Jewish Princess Was a New Woman." NYPL Bull 78 (Fall 1974): 95-113. il. refs.

An interpretation of Oscar Wilde's Salome sees the heroine as a biblical Hedda Gabler. John the Baptist as a principled, autonomous, creative artist evoked the same fury and jealousy in her, the prisoner of a socially determined sex role, as Loveborg did in Hedda. Also the men artists are punished by the society for non-

conformity. Wilde thus links the suffering artist and the
aspiring woman both bound in society's image of them in
stereotyped roles.

923   Martin, Almire. "Telle une Deesse Exigeante, la Mere
dans Quelques Drames Anglo-irlandais." Cahiers de Centre d'
Etud Irland 4 (1979): 69-86. refs.

    Includes a discussion of Synge's Riders to the Sea and On
    the Hill by Dermot O'Byrne.

924   Mease, Rev. James. "Sheela na gig from the Old Church
of Ballylarkin, County Kilkenny." Kilk Arch Soc J Ser 2 III
(1860): 7.

925   Miles, Rosalind. The Fiction of Sex. Themes and
Functions of Sex Difference in the Modern Novel. New York:
Barnes and Noble, 1974. 208pp. bibl.

    Considers definitions of sexuality, creativity and sex,
    the writer as woman in the 20th century, sexual themes,
    moral themes and romance, women's liberation, sexual
    stereotypes and the image of woman. Among the women
    briefly discussed are the Irish writers Edna O'Brien,
    Elizabeth Bowen and Iris Murdoch.

926   Molnar, Joseph. "Shaw's Four Kinds of Women." Theatre
Arts 36 (Dec. 1952): 18-21. il.

    Notes unfavorable critical opinion of Shaw as a
    playwright and refutes the accusation that he was unable
    to create credible characters. (An adaptation of this
    article later published in the June 1953 issue of the
    Shaw Society Bulletin.)

927   Molnar, Joseph. "Shaw's Living Women." Shaw Soc Bull 49
(June 1953): 7-11.

    An analysis of Shaw's women characters and the types they
    represent. These include the "Womanly Woman" type, the
    "Emancipated Woman," the "Life Force Woman" and the "New
    Woman." Molnar argues that these are not simply types but
    individual personalities differing within any given
    category with manifold real-life counterparts. (Adapted
    version of the article by the same author published in
    Theatre Arts, December 1952.)

928   Murphy, Michael J. "Four Folktales About Women." Ulster
Folk 13 (1967): 1-8. refs.

    Four Folktales collected in modern Ulster illustrating
    various facets of woman's character: (1) intuitive
    cunning, (2) ruthlessness, (3) the butt and dumb victim

of male obtuseness, (4) pre-occupation with life and the
love of a virile mate. Brief mention of variant versions
and distribution of the stories.

929   Murray, M.A. "Female Fertility Figures." J Roy Anthr
Inst IXIV (1934): 93-100. plates.

A classification of fertility figures divides these into
three groups: the Universal Mother or Isis type; the
Divine Woman or Ishtar type and the Personified Yoni or
Baubo type. The latter, in whose representation the
genitalia are the essential part are represented in the
modern period by Sheila-na-gigs, peculiar to the British
Isles and several examples have been located in Ireland.
Origin of the legends surrounding Baubo and descriptions
and locations of the known Sheila-na-gigs included.

930   "My Fair Lady - G.B.S. On Women" Shaw R 17 (1) (Jan.
1974): 61. il.

Random quotations from Shaw on women and illustrations
from the New York production of My Fair Lady.

931   Nathan, Rhoda B. "The Shavian Sphinx." Shaw R XVII (1)
(Jan. 1974): 45-52. refs.

Discusses how Shaw embodies the two distinct traditions
of the Sphinx legend - e.g. the Greek and the Egyptian -
in his characterization of women - powerful, vital, free
from restrictive convention, instinctive guarded
intelligence and unequivocal authority.

932   Neville, Grace. "Medieval Irish Courtly Love Poetry: An
Exercise in Power Struggle?" Etud Irland 7 (Dec. 1982):
19-30. refs.

Male-female relations as portrayed in the "Danta Gradha"
(medieval Irish love poems) viewed as one of male
dominance/female subordinance.

933   Ni Bhrolchain, Muireann. "Women in Early Irish Myths
and Sagas." Crane Bag 4 (1) (1980): 12-18. refs.

Discussion of three aspects of the role of woman as
portrayed in Irish mythology: (1) the goddess of
sovereignty, (2) extraordinary conceptions and births
attributed to these women's children and (3) their
association with love and the death of their lovers.

934   NiChuilleanain, Eilean. "Love and Friendship." In The
Pleasures of Gaelic Poetry, ed. by Sean MacReamoinn,
pp.49-62. London: Allen Lane (Penguin), 1982.

Discussion of the paradoxical treatment of love and friendship in Gaelic poetry from the 14th to the 18th century.

935   Norman, Henry. "Sheela-na-gigs at Donamon and Tullivin Castles." Roy Hist & Arch Assoc J Ser. 4 III (1874): 17.

936   Nussbaum, F. "Juvenal, Swift and the Folly of Love." 18th Cent Stud 9 (Summer 1976): 540-552. refs.

Examines the literary tradition of satire against women as a context for Swift's "A Beautiful Young Nymph Going To Bed." Swift's poems in this vein viewed as less warnings against marriage than as warnings of the folly of love — the danger of madness which passion entails.

937   O'Connor, Barbara. "Aspects of Representation of Women in Irish Film." Crane Bag 8 (2) (1984): 79-83. refs.

Brief note on some recent films by independent filmmakers in Ireland.

938   O'Connor, Barbara. "The Presentation of Women in Irish Television Drama." In Television and Irish Society: 21 Years of Irish Television, ed. by Martin McLoone and John McMahon, pp. 123-132. Dublin: R.T.E./ I.F.I., 1984. refs.

Discussion of portrayal of women in the Reardons, Bracken and the Ballroom of Romance and class/gender differences in viewing audience.

939   O Fiannachta, Padraig. ed. Leachtai Cholm Cille XII: Na Mna sa Litriocht. Maigh Nuad: An Sagart. 1982. 198pp.

Includes essays on An Banshenchas, St. Bridget, Cain Adamnain, Women's Liberation in "Bean Ruadh de Dhalach," new women poets, and the Women's Parliament in the "Midnight Court."

940   O Seaghdha, M. "Stair an Sile-na-Gig." Feilscribinn Torna (1947): 50-55. refs.

941   Partridge, Angela. "Wild Men and Wailing Women." Eigse 18 (1) (1980): 25-37. refs.

A comparison of the "bean caointe" — bereaved women mourning their dead men — with "madmen." Author sees both categories as in transitional status and temporarily outside the normal structure of society.

942   Pedersen, Lise. "Shakespeare's The Taming of the Shrew

versus Shaw's _Pygmalion_. Male Chauvinism versus Women's
Liberation?" _Shaw R_ 17 (1) (Jan. 1974): 32-39. refs.

> Argues that in the _Taming of the Shrew_, Shakespeare
> supports the conventional morality of his day and male
> chauvinism whereas Shaw in _Pygmalion_ substitues an
> original view of morality by repudiating the male
> chauvinism of his and Shakespeare's day. It is further
> suggested that Shaw clearly used his play, not only to
> support women's liberation, but also to dramatize his
> criticism of Shakespeare's failure to create and espouse
> an original morality in his drama.

943   Radner, John B. "The Youthful Harlot's Curse: The
Prostitute as Symbol of the City in 18th Century English
Literature." _18th Cent Lit_ 2 (Mar. 1976): 59-64. refs.

> A discussion of the prostitute as a symbol of the radical
> perversity of human relations in the city considers
> primarily the work of Goldsmith, Fielding, Wordsworth and
> Blake and to a lesser extent, Steele, Boswell and
> Johnson.

944   Rafroidi, Patrick. "James et Nora; Gabriel et Gretta;
Richard et Bertha: Autobiographie et fiction dans 'The Dead'
et 'Exiles' de Joyce." _Etud Irland_ No. 5, New Series. (Dec.
1980): 37-51. refs.

945   Rafroidi, Patrick. "Bovaryism and the Irish Novel." _Ir
U R_ 7 (2) (Aug. 1977): 237-243. refs.

> The author states that for the purposes of this paper
> Bovaryism "signifies the dual forces of provincialism and
> feminism" and he discusses the presence of these
> characteristics in the work of Irish novelists.

946   Randolph, M.C. "Female Satirists of Ancient Ireland."
So Folk Q 6 (2) (June 1942): 75-87. refs.

> Discussion of status, role and characteristics of female
> satirists as portrayed in ancient Irish literature and a
> comparison of these with druidesses with whom they shared
> some features.

947   Robinson, Marian. "Woman Will Water the Wild World
Over." _Wake News_ 15 (2) (Apr. 1978): 19-23. refs.

> Discusses the influence of Medb Cruachan, the great
> goddess of Irish mythology on the characterization of
> Anna Livia Plurabelle in Joyce's _Finnegans Wake_.

948   Ross, Anne. "The Divine Hag of the Pagan Celts." In _The
Witch Figure: Folklore Essays by a Group of Scholars in_

England Honouring the 75th Birthday of Katherine M. Briggs. ed. by Venitia Newall, pp.130-164. London: Routledge and Kegan Paul, 1973. refs.

A fascinating study of the Celtic goddesses with their dual form of beauty and fertility, ugliness and destruction describes specific figures and types in Irish mythology - the Cailleach Bheara, Boand, wife of the Dagda, the Morrigan, Sheelagh-na-gigs, etc. The survival in modern Irish folk tradition of these powerful, diverse yet basically homogenous goddesses is traced.

949   Rule, Jane. Lesbian Images. Garden City, N.J.: Doubleday, 1975. 246pp. bibl.

Examines the changing images of women as expressed through the lives and writings of more than a dozen widely read novelists. Four categories of women described: (1) women who wanted to be men (2) women who were emotionally but not sexually engaged with other women (3) women who recognized and tried to suppress the lesbian sides of their nature (4) women who were proud to be women and lesbians. A brief consideration of Elizabeth Bowen and her work (grouped in the second of the categories listed).

950   Ryan, Joan. "Women in the Novels of Kate O'Brien: The Mellick Novels." In Studies in Anglo-Irish Literature, ed. by Heinz Kosok, pp. 322-332. Bonn: Bouvier, 1982.

Discussion of female characters in Pray for the Wanderer and The Land of Spices seen as very much of their time and context, whose characters are defined through O'Brien's major themes - love, pain and departure.

951   S, G.T. (i.e. Rev. George T. Stokes?) "Figures Known As Hags of the Castle, Sheelas, or Sheela na gigs." With note by W.F. i.e. William Frazer on one found in Iona. Roy Soc Antiq Ire J Ser. 5 IV (1894): 77-81, 392-394.

A tabulated list of the figures cut in stone known as 'Sheelas' with descriptions and locations.

952   Scanlon, Leone. "The New Woman in the Literature of 1883-1909." U Mich Pap Wom Stud 2 (2) (1976): 133-159. bibl. refs.

Examines briefly the course of the Feminist Movement in England and the development of the real life "New Woman" who was the model for the fictional heroine. The characteristics of that heroine in the work of some major and minor writers of the period 1883-1909 examined. A brief consideration of Shaw's Man and Superman and Mrs. Warren's Profession included.

953   Scott, Bonnie Kime. _Joyce and Feminism_. Indiana:
Indiana University Press, 1984.

A discussion of Joyce's complex approach to women seen as
involving misogynist elements but also feminist strains.

954   _The Seventh of Joyce_. Ed. by Bernard Benstock
Bloomington. Sussex: Indiana University Press and the
Harvester Press, 1982. 267pp. bibl. refs.

A selection of papers from the seventh International
James Joyce Symposium held in Zurich, in June 1971. The
final chapter titled "Re-Joycing in Sex (Or, Come
Again?)" examines the treatment of sexuality in Joyce's
work (pp.241-266).

955   [Shaw, George Bernard] "As Bernard Shaw Sees Woman." _N
Y Times Mag_ (June 19, 1927): 1-2. il.

The full text of an address delivered by Shaw on behalf
of the Cecil Houses Fund to provide resources for the
maintenance of public lodging houses for women. Shaw
argues that men and women are fundamentally alike and
should be accorded similar rights.

956   Shaw, George Bernard. "G.B.S. on Women: Quotations."
Vogue LXXVII (June 1956): 53.

Random quotations from the dramatic and other writings of
George Bernard Shaw dealing with women.

957   "Sheela-na-Gig at Fethard Abbey: Illustration of." _J
Cork Hist Arch Soc_ Ser.2 IX (1903): 207.

958   Smith, R. O'Brien. "Sheela-na-gig, Ballyfinboy Castle,
near Borrisokane." _Roy Soc Antiq Ire J_ Ser.5 XVI (1906): 88.

959   Spangler, Ellen B. "Synge's Deirdre of the Sorrows as
Feminine Tragedy." _Eire_ 12 (4) (1977): 97-101. refs.

Spangler argues that in feminine tragedy as opposed to
masculine the dramatic tension comes exclusively from
within, from opposing impulses toward creation and
destruction, life and death, humanity and divinity.

960   Sporn, Paul. "Marriage and Class Conflict: the
Subversive Link in George Moore's 'A Drama in Muslin.'" _Clio_
3 (1) (1973): 7-18. refs.

An analysis of Moore's novel A Drama in Muslin as a
dialectical study of the class conflict between tenants

and landlords in Ireland which has as its analogy the
less titantic struggle between the young heroines of the
Irish gentry and the society which forces them to be the
lures and playthings of men.

961   Stanrou, C.N. "The Love Songs of J. Swift, G. Bernard
Shaw and J.A.A. Joyce." Midwest Q 6 (Winter 1965): 135-162.
refs.

An attempt to find a "common denominator" in the three
writers' comments on love. Swift and Shaw are judged to
have more in common with each other than they do with
Joyce. However, Stanrou concludes that "love's
fundamental truth eluded all three."

962   Stein, Joseph. "The New Woman and the Decadent Dandy."
Dalhousie R 55 (Spring 1975): 54-62. refs.

An analysis of the decline of dandyism and the rise of
feminism during the decadent era - the 1890's - through
an examination of the writings of three of the major
"dandies" e.g. Beerbohn, Wilde and Beardsley. Their work
briefly analyzed in terms of their portrayal of the
relationship between the effete dandy and his more vital
antagonist, the "new woman."

963   Stern, Ludw. Chr. "Das Marchen von Etain." ZCP 5
(1905): 522-534. refs.

964   Stopford Green, Alice. Women's Place in the World of
Letters. London: Macmillan and Co., 1913. 32pp. [Reprinted
from 19th Century, June 1897.]

Brief impressionistic survey of subject matter and style
of literary women in England in the 19th century -
actually a philosophical consideration. The author
perceives woman's nature as anarchic, complex, and
passionate to which political philosophy, metaphysics and
theology are alien but which is concerned with the newer
fields of science and the novel.

965   Szoverffy, James. "The Well of the Holy Women: Some of
St. Columba Traditions in the West of Ireland." J Am Folk 68
(1955): 111-122. refs.

A critical examination of context and sources of the
basic tradition of the three Holy Women linked with St.
Columba as his legendary sisters and the Well in
Glencolumcille, County Donegal, called after them; local
legends about these and the rites and rituals associated
with the cult of the well.

966   Timpe, Eugene. "Ulysses and the Archetypal Feminine" In

Perspectives in Literary Symbolism, ed. by Joseph Strelka, pp.199-213. University Park, Pennsylvania: Pennsylvania State University Press, 1968. il. refs.

Uses the archtype of the Feminine or Great Mother as an explanatory device for Ulysses. Joyce seen as beginning with the initiation of the elementary Good Mother concept and from there developing gradually into contradictory concepts which define the Terrible Mother.

967   Tochmarc Etaine. Eriu 12 Part2 (1938): 137-196. refs.

Text translation and indexes of the versions of the "wooing of Etain", a principal tale of the mythological cycle which is concerned with Midir, King of the effmounds of Bri-Leith.

968   Topliss, Iain. "Mary Wollstonecraft and Maria Edgeworth's Modern Ladies." Etud Irland n.b. (n.s.) (Dec. 1982): 13-31. refs.

Argues that Maria Edgeworth was profoundly influenced in a positive way by Mary Wollstonecraft's writings and that she attempted in her own literary endeavor to affect a rapprochement between Jacobin and anti-Jacobin thought, particularly as it related to the position of women.

969   Unkeless, Elaine Rapp. "Leopold Bloom as A Womanly Man." Mod Stud 2 (1) (1976): 35-44. refs.

A study of Joyce's use of traditionally female characteristics with which the author claims he imbues the male hero of Ulysses, Leopold Bloom.

970   Vieth, David M. "A Symposium on Women in Swift's Poems: Vanessa, Stella, Lady Acheson, and Celia." Papers Lang & Lit 14 (2) (1978): 115-151.

Five papers written for the 1976 Modern Language Association Conference focus on Jonathan Swift's artistic response to a series of women, three of them real (Vanessa, Stella, Lady Acheson) and one, a fictitious composite (Celia).

971   Voelker, Joseph Craig. "'Nature it Is.' The Influence of Giordano Bruno on James Joyce's Molly Bloom." James Joyce Q 14 (Fall 1976): 39-48. refs.

Claims that James Joyce was remarkably consistent in his portrayal of women. Joyce's women are sensuous, irrational and rather than fictional representations of actual women are personifications of nature. Molly Bloom, the archtype female is, at once, religious and amoral; an adultress and piously faithful.

972   Wallace, J.N.A. "Sheela-na-gig. Clenagh Castle, County Clare." Roy Soc Antiq Ire J Ser. 7 VII (1937): 128.

973   Wallace, J.N.A. "Sheela-na-gig at Bunratty Castle, County Clare." No Munst Antiq J I (1936-1939): 39.

974   Watkins, Charles A. "Modern Irish Variants of the Enchanted Pear Tree." So Folk Q 30 (June 1966): 202-213. tables. refs.

     The Irish Folklore Commission has twenty-one modern
     variants of Chaucer's "Merchant Tale." These are from
     oral tradition and cluster in two groups: in Group A a
     wife surprised by her husband with another man — usually
     "flagrante delicto" — is enabled to convince the husband
     that he is the victim of an optical illusion; in Group B
     her task is to convince the husband that her being "in
     flagrante delicto" is for his sake.

975   Watson, Barbara Bellow. "The New Woman and The New Comedy." Shaw R 17 (1) (Jan. 1974): 2-16. refs.

     Discusses the Shavian woman — the quintessence of the New
     Woman — and her position as subject at the center of
     Shaw's dramatic structure. This represents a radical
     departure from the traditional comic pattern and reflects
     an essentially changed society. In Shaw the nature of the
     conflict involves the individual woman's humanity and the
     rigidity of the sex role assigned to her. Shaw recognized
     that woman's rebellion against her attributed role would
     be the model for all such rebellion against roles, duty,
     cant.

976   Watson, Barbara Bellow. A Shavian Guide to the Intelligent Woman. New York: Norton, 1964. 250pp. refs.

     Considers Shaw's treatment of women, marriage and love in
     his work and his attitude towards the struggle for
     women's suffrage. Watson argues that the apparent
     ambivalence in Shaw's attitude to the suffragists was his
     view that the vote, as such, though necessary, was an
     inadequate and misguided final goal.

977   West, Rebecca. "And They All Lived Unhappily Ever After." Times Lit Supp (July 26, 1974): 779. il.

     Comment on unhappy endings in modern women's fiction but
     with more detailed discussion of Iris Murdoch, Edna
     O'Brien, Margaret Drabble and Doris Lessing.

978   Whelan, Fae and Keith N. Hull. "There's Talkin for a Cute Woman! Synge's heroines." Eire 16 (1980): 36-46. refs.

Argues that Synge's principal women characters think and
behave in a basic pattern that acts as a unifying theme
in his plays: all suffer from some sort of dissatisfaction
with their lives, seek escape and in the process initiate
the dramatic action.

979   Williams, B. "Molly Bloom: Archetype or Stereotype." J
Marr & Fam 33 (Aug. 1971): 545-546. refs.

Discussion of Joyce's treatment of women in Ulysses. Sees
the character of Molly Bloom as one instance of a general
stereotyped view of women which reflects not simply the
prejudices of the male characters in the novel but those
of Joyce himself.

980   Women in Irish Legend, Life and Literature. Ed. by S.F.
Gallagher. Gerrards Cross, Bucks; Totowa, N.J., Colin Smythe,
Barnes and Noble Books, 1983. 157pp. refs. (Irish Literary
Studies 14.)

Essays in this volume discuss the portrayal of women in
Gaelic, Anglo-Irish and Irish poetry, prose and drama.
Includes discussion of the work of Yeats, Synge, Shaw,
O'Casey, Joyce; also, the dramatic treatments of Sarah
Curran in plays about Robert Emmet and a historical essay
about Anna Parnell.

981   Women in Joyce. Ed. by Suzette Henke and Elaine
Unkeless. Chicago: University of Illinois Press, 1982. 216pp.
refs.

A collection of essays which discuss Joycean women
characters from a realistic perspective and focus on "the
debilitating patterns of cultural oppression that
restrict their lives and the specifically patriarchal
nature of the authoritarian institutions which Joyce
challenges in his work." Some essayists in this
collection praise him for depicting the situation of
Irish women accurately and, for the most part,
sympathetically while others object that he never
envisions a female character who can transcend the
limitations imposed by Irish culture.

FICTIONAL TREATMENTS

This category is comprised of fictional renditions of
events and characters with real life counterparts. For
factual accounts see section on BIOGRAPHY AND
AUTOBIOGRAPHY.

982   Barry, Michael. The Romance of Sarah Curran. Eigse
Books, 1985. 140pp. il.

983   <u>A Beautiful Irish Heiress of the Penal Days</u> (Miss
Catherine McAuley, Foundress of the Order of Mercy.) A drama
in four acts by a lover of "The Little Flower." Dublin: The
Juverna, 1931. 47pp.

   A dramatized version of the life of Catherine McAuley.

984   Beck, Mrs. Lily (Moresby) Adams. <u>The Irish Beauties</u>.
Garden City, New York: Doubleday and Co. Inc., 1931. 310pp.

   Novel based on the lives of the Gunning sisters by the
   former E. Barrington.

985   Brophy, John. <u>Sarah: A Novel</u>. London: Collins, 1948.
320pp.

   A historical novel based on the life of Sarah Curran, the
   fiancee of Robert Emmet.

986   Butler, Margery Bayley. <u>A Candle Was Lit: Life of
Mother Mary Aikenhead</u>. Dublin: Clonmore and Reynolds, 1953.
183pp. il. plates. portrs.

   A novelized version of the life of Mary Aikenhead
   foundress of the Irish Sisters of Charity.

987   Clewes, Winston. <u>The Violent Friends</u>. New York and
London: D. Appleton Century Co., 1945. 191pp.

   A fictional treatment of the friendship of Dean Swift,
   Stella and Vanessa.

988   Conolly, Muriel. <u>For Ireland: A One Act Play for Four
Women</u>. London: Evans. [1973] 15pp.

   Dramatization of the situation of women friends on
   opposite sides in the Northern Ireland struggle.

989   Cove, Joseph Walter (pseud. Lewis Gibbs). <u>Vanessa and
the Dean, the Ironic History of Esther Vanhomrigh and
Jonathan Swift</u>. London: J.M.Dent and Sons Ltd., 1938. 271pp.
facsim. front. plates. portrs.

   A fictionalized account of the relationship between
   Jonathan Swift and Esther Vanhomrigh based on their
   letters, the poem "Cadenus and Vanessa," the
   correspondence and prose works of the Dean. Cove
   considers his "fiction" a valid interpretation of the
   facts.

990   Grumbach, Doris. <u>The Ladies</u>. New York: E.P. Dutton,
1984. 210pp.

Fictional biography of Lady Eleanor Butler and Sarah
Ponsonby.

991   Iona. (pseud.) <u>The Story of Saint Brigid</u> (in the form
of a dialogue between St. Blath, 6th century and a novice in
one of Saint Brigid's convents). Dublin: Talbot Press, 1929.
94pp. il.

Offers a brief overview of the various old lives of St.
Brigid which range from the 7th to the 12th centuries.
Suggests that the same miracles and many of the
incidences in St. Brigid's life are repeated in these
works except for divergence on the circumstances of her
birth.

992   Jacob, Rosamond. <u>The Rebel's Wife</u>. Traler, Co. Kerry.
The Kerryman Ltd., 1957. 216pp.

Semi-fictionalized biography of Matilda Witherington,
later wife of Wolfe Tone based on the writings of Tone,
Matilda and Mary Ann McCracken.

993   Leslie (Doris). <u>Notorious Lady: The Life and Times of
the Countess of Blessington</u>. London: Heinemann, 1976. 273pp.
bibl.

A biography based on Lady Blessington's journals and
diary presents in novelized form the principal characters
and events in her life.

994   Lyttle, W.G. <u>Betsy Gray or Hearts of Down: A Tale of
Ninety-Eight</u>. Newcastle, County Down: Mourne Observer, Ltd.,
1968 reprint. (c.1896) 191pp. il.

Historical novel dealing with the rebellion in County
Down in 1798 and the events which led to this. The title
character is a girl, Betsy Gray who is possibly a real
personage who was murdered after the Battle of
Ballynahinch with whose biography the novelist has taken
poetic license.

995   McKown, Robin. <u>The Ordeal of Anne Devlin</u>. London:
MacMillan & Co. Ltd., 1964. 190pp.

A historical novel based on the life of Anne Devlin,
servant to Robert Emmet, who because of her refusal to
divulge her master's whereabouts after the abortive
rebellion in 1803 was imprisoned for three years by the
British, tortured and half hanged.

996   MacMahon, Bryan. "The Death of Biddy Early." J Ir Lit 1
(2) (May 1972): 30-44.

One act play incorporating elements of the legends about
Biddy Early, the Wise Woman of Clare, including her
marriage to a much younger man; her feud with the
Catholic Church; her ability to foresee the future and
the circumstances of her death.

997   Moore, Frank Frankfort. The Fatal Gift. New York: Dodd,
Mead and Co., 1898. 380pp.

A novel based on the lives of the Gunning sisters.

998   N. A. P. Lantern Beams on the Lee: A Tribute to Nano
Nagle. Bailieborough: The Presentation Sisters, [1956]. 76pp.
il. portrs. (Serialized in Presenting Christ)

Novelized account of the life of Nano Nagle, founder of
the Presentation Order.

999   Reade, Charles. Peg Woffington: a Novel. London:
Bentley, 1857. 256pp. frontis.

Novel based on the life of the Irish actress.

1000   Skidmore, Harriet. "The Angel of Mercy: Catherine
McAuley, Foundress of the Sisters of Mercy." Ir Mon 9
(Dec.1881): 636-643.

A tribute to Catherine McAuley in the form of a play
featuring Europe, Erin (accompanied by the 12 Irish
foundations made by her) England, Scotland, Asia, Africa,
Oceania and America.

1001   [Wadleton, Mrs. Maggie Jeanne (Melody)]. The Book of
Maggie Owen. New York: Gosset and Dunlap, 1941. 262pp. portr.

"Autobiography" of a year in the life of a twelve year
old orphan in Ireland written as a journal in 1908
recounts her day to day activities, observations on
people and things, her friendships, family and a voyage
to America.

1002   Wailly, Armand Francois Leon de. Stella and Vanessa: A
Romance of the Days of Swift. Translated by Lady Duff Gordon.
London: Richard Bentley, 1853. 278pp.

A novel based on the lives of Jonathan Swift, Esther
Johnson and Esther Vanhomrigh.

1003   Woman's Part: An Anthology of Short Fiction by and
About Irish Women 1890-1960. Selected and edited by Janet

Madden - Simpson. Dublin, London; Arlen House, M. Boyars, 1984. 223pp.

A selection of short fiction written by Irish women between 1890 and 1960 seen as reflecting facets of Irish female experience and its evolution during the period.

Education

The entries in this section represent a very small sub-section of the total educational literature since only works that specifically refer to female education are included. Also most secondary Catholic education of girls in Ireland has traditionally been primarily in convent schools and inseparable therefore from histories of those institutions. For these see RELIGION and for accounts of individual educators see BIOGRAPHY AND AUTOBIOGRAPHY - RELIGION AND EDUCATION. The publications listed below mainly deal with higher education for women including the struggle for admission to the University and ideological arguments on appropriate education for women. There is also some material on primary, secondary, vocational, technical and adult education. For education for home-making see MARRIAGE AND THE FAMILY.

1004   "Alexandra College and its Schemes: an Editorial on the Protestant Activities of the Alexandra College Guild, Criticising Catholics Who Attended the Guild Dinner Including Mrs. James Mc Neill and Prof. Mary Hayden." Cath Bull 21 (June 1931): 534-40.

1005   Alexandra College, Dublin: its History and its Work With a History of Alexandra School and a Record of the Work of the Guild and Other College Societies. Jubilee 1866-1916. Dublin: Alexandra College [n.d.] 67pp. il. ports.

   A brief history of the Protestant women's college with details on scholarships, exhibitions, lectures, programs, connection with Trinity College and the Royal University of Ireland, societies and publications.

1006   Alexandra College, Dublin. Students' Union... Rules. Dublin: Printed by R.D. Webb & Sins, 1888. 7pp.

Goals and Constitution of the Students' Union
Association.

1007   Breatnach, Eileen. "Women and Higher Education in
Ireland:1879-1914." Crane Bag 4 (1) (1980): 47-53. refs.

A detailed examination of the evolution of female
education from the early goal of rescuing distressed
gentlewomen through the ultimate accomplishment of
securing the admission of women to the University on the
same terms as men. The crucial role of educational
developments in England including the High School
Movement for girls, The Intermediate Education Act of
1878 and the Royal University Act of 1879, discusssed.

1008   Brooke, William G. (M.A.) "Educational Endowments and
Their Application to the Middle Class and Higher Education of
Girls and Women." Stat & Soc Inq Soc J (Nov. 1872): 114-124.

Presents arguments for the extension to Ireland of
legislation permitting girls to benefit from educational
endowments recently recognized as their right in England
and Wales. Details how the present system totally
excludes Irish women from these benefits with
particularly detrimental consequences for teacher
training. Offers suggestions for improving the existing
situation even while awaiting legislative change.

1009   Byrne, Eileen M. Equality of Education and Training
for Girls (10-18 years) Collection Studies.   Education
Series. No. 9. Luxembourg: Commission des Communautes
Europeenes, July 1978. 90pp. (Eric ED 194692: available in
fiche only)

Based on an in-depth inquiry undertaken in 1977-78, this
report identifies the extent, type and character of
inequalities in the education and training of girls in
the second level of education, ages 10-18. Chapter 1
gives background of this report sponsored by the nine
European communities (Ireland included). Suggestions on
how to further real equality in education and training
offered.

1010   "Catholicus." "The Nursing Profession and the Catholic
Nurse." Ir Mon LXX (Nov. 1942): 441-445.

Advocates a revision of the syllabus for nursing and
midwifery to incorporate Catholic teaching on ethics and
medical ethics.

1011   Clancy, Patrick. Participation In Higher Education: A
National Survey. Dublin: Higher Education Authority, 1982.
86pp.

The findings of the survey in regard to women, broadly
summarized, indicate a significant increase in the
proportion of women in third-level education over the
decade from 35% in 1971/72 to 44% in 1981/82. The most
dramatic increases have been in Law, Science, Dentistry
and Veterinary Medicine. They are still under-represented
in the technological sector, decidedly over-represented
in colleges of education, decidely under-represented in
English, Commerce, Agriculture and over-represented in
the Humanities, Education, Science, Art and Design.
Despite their predominance in the Arts and Social
Sciences at undergraduate level, they constitute only 25%
of full time postgraduate degree students.

1012   Clancy, Patrick and Ciaran Benson. Higher Education in
Dublin: A Study of Some Emerging Needs. Dublin: The Higher
Education Authority, 1979. 46pp.

Based on data gathered from the Department of Education
and the institutions of higher education in Ireland
offers an educational profile of students in the Dublin
area - type of post - primary school attended, subjects
taken at the leaving Certificate, participation rates in
second-level and third-level education and for Dublin
entrants to higher level education, particulars as to
sex, and socio-economic status.

1013   Clarke, M.T. Men, Women and Post-primary Principalship
in Northern Ireland. Belfast: Equal Opportunity Commission
for Northern Ireland, 1978. 14pp. tables. (Also published in
Core 3 (1+) March 13, 1979.)

This study attempts to correlate the disproportion of
women principals to men in post primary education in
Northern Ireland (75.6% are men) - despite the fact that
equal numbers of men and women follow this occupation -
with other possibly relevant factors such as school
management and religious status criteria; incidence of
single sex and co-educational schools, and some
sex-distributed features in the total postprimary teacher
population. Findings indicate that experience and
education alone do not fully account for the disparity
between male and female principals.

1014   Concannon, Eileen."Our Dress Problem: A Proposed
Solution." Cath Bull 1 (1911): 66-69. portr.

Suggests that government funds should be expended on
training of dress designers and dressmakers and a
scholarship fund established for student trainees.

1015   Crowther, Alice Christabel. "Review of Work Done by
Queen Victoria's Jubilee Institute for Nurses in Ireland."
Dublin J Med Sci CXLV (April 1918): 236-240.

An address delivered by the Lady Superintendent, St
Patrick's Nurses' Home, Dublin, Friday, February 22, 1918
gives a brief overview of the six month training course
for nurses at the home to prepare these for careers as
district nurses throughout the country.

1016   Cullen, Rose. "Women and Education in Ireland." Ed
Matters 1 (Sept. 1976): 29-30.

Notes that despite the superior achievement of girls at
second level schools, subjects which have direct bearing
on choice of disciplines in universities and high
prestige work are often excluded from the curriculum in
girls schools. Also the apprenticeship system
discriminates against women. At third level education
women are significantly underrepresented. Statistics
included taken from the OECD survey of the Irish
educational system.

1017   Cumann Bancheimithe Colaiste na h Ollscoile Baile
Atha Cliath: University College, Dublin Women Graduates'
Association, 1902-1982. Compiled on behalf of the
Association by Mary J. Higan. [Dublin: University College
Dublin Women Graduates' Association, 1982.] 78pp. il. photos.
bibl.

Brief history of the Association and the Irish women's
struggle for full parity with men in University
education. Includes biographical sketches of Officers of
the Association and a list of meetings with titles of
papers presented.

1018   Cusack, M.F. Women's Work in Modern Society. London:
Kenmare Publications, 1874. 37pp.

A treatise detailing how women should be educated and
what their role should be in society. Women are judged
inferior to men in physical strength and to some extent
in mental power. Argues against the classical education
of girls and advocates teaching them useful skills; the
poor should be given a good, common sense practical
education while girls of the upper middle class should be
given a good "thorough" and technical education. Presents
arguments for some rights for women, but advocates of
women's liberation viewed as extreme.

1019   Daly, Lilian. "Women and the University Question." New
Ire R XVII (April 1902): 74-80.

Expresses the opinion, which it is claimed John Stuart
Mill also advocated, that the true vocation for women is
to be a fit helpmate for man. Argues against the idea
that women should be trained by the same means and for
the same responsibilities and duties as men. Claims that
women students are wanting in physique and that women by

competing with men in the employment market, are tending
to lower wages. However, argues that the final choice
should be left to women.

1020   Downes, Margaret Tierney. The Case of the Catholic
Lady Students of the Royal University. Dublin: E.Ponsonby,
1888. 24pp.

A plea for the extension of the right to attend Fellows
lectures to the lady students. Downes cites the
Constitution of the University which pledges equal
educational advantages for men and women and reproaches
the Senate for its failure to implement this by requiring
Fellows to hold their lectures in locations from which
women are not excluded.

1021   Dublin University: Statement of the Proceedings from
1892 to 1895 in Connection with the Movement for the
Admission of Women to Trinity College, Dublin and
Correspondence in Reference Thereto. Dublin: University
Press, 1895. 48pp.

Consists of the correspondence which appeared in the
Irish press on the admission of women to Trinity College
for the years stated arranged in consecutive order and in
narrative form.

1022   Edgeworth, Maria. Letters for Literary Ladies. New
York and London: Garland, 1974. (Reprint of 1795 ed.) 47pp.
bibl.

This, Maria Edgeworth's first published work stemmed from
a correspondence between her father, Richard Lovell
Edgeworth and his friend Thomas Day over the issues of
higher education for women and the propriety of female
authorship. In her first letter Maria presents Day's
arguments against female authorship while it also
presents some of the commonly held misconceptions
concerning the status of women in Maria Edgeworth's time.
The following letter takes up most of these assumptions
and refutes them and suggests what might be appropriate
education for women. The remaining letters contrast two
types of women and present views on marriage and social
coventions.

1023   "The Education of Women." Dublin U Mag LXXXIII (May
1874): 583-591.

Decries the type of education commonly offered to women -
music, drawing, French - and argues that these should be
exposed to systematic study of English language and
literature.

1024   Employment Equality Agency. Schooling and Sex Roles:

Agency Commentary, Recommendations and Summary Findings of
Report. Dublin: Employment Equality Agency, 1983. 39pp. il.

   Endorsement by the Employment Equality Agency of the ESRI
   Report, "Schooling and Sex Roles," includes a summary
   version of the general findings and policy implications
   of the Report and an outline by the Employment Equality
   Agency of priorities for action.

1025   Equal Opportunities Commission of Northern Ireland.
Start Again: Make a Fresh Start Through Education and
Training. Belfast: The Commission. [1984?] 17pp.

   A handbook designed for people who want to change their
   employment, return to employment after a gap or to
   improve their existing prospects. Expected to be of
   special interest to women. Details on education and
   training programs, financial aid, etc.

1026   Equal Opportunities Commission for Northern Ireland.
Girls and Education: A Northern Ireland Statistical Analysis.
Belfast: The Commission, 1981. 15pp. tables.

   Figures for representation and attainment by females in
   examinations (O and A levels); destination of school
   leavers, training opportunities and day release, and the
   position of women as teachers and lecturers.

1027   F. (F.J.) "The Education of Girls." Univ Mag LXXVII
(Jan. 1871): 42-49.

   Presents arguments for the education of women to prepare
   them for the moral governance of the society.

1028   Fahy, Betty. "Education for Living: the Rural Woman."
Admin 23 (1) (Spring 1975): 54-60.

   Discusses the kind of education needed by rural women and
   what is currently available through the Department of
   Agriculture and Fisheries and the Irish Countrywoman's
   Association. United Nations and E.E.C. activities on
   behalf of rural women briefly outlined and further unmet
   needs indicated.

1029   Fleming, J.B. "The Teaching of Midwifery in the
University of Dublin." Hermathena 103 (1966): 66-82.

   A review of the teaching of midwifery in the University
   of Dublin, 1749-1966, and an outline of plans for its
   future development.

1030   Forbes, Isabel F. "1866 and 1906. a Memory." Alex Col
Mag (June 1906): 3-7.

Reminescences by a Foundation student of the early days of the college and the sharp contrast provided by the current facility with the then poorly furnished rooms and almost empty library shelves. Brief comment on status of female education in Ireland in the 1860's and the founding of Alexandra College.

1031   Friedman, Harold and Helen Friedman. "Four Exceptional Women in British Education." Integrated Ed 15 (4) (July-Aug. 1977): 10-17. il. refs.

Kathleen Day, headmistress of Rockland Street School in Dublin is one of the "exceptional" women of the title. Rockland Street is an experimental school founded as a research project as well as being a co-operative nursery school. Ms Day's academic background, her skill and dedication, her research efforts on children's intelligence, her administrative ability and the school's outreach efforts to involve local mothers are detailed.

1032   Hannan, Damien. Schooling and Sex Roles: Sex Differences in Subject Provision and Student Choice in Irish Post-Primary Schools. Dublin: The Economic and Social Research Institute, May 1983. 446pp. graphs. tables. bibl.

A highly technical report of the results and conclusions of a very detailed investigation of the extent, nature and causes of sex differences in second-level educational provision and subject specialization of girls and boys in Irish post primary schools carried out in response to a request from the Employment Equality Agency and the Department of Labour. Consequences of findings explicated and recommendations for changing the present structure presented. Major finding showed that while there were often pronounced sex differences in the provision and allocation of subjects these were generally less than the sex differences in the pupils own rates of choice.

1033   Houston, D. "Gardening by Women." Ir Mon XLV (March 1917): 176-179.

Brief note on formation and goals of the Irish School of Gardening for Women.

1034   Irish Women United. Education Workshop. Education Widens The Gap Between The Sexes. Dublin: Irish Women United, 1979. 21pp. il.

Discusses the differences in the education offered to girls and boys: at primary school, there is differential emphasis on subjects taught to girls versus boys within a similar curriculum; at vocational schools girls are directed toward courses which do not fit them for apprenticeships; at academic colleges girls are channeled

into domestic science, language and art courses rather
than mathematics or science. The consequences for higher
education and professional careers for women analyzed.

1035   Knight, William (L.L.D.). "The Higher Education of
Women." Belf Hist & Phil Soc (1894): 88-96.

Text of lecture by Professor Knight giving a historical
overview of education of women in earlier times and in
modern day England with comment and clarifications
regarding the education of women in Northern Ireland by
other participants.

1036   Leydon, Ita. "Development of Nurse Education in
Ireland: Training to Meet Challenges of the Future." Int J
Nurs Stud 10 (2) (May 1973): 95-101. refs.

A brief historical overview of the Irish general hospital
system and the development of nurse training. Considers
content of courses, duration, numbers in training,
levels, specializations, standards and probable effects
of E.E.C. entry and planned major reorganization of the
hospital services on the future of Irish nusing
education.

1037   Lovett, Tom and Libby Mackay. "Adult Education and the
Working Class: a Case Study." Urb R 9 (3) (Fall 1976): 193-
200. refs.

A report on a pilot scheme devised by a member of the
staff of the Institute of Continuing Education,
Londonderry, to help combat the failure of adult
education to reach the working class women in that city.
The scheme centered on the employment of a part-time
tutor organizer whose responsibility was the creation of
study/action groups in the community offering an
alternative educational experience. Rationale, method of
recruitment of "students" and "experts" for the study
groups, and programs offered are described with
conclusions and recommendations.

1038   M.M. "Education of Girls in Housewifery." Ir Mon 54
(Apr. 1926): 174-176.

Questions whether an education which gives insufficient
attention to housekeeping duties can be morally sound.

1039   MacCurtain, Margaret (Sister Benevenuta). "St. Mary's
University College." Univ R 111 (4) (1963): 33-47. refs.

A review of University Catholic education in Ireland with
special reference to the education of women, Dr. Walsh,
Archbishop of Dublin's handling of women's colleges in

the University scheme and an account of St. Mary's
University College and its role in preparing women
students for University exams and its subsequent history
through 1911.

1040   McKenna, Anne. "Achievement and the Adolescent Girl."
Chr Rex XXV (1) (Jan.-Mar.1971): 38-42.

A discussion of the differences in career planning
between adolescent boys and girls poses the question
whether society is educating its female members in ways
that are antithetical to their intellectual development.

1041   Macken, Mary M. (Professor) "Women in the University
and the College." In Struggle With Fortune: A Miscellany for
the Centenary of the Catholic University of Ireland
1854-1954. ed. by Dr. Michael Tierney, pp. 142-165. Dublin:
Browne and Nolan, Ltd. [1954?]   il. portrs. front.

A brief overview of the struggle by women for equal
access to the University which had two distinct phases:
1879-1909 when the Royal University of Ireland admitted
these to degree programs while still barring them from
full University privileges and the second phase 1909-1954
when the National University accorded them equal
treatment with male students. Brief account of prominent
women scholars and activists who led the fight for
equality and an overview of the academic careers of
subsequent female graduates.

1042   Malone, Conor. "Academic Rights of Women: the Sorry
Example Shown at Protestant Centres." Cath Bull XXVII (July
1837): 530-534.

Review of second class status of women students at
Trinity College Dublin where these are denied admittance
to fellowships or professorships, may not hold positions
on the governing body, scholarship restrictions, etc.
contrasted with full equality for those at National
University and its constituent colleges.

1043   Morrissey, Thomas J. Towards a National University:
William Delany, S.J. (1835-1924). Dublin and Atlantic City,
N.J.: Wolfhound Press, Humanities Press, 1983. 425 pp. il.
portr.

Chapter XV has a brief account of the women's struggle
for equal advantage with men in university education and
President Delany's attitudes and actions in this
connection (pp. 279-287).

1044   Murphy, Michael. "Adult Education and Women." Admin 23
(1) (Spring 1975): 49-53.

The author, who is Director of the National Association
of Adult Education discusses categories of women who are
not involved in adult education and suggests possible
ways of involving these.

1045   Nevin, Monica. "Sex Differences in Participation Rates
in Mathematics and Science at Irish Schools and
Universities." Int R Ed 19 (1) (1973): 88-91. il. refs.

Study of a sample of women students in various subject
fields indicates that women are significantly under-
represented in the fields of mathematics and physical
science at secondary school and at University. Some
possible explanations suggested.

1046   "Novels in Relation to Female Education." Dublin U Mag
LXXXV (May 1875): 513-528.

The author decries one result of popular education which
has been to create a new and large class of readers who
have not been trained in discrimination and who thus
become avid readers of cheap and sensational publications
which work to their moral detriment. Suggests parental
censorship and guidelines for alternative reading
material to be made available to young girls for their
leisure entertainment and edification.

1047   O'Brien, Mrs. William. "Intellectual Pride and the
Women of Our Day." Ir Mon 58 (Dec.1930): 645-650.

A warning to women students not to overvalue intellect.

1048   O'Connor, Anne V. and Susan M. Parkes. Gladly Learn
and Gladly Teach: Alexandra College and School 1866-1966.
Tallaght, County Dublin: Blackwater Press, 1984. 279pp. il.
portr. bibl.

A two part history of the College covering the periods
1860-1914 and 1914-1966 which represent distinct stages
in its development. The first was one of continuous
struggle for the recognition of women's rights to higher
education - and Alexandra College played a major role in
this campaign. The second stage deals with its
consolidation as a secondary school while offering a
broad course of studies in other areas.

1049   O'Connor Eccles, C. "The Girls of Today and Their
Education." Ir Mon XXV (Aug. 1897): 419-433.

Decries the inadequate and unrealistic education offered
to most girls and argues that these should be trained in
childrearing and given a preparation for the real world
in which many will have to be self-supporting.

1050   O'Flaherty, K. "Admission of Women Students to Q.C.C."
Cork U Rec No.15 (Easter 1949): 16-21.

     Traces the development of the issue of admission of women
     students to Queens College, Cork (Q.C.C.) from 1876 when
     it was found "inexpedient" to 1883 when the Council of
     Q.C.C. voted to admit women students to art courses. In
     1892 the question of admitting females to the Faculty of
     Medicine arose and was carried despite some opposition.
     The first woman was appointed to the Q.C.C. staff in 1905
     and in 1910 the first professor.

1051   O'Flynn, Grainne. "Some Aspects of the Education of
Irish Women Through the Years." Capu An 44 (1977): 164-179.
refs.

     Brief historical overview of the education of Irish women
     from the earliest times to the end of the 19th century.
     The role of the Church and State in creating and
     preserving male elitism in the educational sphere
     discussed.

1052   O'Hanlon, Terence. "Pioneers of Irish Catholic
Education." Ir Eccl Rec 14 (1919): 200-214.

     A brief discussion of the Penal Laws in Ireland and the
     strictures against Catholic education imposed by these.
     Nano Nagle was therefore educated at a convent school in
     Paris; later she returned to Ireland and began the
     instruction of the children of the poor first in Dublin
     and later in Cork. She later founded the Presentation
     Order so that this work could be continued and expanded.

1053   Oldham, Alice. "Women and the Irish University
Question." New Ire R 6 (5) (Jan. 1897): 257-263. table.

     Details the disadvantages suffered by women in the area
     of higher education. Presents arguments for the securing
     for women of access to University examinations -
     including honors and prizes - and the endowment of
     women's colleges.

1054   Owen, Mrs. Rachel. Reasons Showing The Necessity of
Extending Free Education to the Female Children of the
Distressed of the Higher and Professional Ranks in Society.
Dublin: Edward Purdon. [n.d.] 16pp.

     Presents the plight of these women whose only options are
     marriage, or perpetual dependency on friends or relatives
     and argues that a successful education could equip these
     for employment as teachers or governesses.

1055   Potter, E. "The Modern Housewife." Alex Col Mag XCII
(Dec. 1938): 19-24.

Lecture read at Alexandra College Guild Conference in
1939 calls for training for homemaking.

1056   Purser, Olive. Women in Dublin University 1904-1954.
Dublin: The Dublin University Press, 1954. 18pp. front.
portrs.

Details the struggle for the admission of women to
Trinity College which was pressed by the Association of
Irish Women Graduates who had obtained their degrees by
examination only in the period 1892-1904. In 1904 women
were admitted as students in the University. A brief
overview of their backgrounds, their reception, their
affiliations and their status in the pre and post war
period.

1057   The Queen's Institute (of Female Professional Schools)
9th Annual Report... Dublin: Printed for the Institute by B.
Underwood, 1871. 23pp. tables.

This Institute, founded in 1861 was designed to train
women for industrial occupations and "to secure
remunerative employment for respectable persons of
limited means." Subjects taught included arithmetic,
bookkeeping, telegraphy, sewing, law-writing, languages,
lithography and illumination, music, and drawing. An
overview of the accomplishments of the past year together
with lists of subscribers, and some observations on the
proper education of women.

1058   Reid, Norma G. and Rosamund Goldie. Northern Ireland
Women in Higher Education. Belfast: Equal Opportunities
Commission for Northern Ireland, 1981. 19pp. tables. refs.

Data on male/female distribution in higher education
including institutions attended, type of course studied
and motivation/attitudes. Data correlated with social
class and religious factors.

1059   Rowlands, David and Liz Haggard. "A Summer School for
Housewives." Adult Ed 48 (6) (Mar. 1976): 380-385.

Two articles discuss the organization and implementation
of a one week Summer School designed for working class
housewives in Belfast. Rowlands describes how the course
was organized, recruitment, staffing, student
characteristics and needs. Haggard discusses planning the
course content and the teaching objectives.

1060   S. (F.) "The Irish University Question as Affecting
Women." Westm R 159 (June 1903): 610-624. tables.

Discussion of the Final Report of the Royal Commission on
University Education in Ireland and the evidence

presented to them by major figures in the educational
field, on the present and future role of women in higher
education.

1061   Sheehy, Hannah (B.A.). "Women and the University
Question." New Ire R XVII (May 1902): 148-151.

A response to an article by Miss Daly in an earlier issue
of this magazine (see #1019) in which Ms. Sheehy offers a
rebuttal to Ms Daly's arguments regarding the higher
education of women.

1062   Sheehy-Skeffington, Francis and James A. Joyce. Two
Essays: A Forgotten Aspect of the University Question by
F.J.C. Skeffington and The Day of the Rabblement by James A.
Joyce. Dublin: Gerrard Brothers, 1901. 8pp.

The essay by Skeffington presents arguments for the
preservation and increase of women's present
opportunities for University education and asserts that
any settlement of the University question must conserve
and increase these rights.

1063   Slowey, Maria. "Aspects of Women's Participation in
Adult Education." Aontas R 1 (2) (1979): 16-24. refs.

Pilot study to explore women's participation in adult
education queried 126 married women who had participated
in some form of this in the previous year. Objective and
subjective aspects including extent, content, motivation
and previous formal education among aspects considered.

1064   Smyth, Ailbhe. Breaking The Circle - The Position of
Women Academics in Third Level Education In Ireland. Dublin:
EEC Action Programme on the Promotion of Equal Opportunities
for Women, 1985. 54pp. il. tables. refs.

The introduction describes the context, rationale and
purpose of this study of women academics; documents their
position by grade and by subject area in the four major
types of third-level institutions in Ireland -
Universities, National Institutes of Higher Education,
VEC third-level colleges, Colleges of Education - ;
offers an analysis of the marked differences in the
representation of women and men academics, raises the
issue of discrimination or sex bias and indicates areas
of further research and possible actions for the
achievement of parity between women and men academics.

1065   Special Issue. Tuarascial 9 (1983).

Report of a seminar concerned with equality in primary
education held in October includes an edited version of
papers presented including results of a survey of

equality among national teachers initiated by the Irish
National Teachers Organization in 1981 and sponsored
jointly by them and the Employment Equality Agency and
carried out by the Education Research Center.

1066   Sutherland, M.B. "Co-education and School Attainment."
Brit J Ed Psychol 31 (June 1961): 158-169. tables. refs.

    Reports the results of a study of the effects of
    co-education on attainment in the Northern Ireland Senior
    Certificate exam 1957 by pupils from mainly Protestant
    schools. Findings showed co-educated girls did less well
    than segregated girls while the opposite situation
    obtained for boys.

1067   Tansey, Jean. Summary of the Hannan Report (E.S.R.I.
Paper No. 113, 1983). Schooling and Sex Roles. Dublin:
Employment Equality Agency, 1983.

    (See item #1024.)

1068   University of Dublin. "Resolution to Grant Degrees to
Women." Ir J Med Sci LXVI (July 1903): 51.

    News item on the opening of degrees in the University of
    Trinity College Dublin to women. The resolution was
    adopted by a vote of 74 to 11.

1069   [W.F.B.] "Trinity College and Lady Students: A Plea
for the Higher Education of Women." Dublin U R (Mar. 1885):
25-26.

    Argues for the opening up of all educational institutions
    in Ireland, including Trinity, to lady students. The
    author reviews institutions who have successfully
    admitted women into programs, i.e. King and Queen's
    College of Physicians, Royal University, and refutes the
    old belief of women's inferior intelligence.

Religion and Witchcraft

        This section contains studies dealing with women's role
in the church, the foundation, history, mission and
achievements of individual religious orders and specific
convents including their major contributions in the fields of
education, health and social welfare, conventual life and
religious vocations. Also included in this section are
accounts of the practice of witchcraft in Ireland and trials
of individuals accused of being witches.
        For biographies of individual nuns or founders of
religious orders see BIOGRAPHY AND AUTOBIOGRAPHY - RELIGION
AND EDUCATION. For related material on religious views of the
role of women in society see PERSPECTIVES ON WOMEN'S
LIBERATION. For material on goddesses, banshees and folk
traditions or practices involving women and supernatural
forces see LITERATURE, FOLKLORE and MYTHOLOGY - DEPICTION OF
WOMEN.

ROLE OF WOMEN

1070   Concannon, Helena. "St. Brigid's League: A
Suggestion." Ir Mon 51 (Mar. 1923): 105-109.

    Brief note on St. Brigid's League, an association of
    Irish Catholic women organized to promote a return to old
    Irish ideals of modesty in dress. Concannon suggests that
    the Association extend its scope to include some form of
    charitable action.

1071   Cullen, Mary. "Women and the Church." Furrow 22 (10)
(Oct. 1971): 632-639.

    Background of the Irish Women's Liberation Movement
    examined and the Catholic Church challenged to take
    seriously this new initiative on the part of women or
    find itself bypassed.

1072   Francis de Sales, Sister. "Are Nuns With it." Reality
33 (5) (May 1969): 15-18.

Details changes in day to day practices and lifestyle of
religious sisters.

1073   McInerney, M.H. "Constructive Work for Catholic
Irishwomen." Ir Mon LII (Apr./May 1924): 188-194; 262-268.

Details opportunities for useful work on behalf of
Catholic literature which could be done by Irish women -
including the creation of a Literature Committee to
ensure maximum Catholic exposure to such literature in
libraries, waitingrooms, etc. and in the censorship of
literature offensive to Catholic standards.

1074   McKenna, L. (Rev.) "An Irish Catholic Women's League."
Ir Mon XLV (June 1917): 353-368.

Arguments for the establishment of an Irish Catholic
Women's League to foster a social sense among Catholic
women and to coordinate the activities of existing
charitable and social work organizations. General outline
of the form such an organization might take.

1075   [National Conference of Priests of Ireland.] Working
Party. The "Role of Women in the Church." Furrow 33 (9)
(Sept. 1982): 579-583. table.

Argues that at levels of the ordained ministry, authority
and decision-making the Catholic Church in Ireland
retains a uniquely rigid exclusion of women. At other
levels it shares in the perpetuation of patterns of a sex
based division of labour which relegates women to lower
status and more menial jobs. Includes recommendations to
clergy and faithful on the promotion of effective and
equal participation for women in the Church and in Irish
society.

1076   O'Conor, Margaret M. "The Role of Religious Sisters
Today." Chr Rex 22 (1) (Jan. 1968): 24-28.

A homily on the roles appropriate to nuns within and
outside the church in the 20th century. Facets of these
include the exercise of charity, cultivation of the
spiritual life, exercise of professional roles toward the
increase of the quality of life, mediator between the
world and God, witness.

1077   "To Protect Girl Emigrants." Ir Mon XLII (Jan. 1914):
52.

News item on the activities of the Catholic Women's
League of Great Britain which is devoted to helping

Catholic girls who are emigrating "to avoid the dangers
to which they might be exposed and to obtain employment
for them in their new homes." Irish girls planning to
emigrate are urged to avail themselves of these services.

1078   Regan, Cronan (Sister). "Why Not Women Priests?" Cross
64 (2) (June 1973): 28-29. il.

The author examines the historical background to
establish whether there is precedent for the ordination
of women. She concludes that further research is needed
to clarify the theological issues involved.

1079   Reynolds, Roger E. "Virgines Subintroductae in Celtic
Christianity." Harv Theo R 61 (Oct. 1968): 547-548. refs.

An essay considering the practice of syneisactism defined
as the chaste living together of a male and female
ascetic and the prevalence of this practice in the early
Christian Church in Ireland. Reynolds examines
explanations both theological and environmental for the
practice and possible sources. He concludes that the
practice was fairly prevalent in Ireland and represented
a Christian practice which dates from the origin of
Christianity and was spread throughout the early Church.

1080   Stevenson, (Robert) S.J. Christ Speaks To Women.
Dublin: Catholic Truth Society of Ireland, 1968. 31pp.

(See Perspectives on Women's Liberation #2088.)

1081   Tynan, Katherine. "Social Work for Catholic Women in
Country Places." Ir Mon XLV (Dec, 1917): 754-760.

Explores reasons for the lack of participation by Irish
Catholic countrywoman in community or charitable
activities and suggests various activities they might and
should engage in to their advantage as well as that of
others.

VOCATIONS

1082   Catholic Communications Institute of Ireland. Research
and Development Unit. "Survey of Catholic Clergy and
Religious Personnel. 1971." Soc Stud 1 (2) (Mar. 1972):
137-234. graphs. tables.

Presents results of a questionnaire circulated to all the
Bishops, to the Provincial of each religious order (male
and female) as well as to the Mother Superior of each
individual convent in 1970. Response rate was 100%. Aim
was to present an accurate and comprehensive statistical
picture of priests, brothers and sisters in Ireland and

overseas attached to Irish institutions. Report #3
(pp.188-210) covers Irish religious sisters and includes
general data as well as a breakdown by age, vocations and
departures 1965-1970; qualifications and occupations, and
a list of Orders/Congregations in Ireland in 1971.
Report #5 includes data on vocations to Orders of Sisters
for 1971.

1083   Loreto, M. (Sister) "The Apostolate and Vocation
Fostering." Chr Rex XXII (1) (Jan. 1968): 29-34.

Brief consideration of the forces militating against
vocations in today's society including materialism,
lessening of respect for the religious life, access of
secular women to higher education, atmosphere of
hesitation surrounding the religious life and religion in
general. Presents a programme for a truly comprehensive
religious education including imparting an appreciation
of the role played by the church in education and
culture, a by-product of which would be the fostering of
vocations.

1084   Newman, Jeremiah. "Vocations to the Sisterhoods in
Ireland." Chr Rex 22 (1) (Jan.-Mar. 1968): 7-16.

Discusses the idea of the religious life in a broad sense
and the need for certain reforms in the way this is
practised by Irish women. Reports on a study by Noonan
published in 1967 covering the period 1961-1965 which
found a considerable decline in entries into the
novitiates of all types of religious institutes of women.
Causes briefly examined.

1085   Newman, Jeremiah. "Vocations in Ireland." Chr Rex 21
(2) (Apr.-June 1967): 105-112.

A qualitative analysis of selected current opinion on the
question of trends in vocation rates over the previous
five years reveals a falling off in the numbers recruited
and their perseverence rates. Respondents included
representative members of the Irish secular clergy, of
male and female religious orders, missionary societies
and clerical students. Causes of decline, doctrinal,
pastoral, pedagocial and practical aspects of vocations
discussed.

1086   Noonan, Francis. "Religious Vocations." Chr Rex 21 (2)
(Apr.-June 1967): 126-132. tables.

Reports results of a survey which included 36 of the 39
Superiors of major religious orders included in the
women's section of the Conference of Major Religious
Superiors, of which 31 responded. Presents statistics on
vocations to the diocesan priesthood and the religious
life in the five years prior to the study. A comparison

of entrants for 1962 and 1966 finds a 26% drop overall
for female institutions and a 46% drop in the case of
teaching institutions.

1087   O'Byrne, Simon. (Father) "Hindrances to Vocations in
Ireland." Chr Rex 22 (1) (Jan.1968): 46-51.

Brief discussion of internal and external obstacles to
obtaining vocations to the priestly or religious life.
These include false public image of religious, austerity
of life, parental opposition, fear of authority,
criticism of training of religious, recruiting methods,
complacency.

RELIGIOUS ORDERS

General

1088   Brady, John (Rev.) "The Nunnery of Clonard."   Riocht
na Midhe 11 (2) (1960): 4-7. refs.

Brief historical note on a group of nunneries in Meath
towards the end of the 12th century including the
Augustinian Abbey of St. Mary at Clonard and its various
abbesses.

1089   Cloch Labhrais. Mna Riaghalta na h Eireann.
Bonaventura 3 (1937): 51-57.

Brief note on some convents in Ireland from the time of
St. Brigid to modern times.

1090   Concannon, Helena (Mrs. Thomas). Irish Nuns in Penal
Days. London: Sands and Co., 1931. 124pp. il. plates.
facsims. portrs. (incl. front.) (Originally serialized in
the Irish Catholic 1928.)

A very brief anecdotal overview of the four female
religious orders in Ireland: Poor Clares, Dominicans,
Carmelites and Augustinians after re-opening of convents
in Ireland in the 17th century after a century of
suppression. Also, a brief account of the founding of the
Presentation Order by Nano Nagle. Based mainly on memoirs
and archives of these orders and secondary sources.

1091   Gwynn, Aubrey and R. Neville Hadcock. (eds.) Medieval
Religious Houses in Ireland: With an Appendix to Early Sites.
London: Longman's Green, 1970. 479pp. tables. refs.

Includes a discussion of communities of nuns and the
difficulty of assessing the size and status of these in
the 16th century by which time several had already become
extinct.

1092   Murphy, Dominick (Rev.) <u>Sketches of Irish Nunneries</u>.
With an Introduction on the Nature and Practice of a
Conventual Life. First Series. Dublin: James Duffy, 1865.
178pp.

  Brief accounts of the Dominican, Poor Clare, Carmelite,
  Presentation, Sisters of Mercy, Sisters of Charity and
  Loretto Orders in Ireland from their foundations.

1093   <u>The Religious Orders and Congregations in Ireland</u>.
(Reprinted from the Irish Jesuit Directory and Year Book,
1933.) Dublin: Irish Messenger Office, 1933. 56pp.

  Lists various orders and congregations including some
  that are not, technically, religious which have houses in
  Ireland. Outline of the history, spirit and work, extent
  in Ireland, place of novitiate, and sources for further
  information for each. List is arranged chronologically by
  foundation date.

1094   Steele, Francesca M. <u>The Convents of Great Britain and
Ireland</u>. London: Sands, 1924. 366pp. il. portrs.

  Brief historical accounts of the 90 distinct
  congregations of Catholic female religious orders in
  Great Britain with notes on branches of these in Ireland.

Brigidine Order

1095   <u>Constitutions of the Sisters of Saint Brigid, Ireland</u>.
Dublin: Browne and Nolan, 1908. 96pp.

  Sets out primary and secondary aims of the congregation,
  the means to achieve these, types and conditions of
  membership, rules, etc.

1096   Gibbons, Margaret. <u>Glimpses of Catholic Ireland in the
18th Century</u>. Dublin: Browne and Nolan, 1932. 386pp. il.
front. refs.

  Mainly an account of the restoration of the Brigidine
  Order in 1807. This was the second Irish Sisterhood in
  the field of active service in Ireland after the period
  of the Penal laws. Special prominence is given to the
  life and work of Dr. Delany who resuscitated the defunct
  Sisterhood. Based mainly on documents, books and
  manuscript records in the archives of the Irish
  Brigidines.

Carmelite Nuns

1097   Kingston, John. "The Carmelite Nuns in Dublin 1644-
1829. Reportorium Novum." <u>Dublin Hist Rec</u> 3 (2) (1964):
331-360. fig. refs.

> Traces the foundation of the Daughters of St. Teresa, The
> Carmelite sisters in Ireland from the earliest days
> estimated around 1644, in Dublin and Galway, subsequent
> dispersal under Cromwell, restoration under Charles II
> and James II and again dispersal under William. By 1730
> they were reestablished in Loughrea and then Dublin.
> Details on the day to day activities of the Dublin branch
> including biographical information on the Sisters and
> details on the subsequent foundation of other branches in
> the City. Includes a chart noting all Carmelite
> foundations in Ireland.

Cistercian Order

1098   Walsh, Kilian (Rev.) <u>Women Who Keep God's Vigil: the
Glencairn Story</u>. Dublin, London: Clonmare & Reynolds, Burns &
Oates, (c. 1964). 125pp. il.

> Brief overview of Cistercian order and an account of the
> foundation of the only Cistercian convent at Glencairn,
> County Waterford in 1932, and its subsequent history,
> including its role in the Boston foundation. Includes
> biographical notes on sisters.

Dominican Nuns

1099   Concannon, Helena. "Historic Galway Convents II - The
Dominican Nuns." <u>Studies</u> 39 (1950): 65-71. refs.

> Brief account of the convent of the Dominican nuns in
> Galway founded in 1644 and subsequent foundations with
> profiles of the members of the original community. Based
> on the convent archives in Galway and Dublin.

1100   Dominican Convent, Cabra. Dublin. <u>Annals. (1647-1912)
with Some Account of Its Origins</u>. [Dublin]: Dominican
Convent. 191pp.

> A detailed account of the origin and growth of the
> Dominican Institute at Cabra with an overview of the
> history of the Order in Ireland. The 1644 Dominican
> foundation in Galway was the first convent of Domincan
> Nuns in Ireland since the Reformation. Subsequent history
> of the Order in Ireland and overseas sketched.

1101   <u>Dominican Convent [Cabra]. Immaculata</u>. Dublin:
Dominican Convent, 1957. 96pp. il.

Yearbook of the Cabra branch of the Dominican Order
includes an account of the Cabra foundation with a brief
note on the coming of the Dominican sisters to Galway in
the 1600's and their subsequent vicissitudes.

1102   Genevieve, Mary (Sr.). "Mrs. Bellew's Family in
Channel Row." (Paper read to the Old Dublin Society, February
22, 1967.) Dublin Hist Rec 22 (3) (Oct. 1968): 230-241.

A detailed account, based on their account books, of the
Dublin Dominican community of nuns from its establishment
in 1717 to its departure from Channel Row in 1808.

1103   Kearns, Sister M. Bede (O.P.) "Irish Dominican Sisters
After Fifty Years." Supp Doct & Life 74 (Mar.-Apr. 1978):
98-106.

Brief overview of the development of Dominican convents
in Ireland on the fiftieth anniversary of their
amalgamation into the congregation of Irish Dominican
Sisters. Includes a note on recent foundations abroad.

1104   The Western Wind. Yearbook of the Dominican Convent,
Taylor's Hill, Galway. 1 (1) Galway: Dominican Nuns, 1922.
21pp.

Brief note on the history of the Dominican Convent from
its foundation in 1644 and the subsequent tribulations of
the Sisters involving several dispersals during the Penal
days.

Franciscan Nuns

1105   Concannon, Helena. At His Feet. The Story of The
Foundation of the Franciscan Convent of Perpetual Adoration,
Drumshambo, County Leitrim. Dublin: M.H.Gill and Son, Ltd.,
1948. 117pp. il. portrs.

Abbreviated edition of below.

1106   Concannon, Mrs. Thomas (Helena). At the Court of the
Eucharistic King. Dublin: M.H.Gill and Son, Ltd., 1929.
292pp. il. front.

A popular history of the Franciscan Convent at
Drumshambo, County Leitrim, Ireland and of its
foundresses compiled by the author from the annals and
records of the convent. This convent forms a branch of
the Third Order of St. Francis of Assisi, an enclosed and
contemplative order which has had women members in
Ireland since mediaeval times according to sources quoted
by the author.

Institute of the Blessed Virgin Mary (Loreto)

1107   Gibbons, Margaret. Loreto Navan. One Hundred Years of Catholic Progress., 1833-1933. Navan: [Loreto]. 173pp. il. portrs.

A brief account of the Institute of the Blessed Virgin Mary in Navan with a note on the foundresses Mother Paul Finn and Mother Frances Murphy. By 1933 22 communities of Loreto had been established in Ireland.

Little Sisters of the Poor

1108   J.M.J. The Romance of Charity: A Brief Story of the Little Sisters of the Poor. Dublin: Gill, 1940. 44pp. portr.

This extremely brief history of the Order has a chapter on the Irish branches. Notes the first foundation at Waterford in 1867, followed by Cork in 1875 and Dublin in 1881.

Medical Missionaries of Mary

1109   The First Decade: 10 Years Work of the Medical Missionaries of Mary 1937-1947. Dublin: Three Candles Press, 1948. 107pp. il. plates. portrs.

A miscellaneous collection of articles dealing with the work of the Medical Missionaries of Mary in Ireland and overseas with a brief account of the founding of the Order by Miss Mary Martin in 1937. Their introduction of qualified doctors and nurses into the Missions seen as the most significant development in Catholic Missionary activity.

Missionary Sisters of Our Lady of the Holy Rosary

1110   Silver Sheaves. A Record of Twenty-five Years at Home and in Africa. The Missionary Sisters of Our Lady of the Holy Rosary, Killeshandra, County Cavan, 1949. 108pp. portrs.

A miscellaneous collection of articles on the ocasion of the Silver Jubilee of the Missionary Sisters includes an account of the origin of the foundation at Killeshandra and brief mention of individual sisters.

Our Lady of Charity of Refuge

1111   A Souvenir of the Golden Jubilee of the Convent of Our Lady of Charity of Refuge and of the Magdalen Asylum, High Park, Drumcondra... Dublin: Printed by M. & S. Eaton, 1903. 79pp. front. plates.

Includes a brief sketch of the Order of Our Lady of
Charity of Refuge, founded in 1641 at Carn in Normandy to
aid "unfortunate" women. In 1853 this Order was invited
to send sisters to take charge of the Asylum in
Drumcondra and they later expanded and founded
"Magdalen." In 1858 they also took over the Reformatory
School — for juveniles. The lifestyle and occupations of
the "Penitents", most of whom became permanent residents,
described with some case histories.

Poor Clares

1112   Arnold, Mavis and Heather Laskey. Children of the Poor
Clares. Belfast: Appletree Press, 1985. 160pp.

The story of an Irish orphanage.

1113   Concannon, Helena. "Historic Galway Convents I — The
Poor Clares." Studies 38 (Dec. 1949): 439-446. refs.

Brief account of the return of the Poor Clares from
Belgium to Dublin in 1629 and their subsequent
foundations primarily in Galway. Profiles of the Browne
sisters and other notable individuals.

1114   Concannon, Mrs. Thomas. The Poor Clares in Ireland
(A.D. 1629- A.D. 1929). Dublin: M.H.Gill and Son, 1929.
181pp. refs.

Detailed account of the order in Ireland based largely on
the work of the Poor Clares Annalists in Galway and other
conventual archives and memoirs. Gives a brief outline of
the foundation of the Order in 1629, the exile of the
Sisters during the Cromwellian persecution, their return
to Ireland after the Restoration of Charles II, the
subsequent reestablishment of the Order in Galway and its
later expansion to Dublin, Carlow and Newry. Includes
brief biographical sketches of individual sisters. .

1115   Poor Clare Ter-Centenary Record 1629-1929; Being a
Brief Account of the Lives and Actions of Certain Devout
Women who Restored the Poor Clare cloister to Ireland. Ed. by
Father Syl. O'Brien. Galway: O'Gorman, 1929. 47pp. plates.
portrs.

A collection of articles by different authors on the Poor
Clare record in Ireland. Includes two brief accounts of
the first return from exile of the Poor Clare Sisters in
1629. After two years in Dublin, again forced to
relocate, they stayed for a period near Athlone, then
took refuge in Galway and later on Nuns Island. Despite
the constant disruption they still managed to survive as
a community and even prospered. Accounts of several of
the early Abbess's and overview of more recent activities
included.

Presentation Order

1116   Galvin, Sister M. Camillus. From Acorn to Oak: A Study of Presentation Foundations 1775-1968. Fargo, North Dakota: The Presentation Sisters. [c.1969] 223pp. il. map. charts. fronts. bibl.

    Details the founding and spread of the Presentation Sisters from the Penal Days in Ireland to the spread of the Order to England, India, Pakistan, Africa, New Zealand, New Guinea, Newfoundland, the Phillipines and the United States with brief accounts of the work of the Sisters in each country.

1117   Murphy, J.N. "Honora Nagle and Presentation Nuns." Am J Ed 26 (1876): 705-720. refs.

    Brief account of Honora Nagle's role in the introduction of the Ursulines to Ireland and the foundation of the Presentation Order.

1118   Presentation Convent, Galway 1815-1965. Sesquicentenary Souvenir 1965. Galway: Presentation Sisters, 1965. 88pp. il. portrs.

    Brief note on the foundation of the Order in Galway in 1815; the establishment of the first Presentation school in 1820 and other Presentation foundations in Ireland and overseas.

1119   Presentation Convent, Limerick. Centenary 1837-1937. Limerick: [Presentation Convent, 1937]. 104pp. il.

    A miscellaneous collection of articles including an account of the foundation of a branch of the Presentation Order in Sexton St. Limerick by Maria Catherine King and a short biographical sketch of Nano Nagle, foundress of the Order.

1120   Walsh, T.J. Nano Nagle and the Presentation Sisters. Dublin: M.H. Gill & Son, Ltd., 1959. 427pp. il maps. charts. portrs. bibl.

    (See Biography - Religion - Nano Nagle #680.)

Sisters of Charity

1121   Congregation of the Irish Sisters of Charity. Sisters of Charity of St. Vincent de Paul. Centenary of the Foundation of the Order in Dublin...1857-1957. Dublin: Capital Press, 1958. 77pp. il. portrs.

    Brief history of the Order with notes on their houses in Dublin and in the country.

1122   Felicity, Sister Mary. <u>All About Us</u>. [Mary Aikenhead's
Daughters] Dublin: Anthonian Press, 1961. 32pp.

    Brief account of the rule, work and lifestyle of the
    Sisters of Charity founded over 150 years ago to work for
    the poor in their homes. At that time most nuns lived
    sheltered lives within the walls of their convents.
    Includes a list of their houses in Dublin and in the
    Provinces.

1123   The Irish Sisters of Charity. <u>Centenary Brochure</u>.
Dublin: Irish Sisters of Charity, 1959. 194pp. il. portrs.

    A miscellaneous collection of articles dealing with the
    work of the Irish Sisters of Charity in Ireland during
    their one hundred year existence. Includes a brief
    biographical sketch of the Foundress, Mary Aikenhead.

1124   <u>Irish Sisters Of Charity: The Irish Sisters of Charity
Giving a Brief Sketch of the Foundations of the Congregation</u>.
Reprinted from "St. Anthony's Annals." Foreward by Rev. J.E.
Caravan, S.J. Dublin: Anthonian Press, 1941. 160pp. plates.
portr.

    Brief overview of the 126 year history of the Irish
    Sisters of Charity from the Foundation of the Order by
    Mary Aikenhead in 1815. Forty foundations have been
    established which include hospitals, convents, asylums,
    etc.: located in Ireland and overseas.

1125   Russell, Matthew. "Woman's Mission." <u>Ir Mon</u> XXI (Sept.
1893): 449-453.

    Excerpts from a collection of papers on women's
    philantropy include an account of the work done at the
    Blind Asylum at Merrion, near Dublin and the Hospice for
    the Dying at Harold's Cross, Dublin, both run by the
    Sisters of Charity.

1126   <u>The Sisters of Charity of St. Vincent de Paul</u>. Dublin:
Catholic Truth Society, 1946. 16pp.

    Very brief general overview of the history of the Sisters
    of Charity from the origin of the Order in France and its
    subsequent extension to many parts of the world. This
    account briefly outlines its history in England, Ireland,
    Scotland and Wales. The Irish foundation was made in
    Drogheda in 1855 by some Irish girls trained as Sisters
    at the Motherhouse in France; later another house was
    established in Dublin in 1857. By 1946, 18 houses existed
    in Dublin alone and 11 in other parts of Ireland with a
    Seminary House at Blackrock. Nature of work performed by
    the Sisters and their dedication to the poor, discussed.

1127   Walsh, James J. "The Irish Sisters of Charity and
Mercy: Reformers of Hospitals." In his These Splendid
Sisters, pp. 111-139. Freeport, New York: Books For
Libraries, [c 1927] [1970].

   An account of the origin and history of the Irish Sisters
   of Charity and the Sisters of Mercy and their role in
   hospital reform at the beginning of the 19th century.

                    Sisters of Mercy

1128   "The Golden Jubilee of the Sisters of Mercy." Ir Mon 9
(102) (Dec. 1881): 668-671.

   Tribute to work of the order on its Golden Jubilee. Note
   on expansion of this at home and abroad.

1129   Leaden, A.H. (Rev.) "The Sisters of Mercy in Kilmore
1868-1968." Breifne 3 (12) (1969): 562-582. refs.

   The order of the Sisters of Mercy founded in Dublin in
   1831 by Catherine McAuley rapidly expanded at home and
   abroad. Father Leaden's account details the foundations
   in Kilmore and briefly summarizes their subsequent
   history and the activities of the Sisters: Belturbet
   (1868), Ballyjamesduff (1869), Ballinamore (1871),
   Cootehill (1880). In 1916 the separate foundations in
   Kilmore diocese were amalgamated.

1130   Leaves from The Annals of the Sisters of Mercy.
[Volume 1 Ireland.] By a Member of the Order of Mercy. New
York: Catholic Publications Society, 1881. 519pp.

   (See Biography - Religion - Catherine McAuley #665.)

1131   Russell, Matthew. "The Golden Jubilee of a Convent."
Ir Mon 39 (1911): 512-521.

   An excerpt from the sermon preached by Very Rev. Bernard
   Brady, P.P. of Dunboyne, on the occasion of the Golden
   Jubliee of the Convent of Mercy at Moate, County
   Westmeath. Recalls the early days of the Foundation and
   describes the daily life of the Sisters.

1132   [Russell, Matthew] (Rev.) "The Sisters of Mercy at
Limerick." Ir Mon XXX (346) (Apr. 1902): 181-189.

   Brief tribute to the work of the Sisters in Limerick
   notes the original foundation of this branch there in
   1838, the 6th foundation of the Sisters of Mercy in
   Ireland and one of the most important. Work of the
   Sisters described with anecdotes on individuals.

1133   Russell, Matthew (Rev.) "The Sisters of Mercy at
Rostrevor." Ir Mon XXX (Mar. 1902): 139-159.

    Comment on the nature of a religious vocation and the
    work of the Sisters of Mercy.

1134   Ryan, E.A.(S.J.) "The Sisters of Mercy: An Important
Chapter in Church History." Theo Stud 18 (June 1957):
254-270. refs.

    Details the role of Catherine McAuley, the Irishwoman who
    founded the Sisters of Mercy and the important
    contribution made by this order to the English-speaking
    Church.

1135   St. Mary's Convent of Our Lady of Mercy. Convent of
Our Lady of Mercy, St. Mary's, Limerick 1838-1938. Limerick:
The Limerick Leader, Ltd., 1938. 84pp. il. portr.

    A tribute to Catherine McAuley, the foundress of the
    Order of the Sisters of Mercy in Ireland; an account of
    religious houses in medieval Limerick and a history of
    the convent at St. Mary's from 1838-1938, including
    schools and branch houses.

1136   Sisters Of Mercy, Ennistymon: Centenary Souvenir,
1872-1972. Ennistymon: Sisters of Mercy, [1972]. 23pp. il.
portrs.

    Brief history of the foundation from its beginning in
    1872.

1137   Walsh, James J. "The Irish Sisters Of Charity and
Mercy: Reformers of Hospitals." In his These Splendid
Sisters, pp. 111-139. Freeport, New York: Books For
Libraries, [c 1927] [1970].

    (See Sisters of Charity #1127.)

Sisters of the Holy Faith

1138   Mary Assisi, Sister.(Ed.) Sisters of the Holy Faith.
Dublin: Sisters of the Holy Faith [1967] 172pp. il.

    A miscellaneous collection of articles to mark the
    Centenary of the Order includes a biographical sketch of
    the Foundress Margaret Aylward (1810-1889), brief
    biographical sketches of other Sisters and a short
    history of the order in Ireland. Includes reminiscences
    of her schooldays by Senator Margaret Pearse.

WITCHCRAFT

1139   Benson, E. F. "The Recent Witch-burning at Clonnel."
19th Cent 37 (1895): 1053-1058. refs.

An account of the murder of a Clonnel woman Bridget
Cleary by members of her family who were "exorcising" the
evil spirit they believed she entertained.

1140   Byrne, Patrick F. Witchcraft in Ireland. Cork: Mercier
Press, 1967. 80pp. refs.

An anecdotal, non-critical account of famous witches/
witchcraft in early Irish literature and folklore and
'historical' witches, including Dane Alice Kyteler (14th
century), Florence Newton, the Witch of Youghall (17th
century), Bridget Cleary burned as a witch by her husband
and relatives (19th century) and other anonymous persons
involved with witchcraft not all of whom were women.

1141   Colgan, Nathaniel. "Witchcraft in the Aran Islands."
Roy Soc Antiq Ire 5th ser. 5 (1895): 84-85.

Account of an instance in which a disease was supposedly
transferred from the victim to another person by means of
witchcraft.

1142   A Contemporary Narrative of the Proceedings Against
Dame Alice Kyteler, Prosecuted For Sorcery in 1324 by Richard
de Ledrede, Bishop of Ossory. Ed. by Thomas Wright. (Camden
Society O.S. XXIV) London: John Bowyer Nichols and Son, 1843.
61pp.

Latin text with notes and introduction in English.

1143   Crone, John S. "Witchcraft in Antrim." Ulster J Archae
XIV (Feb.1908): 34-37.

Account of the supposed bewitching of a 19 year old girl
in Antrim in 1698. The girl ate sorrel which she obtained
from a witch and became gravely ill; the witch was
arrested, strangled and burned to death. [Reprinted from
"Satan's Invisible World Discovered" by General
Sinclair.]

1144   Dent, J.G. "The Witchstone in Ulster and England."
Ulster Folk 10 (1964): 46-48. refs.

A discussion of protective devices - especially the
naturally-holed pebble - used by country people against
the blighting influence of witchcraft.

1145   F[inlay], P[eter]. "Witchcraft." <u>Ir Mon</u> 2 (1974): 523-529. refs.

    Includes a brief note on the accusation launched by
Bishop Ledrede, an Englishman in 1327 against Lady Alice
Kyteler and her son, William of practising black magic in
Kilkenny. Her stepson, Sir Roger Outlaw, Prior of
Kilmainhan took up her defense but he too was included in
the accusation. The result was the acquital of the
accused and the forced retirement of Bishop Ledrede to
his native England.

1146   Fuller, James F. "Trial of Florence Newton for
Witchcraft in Cork, 1661." With note by R.D. Journal of the <u>J
Cork Hist & Arch Soc</u> Ser. 2. X (1904): 174-183.

    Detailed account of evidence presented at the trial at
which Florence Newton was committed to Youghall Prison
for having bewitched a local woman Mary Langdon and also
a prison guard, David Jones.

1147   H. M.S. "Witchcraft in Ireland." <u>Dublin U Mag</u> 82 (Aug.
1873): 218-223.

    An account based on the History of Carrickfergus (not
further identified) and a contemporary manuscript by a
local antiquary of the last witchcraft trial in Ireland
at Island Magee, near Belfast in 1710/11. Eight women
were found guilty and sentenced to prison for 12 months.
Their accuser, Mary Dunbar did not appear at the trial
claiming to have been struck dumb through their agency.

1148   Jones, Bryan J. "Corp Chre: a Notice of Witchcraft
Practiced in Louth in the 19th Century." <u>Co Louth Arch J</u> 13
(3) (1955): 288. [Reprinted from <u>Folklore</u> VI (1895): 302.]

    Details on certain superstitions in County Louth.

1149   Jones, Bryan J. "Correspondence: Folklore Objects
from Argyleshire. Corp Chre." <u>Folklore</u> VI (1895): 302.

    An account of the witchcraft belief known as "burying the
sheaf" used to bring about the death of one's enemies.
This belief according to Jones, still survives among
residents of the Bog of Ardee, County Louth.

1150   Kennedy, Patrick. <u>Legends Of Irish Witches and
Fairies</u>. Dublin: Mercier Press, 1976. 90pp.

    Excerpts of folktales from his anthologies <u>Legendary
Fictions of the Irish Celts</u>, <u>The Fireside Stories of
Ireland</u> and <u>The Banks of the Boro</u>.

1151   Milligan, Seaton F. "Witchcraft in County Tyrone in
the Nineteenth Century." Roy Soc Antiq Ire J Ser.5. 1 (1891)
Part 2 (vol.21 of consecutive series): 406-407.

An 1890 report of a case tried at Dungannon where one
farmer sued another for breach of warranty arising out of
his purchase of a cow which had been put under an evil
spell ("blinked") by the original owner.

1152   Morrin, James. "The Kilkenny Witchcraft Case." Ossory
Arch Soc J 1 (1874-1879): 213-239. refs.

Report of the celebrated witchcraft trial of Lady
Kyteler, 1324/5, four times married, charged with
poisoning her husbands. Also, seen as a record of a
struggle between the secular and ecclesiastical powers in
the society.

1153   Murphy, J.C.J. (Mrs.) "Alice Kyteler." Old Kilk R No.
6 (1953): 9-14.

Recounts how the step-children of the four times married,
Alice Kyteler complained to the Bishop of Ossory, Richard
de Ledrede alledging that by sorceries she slew some of
their fathers or seduced from them their wealth. Details
how the Bishop accused her and two accomplices and later
her son and the political opposition he encountered from
her son's cousin, the King's Chancellor and other
powerful personages. Eventually Petronilla of Meath was
burned, her son William was absolved and Dame Alice
escaped to England.

1154   Neary, Anne. "The Origins and Character of the
Kilkenny Witchcraft Case of 1324." Roy Ir Acad Proc 83 (13)
(1983): 333-350. refs.

Suggests that the trial of Alice Kyteler in 1324 in
Kilkenny displays some of the demonic features
deliberately introduced into trials for heresy and ritual
magic in early 14th century France. The French ideas were
imported directly into Kilkenny by the instigator of the
affair, Richard Ledrede, Bishop of Ossory.

1155   Riddell, William Renwick. "The First Execution for
Witchcraft in Ireland." J Crim Law 7 (Mar.1917): 828-837.
refs.

Conflict between religious and secular authority and the
importance of kinship ties in the Ireland of 1324
detailed in this account of the first 'auto de fe' in
Ireland.

1156   Saunderson, G.W. "Butterwitches and Cow Doctors."
Ulster Folk 7 (1961): 72-74.

Beliefs and legends surrounding the production of milk
and butter; the vulnerability of the churning process to
"butterwitches" and remedies.

1157   Seymour, St.John D. _Irish Witchcraft and Demonology_.
New York: Causeway Books, 1973. 156pp. bibl. refs.

A reprint of below.

1158   Seymour, St.John D. _Irish Witchcraft and Demonology_.
Dublin, London: Hodges, Figgis & Co. Ltd., Humphrey Milford,
1913. 256pp.

Described as the first connected study of the history of
witchcraft in Ireland from its earliest recorded
appearance to modern times. Notes the relative freedom of
Ireland from the worst excesses of this and advances as
explanation the Catholic/Protestant division in this
country. Major part of the book concerned with details of
celebrated cases.

1159   Walsh, R.A. "Kyteler's Inn." _Old Kilk R_ No. 18 (1966):
94-96.

News item on the reopening of "Kyteler's Inn" as a
gourmet restaurant. Recounts the main outlines of the
career of Dame Alice Kyteler.

1160   "Witchcraft in County Limerick." _Roy Soc Antiq Ire J_
5th Ser. 2 (1892): 291.

At New Pallas Petty Sessions a Mrs. Breen prosecuted a
Mrs. Bowles for breaking her arm as she tried to retrieve
her geese who had trespassed onto the latter's property.
Mrs. Bowles' defense was that she suspected Mrs. Breen of
trying to "charm" away her butter.

Community Studies

This section contains a sampling of mainly
anthropological studies of specific areas or communities
which, while they do not focus specifically on women,
nevertheless provide much information on life-styles /
life-chances of these. For related material on family roles
and relationships and marriage patterns see MARRIAGE AND THE
FAMILY; for related material involving relations between the
sexes and women's reproductive role see HUMAN SEXUALITY,
REPRODUCTION AND HEALTH; for the sexual division of labour
see EMPLOYMENT AND ECONOMIC LIFE.

1161   Arensberg, Conrad M. and Solon T. Kimball. Family and
Community in Ireland. Cambridge, Mass.: Harvard University
Press, 1959. 216pp.

    Detailed social-anthropological study from a
    functionalist perspective of certain aspects of social
    life in rural County Clare, seen as an instance of Irish
    rural life in general. Partially based on the author's
    previous research primarily, The Irish Countryman by
    Arensberg. Topics covered include the central position of
    marriage and the family in the social structure, the
    complementary nature of male/female roles in the farm
    economy, sex relations and the subordinate position of
    women, kinship and community.

1162   Barnes, Bettina. "Irish Travelling People." In
Gypsies, Tinkers and Other Travellers. ed. by Farnham
Rehfisch, pp. 231-255. London, New York, San Francisco:
Academic Press, 1975. il. bibl. refs.

    This essay details the physical appearance, kinship
    structure, courtship, marriage customs and sexual roles
    of the Irish itinerants and discusses their relationship
    with the settled society.

1163   Bovenkerk, Frank. "On the Causes of Irish Emigration."
Sociol Rur 13 (3-4) (1973): 275-288. tables. refs.

Author examines various theories regarding the causes of
Irish emigration. He discounts the role of high
population density, poor prospects of marriage for
females and, to some extent, alterations in the family
structure, all of which have been advanced as explanatory
variables and sees economic factors as having much more
importance. But author stresses that "push" factors are
no longer the only variable to be considered and
underlines the importance of "adventure" motives.

1164   Brody, Hugh. Inniskillane: Change and Decline in the
West of Ireland. New York: Schocken Books, 1974. (c.1973)
226pp.

A sociological analysis by a participant observer of the
demoralization and depopulation occuring in the West of
Ireland. The author takes issue with recent scholarly
writing about this region which stresses the autonomy,
permanence and strength of the traditional culture. He
sees instead the devaluation of the traditional mores and
the breakdown of community mainly as a result of direct
and indirect contact with urban values. Women, because of
their subordinate role and status in the traditional
culture are emotionally freer to emigrate and less
anxious to assume the inferior status which farm life
imposes. Their disproportionate emigration results in a
male/female imbalance which further hastens the decline.

1165   Buchanan, Ronald H. "The Drift from the Land." Ulster
Folk 6 (60) (1960): 43-61. tables. refs.

Discussion of rural depopulation in Ulster and a
comparison of the situation there with the results of a
study of rural migration in England and Wales during the
past century. Aspects of the problem analyzed include the
demographic structure of the population in the various
counties, age and sex characteristics of migrants and
causes of rural depopulation. Conclusions and
recommendations offered.

1166   Clark, William E. and Michael Gordon. "Distance,
Closeness and Recency of Kin Contact in Urban Ireland." J
Comp Fam Stud X (2) (1979): 271-275.

A study designed to consider the effects of distance on
kin contact. Data were collected from 686 married women
representing a random sample in Cork City during the
Spring of 1974. Findings indicate that distance is the
single most powerful predictor of recency of contact;
however where mother-in-laws were concerned the quality
of the relationship was also a significant factor.
Possible future research avenues are indicated.

1167   Clarkson, L.A. "Household and Family Structure in
Armagh City, 1770." Local Pop Stud No. 20 (Spring 1978):
14-31. tables. refs.

      (See Marriage and the Family #1216.)

1168   Cooper, Ronald and Theresa O'Shea. "Northern Ireland:
A New Society Survey of the Social Trends." New Soc 24 (557)
(June 7,1973): 552-558. il. tables. refs.

      Factual report on major social trends in Northern
      Ireland. Areas covered include demography (population and
      marriage rate increasing), health/welfare, housing, work,
      education (ratio of females to males in full time further
      education - e.g. 18+ - has declined from 1965/6),
      religion (Roman Catholic population increasing due to
      higher fertility ratio of this group) and crime and law.

1169   Crawford, Michael and George Gmelch. "The Human
Biology of the Irish Tinkers: Demography, Ethnohistory and
Genetics." Soc Bio 21 (4) (Winter 1974): 321-331. il. refs.

      A description of the demographic structure of the Irish
      tinker population. Data on age structure, male/female
      ratio, mate selection, age at marriage, fertility and
      mortality rates, blood group and genetic distances. The
      genetic and evolutionary implication of the findings
      discussed.

1170   Cresswell, Robert. Une Communaute Rurale de l'Irlande.
Paris: Institut d'Ethnologie, Musee de l'Homme, 1969. 573pp.
il. bibl.

      Author conducted an anthropological analysis of an Irish
      rural community, Kinvarea, in County Galaway. Background
      on historical development of the parish; its high rate of
      population loss (80% between 1841 and 1956) detailed with
      an examination of causes and consequences, and an
      analysis of its social and economic life. Conclusions and
      suggestions for further research offered. Issues of
      methodology, role of anthropologist in the society he
      studies, validity of the unit of study are raised in the
      discussion following the precis.

1171   Diner, Hasia R. Erin's Daughters in America. Baltimore
and London: John Hopkins University Press, 1983. 192pp. il.
refs.

      Pages 1 - 29 examine women's life in 19th century Ireland
      particularly her place in Irish culture and family life
      and the economic and social lures that led many of these
      to emigrate to the U.S.

1172   Drucker, Amy J. "Simple Life on the West Coast of

Ireland." Engwoman (Feb. 1917): 138-146.

Brief account of daily life among the peasants in a village on the West Coast of Ireland. Description of cabins, furniture, meals, social intercourse.

1173   Fox, J.R. "Kinship and Land Tenure on Tory Island." Ulster Folk 12 (1966): 1-14. charts. tables. refs.

A study of the connections between kinship ties and the inheritance of land on Tory Island, 9 miles Northwest of Donegal. Inheritance of land is bilateral — both men and women can own and transmit land and all of a person's children have a claim on his/her land. Implications of this pattern discussed.

1174   Fox, J.R. "The Vanishing Gael." New Soc 1 (2) (Oct. 11 1962): 17-19. il. table.

An examination of acculturation on Tory Island of the coast of Donegal, and the crucial role of migrant labour now engaged in by both sexes, in this process.

1175   Fox, Robin. "The Visiting Husband on Tory Island." J Comp Fam Stud 10 (2) (Summer 1979): 163-190. tables. refs.

A detailed examination of marriage patterns on Tory Island off the Irish coast. Ten marriages in which husband and wife did not live together analyzed. Factors involved in this pattern include the strong attachment to parents and siblings on the one hand and the possessiveness of parents towards children on the other which both militate against marriage and even when marriage does occur, ensures that the couple continue to live in their natal residences.

1176   Gabriel, Tom. "The Farmers of the 'Western World.'" New Soc 39 (755) (Mar. 24, 1977): 596-598. il. refs.

Details on socio-economic changes affecting farm families in Western Ireland. Data collected in social/cultural anthropological research during 1973 and 1974 and an archival study involving 206 households. Change in socio-economic environment as a result of new technological developments and changing markets are accompanied by higher emigration patterns, rural depopulation, break-up of kin, neighborhood and older communal systems. Declines in marriage rates and household size also part of the new pattern.

1177   Gibbon, P. and C. Curtain. "Stem Family in Ireland." Comp Stud Soc & Hist 20 (3) (1978): 429-453. il. refs.

This study re-examines the evidence for the normative

character of the stem family in Ireland as set forth by
Arensberg and Kimball in their classic study and restated
by other anthropologists (e.g. Solon and Humphreys). Data
for this study taken from later historiography,
anthropological fieldwork and the results of a sample of
household schedules from the 1911 Census of Ireland. The
conclusion reached is that while the stem family did
exist as a norm for a very substantial proportion of the
rural population, Arensberg and Kimball's small/large
farm dichotomy was a misrepresentation of reality.

1178   Gmelch, George. The Irish Tinkers. The Urbanization of
an Itinerant People. Albany: State University of New York,
1977. 178pp. il. bibl.

Chapter 6 "Family and Marriage in the City" (pp.113-134)
discusses the important changes brought about in marriage
and family patterns by the new social environment of the
urban camp and the economic adaptation tinkers have made
in the city. Chief of these is the shift in sex roles,
specifically the increasing independence of women and the
concomitant decline in the male's authority in the
family.

1179   Gmelch, Sharon Bohn. "Economic and Power Relations
Among Urban Tinkers: The Role of Women." Urb Anthrop 6 (3)
(1977): 237-247. refs.

The author, by participant observation, examines the role
of women in the economic and social organization of a
marginal itinerant population in Dublin. Focuses on the
influences of both age and life cycle events upon
authority and power relationships between the sexes.
Findings indicate that while tinker society is clearly
male-dominated, women's roles follow a developmental
cycle. Their authority and power change during the course
of the life cycle. Also discussed are some of the changes
in role relations wrought by recent urbanization.

1180   Gmelch, Sharon. Tinkers and Travellers. Montreal:
McGill - Queens University Press, 1975. 144pp. il. refs.

Description of the life style of the tinkers in Ireland
by an anthropologist husband/wife team who spent thirteen
months living with a group of these while researching
their doctoral dissertations. Chapter four focuses on the
family, marriage practices, child-rearing, husband-wife
relations, etc. while chapters two and three provide some
detail on the women's economic role.

1181   Gordon, Michael. "Primary-group Differentiation in
Urban Ireland." Soc Forces 55 (3) (Mar. 1977): 743-752. il.
refs.

A replication and extension of the work of Latwak and

Szelyeri on primary group structures. Their findings
indicated that proximity of kin and occupation affected
primary group relationships. The study by Gordon which
employed data from interviews with 686 Irish women
generally confirmed their findings.

1182   Hannan, Damien F. Displacement and Development: Class,
Kinship Social Change in Irish Rural Communities. Dublin:
Economic and Social Research Institute, 1979. 231pp. tables.

Details the result of a study to assess the extent to
which a "peasant model" (Arensberg and Kimball) can
validly be used to describe the small farm communities of
Western Ireland in the 1920's and 1930's and a
description and analysis of the disintegration of that
peasant economy in the 1970's. Data collected from census
and economic records and ethnographic studies for the
period 1926-1971 and a study of farm families in 1970/71.

1183   Hannan, Damian F. "Patterns of Spousal Accomodation
and Conflict in Traditional and Modern Farm Families." Econ
Soc R 10 (1) (1978): 61-84. tables. refs.

This paper reports the results of interviews with a
random sample of 408 couples operating family farms in
the West of Ireland. Attention is focused on the extent
of concensus on values between husbands and wives, the
process of accomodation to each other's values, as well
as some of the bases of conflict of values that occur as
families modernize. In the light of these results, the
relative validity and utility of a number of theoretical
orientations in family sociology are assessed. [Author's
precis]

1184   Hannan, Damien F. and Louise A. Katsiaouni.
Traditional Families? From Culturally Prescribed to
Negotiated Roles in Farm Families. Dublin: The Economic and
Social Research Institute, 1977. 222pp. tables. refs.

A study of the changing structure of the Irish farm
family sets out to discover the contempoary validity of
the "traditional" model of family interaction as posited
by Arensberg and Kimball (1940). Data derived from
extended interviews with 408 husband-wife pairs living on
small farms in the West of Ireland in the early 70's and
participant observation in one small community. Findings
indicate substantial variation both in actual interaction
patterns and in the economic, technological, social and
cultural environments as opposed to the homogenous
environment posited by the traditional model. Causes of
these variations discussed.

1185   Hannan, Damien F. "Changes in Family Relationship
Patterns." Soc Stud 2 (6) (Dec. 1973): 559-563. refs.

Report of a study by the author which found that
interrelationships among families in the 10 Western
counties of Ireland has changed considerably from the
rigid sex role and patriarchal decision making patterns
found by Arensberg and Kimball in the 1930's. Change
attributed to increased communications between urban and
rural sectors and to economic and technological factors.

1186   Hannan, Damien F. "Kinship, Neighbor and Social Change
in Irish Rural Communities." Econ Soc R 111 (2) (Jan. 1972):
163-188. refs.

Describes fundamental changes in rural social
organization since the end of World War I or by
mid-1950's in many areas caused by changes in farm
technology, transportation and household economy, extent
and frequency of contact with outside groups as well as
with Government agencies directly trying to affect
change. Changes in kinship patterns noted.

1187   Hannan, Damien F. Rural Exodus: A Study of the Forces
Influencing the Large Scale Migration of Irish Rural Youth.
London: G. Chapman, 1970. 348pp. tables. append.

Presents and analyzes interview data on migration
intentions in 1965 of 556 adolescents, girls and boys,
from Cavan, Ireland and follow-up data collected in 1968
from 269 of the respondents. Considers the interrelation
of migration motives (related to beliefs about local
opportunity, community satisfaction, work obligations and
family expectations) and structural factors such as sex,
education, level of occupational and income aspiration,
remoteness of respondents homes and kinship networks.

1188   Hannan, Damian F. "Migration Motives and Migration
Differentials Among Irish Rural Youths." Sociol Rur 9 (3)
(1969): 195-220. tables. refs.

A study of 556 rural youth in a typical rural trade
center regarding their migration plans and motivation
found that beliefs about one's ability to fulfill
occupational and income aspirations locally were the most
crucial factor. Other important factors were community
satisfaction and family obligations. Social structural
differentials in migration rates as a result of education
level, occupation, sex and ecological location also
examined. More females than males planned to migrate - a
finding consistent with most other rural-urban studies in
the West. Factors operative in this imbalance detailed.

1189   Harris, Rosemary. Prejudice and Tolerance in Ulster: A
Study Of Neighbors and Strangers in a Border Community.
Manchester University Press, 1972. 234pp. plates. charts.

An anthropological study of prejudice in the community of

Ballybeg in Northern Ireland located in the rural west of
the Province. The study is based on participant
observation during ten months, 1952/53, and periodic
contact up to 1965. Findings indicate that both
communities (e.g. Catholics and Protestants) share a
common culture in certain respects e.g. share ideas of
the role of the sexes, but have different social fields.
Ties with co-religionists are very strong as are kin ties
and these re-inforce each other as there are few inter-
religious marriages. Both sides engage in stereotyping.
Class differences and economic factors contribute to
prejudice.

1190   Hooton, Earnest A. and C. Wesley Dupertuis. The
Physical Anthropology of Ireland: With a section on the West
Coast Irish females by Helen Dawson. (Papers of the Peabody
Museum 30 (1-2)) Cambridge, Mass. Peabody Museum of
Archaeology and Ethnology 1955. 299pp. maps. tables. figs.
refs.

The section on the West Coast Irish females (pp.251-299)
covers sociological observations, measurements and
indices, morphological observations, morphological types,
and age changes. Eighteen hundred women were included in
the sample studied. Comparison of findings for West Coast
females and males included in the national sample with
discussion of observed differences.

1191   Humphreys, Alexander J. New Dubliners: Urbanization
and the Irish Family. London: Routledge and Kegan Paul, 1966.
298pp. maps. graphs. tables. bibl.

A sociological analysis of the effects of urbanization
upon the structure of inter-familial and family/community
relationships within first generation Dublin families
based on a sample of 29 families. Decline in community
solidarity, weakening of the extended family ties,
evolution of the husband/wife relationship to one of
equal authority, changes in parent-child
relationships,... all of these and other changes seem to
stem from the economic reorganization of the family in
the urban situation.

1192   Humphreys, Alexander J. "Evolving Irishmen." Soc Order
4 (2) (Feb. 1954): 59-64.

This article, a summary of the research on which the
author's PhD was based describes the family
transformations which urbanization has produced. The full
study has since been published. (See item #1191.)

1193   Kane, Eileen. "The Changing Role of the Family in a
Rural Irish Community." J Comp Fam Stud 10 (2) (Summer 1979):
141-162. tables. refs.

An analysis of the effect of economic changes on family
life in the Gaeltacht based on an ethnological
description of a rural Irish community, Cluain, County
Galaway one of six communities studied by the author over
a six year period. Findings compared with those of
Arensberg and Kimball for County Clare in the 1930's and
topics covered include kinship system, married women's
economic status, marriage and child-rearing patterns,
courtship, etc. Changes since 1968 - the year of this
study - briefly noted.

1194   Kane, Eileen. "Man and Kin in Donegal: a Study of
Kinship Functions in a Rural Irish and Irish American
Community." Ethnology 7 (1968): 245-258. il. refs.

A study of the kinship organization of Cashel, County
Donegal. Findings indicate that it is a matri-centered
community in spite of the fact that most of the wives
come from outside the area but that it is less so than
the Irish American community in the study.

1195   Leyton, Elliott. The One Blood: Kinship and Class in
an Irish Village. St. John's, Newfoundland: The Institute of
Social and Economic Research, Memorial University of
Newfoundland, 1975. 103pp.

A study of kinship patterns in Aughnaboy, a small
Protestant community in Northern Ireland, emphasizes the
interrelationships between kinship and class. The
"elites" deemphasize the concensual model of kindred
obligations while the "masses" maximize relations with
kin. Sexual segregation of occupational roles exists in
all social classes. Also examines marriage patterns and
reasons for late age at marriage.

1196   Messenger, John C. Inis Beag: Isle of Ireland. New
York: Holt, Rinehart and Winston, 1969. 136pp. bibl.

This case study, one of a series in cultural
anthropology, provides a detailed descriptive analysis of
the culture and social structure of one of the Aran
islands. Data on family life, courtship and the position
of women.

1197   O'Crohan, Tomas. The Islandman. Translated from the
Irish by Robin Flower. London, New York: Oxford University
Press, 1978. 245pp. il. fronts.

Life story of a relatively uneducated - "in the modern
sense, though highly trained in the tradition of an
ancient folk culture" - native of the Great Blasket, one
of a remote group of islands off West Kerry. Social life
and customs of the people vividly evoked.

1198   O'Neill, Kevin. <u>Family and Farm in Pre-Famine Ireland:</u>
<u>the Parish of Killeshandra</u>. Madison, Wisconsin: University of
Wisconsin Press, 1984. 232pp. bibl.

Study of a single parish, Killeshandra in County Cavan,
for the period 1780-1845 - the only parish whose records
from the 1841 Census exist intact (the fullest and most
reliable pre-Famine Census) - based on a file of all
12,529 parish inhabitants, contemporary published works,
estate records and parliamentary accounts. Examines
tenure, rents, farm size, markets, capital and
production, labour and family structure. Conclusions
challenge previous scholarly interpretations of the
interrelationships of family size, the single-crop potato
and the Famine.

1199   Robinson, H.W. "A Study of the Church of Ireland
Population of Ardfert, County Kerry, 1971." <u>Econ Soc R</u> 4 (1)
(1972): 93-139. il.

A detailed analysis of the approximately one thousand
Church of Ireland members in Ardfert and the reasons why
membership in this group has declined from a peak of six
thousand in 1881. Three major causes of the decline
posited: structure of population, emigration and mixed
marriages. Data based on a special 1971 Census collected
by local clergy. Information on male and female
occupations, marriage and fertility rates, marital
status, education, family size, birth and death rates,
male/female sex ratio, etc. provided.

1200   Scheper-Hughes, Nancy. "Inheritance of the Meek: Land,
Labor, and Love in Western Ireland." <u>Marx Persp</u> 2 (1) (Spring
1979): 46-76. tables. refs.

Documents the malaise and demoralization in Ballybran, a
mountain parish in the Irish speaking Gaeltacht of West
Kerry.

1201   Symes, D.G. "Farm Household and Farm Performance: A
Study of 20th Century Changes in Ballyferriter." <u>Ethnology</u> 11
(1) (Jan. 1972): 25-38. tables. figs. refs.

This paper examines underlying changes in the structural
form of the rural household which accompanied the massive
rural depopulation in Ireland between 1841 and 1961. In
the 19th century reduction in the number of households
was the most important factor. In the 20th century,
however, contraction within the household was the
important factor. Through a detailed case study of a
small community in Kerry, the author compares the size,
structure, and life cycles of 91 matched households in
1911 and 1969. Implications of these structural factors
for optimal efficiency of farm holdings and government
policy, examined.

Marriage and the Family

This section contains publications on courtship or dating patterns including matchmaking; marriage customs, structures and patterns; intermarriage; family and kin relations including family roles (husband-wife, parent-child); socialization of children and child care; family breakdown including divorce or separation; unwed mothers and status of illegitimate children and ideological statements on the social role of the family.

Additional material on family and kinship will be found in the section on COMMUNITY STUDIES. Various legal issues relating to the family are covered under LAW - GENERAL LEGAL STATUS. For studies of the reproductive role of women, sexual relations, family planning and fertility see HUMAN SEXUALITY, REPRODUCTION AND HEALTH. For material on women as homemakers and their economic contribution; also material on wives in employment outside the home see EMPLOYMENT/ECONOMIC CONDITIONS.

1202   Baggot, Patrick A. Unspoken Problems of Married Life. Dublin: Irish Messenger. n.d. 46pp. [1965?]

    Brief outline of right and wrong attitudes to one another and the marriage relationship written from a Catholic viewpoint.

1203   Baggot, Tony. To Have And To Hold: Marriage Relationship. Dublin & Cork: Mercier Press, 1977. 64pp.

    Talks on male/female relationships which are part of a premarriage course for engaged couples.

1204   Barnes, James. "Non-consummation of Marriage." Ir Med J 74 (1) (1981): 19-21.

A discussion of the effects on the personality induced by non-consummation of marriage. (The author is on the staff of the Catholic Marriage Advisory Council in Dublin.) He comments on the incidence of non-consummation in Ireland, the implications for the couples involved and various adaptations to the situation. Barnes offers some conclusions on the appropriateness of treatment programmes.

1205   Bestic, Alan. The Importance of Being Irish. London: Cassell & Co. Ltd., 1969. 199pp.

Chapter 9, "Love and Marriage," discusses Irish marital breakdown and its causes. Bestic sees ignorance and sexual guilt as major factors combined with a lack of companionship between husbands and wives. Extra-marital relationships, prostitution, birth-control and other issues touched upon briefly.

1206   Binchy, William. Is Divorce the Answer? Dublin: Irish Academic Press, 1984.

Rejects divorce as a solution to marriage breakdown in Ireland.

1207   Birch, Peter (Bishop of Ossory). "The Irish Family in Modern Conditions." Soc Stud 2 (5) (Oct./Nov. 1973): 485-497.

Examines evidence of strain in traditional notions of the family and explores the factors necessary to a happy marriage under modern conditions.

1208   Bond, C.J. "Eugenics and Bernard Shaw." Eugenics R 21 (July 1929): 159-161.

A letter to the editor commenting on Shaw's views on eugenics as put forth in his book, The Intelligent Woman's Guide to Socialism and Capitalism. Bond argues that the main factors which determine choice in marriage are biological and psychological rather than environmental and that Shaw's theory that equalization of income would produce more free choice in marriage and hence a better race is not sound eugenically.

1209   Breen, Richard. "Dowry Payments and the Irish Case." Comp Stud Soc & Hist 26 (2) (1984): 280-296. refs.

Examines the inter-relationship of dowry payments and other social variables such as status, kinship and economics. The study is based on fieldwork in the small community of Beaufort, County Kerry and secondary analysis of the work of other anthropologists.

1210   Burke, Helen. "The Family - Do We Take its Tasks for
Granted." Soc Stud 2 (6) (Dec. 1973): 573-579. refs.

    In this article the ability of the family to meet the
    emotional and social needs of its members is considered.
    Burke recommends education for homemaking for both men
    and women to meet the various "tasks" of the marriage at
    different stages of the family's life cycle: achievement
    of mutuality of the couple; relating well to other groups
    in their circles and their parental families; opening up
    their relationship to include a child; letting children
    go; coping with normal and exceptional stress situations.

1211   Cahill, Edward (S.J.). "Notes on Christian Sociology
(V.) The Family, (A) General Principles (B) Husband and Wife.
(VI.) Social Status of Woman, (A) The Christian Woman (B) The
Feminist Movement and the Modern Woman." Ir Mon 52-53
(1924-1925): 408-420; 473-483; 537-541; 646-654; 28-34.

    Statement of orthodox Catholic position on the nature of
    the family, marriage, roles of husband and wife. Brief
    overview of the political status of women in various
    Western societies and the causes of the Feminist
    Movement. Cahill deplores the threat to Christian ideals
    of feminine modesty and decorum and the foundations of
    family life posed by radical feminism.

1212   Chadwick, Nora K. "Pictish and Celtic Marriage in
Early Literary Tradition." Scott Gael Stud 8 (1958): 56-155.
refs.

    Discussion of Greek and Latin writers' observations on
    marriage customs among the Celtic races in Ireland,
    Scotland and Wales. Chadwick argues that the classical
    scholars ultimately misunderstood the practices they
    observed and she seeks to elucidate the norms regulating
    these. Aspects considered include practices regarding
    marriage within the family and temporary unions.

1213   Chester, Catherine. "Fund Raising Fashion." Status 6
(2) (Apr. 1981): 39-40.

    News report on a fund-raising fashion show organized by
    Cherish, a self-help group for unmarried mothers.

1214   Clancy, Patrick, Sheila Drudy, Kathleen and Liam
O'Dowd. (Eds.) Ireland: A Sociological Profile. Dublin:
Institute of Public Administration, 1986. 434pp.

    Contains essays by 21 contributors. Chapter eight deals
    with marriage and family; chapter 14 covers the social
    dimensions of sex roles.

1215   Clark, William E. and Michael Gordon. "Distance, Closeness and Recency of Kin Contact in Urban Ireland." J Comp Fam Stud X (2) (1979): 271-275.

    (See #1166.)

1216   Clarkson, L.A. "Household and Family Structure in Armagh City, 1770." Local Pop Stud No.20 (Spring 1978): 14-31. tables. refs.

    Detailed study of the population of Armagh, the ecclesiastical capital of Ireland, based on a 1770 Census compiled by Dr. Lodge. An analysis of Dr. Lodge's methodology is presented along with a discussion of his findings and their implications.

1217   Conference on the Unmarried Parent and Child in Irish Society. Dublin: Cherish, 1974. [1975]. 59pp. refs.

    Proceedings of a seminar organized by Cherish, an organization to aid illegitimate children and their parents. Describes the current legal situation in Ireland regarding illegitamacy and available services.

1218   Connell, Kenneth H. Irish Peasant Society: Four Historical Essays. Oxford: Clarendon Press, 1968. 167pp. il. maps. tables. bibl. refs.

    Includes (Chapter 2) a study of illegitimate births in Ireland before the Famine with details on incidence, outcome for mother and child, incidence of infanticide and induced abortion. Data mainly derived from the First Report of Commissioners for Inquiry into the Condition of the Poorer Classes in Ireland [1835-36]. Chapter 4 discusses the post-famine trend toward later marriage or permanent celibacy and the role of the Catholic Church in this development.

1219   Connell, Kenneth H. "Peasant Marriage in Ireland after the Great Famine." Past & Pres No.12 (1957): 76. tables. refs.

    Summary of below.

1220   Connell, Kenneth H. "Marriage in Ireland after the Famine: the diffusion of the Match." Stat & Soc Inq Soc J XIX (1955-56): 82-83. [Discussion p. 95-103.] tables. refs.

    This paper read before the Society in December 1955 is part of the argument of a wider discussion of the history of Irish population since the Famine. The author explores the causes and consequences of the trend to later and less frequent marriage after the Famine. Consolidation of

holdings leading to an unaccustomed scarcity of land,
land legislation and emigration all seen as factors.

1221   Connell, Kenneth H. "Peasant Marriage in Ireland: its
Structure and Development Since the Famine." Econ Hist R 14
(April 1962): 502-23. refs.

A detailed look at the "match" - e.g. the system of
arranged marriages in Ireland which the author sees as
the principal form of marriage among farmers over the
last century. The "match" is contrasted with the
pre-Famine pattern of early "romantic" marriage, and its
diffusion after the Famine is seen as the outcome of
consolidation of holdings and a son's economic dependence
on his father. Factors leading to a modification of this
pattern in recent decades suggested.

1222   Connery, Donald S. The Irish. London: Eyre and
Spottiswoode, 1969. 256pp. il. maps. plates. portrs.

Chapter six has a journalistic discussion of love and
marriage in Ireland. Touches on power relations between
the sexes, the importance attached to marriage and
home-making, the sex ratio which favors men in the
cities, economic disabilities of women in the workforce,
role of the Catholic Church in sex role definition,
family planning and the increased sexual candor which for
Connery, co-exists with a lack of tolerance of premarital
sexual relationships and a lingering Puritanism and
hypocricy about sexual matters.

1223   Corish, Brendan (Tanaiste and Minister for Health and
Social Welfare). Soc Stud 2 (Feb.-Mar.1973): 605-612.

A discussion of income maintenance and community social
service policy in Ireland by the then Minister for Health
and Social Welfare. He calls for radical structural
reform of the existing system and the development of
family-oriented rather than individual-oriented social
services.

1224   Coulter, Carol. "Cherish, Ally, and Adapt Care for
Women, Why Doesn't the State?" Hibernia 42 (Feb. 23, 1978):
8.

Criticizes the lack of Government response to the plight
of unmarried mothers and the inadequacy of voluntary
programs such as "Cherish", "Ally" and "Adapt" to
adequately meet their needs because of money and staff
shortages.

1225   Coward, John. "Ideal Family Size in Northern Ireland."
J Biol Sci 13 (Oct.1981): 443-454. tables. refs.

Data from a survey of 1699 currently (once) married males
used to examine ideal family size in Northern Ireland.
Northern Irish family size ideals (mean 3.6) are
considerably greater than those of many West European
countries and these also vary within Northern Ireland.
Religious grouping is the major factor in these
variations with Roman Catholics generally expressing an
ideal (mean 4.4) for large families. Other factors also
associated with variation include education, age,
occupation, region of residence and religiosity.

1226   Craig, Rose. "Testimony on Unwaged Housework."
ISIS:International Bulletin. Women's International
Information and Communication Service. International Tribunal
on Crimes Against Women. (March 1976): 16-17.

Argues that women should be paid for housework and child-
rearing so it will not be necessary to seek work outside
their homes.

1227   Darling, Vivienne. And Baby Makes Two. Dublin:
Federation of Services for Unmarried Parents and Their
Children, 1984.

Seeks to "provide a descriptive account of the life-style
of a group of unmarried mothers and the special
difficulties they meet" based on interviews with 94 of
these.

1228   Delany, Colette. "Stress in the Family." Soc Stud 2
(6) (Dec.1973): 581-587.

A social worker comments on causes of stress within the
family. Normal stress arises from the interaction of
different personalities in a group situation. Other
stress factors arise in crisis situations: deserted wives
have economic and psychological pressures; many married
women fear additional pregnancies or assault by their
husbands; alcoholism, incest, mental incapacity are all
occasions of high stress. Relative intensity of stress
and various coping mechanisms including the role of the
social worker briefly considered.

1229   Divorce Action Group. Social Reform of Marriage in
Ireland: Practical Steps for Legal Change. ed. John O'Connor.
Dublin: Divorce Action Group, 1983. 24pp.

Presents statistics to support thesis that marital
breakdown in Ireland is increasing and advocates
relaxation of the legal prohibition on divorce.

1230   Dixon, Ruth Bronson. "Late Marriage and Non-marriage
as Demographic Responses: Are They Similar." Pop Stud 32 (3)
(1978): 449-466. tables. refs.

Examines reasons for the divergence of Ireland and Japan
from the general pattern of high congruence between
timing and prevalence of nuptiality; e.g. the social,
economic and demographic factors which cause large
numbers of men and women to delay their nuptials, also
cause high proportions to remain unmarried. In Japan,
marriage was increasingly postponed between 1920 and 1950
but almost everyone married before age 45. In Ireland
between 1850 and 1950 the timing of male nuptiality
varied little yet the proportion of permanent bachelors
rose and fell dramatically. Economic rather than
demographic factors seen as primary explanation for the
Irish pattern.

1231   Duncan, W.R. "The Domicile of Married Women." Dublin U
Law J 1 (1977): 38-45. refs.

(See Law - Marriage and Divorce #1538.)

1232   Duncan, W.R. "Illegitimacy and Law Reform." In
Conference on The Unmarried Parent and Child in Irish
Society. Saturday, October 26th, 1974. pp. 11-19. Dublin:
Cherish, 1975. refs.

(See Law - Family Law #1539.)

*1233   Evason, Eileen. Hidden Violence: A Study of Battered
Wives in Northern Ireland. Belfast: Farset, 1982. 80pp. il.
tables. refs.

(See Law - Penal Law #1596.)

1234   Evason, Eileen . "Just Me and the Kids: Single Parent
Families in Northern Ireland." Women's View 5 (Spring 1981):
10-11.

Case histories of divorced or separated wives, widows and
single mothers. Ten percent of families in Northern
Ireland are headed by a single parent - usually female.

1235   F.W.H. "Marriage and Abduction." Dublin U Mag LXXXV
(Feb. 1875): 174-184.

Includes accounts of several episodes, mostly 18th
century and onwards, in which Irish women of good family
- heiresses - were forcibly abducted and forced to go
through a form of marriage with their abductors. The
practice was, in the main, condoned by society despite
this being a capital felony from 1707.

1236   Fennell, Nuala, Deirdre McDevitt and Bernadette Quinn.
Can You Stay Married: A Self Help Guide for Women. Dublin:
Kincora Press, 1980. 117pp. portrs.

A brief manual compiled by three volunteer members of
AIM, an organization founded in 1972 to campaign for law
reform in areas related to women and the family, offers
advice on making marriages work and the legal options
available in situations of marital breakdowns.

1237   Fennell, Nuala. "Divorce." Image 4 (1) (Jan. 1978):
63. portr.

Discussion of the tendency of Irish people to get
divorces in England, the resulting problems and future
implications.

1238   Fennell, Nuala. Irish Marriage - How Are You! Dublin:
The Mercier Press, 1974. 82pp.

The author, founder of AIM (a Dublin Women's Centre
providing legal advice to those with marital problems)
utilizes data from organization's files to consider the
causes of marital breakdown in Ireland, the emotional,
financial and legal problems faced by the wife in such
situations and the reasons why the existing social
structures are not coping adequately with the problem.

1239   Finlay, Peter. "Divorce in the Irish Free State."
Studies 13 (1924): 353-362.

Outlines the Catholic position on divorce in view of the
renewed discussion of this issue in the Irish context.
Concludes that Catholics are bound morally to resist
legislation allowing divorce.

1240   Geary, J.A. "The Celtic Family." Prim Man 3 (1-2)
(Jan/Apr. 1930): 22-31. il.

Discusses the sources from which our knowledge of Celtic
customs derive, namely Greek and Latin writers and the
Irish and Welsh literatures - the latter seen as more
reliable. Marriage patterns, wedding ceremonies, divorce,
temporary marriage, married women's rights, joint
families, matriarchy, etc. briefly discussed.

1241   Geary, Robert Charles. "The Family in Irish Census of
Population Statistics." Stat & Soc Inq Soc J 19 (1954-55):
1-30. tables.

Statistical data on the Irish family derived from a
special analysis of a sample of 6,280 families taken from
the Census of Population of 1951 with discussion.

1242   Geraghty, Mary. "Who'll Look After the Children."
Women View 1 (Mar. 1980): 8-10. il.

Argues for a viable policy of integrating paid employment
with parenthood - with emphasis on parenthood. Both sexes
should assume responsibility for children. Offers a
variety of options all of which should be allowed to suit
individual circumstances.

1243   Gillman, Con. "Recent Marriage Patterns in Ireland."
Chr Rex 23 (1) (Jan. 1969): 49-53. tables.

An analysis and discussion of marriage rate figures from
1957 with some comparable data from 1926 and 1946 Census
figures.

1244   Gordon, Michael. "Primary-group Differentiation in
Urban Ireland." Soc Forces 55 (3) (Mar. 1977): 743-752. il.
refs.

A replication and extension of the work of Latwak and
Szelyeri on primary group structures. Their findings
indicated that proximity of kin and occupation affected
primary group relationships. The study by Gordon which
employed data from interviews with 686 Irish women
generally confirmed their findings.

1245   Gordon, Michael and Helen Downing. "A Multivariate
Test of the Bott Hypothesis in an Urban Irish Setting." J
Marr & Fam 40 (3) (Aug. 1978): 585-592. il. refs.

Using a sample of 686 married Irish women in Cork city,
the Bott Hypothesis (Family and Social Network 1971)
which argues that the connectedness of a married person's
social network was negatively related to his/her marital
integration, was tested and the results of a multivariate
regression analysis revealed that neither network
connectedness nor the strength of the respondent's
emotional ties to the network had any explanatory power.
The crucial variables were the number of the wife's
network members shared by her husband, and the family's
socioeconomic status.

1246   Gray, Tony. The Irish Answer. Boston, Toronto: Little,
Brown and Co., 1966. 429pp.

Chapter 15 presents a journalistic account of love and
marriage in Ireland. Topics include the Irish woman's
reputation for chastity with a discussion of possible
factors involved in her sexual restraint; the late age at
marriage and its economic basis and birth control.

1247   Hanaghan, Jonathan. The Courage to be Married. With a
Preface by Ludovic Kennedy. Compiled and edited by John
McCann. Cork and Dublin: Mercier Press, 1973. 132pp.

Author discusses the psychological difficulties in

getting to know the marriage partner intimately and
stresses the importance of risk-taking and confrontation
in plumbing the spiritual depths of another human being.

1248   Harris, Maura. Planning Your Wedding. Dublin: Catholic
Truth Society, 1970. 26pp.

    Described as a practical guide for wedding preparation,
    this manual covers practical details as well as Catholic
    religious prescriptions.

1249   Humphreys, Alexander J. "The Family in Ireland." In
Comparative Family Systems. Ed. by Meyer Francis Nimkoff.
Boston: Houghton Miflin, 1965. bibl.

    A study of family life in the Republic of Ireland. The
    section on the rural family relies heavily on Arensberg
    and Kimball's Family and Community in Ireland (see
    #1161). Humphreys adds a section on religious values. His
    description of the urban (Dublin) family is a summary of
    the major points of his thesis (see #2181) and shows the
    changes urbanization has wrought in the family's economic
    and social roles.

1250   Hutchinson, Bertran A. Social Status in Dublin:
Marriage, Mobility and First Employment. Dublin: Economic and
Social Research Institute, 1973. 66pp. [Paper 67] tables.
bibl. refs.

    This paper is based on studies of some aspects of social
    inequality among the population of Dublin. Data analyzed
    under the headings: Class Endogamy and Mate Selection in
    Dublin; Observations on Age at Marriage Related to Social
    Status and Mobility; First Employment, Social Status and
    Mobility in Dublin.

1251   Hutchinson, Bertran. "Observations on Age at Marriage
in Dublin, Related to Social Status and Social Mobility."
Econ Soc R 2 (2) (Jan. 1971): 209-221. tables. refs.

    The purpose of this study was to relate age at marriage
    in Ireland to social status and to social mobility: the
    data derived from a sample of male adult residents of
    Dublin (2540). Findings support other studies showing
    that upper status categories have a tendency to marry
    later than lower - age at marriage falls with decreasing
    social status. Overall, age at marriage for men remains
    widely dispersed (unlike Western Europe where there is
    concentration around the mean) and still remains
    significantly higher than the European norm, but there
    has been a trend towards younger marriages since World
    War II.

1252   Ireland: A Sociological Profile. Dublin: Institute of
Public Administration, 1986.

    Includes chapters on "Marriage and the Family" (chapter
    8) and the "Social Dimensions of the Sex Roles" (chapter
    14).

1253   The Irish Housewife: A Portrait. Dublin: Irish
Consumer Research, Ltd. 1986. 93pp.

    Using quantitative data from secondary sources and
    interviews with a selected sample, offers a digest of
    facts and figures and qualitative impressions regarding
    work, leisure activities, family and social values of
    housewives.

1254   Jackson, Donald. Intermarriage in Ireland 1550-1650.
Minnesota: Cultural and Educational Productions, 1970. 84pp.
bibl.

    A study of the assimilation of the English colonists to
    Irish ways through an examination of intermarriages
    between these and indigenous families. Data is taken from
    genealogical records. An attempt is made to indicate the
    politico-religious evolution of individual families as a
    result of such alliances.

1255   de Joubainville, H. d'Arbois. "L'Achat de la Femme
Dans la Loi Irlandaise." R Celt 3 (1876-78): 361-364. refs.

1256   Joyce, P.W. A Social History of Ancient Ireland.
Dublin: M.H. Gill and Son, Ltd., 1913. 2 vols. il. maps.

    Chapter 19 on the family includes material on marriage
    and the position of women.

1257   Kain-Caudle, P.R. "Family Allowances in Ireland."
Admin 12 (2) (1964): 140-145. tables.

    Classification of types and purposes of assistance
    offered by the State to parents in the rearing of their
    children. The importance of this aid in the Irish
    context, characterized by high celibacy rates, late age
    of marriage, large families and low income per head,
    discussed.

1258   Keane, John B. "Marriage Irish Style." Reality XXXIII
(5) (May 1969): 12-14. portr.

    Comment on the finding by Nuala Fennell in her book
    Irish Marriage - How Are You that there exist a large
    number of unsuccessful marriages in Ireland. Keane

presents his diagnosis of causation — not enough women
are conscientious in their sexual response to their
husbands — and offers his recipe for a happy marriage —
total openness between the spouses.

1259   Kennedy, Robert E. Jr. The Irish: Emigration, Marriage
And Fertility. Berkeley: University of California Press,
1973. 236pp. tables. bibl.

A social demographic analysis of marriage patterns,
fertility rates and celibacy in Ireland during the period
1840-1960. Causes and consequences of these patterns and
differential emigration rates between male/female and
Catholic/Protestant analyzed. Author concludes that
emigration and celibacy were means to the same end — the
achievement of a higher standard of living. Women
accounted for a higher percentage of both rural, urban
and overseas migration to escape a male dominated society
as well as to enhance their social and economic position.

1260   Kenny, Mary. "Two Kinds of Family: Family Life in
London and Dublin." New Soc (May 3, 1979): 271. il.

Journalist, Mary Kenny, compares her family situation
when she lives in London — (casebook lifestyle of urban,
nuclear family) — and a Dublin suburb (almost classic
extended family situation) and benefits and drawbacks of
each.

1261   Kilkenny Social Services, Kilkenny. The Unmarried
Mother in the Irish Community: A Report on the National
Conference on Community Services for the Unmarried Parent.
[Kilkenny]: Kilkenny People, Ltd., 1972. 65pp.

Proceedings of a conference held in Kilkenny in 1970
as a result of the Council of Europe's recommendations
for the protection of single, pregnant women. The purpose
of the Conference was to review the situation in regard
to unmarried mothers in Ireland in light of these
recommendations and to highlight gaps in services.
Aspects covered include the philosophy of care of the
unmarried mother and her child, medical care, the role of
the father, delivery of services. Suggestions for
improved services offered.

1262   Kirke, Deirdre. "Unmarried Mothers: A Comparative
Study." Econ Soc R 10 (2) (Jan. 1979): 157-167. refs.

Results of a study designed to identify factors
associated with unmarried motherhood in Ireland. One
hundred unmarried mothers and a control group of the same
number of married mothers were interviewed in the
National Maternity Hospital, Dublin in 1973. The results
showed that there was no difference betweeen the two
groups in their family background or lifestyle but

significant differences emerged in three areas:
e.g.parental control of dating, attitudes towards
premarital sexual intercourse and religious practice.

1263   Latterson, Laurie. "Marriage Irish Style." Woman Ch 7
(47) (Aug. 7, 1975): 12-13.

A brief discussion of some of the reasons for marital
discord and breakdown in Ireland and the lack of real
solutions.

1264   LeBras, Herve. Child and Family: Demographic
Developments in the OECD Countries. Paris: Organization for
Economic Co-operation and Development, 1979. 219pp. tables.
refs.

This two part analysis of the demographic evolution of
OECD countries since 1945 (including Ireland) contains in
Part I comparative data on vital statistics, fertility
patterns, nuptiality, divorce, illegitimacy, abortion,
etc. Part II has separate chapters on individual
countries: chapter IV details demographic developments in
Ireland.

1265   Lees, Lynn. "Mid-Victorian Migration and the Irish
Family Economy." Vict Stud 20 (1) (Autumn 1976): 25-43. il.
refs.

This article explores the impact on Irish households of
migration to London in the Mid-19th century by focusing
on the nature of the Irish family economy and of female
work roles both before and after movement into the
English capital. Findings indicate that moving to the
city affected the sort of work done and led to
substantial alteration in the familial division of labour
and in contact with the market place. Married women were
most affected and suffered a loss of status within the
family.

1266   Lewis, Ruth. "The Adolescent and the Family." Soc Stud
2 (6) (Dec. 1973): 593-597.

General discussion of the special problems of adolescents
and some that are socially produced such as the
differential treatment of boys and girls and the
unnatural segregation of the single sex boarding school.

1267   Lueschen, Gunther and others. "Family, Ritual and
Secularization - A Cross-National Study Collected in
Bulgaria, Finland, Germany and Ireland." Soc Compass 19 (4)
(1972): 519-536. il. refs.

A cross national study in five metropolitan areas
representing five societal areas each with a different

degree of modernization. The study found that family ritual functions to strengthen family bonds and reinforces the nuclear family. The specific ritual of Christmas becomes oriented more towards the family than towards the Church and loses some of its meaning and function. In spite of changes a fundamental interest in the sacred makes it predominate over modernization. Secularization then appears as a relocalization and privalization of the sacred rather than a movement of desacralization of "more traditional" societies towards "more modern" ones.

1268   Lueschen, Gunther and others. "Family Organization, Interaction and Ritual: A Cross-Cultural Study in Bulgaria, Finland, Germany and Ireland." J Marr & Fam 33 (1) (Feb. 1971): 228-234. il. refs.

This study examines the role of family rituals in maintaining kin relationships in four societies which vary in their degree of modernity. Preliminary results show that in the more modern societies there is a slightly higher frequency of ritual interaction and visits with kin.

1269   Lynd, Robert. Home Life In Ireland. Chicago: A.C. McClung and Co.; London: Mills and Boon, Ltd. [1909] 317pp. il.

Chapter three deals with marriage rates and the custom of arranged marriages called "Matchmaking," while chapter 14 overviews the exceedingly low wages paid to women in the spinning and weaving mills, in warehouses and as outworkers in the cottage industries.

1270   McCarroll, Joseph. Marriage or Divorce: the Real Issue. Dublin: Four Courts Press, 1986.

Argues that the State has a duty - not Catholic, Christian or even religious as such - but human - to uphold life-long monogamy.

1271   McCarroll, Joseph. "The Report on Marriage Breakdown." Doc & Life 34 (July-Aug. 1985): 314-325.

Comment on the Report of the Oireachtas Joint Committee on Marriage Breakdown (1983). McCarroll claims that the principal defect of the Report is the absence of a full and adequate understanding of the true nature of marriage and that the Report functions to serve the interests of the advocates of divorce.

1272   McCarthy, Michael D. "Some Family Facts in Ireland Today." Chr Rex 5 (1) (Jan. 1951): 49-50.

Demographic facts relating to the family in Ireland —
mainly in the Republic. Data derived from official
reports (1946 Census) include overall population trends,
age distribution, sex ratio, marital status, age at
marriage, birth and fertility rates and family
composition.

1273   McElhone, Patricia. When The Honeymoon Is Over. Seven
True Accounts of the Experience of Marriage. Dublin: Veritas
Publications, 1977. 112pp.

A first person account of the experience of widowhood and
the pain of loss by the author, and her description based
upon interviews with the respondents of the happy
marriages of six other couples.

1274   Mc Farlane, W. Graham. "Mixed Marriages In Ballycuan,
Northern Ireland." J Comp Fam Stud 10 (2) (Summer 1979):
191-205. tables. refs.

Presents data collected during 1975-1976 on the extent
of Protestant — Catholic marriages in Ballycuan and
analyses factors which make for the relatively greater
acceptability of some of these versus others. The crucial
factor seen as involving the potential religious
affiliation of children of such marriages and the
religion of the mother seen as central to this. The type
of mixed marriage which is least negatively evaluated by
Protestants is most negatively evaluated by Catholics and
vice versa.

1275   McKenna, Anne. "Attitudes of Irish Mothers to Child
Rearing." J Comp Fam Stud 10 (2) (Summer 1979): 227- 251.
tables. refs.

A study utilizing the Parental Attitude Research
Inventory of childrearing/childbearing attitudes of Irish
mothers. Four hundred and eighty women who had given
birth within the previous one to seven days in maternity
hospitals were surveyed. Results indicate that Irish
mothers endorse attitudes unfavorable to childrearing and
favorable to control over their children more frequently
than do American mothers. Data correlated with other
variables including social class, education, help from
husband, size of family, etc.

1276   McKenna, Edward E. "Age, Region and Marriage in Post-
Famine Ireland: An Empirical Examination." Econ Hist R 31
(May 1978): 238-256. tables. refs.

This article examines the connections between conditions
in the rural economy of Ireland and marriage patterns
during the post-famine period from 1851 to 1911. McKenna
concludes that for the period in question the largest

single influence on marriage patterns was land pressure
with non-agricultural engagement exercising secondary
influence.

1277   Maher, Mary. You and Your Baby. Dublin: Gill and
Macmillan, 1973. 184pp. tables.

A popular manual offers practical advice and basic facts
on pregnancy, childbirth, child care and development.
Includes a directory of maternity services, broadly
defined, including health boards, pediatric services,
pre-school education, etc.

1278   Malcomson, A.P.W. The Pursuit of the Heiress:
Aristocratic Marriage In Ireland 1750-1820. Antrim: Baird,
1982. 70pp. il. bibl. refs.

A study based on primary and secondary sources of the
extent to which marriage in Ireland was an agent of
dynastic aggrandisement and the relevance of personal,
human and non-economic factors e.g. an exploration of the
mores of aristocratic marriage on a country-wide basis
and over a significant period of time. Author concludes
that heiresses had not been a conscious and deliberate
pursuit among the Irish peers who were more likely to
marry the averagely portioned daughters of other Irish
aristocratic families. Role of marriage settlements which
protected rights of younger children, and or, their
mother, analyzed as a causal factor.

1279   Market Research Bureau of Ireland. "Religious Practice
and Attitudes Toward Divorce and Contraception Among Irish
Adults." Soc Stud 3 (3) (June 1974): 276-285. tables.

Report of a survey carried out by the Market Research
Bureau in 1974 based on a random probability sample of
600 households. Five hundred and seventy one persons aged
18 to 60 were interviewed. Single women were about evenly
divided on the divorce issue while a majority of married
women were against divorce. The majority of both single
and married women favored the legalization of the sale of
contraceptives. Data analyzed by age, sex, marital
status, region, social class and religion.

1280   Marriage in Ireland, ed. by Art Cosgrove. [Dublin]:
College Press, 1986.

A series of papers delivered to the Dublin Historical
Society, 1983-84 provide an historical overview of the
status of marriage in Ireland from the 5th to the 20th
century.

1281   Masterson, J.C. "Consanguinity in Ireland." Hum Hered
20 (4) (1970): 371-382. map. tables. refs.

Inbreeding in Ireland studied through an analysis of
ecclesiastical dispensations from the impediment of
consanguinity for Catholic marriages in Ireland for the
period 1959-1968. Data based on approximately 71% of all
marriages in the period for the whole of Ireland and on
91% of all marriages in the Republic of Ireland.
Limitations on data discussed with findings.

1282   Meenan, James. "Some Causes and Consequences of the
Low Irish Marriage Rate." Stat & Soc Inq Soc J 15 (1932/33):
19-27. tables.

Detailed discussion of changes in the Irish marriage rate
throughout the period 1864-1930 and corresponding socio-
economic events in the country. Meenan argues that the
low marriage rate was a result of poor economic
conditions rather than of emigration which itself was a
product of these conditions.

1283   Moore, David. Some Tax Implications of Marriage
Breakdown. Belfast: Queen's University, Belfast, Faculty of
Law Servicing the Legal System, 1981. 26 leaves. refs.

Existing tax options for married couples explicated as
background for a discussion of effects and implications
of separation and divorce actions.

1284   Murray, Donal. "The Ideology of the Family." Soc Stud
2 (6) (Dec. 1973): 537-547.

This article by a professor of moral theology presents
the traditional Catholic teaching on the role of the
family in society and in the church in terms of how it
contributes to human, social and religious development.

1285   N.G. "Wanted! Home Makers." Ir Mon 56 (1928): 70-74.

Decline in teaching and practice of homemaking skills
lamented and a warning that men not finding a happy haven
in the house will seek their pleasures elsewhere (!)

1286 Newman, Jeremiah. Ireland Must Choose. [ ]: Four Courts
Press, 1984.

Essays by the Bishop of Limerick on Church-State
relations, public and private morality, divorce and other
topics written from a conservative Catholic viewpoint.

1287   Newman, Jeremiah. "Social-political Aspects of
Divorce." Chr Rex 23 (1) (Jan. 1969): 5-14.

(See Law #1564.)

1288   O'Beirne, Michael. People People Marry - People People Don't. Dublin: Veritas Publications, 1976. 142pp.

   Author discusses the reason for his setting up a marriage bureau in Dublin and his initial difficulties. Reviews the attitudes towards marriage prior to 1960 in Ireland and the major underlying cause - the male/female imbalance in different geographic areas. Book includes brief profiles of clients and anecdotes of successful matches.

1289   O'Bryne, Simon. Civil Divorce for Catholics...Why Not? 365 Questions and Answers. [Dublin: The Author] 1982. 130pp.

   Presents the theological teaching of the Catholic Church in simple language and exhorts Catholics to be loyal to religious authority on moral issues.

1290   O'Connor, Richard. The Irish: Portrait of a People. New York: G.P. Putnam's Sons, 1971. 384pp.

   Chapter seven entitled "The Bachelor Boys" discusses in a popular, journalistic style the factors which operate negatively on romantic love in Ireland, the presumed unwillingness of Irish males to marry and the past and current status of women in Irish society.

1291   O'Danachair, Caoimhin. "The Family in Irish Tradition." Chr Rex 16 (Sept. 1962): 185-196.

   Discussion of family life, male and female roles and responsibilities, marriage, matchmaking, and kinship ties in the farming community in Ireland around the turn of the century with some consideration of the declining importance of the extended family in the modern context.

1292   O'Faolain, Sean. "Late Marriage in Ireland." Monat 6 (61) (Oct. 1953): 38-44.

1293   O'Hagan, John. "Irish Marriage Trends." Mgt 21 (10) (Oct. 1974): 20-21. tables.

   Statistics from the Census Report on Vital Statistics 1971 include numbers married, marriage rate, age at marriage broken down by occupatinal group. Figures reveal a significant change upwards in the last 10 years and the marriage rate at 7.4 per 1000 is the highest ever recorded in Ireland. Brief discussion.

1294   O'Hare, Aileen. Directory of Services in Ireland for the Unmarried Mother and her Child. Dublin: The Medico-Research Board, 1973. 48pp.

Covers accomodation, services - medical, social and
financial - available to the unmarried mother and legal
aspects of her status.

1295   O'Higgins, Kathleen. Marital Desertion in Dublin: An
Exploratory Study. Dublin: Economic and Social Research
Institute, 1974. 183pp. [Broadsheet Series #9.]

Presents findings of a study of marital desertion in
Dublin based on records of various agencies. Forty
respondents were interviewed. Social origin, age, social
status, courtship patterns, religion, number of children,
sex, wife's opinion of where problem occurred, source of
income after desertion, whereabouts of children are among
the factors examined. Various hypotheses for desertion
considered.

1296   O'Higgins, Kathleen. "Marriage - the Dialogue of the
Deaf." Soc Stud 2 (6) (Dec. 1973): 590-591. refs.

O'Higgins suggests that lack of real communication is a
primary factor in marriage breakdown and recommends
"education for marriage" to teach young people how to
talk and listen so that each can understand the views and
feelings of the other.

1297   O'Reilly, James. "Marital Privacy And Family Law."
Studies 66 (261) (Spring 1977): 8-24. refs.

(See Law #1566.)

1298   Park, G.K. "Sons And Lovers. Characterological
Requisites of the Roles in a Peasant/Ireland, Norway/
Society." Ethnology 1 (4) (1962): 412-424. refs.

A comparison of marriage/succession systems, sexual
morality and the institution of courtship in County Clare
(as reported by Arensberg and Kimball) and the region of
Dunderlandsdat in Northern Norway. The social structure
in the Irish setting calls only for a man to play the
role of son whereas the Norwegian youth has two role
relationships that are critically important - those of
son and lover.

1299   Pentrill, Mrs. Frank. "Old Maids." Ir Mon 13 (Aug.
1885): 42-415.

Describes the lonely lot of those women who have not
married while praising those who, resigned to their fate,
have busied themselves caring for others.

1300   Pentrill, Mrs. Frank. "Teapots and Kettles." Ir Mon 10
(Aug. 1882): 525-528.

Suggests that Irish men are frequently driven to the public house as a result of their wife's bad household management and cooking skills.

1301   Peskett, Clare and Helen Roberts. "A Pilot Study of Child-Rearing Practices Among Mothers of Young Children in Dublin." Econ Soc R 3 (2) (Jan. 1972): 277-284. tables.

Survey of mothers in hospital post-natal wards and follow-up questionnaires at home cover a range of child rearing practices categorized by social class backgrounds of parents.

1302   Power, Patrick C. Sex and Marriage in Ancient Ireland. Dublin, Cork: Mercier Press, 1976. 87pp.

In this superficial overview Power acknowledges that he is mainly dealing with post Christian Ireland because of the lack/unreliability of earlier records. His main sources are the Brehon laws for the pre-Christian period and The Synod of St. Patrick, Finnian's Penitential, etc. for the Christian era. The relative equality of women under the Brehon laws - within the family context - stressed.

1303   Prendergast, Mary Claire. (B.A. M.S.N.) "The Family That Isn't." Chr Rex 14 (Apr. 1960): 92-184.

Comments on the negative aspects of family life in Ireland with constructive suggestions as to how behavior and attitudes might be changed, principally by education.

1304   Rohan, Dorine. Marriage Irish Style. Cork: Mercier Press, 1969, 128pp.

A short summary of Irish marriage problems.

1305   Ryan, Dermot. Archbishop of Dublin. Marriage and Pastoral Care. An Invitation to Priestly Concern with Appropriate Directives, Issued by the Archbishop of Dublin to his Priests. Dublin: Diocesan Press Office, 1975. 40pp.

In this pastoral letter, the Bishop exhorts his priests to help couples realize a happy marriage. Marriage and the family are seen as the basis of society; the Catholic teaching on marriage is defined, the causes of the recent increase in marital breakdown examined.

1306   Sargent, Maud E. "How Marriages Are Made Among the Irish Peasantry: Some Curious Shrove-tide Customs." Leis Hour 4 (1905): 458-463. il.

Matchmaking activities on the eve of Lent in Munster and Connaught briefly mentioned.

1307   Scully, Lean. "The Marriage Rate in Ireland." <u>Furrow</u> 11 (Apr. 1960): 257-259.

     Brief article summarizing the proceedings of a study week-end examining the low marriage and high celibacy rates prevailing in Ireland. Causative factors in the economic position of the country and its educational system discussed.

1308   Shaw, Bernard. <u>Prefaces</u>. London: Constable and Company, 1934. 802pp.

     Preface to "Getting Married" argues Shaw's position that under existing law, marriage is distinctly preferable to any kind of illicit union but that the law needs reform. Various problems with marriage as an institution detailed. Root of problem seen as economic dependence of women on men.

1309   "She Has Eleven Children and The Eldest is Twelve." <u>Th Wk Ire</u> (Nov. 21, 1969): 4. il.

     Brief article on a Ballyfermot mother who was chosen for the Housewife of the Year award.

1310   Sheridan, John D. "A Dublin Family At Work and Play." <u>Sign</u> 36 (Mar. 1957): 18-22. il. photos.

     Profile of a typical Dublin (typical Irish) family and its lifestyle as illustrated by an actual family visited by the author in the fifties.

1311   <u>Singled Out: Single Mothers In Ireland</u>. Dublin: Women's Community Press, 1983. 52pp. il. bibl.

     A publication of Cherish, a self-help group of single mothers founded in 1972, details briefly resources available to single parents. Also suggests inadequacies of these.

1312   Smith, Elizabeth. "Working Wives' Tax - The Battle Won and Lost." <u>Image</u> 6 (4) (Apr. 1981): 55-56.

     Report on the aftermath of the 1980 Supreme Court ruling that it was unconstitutional for a married couple to pay more income tax than two single people.

1313   Somerville, E. OE. and Martin Ross. "For Richer For Poorer." <u>Cornhill Mag</u> 148 (Sept. 1933): 343-351.

     Discusses the sound business principles on which most country marriages in the South of Ireland are based and

how they more often than not make for a happiness that
love matches do not invariably achieve. Various anecdotes
regarding some examples are given.

1314   Stanislaus, Sister. "The Plight of the One Parent
Family." Cross 64 (2) (June 1973): 24-26. il.

Highlights the difficulties facing widows, unmarried
mothers and deserted wives in Irish society.

1315   Tarrant, Con. "Matchmaking in Duhallow at the Turn of
the Century." Seanchas Duthalla 4 (1980/81): 14-16. il.

A discussion of matchmaking details conventions followed
by both families in arranging the marriage of their
offspring and the role of the matchmaker.

1316   "Thumbs Down for Belfast Women's Aid." Women View 3
(Autumn 1980): 16-17. il.

Belfast Women's Aid run a hostel for battered wives but
encountered problems with the Housing Aid Association in
their efforts to enlarge their facility.

1317   Timson, Oonagh. "To Live a Normal Life." Cross 64 (2)
(June 1973): 6-7. il.

Interview with the mother of a Thalidomide child who
discusses the problems faced by her and the rest of the
family in coping with this handicapped child.

1318   University College Dublin. Department of Social
Science. Family Studies Unit. The Changing Family. Papers
presented at seminar 15th - 16th June, 1984. Dublin: Family
Studies Unit, University College, Dublin, 1984. 193pp. il.
tables. bibl.

Relevant chapters include "demographic changes and the
Irish family" (pp.1-38) and "continuity and change: the
life cycle of Irish women in the 1980's" (pp.39-57).

1319   Viney, Michael. The Broken Marriage: A Study In Depth
of a Growing Social Problem. Dublin: Irish Times, 1970.

A series of five articles originally published in the
Irish Times 26-30 October, 1970 examines the greater
incidence of broken marriages in Ireland, identifies
possible contributory causes, the problems of deserted
wives and the difficulty of enforcing maintainance
orders, or obtaining legal separation. Use of the
Guardianship of Infants Act as a means of securing a de
facto judicial separation is discussed and use by the
Irish of British divorce law.

1320   Walsh, Brendan M. "Ireland's Demographic Transformation, 1958-1970." Econ Soc R 3 (2) (Jan. 1972): 251-275.
tables. refs.

An analysis of registration statistics for births and
marriages in Ireland for period indicated. Findings
indicate a strong upward trend in the marriage rate since
1958 and especially after 1966. Birth rate peaked in 1964
and fell by 6%, 1964-1968. By 1970 had regained its 1964
peak, but this was a result of higher marriage rate.
Number of children per family continues to decline. Role
of economic and social factors in changing pattern and
future outlook discussed.

1321   Walsh, Brendan M. "Trends in Age at Marriage in Post-
War Ireland." Demography 9 (2) (May 1972): 187-202. il. refs.

This study of marriage trends in post-war Ireland
indicates that age at marriage has declined substantially
since 1946. Also, the age differential between brides and
grooms has narrrowed. The greatest age differentials are
in rural counties. Explanation of trends suggested.

1322   Walsh, Brendan. "A Study of Irish County Marriage
Rates, 1961-1966." Pop Stud 24 (2) (July 1970): 205-216. il.
refs.

A detailed examination of inter-county variation in
marriage rates in Ireland over the intercensal period,
1961-1966. Male and female rates compared and analyzed.
Findings indicate that the sex ratio plays a critical
role in the determination of Irish county marriage rates.
Role of other factors, e.g. economic conditions, female
participation in labor force, also discussed.

1323   Walsh, Dermot. "The Unmarried Mother and Her Child in
Ireland" In Conference on the Unmarried Parent and Child in
Irish Society, pp. 32-42. Dublin: Cherish, 1975. tables.
refs.

The increased incidence of illegitimate births in Ireland
- a doubling of these in the 1961-1971 period - and the
numbers of Irish women seeking abortions in England
highlight the problem examined by the Conference. The
most serious problem is the almost complete absence of
facilities to enable the unmarried mother to keep her
child and the difficulty of obtaining housing. Other
problems detailed and solutions suggested.

1324   Walsh, Laurence. "Marriage In Rural Ireland." Reality
33 (1) (Jan. 1969): 2-6. tables. portrs.

Decries the paucity of marriages in rural Ireland and the
late age at which these take place. The problem seen as

most acute in the West of Ireland, partly because of a
scarcity of girls but even where females are available,
too many men remain permanent bachelors. Discusses the
efforts of Catholic Action and the clergy to solve the
problem, notably by the organization of a Marriage
Introduction Bureau.

1325   Walsh, Susan. "The Family: A Sociological
Perspective." Soc Stud 2 (6) (Dec. 1973): 550-557. refs.

A brief consideration of the family from a functionalist
perspective sees its task as meeting the affectional,
reproductive and socialization needs of society. Changes
affecting the modern family in Ireland (more people
marrying and at earlier ages; slight decrease in average
family size; change in women's role and ideology of the
family) and future outlook briefly discussed.

1326   Wilson Davis, Keith. "Ideal Family Size in the Irish
Republic." J Biosoc Sci 12 (1) (Jan. 1980): 15-20. tables.
refs.

Reports data from a 1973 survey in which a national
sample of Irish, Roman Catholic wives aged under 44 years
had been questioned on their knowledge, attitudes and
practice of family planning and on related fertility
topics - in this case ideal family size. Irish wives have
high family size preferences; the overall mean ideal
family size being 4.3 children, significantly higher than
the ideal of Americans and West Europeans.

Human Sexuality, Reproduction
and Health

This section contains material on female sexuality, reproduction, fertility — including the relationship of this to socio-economic and religious factors — family planning and health. Also includes the statements of official religious positions on issues of abortion/birth control. Some general studies on population patterns including fertility are grouped here and cross referenced to other relevant areas, such as MARRIAGE AND THE FAMILY, etc. Studies which are primarily medical treatises on female diseases have been excluded. Legal aspects of contraception and abortion, including material on the recent Anti-Abortion Amendment will be found under LAW. Additional material on women's psychological functions will be found in the section on PSYCHOLOGY.

1327   Aalen, F.H.A. "A Review of Recent Irish Population Trends." Pop Stud 17 (1) (July 1963): 73-78. refs. tables.

Overview of 20th century demographic trends in Ireland with detailed analysis of the latest Census figures (1961). High emigration, low marriage rate, late age at marriage, high fertility combined to produce an average rate of natural increase (by European standards) and an overall decline in population. Regional differences, especially urban/rural contrasts in male/female sex ratio, marriage and fertility rates, age at marriage, migration patterns and overall population loss analyzed.

1328   Aberdeen, (Countess). "The Sphere of Women in Relation to Public Health." Dublin J Med Sci CXXXII(477) 3rd series. (Sept. 1, 1911): 161-170.

The Presidential Address to the Health Congress held in Dublin under the auspices of the Royal Institute of Public Health treats the founding of the Women's National

Health Association in Ireland and their central role in combating tuberculosis. Makes a case for University courses in health and home economics for women.

1329   Abortion Now. <Produced by Life Education and Research Network ...> Dublin: Life Education and Research Network, 1983. 93pp. bibl.

Presents arguments justifying the need for specific anti-abortion legislation.

1330   Ahearne, P. (Rev.) "The Confessor and the Ogino-Knaus Theory." Ir Eccl Rec 5th Ser. LXI (Jan. 1943): 1-14. refs.

An outline of working principles to be applied by the Catholic clergyman when counseling in the confessional on use of the infertile or "safe" period within marriage.

1331   Alert: Oral Contraception. Dublin: Irish Family League. [ca 1975] 14pp.

Medical hazards of the contraceptive pill presented in alarmist terms. Also discussion of the immorality of artificial contraception.

1332   Anderson, Barbara A. "Male Age and Fertility: Results From Ireland Prior to 1911." Pop Index 41(4) (Oct.1975): 561-566. tables. refs.

An analysis of the effect of male age on fertility patterns utilized data from the Census of Ireland 1911 (Ireland, 1913). Findings indicate that the age of husband did affect fertility showing a pattern of almost linear decline after 45. Others factors which might be associated with age of husband and with a downward influence on fertility are noted and the dangers of generalizing data to other populations.

1333   Bark, N. "Fertility and Offspring of Alcoholic Women - Unsuccessful Search for the Fetal Alcohol Syndrome." Brit J Addict 74 (1) (1979): 43-49. tables. refs.

Reports results of a study designed to test the Fetal Alcohol Syndrome. Forty married women in a psychiatric hospital in Dublin diagnosed as alcoholics were compared with a control group matched by age who had been diagnosed as suffering from endogenous depression. No significant differences were found in the fertility, outcome of pregnancy or state of the children. Probable reasons for this finding e.g. age at which mother became an alcoholic briefly discussed and the implications for future research.

1334   Barnes, J. "Psychosexual Problems and Infertility." Ir J Med Sci 148 (51) (1979): 6-10. tables. refs.

The author, on the staff of the Catholic Marriage Advisory Council in Dublin, details the modus operandi of a sexual dysfunction clinic in Dublin. Also discussed is the aetiology and treatment of vaginismus and results of a study of 30 vaginismic women presented.

1335   Barwin, B. Norman. "Pregnancy in the Unmarried Mother." Ulster Med J 39 (Part 2) (1970): 143-146. tables. refs.

A study designed to assess all the cases of illegitimate births during 1969 in two maternity hospitals in Belfast compared these with a control group of 150 married primigravida during the same period. Three major obstetrical problems were identified: the unmarried group had higher incidence of pre-eclampsia, anaemia and prematurity rates; also perinatal and neonatal mortality was considerably higher in the unmarried group. Social implications of these findings briefly considered.

1336   Bates, Tom. "Contraception: a Straight Answer to the Bishops." Church & State 1 (4) (Summer 1974): 20-23.

Comment — polemical in tone — on position of Irish Bishops on the issue of contraception. While still maintaining that contraception is morally wrong and would be even if use should be legalized, Bishops no longer maintain that the Irish government can not morally make these legally available. Bates agrees with the Bishops' position that the issue of contraception is a public as well as a private concern but he disagrees with their arguments on the deleterious social effects of widespread contraceptive use.

1337   "Bishops and Family Planning." Magill Mag 2 (4) (Jan. 1979): 21. portrs.

A note on the latest position of the Irish Bishops Conference on the issue of family planning legislation contrasts this with the tone and emphasis of previous statements by the hierarchy on this issue.

1338   Blake, Carla. The Irish Mother's Baby Book. Dublin: The Mercier Press, 1974. 135pp. il.

A practical manual about pregnancy and the everyday life and requirements of a baby from birth to about four years. Written by a mother and a registered nurse.

1339   Blaney, Roger and Inge S. Radford. "The Prevalence of Alcoholism in an Irish town." J Stud Alcohol 34 (4A) (Dec.1973): 1255-1269. il. refs.

Interviews with 181 male and 179 female residents of Larne, Northern Ireland aged 18 years and over revealed that 82% of the men and 59% of the women drink. However none of those (3.6%) who scored high on the Mulford and Miller's 1960, Preoccupation with Alcohol Scale were women, 12.7% had low scores on this test and 83.7% had no preoccupation. The reproducibility of the methodology and its ability to detect alcoholism are discussed.

1340   Boland, Hazel G. (M.D.) "Rape and How to Avoid it." Image 3 (3) (Feb. 1978): 10-11. il.

Comment on the increased incidence of rape in Irish society and ways to avoid it.

1341   Bond, C.J. "Eugenics and Bernard Shaw." Eugenics R 21 (July 1929): 159-161.

(See Marriage and the Family #1208.)

1342   Bowman, Eimer Philbin. "Sexual and Contraceptive Attitudes and Behaviour of Single Attenders at a Dublin Family Planning Clinic." J Biol Sci 9 (4) (Oct.1977): 429-445. il. refs.

A preliminary breakdown of the characteristics of all new attenders at a Dublin family planning clinic during the first six months of 1974 showed that just under half of those attenders were unmarried at the time of their first visit. Of these, three in five planned to marry shortly and two in five had no marriage plans. A sample of 50 of these single women not then planning to marry were interviewed. Data are presented on their family and educational backgrounds, their sexual and contraceptive behaviour and their attitudes to related issues.

1343   Brahimi, Michele. "Nuptialite et Fecondite des Mariages en Irlande." Pop 33 (3) (June 1978): 663-703. (English summary.) charts. tables.

A detailed study of marriage and fertility patterns in Ireland indicates that while at the beginning of the century Ireland demonstrated a unique demographic profile in Europe characterized by a low marriage rate and a late age at marriage, today the differences are much less pronounced although nuptiality is still slightly lower than in other parts of Europe while marital fertility still remains relatively higher despite a general decline in the decade 1960-1970.

1344   Brennan, Pat. "Blacklash and Blackmail: How a Tiny Catholic Pressure Group Privately Won a Commitment to a Constitutional Amendment on Abortion." Magill Mag 5 (10) (July 1982): 14-24. il.

Background on the introduction of the constitutional amendment outlawing abortion in Ireland passed in the Fall of 1983. Identifies the various groups who conducted the pro-Amendment campaign.

1345   Brennan, Pat. "The Family Planning Clinics." Magill Mag 2 (9) (1979): 4-5. il.

A discussion of the negative impact of the proposed Family Planning Bill on the operation of these clinics.

1346   Brooker, David and A. Douglas Roy. "Breast Disease in Women Under Thirty: Ten Year Review and Assessment of Clinical Screening." Ulster Med J (Belfast) 51 (2): 151-160. tables. refs.

Reports results of a study designed to evaluate breast screening in women under the age of 30 and to relate this to the incidence of breast biopsy in hospital practice. Records of all women who had undergone surgery in the Royal Victorian Hospital 1970-1979 were assessed and information was also collected from women seen at screening clinics 1978-1980.

1347   Campbell, Flann and Mary Campbell. "Society at Work: Ireland's Durex Politics." New Soc 17 (452) (May 27, 1971): 913-914.

This article discusses the issue of birth control in Ireland and the growing volume of organized lay agitation against the official Catholic and Government positions on this issue. The different pressures on both the Church and the Government to rethink their positions analyzed.

1348   Carr, C.J. "A Family-Planning Survey." J Ir Med Assoc 73 (9) (1980): 340-341. tables.

Report of a survey of patients attending the public and private ante-natal booking clinics in Portiuncula, County Galway during the period November 1979 - February 1980. Respondents were queried as to the intentionality of their pregnancy, their method of family planning and pill usage. Results suggest that many of these couples attempting to plan their families are not succeeding while over one third are not planning at all.

1349   "The Characteristics and Responses to Treatment of Female Patients Under Forty-five Admitted to Holywell Hospital on Account of Depressive Symptoms." J Ir Med Assoc LXIII (1970): 290-292. tables.

A retrospective study utilizing case records and follow up interviews of all female patients under 45 normally resident in North and South Antrim hospitalized during

the period March 1, 1968 to February 28, 1969. Purpose of
the study to distinguish psychological from physiological
depressions; to discover the presence of environmental
stresses and their nature and to evaluate previous
treatment. Findings include a high incidence of
psychological depression; a large percentage had previous
hospital admissions, a high representation of social
classes IV and V and a high incidence of marital discord.

1350   Churchill, Fleetwood (Dr.) Obstetric Morality Being a
Reply to an Article in No.LXXXVII of the Dublin Review.
Dublin: H.M. Gill, 1858. 24pp. refs.

Author disagrees with the theological and obstetrical
reasoning of the author of the earlier article who had
argued that the operation of craniotomy under any
circumstances is immoral if the child is alive. (See
#1432.) Churchill presents moral, theological and
obstetrical arguments to support his opinion.

1351   Cleary, M.P. (Rev.) "The Church of Ireland and Birth
Control." Ir Eccl Rec 38 (768) (Dec. 1931): 622-629. refs.

Strong statement of condemnation by an Irish Catholic
priest of the action of the Lambeth Conference in
accepting birth control as permissable in certain cases.
Singled out for special denunciation are the 13 Irish
Bishops who participated in that Conference and have not
disassociated themselves from its position.

1352   Coffey, Victoria. "Maternal Influenza and Congenital
Deformities. A Prospective Study." Lancet 2 (1970) (Nov. 28,
1959): 935-938. tables. refs.

During the 1957-58 epidemic of Asian influenza in Dublin
663 pregnant women attending antenatal clinics in the
three maternity hospitals stated that they had had
influenza during their pregnancy. The incidence of
congenital deformities in the children born to these
women was 2.4 times that in the children of the control
group. The abnormalities were almost entirely of the
central nervous system; the commonest was anencephaly.

1353   Compton, Paul A. "An Evaluation of the Changing
Religious Composition of the Population of Northern Ireland."
Econ Soc R 16 (3) (Apr. 1985): 201-224. tables. refs.

Because of the rapid growth of the number of Catholics in
recent decades these now (1981) make up 38% of the
population in Northern Ireland in contrast to a former
33%. If trend continued Catholics would attain majority
status but declining Catholic fertility and a lower rate
of natural increase prevent this.

1354   Compton, P.A. "Fertility Differentials and Their
Impact on Population Distribution and Composition in Northern
Ireland." Environ & Plan 10 (12) (Dec. 1978): 1397-1411. il.
refs.

Describes the geographical variability of fertility in
Northern Ireland and its relationship to the factors of
religious denomination, social class and proportion of
the population married. Internal migration is seen as
more important than natural increase in changing
population patterns.

1355   Compton, P.A. and F.W. Boal. "Aspects of the
Intercommunity Population Balance in Northern Ireland." Econ
Soc R 1 (4) (July 1970) 455-476. il. refs.

An attempt to establish the existing and likely future
proportions of Protestants and Catholics in the
population of Northern Ireland. Differentials in
fertility and migration of both groups examined and
implications of findings for the political future of the
province discussed.

1356   Compton, Paul A., Lorna Goldstrom and J.M. Goldstrom.
"Religion and Legal Abortion in Northern Ireland." J Biol Sci
6 (4) (Oct. 1974): 493-500. il.

Details the results of a study of 522 women who sought
abortion through the Ulster Pregnancy Advisory
Association between January 1971 and August 1973.
Analysis of the religious factor indicates that the
incidence of abortion among Roman Catholics seems to be
remarkably high and it is expected that it will rise
still further in both relative and absolute terms.

1357   Condron, Mary (ed.) Abortion: The Tragic Dilemma.
Dublin: Student Christian Movement Pamphlet No.37, 1979.
23pp.

Brief outline of the history of abortion and
contraception. Presents some statistics on the incidence
of abortion in Ireland.

1358   Connell, Kenneth H. "The Land Legislation and Irish
Social Life!" Econ Hist R 2nd Series XI (1) (1958): 1-7.
(Substantially the text of the Thomas Davis lecture broadcast
by Radio Eireann on St. Patrick's Day, 1957.)

A popular restatement of the author's points about
population patterns in Ireland. Pre-famine jump in
population attributed to early marriage patterns and a
potato diet, a result of landlord exploitation of
peasantry and subdivision of holdings. By the end of the
century this pattern replaced by the "match." Principle
factors in the change were the famine, land legislation

and related factors.

1359   Connell, Kenneth H. The Population of Ireland. 1750-1845. Oxford: The Clarendon Press, 1950. 293pp. tables. refs.

This study measures the rate of population growth in Ireland in the century and a half before the Famine and examines factors responsible for the steep expansion in the rate of growth beginning in the 1770's. This seen as mainly due to a rising birth and fertility rate, the outcome of a preference for large families and a trend towards early marriage. Agricultural and economic factors responsible for these trends analyzed; also, the causes of regional variations.

1360   Cooney, John. "Contraception in God's Green Isle." Commonweal 100 (May 24, 1974): 276-277.

Brief discussion of the issue of birth control in the Republic of Ireland. Recent legal and political developments and future prospects examined.

1361   Courtney, Angela. "The Feminist Case Against Abortion." Scope 45 (1981): 9-10. refs.

Feminist case against abortion argues that this escalates the pressures on young girls to be sexually compliant. Feminists should fight for self-determination for all women at the personal level.

1362   Cousens, S.H. "Population Trends in Ireland at the Beginning of the 20th Century." Ir Geo 5 (5) (1968): 387-401. maps. graphs. refs.

This article reviews the major outlines of the regional variations in population trends in Ireland for the 19th century. Change and continuity of these trends in the early years of the 20th century examined and causes and consequences discussed.

1363   Cousens, S.H. "The Regional Variation in Population Changes in Ireland, 1861-1881." Econ Hist R 2nd Series. 17 (2) (Dec. 1964): 301-321. il. refs.

Cousens' findings indicate that regional variation in natural increase dominated the pattern of population change. Natural increase was much greater in the West than in the East. These regional differences in natural increase were largely the result of remarkable variation in the degree of celibacy and the age of marriage which were to some extent connected with the availability of land. Marriage was most restricted where the standard of living was higher. Unlike Connell, Cousens sees regional

variation as of long standing and not a post Famine
phenomena e.g. areas of early and numerous marriages
persisted with areas of late and few marriages.

1364   Coward, John. "Recent Characteristics of Roman
Catholic Fertility in Northern and Southern Ireland." Pop
Stud 34 (1) (1980): 31-44. tables. refs.

   An examination of post 1961 Census vital registration
   figures to investigate differences in fertility patterns
   of Catholics in Northern Ireland versus those in the
   Republic and the relative influence on those of various
   socio-economic factors, especially minority status. The
   findings indicate that fertility is high, by Western
   European standards for both North and South; in addition
   both groups have experienced broadly similar changes
   since 1961 with declines in marital fertility and
   increases in nuptiality for similar reasons. However, the
   fertility rates of Catholics in Northern Ireland are
   slightly higher than that of Catholics in the Republic
   and this is attributed to their minority status.

1365   Coward, John. "Regional Variations in Family Size in
the Republic of Ireland." J Biosoc Sci 12 (1) (1980): 1-14.
maps. graphs. tables. refs.

   Data from the Census Fertility Reports are used to
   investigate social and regional variations in family size
   in the Republic of Ireland. Average family size declined
   by approximately 10% between 1946 and 1971. There are
   distinct socioeconomic variations in family size with
   religion and class key variables. There are also marked
   regional differences in family size. These can be
   influenced by a variety of factors such as differences in
   religious affiliation, infant mortality and the degree of
   selection through emigration, but are most strongly
   affected by economic and occupational changes.

1366   Coward, John. "Changes in the Pattern of Fertility in
the Republic of Ireland." Tijd Schrift Voor Economische en
Sociale Geografie. J Econ & Soc Geo 69 (6) (1978): 353-361.
il. maps. tables. bibl. refs.

   An examination of regional variations in fertility in
   Ireland for 1926 to 1976 using Census data sees the high
   level of Irish fertility as essentially a product of high
   rates of marital fertility and that compared with England
   and Wales, proportions married are relatively small. Over
   the period of study there has been a general increase in
   fertility as a result of increases in proportions married
   outweighing declines in marital fertility. The spatial
   pattern of high overall fertility has changed markedly
   during the last fifty years - relationship of this with
   occupational and religious structure of the population
   and variation in the incidence of family limitation are

analyzed and future trends predicted.

1367   Coward, John. "Family Planning Clinics in the Republic
of Ireland." Ir Geo 16 (1978): 186-190. maps. tables.

An overview of the confused situation regarding family
planning in Ireland. Notes that while the advertising and
sale of contraceptives are prohibited, importation of
these for personal use has been permissable since 1973.
Two family planning clinics were opened in Dublin in 1970
and 1972 under the auspices of the Fertility Guidance
Council followed by the creation in 1973 of Family
Planning Services, an organization specializing in the
distribution of contraceptives by post. Data on number,
characteristics and spatial distribution of persons using
these services presented.

1368   Cullen, Mary and Terri Morrissey. Women and Health:
Some Current Issues. Dublin: Women's Studies Unit, Irish
Foundation for Human Development, 1985. 104pp. il. tables.

A two part report relates available data on Irish women's
lives, occupations and health to current findings and
concerns in the literature on health. The second part of
the report concentrates on issues pertaining specifically
to women's mental health.

1369   Dalen, Per. "Maternal Age and Incidence of
Schizophrenia in the Republic of Ireland." Brit J Psych 131
(Sept. 1977): 301-305. refs.

Detailed results of a survey of studies that show a high
incidence of schizophrenia in Ireland discussed. Maternal
age at birth seen as the major explanatory variable.

1370   Dean, Geoffrey. Termination of Pregnancy, England
1983, Women From the Republic of Ireland. Dublin:
Medico-Social Research Board, 1984. 33 leaves. tables.

Pilot study by Medico-Social Research Board to
ascertain in greater detail than previously available
characteristics of Irish women seeking abortions in
England. Based on a survey of nursing homes and referral
agencies and interviews with women all giving Irish
residences. Characteristics include social class, use of
contraception, age groups, area of residence, marital
status. Study to be continued in 1984 and findings to be
compared with data on these Irish unmarried mothers who
elected to have their children.

1371   Devane, R.S. (Rev.) S.J. "The Dance Hall." Ir Eccl Rec
5th Series 37 (Feb. 1931): 170-194.

The author presents his case for control of the dance
hall citing the moral dangers these present (located in
isolated places, run without supervision, open to all,
near public houses). Suggests that immorality is a
logical outgrowth and cites the increased incidence of
unwed motherhood, and infanticide as reported in the
daily press. Points out that precedent exists for
licensing inspection and urges that Irish Public Bodies
exert this control. Suggests conditions for dance hall
licenses.

1372   Dooley, Maurice (Rev.) "Contraception and the Irish
Constitution." Soc Stud 3 (3) (June 1974): 286-315. refs.

This article by a Catholic clergyman questions the
Supreme Court's interpretation of the Constitution which
allowed it in the McGee Case to legalize the importation
of contraceptives. Possible implications and consequences
of this decision analyzed.

1373   Drake, Michael. "Marriage and Population Growth in
Ireland, 1750- 1845." Econ Hist R 2nd Series 16 (2) (Dec.
1963): 301-313. il. refs.

A response to and critique of Dr. K.H. Connell's studies
in Irish population history. Essentially Drake challenges
Connell's conclusions regarding the early age at marriage
before the Famine and its role in bringing about rapid
population growth. His objections center on the accuracy
of Connell's sources (mainly literary rather than
statistical) and assumptions based on these. Drake
suggests a reinterpretation of Irish population history
for this period is needed and suggests possible areas for
research. (For comments and critique see Lee, J. #1409.)

1374   Dreifus, C. "Ireland: Saved From an Epidemic of
Fornication? The Great Contraceptive Debate." MS 3
(Feb.1975): 19. il.

Brief note on the Supreme Court Decision in the McGee
case to legalize the importation of contraceptives into
the Republic of Ireland. Failure of the Government to
pass a limited measure designed to permit sale of these
to married couples briefly discussed.

1375   Dupaquier, Jacques. "Les Aventures Demographiques
Compares de la France et de l'Irlande." Annales 33 (1)
(Jan.-Feb. 1978): 143-155. tables. refs. [English summary
p.202]

Presents comparative demographic circumstances in France
and Ireland during the period 18th to 20th century.
Analysis of data on emigration, fertility and celibacy in
Ireland before and after the Great Famine and in France

before and after the Revolution.

1376   "Durex Politics." Economist 242 (Feb. 19, 1972):
37-38.

Discussion of the arguments pro and con for the private
members' bill introduced in the Dail which would permit
the sale of contraceptives in Ireland and the circulation
of advice on family planning. The majority of the
deputies voted against the proposed measure.

1377   "Editorial." Magill Mag 5 (10) (July 1982): 4.

Argues that the proposed constitutional amendment on
abortion has very little to do with the actual issue of
abortion but a great deal to do with re-asserting the
Catholic nature of the Irish State and reversing recent
trends towards a pluralist society.

1378   Eithne. "Retreats for Working Girls." Ir Mon 51
(1923): 324-330.

"Boy-mad" working class girls deplored. Possible remedies
considered include education, recreation, and religious
instruction. The latter seen as most viable alternative
and enclosed retreats advocated.

1379   Family Planning. A Guide for Parents and Prospective
Parents. Dublin: Fertility Guidance Co., Ltd. [n.d.] 16pp.

Outlines the various methods of contraception with a
discussion of their relative effectiveness and
suggestions as to how to choose the most suitable
approach. Includes a list of centers offering advice on
family planning.

1380   "Family Planning in Galway." Fortn R No. 128 (June 4,
1976): 5.

Brief news item on activities of anti-family planning
lobby in Galway.

1381   Family Planning for Ulster: Conference Held in the
Conway Hotel, Dunmurry, Co. Antrim on Friday, May 31st 1968.
Sponsored by Ortho Pharmaceutical Ltd. Bristol: Wright, 1969.
72pp. il. portrs.

Speakers at the Conference focused on family planning as
a public health service, the need for marriage guidance,
organization and operation of family planning clinics,
and client counseling.

1382   Fennell, Nuala. "Contraception: The Facts After the
Act." Image 6 (1) (Jan. 1981): 47-50. portr.

The practical implications of the Health, Family Planning
Act of 1979 are discussed.

1383   Fertility Guidance Co. Ltd. Education Committee.
Family Planning: A Guide for Parents and Prospective Parents.
Dublin: Family Planning Services. [1977] 16pp.

Discusses the various methods of family planning and the
relative efficacy of these. Includes a directory of
counseling services.

1384   Fitzgerald, Barbara. "The Image Makers." Status 6 (2)
(Apr. 1981): 14-20. il.

General information on types, costs, risks of cosmetic
surgery available to Irish women in either Ireland or
England with some case histories.

1385   Flannery, Austin. Abortion and the Law. (A Doctrine
and Life Special) Dublin: Dominian Pub., 1983. 74pp.

Statements from the Irish and English hierarchies,
articles on medical ethics and pro and con abortion
statements from other contributors.

1386   Freedman, D. and others. "Sexually Transmitted
Diseases Seen by General Practitioners in Ireland - Use of a
Telephone Survey." Sex Transm Dis 8 (1) (1981): 5-7. tables.
refs.

Reports the results of a telephone survey of a sample of
general practitioners in Ireland during July 1978 for the
purpose of establishing the frequency of diagnosis of
venereal disease during the preceding year. The national
frequency (per 100,000 population) was estimated to be
7.7 for syphilis, 97 for gonorrhea and 2000 for
nonspecific venereal diseases. The disproportionate
male-to-female ratio of cases seen by physicians is
considered to be associated with underreporting and may
indicate a higher endeminity of disease than that
suggested by the data. However the incidence of sexually
transmitted diseases in the Irish Republic is relatively
low.

1387   Friel, Brian. "Sex in Ireland." Critic 30 (Mar.- Apr.
1972): 20-21.

Comments on sexual attitudes and behavior in Ireland by
the well known playwright.

1388   Geary, R.C. "Irish Population Prospects Considered
from the Viewpoint of Reproduction Rates." Stat & Soc Inq Soc
J 16 (1940-41): 91-122. tables. refs. appendix. (Read before
the Society March 1941.)

The primary purpose of this paper is to revise and
elaborate, using 1936 Census data, prognostics of
population made by the author in 1935. The significance
of gross and net reproduction rates are examined from a
theoretical and practical viewpoint. Geary also computes
gross reproduction rates for each Census year back to
1871 and the rates for different areas of the country in
1935-1937 are compared. He offers three series of
prognostics based on a detailed analysis of trends in
births, deaths and emigration. Comments on Dr. Geary's
paper included.

1389   Greer, Angela E. "Family Planning in Northern
Ireland." Fam Plan 11 (2) (July 1962): 40-43. tables.

Report of a survey carried out in two areas of Belfast
in 1961 to discover the extent of knowledge about methods
of family limitation. In the general practice area on the
outskirts of Belfast, a random sample of 100 married
women under 51 were chosen; information about the clinic
attendees in the city was extracted from a sample of
records. Findings indicate a high incidence of
contraceptive knowledge and practical use of
contraception but indicate that there is still an unmet
need in the community for more information on this
subject.

1390   Greer, H.L. and others. A Report on an Enquiry into
Maternal Deaths in Northern Ireland, 1960-1963. Ministry of
Health And Social Services. Belfast: H.M. Stationery Office,
1965. 41pp. graphs. tables.

An examination of causes of all deaths of women in
Northern Ireland which occurred during pregnancy or
childbirth for the years indicated. There were 63 such
deaths. Includes details of avoidable factors in these
deaths and lists the categories of persons who appear to
have been responsible. The report notes a reduction in
such deaths from an earlier study covering the years
1956-1959.

1391   Grogan, Richard. "Our Doctors Dither, Our Laws
Discriminate." This Week Ire (Nov. 7, 1969): 21-23+. il.

A three part article on birth control in Ireland
discusses doctors' ambivalence about prescribing the pill
as a result of the Papal Encyclical, current legislation
in this area, actual practice, and the operation of the
Fertility Guidance Clinic in Dublin.

1392   Hall, Richard. "Progress at Last." Hew Humanist 89
(April 1974): 44-406. il.

An account of two recent court cases which, it is
claimed, auger well for the ultimate legal availability
of contraceptives in the Republic of Ireland. Discussion
of factors which have contributed to the new climate of
opinion.

1393   Harper, K.W. "Maternal, Infant and Social Factors
Associated With Birthweight." Ulster Med J 45 (2) (1976):
210-215. tables. refs.

Data on all singleton livebirths in the Royal Maternity
Hospital, Belfast from January 1st 1974 until May 31st
1974 were analyzed. Age, height, parity, religion and
social class of the mother were among the factors
significantly associated with birthweight. Implications
of findings discussed.

1394   Hayes, John. "Aspects of the World Population
Problem." Soc Stud 3 (3) (1974): 229-253. refs.

An analysis of the world population problem in terms
of (1) causes, (2) dimensions, (3) socio-scientific
approaches to the problem, (4) population policies and
(5) ethics and population. The situation in Ireland
considered briefly under these various categories.

1395   Herity, Bernadette A. and others. "A Study of Breast
Cancer in Irish Women." Brit J Prev Soc Med 29 (3) (Sept.
1975): 178-181. tables. refs.

A random sample of 100 breast cancer patients attending
St. Luke's Hospital, Dublin were compared with 200
control patients during the period 1972-1973. Main
finding: an excess of nonparous women among cases as
compared to controls was not observed. Possible
explanations for this unusual finding discussed; also
findings regarding breast cancer and other variables e.g.
socioeconomic status, marital status, age at marriage, at
first pregnancy, natural menarche, hysterectomy, etc.

1396   "Ireland: Emigration and Education." Round Tab 45
(1954): 64-68.

Commentary on the report of the Commission on Emigration
and Population Problems appointed in 1948 "to investigate
the causes and consequences of the present level and
trend in population and to consider the desirability of
formulating a national population policy." Findings of
the Commission and other factors involved in the
demographic picture discussed.

1397   "Irish Bishops' Conference on the Proposed Legislation
Dealing With Family Planning, Contraception." L'Osservatore
Romano (Weekly edition) (Apr. 27, 1978): 11. (Statement
issued Apr. 4, 1978.)

    States Catholic Church's position on above issues: not
    opposed to family planning as such but use of artificial
    contraceptives is viewed as morally wrong. While it does
    not follow from this that the Irish State is therefore
    bound to prohibit the distribution and sale of
    contraceptives legalization would affect the moral tone
    of the society and lead to a lowering of standards of
    sexual morality.

1398   "Irish Rebellion." Newsweek 77 (June 7, 1971): 65. il.

    News item on women's demonstration in favour of
    legalization of contraceptives in Ireland.

1399   Johnson, James H. "Population Changes in Ireland.
1951- 1961." Geo J 129 (2) (June 1963): 167-174. il. refs.

    An analysis of 1961 preliminary Census reports of both
    Northern Ireland and the Republic of Ireland. Northern
    Ireland had a population of 1,425,000 which was the
    highest recorded since 1851; in the Republic of Ireland
    there were 2,815,000 people, the smallest number ever
    enumerated. Rural- urban and regional variation in
    population analyzed; also role and causes of emigration
    and varying patterns of natural increase.

1400   Johnson, James H. "Marriage and Fertility in 19th
Century Londonderry." Stat & Soc Inq Soc J 20 (1) (1957-58):
99-117. maps.

    Data from Census figures from 1841 to 1901 examined for
    the county of Londonderry and Ireland as a whole.
    Findings indicate a drop in the population of married
    women of fertile age in the population of 19th century
    Londonderry occuring particularly between 1841 and 1851
    and again 1881-1900. Except for these periods fertility
    remained stable but with considerable regional variation
    in the country as a whole. Causes of these findings
    analyzed.

1401   Kammeyer, K.C.W. "The Dynamics of Population." In
Irish History and Culture. ed. by H. Orel, pp.189-223.
Witchita, Kansas: University Press, 1976.

    A discussion of demographic patterns in Ireland during
    the last two centuries. Various explanations of the rapid
    growth of population in the 18th century and the
    subsequent decline after 1841 evaluated. The role of late
    marriage, permanent celibacy and emigration in this
    decline stressed.

1402   Kaser, Clyde V. "Current Mating and Fertility Trends."
Eugenics Q 6 (2) (June 1959): 66-69. il. refs.

Describes recent trends in and current patterns of mating
and fertility in modern Western countries. Ireland has
the lowest proportions married among women under 25. The
fertility rates of the women who do get married, however,
outrank those of any other country in the Western world.
Causes of findings briefly discussed.

1403   Kennedy, Robert E. Jr. "Minority Group Status and
Fertility; the Irish." Am Sociol R 38 (1) (1973): 85-96. il.
refs.

This study compares the fertility of Catholics in
Northern Ireland where they are the minority with that of
Catholics in the Republic of Ireland where they are the
majority and makes a similar comparison of the fertility
of nonCatholics in the two parts of Ireland. He suggests
that minority group status can exert an independent
effect on fertility under certain specific circumstances.
Even when these circumstances exist as they do in
Northern Ireland the impact of minority group status on
fertility is less important than such factors as
religion, rural/urban residence or the selective impact
of migration.

1404   Kennedy, Robert E. Jr. "The Social Status of the Sexes
and Their Relative Mortality Rates in Ireland." In Readings
in Population ed. by William Petersen, pp.121-135. New York:
MacMillan, 1972. tables. refs.

An examination of male and female mortality rates in
Ireland over the last century which is seen to illustrate
how male dominance is associated with relatively high
female mortality, a linkage that before the 20th century
may have been common in some European societies. In
Ireland these social customs sustaining male dominance
persisted into the mid-20th century.

1405   Kennedy, Robert E. Jr. and Edward E. McKenna.
"Commentary and Debate: 'Marriage and Fertility in Post-
Famine Ireland': A Comment on McKenna's Interpretations." Am
J Sociol 81 (2) (Sept. 1975): 413-415. il. refs. (Note reply
415-416.)

Kennedy takes issue with McKenna's interpretations of
marriage and fertility patterns in post Famine Ireland
claiming that McKenna does not explain why the sex ratio
was so closely tied to male marriage patterns or why the
ratio itself should have changed during the period.
Kennedy explains the change in the sex ratio as the
result of a relative worsening of female mortality and
more importantly, a greater out-migration of single
females from rural areas.

1406   Kenny, Mary. "Is This the End of the Change of Life?"
Image 1 (10) (July 1976): 27-28+.

    Discussion of physiological and psychological effects of
    the menopause.

1407   Kilpatrick, S.J., J.D. Mathers and A.C. Stevenson.
"The Importance of Population Fertility and Consaguinity Data
Being Available in Medico-Social Studies." Ulster Med J 24
(1955): 113-122. tables.

    Presents arguments in favour of accumulation of data on
    fertility and "inbreeding" in the population of Northern
    Ireland. Such data seen as essential for population
    genetic studies. Also presents some data on prevailing
    consanguineous marriage rates in Northern Ireland.

1408   Knaggs, J.F. "Natality in Dublin in the Year 1955."
Stat & Soc Inq Soc J 20 (1) (1957-58): 37-55. tables. refs.

    The author explains the modification made in 1955 in the
    system of recording births. He presents and discusses
    such data as month of occurrence, age at maternity, order
    of birth, duration of marriage, social group, place of
    occurrence, exnuptial births, etc. The increase in births
    recorded in 1955 are seen to be a result of an increase
    in the relevant population (e.g. women of child-bearing
    age) and not a reflection of higher fertility, per se.
    His findings indicate a slight rise in average age at
    marriage over the 1945-1955 interval; also that Irish
    women have more children than in other countries.

1409   Lee, Joseph. "Marriage and Population in Pre-Famine
Ireland." Econ Hist R 21 (2) (Aug.1968): 283-295. tables.
refs.

    Analysis of Dr. Michael Drake's critique of Dr. K.H.
    Connell's interpretation of pre-famine Irish population
    history. (See item #1373.) Lee agrees with Drake's main
    conclusion that median age at marriage in the 1830's was
    higher than hitherto accepted but challenges most of his
    other conclusions.

1410   "Life Expectancy in Ireland and Comparison With Other
Countries." Pub Health Rept 47 (23) (June 3, 1932): 1248-
1250. charts. tables.

    Comparative figures for male and female life expectancy
    in Ireland, the United States, England, Wales and Germany
    for the years 1911 and 1926. Ireland has a distinctive
    pattern in being the only country where the female life
    expectancy was not higher than the male. For Irish
    females life expectancy is one and one half to two years
    lower at birth than in any of the other countries.

1411   Lukianowicz, N. "Suicidal Behaviour: An Attempt to
Modify the Environment." Psychiatr Clin 6 (3) (1973):
171-190. refs.

A comparative study of 91 women who were admitted to a
psychiatric hospital in Antrim, Northern Ireland in 1971
following a suicide attempt and another group of 100
female patients treated in the same hospital after a
suicidal attempt in 1962 and 1963. Findings suggest that
the incidence of suicidal attempts has almost doubled in
the last decade, that drugs are more heavily used in the
attempts and with the exception of psychotic patients,
suicidal behavior in both groups was goal and gain
directed and aimed at changing the environment to the
patient's benefit.

1412   McCarthy, Desmond P. and Dermot Walsh. "Suicide in
Dublin." Brit Med J No. 55 (June 4, 1966): 1393-1396. maps.
tables. refs.

A study of suicide in Dublin over the 10 year period
1954-1963 based on coroners records. Data on 315 cases
analyzed by age and sex distribution, area of residence
and social status, time of year, method and causes. A
mean annual suicide rate of 4.5 per 1000 population was
established. At all ages male rate exceeded the female
rate. Rates were highest in the central city areas -
regions of low social cohesion.

1413   MacKay, D.N. "Mental Subnormality in Northern
Ireland." J Ment Defic Res 15 (12) (1971): 12-19. tables.
refs.

A prevalence study of mental subnormality in Northern
Ireland based on the registers of the three Management
Committees at the end of 1968 revealed that in a general
population of 1,502,000 there were 6,117 ascertained
subnormals - e.g. 4.07 per 1,000. Of these 3,253 were
male and 2,864 female. Twenty two percent were under 14
years of age. Approximately one in three were in
residential care. Between the ages of 35 and 54 female
subnormals outnumber males and their prevalence rates are
higher. In all the other age groups (except 70+) the
prevalence rates for males exceed those for females.

1414   McKenna, Edward E. "Marriage and Fertility in Post-
Famine Ireland: A Multivariate Analysis." Am J Sociol 80 (3)
(1974): 688-705. il. refs.

Using data from the Censuses of 1851, 1871, 1891 and
1911 and a multivariate regression analysis this study
tests Connell's theory of post-famine demographic trends
in Ireland which links declining fertility and declining
marriage rates. The theory further ties declining
marriage rates to economic hardship. McKenna's
conclusions are that the theory is only marginally

successful in explaining marriage-rate variations among the counties of Ireland; also, that there are indications that variations in marital fertility were not more important than variations in marriage rates in the structuring of general fertility during certain portions of the post- famine period. (Comments: See #1442.)

1415   McLaughlin, Patrick J. (Fr.) "Ireland and the World Population Problem." Capu An (1962): 147-163. refs.

Argues against the idea that the world population problem can only be solved through the use of contraceptive measures, abortion and sterilization - viewed as immoral - and suggests that it is possible to increase supplies sufficiently to cope with the likely population increase in the future. The author outlines ways in which Ireland can contribute to a solution to the world population problem.

1416   MacNamara, Angela. Living and Loving. Dublin: Catholic Truth Society, 1969. 42pp.

A brief instruction manual for Catholic teenagers offers advice on sexual behavior and elementary information on the facts of life.

1417   McQuaid, [Most Rev.] John Charles. Contraception and Conscience: Three Statements. [n.p. n.d.] 7pp.

States that any contraceptive act is bad in itself - this has been the constant teaching of the Catholic Church. It is a violation of the moral law as is civil divorce.

1418   Maguire, Catherine. "Catholics for a Free Choice." Women View 2 (Summer 1980): 10-12. il.

Reports on the organization, Catholics for a Free Choice, who are opposed to anti-abortion legislation and who campaign for medically safe abortions for all women. Explains their viewpoint and its rationale.

1419   Market Research Bureau of Ireland. "Religious Practice and Attitudes Toward Divorce and Contraception Among Irish Adults." Soc Stud 3 (3) (June 1974): 276-285. tables.

(See Marriage and the Family #1279.)

1420   Marshall, John. Catholics, Marriage and Contraception. Dublin: Helicon, 1965. 212pp.

An overview of the issue of birth control from a Catholic perspective. Reviews the Judaic tradition, discusses the meaning of love and marriage, the nature of sexuality,

Church teaching on procreation, current methods of birth control, the natural law, etc. Concludes that contraception is not an acceptable solution but periodic continence may be practiced.

1421   Messenger, John C. "Sexuality - Two Anthropological Studies, The Lack of the Irish." Psychol Today 4 (Feb. 1971): 41, 42, 68.

Report of ethnographic research conducted by the author and his wife over a 19 month period beginning in 1958 in a small island community off the Irish coast. Data on sexual knowledge and activity of islanders.

1422   Miller, J.F. and others. "Comparison of Use of the Dalkon Shield in Dublin and Southhampton." Brit Med J No.5971 (June 16, 1975): 519-601. tables. refs.

Two groups of women - 2729 in Dublin and 510 in Southampton - fitted with the Dalkon Shield I.U.D.'s in 1974 are compared on continuation rates at twelve months, complications leading to expulsion or removal and reasons for discontinuence. The Southampton population had higher event rates on all variables.

1423   Mooney, Michael I. "The Parish Hall." Furrow 4 (1) (Jan. 1953): 3-7. Comment 8-15+.

Discussion of the parish hall and its emergence as a clerical response to the spread of commercial dance halls with the introduction of licensing legislation. Clerical control of these viewed favorably.

1424   Moore, Angela and Patricia Murphy. "Attitudes, Knowledge and the Extent of Artificial Contraception in Classes IV and V in Ireland." Ir Med J 73 (9) (1980): 342-347. tables.

A survey of a random sample of 100 lower class recent mothers before their discharge from the Rotunda Hospital, Dublin and 50 male visitors - husbands or boyfriends of these. The results indicated that 53% of the participating women and even more of the men had used some form of artificial contraception in the past. The majority had not had any medical advice on the subject. Only a small minority of both men and women felt the use of artificial contraception to be wrong. While 92% of the men considered family planning to be the joint responsibility of both partners, in practice many showed less responsibility.

1425   Murphy, H. and others. "Post-Natal Mothers on Family Planning." J Ir Med Assoc 72 (2) (Feb. 16, 1979): 49-52. tables. refs.

Results of a survey of 120 recently delivered mothers at
the Maternity Hospital, Wexford. Patients were queried on
family planning practice and outcomes and results
correlated with age, parity, socio-economic group, prior
family planning history, ideal number of children and
source of information on family planning. Results showed
that most pregnancies were unplanned and most patients
stated they were poorly informed.

1426   Murphy, J. " The Effects of Smoking, Maternal Age and
Parity on the Outcome of Pregnancy." J Ir Med Assoc 67 (June
15, 1974): 309-313. tables. refs.

The influence of maternal cigarette smoking on foetal
survival was studied in 12,013 patients who attended the
Coombe Lying-In Hospital in Dublin. Abortion and
stillbirth were found to be significantly commoner among
patients smoking five or more cigarettes daily. The study
also confirmed the association between advanced age and
high nulliparity on foetal wastage.

1427   Murphy, Thomas, Nessa Joyce and Keith Wilson-Davis.
"Perinatal Mortality Study at the National Maternity
Hospital, Dublin. 1968- 69." J Ir Med Assoc 65 (6) (Mar.18,
1972): 125. tables. refs.

A pilot study of all perinatal deaths at the National
Maternity Hospital for the period indicated which totaled
179. Mothers who lost their babies were matched with a
control group of mothers who had live births. Information
was collected by personal interview on socioeconomic
status, hospital booking, source of referral and
antenatal care. Findings indicated that while the
socioeconomic status of both groups were substantially
similar, the control group had significantly better
antenatal care despite the fact that the other group were
significantly more at risk because of their age and
medical history.

1428   Neil, Joyce. "Comparison of Continuation Rates in Oral
Contraceptive and I.U.C.D." Med Gynaec 8 (1) (1974): 10-11.
table.

All patients who attended the Royal Maternity Hospital,
Belfast, post natal and family planning clinics during
1969 who chose either oral contraceptives or I.U.C.D.'s
as a contraceptive method were followed up to find out
how many were still using the method at the end of one
and two years. The findings showed that despite the fact
that more women initially chose oral contraceptives, the
continuation rate was significantly better for I.U.C.D.
users. The implications of this finding for the long term
efficiency of contraceptive services noted.

1429   Nowlan, David (Dr.). "Family Planning in Ireland." Fam
Plan 20 (3) (Oct. 1971): 52-53. refs.

A brief article by the Medical Correspondent of the Irish
Times detailing the then situation regarding
contraceptives in Ireland. Role of The Fertility Guidance
Company and the Irish Family Planning Rights Association
discussed.

1430   O'Brien, John A. (Ed.) The Vanishing Irish. New York:
McGraw Hill, 1953. 258pp. maps. tables.

A collection of essays dealing with the causes and
consequences of Ireland's declining population over the
previous century and possible measures to reverse the
trend. Contributors include scholars, playwrights,
novelists, biographers, historians, sociologists,
educators and journalists. A brief biographical sketch of
each included. Sexual attitudes, male-female roles and
status, tradition, puritanism, economics are among the
causative factors discussed.

1431   "Obscene Publication." Economist 262 (Mar. 5, 1977):
62.

Brief mention of two cases pending in the Irish high
court involving the Irish Censorship of Publications
Board's ban on a booklet published by the Family Planning
Association; also mention of a Family Planning Bill
pending in Parliament whose aim is to liberalize the law
so that information on contraceptives can be more freely
available.

1432   "Obstetric Morality." Dublin R LXXXVII (Apr. 1858):
100-130. refs.

An examination of texts on midwifery takes issue with
instructions which are premised on the condition of the
mother's health at the expense of the life of the child.
Author claims that the principles of Christian morality
oppose any actions which endanger the child even if the
mother's life is at stake. For reply see #1350.

1433   O'Bryne, Simon. Should Abortion Be Legalized? What
Catholics Should Know: Questions and Answers. NAAS: The
Leinster Leader, 1982. 54pp.

Explains in simple language Catholic teaching on the
abortion issue.

1434   O'Donnell, Michael. (Dr.) "Dublin's Lonely Outpost: A
Land of Saints and Hypocrites." Fam Plan 19 (2) (July 1970):
47-52. il. (Reprinted from February 10th issue of World
Medicine.)

Author points out the inconsistencies between Irish
ideology and law on contraception and actual behavior.

The Catholic Church, the State and the Irish medical
profession are charged with hypocricy in their rulings on
this issue.

1435   O'Mahony, Nora Tynan. "In a Magdalen Asylum." Ir Mon
24 (1906): 374-377.

Brief account of a visit to a home for "fallen" women in
St. Mary's High Park, Drumcondra.

1436   O'Mahony, T.P. "The Pill and Irish Politics." America
130 (1) (Jan. 1974): 9-11.

An analysis of religious and political issues surrounding
the question of contraception in Ireland and the
relevance of events in Northern Ireland to this issue.
Review of recent events - the McGee Case, Senator
Robinson's Family Planning Bill - and further propects
discussed.

1437   O'Sullivan, Karl. "Observations on Vaginismus in Irish
Women." Arch Gen Psych 36 (7) (1979): 824-826. tables. refs.

A report on 23 Irish women with vaginismus. The author
describes social and cultural factors unique to Ireland
which he believes are of importance in the clinical
presentation of this form of sexual dysfunction. Women
diagnosed as suffering from vaginismus are compared with
those complaining of orgasmic dysfunction. The
differences between the two groups are seen as relating
to childhood experience, their perception of their
marriage and their sexual dysfunction. Details on success
rate, number of sessions required for treatment and
recovery rate at follow-up are described for vaginismus.

1438   The Ovulation Method of Natural Family Planning.
[Based on a lecture of Dr.J.J. Billings K.C.S.G. M.D.
(Melbourne) F.R.A.C.P., F.R.C.P. (London)] Cork: Ovulation
Method Advisory Service. n.d. 16pp.

Description of the method of family planning developed
over the past 15 years in Melbourne by Dr. John J.
Billings, a neurologist and associates. The method is
now widely used in Australia and has spread to many other
countries including Ireland where there are now several
centers of instruction.

1439   Park, A.T. "An Analysis of Human Fertility in Northern
Ireland." Stat & Soc Inq Soc J Part 1. 21 (1962-63): 1-13.
tables.

An examination of fertility utilizing a measure of
"fertility ratio" designed to equalize the effect of
different age compositions in comparative studies.

Findings indicate an overall decline in fertility in
Northern Ireland as a whole during the years 1871-1911
and a dramatic decrease between then and 1951. Rates
compared with those in Great Britain and explanations for
Northern Ireland's higher fertility patterns presented.

1440   "Pill Was Bitter." Economist 252 (July 27, 1974):
36-37.

News item on the failure of the Irish Government's Bill
which would have legalized the sale of contraceptives.
Liam Cosgrave, the Prime Minister voted against his own
party's bill. Implications of this for the future of the
Coalition Government discussed.

1441   "Pregnancy: A Testing Business." Th Wk Ire (Nov. 21,
1969): 16. il.

Brief article on the unavailability of a pregnancy
testing service in Ireland which does not involve a
doctor and a hospital.

1442   Pullum, Thomas, Eric Almquist and Edward E. McKenna.
"Comment on McKenna's 'Marriage and Fertility in Post-Famine
Ireland.'" Am J Sociol 81 (6) (May 1976): 1472-1476. (Comment
1476-1477. Reply 1477-1481.) il. refs.

Pullum raises methodological issues regarding the
calculation of the general fertility ratio and proposes
various methods of assessing the relative impact of the
two determinants of this ratio. These methods then
applied to McKenna's data and compared with his results.
Almquist argues that changes in the rural economy began
earlier in the 19th century than 1951, McKenna's earliest
year of analysis. He points out the possible importance
of the home spinning industry run by females in marriage
decisions and consequent demographic trends. (See #1414.)

1443   Rose, R.S. "Induced Abortion in the Republic of
Ireland." British J Crim 18 (3) (July 1978): 245-254. il.
refs.

Results of a comparative study of abortions known or
reported to the police in the Republic of Ireland,
Northern Ireland, England, Wales and Scotland, indicate
that the Republic of Ireland had, as expected, the lowest
rate of induced abortion and that this pattern exists for
at least 106 years. A further study of other offences
dealing with fertility regulation indicate that the
Republic of Ireland also had, during this same period,
higher rates of infanticide, concealment of childbirth
and abandonment of children than the other countries
studied.

1444   Rose, R.S. "Abortion and Irish Women." Soc Stud 6 (1)
(Nov. 1977): 71-119.

The author describes the social characteristics of 190
women usually resident in the Republic of Ireland whose
pregnancies were terminated between 1973 and May 1975,
through the Pregnancy Advisory Service, London.

1445   Russell, W.T. "A Study of Irish Fertility Between 1870
- 1911." Metron 7 (1928): 101-113. tables.

A detailed examination of fertility rates in Ireland
compares the situation there with data on Swedish
fertility rates. Main findings: (1) fairly constant
higher rates for Irish women; (2) a decline occurred in
the period 1880-1882; (3) the fertility rates in the
counties of Antrim and Down had not declined to any
appreciable extent despite the fact that the Catholic
population accounted for only 25% of the total
population. A political or economic basis thus
postulated. Data abstracted from the Annual Returns of
the Registrar General for Ireland.

1446   Ryan, W.J.L. "Some Irish Population Problems." Studies
9 (2) (1955-56): 185-188. refs.

A summary and analysis of the report of the Commission on
Emigration and other Population Problems [1948] dealing
with demographic trends in Ireland from the 18th century.
The two great population problems of the Irish Republic
identified as the low marriage rate and emigration.
Causes and consequences of these discussed.

1447   Rynne, Andrew. Abortion. The Irish Question. Dublin:
Ward River Press, 1983.

(See Law #1605.)

1448   Scheper-Hughes, Nancy. Saints, Scholars and
Schizophrenics. Berkeley, Los Angeles: University of
California Press, 1979. 245pp. tables. refs.

Chapter four (pp.95-130) deals with marriage, celibacy
and relations between the sexes in rural Ireland within
the context of mental illness. Findings and conclusions
based on a year of fieldwork in a representative small
isolated rural community in the Kerry Gaeltacht area.
Chapter six includes the author's previous article on sex
roles, birth order and the Irish double bind.

1449   Shaw, George Bernard. "Morality and Birth Control."
Inde Shavian 10 (3) (1972): 33-36.

Reprint of an article written by George Bernard Shaw in

1919 as a contribution to the Birth Control Movement.
Argues that everyone should be taught that reproduction
is a controllable activity but the application of that
knowledge should be left to the discretion of the couples
involved. (Originally published in _Physical Culture_ July
1919.)

1450   Shaw, George Bernard. "The Need for Expert Opinion in
Sexual Reform." In _Platform and Pulpit_. ed. by Dan H.
Lawrence, pp. 200-207. London: Rupert Hart-Davis, 1962.
portr. (Address delivered before the 3rd International
Congress of the World League for Sexual Reform, held in the
Wismore Hall, 13 September 1929. Sexual Reform Congress, ed.
Norman Haire, London, 1930.) (An authorized verbatim report
at variance with the official text as approved by Shaw
appeared in _Time and Tide_ September 20, 1929.)

Shaw recommends that one seek expert opinion,
psychological and political, on the probable results of
any intended course of sexual reform.

1451   Sklar, June. "Marriage and Non-Marital Fertility:
Comparison of Ireland and Sweden." _Pop & Devel R_ 3 (4)
(1977): 359-377. il. refs.

A study of the relationship between age at marriage and
illegitimacy rates through a detailed analysis of
marriage behavior and non-marital fertility in the Irish
Republic and Sweden in the 19th and early 20th centuries.
Findings indicate that while a rising age at marriage may
have some effect in increasing the level of illegitimate
fertility, it is the institutional structure motivating
reproduction outside marriage that is of primary
importance. Implications of findings for population
policy in developing nations indicated.

1452   Smith, Louis P.F. "Observations on a Declining
Population." _Chr Rex_ XIV (1) (Jan. 1960): 23-33.

Brief analysis of the causes and consequences of
population decline in Ireland. The decline in rural
population was not offset by the increase in town
population as observed in other countries because of the
high rate of emigration: the Famine of 1846 made a clear
break in Irish population history. The economic
consequences include a reduced standard of living and
reduced investment; the social consequences include a
marriage rate that is the lowest in Europe.

1453   Spellman, M.P. "Mongolism - Survey in Cork City and
County." _J Ir Med Assoc_ 59 (July 1966): 12-13. tables. refs.

Reports the results of a survey in Cork city and county
of the incidence of Mongolism during the years 1962 and
1963. Age of mother and socio-economic factors

considered. Findings indicate that the average age of the mothers of Mongol children were higher than the average age of mothers of normal babies as was the age at marriage.

1454   "Statement from the Irish Bishops' Conference on Proposed Legislation Dealing With Family Planning and Contraception." L'Osservatore Romano 17 (526) (Apr. 27, 1978): 11. [English Edition.] (Statement also reproduced in The Furrow 29 (August 1978): 525-527.)

(See Human Sexuality, Reproduction and Health #1397.)

1455   Stockley, William F.P. "Catholic Protestantism." Ir Eccl Rec 5th Ser. XLII (Dec. 1933): 607-629.

Presents Catholic position in opposition to birth control and abortion.

1456   Stronge, John. "Modern Concepts in Obstetrics: Modern Standards of Antenatal Care." J Ir Med Assoc 66 (6) (1973): 163-165.

The crucial importance of the first antenatal visit in which the pregnant woman is most receptive to antenatal education regarding use of drugs, weight etc. stressed. Stronge recommends continued medical supervision, minimally, visits every four weeks until the 28th week thence every two weeks until the 36th week and weekly thereafter until conception and specifies specific examinations at these.

1457   Sweetman, Rosita. On Our Backs: Sexual Attitudes in a Changing Ireland. London: Pan., 1979. 230pp.

A series of 27 interviews with unmarried working class young men and women and married women in Ireland regarding their sexual attitudes and behavior; also interviews with professionals in various fields and representatives of various groups and organizations discussing various sex related issues in the Irish context. Introduction, conclusion and comments by journalist Sweetman.

1458   Thomas, E. Gwyn. "Demographic Problems of the Irish Free State." Geography 20 (Mar. 1935): 28-37. graphs. tables. refs.

An analysis of economic and demographic factors which in the early years of the Irish Free State brought about a decline in emigration and a tendency to population equilibrium.

1459   Trench, Brian. "The Knights of the Long Knives Against Contraception." _Magill Mag_ (Jan. 1979): 17-21.

An analysis of the vigorous opposition to a bill to liberalize sale of contraceptives in Ireland mounted by the Knights of Columbanus and the Opus Dei.

1460   Trench, Brian. "Taking Precautions." _New Statesm_ 17 (Jan. 5, 1979): 2-3.

Brief discussion of the Irish Government's _Family Planning Bill_ which would require a doctor's prescription for all forms of artificial contraception and gives doctors the onus of deciding that these be used for "bona fide family planning."

1461   Tucker, G.S.L. "Irish Fertility Ratios, Before the Famine." _Econ Hist R_ 2nd Series 23 (2) (Aug. 1970): 267-284. il. refs.

An analysis of former attempts to measure Irish fertility for the pre-Famine period. Tucker argues that the data on which these earlier studies were based rested on the age distribution reported in the Census of 1841 which, he claims, was in serious error at critical points. Tucker challenges previous estimates of the average crude birth rates and the derived fertility ratios and offers possible alternative figures.

1462   Viney, Michael. _No Birthright: A Study of the Irish Unmarried Mother and Her Child_. Dublin: Irish Times, 1964. 56pp. tables.

Numbers, attitudes - parental and social, - assistance available including adoption facilities and foster homes included in this overview of the situation of the unmarried mother in Ireland in 1963.

1463   Walsh, Brendan. "The Male/Female Differential in Life Expectancy in Ireland - a Note." _J Ir Med Assoc_ 71 (14) (1978): 475-480. tables. refs.

A retest of the hypothesis of the association between life expectancy and level of income in the Irish context finds that the correlation holds. A further examination of the male/female differential in life expectancy finds that in Ireland female life expectancy exceeds male to a relatively small extent compared with O.E.C.D. countries in the late 1960's and this differential is seen as consistent with Ireland's state of economic development.

1464   Walsh, Brendan M. "Ireland's Population Prospects." _Soc Stud_ 3 (8) (1974): 254-260. graphs. tables.

An analysis of recent demographic trends finds a change from a history of emigration, population decline and late marriage to a situation of population growth, zero emigration (or even net in migration), early marriage and a reduced prevalence of celibacy. The implications of these changes and future trends assessed.

1465   Walsh, Brendan M. "Post-War Demographic Developments in the Republic of Ireland." Soc Stud 1 (June 1972): 309-317. tables. refs.

Details the changing population pattern in Ireland in the decade since 1961 when for the first time in 115 years population decline was halted and the population increased by 5%. Regional nature of this pattern, its causes, future trends and their implications discussed.

1466   Walsh, Brendan. "The Need for Change." Fam Plan 20 (3) (Oct. 1971): 69-71.

This article by the Chairman of the Irish Family Planning Rights Association presents a case for change in the anti- birth control laws in Ireland in view of the country's demographic problems.

1467   Walsh, Brendan M. "Marriage Rates and Population Pressure: Ireland 1871 and 1911." Econ Hist R 2nd Series 23 (1) (Apr. 1970): 148-162. tables. refs.

An exploration of the regional pattern of Irish demographic change and the role of economic factors in these developments including a consideration of the relationship between fertility and nuptiality levels.

1468   Walsh, Brendan M. "An Empirical Study of the Age Structure of the Irish Population." Econ Soc R 1 (2) (Jan. 1970): 259-279. il. refs.

An analysis of the roles of birth, death and migration rates in the determination of the age structure of the Irish population. Data taken from the 1966 Census of Population. Causes of the high levels of both young and old dependency examined and future trends explored.

1469   Walsh, Brendan M. Religion and Demographic Behavior in Ireland. Dublin: Economic and Social Research Institute, 1970. 50pp. tables. refs. (Paper No.55.)

A detailed comparative analysis based on published Census and Vital statistics of the demographic behavior of the religious groups in Ireland both in the Republic of Ireland and in Northern Ireland focused mainly on the period 1946-1961. Includes data on birth rates, marriage, fertility, nuptiality, age structure, migration rates, occupational distribution, mixed marriages, recent trends. The findings indicate that Ireland is composed of two religious communities: Roman Catholic and Other Denomination with strikingly different patterns of demographic behavior. Implications of the findings and future trends discussed.

1470   Walsh, Brendan. Some Irish Population Problems Reconsidered. Dublin: Economic and Social Research Institute, 1968. 36pp. tables. (Paper No.42.)

Walsh argues that the low level of Irish marriage rates is an archaic method of population control which has allowed the country to maintain a high marriage fertility rate without the consequences of a high birth rate. Some social costs of this demographic pattern are examined and future trends explored.

1471   Walsh, Dermot. [M.B.M.R.C. Psych D.P.M.] "A Century of Suicide in Ireland." J Ir Med Assoc 69 (6) (Mar. 27, 1976): 144-152. graphs. tables. refs.

An analysis of suicide rates for Ireland from 1864 to 1976 indicate an increase in suicide for the first part of the century followed by a steady decrease in the 25 years prior to this study. Male - female ratios documented and an analysis of differing urban/rural patterns and possible influence of marital status on these patterns explored. Causes of suicide and effects of warfare and civil strife on suicide rate discussed.

1472   Walsh, Dermot. "Medical and Social Characteristics of Irish Residents Whose Pregnancies Were Terminated Under the 1967 Abortion Act in 1971 and 1972." J Ir Med Assoc 68 (6) (Mar. 22, 1975): 143-149.

1473   Walsh, Dermot. "Pregnancies of Irish Residents Terminated in England and Wales in 1973." J Ir Med Assoc 69 (1) (Jan. 17, 1976): 16-18.

Author presents his findings regarding the medical and social characteristics of Irish residents who in the years 1971-1973 availed of the Abortion Act of 1967 to terminate their pregnancies in England. The vast majority are single and the number is increasing each year. The age group 20-24 had the highest proportion of abortions followed by the 25-29 age group. Most of the over 35 women who had abortions were married.

1474   Walsh, Dermot. "Patients in Psychiatric Hospitals in 1963. A Comparison with England and Wales." Brit J Psych 118 (1971): 617-620. il. refs.

Analyzed 1963 Irish psychiatric hospital census returns

and compared them with those of a similar census carried
out in England and Wales. Findings indicate that the
Irish male hospitalization rates were triple and the
female rates double the English and Wales rates. Irish
ratios are higher for all ages and both sexes in various
diagnostic groups. An analysis of the effect of Ireland's
abnormal demographic structure is presented.

1475   Walsh, Dermot. "Alcoholism in Dublin." J Ir Med Assoc
61 (371): (May 1971): 153-156. tables. refs.

This study examines records of all persons first admitted
to Dublin psychiatric facilities from Dublin city and
county during 1962 with the diagnosis of either alcoholic
addiction or alcoholic psychoses. Also examines total
admissions and readmissions and compares the rates with
the United States, Scotland, England and Wales. Findings
indicate Dublin has a very high rate of hospitalized
alcoholics and both male and female admission rates in
Dublin are greater than in the other countries. The
female married rate in Ireland is twice that of the
unmarried.

1476   Walsh, Dermot. "Alcoholism in the Republic of
Ireland." Brit J Psych 115 (526) (1969): 1021-1025.

A study of first admissions for alcoholism in the
Republic of Ireland in 1964. Of 690 admissions, 87 were
female. Some social, demographic and geographical
characteristics of the data are examined. All admission
rates for women were lower than those for men by social
group but in certain higher socio-economic groupings,
female rates were a significantly higher fraction of the
corresponding male rates.

1477   Walsh, Dermot. "Mental Illness in Dublin - First
Admissions." Brit J Psych 115 (1969): 449-456. il. refs.

Details the results of a one year study of first
admissions to Dublin Psychiatric Facilities. Analysis of
rates in terms of age, sex, marital status and area of
residence presented.

1478   Walsh, Noel. "In Defense of the Unborn." Studies 61
(1972): 303-314. refs.

Observations and opinions of a practising psychiatrist on
the harmful psychological effects, frequently suppressed,
of abortion on women.

1479   "The War and the Wombs." Hum Beh 3 (Oct. 1974): 50-51.

Brief journalistic note on the demographic situation in
Northern Ireland where the Catholic birthrate exceeds

the Protestant whereas in Eire, these rates are similar.
Implications and explanations of this situation briefly
explored.

1480   Ward, C.K. "Sociological Aspects of Family Planning
Programmes." Ir Nurs News (July/Aug. 1961): 7-8.

Comment on two aspects of family planning which must
concern Catholics e.g. (1) the relation of world
population to world food resources (2) a social climate
favoring family planning. Citing U.N. Reports, Ward
argues that there is no question of the adequacy of world
resources to meet population needs though there is a
problem of distribution. Catholics should adopt a
positive approach and concentrate on research to refine
knowledge of the infertile period, home assistance
programs for mothers and advisory and support services
for couples.

1481   Whither Ireland? A Study (August 1974) of Recent
Trends, Contraception - and Associated Issues. Dublin: Irish
Family League, 1975. 14pp.

Negative summary of recent press items and other
expressed opinion which are viewed as threatening the
basic values and character of Irish society. These
include the call for a secular constitution and the
proposed legalization of contraceptives.

1482   Whyte, J.H. The Church and State in Modern Ireland,
1923-1970. Dublin: Gill and MacMillan, 1971. 466pp. bibl.

An examination of the influence of the Catholic church on
Irish Government policy since 1922. Chapters 7-8 discuss
in detail the mother and child scheme, the controversial
measure introduced by Dr. Noel Browne to provide health
benefits for expectant mothers and their children. The
full text of the proposal is included in the appendix.
Chapter two discusses the influence of the Church on
sexual morality and the extent to which the State
implemented legislation to safeguard Catholic moral
standards regarding birth control and divorce.

1483   Williamson, B. "Thou Shalt Not Dance." Spectator 191
(Oct. 9, 1953): 392.

Brief comment on opposition by some Irish Catholic
bishops to the granting of licenses to dance hall
proprietors.

1484   Wilson-Davis, Keith. "Some Results on an Irish Family
Planning Survey." J Biosoc Sci 7 (4) (Oct. 1975): 435-444.
il. refs.

Results of a 1973 survey of 754 married women and 194 husbands in the Republic of Ireland regarding the Government ban on and the desired availability of contraceptives. Data on the extent of family planning, socio-economic differences between the planners and methods used are presented. Only 25% of respondents were in favor of the Government ban.

1485   Wilson-Davis, Keith. "The Contraceptive Situation in the Irish Republic." J Biosoc Sci 6 (1974): 483-492.

Discusses the legal prohibition of the sale, importation and advertising of "unnatural methods" of contraception in the 1935 Criminal Law Amendment Act and the repeal in 1973 of the ban on the importation of contraceptives. Other factors which indicate a changing climate of opinion such as family planning clinics in Dublin and usage of the pill are discussed and the possibility of further legal changes weighed.

1486   Wilson-Davis, Keith. "Irish Attitudes to Family Planning." Soc Stud 3 (3) (June 1974): 261-275. tables. refs.

Preliminary analysis of a fertility survey carried out by the author in 1973 based on a national three stage sample of married women aged 15-44 years. Eight hundred wives and 200 husbands were interviewed. Data analyzed by age, region, sex and husbands occupation. Attitudes toward the Government ban on contraceptives, availability of contraceptives if ban were removed and actual family planning practices among topics explored.

1487   Wright, P. "Fertility Behavior of a Minority Population: the Catholics in Northern Ireland." Ekistics 37 (221) (1974): 249-256. maps. tables. refs.

An attempt to explain the higher Catholic birthrate in Northern Ireland compared to the Republic of Ireland. Various explanations are considered but the conclusion is that it is their minority status per se, that is the most crucial factor.

1488   "Yeats and the Yogi on Birth Control: An Editorial." Cath Bull XVIII (Oct. 1928): 991-992.

Bitter attack on W.B. Yeats for expressing opposition to a policy which would ban all books dealing with birth control and all journals carrying reviews of books on this subject.

Psychology

This section contains publications dealing with sex roles including socialization, stereotyping, behavior, differences, conflict and with female identity, attributes, attitudes or values. Additional material on family roles and socialization within the family will be found under MARRIAGE AND THE FAMILY. For material on psychological or psychiatric impairment see HUMAN SEXUALITY, REPRODUCTION AND HEALTH.

1489   Bender, David S. "Sex Role Development and Achievement of Adolescents in Ireland." Paper Presented at the Annual Meeting of the American Educational Research Association, San Francisco, April 1976. Eric ED 177168 26pp. tables. refs.

   Presents results of a questionnaire administered to 750 Irish adolescents. Sex differences were found for the following variables: academic achievement, educational and occupational aspirations, assertiveness, stereotypes of adult role.

1490   Best, Deborah L. and others. "Development of Sex-Trait Stereotypes Among Young Children in the United States, England and Ireland." Eric [ED 135491]

   Reports results of two studies one using the sex stereotype measure II, a 32-item picture story technique to assess children's knowledge of sex trait stereotypes and another, the sex attitude measure, to assess general evaluative bias towards male and female persons. Both techniques administered to preschool, third and sixth grade Euro-American children. Cross nationally there was found to be a high degree of similarity in the nature of the sex stereotypes being learned.

1491   Bolger, Niall. "Sex Roles, Hopelessness and Locus of

Control." Brit Psychol Soc Bull 33 (May 1980): 214. refs.

Samples of Trinity College undergraduates examined in a
replication of a study which found significant
correlation between scores on Beck's Hopelessness Scale
and Rotter's Internal-External Locus of Control Scale
confirmed that this correlation held for males. A further
study using, in addition, the Bem Sex role inventory,
found sex role variables to be systematically related
with inter-scale correlation.

1492   Brown, W. P. and G. M. Davies. "Studies in Word
Listing: Testing for Group Differences in Category Norms." Ir
J Psychol 3 (2) (Winter 1976): 87-120. tables. refs.

Category norms for fifteen categories were collected
from university students in Scotland and Northern
Ireland. Various techniques were used to compare the
norms derived from the responses of these two groups. The
same techniques were applied to a comparison of the norms
for men and women students. The results indicated that
category norms can be very substantially affected by the
"nationality" or the sex of the normative group.
Difficulties in the evaluation of the analytic techniques
are discussed.

1493   Browne, Maureen. "The Casualities of Freedom." Image 6
(5) (May 1981): 36-38.

Report on increase in drug-taking and suicide among
women.

*1494   Cartin, C; P. Jackson and B. O'Connor. Gender in
Irish Society. Galway: Galway University Press. (forthcoming)

1495   Cooper, Bruce. "If Only a Woman Were Like a Man or
Don't Put Your Daughter Down the Mine, Mrs. Worthington." Ind
& Comm Tra 7 (6) (June 1975): 250-251.

Bruce Cooper, dean of Management and Continuing Education
at the Northern Ireland Polytechnic, reflects on male/
female stereotypes occasioned by his participation in an
affirmative action programme in an International Summer
School in The United States.

1496   Davis, E.E. [Fine-Davis, Margret,] and others. "A
Study of the Factor Structure of Attitudinal Measures of
Major Social Psychological Contructs in an Irish Sample."
Econ Soc R 9 (1) (1977): 27-50. tables. refs.

A study designed to test the validity cross-culturally of
certain measures of social psychological and quasi
personality constructs. A questionnaire was administered
to a random sample of 412 subjects resident in Dublin,

Ireland. Many of the factors which emerged from the study
replicated measures of the same construct obtained in
previous, largely American, studies and therefore lend
support to the construct validity of these. A further
modified questionnaire found a significant positive
correlation between religiosity and traditional sex role
orientation.

1497   "Do Women Think Like Men? Part of a Discussion Between
G.M.Young, John Mabbott, Elizabeth Bowen and Phyllis
Vallance." Listener 26 (Oct. 30, 1941): 593-594.

General discussion of principles of thinking and how men
and women exercise this function. Elizabeth Bowen defines
women's strength of mind as flexibility, quickness on the
uptake, sensitiveness and a sympathetic attitude towards
the other person's point of view; drawbacks may be the
introduction in debate of irrelevant and personal details
whereas men frequently make an argument unreal by being
too abstract.

1498   Dunne, Elizabeth A. "Sex Differences in the
Anticipation of a Real-life Stressor." Ir J Psychol 1 (9)
(1981): 40-44. refs.

Eleven female and eleven male undergraduates at
University College, Cork tested under the stress factor
of anticipation of a University exam. Results did not
reveal the expected differences in psychophysiological
reactions even though the 72 hour pre-examination period
was significantly more disturbing for the females in
terms of their self-rating of "tension" "unhappiness" and
"irritability". Interpretations of the data offered.

1499   Elliott, A.G.P. "Sex and Decision-Making in the
Selection Interview - A Real-Life Study." J Occ Psychol 54
(4) (1981): 265-273. tables. refs.

Report on a study of the effects of sex on the judgements
made in the employment interview examined the interview
results of 200 male and 200 female candidates for work in
an Irish bank. Interview records showed significant
differences between male and female interviewers'
perceptions of applicants. The implications of the
findings are discussed.

1500   Fields, Rona M. Society Under Siege: a Psychology of
Northern Ireland. Philadelphia: Temple University Press,
1976. 266pp.

Chapter five has a brief overview of the status of women
in Ireland under the Brehon laws as a contrast to their
current subordinate status. Emphasis on situation in
Northern Ireland and the factors which have exacerbated

sexism during the preceding decade of violence.
Individual women who have led the civil rights movement
seen as exceptions who have transcended stereotypes.

1501   Fields, Rona M. A Society on the Run: a Psychology of
Northern Ireland. Harmonsworth: Penguin, 1973. 216pp.

This book examines the long term effects of stress on
the population of Northern Ireland. Using the case-study
method, the author, a psychologist and sociologist,
administered various tests such as personality
measurements, psycho-motor functioning, evaluation
through counseling and interviews. Includes qualitative
analysis of media and documents. A chapter focuses on the
position and behavior of women.

1502   Fine-Davis, Margret. Women and Work in Ireland: A
Social Psychological Perspective. Dublin: Council for the
Status of Women, 1983. 239pp. tables. bibl.

(See Employment #1669.)

1503   Fine-Davis, Margret. "Personality Correlates of
Attitudes Toward the Role and Status of Women in Ireland." J
Pers 47 (3) (1979): 379-396. tables. figs. refs.

Presents results of a study designed to examine the
possible relationships between personality and related
social- psychological characteristics on the one hand and
attitudes toward sex roles and issues relevant to the
status of women on the other. The random stratified
sample consisted of 420 male and female Dublin adults
aged 18 to 65. Findings indicate that traditional
sex-role attitudes and less favorable attitudes to equal
pay, contraception and maternal employment were
correlated with measures of religiosity, distrust,
self-deprecation, powerlessness and a need for order and
predictability.

1504   Fine-Davis, Margret. "Social-Psychological Predictors
of Employment Status of Married Women in Ireland." J Marr &
Fam 41 (1) (Feb. 1979): 145-158. tables. refs.

A study designed to investigate several sets of
personality and attitudinal variables together to assess
their relationship to one example of sex-role behavior,
e.g. labour force participation on the part of married
women. Two hundred and forty Irish married women
stratified by employment status, age, socioeconomic
status and presence or absence of dependent children
comprised the sample. Findings showed that employed and
non-employed married women differed significantly on a
number of characteristics.

1505   "In Praise of Women." Intercom 6 (8) (Aug. 1975):
2-10.

   Reflections by seven Catholic priests on friendship with
   women as they have personally experienced it. Reflections
   on the same theme by seven women - two married, two
   single and three nuns.

1506   Kelleher, M.J. and J.R. Copeland. "Assessment of
Neurotic Symptoms in Irish Female Patients." Brit J Psych 124
(June 1974): 554-555. tables. refs.

   An abstract of a paper reports higher scores on neurotic
   scales by Irish females found by the authors in three
   separate comparative studies of Irish and British
   psychiatric patients using three different instruments of
   diagnosis. Authors stress caution in interpreting scores
   of Irish females on scales which were standardized with
   reference to different populations.

1507   Kelleher, M.J. "Cross-national
(Anglo-Irish)Differences in Obsessional Symptoms and Traits
of Personality." Psychol Med 2 (1972): 33-41. il. refs.

   A comparative study utilizing the Leyton Obsessional
   Inventory, part of the Cornell Medical Index and a short
   version of the Maudsley Personality Inventory of a group
   of Irish, English and Irish immigrant orthopedic
   patients. Results indicated that the Irish subjects had
   more obsessional symptoms and traits than did the
   English. Rural dwelling Irish females and bachelor Irish
   males had highest obsessional scores. Relationship of
   cultural background to development of obsessional
   symptoms and implications discussed.

1508   McCafferty, Nell. "Woman in the House." Status 6 (1)
(Mar. 14, 1981): 11.

   Brief note on the Report to the Joint Committee on State
   sponsored Bodies regarding the treatment of women on T.V.
   Fourteen women's groups were invited to make submissions:
   Irish Countrywoman's Association sent a written
   testimonial; the Rape Crisis Centre made an oral
   submission.

1509   McKernan, J. and J.L. Russell. "Differences of
Religion and Sex in the Value-systems of Northern Ireland
Adolescents." Brit J Soc Clin Psychol 19 (June 1980): 115-
118. tables. refs.

   A study designed to investigate similarities and
   differences in the value systems of Northern Ireland post
   primary pupils. Form E of the Rokeach Value Survey
   administered to all 4th year post primary students
   attending second level schools in the counties of Antrim

and Londonderry. Findings indicated that females placed a higher value on "domestic" values than did males suggesting that female students may be socialized into adopting a subservient role in Irish society.

1510   Muir, Erica. "Teaching Borstal Girls to Relax." Int J Offend Ther 19 (3) (1975): 237-240. il.

Description of a relaxation program instituted at a Borstal serving Scotland and Northern Ireland. Since aggression is viewed as an outcome of tension, which is also associated with the use of alcohol and drugs, girls are trained in basic relaxation techniques as a more positive alternative to relieve tension. They are also provided with training in non-verbal communication and social skills.

1511   O'Connor, Noreen. "Human Encounter: Beyond the Philosophy of Male and Female." Crane Bag 4 (1) (1980): 20-25. refs.

A philosophical consideration of what it means to be female/male and the encounter of self and other.

1512   Offer, Daniel and others. "The Self-Image of Adolescents: a Study of Four Cultures." J Youth & Adol 6 (3) (Sept. 1977): 265-280. tables. refs.

This paper discusses the effectiveness of the Offer Self Image Questionnaire in meaningfully separating normal, juvenile delinquent and emotionally disturbed adolescents; older and younger teenagers, males and females. The results of administering this test in four different cultures including Ireland are described as are some of the methodological problems inherent in doing cross-cultural research. Irish females saw themselves as healthier than their male counterparts on several items: social relations, morals, mastery of the external world, vocational/educational goals but less so in the case of sexual attitudes and behavior.

1513   Scheper-Hughes, Nancy. "Breeding Breaks Out in the Eye of the Cat: Sex Roles, Birth Order and the Irish Double-bind." J Comp Fam Stud 10 (2) (Summer 1979): 207-226. tables. refs.

A study of the effect of sex and birth order on the quality of adolescent's socialization experiences. The study was carried out in Ballybran West Kerry between May 1974 and April 1975 and consisted of a series of interviews with 28 parents and 36 adolescents (22 girls and 14 boys). Psychological projective tests were administered to the adolescents. Study found that the dynamics of rural Irish socialization is weighted in favor of the mental health of daughters and earlier born sons. Causes and consequences of this pattern analyzed.

1514   Scheper-Hughes, Nancy. <u>Saints, Scholars and Schizophrenics</u>. Berkeley, Los Angeles: University of California Press, 1979. 245pp. tables. refs.

(See Human Sexuality, Reproduction and Health, #1448.)

1515   Williams, John E. and others. "Sex Trait Stereotypes in England, Ireland and the Unites States." <u>Brit J Soc Clin Psychol</u> 16 (4) (Nov.1977): 303-309. tables. refs.

Using the item pool of the adjective check list (ACL) the responses of 50 male and 50 female English and Irish University students were compared to those of U.S. students previously studied in 1975 to assess sex-trait stereotypes in the three countries. The results showed a remarkable degree of similarity in the stereotypes common to all three. These male and female stereotypes were less sharply differentiated in Ireland - possible explanation suggested.

1516   Woman (a pseud.) "Are We Inferior." <u>Univ Mag</u> LXXX (Sept.1872): 344-348.

Argues that men and women differ radically in their modes of reasoning; that the mind of man moves analytically, that of woman synthetically. Man's intellectual faculty as applied to practical life is stronger but woman's is really of a higher order - transcendental.

Law

This section contains publications dealing with women's legal status and efforts to promote or enhance this. The material is grouped in two main sections: GENERAL LEGAL STATUS (including continuing anomalies which discriminate against women in various categories or affect her control over her own body) and PENAL LAW (studies of women as subject or agent of criminal activity including rape, violence against women, prostitution, abortion - viewed as a crime). The attempt is to include only discussions dealing with specifically legal aspects of various issues. For additional material involving other considerations in family break-up, contraception or abortion see the sections on MARRIAGE AND THE FAMILY and HUMAN SEXUALITY, REPRODUCTION AND HEALTH. For accounts of women's efforts to achieve full legal equality including the right to suffrage see POLITICS; for ideological statements on their right to equality under law see PERSPECTIVES ON WOMEN'S LIBERATION.

A third major category of legal materials involving women - e.g. studies dealing with employment legislation - are grouped in the section on EMPLOYMENT AND ECONOMIC LIFE.

GENERAL LEGAL STATUS

1517   Aim Group. Report Number Two: Legal Separation in Ireland. Dublin: [Aim Group], 1976. 59pp. tables.

Details results of a study designed to assess the effects on respondents of obtaining legal separations in Ireland. Some of the problems cited by the participants were: the lack of divorce legislation; the status problem and half-life of the separated; the need for job retraining for wives, full legal rights for women, joint ownership of the matrimonial home and machinery for the enforcement of maintenance payments. The study concludes with specific recommendations for reform.

1518   Barrett, Sean. "Divorce Irish Style." Church & State 1
(2) (Autumn 1973): 22-29.

A brief review of some of the arguments presented on both
sides in 1925 during the government debate on whether to
allow divorce in Ireland. While the constitutionality of
making this legally unobtainable was questioned, Barrett
claims that the only real opposition came from William
Butler Yeats who defended the rights of the non-Catholic
groups to freedom of conscience on this issue to no
avail.

1519   Binchy, William. "Divorce in Ireland: Legal and Social
Perspectives." J Div 2 (1) (Fall 1978): 99-108. refs.

Ireland is one of the few countries where divorce is
constitutionally prohibited. In this article, Binchy
succinctly presents the present legal remedies for broken
marriages - nullity decrees or judicial separation - and
places this in the context of the historical background.
He further analyzes the problems between Church and State
in this area and the social effects of the prohibition of
divorce including public attitudes. Proposals for reform
of the divorce law discussed.

1520   Binchy, William. "Marital Privacy and Family Law: A
Reply to Mr. O'Reilly." Studies 66 (264) (1977): 330-335.
refs.

Argues that the decision by the Supreme Court in the
McGee case has eased the path toward constitutional
recognition of a "right" to abortion. [See O'Reilly
#1566.]

1521   Binchy, William. "New Vistas in Irish Family Law." J
Fam Law 15 (4) (1977): 637-673. refs.

Principal aspects of Irish family law and recent changes
summarized. Aspects of family law included are marriage,
sex discrimination in jury service, contraception and
abortion, child custody and guardianship.

1522   Bromley, P.M. and B. Passingham. Divorce Law Reform in
Northern Ireland. Belfast: Queens University, Department of
Law, 1978. 71pp.

Historical background and current legal situation
explicated including grounds for divorce action,
financial and property considerations, child custody and
costs.

1523   Brooke, William G. "Report on the Differences in Law
of England and Ireland as Regards the Protection of Women."
Stat & Soc Inq Soc J 6 (April 1973): 202-229. refs.

Detailed discussion of the anomalies in the law which
denies Irish women protection enjoyed by English women in
the areas of maintenance of illegitimate children, rights
of married women, education, poor relief, municipal and
other franchise, and other areas.

1524   de Burca, Mairin. "Criminal Conversation - Another
Irish Solution." Women View 4 (Winter 1980): 15. il.

A discussion of the criminal conversation tort whereby a
man can sue another man for financial "damages" for the
seduction of his wife. Reviews the recommendations of the
Law Reform Committee on this. Offers suggestions for
improving the law covering deserted wives and children.

1525   de Burca, Mairin. "Equality Before the Law." Cross 64
(2) (June 1973): 10-11. portr.

Listing of disabilities suffered by Irish women. The
capitalistic system seen as the root cause of this
discrimination.

1526   "Chemical Job." Economist 250 (Feb. 16, 1974): 42.

Brief discussion of proposed changes in the law regarding
the importation of contraceptives to Ireland made
necessary by the recent Supreme Court decision that the
existing prohibition of the import of these was
unconstitutional.

1527   Clarkin, James. "Ireland's Catholics and the
Contraceptive's Bill." Chr Cent 91 (June 12, 1974): 629.

Discusses the impending legislation relating to "Control
of Importation, Sale and Manufacture of Contraceptives"
in the wake of the Supreme Court ruling that the
prohibition of the importation of contraceptives was
invalid.

1528   Colum, Padraic. "An Irish Champion of Women." Cath W
100 (1915): 500-503.

The title refers to St. Adamnan whose fame rests on "Cain
Adamnain," or law of Adamnan which later generations
regarded as the charter of women's freedom in Ireland.
Colum recounts the legend of how this law was passed.
Regardless of the truth of the legend a woman
unquestionably had extensive rights under the Brehon laws
including the right to alimony, property and contract
rights and legal equality (in some cases superiority) to
her husband.

1529   Costello, Declan. "Legal Status of Women in Ireland."

<u>Admin</u> 23 (1) (Spring 1975): 68-70.

This article by the then Attorney General details the
major legal changes affecting women suggested by the
Committee on the Status of Women and the 19th Interim
Report of the Committee on Court Practice and Procedure
and the action taken on these recommendations.

1530   Creighton, W.B. "The Sex Discrimination (Northern
Ireland) Order 1976." <u>No Ire L Q</u> 29 (3/4) (1978): 316-338.
refs.

Detailed exposition of provisions of the Act with a
critique of its limitations, notably its complexity and
limited remedies for proven infractions.

1531   Davitt, Cahir. "Some Aspects of the Constitution and
the Law in Relation to Marriage." <u>Studies</u> 57 (Spring 1968):
6-19. (Comments 20-33). refs.

Jurisdiction of the Irish High Court in regard to
matrimonial issues specified. Historical evolution of the
law in this area discussed and its current application in
regard to voidable marriages, clandestine marriages,
foreign divorce judgements and divorce. Anomalies in
current situation and the possibility of a Constitutional
Amendment raised.

1532   "Dialogue. Senator Mary Robinson and Mary McAleese
Speak to Betty Purcell." <u>Crane Bag</u> 4 (1) (1980): 60-65.

A free ranging, informal discussion of the main legal
anomalies for women in the general area of family law and
the dilatoriness of the Law Reform Commission in
remedying these; lack of day care and creche facilities
for working mothers; contraception and abortion in
Ireland.

1533   "Difficult Birth." <u>Economist</u> 270 (Jan. 6 1979): 28,30.

Discussion of the health/family planning bill which would
legalize the importation, advertising and sale of
contraceptives in Ireland but would allow these to be
made available only on a doctor's prescription.
Background of proposed legislation and opposition to this
briefly discussed.

1534   Downey, Raymond V. "Till Death Do Us Part." <u>Inc Law
Soc Gaz</u> 69 (1) (Jan.-Feb. 1975): 23-25.

The Presidential address of November 27, 1974 to the
Medico Legal Society presents arguments for full equal
rights and opportunities for women within marriage and

outlines legal changes necessary to protect these.

1535   "Draft Matrimonial Causes (Northern Ireland) Order
1978." Furrow 29 (Aug. 1978): 527. (Statement issued by the
six Catholic Bishops who have jurisdiction in Northern
Ireland on the Draft Matrimonial Causes (Northern Ireland)
Order.)

    Reiterates Catholic teaching on the indissolubility of
    marriage in light of the proposal to introduce new
    divorce legislation in Northern Ireland which would make
    divorce easier to obtain.

1536   Dublin Founding Group. "The Civil Wrongs of
Irishwomen." IDOC International (North American ed.) 30 (Aug.
28, 1971): 48-77. il. (Originally published by the Founding
Group of the Irish Women's Liberation Movement.)

    Documents legal inequalities and other forms of
    discrimination suffered by women in Ireland. Covers
    education, employment, marital status, child care and
    responsibilities, family planning, divorce, etc. Special
    plight of widows, deserted wives and unmarried mothers
    also discussed.

1537   Duncan, W.R. "Supporting the Institution of Marriage
in Ireland." Ir Jur 2 (Winter 1978): 215-232. refs.

    Examines the origins, nature and efficacy of the policy
    of supporting the institution of marriage and the family
    founded on marriage in the family law of the Irish
    Republic and the role of the Roman Catholic Church in
    this development. The gap between formal law and social
    practice and its implications for the future analyzed.

1538   Duncan, W.R. "The Domicile of Married Women." Dublin U
Law J 1 (1977): 38-45. refs.

    In this submission to the Law Reform Commission the
    author, a lecturer in law at Trinity College, Dublin
    presents arguments for the abolition of the
    wife/dependency rule (i.e. that a wife's domicile during
    marriage is the same as and changes with that of her
    husband) and the substitution of a rule that a married
    woman's domicile should be decided in the same way as
    that of a single woman.

1539   Duncan, W.R. "Illegitimacy and Law Reform." In
Conference on the Unmarried Parent and Child in Irish
Society, pp.11-19. Dublin: Cherish, 1975. tables. refs.

    Presents a summary of the legal disabilities of
    illegitimate children: no legal right initially even to
    mothers name; no rights in the estate of natural father

and only very limited rights in relation to the natural
mother; right to parental support limited. Describes the
stigma surrounding illegitimate status and the historical
sources of existing law. Presents and refutes arguments
for the preservation of the concept of illegitimacy, and
suggests needed reforms.

1540   Equal Opportunities Commission for Northern Ireland.
Report of the Seminar on Sex Discrimination: 25th April,
1980. Belfast: The Commission, 1980. (n.p.)

First legal seminar organized by the Commission and also
the first seminar of its kind presented in Northern
Ireland on the implementation of the sex discrimination
legislation.

1541   Eve, Judith. Financial Provision on Divorce: A
Discussion of the Provisions Relating to Ancillary Relief on
Divorce Contained in the Matrimonial Causes (Northern
Ireland) Order 1980. Belfast: Queens University, Belfast,
Faculty of Law. Servicing the Legal System [1980] 28 leaves.
refs.

An explication of some of the complexities pertaining to
distribution of family assets following a reform of
matrimonial law in Northern Ireland simplifying the
process of obtaining a divorce but introducing extensive
discretionary powers to the court in financial provision.

1542   Fennell, Nuala. "Divorce Irish Style." Image 1 (12)
(Sept. 1976): 3-5; 2 (1) (Oct. 1976): 11-12.

Non-technical presentation of available options to cope
with irretrievably broken marriages in Ireland. Proposed
reforms in the area of family law also discussed.

1543   Gilchrist, Carol Anne. "Ireland's Deserted Wives."
Cross 64 (2) (June 1973): 12-13. il.

Brief discussion of social and legal changes needed to
improve the situation of the deserted family in Ireland.

1544   Haderman, Mary. "Irish Women and Irish Law." Crane Bag
4(1) (1980): 55-59. refs.

Details on status of women under English common law which
made a wife practically the property of her husband and
which was imposed in Ireland with the destruction of the
Brehon laws. While most of the restrictions on married
women have been removed there persist some legal
anomalies, mainly remedies open to husbands but not to
wives. These are being considered by the Law Reform
Commission which has already issued a paper recommending
abolition of some of these.

1545   Hancock, W. Nealson. "The Difference Between the
English and Irish Poor Law, as to Treatment of Women and
Unemployed Workmen." Stat & Soc Inq Soc J III (June 1862):
217-235.

   Presents an historical overview of the Irish Poor Law
   noting why and wherein it differs from the English Poor
   Law. Deplores the negative effect of this differential
   treatment especially in the case of female minors,
   widows, women generally , the old, the infirm and the
   unemployed — in Ireland all are met with the same
   stringent test of destitution as the able bodied male.

1546   Hannon, Patrick. "Nullity and Divorce." Tablet 231
(7132) (Mar. 19, 1977): 278-281.

   The author, a lecturer in moral theology at Maymooth
   discusses the limitations of existing remedies for
   marriage breakdown in Ireland e.g. separation and
   annulment, and briefly reviews arguments on proposed
   changes which include a reformed nullity law or divorce
   legislation. The central concern in the Irish context is
   the social impact of a change in the law. Hannon suggests
   that a discretionary divorce law might be a possible
   method of lessening the threat of adverse social
   consequences.

1547   Horgan, J. "Binding and Loosing in Ireland."
Commonweal 87 (Feb. 16, 1968): 578-9. [Reply 88: 158-9.]

   Discussion of divorce and the Irish Constitution and
   recent attempts to reform divorce provisions which are
   seen as discriminating against both non-Catholics and
   Catholics who have had their marriages annuled by the
   Church.

1548   Ignota. "The Present Legal Position of Women in the
United Kingdom." Westm R 163 (May 1905): 513-529.

   Discussion of provisions of the successful Married
   Women's Property Acts affecting England and Ireland,
   (passed 1870- 1893) and other legislation relevant to
   women's position. Argues for their admission to the
   practice of law and their right to the Parliamentary
   franchise; also notes continuing anomalies in laws
   relevant to them.

1549   "Ireland Declines to Ratify the Convention on the
Elimination of Discrimination Against Women." Women View 3
(Autumn 1980): 15.

   A brief note on the articles of this Convention which set
   forth in legally binding form internationally accepted
   principles and measures to achieve equal rights for women

everywhere.

1550   Ireland (Eire) Office of the Attorney General. The Law
of Nullity in Ireland. Dublin: Stationery Office. 1976 57pp.

A memorandum and a draft bill on the law of nullity
prepared to facilitate discussion of reform legislation.
Detailed analysis of grounds of nullity, void and
voidable marriages, bars to relief, consequences of a
nullity decree, ancillary orders, nullity proceedings,
collusion, etc. Concludes with specific recommendations
for appropriate modifications and amendments.

1551   Irish Women's Franchise League. Facts for Irish Women.
[Dublin. Reprinted from the Irish Citizen 1912.] 1 fold.

Presentation of some legal disabilities suffered by
women: not legally a person, not recognized as a parent,
must prove cruelty to get a divorce even if her husband
has a mistress, employment discrimination.

1552   [Kerr, A.] "The Need for a Recognition of Divorces
Act." Dublin U Law J No.1 (1976): 11-17. refs.

Irish residents who have obtained foreign divorces may
not have these recognized under Irish law. Resulting
problems could involve statutory rights of persons under
the Succession Act, interstate succession, deserted wives
allowances, prosecution for bigamy, nullity suits, tax
liability, legitimation of children of subsequent
marriage, etc. A Divorce Recognition Act or some
definitive ruling by the Irish Supreme Court seen as
necessary to clarify which foreign divorces will be
recognized in the Irish Republic.

1553   Kerr, Gillian (ed.). Custody of Children on Breakdown
of Marriage in Northern Ireland: report of the proceedings of
a seminar held in the Queen's University, Belfast on June 12,
1981. Belfast: Queen's University, Belfast. Faculty of Law.
Servicing the Legal System, 1982. 37pp. (Cover title SLS
Conference Report) refs.

Covers definition of terms, existing law, trends in
custody and access disputes and role of social worker
reports in these.

1554   Law Students Debating Society. The Legal Position of
Women in England and Ireland. An address delivered in the
Kings Inns October 29, 1878 by the auditor Seymour Bushe.
Dublin: Printed by Charles Chambers, 1878. 35pp.

A brief review of legal disabilities of women under
British Law. Heritage of Common Law ideas still reflected

in the legal discrimination suffered by women. Presents
arguments for the complete proprietary rights of married
women.

1555   Lawson, William. (L.L.D. Barrister-at-Law) "The
Liability of Married Women to Income Tax." Stat & Soc Inq Soc
Ire J 10 (Aug. 1899): 432-436.

Calls attention to the anomalous state of the law as
regards the liability of married women to Income Tax
under the 1842 Income Tax Act (extended to Ireland in
1853) and argues for the elimination of this aspect of
discrimination against married women.

1556   Lee, Gerard A. "Aspects of the Irish Constitution. IV
Irish Matrimonial Laws and the Marital Status." Chr Rex 23
(1) (Jan. 1969): 65-74. refs.

The Irish Constitution guarantees the protection of the
family and the civil and ecclesiastical authorities in
the Republic prohibit divorce. There is however some
ambiguity regarding the legal recognition of foreign
divorces. Lee argues that there is a conflict not merely
between canon and civil law relating to marriage in the
Republic of Ireland but also between the Irish and
British civil law of marriage relating to the effect in
Ireland of a divorce a vinculo lawfully decreed by the
courts in England under their domestic law.

1557   Lee, Gerard. Irish Matrimonial Laws and the Marital
Status. [Reprinted from the Northern Ireland Legal Quarterly
16 (3) Sept. 1965: 387-398.) Belfast: Newry: W&S Magowan,
Ltd., 1965.

A discussion of the conflict between civil and
ecclesiastical rules relating to marriage validity in the
Republic of Ireland and the problems faced by the Irish
courts in forming judgements regarding the status of
residents divorced in other territories.

1558   The Legal Rights of Women in Ireland. [San Francisco,
Consulate General of Ireland, 1975?] 1p.

1559   Lynch, J. "Legal Status of Women in Ireland." Admin 23
(1) (Spring 1975): 61-67.

An article by the then leader of the Opposition party
discusses pre-existing anomalies in the law which worked
against women and which have been removed by recent
legislation e.g. the Woman's Status Act, 1957, the
Guardianship of Infants Act 1957, the removal of the
Marriage Bar against teachers in 1957 etc. Notes
persisting anomalies in the area of social welfare
legislation.

1560   MacAonghusa, Proinsias. "Ireland's Divorce Battle."
New Statesm 74 (Dec. 22, 1967): 874-5.

    A discussion of proposed changes in Ireland's divorce
    laws which would give non-Catholics the freedom to
    divorce. Reaction from various clerical figures: Cardinal
    Conway, head of the Catholic Church opposed; Presbyterian
    and Church of Ireland spokesmen welcomed the proposed
    change in principle even though the latter do not
    recognize divorce within the Church. Constitutional
    problems of allowing divorce to some categories of
    citizens while denying this to others, noted.

1561   "Maternity Provisions in Ireland: a Review of Current
Practice." Eur Ind Rel R No.30 (June 1976): 10-12.

    Overview of the situation regarding maternity leave in
    Ireland includes an account of the statutory provisions
    and current practice in both the public and private
    sectors. Maternity leave is not specifically dealt with
    other than in general social welfare legislation in
    Ireland.

1562   Murphy, Yvonne. "Family Law in Ireland - A Guide."
Trib Mag 2 (28) (Aug. 1, 1982): 4-7.

    An overview by a lawyer of recent changes in family law
    in Ireland. Areas covered include capacity and
    entitlement to marry; ending the marriage or deciding it
    never really existed; children; maintenance of spouses
    and children; family home; succession; legal aid and
    other help. Not covered - the family outside marriage,
    the adoption acts and the whole area of procedure.

1563   "New Irish Anti Discrimination Bill (London)." Ind Rel
R & Rep No.118 (Dec. 1975): 21-22.

    An examination of the main provisions of the proposed new
    Irish legislation e.g. the Anti-Discrimination
    (Employment) Bill 1975, intended to complement the Anti
    Discrimination (Pay) Act already on the State Book,
    compares this new bill with the equivalent section of the
    United Kingdom Sex Discrimination Act.

1564   Newman, Jeremiah (Rev.) "Socio-Political Aspects of
Divorce." Chr Rex 23 (1) (Jan. 1969): 5-14.

    Refutation of the arguments for legalizing divorce in
    Ireland presented in the recently published Report on the
    Constitution e.g. (1) the existence of minorities who
    favor this (2) the anomalous situation of those Catholics
    to whom the Church grants decrees of nullity which have
    no force in civil law. The author concludes with a
    restatement of the traditional Catholic position against
    divorce.

1565   O'Neill, Gregory. "Maintenance. Making A Reasonable Effort?" Case (Apr. - June 1979): 13-14.

Examines the philosophical background of family law in Ireland which rests on the premise that the State's interest in the maintenance of the wife and children of a broken marriage stems from its concern that they might become a charge on public funds.

1566   O'Reilly, James. "Marital Privacy and Family Law." Studies 66 (161) (Spring 1977): 8-24. refs.

This article treats the 1973 Supreme Court decision in McGee versus Attorney General which established a right of marital privacy including access to contraceptives. Background and implications of Supreme Court action discussed. Author states that this constitutional right of marital privacy while protecting family planning does not mean a right to abortion.

1567   O'Reilly, James. Custody Disputes in the Irish Republic: the Uncertain Search for the Child's Welfare?" Ir Jur 12 (Summer 1977): 37-70. refs.

An incisive analysis of difficulties in the application of the Guardianship of Infants Act 1964. These concern (1) lack of finality in custody decisions, (2) difficulties in interpretation caused by differing treatment of matrimonial misconduct, (3) lack of a coherent philosophy or approach that would ensure consistency in application. Guidelines to help resolve these problems suggested and the need for a child centered approach strongly argued.

1568   O'Reilly, James. "Illegitimacy and the Law." In Conference on the Unmarried Parent and Child in Irish Society, pp. 21-31. Dublin: Cherish, 1975. refs.

A review of the present legal situation in Ireland considers the status of bastardy, the almost non-existent succession right of the illegitimate child, lack of procedures to establish proofs of paternity, problems of affiliation proceedings, unmarried mother's allowance. Calls for abolition of legal discriminations between legitimate and illegitimate and points to the example of many countries.

1569   O'Reilly, James. "Family Law in Ireland." Soc Stud 2 (6) (1973): 599-604.

Examines the currrent state of family law in Ireland and notes various shortcomings in the areas of legal aid, maintenance provisions, broken marriages, etc.

1570   Osborough, Nial. "Commission on the Status of Women."
Ir Jur 4 (1969): 327-329.

A discussion of recent legal reforms in the status of
married women, including the Married Women's Property
Act. Includes suggestions for further beneficial changes.

1571   Palley, Claire. Wives, Creditors and the Matrimonial
Home." No Ire L Q 20 (2) (1969): 132-140.

Argues that the Parliament should enact legislation
making spouses joint tenants of the matrimonial home on
marriage or purchase to protect deserted wives, avoid
disputes over spouses' rights in the matrimonial home and
eliminate many of the financial objections to divorce.

1572   Parent Versus Parent. North West Region Irish
Association of Social Workers, 1984.

Papers of a conference held in July 1983, following the
transfer of jurisdiction of applications under the
Guardianship of Infants Act from the High Court to the
Circuit and District Courts, to explore the legal,
psychological and social implications considered by
courts in dealing with disputes between parents over
custody, access and maintenance of their children
following marital breakdown.

1573   Phelan, Andrew. "The Proof of Irish Marriages." Law J
106 (July 6, 1956): 422.

Comments on the implications of Ireland's departure from
the British Commonwealth in 1949 for procedures for the
proof of public documents such as marriage certificates.
Concludes that no change is necessary in these
procedures.

1574   Quekett, Arthur S. (Sir). "Divorce Law Reform in
Northern Ireland." J Comp Leg 3rd Series. 22 (1) (1940):
32-35.

Background and scope of Matrimonial Causes Act of 1939
which substituted a judicial for a legislative system of
divorce.

1575   Quinn, Bernadette. "A.I.M. for Women." Reality 36 (8)
(Aug. 1972): 44-46. il.

Brief note on formation and goals of A.I.M., a group
organized to lobby for legislation giving a wife a legal
right to a percentage of her husband's income if he fails
to suppport her or their family.

1576   Redmond, Mary. "The Law and the Marital Breakdown." Ir Theo Q 45 (3) (1978): 191-200. refs.

An attempt to offer a new solution to the problems caused by Irish marriage laws other than the remedies traditionally suggested e.g. divorce or wider nullity laws.

1577   Robinson, Mary T. "Reform of the Law Relating to Family Planning." Dublin U Law J 2 (1976):12-14.

Review of history and content of three bills related to family planning all of which were defeated in the Irish Parliament: The Criminal Law Amendment Bill 1971, Family Planning Bill 1973 and Control of Information, Sale and Manufacture of Contraceptives Bill, 1974. Yet another bill, Family Planning Bill, 1974 which received its first reading in November 1974 was still pending in July 1976.

1578   Samuels, Alex. "Remarriage and the Widow's Damages." No Ire L Q 18 (4) (1967): 422-427. refs.

Discussion of the Fatal Accidents Acts 1946-1959 which require the court in assessing damages for the widow to take into account the fact of remarriage or the prospects of such on the grounds that remarriage would almost inevitably reduce the financial loss otherwise resulting from the death of the first husband.

1579   Shatter, Alan. Family Planning Irish Style. Dublin: Artifacts, Ltd., 1979. 30p. il.

The Health (Family Planning) Bill 1978 was given its first reading in Dail Eireann on December 13, 1978. This book briefly examines and illustrates the way in which the Bill may affect certain categories of persons and bodies who come within its ambit.

1580   Shatter, Alan. Family Law in the Republic of Ireland. Dublin: Wolfhound Press, 1977. 360pp. tables.

Designed for the law practitioner and law student, this is described as "the first comprehensive book written by an Irish lawyer on this particular branch of the law." The major areas of family law are covered. Author offers criticism of existing system and concrete suggestions for reform; he also analyzes the effect of the special status accorded to the family in the Constitution.

1581   Simms, K. "The Legal Position of Irishwomen in the Later Middle Ages." Ir Jur New Series. 10 (1975): 96-111. refs.

A detailed scholarly study based on literary, legal,

church and administrative records examines Irish
Matrimonial practices and the status of women for the
period 12th to 16th century. Findings indicate that canon
law was frequently ignored by the Irish aristocracy and
recognized male/female unions often preceded a valid
church marriage. During the course of the 16th century
these practices gradually ceased. Overall the status of
Irish women in this period did not compare favorably with
women in the rest of Europe.

1582   Thurneysen, Rudolf and others. Studies in Early Irish
Law. Dublin: Royal Irish Academy, 1936. 286pp. refs.

A group study of the legal status of women in early Irish
law based mainly on the Cain Lanamna consists of a German
translation and interpretation of the text and chapters
on special branches of the law relating to women e.g.
classes of women described in the Senchas Mar; the
relationship of Mother and Son, Father and Daughter, law
of inheritance, education of children, women's legal
capacity.

1583   V.T.H.D. "The Legal Status of Married Women." Ir Jur
21-22 (1955- 1956): 49-52. refs.

The issues raised by the legislation introduced in Dail
Eireann on October 31, 1956 under the short title of "The
Married Women's Status Bill." Details on the then current
situation regarding legal proceedings between spouses: as
governed by the common law, as modified by the Married
Women's Property Acts 1882-1907 and the effect of changes
envisioned in the pending legislation.

1584   Veitch, Edward. "A Law Reform (Bereaved Spouses) Act."
No Ire L Q 22 (3) (Autumn 1971): 319-332. refs.

Discussion of provisions of the English Law Reform
(Miscellaneous Provisions) Act, 1971 known popularly as
the Widows Damages Act points out serious errors of
omission in this which should be addressed if this were
to be re-enacted for Northern Ireland.

1585   Vereker, J.P. "Judgement Mortgages by and Against
Females." Ir Law Times & Sol J 6 (1872): 204-205.

Explication and discussion of titles "spinster" and
"widow" in legal terminology especially as applied to
judgement mortgages by or against females.

PENAL LAW

1586   Abortion and Law. A Doctrine and Life Special. Dublin:
Dominican Pubs., 1983. bibl. refs.

A collection of essays centering on the issue of abortion
in response to the Anti-Abortion Amendment campaign. The
contributors, opposed to abortion, but also to the
Amendment, discuss the difficulties and the legal and
social implications of such a Constitutional change.

1587   "The Abortion Referendum" : The Case Against. Ed. by
Mavis Arnold and Peadar Kirby. Dublin: AntiAmendment
Campaign, 1983. 83pp.

Overview of the arguments, including discussion of legal,
ethical, medical and political aspects, against the
referendum on abortion with background information on the
campaign.

1588   Belfast Women's Aid. "Belt Tightening or Suffocation?
The Case of Belfast Women's Aid and the E.H.S.S.B." Scope 29
(Nov. 1979): 17. il.

Brief note on purpose, operation and funding of the
voluntary organization which acts as a refuge and support
for battered women.

1589   Boyle, Christine. "Violence Against Wives: the
Criminal Law in Retreat?" No Ire L Q 31 (1) (Spring 1980):
35-57. refs.

Considers various possible explanations for the growing
reluctance to apply the law in the domestic sphere:
tendency to regard family violence as cases of civil
rather than criminal law; inherent difficulties in
enforcing the law inside the home; privacy considerations
and male attitudes. Author calls for consistency both in
structure and enforcement of criminal law to demonstrate
seriousness and validity of complaints of wife abuse.

1590   Carne, Ros. "Dublin's Prostitutes." Magill Mag 2 (6)
(1979): 29-31. il.

Presents statistics for 1977 on arrests/convictions for
street prostitution in Dublin with excerpts from case
histories and brief discussion on sanctions, areas of
operation and role of police.

1591   Coolock Community Law Centre. "Barred." Report on a
Survey into the Operation of Section 22 of the Family Law
(Maintenance of Spouses and Children) Act, 1976. Dublin:
Coolock Community Law Centre, 1979. 31pp.

Report of a survey conducted between December 1st, 1977
and March 23rd, 1978 of free Legal Advice Centres on the
operation and effectiveness of the law barring a violent
spouse from the home. Includes an analysis of all cases
coming to court during period of the survey.

1592   Corea, Gena. "The Violence Isn't All in the Streets."
Ms 8 (July 1979): 94+.

A brief discussion of violence toward women - wives and
daughters - in Northern Ireland. Includes some case
histories of father/daughter incest, wife-battering and
other forms of domination/cruelty.

1593   Council for the Status of Women. Submission on Rape in
Ireland. Dublin: The Council. [n.d.] 19pp.

The Report describes the procedure for reporting rape in
Ireland. Covers pretrial and preliminary procedure,
trial, evidence, consent, degree of proof, indecent
assault etc. Offers specific recommendations for reform
of the law in definition of what constitutes rape,
evidence, the anonymity of complainant and accused, women
on juries, legal aid. Also offers recommendations in
regard to medical, police and scientific investigation.

1594   Devane, Richard S. "The Legal Protection of Girls." Ir
Eccl Rec 37 (1931): 20-40. tables.

Discussion of a Departmental Committee established by
the Ministry for Justice in Ireland to review the
Criminal Law Amendment Act of 1815 which concerns the
protection of women and girls, particularly in relation
to procuration, seduction, abduction, rape and brothel-
keeping.

1595   Dublin Rape Crisis Centre. First Report. Dublin: Rape
Crisis Centre. Jan. 1979. 12pp. refs.

Offers a definition of rape, describes social attitudes
and myths that encourage this, details the law and
police/court procedures in this area and explains the
aims and services of the Centre.

1596   Evanson, E. Hidden Violence: A Study of Battered Wives
in Northern Ireland. Belfast: Farset Press, 1982. 80pp. il.
tables. refs.

Reports results of a survey of battered women in Northern
Ireland, part of a wider study of single parent families
conducted in 1978/9. Also, includes interviews with women
from refuges for victims of wife abuse. Covers a range of
social and interpersonal data relating to wife battering
including incidence, causes and support services.

1597   "Family Law: Barring Orders." Ir Law Times VI (6)
(Oct. 1983): 96-97. refs.

Discussion of two recent cases involving barring orders
questions whether the consideration of children's
interests should take precedence over the safety or

welfare of a spouse in deciding such cases. Argues that
barring orders should only be made in cases of serious
misconduct.

1598   Finegan, John. The Story of Monto: an Account of
Dublin's Notorious Red Light District. Cork: Mercier Press,
1978. 48pp.

An account of an area of Dublin where for about 100
years, prostitution was not only tolerated but openly
flaunted and liquor was available 24 hours a day. Most
active period 1860-1900. Details on clientele, Madames
and prostitutes, fees, literary references, etc. and role
of Frank Duff and the Legion of Mary in reform activity.
By 1930 the area had been totally cleared. Some
discussion of subsequent commerical sex activities in
other areas of Dublin.

1599   Gannon, Ita and Jack Gannon. Prostitution: The Oldest
Male Crime. Dublin: Jig Pubs., 1980. 24pp.

A denunciation of prostitution as a social evil by which
women are economically and sexually exploited by men.
Offers suggestions on how this might be eliminated,
including penal sanctions against clients.

1600   "Homicide and Abortion in England and Ireland." J Crim
Law 21 (Oct.-Dec. 1957): 362-365.

Comment and interpretation regarding the decision of the
Court of Criminal Appeal in Eire in the People (A..G.) v.
Cadden (91I.L.T.R.97) in which a midwife was convicted of
murder by the use of an instrument in an attempt to
procure an abortion. Author points out the differing
interpretation by the courts in England and Ireland of
old common law doctrine.

1601   McCafferty, Nell. A Woman to Blame. Dublin: Attic
Press, 1986. il.

Kerry babies case.

1602   Mathews, Mary. "Abortion and Irish Law." Law & Justice
No. 58/59 1978: 81-98. refs. (Originally appeared in the
Catholic Lawyer 22 (Autumn 1976) with a longer title.)

Examines existing statutory provisions upon which the
crime of abortion rests in Ireland, the rights of the
fetus at law and discusses the relevant constitutional
provisions.

1603   Middleton, Audrey. "Belfast Women's Aid." Quest No. 6
(Mar. 1977): 5-6.

Account of the operation and philosophy of the refuge for battered women in Belfast.

1604   O'Donnell, Rory and Teresa Brannick. "The Influence of Turnout on the Results of the Referendum to Amend the Constitution to Include a Clause on the "Rights of the Unborn": A Review of Walsh's Findings." Econ & Soc R 16 (1) (1985): 59-69. tables. refs. (Reply by Walsh pp. 71-78.)

Challenges the validity of Walsh's attempt to assign a preference either for or against the Amendment to those who abstained from voting in the 1983 Referendum.

1605   Rynne, Andrew (Dr.) Abortion: The Irish Question. Dublin: Ward River Press. [1982]   220pp.

Current law on abortion, statistics on number of Irish women who had legal abortions in England, background of events surrounding the Irish Anti-Abortion campaign, major groups involved and arguments on both sides of this complex issue briefly summarized by an Irish doctor who makes clear his own Anti-Abortion position.

1606   Wardell, J. "Notes from the Dublin Intelligence Regarding Rapparees, and the Forcible Abduction in 1707, of Margaret Mac Namara, County Clare, by John O'Brien." Roy Soc Antiq of Ire J Ser. 5 13 (1903): 91.

Note on news item in the Dublin Intelligence of May 27, 1707 of the abduction of a 13 year old gentlewoman with a reward of 20 guineas for anyone who would rescue her.

1607   Women Against Violence Against Women. [Dublin: Dublin Rape Crisis Group, 1978]. 3 leaves.

Two leaflets, one asking support for an anti-rape march organized by the Dublin Rape Crisis Group for the 13th of October 1978, and the other a press statement about the march.

1608   Women Against Rape Action Group. Rape: A Crime of Violence. Dublin: W.A.R.A.G., n.d. 1 leaf.

Employment and Economic Life

This section contains publications dealing with the economic situation of women, primarily outside the family context - e.g. women in the recognized labour force, including overwhelmingly works dealing with disparities between male and female workers in terms, conditions and types of employment and career prospects. Because of the large volume of material on the single issue of EQUAL PAY, these studies have been grouped here as a single sub-category. All discussions of legal decisions affecting women's employment, including protective legislation are grouped here because of the direct connection between these and women's status in the labour force. Also included in this section are works dealing with factors inhibiting female employment including social attitudes towards women workers and/or working mothers; also accounts of women's organized economic activity in cooperative movements or trade unions. Some material on women's work within the home is included where this had a recognized financial return as are other family-related remunerated activity such as begging by female "travellers." Also included in this section are studies of the financial situation of widows or deserted wives. More traditional anthropologic discussions of women's family work roles will be found under COMMUNITY STUDIES; for studies of role conflict experienced by working mothers see the sections on PSYCHOLOGY and MARRIAGE AND THE FAMILY; see also the latter for materials on economic aspects of family life e.g. family allowances, dowries. For ideological statements on women's right to independent economic careers see PERSPECTIVES ON WOMEN'S LIBERATION. Material on commercial sex activity is located under LAW - PENAL LAW.

GENERAL

1609   "Access to Employment, Job Interviews and Discrimination." Ir Law Times VI (6) (Oct. 1983): 94-101.

Analysis and discussion of the recommendation of the
Equality Officer in the case of Chaney versus University
College, Dublin (EE 15/83). Issues involved a female
applicant for employment considered to have been
discriminated against by being asked questions regarding
her children during the job interview that were not asked
of male applicants. Nominal nature of compensation noted.

1610   Anco. Training for Women - Adult and Apprentice
Courses. Dublin: Anco, 1975. 13pp.

Pamphlet introducing the Industrial Training Authority
(Anco- An Chomhairle Oiliuna) established by the
Government in 1967 to provide and promote the provision
of training at all levels in commerce and industry with
details on what courses are open to men and women and
those geared specifically to women.

1611   Anti-Discrimination (Pay) Act, 1974. Explanatory
Booklet for Employers and Employees. Dublin: Department of
Labour, 1977. 8pp.

General guidance about the provisions of the Act in
non-legal language.

1612   "Army Commissions For First Women Officers." Ire Today
977 (June 1981): 15.

News item on the first eight women officers commissioned
as Second Lieutenants at the Curragh Camp, Co. Kildare,
Ireland.

1613   Barry, Bernadette. Women at Home: a Report on
Nationwide Get-togethers of Women. Dublin: Council for the
Status of Women [1982] 28pp.

Report on a series of discussions held in eight rural
venues in 1981 at which women working full time within
the home voiced their concerns. (See Walsh, M. #1776.)

1614   Bell, Cecil A. "A Businessman's View of Women in
Management." Admin 23 (1) (Spring 1975): 84-88.

The author who is managing director of a firm which
employs three hundred people discusses the reasons so few
women occupy managerial positions and possible measures
to correct this imbalance.

1615   Bennett, Don, "Maggie Feathers and Missie Reilly:
Hawking Life in Dublin's City Quay." In Culture and Ideology
in Ireland, C. Curtain et al, eds., pp. 136-152. Galway:
Galway University Press, 1984. refs.

An account of daily life among one extended family of
street traders based on 80 oral interviews with
approximately 60 persons as part of a broad based study
of Irish urbanism and working-class history.

1616   Bhroin, Noirin Ni. _The Motivation and Productivity of
Young Women Workers_. Dublin: Irish National Productivity
Committee, 1969. 151pp. il. tables. bibl.

(See Ni Bhroin Noirin, #1735.)

1617   Bhroin, Noirin Ni and Gillian Farren. _The Working and
Living Conditions of Civil Service Typists_. The Economic and
Social Research Institute, 1978. 164pp. tables. refs. (Paper
93.)

(See Ni Bhroin Noirin, #1736.)

1618   Blackburn, Helen. (ed.) _A Handbook of Reference for
Irishwomen_. London: The Irish Exhibition, 1888. 112pp. map.
tables.

An analysis of certain cottage industries in Ireland,
traces the role of convents and of benefactors in
forwarding this work and stresses the need for technical
and industrial training and greater coordination.

1619   Blackwell, John. "Women in the Irish Civil Service: A
Comment." _Seirbhis Phoibli_ 6 (1) (Eanair 1985): 9-16.

Reaction to previous articles by Meehan (see #1723) and
Lenihan (#1707). Blackwell suggests that more data is
needed on speed of progress through grades in the Civil
Service and on numbers who apply for and are successful
in obtaining more specialized positions to get total
picture of equality of opportunity and treatment of women
in the Service.

1620   Bolger, Pat (ed.) _And See Her Beauty Shining There_.
Dublin: Irish Academic Press, 1986. 96pp. il.

Essays by Horace Plunkett, A E and others on the Irish
Countrywomens' Association 75th Anniversary.

1621   Boyle, Elizabeth. _The Irish Flowerers_. Belfast: Ulster
Folk Museum and Institute of Irish Studies, Queen's
University, Belfast, 1971 160pp. map. plates. portr. bibl.

A history of the Irish embroidery and lace industries
describes the working lives of the mostly female,
embroiders, their patrons and agents. Also attempts to
estimate the importance of Irish lacemaking at various
periods, the views the workers themselves took of their
skills and the value of earnings.

1622   Boyle, Elizabeth. "Embroidery and Lacemaking in Ulster." Ulster Folk 10 (1964): 5-22. plates. refs.

   Overview of development and present status of above industries, salary levels and future prospects.

1623   Bradshaw, Myrrha, ed. Open Doors for Irishwomen: A Guide to the Professions Open to Educated Women in Ireland. [Foreward by the Countess of Dudley.] Dublin: Irish Central Bureau for the Employment of Women, 1907. 80pp.

   Lists careers open to women with details on personal qualifications, preliminary education, professional training, remuneration and prospects for advancement.

1624   Breen, Richard. "Farm Servanthood in Ireland 1900-1940." Econ Hist R 36 (1) (1983): 87-102. tables. refs.

   Brief account of recruitment, working conditions and class background of male and female servants in Ireland based on fieldwork in Beaufort, a rural community in County Kerry, including testimony of informants (1925+) and Census schedules for 1901 and 1911. Overall these appear to have been treated less well than their counterparts elsewhere in the British Isles.

1625   Brennan, Niamh. "Women in the Profession - A Changing Profile." Acct Ire 16 (5) (Nov. 1984): 16-17. portrs. tables.

   Comment on female membership of the Institute of Chartered Accountants in Ireland (ICAI) which in 1984 represented 4.5% of the total membership. 70% of these have qualified in the last five years. Their distribution and future trends briefly discussed.

1626   Bryans, Hilary. "Women Power." Scope 26 (1929): 10-12. il.

   Comment and popular survey of "Women Power," the series on Women and Work in Northern Ireland by Janet Trewsdale and Mary Trainor. (See #1782-1784.) Claim that this statistical survey does not really sttempt to place the statistics in any broader social context and does not raise the issues of women's own perceptions of employment opportunities available in Northern Ireland and their own attitudes towards careers.

1627   de Burca, Mairin. "Feminist Battle at Dublin Airport." Hibernia 43 (June 21,1979): 9. il.

   Report on women aircraft cleaners at Dublin Airport seeking employment despite bitter opposition from the Irish Transport and General Workers Union and pusillaminity on the part of Aer Lingus.

1628   Cahill, Bernadette. "As Others See Us." Cross 64 (2)
(June 1973): 32-33. il.

    Brief critical discussion of the obstacles to employment
    married women in Ireland encounter.

1629   Carroll, Mary. "Are Irish Women Free?" Cross 61 (9)
(Jan. 1971): 11-12. il.

    Catalog of disabilities suffered by Irish women in work
    and in educational opportunities.

1630   Charter of Rights for Women. Dublin: Irish Congress of
Trade Unions, 1976. 1p.

1631   Commission of the European Communities 1975. Women and
Employment in the United Kingdom, Ireland and Denmark.
Cranfield: R.B.Cornu, 1974. 63pp. tables. refs.

    The second part of this study entitled "Women and
    Employment in Ireland" (pp.1-56) presents statistical
    information on the actual distribution of female
    employment by occupation, age, region, etc. and the
    social factors affecting this distribution: e.g. the
    economic and demographic background, education,
    unionization, social welfare legislation, marital status,
    maternity benefits and leave, marriage bar, pension
    schemes, etc. The data has been derived from the Report
    of the Commission on the Status of Women issued in
    December 1972 (See #1822), the Census of Population 1961,
    1966 and 1971, and the study, Women and Employment in
    Ireland: Results of a National Survey. (See #1773.)

1632   Connolly, James. Labour in Ireland. The Re-Conquest of
Ireland. With an introduction by Robert Lynd. Dublin and
London: Maunsel and Co. Ltd., 1917. 346pp.

    Chapter VI entitled "Woman" discusses the revolutionary
    value of woman's enfranchisement. The critique of
    capitalist society presented sees the worker as the slave
    of that society and the female worker as the slave of
    that slave. The system of private property and the law of
    primogeniture oppresses women. Peasant women and
    industrial women workers are viewed as equally oppressed
    being required to carry the double burden of work both
    inside and outside the home.

1633   Cornu, R.B. Women and Employment in the United
Kingdom, Ireland and Denmark. Cranfield: Commission of the
European Communities, 1974. 63pp. tables. refs.

    The chapter on Ireland details the distribution of female
    employment and factors affecting this. The major findings
    include (1) the overall low level of female participation

in the work force (26% in 1971) and the still lower
proportion of married women;(2) the occupation and
industry distribution of female workers reveals
pronounced patterns of sex segregation; (3) Women earn
generally far less than their male colleagues; (4) While
legislation has been initiated to remedy some of the more
blatant discrimination practices other areas still remain
to be addressed.

1634   Cromie, Stanley. "Women as Managers in Northern
Ireland." J Occ Psychol 54 (2) (1981): 87-91. tables. refs.

Forty percent of the employed work force in Northern
Ireland in 1979 were female; only 4.6% of these occupied
managerial positions. This study explores job involvement
of both men and women and attitudes toward women as
managers. Ninety nine women and 79 men in the Belfast
area were surveyed. Results indicate that there are no
differences in job involvement of men and women at the
same job level; however, men are less predisposed to
accept women as managers than are women.

1635   Crummey, Elizabeth. "A Woman's Work." Women View 5
(Spring 1981): 12.

Note on women conductors in C.I.E. (Corus Iompair
Eireann: the Irish Transportation System).

1636   Daly, Mary E. "Women in the Irish Workforce from
Preindustrial to Modern Times." Saothar 7 (1978): 74-82.
tables. refs.

Detailed analysis of the place of women in the Irish work
force over approximately two centuries and correlation of
this with social, economic and technological changes in
society. The role of full time homemaker as the ideal
occupation for all women had become enshrined by 1900 and
was not seriously challenged until the mid 1960's.

1637   Daric, Jean. "Quelques Vues sur le Travail Feminim non
Agricole en Divers Pays." Pop 13 (1) (Jan.-Mar. 1958): 69-78.
tables. refs.

Tables provide data on the evolution of labour force
participation by women from 1900-1950, and their relative
concentration by area of employment in many countries
including Eire. (Text in French.)

1638   Deeny, James. The Irish Worker: A Demographic Study of
the Labour Force in Ireland. Dublin: Institute of Public
Administration, 1971. 97pp. tables. refs.

Statistics from various official sources are combined and
analyzed to present a demographic picture of the labour

force in Ireland as of 1966. The overall demographic
patterns from 1926-1966 also briefly summarized.
Characteristics of the female labor force include a low
participation rate, a large proportion of young workers,
a large annual loss through marriage and emigration and
minimal employment of married women.

1639   Delap, Kathleen. "Women in the Home." Admin 23 (1)
(Spring 1975): 89-93.

An article by a member of the Executive Committee of the
Irish Countrywomen's Association on the social
contribution of married women as homemakers.

1640   Devine, Francis. "Early Slaves of the Linen Trade."
Liberty (Feb. 1976): 3. il.

Overview of early attempts to organize women in the
textile industry.

1641   Dickson, Emily W. "The Need for Women as Poor Law
Guardians." Dublin J Med Sci XCIX (April 1895): 309-314.

Presents arguments in favor of women serving as Poor Law
Guardians: women serve in that capacity in England,
management of a workhouse is very similar to household
management. Lists those activities which have been
successfully performed by women Guardians in England.

1642   Dublin Women's Suffrage and Local Government
Association. Suggestions for Intending Women Workers Under
the Local Government Act. Dublin: The Association. n.d.
(c.1901) 8pp.

Outlines the openings in public work for philanthropic
Irishwomen as a result of the Local Government Act of
1898 and the Women Poor Law Guardians Act of 1896.

1643   Duffy, Maureen. "The Working Wife in Dublin." Reality
38 (2;3) (Feb. 1974; Mar. 1974): 14-17; 17-20. il.

Report of a survey aimed at discovering the attitudes of
married women toward working wives. Respondents were a
random sample of 152 middle class housewives. Findings
indicated a mixture of approval and apprehension with
growing support for women at work - 64% believed roles of
mother and working wife were compatiable. But majority
felt that the working mother generally produces negative
effects on her children.

1644   du Lac, Pere (S.J.). "A Needle-worker's Trade Union."
Ir Mon 44 (Dec. 1916): 749-65.

Brief sketch of the life of Pere du Lac and his activities on behalf of the needle-workers of Paris with a partial excerpt in English of his writings on their behalf. A parallel is drawn between their situation and that of the women in the garment industry in Dublin with a brief outline of the dismal situation of the latter. du Lac argues for unionization of these.

1645   Eccles, Charlotte O Connor. "A Plea for the Modern Woman." Ir Mon 32 (May/June 1904): 241-248; 319-323.

A consideration of prejudice and other problems faced by women in the employment market. Author argues for an understanding of the economic motives that impel many women to work and insists they should not be disdained on this account. Argues furthermore that they should be allowed to work in whatever occupation they are fitted for not simply traditional "women's work".

1646   Employment Equality Agency; its Role in Eliminating Sex Discrimination and Promoting Equality of Opportunity Generally Between Men and Women in Employment. Dublin: Employment Equality Agency. n.d. 2pp.

1647   Employment Equality Agency. Women's Place in the Irish Economy, Present and Future: Report of a Seminar [held] in Trinity College, Dublin, November 25th, 1978. Dublin: Employment Equality Agency, 1978. 46pp.

Text of papers presented at the seminar dealing with women in the Irish economy: equal treatment in employment, recent legislation, training for a changing world, the European dimension, with discussion and summary.

1648   Employment Equality Act, 1977. Explanatory Booklet. Dublin: Department of Labour, 1977. 28pp.

Covers the scope of the Act, enforcement procedures and the role and function of the Employment Equality Agency.

1649   "Employment Equality Act." Trade Un Info (Autumn 1977): 4-6.

Summary of the main provisions of the Employment Equality Act 1977 which came into operation on July 1st, 1977.

1650   Employment Equality Act 1977. Guidelines for Employees. Dublin: Employment Equality Agency. n.d. 6pp.

1651   Employment Equality Agency. Report of a formal investigation under Section 39 of the Employment Equality

Act, 1977 in regard to the recruitment of air hostesses by
Aer Lingus. Dublin: Employment Equality Agency, 1978. 15pp.
tables.

> The findings indicated that there had been unlawful sex
> discrimination by Aer Lingus, Ireland's national airline,
> in relation to employment of men and in the
> classification and advertising of positions. However,
> revised advertising and subsequent recruitment of men as
> stewards seen as proof of a change of policy consistent
> with the Employment Equality Act of 1977 and formal
> investigation was concluded.

1652   Employment Equality Agency: Review of the Ban on
Industrial Nightwork for Women. Report to the Minister for
Labour under Section 38 of the Employment Equality Act 1977,
following a review of the prohibition in the Conditions of
Employment Act 1936 on the employment of women in industrial
work at night. Dublin: Employment Equality Agency, 1978.
38pp.

> The report found that the discrimination situation caused
> by the ban on nightwork for women should be rectified by
> abolition of this legislation.

1653   Employment Equality Agency: Guidelines for Eliminating
Discrimination from Job Advertisements. Dublin: Employment
Equality Agency, 1977. 1 fold leaf.

1654   Equal Opportunities Commission for Northern Ireland.
The Industrial Tribunals System - Recommendations for Change.
Belfast: The Commission, 1981. 34pp.

> The Commission supports the view that an Industrial
> Tribunal is the proper forum for the hearing of Equal Pay
> cases and Sex Discrimination cases concerning employment
> but recommends certain changes in the Industrial Tribunal
> System so as to ensure that the public feel confident
> that cases are handled in a manner consonant with the
> aims of the legislation.

1655   Equal Opportunities Commission for Northern Ireland.
Report of the Equal Opportunities Commission for Northern
Ireland. Belfast: H.M.S.O., 1977.

> Reports to Parliament pursuant to Article 54 and Schedule
> 3 of the Sex Discrimination (N1) Order 1976.

1656   Equal Opportunities Commission for Northern Ireland.
Sex Discrimination (Northern Ireland) Order 1976. Job
Advertisement Checklist. Belfast: The Commission. n.d. 1p.

> Emphasis on sexist terminology to be avoided in placing
> job advertisements.

1657   Equal Opportunities Commission for Northern Ireland.
Equal Opportunities: A Guide for Employees. Belfast: The
Commission. 1 leaf.

1658   - - - Equal Opportunities: Education. Belfast: The
Commision, 1976. 1 leaf.

1659   - - - Equal Opportunities: A Short Guide to the Sex
Discrimination (Northern Ireland) Order. Belfast: The
Commision, 1976. 1 leaf.

1660   - - - Equal Opportunities: A Guide for Employers.
Belfast: The Commision, 1976. 1 leaf.

1661   - - - Equal Opportunities: Housing, Goods, Facilities
and Services. Belfast: The Commision, 1976. 1 leaf.

1662   - - - Find Out About the Equal Opportunities
Commission for Northern Ireland. Belfast: The Commision,
1976. 1 leaf.

1663   - - - The Employers Guide to Equal Opportunities for
Men and Women. Belfast: The Commision. n.d. 32 pp.

1664   - - - Employment Advertising - The Equal Opportunities
Handbook. Belfast: The Commission, 1976. 8pp.

    Pamphlets outlining the provision of the Sex
    Discrimination (Northern Ireland) Order 1976 as it
    relates to employers, employees, provision of housing,
    goods, facilities, services, education and the role of
    the Commission in eliminating sex discrimination.

1665   Equal Status for Men and Women in Occupational Pension
Schemes. London: H.M.S.O., 1976. 232pp. refs.

    This extremely detailed and comprehensive 3 part
    Government report considers the existing pension
    legislation in the United Kingdom (including Scotland and
    Northern Ireland); existing legislation on equal status
    (the Equal Pay Act, 1970; the Sex Discrimination Act
    1975) and enforcement procedures, and concludes with a
    summary of conclusions and recommendations.

1666   Equality for Women: A Discussion Paper Presented to
Annual Delegate Conference 1980. (Prepared on behalf of the
National Executive council by the Research Department
Development Services Division, ITGWU.) Dublin: [Irish
Transport and General Workers Union, 1980.]   58pp.

1667   Evanson, Eileen. Who Needs Day Care: A Study of
Services for the Under Fives in Northern Ireland. Belfast:
Equal Opportunities Commission for Northern Ireland, 1983.
47pp. refs.

    Background on day care provision in both England and

Northern Ireland and the development of and response to a
day care service for children under five provided by a
voluntary organization - Foyle Day Care Association
(FDCA). Main aim of FDCA is to respond to parental needs
and to cater, in particular, for a group (working women)
discriminated against in the development of statutory
provision.

1668   Fairweather, Margaret I. "Quantity Surveying as a
Profession for Women." Alex Col Mag XCI (June 1938): 14-18.

A chartered quantity surveyer, then the only female in
the profession in Ireland discusses qualifications
required, the nature of the work and employment
opportunities.

1669   Fine-Davis, Margret. Women and Work in Ireland: A
Social Psychological Perspective. Dublin: Council for the
Status of Women, 1983. 239pp. tables. bibl.

Results of a nationwide survey on the quality of Irish
women's working lives in various roles - employee,
homemaker, retiree - ; the effect of their work on their
overall well-being and the societal context e.g. the
general attitudes and belief systems surrounding women's
roles. Data collected from a representative sample of
1862 male and female adult respondents interviewed in
1978. Data compared with 1981 and 1975 findings to
analyze trends. Includes summary of findings and
implications/recommendations for social policy.

1670   Fine-Davis, Margret. "Mothers' Attitudes Toward Child
Care and Employment: A Nationwide Survey." In Working Party
on Child Care Facilities for Working Parents. Report to the
Minister for Labour, pp. 73-168. Dublin: The Stationery
Office, 1983. tables. refs.

Reports results of a nationwide survey designed to elicit
accurate and systematic data on the actual and preferred
child-care arrangements used by working mothers and the
relationship of child care resources to employment for
currently non-employed mothers. Based on a 1981
nationwide representative sample of 1021 mothers (581
employed and 440 non-employed). Recent trends and events
influencing labour force participation of married women
described and policy recommendations advanced.

1671   Geary, R.C. and F.S. O Muircheartaigh. Equalization of
Opportunity in Ireland: Statistical Aspects. (ESRI Broadsheet
No. 10) Dublin: Economic and Social Research Institute, 1974.
122pp. tables. refs.

A detailed statistical analysis of factors central to
equalization in its relation to jobs and incomes based
mainly on 1966 Census figures and a 1972 study. Authors

conclude that employed women's significantly lower
earnings are primarily a result of their concentration in
specific industrial sectors and industries.

1672   Gibson, Edward. "Employment of Women in Ireland." Stat
& Soc Inq Soc J (April 1862): 138-143.

A Report on the founding in 1861 of an Irish branch of
the Society for promoting the employment of educated
women and its accomplishments, viz, the training of women
in such areas as bookkeeping, arithmetic, writing,
supervision, sewing, engraving, lithography, etc. and
their placement in industry. Other kinds of occupations
deemed suitable for women - who are neither wives nor
heads of families - briefly discussed.

1673   Gmelch, George. "The Effect of Economic Change on
Irish Traveller Sex Roles and Marriage Patterns." In Gypsies,
Tinkers and Other Travellers ed. by Farnham Rehfisch, pp.
257-269. London: Academic Press, 1975. il. refs.

A discussion of the causes and consequences of the
disruption of the Travellers traditional way of life.
Women derive a benefit from these changes which give them
economic power as breadwinners and thus control of family
finances and consequently a greater role in family
decision making. Other related changes include an earlier
age at marriage and an increase in cousin marriages.

1674   Gmelch, G. and S.B. Gmelch. "Begging in Dublin: The
Strategies of a Marginal Urban Occupation." Urb Life 6 (Jan.
1978): 439-454. refs.

An account of the begging strategies employed by Dublin
tinkers. This activity is exclusively reserved for the
female members of this migrant group, an outgrowth of
their traditional task of door to door peddling.

1675   Gorman, Liam. Managers in Ireland. Dublin: Irish
Management Institute, 1974. 228pp. charts. tables. il.

A study of the characteristics of managers employed in
the transportable goods industries in the Republic of
Ireland. Chapter 6 "Women in Irish Management" presents
data pertaining to women who comprise 30% of total
employees in manufacturing but are poorly represented in
managerial positions and mainly in the lower ranks.
Comparative data for Western Europe and the U.S. noted.

1676   Graecen, Lavinia. "Careers for Women: Law." Image 3
(4) (Mar. 1978): 30-31. portr.

1677   - - - "Careers for Women: Medicine." Image 3 (5)
(April 1978): 22-24. portrs.

1678   - - - "Careers for Women: Architecture." Image 3 (6)
(May 1978): 32-33. portr.

1679   - - - "Careers for Women: The Diplomatic Corps." Image
3 (7) (June 1978): 43-44. portr.

Brief overview of opportunities/qualifications for above
fields.

1680   Greacen, Lavinia. "Women in Business." Mgt 22 (3)
(Mar. 1975): 23-25. portrs.

Brief comments by some women executives on management
opportunities for women in Ireland and their own career
experiences.

1681   Great Britain. Royal Commission on Labour. The
Employment of Women. London: Printed for H.M. Stationery
Office of Eyre and Spottiswoode, 1893. 352pp. tables.

Chapter VI has an extremely detailed analysis of
industrial conditions of Irish women in 156 factories,
workshops and convent industries throughout Ireland.
Occupations include shop assistants, clothing industry -
including linen, woolen, poplin and tweed manufacture -
and trade, dairy, poultry and pig farming etc. with
details on distribution of workers, hours, salaries,
health, sanitation and other aspects minutely recorded.

1682   Groneman, Carol. "Working Class Immigrant Women in Mid
19th Century New York - Irish Woman's Experience." J Urb Hist
4 (3) (1978): 255-273.

An analysis of the distinct patterns of work, family and
leisure which the immigrants brought with them to the New
World focuses on Irish female emigration to pre-Civil War
New York City. Discusses the reasons for emigration:
increased use of land for tillage resulted in increase in
number of small farms, decline of domestic industries and
a phenomenal increase in population.

1683   Harris, Lorelei. "Industrialization, Women and
Working- Class Politics in the West of Ireland." Capital &
Class 19 (1983): 100-115. il. refs.

State sponsored industrialization in Ireland has created
a mass entry of women into industry. This study examines
the implications for trade unionism of the influx of
women into multi-national enterprises in County Mayo.
Concludes that women have weakened the possibilities for
trade-union militancy in the private sector but they will
have a positive long term effect on working class
politics in the Republic having now a voice outside the
home.

1684   Harris, Lorelei. "Class Community and Sexual Divisions in North Mayo." In Culture and Ideology in Ireland, C.Curtain et al, eds., pp.154-171. Galway: Galway University Press, 1984.

   Incorporates an analysis of the increase in women's participation in manufacturing industry in North Mayo between 1966 and 1979 and the effects of this on patriarchal relations within both the domestic and public spheres.

1685   Haslett, Deirdre. Discriminatory Aspects of the Social Welfare System. (Paper read to the I.C.T.U. One-day Conference on "Irish Women and Social Welfare," April 12, 1975.) [Dublin: Economic and Social Research Institute, 1975.] 207pp.

   A detailed analysis of two aspects of the Social Welfare System: the Social Insurance Contribution Scheme and the coverage of the Unemployment Service. Details the short-comings of these in relation to various categories of women, and the underlying philosophy which classes all women as dependent.

1686   Hayes, Dermott. "Women in the Public Service." Ind & Comm Tra (Mar. 1985): 25-30. il.

   Discussion of the status of women in the Civil Service. Disputes assertions by Meehan (see #1723.)

1687   Houston (Professor). "The Extension of the Field for the Employment of Women." Stat & Soc Inq Soc J IV (Nov. 1866): 345-353.

   Presents and refutes arguments against extending the field of employment for women while also indicating the real hardships suffered by women excluded from gainful employment or training. Opposing viewpoints presented in the discussion following the main paper.

1688   Humphreys, L.J. "Market Gardening as a Career for Women." Dept Agric & Fish J XVII (1) (Oct.1916): 36-39.

   Some general observations on market gardening and its possibilities as a career for educated women in Ireland.

1689   Hynes, Ita. Careers For Women. Dublin: Pillar Publishing Co., 1946. 79pp.

   Details on approximately 20 careers open to women specifying type of education and training required by each. Many represent new fields opened up to women during the 2nd World War.

1690   "Industrial Earnings." <u>Trade Un Info</u> (Feb.-Mar. 1970):
4-5. tables.

    Report of average earnings and hours worked by men and
women in industry September 1969. Women's hourly earnings
represented 55% of men's.

1691   "Industrial Earnings." <u>Trade Un Info</u> 12 (72) (Oct.
1956): 10-12. tables.

    Presents statistics on average weekly earnings of men and
women in industry October 1954. Points out that "average"
has little meaning since it conceals wide variations due
to the differing proportions of men, women and juveniles
employed; also average earnings are higher in industries
where the labour force is almost wholly male. Women's
earnings averaged 55% of men's earnings in all industries
taken together.

1692   The Institute of Chartered Secretaries and
Administrators. <u>Law and Current Affairs Committee. Republic
of Ireland Region. Employment Legislation in Ireland: A
Practical Guide and Handbook</u>. Dublin: Institute of Chartered
Secretaries and Administrators, 1978. 104pp.

    Includes a synopsis of the provisions of the Anti-
Discrimination (Pay) Act 1977; the Employment Equality
Act 1977 and the Family Law (Maintainance of Spouses and
Children) Act 1976.

1693   "Ireland. Child Care and Working Parents." <u>Eur Ind Rel
R</u> (May 1983): 26-27.

    Account of a major government-commissioned Report to the
Irish Minister for Labour which includes a series of
proposals aimed at easing the pressure on working parents
through improved day care facilities, reorganization of
work, flexible scheduling, part-time and temporary
employment. Background and recommendations of Report
discussed in detail.

1694   Irish Conference of Professional and Service
Associations. <u>Women in Employment: A Report by the Irish
Conference of Professional And Service Associations. Compiled
by Charles H. Smith</u>. Dublin: Irish Conference, 1982. 40pp.
tables. refs.

    Reports results of a survey carried out by the Irish
Conference of Professional and Service Associations of
their affiliated organizations to establish quantitative
data on women in employment especially in areas of
possible discrimination. 35,000 white collar employees in
target population. Areas covered include status of female
employees, promotion opportunities, maternity leave,

child-care, training, pension schemes, union
membership/officerships. Includes recommendations for
management, unions and women employees.

1695   Irish Congress of Trade Unions. Equality for Women
Workers: A Guide for Union Negotiators and Shop Stewards.
Dublin: Irish Congress of Trade Unions, [1978?]. 20pp.

    Brief note on the principle of equality, the provisions
    of the Employment Equality Act 1977, the issue of equal
    pay and women in trade unions.

1696   Irish Congress of Trade Unions. Submission by Irish
Congress of Trade Unions to Commission on the Status of
Women. Dublin: Irish Congress of Trade Unions, 1970. 29pp.
bibl.

    Statistical data on women in the labour force based on
    the 1966 Census. Discusses employment opportunities,
    including education; employment of married women, equal
    pay and trade union organization.

1697   Irish Textile Workers Union. [Textile Section: Irish
Women Workers Union] To The Linen Slaves of Belfast. Liberty
Hall, Dublin. (n.d.) 3pp.

    Call to the Belfast linen workers to organize to fight
    their miserable working conditions.

1698   The Irish Women Workers' Union. The Right To Work But
Not For Women. Dublin: Irish Women Workers Union, 1935. 4pp.

    Gives reasons for their opposition to the proposed
    government legislation which would prohibit the
    employment of women in certain forms of industrial work
    or restrict the number of women employees.

1699   The Irish Women Workers' Union. Memoranda [by the
Dublin Typographical Provident Society, the Irish Bookbinders
and Paper Rulers' Union, the Irish Women Workers' Union and
the Dublin branch of the Amalgamated Society of
Lithographers] submitted to the Minister of Industry and
Commerce in support of the claim for protection for printing.
n.p. 1925. 19pp.

1700   The Irish Women Workers' Union. The Wooden Horse: A
Reply to Fascists. [Dublin?]: Irish Women Workers Union. n.d.
8pp.

    Rejects policy of Fine Gael seen as a Fascist program
    where workers and women are denied their rights and
    advocates a strong trade union.

1701   The Irish Women Workers' Union. [Handbill urging women
workers to join the union.] Dublin: Irish Women Workers
Union. n.d. 1 leaf.

1702   Jackson, Karen. A Guide to Sex Discrimination and Fair
Employment Legislation in Northern Ireland. London: The
Industrial Society, 1977. 63pp.

        Covers in detail the Sex Discrimination (Northern
        Ireland) Order 1976, Fair Employment (Northern Ireland)
        Act 1976, including definition of terms, provisions,
        exceptions, enforcement, the Equal Opportunity
        Commission, Fair Employment Agency and the Fair
        Employment Appeals Board.

1703   Jackson, K.O. "Role of Voluntary Association in
Development of the Rural Community." Int R Com Devel 21
(1969): 199-220. il. refs.

        Description of the Irish Countrywoman's Association (ICA)
        as one of a number of Voluntary Associations in County
        Galway. Objectives and activities of organization
        detailed and its potential for implementation of
        development planning assessed.

1704   Jackson, Pauline and Ursula Barry. "Women Workers and
the Rationalization of Services." Soc Stud 8 (1-2) (Spring -
Summer 1984): 69-80. tables. refs.

        New services based primarily on developments in
        information technology are viewed as changing and
        contracting the service sector of the economy.
        Implications of these developments for women workers
        include reduced employment opportunities and
        deskilling/dehumanization of work environment.

*1705   Kennedy, Stanislaus. But Where Can I Go - Homeless
Women in Dublin. Dublin: Arlen House, 1985.

1706   Landau, Eve C. The Rights of Working Women in the
European Community. Brussels: Commission of the European
Community, 1985. 224pp. refs.

        Overview of positive developments at the close of the
        UN decade for women. Marked progress seen in the field of
        legislation and in judicial decisions concerning the
        equality of men and women in employment.

1707   Lenehan, Brian. "Leading Women Astray." Seirbhis
Phoibli 5 (1) (Bealtaine 1984): 15-22. il. tables.

        Response by the Principal Officer in the Management

Services Directorate of the Department of the Public
Service to article by Meehan (#1723) regarding status of
women in the Civil Service. While Lenehan accepts as true
the facts on actual status of women in the Service he
attributes this to the Marriage Bar (now discontinued)
and past discrimination in favour of women in
recruitment.

1708   Lentin, Ronit and Geraldine Niland. Who's Minding the
Children. Dublin: Arlen House, 1980. 137pp. bibl.

A description of child-minding facilities with a
discussion of attitudes towards working mothers and legal
considerations. Lack of governmental control of day care
centers and inadequate provision of these decried.

1709   Leydon, Mary. A Study of Young Women Industrial
Workers in the West of Ireland. (Dublin: ANCO Industrial
Training Authority), 1980. 102pp. bibl.

Reports results of interviews with 166 young unmarried
women workers in the greater Galway and Sligo areas
conducted in the period August 1977 - February 1978.
Pre-employment or on the job training of these almost
totally absent as was their trade union awareness. While
the vast majority had received a considerable amount of
post-primary education, they saw this as non-relevant to
their present employment and gave negative reasons for
taking factory work.

1710   Lindsay, Pauline. "Can Science Remain A Male
Preserve." Tech Ire 15 (9) (Feb. 1984): 25-28. il. tables.

Brief consideration of the role of education in the
representation of women in scientific and engineering
positions. Implications of this pattern in an
increasingly technological environment discussed with
excerpts from the Economic and Social Research Institute
report "Schooling and Sex Roles" commissioned by the
Employment Equality Agency.

1711   Lucey, Cornelius (Rev.) "The Problem of the Woman
Worker." Ir Eccl Rec 5th Ser. 48 (Nov. 1936): 449-467. table.

Discusses the effects of capitalism and industrialization
in opening up the labor market to women, the reasons
women engage in this work and the social and moral
consequences. Catholic doctrine on family life, a living
wage and on women's role presented and various proposals
offered to eliminate the economic necessity of women
working outside the home.

1712   Lynd, Robert. Home Life In Ireland. Chicago: A.C.
McClung & Co.; London: Mills and Boon, Ltd. [1909] 317pp. il.

(See Marriage and the Family #1269.)

1713   McCarthy, Eunice. "Work Orientations of Female and
Male Clerical/ Administrative Employees." Ir J Bus & Admin
Res 1 (1979): 86-98. tables.

   McCarthy reviews previous studies which have concluded
   that female employees do not seek satisfaction from
   intrinsic job factors but work primarily to fulfill
   financial and social needs. McCarthy in her study sought
   to control for another independent variable, e.g. job
   level. She chose a job importance model which consisted
   of 10 job characteristics which was administered to 228
   male and female employees. The findings revealed no sex
   differences between males and females at the same job
   level.

1714   McCool, Joe. "The Impact of Women on Irish Technology."
Technology 9 (12) (Mar. 1978): 11-18. il. graphs. refs.

   Presents a statistical breakdown of female engineers
   employed in Ireland and of female students studying
   engineering in college and at urban/regional technical
   schools. Despite a small gain in recent years, McCool
   concludes that women are not significantly participating
   in engineering and technical careers. Causes and future
   prospects briefly analyzed.

1715   McDermot, Derry. "Women in Trade Unions and Positive
Action." Women View 2 (Summer 1980): 7-9. il.

   Discusses the poor representation of women at executive
   levels in trade unions. Argues for reserved seats for
   women.

1716   McGuinness, Catherine. "Women - Living Down the
Stereotypes." Mgt 22 (3) (Mar.1975): 20-25. il.

   Overview of women's position in the workforce in Ireland:
   one third of the work force, they are generally
   concentrated in the lowest positions in all sectors. The
   role of stereotyped thinking about women's abilities,
   desires and opinions in creating or maintaining this
   position discussed. Included are interviews with four
   women who have made some progress in their careers.

1717   McKenna, Anne T. "Women in Public Administration."
Admin 12 (1) (Summer 1964): 61-66. tables. refs.

   This article presents data on the distribution of women
   in the Irish Civil Service. While the author suggests
   that the percentage of women employed in this sector is
   consistent with the employment ratio in this country as a

whole, the proportion of women in administrative and executive grades is low compared with similar figures for other countries. Possible explanations for this pattern, prospects and proposals for change discussed.

1718   McKenna, L. (Rev.) "A Plea for Mothers' Pensions." Ir Mon 47 (1919): 121-133.

Points out the difficulties of rearing children and also being a breadwinner and argues for state subsidies for mothers.

1719   McKeon, Barbara. "How To Succeed in Business Without Being a Man." Image (Sept. 1982): 74+. portrs.

Success stories of Anna Costello, dress designer-manufacturer, Rhona Techan, proprietor of a wine bar.

1720   Mallow, Ita. "Widows of Ireland Unite." Word (Nov. 1971): 17-19. il.

An account of the formation, achievements and objectives of the Association of Widows in Ireland founded in 1967.

1721   Martin, Mrs. Charles. "St. Martha's Home." Ir Mon 9 (1881): 57-60.

Description of a Catholic residence designed for female shop assistants, seamstresses, governesses, etc. Includes a plea for volunteers and benefactors.

1722   Matthews, Alan. "Women in the Farm Labour Force." Ir Farm Mon (Mar. 1981): 11-12.

Reviews various attempts to measure Irish women's actual participation in agriculture, roles available to farm women and changes in these.

1723   Meehan, Ita. "Women in the Civil Service." Seirbhis Phoibli 4 (2) (Nollaig 1983): 5-20. tables. portr.

Overview by the then Deputy Head of the Department of Posts and Telegraphs of the position of women in the non-industrial Civil Service and specifically of the negative effects of the removal of the "Marriage Bar" and the Employment Equality Act on their overall numbers and status despite the intent of these measures. Continued discrimination and prejudice against women seen as cause.

1724   Messenger, Betty. "You Will Easy Know a Doffer: The Folklore of the Linen Industry in Northern Ireland." Eire Ire 16 (1) (1979): 6-15. refs.

A slightly revised version of a paper read at a regional meeting of the American Committee for Irish Studies in October 1977. Preliminary research on the spinners and their work environment later expanded into a monograph on entire industry.

1725   Messenger, Betty. Picking Up the Linen Threads: A Study of Industrial Folklore. Austin: University of Texas Press, 1975. 265pp. il. bibl.

Detailed study of the Northern Ireland linen industry in the first decades of this century based on an extensive program of interviews with 84 people (24 male) who had worked in the factories or mills in Belfast. Topics covered include attitudes to work, work discipline, management practice, labour mobility, status and general conditions of work supplemented by songs, anecdotes, rhymes, narratives, riddles, nicknames and sayings that emerged from this work. In spinning and weaving the overwhelming majority of workers were female and this is primarily their own account of the quality of their lives.

1726   Messenger, Betty. "Picking Up the Linen Threads: Some Folklore of the Northern Irish Linen Industry." Folk Inst J 9 (1975): 18-27.

(See more extensive discussion in #1725.)

1727   Moran, Mairead. "Women and the Co-operative Movement." Coop Ire 37 (May 1979): 37-38; 38 (June 1979): 38-39.

An inclusive review of the part women have failed to play in the Irish Co-operative Movement and a program of how farm men and women might be re-united in a co-operative development program. Moran argues that the formation of the United Irishwomen as a separate female organization within the Co-operative Movement was a mistake. Neither the Co-operative Movement nor the political parties harnessed women's efforts in the development of the new state.

1728   "Mr. Thomas Johnson and the Strike. An Bhean - Oibre: the Woman Worker." Lughnasa (1928): 3.

News item regarding support given by Mr. Thomas Johnson, Secretary of the Irish Trade Union Congress to the Women Workers Union.

1729   Murie, Alan. "Family Income Supplement and Low Incomes in Northern Ireland." Soc & Econ Admin 8 (1) (Spring 1974): 22-42. il. refs.

An analysis of the Family Income Supplement scheme as it

operates in Northern Ireland as a limited anti-poverty
measure. The maximum benefit level prevents many families
from receiving an "adequate" benefit or achieving an
income position comparable to that of other F.I.S.
recipients where family composition is similar but
earnings differ. Implications of findings for F.I.S. and
other such schemes in other contexts and situations
discussed.

1730   Murphy, Christina. "Women in the Public Service." Pub
Affairs 6 (1) (Sept. 1973): 2-3. il. refs.

A discussion of the implications for women's status of
the removal of the marriage bar in the Civil Service and
other statutory bodies. Equal pay, maternity leave,
recruitment and promotion in this sector briefly
considered.

1731   Murphy, L. "Women's Sphere in the Poultry Industry
with Special Reference to Ireland." Dept Agric & Fish J XIX
(3) (May 1919): 293-7. tables.

Describes the unique role of women in the poultry
industry in Ireland. With the exception of the shipping
of the produce, almost the entire industry is controlled
by them. Their role and success in the different branches
of this industry are described; also a brief historical
background, including an account of the training of
teachers, the role of competitions and the appointment of
Marketing Inspectors all of which have been co-ordinated
by the Department of Agriculture.

1732   National Women's Talent Bank. Dublin. [n.d.] 4pp.

Established by the Government in December 1974 in
consultation with the Women's Respresentative Committee,
the Bank concerns itself with the identification of
qualified women with appropriate credentials which would
equip these for possible service on Governmental
committees and commissions or on boards of professional
organizations.

1733   "New Equal Opportunity Legislation for Ireland." Eur
Ind Rel R No. 43 (July 1977): 6-9.

A brief report on the establishment of Ireland's newest
statutory body, the Employment Equality Agency, which is
charged with the duty of promoting equality of
opportunity between men and women in employment and of
investigating and taking action to eradicate existing
discriminatory practices.

1734   "New Irish Anti-Discrimination Bill (London)." Ind Rel
R & Rep No. 118 (Dec. 1975): 21-22.

(See Law - General Legal Status #1563.)

1735   Ni Bhroin, Noirin. The Motivation and Productivity of Young Women Workers. Dublin: Irish National Productivity Committee, 1969. 151pp. il. tables. bibl.

Originally the authors MA thesis in 1967 this study examines job attitudes and motivation among female piece workers in a clothing factory in Dublin and the relationship of these and age of workers to job performance. Findings are related to organizational and technological factors, supervisory and training practice and the communication system. The importance of informal structures in industry and the perception by employees of incentive schemes are highlighted.

1736   Ni Bhroin, Noirin and Gillian Farren. The Working and Living Conditions of Civil Service Typists. The Economic And Social Research Institute, 1978. 164pp. tables. refs. (Paper # 93.)

Presents the results of a study that included practically every Civil Service typist working in Dublin in 1972. Includes descriptive data on their sex (all females), their age distribution, counties of origin, office skills, relevant Civil Service examination results, organization of their work, their attitudes to it, the correlation between this and organizational factors. Also their evaluation of their rented accomodation and their attitudes to city life are discussed.

1737   Ni Chuilleanain, Eilean. "Women as Writers: the Social Matrix." Crane Bag 4 (1) (1980): 101-105.

Discussion of the relationship of the woman writer to the social structure: class, community, professional/amateur categories. Risks for the artist include becoming embedded in her material, professionalism, mediocrity.

1738   "Nightwork for Women." Trade Un Info 242-246 (Spring 1979): 17.

A news item on the review of the ban on industrial nightwork for women by the Employment Equality Agency. Their report details the current legislation in this area; presents a summary of the relevant situation in other countries and recommends repeal of the legislation which imposes restrictions on women that do not apply to men.

1739   "No Token Women Here." Mgt 22 (4) (Apr. 1975): 9.

News item discussing Allied Irish Banks formation of a

committee to do a thorough overhaul of the whole question
of women in banking and ensure that equal opportunities
are available to all.

1740   Noel, Felicia."Why So Many Women Cannot Find Work." Ir
Mon XXXII (July 1904): 389-391.

Explanations include an inadequate educational system and
lack of appropriate training for available opportunities.

1741   O'Brennan, Lily. "An Appeal to Irishwomen." Capu An
(1933): 239- 240.

Appeal to women of Ireland to purchase Irish made goods.

1742   O'Connell, Joan. "Discrimination for a Woman Starts
The Day She Is Born." Th Wk Ire (Nov. 7, 1969): 9.

Brief note by the newly appointed Education Officer of
the Irish Congress of Trade Unions on the current status
of women and employment in Ireland and how the situation
might be improved.

1743   O'Keefe, Susan. "EDP -Why Women Have Not Stepped into
the Limelight." Bus & Fin 21 (32) (Apr. 1985): 26-27. il.

The Irish Industrial Development Authority launched an
Enterprise Development Program to encourage individual
entrepreneurship. Of the resulting 130 projects none were
instigated by women. This article advances some
explanations, primarily built-in eligibility criteria in
enterprise development which adversely affect female
applicants and social attitudes toward women in business.

1744   O'Leary, Michael. "Gentle Revolution." Admin 23 (1)
(Spring 1975): 4-7.

This article by the then Minister for Labour documents
recent and forthcoming legislation designed to eliminate
discrimination against women. Author also discusses
current activities of the Council for Social Affairs of
the E.E.C. in connection with the role of women in
society.

1745   - - - "Ireland's Own Efforts." Cross 66 (1) (May
1975): 9-10. portr.

This article presents economic arguments for giving women
a greater role in society. Details of recent and
forthcoming legislative measures to improve the situation
of women in Ireland presented.

1746   Owens, Evelyn. "The Slave of the Slave?" Cross 63 (10)
(Feb. 1973): 6-8. il.

The author, an Irish Senator, examines the position of
women in the trade unions and stresses the importance of
worker organization to remedy discrimination against
women in the labor market.

1747   de Paor, N. "Women in the Civil Service." Admin 3
(2-3) (Summer 1955): 141-147.

Of the 9000 women in the Irish Civil Service, most are in
the lower ranks. Promotion to higher ranks proceeds
slowly, and a woman who is promoted needs to be greatly
superior to her male competitors. Two arguments are
brought into every discussion on the position of women in
the Civil Service: (1) the average woman takes more sick
leave than a man and (2) the retirement of women on
marriage makes it wasteful to train them for higher
posts.

1748   Patterson, Patricia. "Aran Kitchens, Aran Sweaters."
Heresies (Winter 1978): 89-92. il.

Discussion of the two crafts executed by the women of
Aran, an island twelve miles off the West coast of
Ireland: interior design and knitting. Various stitches
illustrated, also the interiors of the kitchens.

1749   Plunkett, Sir Horace Curzon. Ellice Pilkington, and
George [W.] Russell ("AE"). The United Irishwomen; Their
Place, Work, and Ideals. With a preface by The Rev. T.A.
Finlay. Dublin: Maunsel and Co. Ltd., 1911. 50pp.

Three essays which document the problems of rural life in
Ireland, the history and goals of the United Irishwomen's
Association and their potential for promoting rural
improvement and fostering co-operative action.

1750   "Position of Women in Pension Schemes. Survey by Irish
Pensions Trust, Ltd." Liberty 32 (7) (Feb. 1978): 1,4.

Report on a two part survey by Irish Pensions Trust which
indicates that women fare much worse than men in existing
pension schemes.

1751   Power, Conflict and Inequality: Studies in Irish
Society. ed. by Mary Kelly, Lian O'Dowd, James Wickham.
Dublin: Turse Press, 1982. 222pp. il. tables. bibl.

Includes two essays dealing with "Women, Industrial
Transition and Training Policy in the Republic of
Ireland" (pp.147-157) by Ann Wickham and "On the Margins

of the Power Elite: Women in the Upper Echelons"
(pp.159-170) by Joy Rudd.

1752   Prone, Terry. "Women in Communications." Cross 64 (2)
(June 1973): 4-5. portr.

Comments by a free lance reporter on the position of
women in Irish television notes their general exclusion
from "hard" current affairs interviewing and news reading
and the tendency not to employ women as producers and
researchers.

1753   "Proposed Equal Opportunities Legislation for
Ireland." Eur Ind Rel R 23 (Nov. 1973): 4-6.

Detailed discussion of the provisions of the proposed
Irish Anti Discrimination (Employment) Act to become
effective in 1976 designed to complement the Anti
Discrimination (Pay) Act in operation since December
1975. Irish bill seen as falling short of the United
Kingdom's recently enacted legislation in this area in
terms of scope and enforcement provisions.

1754   Punch, Mary C. "Womanagers." Mgt 19 (5) (May 1972):
63- 67. portrs.

Brief overview of women in managerial positions in
Ireland considers women's education and employer's
attitudes as factors responsible for their low
representation in these. Includes excerpts from
interviews with some women holding responsible positions.

1755   Purdon, K.F. "The United Irishwomen." Engwoman No. 120
(Dec. 1918): 108-113.

Brief article discussing the formation, aims and
achievements of the United Irishwomen organization.
Activities include the encouragement of cottage
industries, and the establishment of milk depots, and
co-operatives.

1756   [Radio Telefis Eireann] Working Party on Women in
Broadcasting. Report to the Radio Telefis Eireann Authority.
[Dublin] [Radio Telefis Eireann] 1981. 56pp. il.

Report of the Working Party set up by the RTE Authority
in Jan. 1979 to examine the position of women in Irish
broadcasting. Aspects considered include representation
of women in programs (actual participation and program
orientation); job opportunities in broadcasting and
portrayal of women in advertising. In all areas women are
at severe disadvantage. Includes a summary of findings
and recommendations.

1757   "Role of the Irish Labour Court: Effectiveness of
Court Called into Question." Eur Ind Rel R No.28 (April
1976): 12-14.

   Outline of structure and functions of the Court
   established under the Industrial Relations Act, 1946, to
   aid employers and unions in solving their differences by
   means other than industrial action. As of January 1976
   the Court's duties have been broadened to include the
   investigation of equal pay claims under the Anti-
   Discrimination (Pay) Act. Criticisms of the Court have
   been increasingly voiced by trade unionists.

1758   Rudd, Joy. "On the Margins of the Power Elite: Women
in the Upper Echelons." In Power, Conflict and Inequality:
Studies in Irish Society, pp.159-170. Dublin: Turse Press,
1982. il. tables. bibl.

   Women are seen as remaining peripheral to the key power
   structuring of Irish society. They are significantly
   under represented in decision making positions even in
   those occupations such as primary teaching and nursing
   where they overwhelmingly predominate despite the growing
   consciousness of women's rights.

1759   Rudd, Joy. "The Economic Dependence of Women in
Ireland." In Dependency: Social, Political, Cultural:
Proceedings of the 5th Annual Conference of the Sociological
Association of Ireland, ed. by A. Spencer, pp. 96-104.
Belfast: Queen's University, Department of Social Studies,
1979. il. graphs. tables. refs.

   Examines the ideology of the family, attitudes toward and
   actual employment status of women in Ireland.

1760   Sandell, Steven H. Monitoring the Labour Market
Progress of Women in Ireland: Statistics Needed for
Employment Equality. Dublin: Employment Equality Ageny, 1980.
36pp. tables. refs.

   A report prepared for the Agency first describes the
   current employment position of Irish women and examines
   the presently available data to monitor that position.
   Then from a review of the position of women and the
   availability of data in other industrial countries, in
   conjunction with policy goals for women in Ireland,
   Sandell derives statistical data needs to monitor
   progress toward equality in employment between the sexes.

1761   Sex Discrimination: A Guide to the Sex Discrimination
(Northern Ireland) Order 1976. Belfast: Department of
Manpower Services, 1976. 52pp.

   Detailed exposition of the Act as it relates to

employment, education, provision of goods, facilities,
services, other areas, enforcement, and the role of the
Equal Opportunity Commission for Northern Ireland.

1762   Sheridan, Rita. "Women's Contribution to Farming, Farm
and Food Research." An Forus Taluntais (Apr. 1982): 46-48.
il. tables.

An examination of the limited data available including a
1975 Employment Equality Commission Farm Structures
Survey and a 1978 Farm Management Survey (Ireland)
concludes that women's contribution to farm work is
neither adequately measured nor recognized.

1763   Smith, Louis P.F. "Women in the Workforce in Ireland."
Allied Ir Bank R (Oct. 1981): 1-3. chart. portr.

Details the social and economic factors which are causing
more married women to work outside the home. These trends
could cause the participation rate of married women in
the female labour force to increase from one third to
over 50% Ability of the market to absorb these increased
numbers given the decline in sectors where women have
been traditionally concentrated and other social
implications briefly discussed.

1764   "Special Objectives for Women's Year 1975." W Ir Nurs
4 (5) (May 1975): 3.

Editorial points out the special relevance to the nursing
field of two of the objectives highlighted by the United
Nations for International Women's Year, e.g. encouraging
women to train for and enter non-traditional occupations;
equalization of pay and non-discrimination in employment
opportunities.

1765   "These Magnificant Girls in Their Flying Machines." Th
Wk Ire (Nov. 28, 1969): 40. il.

Brief article on the changing role and image of the air
hostess and excerpts from interviews with some of the air
hostesses employed by Aer Lingus.

1766   "Towards Equal Pension Rights for Women." Liberty
(Sept. 1977): 9.

Report of an Equal Pay Officer's decision and Labour
Court agreement on a claim on behalf of 24 workers at
Linson Ltd Swords which held that, as women are entitled
to equal pay, they should also be entitled to any other
fringe benefits which employees enjoy and so should have
equal pension rights.

1767   Trewsdale, J. "The Role of Women in the Northern
Ireland Economy." In Religion, Education and Employment, eds.
R.J. Cormack and D. Osborne, pp. 100-117. Belfast: Appletree,
1983. refs.

   While overall female participation in the labour force in
   Northern Ireland is relatively low and concentrated in a
   lower-paid sector, the author asserts that any
   significant difference in the employment of Roman
   Catholic versus non-Roman Catholic women in 1971 can be
   attributed to the geographic distribution of the
   population and social practice rather than directly to
   any form of religious discrimination. Recent trends in
   part-time employment explored.

1768   "U.K." Eur Ind Rel R No. 27 (Mar. 1976): 18.

   Includes a note on the draft order - Sex Discrimination
   (Northern Ireland) Order 1976 - which has been prepared
   and on which comments of interested parties are sought by
   March 25th, 1976. The Order is then to be presented to
   the British Parliament for approval. Provisions of the
   draft order mirror those of the British Sex
   Discrimination Act (EIRR IS) and include provision for
   the establishment of a separate Equal Opportunities
   Commission for Northern Ireland.

1769   "The United Irishwomen." Spectator 106 (May 27, 1911):
801-802.

   A brief account of the United Irishwomen Movement and
   their efforts to improve the rural scene in Ireland.

1770   Walsh, Brendan. The Impact of Employment Equality
Commission Membership on Women in the Labour Force. Dublin:
Centre for Economic Research, Univesity College, Dublin,
1982. (Policy Paper # 1.) 19pp. tables. refs.

   An analysis of the main changes that have taken place in
   the labour force status of Irish women in the years
   immediately prior and subsequent to Ireland's accession
   to the Employment Equality Commission.

1771   Walsh, Brendan M. and B.J. Whelan. "The Determinants
of Female Labour Force Participation: an Econometric Analysis
of Survey Data." Stat & Soc Inq Soc J 23 (1) (1973-74): 1-34.
tables. [Includes discussion.]

   An analysis of survey data using a statistical technique
   to assess the impact of certain economic variables on the
   decision by women to work outside the home. Findings
   indicate that single women are more likely to work if
   jobs are available in the vicinity of their homes, if
   their potential income is high and if they are the head
   of the household. Married women's labor force

participation is influenced by the number and ages of
their children, their actual and potential income and
their husband's approval.

1772   Walsh, Brendan M. "Married Women, Employment and
Family Size." Soc Stud 2 (6) (Dec. 1973): 565-572. refs.

A theoretical consideration from an economic perspective
of the interrelationship of fertility patterns and labour
force participation. Author points out the need for such
an overall theory in evaluating the issues of equity in
taxation of married women or state subsidies to child
care centers in Ireland.

1773   Walsh, Brendan M. and Annette O'Toole. Women And
Employment in Ireland: Results of a National Survey. Dublin:
Economic and Social Research Institute, 1973. 156pp. tables.
refs. (Paper # 69.)

Presents the results of a national survey conducted
during March-May 1971 on topics related to the employment
of women in Ireland. The sample was composed of 5000
women aged between 14 and 65. Topics covered include
reasons for working/not working, attitudes towards women
workers, occupational distribution of employed women,
work patterns, child care facilities. Women comprised one
quarter of the labour force in both 1961 and 1966, the
latest dates for which Census figures were available.
Some conclusions on employment policy based on survey
findings are included.

1774   Walsh, Brendan M. "Women and Work." Pub Affairs 4 (7)
(Mar.1972): 8-9.

A socio-economic analysis of the causes of the low
participation of married women in the labor market in
Ireland in the past, and factors which are now becoming
operative to increase demand and hence opportunities for
this group.

1775   Walsh, Brendan M. "Aspects of Labour Supply and Demand
With Special Reference to the Employment of Women in
Ireland." Stat & Soc Inq Soc J 125th Session. Part 3.
(1970/1971): 88-118. tables. refs.

A detailed examination of the labor force participation
of women in Ireland considers factors affecting their
participation, the structure of total employment
opportunities, the sex ratio overall and in individual
sectors of the economy. Data are derived from Census of
Population figures for the years 1961-66. The high degree
of sex segregation of occupations in Ireland is not
expected to change radically in the short term.
Implications and limitations of the data discussed.

1776   Walsh, Mary Ena. <u>Women in Rural Ireland: A Report of the Get-togethers Held in 1982</u>. Dublin: Council for the Status of Women, 1983. 50pp.

 A companion volume to "Women at Home" report published in 1982 detailing discussions held throughout 1982 in centres of rural population in Ireland where women working full time in the family home/farm/business voiced their opinions, needs and/or problems. (See Barry, B. #1613.)

1777   Weir, Hilary. "The New Women." <u>Scene</u> 2 (4) (Apr. 1968): 58-63. il.

 Brief profiles of women who have succeeded in making it in the world of business and their comments on male attitudes to their success, their feelings about themselves and independence.

1778   Whittey, St. J. "A Constructive Criticism of the Work of the United Irishwomen." <u>Bet Bus</u> (Apr. 1916): 260-270.

 Considers the aims of the United Irishwomen's Society, their achievements, their overlap with other organizations and the obstacles they must deal with. Author suggests that they concentrate their energies on the organization of women's co-operative societies for the marketing of farm products.

1779   Whyte, Anne. "The Irish Countrywomen's Association." <u>Reality</u> 35 (9) (Sept. 1971): 7-9. portr. il.

 Brief account of founding, organizational framework and activities of the Irish Countrywomen's Association founded in 1910 with the name United Irishwomen with the goal of promoting better living conditions in rural Ireland.

1780   <u>Who Makes the Decisions: Women on the Boards of State Sponsored Bodies</u>. 2nd Ed. Dublin: Council for the Status of Women, 1982. 34pp. tables.

 A follow-up to a 1980 report by the Council documenting the extent of participation by women on the boards of state-sponsored bodies with the intention of highlighting the inadequate and disproportionate number of women on these boards. The current report shows that the situation is still unsatisfactory - out of 90 boards, 49 had no women appointees. Role of government in correcting this imbalance stressed and other recommendations offered.

1781   Wickham, Ann. "Women, Industrial Transition and Training Policy in the Republic of Ireland." In <u>Power, Conflict and Inequality: Studies in Irish Society</u>, pp.147-157. Dublin: Turoe Press, 1982. il. tables. bibl.

An examination of the role of women in Irish
manufacturing industry up to 1971 with particular
reference to their exclusion from government training
policies in the 1960's and early 1970's, despite their
significant representation in the traditional
manufacturing workforce and their growing importance in
other sectors.

1782   Womanpower No. 1: A Statistical Survey of Women and
Work in Northern Ireland. Belfast: Equal Opportunity
Commission for Northern Ireland, 1979. 42pp. bibl. append.

1783   Womanpower No. 2: Recent Changes In the Female Labour
Market in Northern Ireland. Belfast: Equal Opportunity
Commission for Northern Ireland, 1981. 53pp. append.

1784   Womanpower No. 3: The Impact of Recession on Female
Employment and Earnings in Northern Ireland. Belfast: Equal
Opportunity Commission for Northern Ireland, 1983. 44pp.
tables. bibl.

Reports commissioned by the Employment Equality
Commission and prepared by members of the Economics
department at Queen's University based on official
statistics including the 1978 and 1979 Labour Force
Surveys, and other sources such as the Department of
Manpower Services Gazette, the Digest of Statistics,
Northern Ireland, and the Census of Population. Reports
are to be issued biennially.

1785   "Women and Social Welfare." Trade Un Info (July-Sept.
1975): 20.

Reports on the status of the fifteen recommendations made
by the Commission of the Status of Women regarding the
Administration of social welfare benefits: 8 of these
have been fully implemented, 3 partially, 3 are under
examination, 1 has not been implemented. Lists instances
of differential treatment of men and women under social
security schemes administered by the Department of Social
Welfare.

1786   "Women at the Top." Ir Bus 4 (Dec. 1978): 8-13.
portrs.

Interviews with some women who have achieved a leading
position in Irish business: the couturier, Pat Crowley;
the public-relations consultant Mary Finan; Margaret
Downs, a senior partner in a leading accounting firm;
stud owner, Frances Wilby; printing specialist, Claire
Browne and investment fund manager Elizabeth Holden.

1787   "Women at Work." <u>Trade Un Info</u> (Spring 1979): 18.

Report on the finding by the Employment Equality Agency
that Aer Lingus was guilty of sex discrimination in its
advertising and recruitment patterns. Evidence of changed
policies led EEA to conclude its formal investigation.

1788   "Women at Work." <u>Trade Un Info</u> (Winter 1978): 16.

Presents statistics from EEC Labour Force Survey
(May/June 1977) on numbers of married women in the work
force and pay scales of men and women in the public
service. Also notes that womens pension rights are
covered by the Anti-Discrimination (Pay) Act 1977.

1789   "Women at Work." <u>Trade Un Info</u> (April/June 1975): 27-
29. tables.

Statistical data on women at work in the Republic of
Ireland derived from various Census reports. Includes
data on numbers employed in the main industrial sectors
1926-1971 and several detailed breakdowns by occupational
group, industry, socio-economic group, age group and
marital status for 1971 with some comparisons with
earlier periods.

1790   "Women in Employment." <u>Trade Un Info</u> (Spring 1979): 2-
4. tables.

A profile of employed women in the Irish economy based on
statistics published by the Central Statistics Office
from the Labour Force Survey carried out in 1977.
Information obtained by means of a personal interview
with a representative sample of 40,000 households.
Includes statistics on numbers and ages of females in
outside employment; status of other females in sample;
distribution, employment status and main occupational
groups of working females.

1791   "Women Workers and the Recession." <u>Liberty</u> (July
1977): 10.

Report of a one day seminar sponsored by the Trade Union
Women's Forum and the Dublin Council of Trade Unions.

1792   "Women's Charter." <u>Trade Un Info</u> (July-Sept. 1976):
24.

Statement of rights for women which the Irish Congress of
Trade Unions supports.

1793   "Women's Earnings." <u>Trade Un Info</u> (Jan.-Mar. 1976): 6.
table.

A comparison of male and female earnings in the manufacturing industry for June 1975 and June 1970.

1794   "Women's Earnings: Survey of Money Earnings and Real Earnings of Women in Industry." Trade Un Info 15 (88) (Oct. 1958): 9-10. tables.

Presents figures on average weekly earnings of women for the period 1945-1956; also figures for 1938 and these analyzed in terms of "real" versus "earned" money (e.g. purchasing power). Also presents Census figures for October 1956 showing the average weekly earnings of women over 18 in all manufacturing and service type industries broken down by industry group.

1795   Working Girls Hostel. Hanbury Lane, Dublin. Annual Report 1915/16 -1932. Dublin: Curtis, 1916-1933.

Annual reports of a hostel or home under lay management "in which respectable working girls and young women could obtain night shelter and partial board at a nominal cost." Aim of the hostel was the provision of temporary shelter pending the obtaining of employment - also provided clothes or clothing repairs and also acted as an employment agency. Reports provide details on "specimen cases" of their guests and lists of their subscribers.

EQUAL PAY

1796   Byrne, Geary. "Will Equal Pay Be All That Bad?" Bus & Fin II (44) (July 24, 1975): 13.

Comment on a report by P E Management which sees opportunities for increased productivity under equal pay and outlines how employers might achieve this objective.

1797   Callender, Roshen. "Equal Pay and Inability to Pay." Liberty (July 1977): 11-12.

Discusses the argument that women should not press for equal pay in situations where this could lead to a closure of the firm and the loss of their jobs and the opposing view that the trade union movement should not prop up firms that are inefficient and depend for survival on being subsidized by the workers.

1798   Creighton, W.B. "Equal Pay Act (N.I.) 1970." No Ire L Q 22 (1971): 533-540. refs.

Background and discussion of the provisions of the Equal Pay Act (Northern Ireland) 970 to take effect December 1975. Problems of definition and limitations explicated and conditions for success outlined.

1799   Equal? Dublin: Irish Congress of Trade Unions, 1976. 1
fold.

>A list of questions prepared for women trade unionists to
enable these to pinpoint areas of discrimination.

1800   Equal Employment Commission for Northern Ireland.
Equal Pay for Women: What You Should Know About It. Belfast:
The Commission, 1984. 1p.

>Describes the amendments to the Equal Pay Act (Northern
Ireland) 1970 as revised in 1984.

1801   "Equal Pay." Civ Serv R (Mar./Apr. 1977): 3.

>The Civil and Public Services Staff Association goes on
record that it refuses to be bound by any agreements
reached by any Unions or Associations with the Minister
which withdraw demands for equal pay.

1802   "Equal Pay." Liberty 32 (7) (Feb. 1978): 6-7.

>Various articles on the disposition of cases referred to
Equality Officers since the Anti-Discrimination (Pay) Act
of December 31, 1975; statistics on women at work
assembled by the Central Statistics Office (part of the

>E.E.C. sample Labour Force Survey carried out in all the
member states in January 1977); and costs of equal pay
and progress toward this in different industries (survey
of Irish Transport and General Workers Union).

1803   "Equal Pay." Post Work (May 1977): 72-73, 83.

>A brief review of the implementation of the Equal Pay
Act, note on pending discussions between the Public
Services Committee and the Minister, review of the status
of equal pay claims by female store assistants, cleaners,
post office clerks, telephonists.

1804   "Equal Pay." Post Work (Oct. 1975): 206-228.

>Includes the final submission of the Post Office Workers'
Union to the Equal Pay Commissioner of the Labour Court
in support of the claim that telephonists in the
Department of Posts and Telegraphs should have equality
of pay with male night telephonists in that department;
the submission by the "Official Side" (e.g. the
Government); the report of the Equal Pay Commissioner,
and the Agreed Statement on pay of the Government and
Irish Congress of Trade Unions of September 23rd, 1975.

1805   "Equal Pay." Relate 4 (2) (Nov. 1976): 2-3,6.

An in depth look at the provisions of the Anti
Discrimination (Pay) Act 1974 and procedures for making
claims under this Act.

1806   "Equal Pay. Commission's Report on Equal Pay in
Denmark, Ireland and the U.K. (London)." Eur Ind Rel R No.5.
(May 1974): 13-20.

The European Commission's Draft Report on the application
of the principle of equal pay in the new member states
surveyed the situation from different vantage points:
equal pay in the public and private sectors, legislative
measures and collective agreements. In the case of
Ireland, significant discrimination was found to persist
in the public and private sectors both in salary scales
and in social security provisions. The Draft Directive on
the application of the principle of equal pay, together
with specific amendments suggested by the Economic and
Social Commission are included in the report.

1807   "Equal Pay and the Accountant." Acct Ire (Dec. 1975):
20.

Points out the substantial additional burdens financial
planners and auditors will face when the
Anti-Discrimination (Pay) Act will take effect.

1808   "Equal Pay and Pensions." Liberty 32 (7) Supplement
(Feb. 1978): 5.

Background and clarification of equal pay legislation, an
overview of the pattern of female employment in Ireland
and estimates of costs of equal pay to Irish industry.

1809   Equal Pay Checklist. Dublin: Department of Labour,
1974. 6pp.

Information leaflet for employers about provisions of
Anti-Discrimination (Pay) Act.

1810   Equal Pay Conference: Speakers Papers. Prepared by the
Research and Information Division (Federated Union of
Employers). Dublin: Federated Union of Employers, 1975. 46pp.
tables.

Covers the present situation as regards equal pay in
Ireland; the use of job evaluation in this context; a
case study of introducing equal pay; problems in the
white collar area; and planned strategy for implementing
equal pay.

1811   "Equal Pay Covers Pensions." Liberty (Mar. 1977): 11.

The crucial importance for women of the ruling by the
Equal Pay Officers that pensions do come within the scope
of the Anti-Discrimination (Pay) Act 1974 noted. Most
pension schemes in Ireland if they cover women at all do
so unequally.

1812   "Equal Pay Determinations." Trade Un Info (Winter
1978): 44.

Summaries of recommendations made by Equality officers
under the Employment Equality Act, 1977.

1813   "Equal Pay Dispute." Post Work 55 (4) (April 1977):
1,37.

Discusses the progress to date of the female telephonists
claim for pay parity with male night telephonists
employed by the Post Office.

1814   Equal Pay for Women; What You Should Know About It.
Belfast: Department of Manpower Services. n.d. 1 leaf.

Explains the provisions of the Equal Pay Act (N1) 1970
which came into force at the end of 1975.

1815   Equal Pay Guidelines. What Women Workers Should Know
About the Provisions of the Anti-Discrimination (Pay) Act,
1974. Dublin: Employment Equality Agency. n.d. 5pp.

1816   "Equal Pay in Ireland: a Progress Report." Eur Ind Rel
R No.11 (Nov. 1974): 5-7.

Discussion of the terms of the National Agreements of
1972 and 1974 in Ireland negotiated by the Employer-
Labour Conference which included provision for movement
toward Equal Pay (Equal Pay legislation to become
effective in 1975). Of primary importance is the
provision for negotiation of pay increases for women
doing work of "equal value" with men but underpaid
relative to these.

1817   "Equal Pay Recommendations." Trade Un Info (Spring
1970): 8,22.

Summaries of recommendations made by Equal Pay officers
under the Anti-Discrimination (Pay) Act, 1974.

1818   "Equal Pay Recommendations." Trade Un Info (Summer
1978): 32.

1819   Federated Union of Employers. Equal Pay Conference:
Speaker's Papers Prepared by the Research and Information

Division. Dublin: Federated Union of Employers, 1975. 45pp.
tables.

Papers cover the present situation regarding equal pay in
Ireland, use of job evaluation, problems in introducing
equal pay in the white collar area and strategies for
implementation.

1820   Federated Union of Employers. Women in Employment:
Implications of Equal Pay. Dublin: Federated Union of
Employers. n.d. (circa 1972) 11pp. tables.

This article represents the submission by the F.U.E. to
the Governmental Commission on the Status of Women in
Ireland. (See Report of the Commission, item #1822.)
Discusses problems of definition, the cost of equal pay,
effect on social security, marriage bar, taxation and
appeals machinery. Offers guidelines to member companies
in preparation for equal pay legislation. Includes
partial texts of Internatinal Labour Organization
Convention Article 119 regarding equal pay.

1821   Henry, E.W. and B.M. Walsh. "Price-change Calculations
Based on Three Forms of the Input-Output Model: An
Illustration from Estimates of the Impact of Equal Pay on
Irish Industry." Econ Soc R 2 (3) (April 1971): 329-336. il.
refs.

Various input-output models defined and applied to an
analysis of the implications of removing the differential
between male and female wage rates in similar occupations
for industry costs and price levels in the Irish
manufacturing sector.

1822   Ireland. (Eire) Commission on the Status of Women.
Interim Report On Equal Pay. Presented to the Minister for
Finance August 1971. Dublin: Stationery Office, 1972. 107pp.
tables. bibl. refs.

Details the establishment of the Commission and its
charge, the concept of equal pay, the pattern of women's
employment and earnings in Ireland, causes of unequal
pay, attitudes towards and criteria for equal pay,
legislative enactment and implementation. Includes a
summary of recommendations.

1823   "Ireland." Eur Ind Rel R No.27 (Mar. 1976): 18.

News item on the rejection by the European Commission of
the Irish Government's application for a temporary
derogation from the European Commission's Equal Pay
Directive (EIRR 26) and it's efforts to press the
Commission for cash subsidies to cover costs of
implementing equal pay.

1824   "Ireland: Interim Report on Equal Pay by the
Commission on the Status of Women." Int Labor R 105 (Feb.
1972): 182-6.

Brief background on formation of the Commission with a
summary of its principal findings and recommendations
regarding womens' social, political and economic status.

1825   "Ireland Attempts to Defer Equal Pay Obligation." Eur
Ind Rel R No.26 (Feb. 1976): 2-4.

A discussion of the application by the Irish Government
to the European Community in Brussels for a "derogation"
from the E.E.C. Treaty of Accession Rules to enable
Ireland to postpone compliance with the terms of the
Equal Pay Directive. Context of new proposals by Irish
government and first reactions to these examined. [Text
of Amendment Bill p 19-20.]

1826   "Irish Equal Pay Act." Eur Ind Rel R No.7 (1974): 26-
28.

Provisions of the Anti-Discrimination (Pay) Act, 1974
(Ireland) designed to ensure equal treatment in relation
to certain terms and conditions of employment between men
and women.

1827   "Irish Proposals to Postpone Equal Pay." Ind Rel R &
Rep No.123 (Mar. 1976): 7.

Brief report on the Irish Government's proposals aimed at
deferring full implementation of equal pay for an
unspecified period because of the economic situation.

1828   "Job Evaluation and Equal Pay." Civ Serv R (Jan.-Feb.
1974): 13-14, 25. portr.

Discusses the role of job evaluation in furthering the
principle of equal pay but points out the necessity for
joint participation of workers and management in any
system of job evaluation and the importance of training
women as assessors.

1829   Larsen, C.A. "Equal Pay for Women in the United
Kingdom." Int Labour R 103 (1971): 1-11.

Background, scope, provisions and implications of the
Equal Pay Act of 1970 discussed.

1830   McDonald, Sean. "The Wages of Sex." Bus & Fin 11 (23)
(Feb. 27, 1975): 10-12. il.

Examines some of the arguments surrounding the equal pay
issue and the recent efforts to have the introduction of

equal pay delayed because of the economic climate. Also looks at the whole issue of discrimination and the experiences of five women who comment on their work situation.

1831   "New Equal Pay Legislation in Ireland." Eur Ind Rel R No. 7 (July 1974): 13-14.

This article lists the main features of the Irish Anti-Discrimination (Pay) Act 1974. The background of the legislation, definitions of "like work" and procedures for its implementation are briefly analyzed. [Text of Act on p.26.]

1832   Northern Ireland. Department of Economic Development. Equal Pay: A Guide to the Equal Pay Act (Northern Ireland) 1970. Revised 1984. Belfast: HMSO, 1984. 19pp.

General guidance for employees and employers about their rights and obligations under the above Act as amended and supplemented by the Sex Discrimination (Northern Ireland) Order 1976, the Industrial Relations (No.2) (Northern Ireland) Order 1982, the Wages Councils (Northern Ireland) Order 1982 and the Equal Pay (Amendment) Regulations (Northern Ireland) 1984.

1833   O'Brien May. "A Look at the Equal Pay Position." Liberty (Oct. 1977): 5.

A look at the various recommendations issued by Equality Officers from their appointment in February 1976 to evaluate women's claims for equal pay; the review of these by the Labour Court and its subsequent treatment of appeals. Problems posed by this entire process - inordinate delay and lack of consultation with the Officers by the Labour Court - discussed.

1834   O'Connor, Judy. "Equal Pay - What Will it Cost?" Mgt (Mar. 1974): 33-34. tables.

A discussion of the financial implications of the new bill which would advance to December 31, 1975 the date for the introduction of equal pay for women doing work of equal value to that of men and thus bring Irish Government policy into line with that of the European Economic Community. The Federated Union of Employers' opposes this measure.

1835   O'Hagen, J.W. The Cost of Equal Pay and Employers Social Welfare Contributions to Manufacturing Industry: An Economic Evaluation. Dublin: European League for Economic Co-operation and Irish Council of the European Movement, 1977. 68pp. tables.

This two part report was prepared at the request of a
study group comprised of members of the European League
for Economic Co-operation and the Irish Council of the
European Movement. Part one of the report presents some
of the issues involved in equal pay, estimates the cost
to the Irish Manufacturing Industry of its implementation
and the unequal impact on different industries and firms
in that sector. A preface by the study group discusses
the findings of the Report and offers recommendations on
policy matters based on these.

1836   O'Mahony, Brian. "Ryan Bursts Equal Pay Balloon." Bus
& Fin 12 (20) (Jan. 29, 1976): 21. il.

Reports on planned Amendments to the Anti-Discrimination
(Pay) Act of 1974 announced by the Government
e.g.indefinite retention of the differential between
married and single; in the industrial sector exemptions
to be allowed where management and unions agree to put a
joint case to the Labour Court showing that job losses
would result if equal pay were introduced.

1837   P.E. Consulting Group Limited, Management Consultants.
Preparing For Equal Pay. Dublin: P.E. Consulting Group, Ltd.,
1975. 14pp. map.

A memorandum prepared by the staff of P.E. Consulting
Group intended to assist employees who will be involved
in implementing the provisions of the Equal Pay Act.
Includes its main provisions, the background, its
implications and implementation.

1838   Stafford, Brigid. "Equal Pay for Women." Ir Mon LXXIV
(July 1951): 308-314.

Data on the law and practice of member countries,
including Ireland, in regard to equal pay for men and
women based on reports of the International Labour
Office, replies by member countries to ILO questionnaires
and statements st the International Labour Conference in
Geneva in 1950.

1839   Stafford, Brigid. "International Labour Conference on
Equal Pay." Ir Mon LXXIX (Aug. 1951): 363-364.

Report on the final discussion of the question of equal
remuneration for men and women workers for work of equal
value, at the 34th session of the ILO in Geneva in June
1950.

1840   Stanbrook, A. "Some Are More Equal than Others."
Economist 263 (April 9, 1977): Survey 13. portr.

Discusses very briefly pay discrimination suffered by
working women in Ireland in both the public and private

sector and the lack of interest displayed by the trade
unions in fighting this issue.

1841   "Symposium on the Interim Report on Equal Pay of the
Commission on the Status of Women." Stat & Soc Inq Soc J
(125th Session) XXII (4) (1971-72): 106-142. tables. figs.
refs.

    Contains an analysis of the ways in which the
    recommendations in the Report would affect women workers
    and trade unionists; the economics of equal pay; relevant
    factors involved in its implementation and possible
    strategies. Includes data on wage rates and numbers
    employed in manufacturing and male/female pay
    differentials.

1842   Walsh, Brendan M. Estimating the Costs of Equal Pay in
Irish Industry. [Dublin]: Economic And Social Research
Institute. [n.d.] 14pp. tables. (Memorandum Series # 71.)

    Includes a range of estimates of overall costs and a
    ranking of industries by the extent of the impact of
    equal pay legislation on their labour costs and output
    prices. Author warns that the avialable wage and
    employment data are very seriously inadequate to the task
    of even rough calculations of probable costs.

1843   Wayne, Naomi. "Equal Pay Hopes Hit by Court." Liberty
(Sept. 1977): 1.

    A report on a negative decision by the Labour Court on a
    claim for equal pay involving three women cleaners and
    one male general labourer. Court accepted the company's
    argument that the male was paid a higher rate on grounds
    other than sex and dismissed women's claim.

1844   "Women and Men's Pay." Trade Un Info (Spring 1977):
7-8. tables.

    An analysis of the average hourly earnings of adult men
    and women as published by the Central Statistics Office.
    Figures for June 1970 and June 1976 compared for evidence
    of progress towards pay equalization between men and
    women. While there has been some improvement women still
    lag behind.

History

This category includes material primarily dealing with women's social history. Historical studies of the suffrage struggle and other political activity by women is located under POLITICS. Historical and contemporary accounts of women involved in Nationalist or protest activities is located under REVOLUTIONARY MOVEMENTS (separated from the section on POLITICS primarily because of the volume of material and contemporary relevance). For biographical material on famous historical personages see BIOGRAPHY AND AUTOBIOGRAPHY — HISTORY, POLITICS AND REVOLUTIONARY MOVEMENTS; for the history of religious orders see RELIGION — RELIGIOUS ORDERS; for historical studies of the family see MARRIAGE AND THE FAMILY; for accounts of women's status under the Brehon laws see LAW — GENERAL LEGAL STATUS; for material on the evolution of university education for women see EDUCATION.

1845   Adamnan, Abbot of Iona. [Saint]. Cain Adamnain. An Old Irish Treatise on the Law of Adamnan. Edited and translated by Kuno Meyer. (Anecdota Oxoniensia, Mediaevel and Modern Series XII) Oxford: Clarendon Press, 1905. 56pp.

Illustrates the social history of ancient Ireland and the treatment of women before Adamnan's time. These suffered various indignities such as having to dwell outside the home, go to war, etc. Legend claims that Adamnan's mother prevailed upon her son to strive for the abolition of these disabilities and the result was "Adamnan's law" passed in 697 A.D., the first legal provision for women's protection. Details on penalties for breaking this.

1846   Atkinson, Sarah. "The Lady Dervorgilla." Ir Mon XV (Feb. 1887): 93-104. refs.

A rebuttal of the widely held belief that the Anglo

Norman invasion of Ireland was an outcome of the
abduction of the Lady Dervorgilla, wife of Tiernan O
Ruark, Prince of Breffny by Dermod MacMurrough.

1847   Bary, Valerie M. "Household Lists 1826-1838 Made by
Lady Godfrey of Kilcoleman Abbey, County Kerry." Ir Ancest
11 (1979): 30-44. il.

Surviving papers from Kilcoleman Abbey, formerly called
Bushfield in the parish of Milltown, County Kerry once
the seat of the Godfrey family includes a record kept by
Lady Godfrey between 1826 and 1838 which notes the books
in the library, the furnishings of the school that she
and her husband supported in Milltown as well as lists of
china, glass, kitchen utensils and bedroom furniture.

1848   Bryant, Sophie. Liberty, Order and Law Under Native
Irish Rule. London: Harding and More, 1923. 399pp. refs.

Chapter five has a passage on the law of social
connections; chapter 15 deals with the rights of women as
owners of property.

1849   Cassidy, James F. The Women of the Gael. Boston: The
Stratford Co., 1922. 208pp.

An effusive tribute to Irish women from Celtic times to
the present. The emphasis is on their piety, purity,
learning and patriotism. While some examples from the
'honor roll' of notable individuals have their claim to
fame in their martial abilities, the emphasis is on the
special spiritual role of women and their indirect
influence on events.

1850   Dillon, Myles and Nora K. Chadwick. The Celtic Realms.
New York: New American Library, 1967. 355pp. il. refs.

Brief section on high status of women in Celtic society,
the importance of Queen Maebh in Irish legend, and the
position of women under the Brehon laws in Ireland.

1851   Dobbs, Maighread Margaret. "The Ban-Shencus." R Celt
47 (1930): 283-339; 48 (1931): 161-234; 49 (1932): 437-489.
refs.

"The Ban-shencus" - History of women - is a list of
famous married women in Irish literature and history.
There are both metrical and prose versions and these vary
in length and in matter. Location of copies of the
original manuscripts is given with transcriptions of the
texts and critical commentary on these.

1852   Dobbs, Margaret E. "Women of the Ui Dunlainge of

Leinster." Ir Geneal 1 (1940): 196-206. refs.

A list of ladies, wives and daughters of leading
families in North Leinster during the period 500 A.D. to
800 A.D. Includes 15 names which, though not arranged
chronologically, can be dated by their husbands or sons.
Composition dates from the 8th century and is in middle
Irish. Sources, translation and detailed textual notes
included.

1853   Hayden, Mary. "Dublin Ladies of the 18th Century."
Alex Col Mag XCI (June 1938): 3-13.

Popular account based mainly on the contemporary diaries
of Mrs. Freke, Mrs. Bailey and Mrs. Delaney, briefly
describes the education, domestic and social activities,
of the wives and daughters of the nobility and the
'county people' of the period.

1854   Hayden, Mary. "Women in the Middle Ages." Ir R 3
(Mar. 1913-Feb.1914): 282-215, 344-358.

Brief undocumented discussion of the status of different
classes of women, their occupations, education and rights
in Western Europe during the Midddle Ages.

1855   Heanue, William. "From Patrick to Brian to
Bernadette." Liguorian 1 (59) (March 1971); 14-17.

A capsule overview of Irish history from the time of St.
Patrick (A.D.431) to the recent troubles in Belfast.

1856   Home Rule for Irishwomen. (Delegates to the National
Convention) (n.p. n.d.) 1p.

(See Home Rule #1900.)

1857   Hull, Vernan. "How St. Adamnan Released the Women of
Ireland from Military Service." ZCP 21 (1939): 335-338.

Text of tale here published for the first time from the
Book of Lecan with critical commentary on this and other
versions and explanatory notes.

1858   de Kay, Charles. "Women in Early Ireland." Cent Mag
16 (1889): 433-442. il. refs.

Brief diffuse discussion of myth and actuality
acknowledges the difficulty of separating these.

1859   de Kay, Charles. "Woman In Ireland of Old." Cath W 43
(June 1886): 372-383.

Brief anecdotal discussion of role of women and family customs in ancient Ireland including the practice of fosterage.

1860   M'Elheran, John. The Condition of Women and Children Among the Celtic, Gothic, and Other Nations. Boston: Patrick Donahoe, 1858. 393pp. il.

An anecdotal, highly partisan account of the relatively favorable treatment afforded to women among the Celts compared to their invidious situation among the barbaric Saxons.

1861   Muddiman, J.G. "Documents About Cromwell's Massacre at Wexford." Notes & Quer (Oct. 27, 1934): 291-293.

Gives sources for the account of the massacre of 200 women by Cromwell at Wexford, Ireland, in 1649.

1862 Ni Chinneide, Maire. Women In Ancient Ireland: A Lecture to the Irish Women's Franchise League, Tuesday, January 18th 1910. Dublin: Irish Women's Franchise League, 1910. 12pp.

Discusses the legal status and general condition of women in ancient Ireland and the professions open to them.

1863   Ni Dhubhghaill, C. Maire (Crissie M. Doyle). Women In Ancient And Modern Ireland. Dublin: Kenny Press, 1917. 40pp. plates.

Brief, popular account of the situation of women in ancient Ireland with details on their education, occupations, property rights, marriage customs and dowries, rights of married women, etc. Author contrasts their central role in the society of their day with the status of women in modern Ireland who are barred from entering many spheres.

1864   O Faolain, Julia and Lauro Martines (Eds.) Not In God's Image. London: Maurice Temple Smith, Ltd., 1973. 362pp.

A chronological exploration of the lives of European women throughout history and attitudes towards woman's nature and role. Sources include literary works, diaries, letters, laws and court cases, religious customs, etc.

1865   Orientalis (pseud.) "Exclusion of Women." Ulster J Archae Series 1. 5 (1857): 155.

Note regarding a certain island in one of the Irish lakes into which no female of any animal (including the human species) was allowed to enter and similar rules in various parts of Europe.

1866   O'Sullivan, M.D. "The Wives of Ulick, First Earl of Clanrickarde." Galway Arch Soc J 21 (1945): 174-183. refs.

An account of matrimonial affairs of Ulick Burke, an Anglo-Irish Christian of the 16th century and descendant of the De Burgh family, who was married to three different women. He deserted his first wife and divorced the second. Political and financial considerations involved in his decisions and subsequent family disputes and claims briefly noted.

1867   Sheehy Skeffington, Hannah. "Some Women in Irish History (and Some Books About Them.)" Ir Lib Bull 111(3) (May-June 1942): 37-40.

Popular discussion of influence of mythological and historical Irish female figures on the imagination of succeeding gnerations.

1868   Simms, Katherine. "The Legal Position of Irishwomen in the Later Middle Ages." Ir Jur 10 (1975): 96-111. refs.

(See Law #1581.)

1869   Tipton, I.C. and E.J. Furlong. "Mrs George Berkeley and Her Washing Machine." Hermathena 1 (Autumn 1965): 38-47. il. refs.

Contents of four pages in the Chapman Manuscript in Trinity Library written by George Berkeley's wife. Includes maxims of conduct, an exemplary day's time table, list of things to be done when bringing family from Oxford to Ireland. Includes first recorded use of term "washing machine."

1870   Walsh, Micheline. "Some Notes Towards a History of the Womenfolk of the Wild Geese." Ir Sword 19 (Winter 1961): 98-106, 133-145.

Brief account of the part played by the female family members of the Irish rebels, who fled to the Continent in the 17th and 18th centuries, in the Europe of their day. Includes some details on their former lives in Ireland.

Politics

This section contains publications pertaining to women in their civic capacity (as voters, office-holders or candidates for political office, members of political parties) and their struggle for full political rights, notably suffrage; also , official party positions on women's issues. Publications dealing with women's participation in various national and international organizations are included but those pertaining to economic and/or trade union activity are located in the section on EMPLOYMENT AND ECONOMIC LIFE. For ideological discussions of the relationship of Nationalism and Feminism see PERSPECTIVES ON WOMEN'S LIBERATION; for women's struggle to obtain access to higher education see EDUCATION; for factual accounts of women's actual or historic legal status see LAW - GENERAL LEGAL STATUS.

1871   Atkinson, Sarah. "Report of the Irish Ladies' Papal Address Committee." Ir Eccl Rec VIII (Apr. 1872): 325-336.

    Detailed account of the campaign which obtained signatures and offerings from the women of Ireland and forwarded these to Pope Pius IX as a gesture of support and solidarity.

1872   All Ireland Conference Committee of Women Delegates. Women of Ireland. [n.p.] 1917. 1p.

    A call to Irish women to avail themselves of the equal rights, liberties and responsibilities granted to them by the Republican Proclamation of 1916 and urging them to avail themselves of these rights by joining Sinn Fein.

1873   Barnes, Monica. "Women in Local Politics: A Note." Admin 23 (1) (Spring 1975): 80-82. tables. (Based on her

article in the Newsletter of the Women's Political
Association for August 1974.)

A comparison of the political fortunes of women
candidates in the 1967 and 1974 local elections. In 1974
there was an increase of 65% in women's representation on
local authorities but this still brings overall
representation only to 5.8% against 3.5% in 1967.

1874   Barry, David. (Rev.) "Female Suffrage From a Catholic
Standpoint." Ir Eccl Rec 4th Series. XXVI (Sept. 1901):
295-303.

Presents arguments for universal enfranchisement of all
adult males without property requirements but argues that
these criteria do not apply to women. Further argues
against female suffrage in the interest of preserving the
Catholic ideal of the unity of domestic life with the
husband at the head.

1875   "Bernadette Bids." Economist (Apr. 19, 1969): 23.
portrs.

Report on the left wing challenge posed by Bernadette
Devlin, candidate of the People's Democracy to Mrs. Anna
Forrest, the Unionist incumbent for the Mid Ulster seat
in the upcoming election. Seat previously held by
Unionists since 1956.

1876   Blackburn, Helen. Women's Suffrage: A Record of the
Women's Suffrage Movement in the British Isles. New York:
Collectors Editions, Sourcebook Press, 1970. (c. 1902).
298pp. il. bibl.

Includes very brief profiles of Ms. Tod and Mrs. Haslam
and their association with the Women's Suffrage Movement
in Ireland. (portrs. pp. 131,216.)

1877   Boyd, Earnest A. "Feminism and Women's Suffrage." Ir R
111 (May 1913): 144-149.

Comments on anti-feminist backlash generated by the
militant tactics of the Suffragists and presents
arguments for the economic independence of women.

1878   Brazil, Paula. "One Nun, One Vote." Reality 33 (6)
(June 1969): 20-21. portr.

A teenager questions why so few nuns exercise their
democratic duty by voting. Points out their civic
responsibility as representing an educated sector of the
body social to help shape educational and cultural policy
and, as educators, the importance of their example and

teaching in developing civic responsibility in the young.

1879   Brennan, Pat. "Toning Up for the General Election."
Status 6 (2) (Apr. 1981): 32-35, 37. il.

Report of a women's political conference held in February
1981 to consolidate and articulate issues on which to
base a unified women's rights campaign in the next
election.

1880   British and Irish Communist Organization. Women's
Liberation in Britain and Ireland. Belfast: British and Irish
Communist Organization, 1974. 12pp. (Policy statement No. 7)

States the official party attitude towards various issues
affecting women. Argues that the Women's Liberation
Movement is not changing society — women's emancipation
is contingent on their involvement in industrial
production and economic factors are the causal agents.
There is no social need for a Women's Liberation Movement
and women abroad should apply their energies toward
participation in general politics.

1881   Burca, Mairin de. "The Women's Vote." Hibernia 43
(June 21, 1979): 8. il.

Brief discussion of the women's vote in recent Dublin and
European elections characterized as minuscule, seldom
crossing party boundaries and making no demands on
feminist issues.

1882   Carty, R.K. "Women in Irish Politics." Can J Ir Stud 6
(1) (June 1980): 90-104. tables. refs.

A descriptive and comparative study of the role of women
in Irish parliamentary politics. Low female representation
in both houses of the Oireachtas and their pattern of
access — mainly family inheritance, especially to the Dail
— is a persistent problem since 1922. Carty examines the
1977 election campaign and its outcome and indicates
factors which indicate a new role for women in Irish
politics.

1883   Clery, Arthur E. "The Religious Aspect of Women's
Suffrage." Ir R 111 (Nov. 1913): 479-484.

Presents arguments for the extension of the vote to women
because of the beneficial effects for religion which
would result.

1884   Comhthrom, dos na Mnaibh. The Will of the People. Are
Irishwomen Under 30 People? [The Republican Proclamation of
1916 says yes, British Law says no. What does Dail Eireann

say? A General Election is at hand; demand Government by
consent women must vote in this election on the same terms as
men.] n.d. n.p.

1885   Cousins, James H. and Margaret E. Cousins. We Two
Together. Madras: Ganesh & Co., 1950. 784pp. portrs.

    Chapters xiv, xv, by Margaret E. Cousins discusses the
    formation of the Irish Women's Franchise League in
    November 1908 with the author as Treasurer, Hannah Sheehy
    Skeffington as Secretary and Mrs. Charles Oldham as
    President. Includes a brief account of its aims and
    activities.

1886   Day, S.R. Women in the New Ireland. Cork: Munster
Women's Franchise League. n.d. (c.1912). 4pp.

    Presents arguments for giving women the franchise on
    democratic grounds.

1887   Democratic Socialist Party. Outline Policy On Women's
Rights. Dublin: Democratic Socialist Party. [1982] 8pp.

1888   Fairweather, Eileen; Roisin McDonough and Melanie Mc
Fadyean. Only the Rivers Run Free. Northern Ireland: The
Women's War. London and Sydney: Pluto Press, 1984. 343pp.

    Taped conversations with women in Northern Ireland -
    Catholics and Protestants, feminists and non-feminists,
    political activists, female political prisoners, mothers
    of sons 'on the blanket', etc. - on a range of issues
    affecting their daily lives in Northern Ireland.

1889   Farrell, Brian. "Markievicz and the Women of the
Revolution" In Leaders and Men of the Easter Rising ed. by
F.X. Martin, pp. 227-238. Dublin, London: Methun and Co.,
1967. refs.

    Brief overview of role of women in Irish political
    affairs notably in the Ladies Land League prior to the
    foundation of Inghinidhe na h Eireann by Maud Gonne in
    1900. Details on activities of that organization, the
    Fianna Eireann founded by Constance Markievicz and the
    role of women during the 1916 Rising.

1890   Fennell, Nuala. Women and the Fianna Fail Government:
Signposts for Change or Stalemate?" Image 3 (5) (Apr. 1978):
36-38.

    Analysis of Fianna Fail party stand on women's issues,
    continuing areas of sexual disadvantage and
    discrimination and need for women's organizations to
    take a more aggressive advocacy role.

1891   Fennell, Nuala. "Women and Politics: The Way Forward."
Image 3 (3) (Feb. 1978): 14-16. portr.

    Considers what women learned in the 1977 election,
    problems of women party members and strategies for the
    future.

1892   Ferguson, Delancey. "Woman of Ulster." Am Scholar 18
(2) (Spring 1949): 193-199.

    Author gives a character sketch of his cousin, an Ulster
    Protestant and the state of that province at the time of
    his visit to her in 1913 - e.g. which was seething with
    agitation over the threat of Home Rule then being
    proposed by the Asquith Government.

1893   Fine Gael Party. National Partnership Through
Equality. Dublin: The Party, 1981. 20pp.

    Fine Gael policy document on women.

1894   Fitzgerald, William G. (ed.) The Voice of Ireland.
Dublin: John Heywood, 1924.

    Includes a chapter "The Woman's Part" (pp.158-174) with
    essays on women's political influence in modern Ireland,
    Cumann na mBan and other topics.

1895   Gassman-Sherr, Rosalie. The Story of the Federation of
Women Zionists of Great Britain and Ireland: 1918-1968.
London: Federation of Women Zionists, 1968. 77pp. il. portrs.

    This account by the then General Secretary details the
    founding and expansion of the Federation and their
    substantial fund raising efforts on behalf of the State
    of Israel. Dublin's membership increased from 80 in 1939
    to 330 in 1967 and in 1966, Eire was represented by one
    delegate, Dr. Hazel Boland, at the 15th Conference of
    World WIZO (Women's International Zionist Organization.)

1896   Gossan, N.J. A Plea for the Ladies. Dublin: William J.
Dunbar, 1875. 31pp.

    Author summarizes the leading arguments in favor of
    enlarging the sphere of female influence, and indicates
    his support of certain limited rights for women e.g. to
    vote, to enter some professions, etc.

1897   Harrison, B. "Men on Women's Side." Times Lit Supp No.
3957 (Jan. 27, 1978): 87.

    A review article discusses Shaw's feminism in the general
    context of male contributions to the feminist struggle in
    England during the years 1860-1920.

1898   Haslam, Thomas J. Some Last Words on Women's
Suffrage. Dublin: The Ormond Printing Co., 1916. 18pp.

    Argument for extension of suffrage to all adult women
    except for criminals and imbeciles.

1899   Haslam, Thomas J. Women's Suffrage from a Masculine
Standpoint. An address delivered in the Mansion House,
Dublin. Dublin: The Ormond Printing Company, 1906. 24pp.

    Refutes arguments against extension of voting rights to
    women and calls on women of high social position to be
    active in the struggle for enfranchisement.

1900   Home Rule for Irishwomen. (Delegates to the National
Convention.) (n.p. n.d.) 1p.

    Calls on delegates to the National Convention to oppose
    the Home Rule Bill which proposes to exclude Irishwomen
    from the rights of representation and citizenship and to
    support women's suffrage.

1901   Irish Women's Franchise League. A Meeting... [every
Tuesday 8p.m.] n.d. 1p.

1902   Irish Women's Franchise League. Report of the
Executive Committee of the Irish Women's Franchise League for
1913. Dublin: Corrigan and Wilson, 1914. 28pp.

    Details activities of the League during the year. Main
    achievement seen as the concession by the Ulster Unionist
    Council of votes to Ulsterwomen. Brief account of
    Suffragist militancy in Ireland and arrest of Hannah
    Sheehy Skeffington.

1903   Irish Women's Franchise League. [Handbills.] Votes for
Women. Why Not Have A Cozy Tea in the Suffrage Tea Room.
Dublin: Printed by Corrigan and Wilson. [c.1912] 1 fold.

    Advertisement for free meetings held in Antient Concert
    Buildings.

1904   Irish Women's Franchise League: Programme of Public
Meetings, Jan-May 1910. Antient Concert Buildings. Dublin,
[1910]. [1p.]

1905   Irish Women's Suffrage And Local Government
Association. Report of the Executive Committee for 1896-1918.
Dublin, 1897-1919.

    Includes a preface overviewing the foundation of the
    Association in 1876 with details on suffrage and other
    activities in Ireland from 1866 onwards.

1906   Irish Women's Suffrage and Local Government
Association. (List of women elected or co-opted under the
Local Government Act, 1902.) [Dublin] n.p. [1902]

1907   Irish Women's Suffrage Federation: Annual Reports 1-6,
1912-1917.

     Includes a note on origins and objectives.

1908   Kingham, N. United We Stood: The Official History of
the Ulster Women's Unionist Council 1911-1974. Belfast:
Appletree Press, 1975. 95pp. il.

     Written by the Organizing Secretary of the Ulster Women's
     Unionist Council (1938-1971) and based on Minute Books,
     Annual Reports, miscellaneous records and Press reports
     details formation, goals, constitution and activities of
     the organization founded in 1911 to resist Home Rule for
     Ireland.

1909   Labour Party. Labour Women's National Council. Towards
Equality: Policy Statements on the Status of Women, Presented
to the 1975 Annual Conference of the Labour Party by the
Labour Women's National Council. Dublin: The Labour Party,
1975. 27pp. tables.

     Review of the progress which has been made in the Labour
     Party and in Irish society generally towards achieving
     equality of opportunity for women. Includes sections on
     education, employment, pensions, social welfare,
     taxation, day care, etc.

1910   Lavery, Rose. "The Future of Irishwomen." New Ire R
(Dec. 1909): 231-234.

     A response to the criticism of the apathy of Irishwomen
     on the question of political enfranchisement. Lavery
     points out that the Catholic Church, whose influence is
     preeminent in Ireland counsels resignation under trial;
     public opinion in Ireland is masculine opinion and
     anti-suffragist; women being economically and socially
     dependent on men are reluctant to express opinions of
     which men disapprove; if women do speak out they are
     characterized as unwomanly; if they remain silent,
     characterized as indifferent.

1911   Law Students Debating Society of Ireland. Women's
Suffrage. An address delivered ... by the auditor, C.O. Kane
Donegan, B.A. Dublin: Printed at the University Press by
Ponsonby and Weldrick, 1892. 39pp.

     Examines claims put forward by the advocates of Women's
     Suffrage and objections commonly raised against this.
     Conclusion advocates the extension of the vote to women.

1912   McCafferty, Nell. "Room for the Ladies." <u>Status</u> 6 (2) (Apr. 1981): 11.

Assesses the progress of women T.D.'s (members of the Dail) and sees their potential for forming common cause on issues affecting women as remaining untapped.

1913   McConnell, Maggie. "Irish Women Poised to Make Breakthrough." <u>Int Cnl Soc Dem Wom</u> 21 (9-10) (1975): 17-18.

Article by the only woman member of the Executive of the Irish Labour Party gives her assessment of the situation of women in the Republic of Ireland. The policy of the Irish Labour Party towards women's rights and the position of women in the party detailed.

1914   McCraith, L.M. "Irishwomen and their Vote." <u>New Ire R</u> 30 (4) (Dec. 1908): 193-198.

Comment on the apparent indifference of Irishwomen to the struggle for the vote for women. McCraith attributes their apathy to the natural conservatism of the Irish race and in addition to the fact that they already possess all the "influence" on events they want.

1915   Martin, Violet Florence. "Not the Woman's Place." In her <u>Strayaways</u>, pp.228-240. London: Longman's Green, 1920. il.

Brief commentary on the importance of sports generally and especially hunting in the enlargement of women's field of action and in creating the climate for the extension of voting rights to these.

1916   Mooney, Mairin. "Women in Ireland." <u>Labour Mon</u> 61 (2) (Feb. 1979): 75-81.

Left wing politics seen as best hope for women especially working class women. Present status of women in Ireland briefly outlined from a left political perspective. Women's Liberation Movement viewed as having had a positive impact in the area of employment but areas of discrimination persist. Role of trade unions discussed.

1917   Mooney, Maureen. "Work on the Women's Question." <u>Ir Socia R</u> 2 (1978): 5-8.

Brief review of developments in the 1971-1975 period which led to the establishment of the National Committee on Women within the Communist Party of Ireland and their Resolution presented to the 16th Party Congress in March 1975 outlining the Party's policy on women.

1918   Owens, Rosemary Cullen and Women in Community
Publishing Course. Did Your Granny Have a Hammer? A History
of the Irish Suffrage Movement 1867-1922. Dublin: Attic
Press, 1985.

   Outline history of the Irish Suffrage Movement in
   portfolio form with facsimile reproductions of original
   material, newspapers, cartoons, letters, photographs,
   etc.

1919   Owens, Rosemary Cullen. Smashing Times: A History of
the Irish Women's Suffrage Movement 1889-1922. Dublin: Attic
Press, 1984. 159pp. il. portrs. bibl.

   Traces the development of the early feminist movement in
   Ireland detailing the historical background,
   personalities involved, objectives, tactics, relationship
   with other groups, notably Labour and Nationalist,
   achievements, and reaction from politicians, religious
   figures and the general public.

1920   Owens, Rosemary Cullen. "Votes for Ladies, Votes for
Women: Organized Labour and the Suffrage Movement 1876-1922."
Saothar 9 (1983): 32-47. refs.

   Examination of the interrelationships between the
   suffrage and the trade union movements including
   ideological, strategic and personal links.

1921   Reports of the Irish Women's Suffrage and Local
Government Association from 1896 to 1918, with a preface by
Miss Dora Mellone.   Dublin: The Ormond Print Co., Jan. 1919.
10pp. front.

   Brief historical background on the Association, its
   political and educational activities on behalf of the
   Parliamentary Enfranchisement of women, membership and
   aims, the work of the Association from 1896 to 1918 is
   fully detailed in the printed reports. (See #1922.)

1922   Report of the Executive Committee of the Dublin
Women's Suffrage (and Poor Law Guardians) Association 1897.
Dublin: R. Chapman. 1898+ (In 1898 name changed to ...and
Local Government's Association. In 1901 name changed to Irish
Women's Suffrage and Local Government Association.)

1923   Report of the Executive Committee of the Irish Women's
Suffrage and Local Government Association. [1901-1918]

1924   Robinson, Mary T.W. (Senator) "Women and the New Irish
State." J Ir Lit 6 (2) (May 1977): 28-38. il.

Article dealing with the underlying causes of the non-
participation of women in the new Irish state and the
consequences for the evolution of the political, legal,
social and economic life of the country. Author
speculates on the future outlook for Irish women.

1925   Ryan, Frederick. "The Suffrage Tangle." Ir R 2 (Sept.
1912): 346-351.

Presents arguments in favor of women's suffrage while
disapproving of action taken by militant suffragists.

1926   Shaw, George Bernard. Sir Almroth Wright's Case
Against Woman Suffrage Answered by Bernard Shaw. Dublin:
Irishwomen's Suffrage Federation, [1914?] 8pp. [Reprinted
from the New Statesman.]

Decries Wright's views that men are more rational than
women.

1927   Shaw, George Bernard. "The Unmentionable Case for
Women's Suffrage." Engwoman No. 2 (Mar. 1909): 112-121.

Argues for the presence of women on public bodies.

1928   Sheehy Skeffington, Hanna. "Women in Politics." Bell 7
(2) (Nov. 1943): 143-148.

Analysis of failed campaign by four women (including the
author) in the recent General Election who had run as
Independents on a platform stressing need for greater
female representation in Government. Political machines
which do not educate the electorate viewed as responsible
for their rejection by the voters.

1929   Sheehy Skeffington, Hanna. "The Women's Movement —
Ireland." Ir R 2 (17) (July 1912): 225-227.

Brief article on the resort to militant tactics on their
own behalf by Irish suffragists and why constitutional
methods employed since 1876 were not sufficient to
persuade Parliament to grant women their rights. (The
author wrote this article prior to beginning a jail term
for her involvement in this struggle.)

1930   Sheehy Skeffington, Hanna. The Duty of Suffragists.
(Reprinted from The Irish Citizen.) [n.p. n.d.] 1p.

An exhortation to women not to be persuaded to abandon
their demand for votes because of the "national crisis"
as the news media advocate.

1931   "Should Women Play a Bigger Part in Irish Public
Life?" Word (Mar. 1968): 7-10. il. portrs.

    Comments by prominent Irish men and women on the role of
    women in public life.

1932   Sinn Fein. An Appeal to the Women of Ireland. n.p.
n.d.

    Eulogistic tribute to Irish women extolls their
    nationalism and asks for their vote.

1933   Sinn Fein. Education Department. Women in Ireland.
Dublin: Sinn Fein. [1984] 9pp. il. (Republican Lecture Series
8.)

    Position paper.

1934   Sinn Fein: The Workers Party. National Women's
Committee. Women in Ireland. Dublin: [Sinn Fein] n.d. 14pp.
il.

    Policy statement on issues affecting women: education,
    employment, legal, financial and social welfare status.

1935   Sjoo, Monica. "Cultures Apart." Peace News 2073 (June
30, 1978): 13. il.

    News item on the first Lesbian Conference in Ireland held
    at Trinity College May 26-28, 1978 by a participant.
    Eighty women attended.

1936   Snoddy, Oliver. "Suffragettes in Carlow." Carloviana 1
(13) (1964): 26. refs.

    Brief note on Mrs. Spring Rice, Mrs. Sheehy Skeffington,
    Helen Chenevix and Louie Bennett. Lists the numerous
    women's organizations in existence in Carlow in 1914 and
    their internal divisions despite their similar
    objectives. All points of view represented in the Irish
    Citizen edited by Mrs. Sheehy Skeffington.

1937   "Sons and Widows." Economist 214 (1965): 1259.

    Brief comment on the practice in Ireland of electing
    widows and sons of former deputies to the Irish
    Parliament.

1938   Story, E.G.M. "National Council of Women of Ireland."
Alex Col Mag 10 (Dec. 1937): 52-53.

Note on activities of National Council - annual meeting,
opposition to draft of new Irish Constitution, Women
Citizens Club afternoons.

1939   Thompson, William. Appeal of One Half of the Human
Race, Women, Against the Pretentions of the Other Half, Men,
To Retain Them in Political And Thence in Civil and Domestic
Slavery. London: Printed for Longman, Hurst, Rees, Orme,
Brown and Green, 1825. [Reprinted 1975.] 221pp.

   A reply to James Mill's dismissal of political rights for
   women in his famous "Essay on Government" in which Mill
   argues that almost all women are adequately represented
   in political matters by their fathers or husbands.
   Thompson refutes this argument and makes the most
   impressive case for women's rights before the publication
   in 1869 of John Stuart Mill's The Subjection of Women.
   Among the targets attacked are the legal disabilities
   suffered by women, their lack of access to education and
   their enslavement to the authority of their fathers or
   husbands.

1940   Timpson, Oonagh. "Matters Affecting Women." Cross 66
(1) (May 1975): 4-5. il.

   Argues that the only way to give full representation to
   women who comprise 51% of the population is to pass a law
   requiring that all Government committees must be 50%
   female.

1941   Trinity College. New Library. Votes for Women,
Exhibition of Documents and Mementos relating to the Irish
Women's Suffrage Movement October 9 - 24, 1975. [Dublin: The
Library, 1975.] 8pp.

1942   [An Ulster Woman] "Why Ulster Women Are Protesting."
Spectator 108 (June 15, 1912): 945-946.

   Presents the rationale for the opposition of Ulster women
   to the Home Rule Bill - their freedom of thought and
   speech will be curtailed by a party the majority of whom
   accept Roman Catholic principles and the Vatican Decrees
   of 1864.

1943   Votes for Women: Irish Women's Struggle for the Vote.
[Published by Andree D. Sheehy Skeffington and Rosemary
Owens. n.p. n.d.] 27pp. il.

   Catalog of an exhibition on the Irish Women's Suffrage
   Movement. Includes a brief historical overview of the
   movement and the previously unpublished "Reminiscences of
   an Irish Suffragette" by Hanna Sheehy Skeffington.
   Includes reproductions of posters and cartoons used in
   the campaign.

*1944   Ward, Margret. <u>Suffrage First Above All Else: An
Account of the Irish Suffrage Movement</u>. London: Pluto Press,
1982.

1945   Ward, Margret. "Suffrage First Above All Else: An
Account of the Irish Suffrage Movement." <u>Femin R</u> 10 (1982):
21-36.

   An incisive analysis of the Suffrage Movement in Ireland
   deliniates the various groups involved and their
   respective ideologies and documents how the separate
   issues of 'Home Rule' and 'Votes for Women' became
   hopelessly entangled. This plus the outbreak of War and
   the threat of Civil War effectively destroyed the
   Suffrage Movement despite the extension of the vote to
   women in 1922.

1946   Webb, Alfred. "The Propriety of Conceding the Elective
Franchise to Women." <u>Stat & Soc Inq Soc J</u> 4 (Jan. 1868):
455-461.

   Presents and refutes arguments against the extension of
   the franchise to women.

1947   <u>Women's Rights in Ireland</u>. Dublin: Sinn Fein: National
Women's Committee, 1975. 24pp.

   Brief overview of disabilities suffered by women in
   taxation, social welfare, education and some problems
   occasioned by the antidiscrimination legislation - Pay
   and Employment - (1975). Outlines policy for the Sinn
   Fein Party on women's issues.

1948   <u>Women's Social and Progressive League (Comluct Ban
Eireann) Annual Report 1937-1938</u>. Dublin: The League, [1938.]

   This first annual report describes the founding of the
   League with a description of its criteria for membership
   - non-party, non-sectarian, open to all women - and aims;
   viz. to promote and protect the political, social and
   economic status of women. (Reports also issued for the
   years 1938-39, 39-40, 41-42, 42-43.)

1949   <u>Women's Suffrage Pamphlets and Handbills</u>. Presented to
the Library of Trinity College Dublin by Mrs. A. Sheehy
Skeffington. [Dublin: n.p. n.d.]

   (See #1941.)

Revolutionary Movements

This section contains historical material on women's participation in the Nationalist struggle as well as contemporary material relating to their role in the ongoing struggle in the six counties of Northern Ireland, including peace efforts spearheaded by women. For material on related constitutional political activity see POLITICS; also for historical accounts of militant suffragette activity. Theoretical perspectives on the effects of revolutionary and/or trade union activity on the Feminist cause are located under PERSPECTIVES ON WOMEN'S LIBERATION.

1950   d'Arcy, Margaretta. Tell Them Everything: A Sojourn in the Prison of Her Majesty Queen Elizabeth II at Ard Macha (Armagh). (London): Pluto Press, 1981. 127pp.

An account of a three month sentence served in Armagh jail by the author rather than pay a fine for demonstrating (on International Woman's Day 1979) against the inhuman and squalid conditions in the prison where 30 young Republican women were engaged in a "no-wash" protest.

1951   Bedarida, Catherine. "Ces Irlandaises au Drapeau Vert." Histoire (Nov. 30, 1981): 86-87. portrs. refs.

Brief comment on Nationalist women in Ireland during the period 1890-1921. Includes a note on Constance Markievicz, Maud Gonne, Sally Allgood and her sister Maire O'Neill. Points out the irony that these women taking part in the Nationalist struggle helped to sever the connection with socially progressive Britain – where women's rights were concerned – and helped create an Irish state with a profoundly reactionary view of the role of women.

1952   "Belfast Women Speak Out." WICCA No. 1 (1978): 11-13.
il.

   Brief article reporting substance of an address by two
   members of the Relatives Action Committee, a Northern
   Ireland Woman's Group to students at Dublin universities.
   Harassment by British Army of civilian population in
   Republican areas, torture of men in prison, goals and
   methods of Relatives Action Committee are briefly
   discussed.

1953   "Bernadette Is Sentenced and Everyone Sleeps Less
Easily." Economist 233 (Dec. 27, 1969): 39. il.

   Analysis of the effects on the political situation in
   Northern Ireland of the six month imprisonment verdict
   accorded to Bernadette Devlin by the Londonderry Court.

1954   Berson, T. "Northern Ireland's Peace People." Chr Cent
93 (Nov. 17, 1976): 995-996.

   Background on formation of the Peace Movement by Mairead
   Corrigan and Betty Williams. Outlook for peace as a
   result of this movement and the ecumenical movement among
   the various churches in Northern Ireland explored.

1955   Bonfante, Jordan. "Fierce Women of Ulster." Life 71
(Dec. 3, 1971): 24B-30D. il.

   Various roles and activities of women in the guerilla
   warfare in Northern Ireland briefly discussed.

1956   Boyle, H. "To Melt a Heart of Stone." Nation 223 (Oct.
2, 1976): 30.

   Brief article describing formation of the Peace
   organization in Northern Ireland and their early rallies
   which united women from both Catholic and Protestant
   areas.

1957   Buckley, Margaret. The Jangle of the Keys. Dublin:
James Duffy and Co. Ltd., 1938. 116pp.

   The author describes her arrest for Republican activities
   in 1923 during the Civil War, her subsequent internment
   in Mountjoy jail, tranfer to the North Dublin Union camp
   where conditions were worse than Mountjoy and a later
   transfer to Kilmainham Jail. Her comrades, daily
   routines, hunger strikes, attempted escapes and final
   release described minutely.

1958   Buckley, Susan and Pamela Lonergan. "Women and the

Troubles" In <u>Terrorism in Ireland</u> ed. by Yonah Alexander and
Alan O'Day, pp. 75-87. London: Croon Helm; New York: St.
Martins Press, 1984. refs.

(See Perspectives of Women's Liberation #2018.)

1959   "A Chance for Peace." <u>Senior Sch Stud</u> 109 (Jan. 13,
1977): 13-15. il.

   Brief background information on outbreak of violence in
   Northern Ireland in 1968 and the factors instrumental in
   the formation of the Women's Peace Movement by Mairead
   Corrigan and Betty Williams.

1960   Concannon, Mrs. Thomas (Helena). <u>Women of
Ninety-Eight</u>. Dublin: M.H. Gill and Co., 1919. 326pp. front.

   Brief sketches of the "obscure heroines" - the mothers,
   wives, sisters and sweethearts of the heroes of the 1798
   rebellion. Activities of these included actual
   participation in the fighting, acting as messengers and
   intelligence officers, recordkeeping, inspiring their men
   and mourning their loss.

1961   Conlon, Lil. <u>Cumann na mBan and the Women of Ireland</u>.
Kilkenny: Kilkenny People Ltd., 1969. 312pp.

   A chronological account by a participant of the
   activities of Cumann na mBan (Irish Women's Council) from
   its founding in 1913 through 1925. Considerable detail on
   activities of rank and file women in the organization.
   Accounts of Black and Tan reprisals against the
   Volunteers and their supporters - including women. The
   split in ranks of Cumann na mBan after the Treaty
   paralleled the split in the country at large between
   supporters and opponents of this.

1962   Conway, Thomas G. "Women's Work in Ireland." <u>Eire Ire</u>
7 (1) (1972): 10-27. refs.

   Brief overview of the contribution of Irish women to the
   National cause either as artists or activists. Most of
   these seen as atypical by contemporary standards being
   mostly liberally-educated, of upper-middle or
   aristocratic background and chiefly Protestant.
   Individual women identified with a brief note on their
   contribution.

1963   Cumann na mBan. <u>Constitution</u>. (n.p. n.d. c. 1915?)
Cumann na mBan. 4pp.

1964   Cumann na mBan. (The Irishwomen's Council). <u>Riaglaca</u>.
Dublin: Cumann na mBan. (n.d.) 4pp.

1965   Cumann na mBan Executive. *The Present Duty of Irishwomen*. Dublin: Cumann na mBan. n.d. 4pp.

Political pamphlet exhorting Irishwomen to vote for Sinn Fein candidates at the next general election. The platform of Sinn Fein and the other parties detailed.

1966   Cumann na mBan. *Manifesto from Cumann na mBan (Irish Women's Council) The Women's Section of the Volunteer Movement*. Dublin: Cumann na mBan, 1914. 4pp.

Pamphlet detailing aims of the organization, criteria for membership, formation, constitution and names of the provisional committee. Includes an appeal to Irishmen to resist conscription.

1967   "Cursed be the Peacemakers." *Time* 108 (Oct. 25, 1976): 42. il.

Report on attacks on leaders of the Peace Movement in Northern Ireland (Mairead Corrigan and Betty Williams) who are striving to walk the thin line between condemnation for British Army brutality and support for the British Army and the Royal Irish Constabulary as legitimate instruments of law.

1968   "The Deadly Sisters." *Newsweek* 81 (Apr. 16, 1973): 46+. il.

Brief article dealing with numbers, recruitment, training and military activities of the present-day Cumann na mBan, the sister organization of the Irish Republican Army.

1969   Dreifus, Claudia. "A Woman of Belfast." *Progressive* 39 (Apr. 1975): 28-31. il.

Profile on an Irish Catholic woman whose husband, a member of the Provisional IRA, is interned in Lough Kesh. Details on her life style, her difficulties in single handedly raising their eight children, her political hopes and fears.

1970   "The Enforcers." *Newsweek* 79 (Apr. 24, 1972): 39. il.

News item regarding IRA "justice" meted out to a pregnant mother who was severely beaten for allegedly using and selling drugs in one of the IRA controlled sectors of Belfast.

1971   Faligot, Roger. *James Connolly et le Mouvement Revolutionnaire Irlandais*. Paris: Francois Maspero, 1978. 333pp. bibl.

Includes a chapter on "Connolly et la luite des femmes irlandaises" (pp.213-249) with discussion of Connolly's views on women's suffrage, female nationlist movements, working-class women, marriage and divorce based on his writings in The Reconquest of Ireland.

1972   Fell, Alison. "And There's Another Side." Spare Rib 3 (Sept. 1972): 11-15, 26.

Interviews with six Northern Ireland women representing Protestant, Official IRA and Provisional IRA on the situation of women in Northern Ireland.

1973   Fox, R.M. Green Banners. The Story of the Irish Struggle. London: Secker and Warburg, 1938. 352pp. il. plates. portrs. bibl.

Chapter 22 "Militant Women" (pp. 285-302) deals with the activities of Republican women in 1916 during the Easter Rebellion. Has a brief background on Cumann na mBan and its predecessor organization, Inghinidhe na h Eireann founded by Maud Gonne.

1974   Franks, Lucinda. "We Want Peace. Just Peace." N Y Times Mag (Dec. 19, 1976): 29-31+. il.

Article discusses the formation of the Peace Movement in Northern Ireland led by Betty Williams and Mairead Corrigan, reactions to it by the general public and various political groupings and its future prospects.

1975   Gretton, John. "Belfast: The Social and Economic Reality." New Soc 16 (431) (Dec. 31, 1970): 1161-1164. il. maps.

Discussion of political situation in Northern Ireland. Includes a brief profile of two families and a discussion of the Women Together Movement.

1976   Haeger, Robert. "Is Peace in Northern Ireland Becoming Possible at Last." U S News 83 (Oct. 24, 1977): 84+. il.

Author examines the possibility of an end to the violence in Northern Ireland. Favorable portents - including the award of the Nobel Peace Prize to two Irish women, leaders of the Peace Movement - and negative ones reviewed and evaluated for a mainly pessimistic conclusion.

1977   Inghinidhe na h Eireann. To the Women of the North Dock Ward. [n.p. n.d.] 1p.

Appeal to women to vote for Thomas Bryne of Donnycarney

on account of the assistance he has always given the
society. Signed by Maud Gonne as President and other
officers.

1978   Inghinidhe na h Eirean. [Membership card, unsigned,
declaring the objects of the Association.] [n.p. n.d.] 1p.

1979   Irishwomen! How To Defeat Conscription. Take The Women
Workers Pledge. n.p. n.d. 1p.

   Call on Irishwomen to refuse to fill places vacated by
   men and to help families of men who suffer through
   refusing military service.

1980   Irishwomen and the Irish Republican Army. [n.p. n.d.
c.1921]

   A declaration of support by the women of Ireland for the
   I.R.A.

1981   Jeffares, Marion. "Women and Easter Week, 1916."
Easter Wk (1966): 24. portrs.

   Brief discussion of the period leading up to and
   including the 1916 Rising described as the Golden Age of
   Irish womanhood. Women identified as having played
   conspicuous parts in the literary, cultural and
   nationalist revival at the turn of the century include
   Maud Gonne McBride, Constance Markievicz, Hannah Sheehy
   Skeffington, Helena Moloney.

1982   "Keepers of the Flame." Newsweek 78 (Nov. 29, 1971):
33-34. il.

   Details terrorist activities on the part of some women in
   Northern Ireland against the British and against Irish
   girls who fraternize with them.

1983   Keerdoja, Eileen. "Ulster's Peace Women." Newsweek 91
(Mar. 27, 1978): 18. il.

   A short report on the present status of the peace
   movement in Northern Ireland six months after the award
   of the 1976 Nobel Peace Prize to its co-founders.

1984   McCafferty, Nell. The Armagh Women. Dublin: Coop
Books, 1981 94pp.

   An exploration of the events leading up to the "dirt"
   protest by thirty female Republican prisoners in Armagh
   jail from February to December 1980 - denial of special
   status, escalating repression - and depiction of
   conditions in and outside the prison.

1985   MaCallion, Edna. "Women of Belfast." America 125 (Nov. 27, 1971); 453-456. il.

An account of the role played by the Women Together Movement in trying to involve women of all denominations to work together to end the violence in Northern Ireland. Goals of the organization and achievements detailed.

1986   McDonnell, Kathleen Hayes. There Is a Bridge at Brandon: A Personal Account of the Irish War of Independence. Cork: Mercier, 1972. 217pp. il.

An account of the Volunteer Corps organized in Brandon, a Unionist stronghold in late 1913 by the author's husband; her own efforts to form a female Auxiliary corps; Easter 1916 and the confusion and lack of information among the Cork branches of the Volunteers, anti-recruitment efforts by her husband, his arrest, her travels to Wakefield Jail to visit him and to publicize prison conditions, and her harassment during the Black and Tan Era.

1987   McGuire, Maria. To Take Arms: My Year With the IRA Provisionals. New York: Viking, 1973. 186pp.

This book explores such questions as how the IRA justifies terrorism tactics, how genuine are the Provos' beliefs in a United Ireland, and the disillusionment of one IRA member with the cause as a whole.

1988   McKay, Mary. "Living With the Army in Your Front Garden." Spare Rib No. 43. (Feb. 1976): 9-13. il.

Brief article discussing the history and political background of the struggle in Northern Ireland and the part played by Catholic women in the context of the overall situation of women in the labor market and their relatively less favored situation versus their counterparts in the United Kingdom.

1989   Markievicz (Constance de). Women, Ideals and the Nation. A lecture delivered to the Students National Literary Society, Dublin by Constance de Markievicz... Dublin: Inginidhe na hEireann, 1909. 16pp.

Discusses role of women in public life in other countries, their relative lack of participation in Ireland and what they could achieve therein. Exhorts Irish women not to join any suffrage society or franchise league that does not include in its program the freedom of the Nation.

1990   Middendorff, Wolf. "Die Persoenlichkert der Terroristen, Insbesondere die Frau als Terroristin." Krimin 30 (7) (1976): 189-196; 30 (8) (1976): 357-363.

Comment on female terrorism in Russia, Ireland, the
United States and West Germany.

1991   Ni Bh (E.) A Call to Irishwomen. [to join Cumann na m
Ban. English and Irish language versions] [n.p. n.d. 1917]
1p.

1992   O h Annrachain, Michael. Irish Heroines being a
lecture written for and delivered before An Ard Craob Cumann
na m Ban, Dublin, during the winter preceding Easter Week,
1916. Dublin: The O Hanrahans. n.d. 35pp.

   Recalls the deeds of famous Irish women in the
   revolutionary struggle and exhorts the women of Cumann na
   m Ban to follow their example.

1993   O'Neill, Marie. "The Ladies Land League." Dub Hist R
35 (4) (1982): 122-133. refs.

   Brief account of foundation and activities of the League
   and its role in the Land War after the arrest of the male
   leaders, controversy surrounding their activities and
   political differences between Anna Parnell and her
   brother, Charles Stewart in connection with this.

1994   "A People's Peace Prize." Time 108 (Sec. 13, 1976):
59. il.

   News item on the award to Betty Williams and Mairead
   Corrigan, co-founders of the Ulster Peace Movement of the
   Norwegian People's Peace Prize.

1995   Pethick-Lawrence, Emmeline. Le Terrorisme Anglais et
les Femmes Irlandaises. Paris: La Delegation Irlandaise
[1921]. (Reprinted from the Daily News, London 27 April
1921.)

   Case history account of British Army outrages against
   women in Ireland during raids.

1996   Phillips, B.J. "Tragedies in Ireland." Ms 1 (Mar.
1973): 39+. il.

   Brief note on how women are affected by the civil strife
   in Northern Ireland with comments by women on both sides.

1997   "Pied Pipers of Peace." Time 108 (Sept. 6, 1976): 27.
il.

   Brief news item on role of Betty Williams and Mairead
   Corrigan in the organization of the Peace Movement in
   Northern Ireland.

1998   "A Playgroup Called Freedom." Spare Rib 41 (Nov.
1975): 17-19. il.

    A group of women from Armagh describe their fight to form
a playgroup on their housing estate.

1999   Reidy, (James). The Influence of the Irish Woman on
the National Movement. Lecture delivered before the Brooklyn
Gaelic Society, March 18, 1906. [Brooklyn, 1906?]. 8pp.

    A roll-call of women active in the cause of Nationalism
invoked to exhort their present day descendants to follow
their example.

2000   "Republicanism - What Our Irish Sisters Think." Spare
Rib 99 (Nov. 1980): 31-34. il.

    Responses by three women's groups in Northern Ireland:
Women Against Imperialism (W.A.I.), Derry Women's Aid and
Belfast Women's Collective to the query posed by Spare
Rib as to whether feminists should support the women in
the Armagh Women's Prison on the "no-wash" protest and
whether they should support the "liberation" struggle
being fought by the IRA.

2001   Reynolds, John J. "Inginide ha h Eireann: The
Daughters of Erin." Gael 21 (Aug. 1902): 257-260. il.

    A brief history of the Society notes its aims, membership
and activities, especially their Nationalist theatrical
productions, classes in Irish language history, music and
dance.

2002   Sheehy, Gail. "The Fighting Women of Ireland." N Y 5
(March 13, 1972): 45-55. il.

    An account of the activities engaged in by Northern Irish
women in the civil rights struggle. These include
organizing groups and demonstrations, guerilla warfare
and undergoing imprisonment. Sketchy profiles of some of
these women and excerpts from their conversations with
Ms. Sheehy. Also a vivid account of "Bloody Sunday."

2003   "Two Peace Prizes from OSLO." Time 110 (Oct. 24,
1977): 54. il.

    Brief news item regarding the award of the 1976 Nobel
Peace Prize to Betty Williams and Mairead Corrigan,
leaders of the Peace Movement in Northern Ireland.
Current status of movement and projects undertaken with
Nobel funds briefly discussed.

2004   Ward, Margaret. <u>Unmanageable Revolutionaries: Women and Irish Nationalism</u>. Kerry: Brandon Book Pub. Ltd., 1983. 196pp. refs.

    A pioneering study of the role played by the small minority of women who participated in the nationalist struggle between the 1880's and the 1940's from a feminist perspective. Focus is on three organizations: The Ladies Land League (1881-82); Inghinidhe na h Eireann (1900-14); the Cumann na m Ban (1914-). Based mainly on previously published sources and a few unpublished memoirs supplemented by some interviews.

2005   Ward, Margaret. "Marginality and Militancy: Cumann na mBan 1914-1936." In <u>Ireland: Divided Nation, Divided Class</u>. ed. by A. Morgan and B. Purdie, pp. 96-110. London: Ink Links, 1980. refs.

    A socialist/feminist analysis of the women's nationalist party, Cumann na mBan argues that the women's marginal status in the Irish Nationalist tradition and exclusion from political decision-making in their mobilization resulted in their uncompromising idealism based more on principle than on an experienced appreciation of political practice. The current status of women in the Republican organizations in Northern Ireland briefly examined.

2006   Willenson, Kim and Anthony Collings. "Two Women of Ulster." <u>Newsweek</u> 90 (Oct. 24, 1977): 61. il.

    News item on the circumstances which gave rise to the "Peace Movement" in Northern Ireland and the award of the 1976 Nobel Peace Prize to the leaders of that Movement - Betty Corrigan and Mairead Williams. Impact of that award on peace prospects briefly discussed.

2007   Willenson, Kay and Malcolm McPherson. "Grandma Venom." <u>Newsweek</u> 88 (Aug. 23, 1976): 55-57. il.

    News item on the arrest of Maire Drumm, 56 years old, a vice president of Sinn Fein (the political arm of the Provisional, IRA) known locally as the 'Fiery Grandmother,' plus details on the British effort to put pressure on the IRA (Irish Republican Army).

2008   <u>The Women of Ninety-Eight</u>. Dublin: M.H.Gill and Son. [n.d.] 326pp. portr.

    Leaflet paying tribute to heroines of the '98 rebellion - names representative of the magnificent contribution made by the women of Ireland. Tone's wife, women of Wexford, Mary Doyle, Betsy Grey, Mary McCracken, Mary Emmet, Anne Devlin among those mentioned.

2009   Yates, Barbara. "Ireland: What Sort of Peace." <u>Union Wage</u> No. 40 (Mar.-Apr. 1977): 6, 13. il.

Attitudes of Northern Irish women explored. Conclusions: The Peace Movement is not exclusively a Women's Movement; many women are actively involved in all aspects of the Republican Movement and their principal aim is the ending of British Imperialism in Ireland. This involvement leaves them no time to fight for women's issues, per se.

Perspectives on Women's Liberation

This section covers ideological debates, pro and con, on feminism; the relationship of this with Nationalist, Socialist or Labour Movements, theoretical or actual; activities, achievements, personalities and groups associated with the Women's Liberation Movement; descriptive, prescriptive and analytic accounts of women's actual status in Irish society generally. For accounts of women's actual status or achievements in major social institutions see those categories, e.g. LAW, EMPLOYMENT AND ECONOMIC LIFE, EDUCATION. Role conflicts arising from new opportunities and other stress factors are treated in the sections on MARRIAGE AND THE FAMILY, and PSYCHOLOGY. For discussion of the struggle for women's suffrage, see POLITICS. The section on REVOLUTIONARY MOVEMENTS contains some additional material on the effects of Nationalism and other political ideologies on Feminism both currently and historically.

2010   The Autonomy of the Women's Movement. Dublin: Movement for a Socialist Republic. Women's Commission, 1977. 10pp.

A discussion of how the Women's Liberation Movement can be made part and parcel of the fight for Socialism and in what sense the Women's Movement has autonomy within that struggle.

2011   Beere, Thelka. "Commission on the Status of Women: Progress Report." Admin 23 (1) (Spring 1975): 31-46.

This paper by the Chair of the Commission details what had been already accomplished, what was in progress and what remained to be done to implement the Report of the Commission. Concludes that 50% of recommendations have been implemented or are in process of being implemented, 30% have been accepted in principle and 20% have not been acted upon.

2012   Bernard, Anne. "Creativity and Procreativity." <u>Crane Bag</u> 4 (1) (1980): 31-41. refs.

Argues that the basic ideology of the feminist praxis rests upon a masculine ideal - a fundamental opposition of creativity and procreativity. Elucidates the origin of that ideology and the anthropological framework upon which it rests and its expression in Simone de Beauvoir's <u>Second Sex</u> which is criticized for sharing the male contempt for the immanence of the female. Presents an outline for a new kind of possibility for the world of feminine imagination - the reconciliation of the male and female principles.

2013   Blackburn, Helen. (ed.) <u>A Handbook for Women Engaged in Social and Political Work</u>. [2nd ed.] Bristol: J.W. Arrowsmith, 1895. 116pp. charts. diag.

A brief overview of the then status of women in England and Ireland. Includes chapters on Franchises open to women, public appointments held by them, their education and employment, legal status, women's organization, and a chart of their progress between 1848 and 1895.

2014   Bluh, Bonnie C. <u>Woman to Woman: European Feminists</u>. New York: Starogubski, 1974. 317pp.

The author, an American feminist records personal comments by women in Ireland, England, Holland, France, Italy, Spain and The United States. Her respondents in Ireland include some of those active in the Women's Liberation Movement - many of whom are journalists. Topics covered include the difficulties of consciousness-raising, sexism in Ireland, feminism and politics, contraception, abortion, etc.

2015   Brennan, Pat. "Government Undermines Women's Council." <u>Status</u> 1 (4) (March 14, 1981): 17-21.

Brief note on the history of the Council for the Status of Women founded in 1973 and headed by Monica Barnes.

2016   Brennan, Pat. "Women in Revolt." <u>Magill Mag</u> (Apr. 1979): 34-46. portrs. refs.

Traces the evolution of the modern women's movement in Ireland and the various groups and organizations concerned with women's issues. Foremost in terms of consciousness-raising was the initial Women's Liberation Movement founded in early 1970 and lasting through 1971 when it dissolved through dissension over ideological and organizational issues. Many smaller offshoots of this and other more mainstream groups some of which are still active are minutely described.

2017   Brennan, Pat. "Women Organize in Dublin." <u>Magill Mag</u> 2 (4) (Jan. 1979): 6.

   Brief note on the formation of a Women's Centre in Dublin outlines aims of the steering collective and considers its prospects for success in reuniting the fragmented Irish Women's Movement.

2018   Buckley, Suzann and Pamela Lonergan. "Women and the Troubles" In <u>Terrorism in Ireland ed. by Yonah Alexander and Alan O'Day</u>, pp. 75-87. London: Croon Helm; New York: St. Martin's Press, 1984. refs.

   Concludes that Northern Irish women's political participation whether for or against terrorist activities in the province have made little contribution to their equality with men nor has it led to any increase in feminist consciousness.

2019   Burca, Mairin de. "Women's Liberation." <u>Teoiric</u> No.4 (1975): 1-5.

   Brief background on the Women's Liberation Movement in the United States and in Ireland. Discusses areas where women's needs are not being met, notably in the areas of day care, and family planning. Position of women in Socialist countries and in left wing revolutionary movements also seen as less than satisfactory.

2020   "The Changing Status of Women Is a Good Thing." <u>Liberty</u> (June 1976): 13.

   A poll of male members of the Employment Equality Commission show that 78% of these approve the changing status of women. Other findings indicate that most women prefer to work outside the home. However, the majority of both sexes regard politics as still a male preserve.

2021   Chester, Catherine. "And Now For Something Completely Different." <u>Status</u> 6 (2) (Apr. 1981): 12-13. il.

   Comments by Irish women on Irish men.

2022   Cullen, Mary. "How Radical Was Irish Feminism Between 1860 and 1920?" In <u>Radicals, Rebels and Establishment</u>. ed. by P.J. Corish, pp. 185-201. Belfast: Appletree Press, 1985. refs.

   An examination of the interaction between ideological and socio-economic forces in the development of Irish feminism in the period.

2023   Derwin, Des. and others. "Women's Struggles." <u>Int</u>

Socia No. 92 (Oct 1976): 37-38. il. refs.

   Brief article on the situation of Irish women. Topics
   touched upon include equal pay, contraception, divorce,
   abortion, Establishment and non-Establishment women's
   organizations and their goals and membership.

2024   Duffy, Maureen. "Irish Women Need Women's Lib."
Reality 36 (12) (Dec. 1972): 37-41. il.

   Brief article documenting some of women's grievances in
   Ireland.

2025   Eire (Ireland). Office of the Minister of State for
Women's Affairs. 100 Years of the Irish Women's Movement.
Dublin: Office of the Minister of State for Women's Affairs,
[1984]. 1p.

2026   Eire (Ireland). Office of the Minister of State for
Women's Affairs. Aims and Framework for Action. Dublin:
Office of the Minister of State for Women's Affairs, [1984].
1p.

2027   Eire (Ireland). Office of the Minister of State for
Women's Affairs. Women and the Law. Dublin: Office of the
Minister of State for Women's Affairs, [1984]. 1p.

   A series of summary pamphlets issued by the newly created
   Office of the Minister of State for Women's Affairs.

2028   Evanson, Eileen. "Women in Northern Ireland:
Employment, Law and Social Provision." New Com 5 (1-2)
(Summer 1976): 59-63. refs.

   Brief overview of status of women in Northern Ireland
   considers rigid sex roles, discrimination in employment
   and training opportunities and other disabilities.

2029   Evason, Eileen and Clara Clark. Women and Social
Policy - North and South. Submission to the New Ireland
Forum, 1983.

   Underlines how Northern women in Ireland would lose out
   if they joined an unchanged Southern Irish state in the
   areas of family allowances, health care, family planning
   services, legal aid, family law protection, right to
   divorce and remarriage. Also indicates some areas where
   the situation is better in the South - parent/child
   rights, Family Home Protection, direct social welfare
   provision for separated wives.

2030   Exile. "Women in Public Life." Bell 4 (1943): 266-271.

Reflections on the condition of Irish society and on what women could contribute to it.

2031   Feminist Federation. "Nothing Beyond the Fragments."
Class Strug No.7 (June-Sept. 1980): 20-21.

Background and critique - from a radical feminist perspective of the Feminist Federation, an umbrella style organization embracing multi-type women's groups founded in June 1979 to fill gap left by dissolution of Irishwomen United.

2032   Fennell, Nuala. "Women's Rights." W Ir Nurs 2 (May 1973): 93. (Summary of address given by the former member of AIM at the February meeting of the Dublin branch of the Irish Nurse's Association.)

Fennell argues that because they were unwilling to be associated with radical ideas in the areas of abortion and divorce embraced by the Women's Liberation Movement in America, Irish women refused to become part of this struggle - even in areas they do consider important: rights of deprived, deserted or mistreated wives, equal pay, contraception, fair family law and reformed adoption legislation. Fennell calls on all women to become politically aware and active.

2033   Fennell, Nuala. "Hold Me Banner While I Feed The Baby." Cross 63 (11) (Mar. 1973): 12-14. il.

The author outlines some of the difficulties faced by women's rights organizations in Ireland and the need for male support. Lack of significant female participation in national or local politics, the professions and public administration is a significant disadvantage in pressing claims for full equality.

2034   "The Fighting Women of Ireland: Women for Irish Freedom." Women 3 (4) (1972/73): 24-29. il.

Reprint of excerpts from the pamphlet, Irish Women Speak. Interviews with women active in the Women's Liberation Movement, the Northern Ireland Civil Rights Association and the Official IRA regarding current and future prospects for Irish women in general and in these organizations.

2035   Flanagan, Donal. "The More Subtle Discrimination."
Studies 64 (255) (1975): 231-242.

Discusses the formation of the Commission on The Status of Women, its findings, recommendations and the practical results of its work to date. Analyses the Commission's Report wherein the roots of discriminatory behavior are

seen as rooted in the socialization process. Flanagan
feels that religion is a key factor in this not
sufficiently noted by the Commission.

2036   Guthrie, (Rev. Hunter). "Woman's Role in the Modern
World." Ir Mon LXIX (May 1941): 246-252. (Condensed from an
article in the Catholic World.)

Suggests three elements which woman can reintroduce
into the world culture: a sense of reverence, the
establishment of the family and the proper evaluation of
suffering. The Feminist Movement seen as being
detrimental to this proper role of women in the world.

2037   Hall, Lynda. "The Sources of Women's Oppression Are
Buried Deep Within The Capitalist System and Legislation
Alone Cannot Uproot Them." Hibernia 42 (Jan. 27, 1978): 9.

Argues that women must organize independently of men;
that feminism is incompatible with capitalism and
requires a revolutionary transformation of society.

2038   Handbook of International Data on Women. New York:
Halsted Press, 1976. 468pp. tables. bibl.

Data arranged in the following categories: general
economic activity, employment status, industry,
occupation, education and literacy, migration, material
status, vital statistics, political and civic
participation taken from existing U.N. statistics on the
status of women in member countries - including Ireland.
Reliability and completeness of the data vary depending
on the reporting systems of the countries involved.

2039   Hayden, Mary. (M.A.D.Litt.) "Woman's Role in the
Modern World." Ir Mon LXIX (Aug. 1941): 392-402. appendix.

Response and critique of Father Guthrie's article (See
#2036.) Positive achievements of the Suffragette
Movement and changed role of modern housewife discussed.

2040   Hogg, Lorna. "Women At War." Image 4 (11) (Nov.
1979): 13-18.

Interview with three women on their attitudes toward
women's liberation in Ireland.

2041   Hussey, Gemma. "Dark Rosaleen Is Waiting." Tablet
(Mar. 21, 1981): 284-288.

A brief overview of the current status and future
prospects of women in Ireland by Senator Hussey who

represents women's issues for the Fine Gael Party.

2042   Hussey, Gemma. Ireland. Dublin: Department of Foreign Affairs, 1977. 3 pp. (Facts Sheet 10/77)

Fact sheet on current status of women in law, education, employment, politics and public life.

2043   "The Inequality of Irishwomen." Image 5 (4) (Apr. 1980): 12-14. portr.

Summary of remaining inequalities suffered by Irish women.

2044   Irish Women Agenda for Practical Action: Working Party on Women's Affairs and Family Law Reform. Dublin: The Stationery Office, 1985. 392pp. tables. refs.

Identifies the main issues affecting women in Irish society and puts forward specific proposals for change in a number of areas.

2045   [Irish Women's Liberation Movement.] Chains or Change: The Civil Wrongs of Irishwomen. Dublin: Irish Women's Liberation Movement, Founding Group, 1971. 31pp.

Fact sheet detailing the disabilities suffered by women in Ireland. Topics covered include legal inequalities, employment, education, women in distress (widows, deserted wives, unmarried mothers) single women, etc. Also covered briefly are family planning, child care, retraining and tax discrimination.

2046   Jones, Gay and Gail Chester. "Women in Northern Ireland: the Peace People." Peace News No. 2073 (June 30, 1978): 9-11. il.

Discussion of women in Northern Ireland from a feminist perspective. Women seen as having a major role in the community and in various organizations but their struggle for Women's Liberation overshadowed by the larger complicated Loyalist/Republican/British Army political struggle.

2047   Kearney, A.P. "All Women Are Not Eegits." Capu An (1973): 335-336.

Tongue in cheek article from a self-styled "male non-practising advocate of women's liberation" criticizes women's susceptibility to television commercials.

2048   Keating, Michael. "Women's Lib and the Humble

Housewife." Market News 2 (Mar. 1980): 43.

    Address by a Fine Gael TD considers ways to improve the
status and economic independence of women working in the
home as wives and mothers.

2049   Kenny, Mary. Woman Times Two. How To Cope With a
Double Life. London: Sidgewick and Jackson, 1978. 179pp.

    An examination of how women approach the two principal
responsibilities in their lives - their families and
their jobs and how they co-ordinate these two dimensions
by a self-proclaimed Women's Liberation Revisionist.
Crucial importance of choice and support structures
stressed.

2050   Kenny, Mary. "Women as Chattels." Agenor 35 (May/June
1973): 7-8.

    Brief catalog of various disabilities and discriminations
suffered by Irish women in the legal, economic,
educational and social spheres.

2051   Larkin, Pauline. "The Status of Women in Ireland."
Eirigh 61 (June 1969): 6-9. portr.

    For the author women's new freedoms will make these
better mothers. Motherhood will lose its obsessive
quality when it is no longer seen as women's only goal in
life.

2052   La Chard, Jeanne. "Injustice to Irishwomen." Listener
91 (2360) (June 27, 1974): 822-823. il.

    Short article on the current situation of women in
Ireland and recent changes in their legal status. Also
brief description of various groups promoting women's
issues: AIM (compaigning for change in matrimonial law),
CHERISH (an organization for single women who want to
keep their babies), and the Women's Liberation Movement.

2053   Levine, June. "The Women Who Started the Women's
Movement - Where Do They Stand Today?" Image 7 (11) (Nov.
1982): 66-68. portr.

    Interviews with Mary Kenny, Nuala Fennell, Nell
McCafferty, Mary Maher, Rosita Sweetman, Mairin de Burca
twelve years after the establishment of the Women's
Liberation Movement in Ireland.

2054   MacCafferty, Nell. "Ireland's Paradox: The Womb and
the Border." Ms 11 (Mar. 1983): 94-98. il. (Excerpt from

book, <u>Sisterhood is Global</u> ed. Morgan, 1983.)

Brief consideration of status of women in Ireland and the
issues posed for feminists by the cultural and political
divisions between North and South.

2055   MacCafferty, Nell. "Why We Don't Need Men." <u>Magill Mag</u>
2 (2) (Nov. 1978): 93-94. portr.

Comment on reaction to the recent march protesting
violence against women and rape.

2056   MacDonagh, W.P. (S.J.) "The Position of Woman in
Modern Life." <u>Ir Mon</u> 67 (June 1939): 389-399.

This article presents arguments against sexual equality
of male and female. Marriage regarded as "normal" and
most rewarding career for a woman; a woman's proper place
is in the home and the husband is the natural head of the
family. The right of a married woman to a career outside
the family is rejected except in cases of economic
necessity. Delayed age at marriage, decline in number of
marriages and a falling birth-rate viewed as evils
resulting from the entry of women into the labor market.

2057   MacCurtain, Margaret. "Women: The Historical Image."
<u>Books Ire</u> 90 (Feb. 1985): 10-11. portr.

Excerpt from <u>Irish Women: Image and Achievement</u> ed. by
Eilean Ni Chuilleanain.

2058   MacCurtain, Margaret. "Women - Irish Style." <u>Doct &
Life</u> 24 (4) (Apr. 1974): 182-197.

A factual presentation on women in various aspects of
their life situation particularly their work choices with
some recommendations as to how their status might be
improved.

2059   McKillen, Beth. "Irish Feminism and Nationalist
Separation. 1914-1923." <u>Eire Ire</u> 17 (3) (1982): 52-67; (4)
(1982): 72-90. refs.

An investigation of the effects of the separatist
movement on the membership, activities and relations
between three important women's groups - the Irish
Women's Franchise League, Irish Women Workers Union and
Cumann na mBan, a women's separatist organization -
between 1914 and 1923.

2060   Meehan, Ita. "Woman's Place in the Community." <u>Chr Rex</u>
XIII (Apr. 1959): 90-133.

An examination of the role of women finds in Scripture a
warrant for the superiority in rank of men as created
first and asserts that women have been subjected to their
husbands as a punishment for Eve's sin of disobedience;
furthermore, Christ taking on human form became a man —
another argument for the superiority in rank of men.
Woman's primary function is motherhood — which can be
spiritual and for the married woman her home is her
primary responsibility. But all women should play a role
in their communities.

2061   Minister of State for Women's Affairs. One Hundred
Years of the Irish Women's Movement. Dublin: Government
Printing Office. n.d. (c.1984) 1p.

2062   - - - Aims and Framework for Action. Dublin:
Government Printing Office. n.d. (c.1984) 1p.

2063   - - - Women and the Law. Dublin: Government Printing
Office. n.d. (c.1984) 1p.

Informational pamphlets issued by the Office of Women's
Affairs established in 1982.

2064   Mooney, Mairin. "Women in Ireland." Labour Mon 61 (2)
(Feb. 1979): 75-81.

(See #1916.)

2065   Morgan (Lady) [Sydney Owenson] Woman and Her Master.
London: Henry Colburn, 1840. 2 vols. refs.

An early feminist analysis of women's contribution to
ancient history which, Morgan asserts, standard texts
written by men ignore.

2066   Murphy, Christina. "The Status of Women in Ireland."
Pub Affairs 2 (7) (Mar. 1970): 8-10. il.

A resume of the remarks of Professor Fogarty (The Irish
Representative) at the Yugoslav conference on the
status of women in the member countries of the U.N. He
points out that Irish practice in the areas of
co-education, equal pay, and rights of married women
falls short of accepted international principles and
offers suggestions for short and long term family
centered policies to upgrade the status of women in
Irish society.

2067   Murphy, Michael W. "Measured Steps Towards Equality
for Women in Ireland: Education and Legislation." Convergence
8 (1) (1975): 91-100.

"This article, by the director of Aontas, the national
association of adult education in Ireland, considers the
celebration of International Women's Year in Ireland from
the viewpoint of legislative measures, and programs
organized at the level of government and by voluntary
organizations." (Author's abstract.)

2068   National Federation of Business and Professional
Women's Clubs of Great Britain and Northern Ireland. Justice
or Prejudice. London: National Federation of Business and
Professional Women's Clubs of Great Britain and Northern
Ireland, 1968. 48pp. bibl.

An updating and revision of the 1965 report on the
inequalities between the sexes in Britain and Northern
Ireland. Includes chapters on discriminations against
women in law, education and training, at work, in public
life, and other inequalities. The report concludes that
while the status of women has improved, they still do not
have full equal rights with men. The causes of this
continued discriminatory pattern are analyzed and
recommendations offered to improve the situation.

2069   Ni Chuilleanain, Eilean. Irish Women: Image and
Achievement. Dublin: Arlen House, 1985. 144pp. front.

A series of essays, all except two based on lectures
delivered as part of a tour known as the "Irish
Fortnight" in various American cities in 1979, and
rewritten to supplement, update and extend the mainly
historical Women in Irish Society (#2104). The image
of women in myth, folklore, history and politics and
their artistic achievement are the primary focus.

2070   "No But Seriously." Status 6 (1) (Mar. 14, 1981):
14-15.

A miscellaneous and light-hearted selection of the views
of some Irish men on the subject of women.

2071   Nolan, Oonagh. "The United Irish Woman?" Cross 64 (2)
(June 1973): 30-31. il.

A brief account of four of the main organizations
involved in improving the lot of women in Ireland: the
Irish Countrywoman's Association, The Women's
Progressive Association, Women's Liberation Movement and
A.I.M. (Action, Information, Motivation).

2072   O Colmain Domhnall. Parliament na mBan [A Didactic
Treatise on Public Morality in Seventeenth Century Ireland]
Edited with introduction, notes and vocabulary by Brian O
Cuiv. Baile Atha Cliath: Instituid Ard-Leinn, 1952. 270pp.

A homily written as an account of the proceedings of a
Parliament of Women held in Cork. Women's non-
participation in public life, the education of girls,
women's authority in the home, and female dress are main
themes but includes a disquisition on public morality.

2073   O Glaisne, Risteard. Saoirse na mBan. Ata Cliath. Clo
Grianreime, 1973. 154pp.

    Overview of Women's Liberation Movement worldwide and in
    Ireland with some historical background on the status of
    women in Irish society.

2074   O'Hanlon, Thomas J. The Irish. New York: Harper and
Row.[1975] 316pp. il.

    Brief popular style discussion (pp.201-204) of the
    subordinate status of Irish women, their low
    participation in the labor force and their almost total
    exclusion from any political influence. Women's
    Liberation seen as having low priority as a serious
    political issue.

*2075   Personally Speaking...Women's Thoughts on Women's
Issues. ed. by Liz Steiner Scott. Dubln: Attic Press, 1985.

2076   Porter, Mary Cornelia and Corey B. Venning.
"Catholicism and Women's Role in Italy and Ireland." In Women
in The World: A Comparative Study. Ed. by Iglitzin, Lynne and
Ruth Ross. pp81-103. Santa Barbara, California: Clio Books.
(c.1976).

    Argues that the status of women in Italy and the Republic
    of Ireland has conformed rather closely to the position
    which has been assigned women within the Catholic Church.
    (Paper originally presented to the Annual Meeting of the
    American Political Science Association, New Orleans,
    September 4 - 8, 1972.) External factors are causing
    changes in that position which may then in turn cause a
    change in the church's view of "woman's place."

2077   Porter, Mary Cornelia and Corey Venning. "Church, Law
and Society: The Status of Women in Italy and The Republic of
Ireland." U Mich Pap Wom Stud 1 (2) (June 1974): 125-141.
refs.

    Notes that Ireland and Italy, despite their different
    historical and cultural foundations exhibit striking
    parellels in the legal and social status of women. These
    parellels, especially in family law a'so run very close
    to the law and teaching of the Roman Catholic Church on
    the role and status of women in the Church and in
    society.

2078   Purcell, Berty. "Ten Years of Progress? Some
Statistics." Crane Bag 4 (1) (1980): 43-46. refs.

    A brief examination of women's status in three major
    areas: economic, sexual and social and an assessment of
    achievements in the preceding decade. Concludes that
    despite some improvements, not much other than women's
    consciousness has changed.

2079   Rose, Catherine. The Female Experience: The Story of
the Women's Movement in Ireland. Galway: Arlen House, 1975.
108pp. bibl.

    A brief overview from a feminist perspective sees the
    teachings of the Catholic Church as primarily responsible
    for the secondary image and status of women in Ireland.
    The lack of industrialization, lack of access by women to
    higher education and the subordination of feminism to
    Nationalism compounded this secondary status. The
    emergence of the Women's Liberation Movement in the
    1960's-1970's and future prospects briefly considered.

2080   Senex. "The New Girl." Ir Mon 54 (Feb. 1926): 738-744.

    Comments on "the so called emancipation of women" in the
    first 25 years of the 20th century and decries the
    resulting vulgarity, licence, smoking, dress, etc. of the
    modern woman.

2081   Shannon, Elizabeth. Up in the Park: the Diary of the
Wife of the American Ambassador to Ireland 1977-1981. New
York: Atheneum, 1983. 358pp. il. portrs.

    Includes an informal and highly sympathetic account of
    some events in the Irish Women's Movement which was then
    actively involved with fund-raising and consciousness -
    raising and had achieved certain gains in women's status.
    Shannon also describes her outreach efforts to itinerant
    girls.

2082   Shaw, George Bernard. "The Menace of the Leisured
Woman." Time & Tide 8 (Feb. 4, 1927): 106-107. (A verbatim
report of a speech made from the Chair at the debate held at
Kingway Hall on January 27th.)

    Shaw comments on motherhood, family and the necessity of
    everyone realizing his/her potential through productive
    work.

2083   Shaw, George Bernard. "The Womanly Woman." In his The
Quintessance of Ibsenism, pp. 33-49. New York: Brentano's,
1913.

    Presents his philosophy on women's liberation: "unless

woman repudiates her womanliness, her duty to her
husband, to her children, to society, to the law, and to
everyone but herself, she cannot emancipate herself."

2084   Sheehan, Helena. Communism and the Emancipation of
Women. Dublin: Communist Party of Ireland, 197-. 22pp.

A standard analysis of women's oppression from a
Communist perspective locates the source of this in the
sexual division of labor inherent in a capitalist
society. Women in Ireland viewed as particularly
oppressed because of general economic undevelopment.
Catalogs some of the disabilities suffered by Irish women
in employment, education, law, etc. and critiques certain
tendencies of the Women's Movement.

2085   Sheehy Skeffington, Francis. War and Feminism.
(Reprinted from The Irish Citizen n.p. n.d.). [c.1915] 8pp.

Sheehy argues that war is necessarily bound up with the
destruction of feminism and that feminism is necessarily
bound up with the abolition of war.

2086   Smyth, Ailbhe. "Women and Power in Ireland: Problems,
Progress, Practice." Wom Stud Int Forum 8 (4) (1985):
255-262.

"Describes the extent to which women in Ireland are
chronically and grossly under-represented in power
elites and analyses some of the barriers which have
precluded... women's equal participation in the decision
and policy-making processes." (Author abstract)

2087   "The Status of Women." W Ir Nurs 1 (May 1972): 94.

An editorial briefly reviews the memorandum submitted by
the Council of the Irish Nurses Association to the
Commission on the Status of Women early in 1972 and oral
evidence submitted at a later date. The main thrust of
their submission was on the necessity of supplying
educational and research facilities to enable nurses to
gain adequate recognition in the limited areas where they
are gaining consultive status and the improvement of
promotional outlets.

2088   Stevenson, Robert. (S.J.) Christ Speaks to Women.
Dublin: Catholic Truth Society of Ireland, 1968. 31pp.

Brief article discussing Christianity's effect on
elevating the status of women.

2089   Sweeney, Maire Claire. "Women in Ireland: Not Yet
Citizens." An Gael (Spring 1984): 12+.

An Irish journalist and an American writer conclude that
the two most powerful forces thwarting the progress of
the Irish Women's Movement are the Catholic Church and
the legal system.

2090   Sweetman, Rosita. On Our Knees: Ireland 1972. London:
Pan Books, 1972. 288pp. plates. portrs.

Chapter three of this journalistic account of present
conditions in the North of Ireland analyzes from a
Socialist perspective the status of women in this society
and catalogs their disabilities.

2091   Swift, Jonathan. The Works of Jonathan Swift
containing additional letters and poems and a life of the
author by Sir Walter Scott. 1824. 19 vols.

Volume IX includes "Letter to a very young lady on her
marriage" (pp.208-220) in which Swift advises her on
modest behavior, against demonstrativeness, frivolity,
all-female company and preoccupation with dress and urges
her to win her husband's esteem by the cultivation of her
powers; "On the death of Mrs. Johnson (Stella)" (pp.
281-293) in which he pays tribute to the character wit,
intelligence, civility, ease, sincerity and brilliant
conversation of his long time friend, Esther Johnson and
"On the education of ladies" (pp. 267-271.) which is a
scathing attack on what passed for education among the
nobility and gentry of the period of both sexes but
especially women.

2092   Tansey, Jean Women in Ireland: A Compilation of Data
and Information Relating to Women in Irish Society. Dublin:
Council for the Status of Women, 1984. 363pp. il. tables.
bibl.

Covers demography, education employment and trade unions,
rural women, Employment Equality Commission, social
welfare, health, law, electoral politics. Each chapter
has a summary of major relevant findings. Includes
extensive tables and appendices.

2093   Tansey, Jean. Women's Studies Unit, the Irish
Foundation for Human Development. Who Makes the Decisions? 1
- Women on the Boards of State-Sponsored Bodies. Dublin:
Council for the Status of Women, 1980.

2094   Tansey, Jean. Women's Studies Unit, the Irish
Foundation for Human Development. Who Makes the Decisions? 2
- Women on the Boards of State-Sponsored Bodies. Dublin:
Council for the Status of Women, 1981. tables.

Discusses the Government's responsibility in public
appointments, the significance of the participation of

women on these, women's actual representation on the
boards of State sponsored bodies and on State Commissions
and Committees. The report demonstrates the low level of
representation of women on these and calls for a specific
commitment by the Government to equalize access.

2095   Van Voris, Jacqueline. "Daniel O'Connell and Women's
Rights: One Letter." Eire Ire 17 (3) (1982): 35-39.

    Brief note on the Liberators role in the beginnings of
    the Women's Rights Movement at the World's Anti-Slavery
    Convention held in London in 1940. This was a letter he
    wrote to Lucretia Mott setting forth his position against
    the exclusion of women delegates from that Convention.

2096   Viney, Ethna. "Woman in Rural Ireland." Chr Rex 22 (4)
(Oct.-Dec. 1968): 333-342.

    Describes the activities, condition and status of the
    wives and daughters of small farmers, small shop-keepers
    and farm laborers. She finds that for these women life
    has improved because of new technologies but a lot of
    sheer drudgery remains. Their lack of political or
    organizational involvement, intellectual pursuits or
    leisure time and their relative isolation deplored.

2097   Ward, Margaret and Marie Theresa McGivern. "Images of
Women in Northern Ireland." Crane Bag 4 (1) (1980): 66-72.
refs.

    A consideration of roles of women in Northern Ireland
    sees these as locked into traditional definitions in a
    patriarchal society. Influence of family, religion and
    the mass media in shaping and defining this constricting
    role examined; also media disregard for actual
    achievements of women in the political arena and their
    stereotyped depiction criticized.

2098   Wilde, [Jane Francesca] Lady. Social Studies. London:
Ward and Downey, 1893. 244pp.

    Chapter one, "The Bondage of Women" has a brief overview
    of the inferior status of women historically with
    scattered examples from different cultures. Some
    contemporary disabilities of women also discussed.

2099   "Womanhood and its Mission. Part I." Univ Mag LIII
(May 1859): 623-640.

2100   "Womanhood and its Mission. Part II." Univ Mag LIII
(June 1859): 696-711.

    Argues against the extreme and in the author's view the
    wrong position (1) that women should seek their destiny

in separatism, apart from men and (2) that women have a
right to all the pursuits and occupations of men. The
proper mission of women in the domestic sphere is the
education of her children and her role as homemaker while
her social duty is the spiritual leavening of society.

2101   [Women and Ireland Group] Irishwomen at War. Papers
from the Feminism and Ireland Workshop June 26, 1977. 2nd ed.
London: Women and Ireland Group, 1977. 49pp. refs.

An analysis of the specific oppression of Irish women by
the Socialist/Feminist wing of the Women's Liberation
Movement in Britain, sees the oppression of Irish women
as an outcome of the influence of the Catholic Church on
the Irish Constitution and the low status of women in
the right wing, Orange Protestant tradition in the North
of Ireland. Specific wrongs suffered by Irish women
detailed. Also attempts an analysis of why Ireland is an
issue for women in the British Women's Movement.

2102   "Women and Work." Univ Mag LXXX (Dec. 1872): 670-682.

Argues that there is a broad difference between the sexes
but that this does not imply female inferiority. Woman is
the complement to man. She should be allowed to do
whatever work she pleases provided she does not thereby
lose any of her "womanly delicacy." She needs other
options in life than marriage as a means of survival.

2103   "The Women of Ireland." Dublin U Mag 13 (May 1839):
591-595.

Effusive tribute to the women of Ireland who are
contrasted with the independent French women to the
latter's disadvantage and the more prosaic English.

2104   Women in Irish Society: The Historical Dimension. Ed.
by Margaret MacCurtain and Donncha O Corrain. Dublin: Arlen
House, 1978. 125pp. bibl. refs.

A collection of studies on the position of women in Irish
society based on a series of lectures delivered over
Radio Eireann between October and December 1975 (The
Thomas Davis Lectures). The essays trace the evolution of
women in Ireland from the 5th century to the present and
analyze how their role was shaped by tradition, laws,
politics and economics and more recently, women's own
search for equality and liberation.

2105   "Women's Attitudes on Their World." Image 5 (11) (Nov.
1980): 10-18. il.

Presents results of a survey carried out by Irish
Marketing Surveys Ltd. Covers women's views on Northern

Ireland, economic priorities, sex discrimination,
divorce, contraception, etc.

2106   "The Women's Movement in Ireland." Agenor 35 (May/June
1973): 7-8.

    Short description of the founding of the Women's
    Liberation Movement in 1969 in Ireland and its influence
    on Government and on other organizations.

2107   Women's (sic) Only Event. [Leaflet announcing a
Women's (SIC) only event to celebrate International Women's
Day on March 8th, 1979.] [Dublin, 1979.] 1 leaf.

2108   Women's Representative Committee. Progress Report on
the Implementation of the Recommendations in the Report of
the Commission on the Status of Women...December 1976.
Dublin: Stationery Office, 1977. 57pp.

2109   Women's Representative Committee. Second Progress
Report on the Implementation of the Recommendations in the
Report of the Commission on the Status of Women. (Final
Report of the Women's Representative Committee). Dublin:
Government Stationery Office, 1978. 96pp. tables.

    Progress Reports discuss actions taken through December
    1978 by the Government, semi-State Bodies, trade unions,
    employers and by women themselves to implement the
    Recommendations and suggestions in the Report of the
    Commission on the Status of Women five years previously.
    While progress continues to be made in eliminating
    discrimination referred to in the Report, particularly in
    employment and working conditions, the Committee is
    concerned about the extent and level of discrimination
    which still remains in other areas. Includes background
    information on the Women's Representative Committee,
    established 1974.

2110   Women's Representative Committee. [Information
brochure.] [Dublin: The Committee, 1976.] 21pp.

    Fact sheet explaining why the committee was created and
    its composition.

2111   Women's Representative Committee. Dublin: The
Committee. [n.d.] 6pp.

    Fact sheet on the nature, composition and function of the
    Committee with details on its accomplishments to date.

2112   Women's Rights in Ireland. Compiled by Ailbhe Smyth.
Dublin: Ward River Press for the Irish Council for Civil

Liberties, 1983. 221pp.

This guide/directory offers a short factual outline of women's rights in Ireland in such areas as education, employment, health, family relations, social welfare etc. including lists of resource organizations and suggestions for further reading.

2113   Working Party on Women's Affairs and Family Law Reform. Irish Women: Agenda for Practical Action. Dublin: Statistical Office, 1985. 392pp. il. tables. graphs. bibl.

The Inter-Departmental Working Party on Women's Affairs and Family Law Reform was established by the Taoiseach in 1983 to review the existing situation in relation to measures affecting women's affairs and Family Law Reform, identifying areas still requiring action, and how best to promote positive opportunities and facilities for women. Their extensive report includes a summary of the main findings with detailed chapters on the Changing Role of Women, Employment, Education, Health Services, Child Care Facilities, Social Welfare, Position of Women in Rural Ireland, Women in the Home, Issues relating to Single Parenthood, Family Law Reform and other issues.

2114   Zoillin, Ziolla. "Ceist na Mban." Hermes No.4 (Feb. 1908): 108.

General—Miscellaneous

HANDBOOKS & DIRECTORIES

2115   Clark, Clara. <u>Coping Alone</u>. Dublin: the Women's Press, (c1982). 192pp. refs.

   Handbook on legal, social and financial aspects of single parenthood. Includes a directory of support services.

2116   <u>Directory of Services in Ireland for the Unmarried Woman and her Child</u>. Dublin: The Working Party for the Further Development of Services for the Unmarried Mother and her Child, 1973. 51pp.

2117   <u>Directory of Services in Ireland for Unmarried Parents and Their Children</u>. 3rd ed. Dublin: Federation of Services for Unmarried Parents and Their Children, 1982. 80pp.

   Covers accomodation, medical care, social work agencies, financial aid, adoption, child care facilities, legal aspects.

2118   Equal Opportunities Commission for Northern Ireland. <u>A Guide to Women's Voluntary Organizations in Northern Ireland</u>. Belfast: The Commission, 1983. (n.p.)

   Social, educational and legal organizations are represented in this listing. Qualifications for membership, aims and contact persons listed for each organization.

2119   Hogg, Lorna. <u>A Handbook For Single Women in Ireland</u>. Dublin, Cork: The Mercier Press, 1981. 128pp.

   Information on renting apartments, buying a car,

investing money, buying a home, restaurants, recreation, volunteer work, travel, working holidays, counseling services, relationships, clothes, money management.

2120   Irish Women's Diary and Guidebook, 1981-. Dublin: Irish Feminist Information, 1981. 204pp.

Contains a directory of women's organizations, health and social welfare agencies and a bibliography on some issues affecting women. Also, includes an overview of women in the work force, child care facilities, the drug industry in Ireland, the reproductive cycle, violence against women, self help and personal health. Updated annually.

2121   Martin, Janet. The Essential Guide For Women in Ireland. Galway: Arlen House, 1977. 141pp. bibl. refs.

This handbook details present day customs and legislation regarding women in Ireland. Covers such topics as equal pay, social welfare and health benefits, position of a wife under Irish law, child-care, income tax, housing, etc. Includes a list of women's organizations.

2122   Neeson, Dee. Maternity Services in Ireland: The Complete Guide. Dublin: Gill and MacMillan, 1986. 239pp.

The first complete guide to the services, support groups, medical options and choices available to pregnant women in Ireland.

2123   Pozzoli, Peter R. Irish Women's Athletics. Enfield, Greater London: Women's Track and Field World, 1977. 303pp. il.

Overview of the participation of 205 Irish women in sports lists the Irish representatives in major games, international results, championship winners 1966-1976 with portraits of 127 international/championship winners (57 of these overlap).

2124   Roper, Anne. Woman to Woman: A Health Care Handbook and Directory for Women. Dublin: Attic Press, 1986.

Offers clear concise information in non-technical language on a variety of topics including sexuality and sexually transmitted diseases; reproduction — including fertility control and pregnancy and the politics of health care. Includes a comprehensive source directory of groups, organizations and individuals in the areas of health care.

2125   "The Who's Who of Women's Organizations." Image 1 (11) (Aug. 1976): 34-36. il. portrs.

Identification of major women's groups with a note on
their origins, goals and locations: Adapt, Aim, Ally,
Association of Irish Widows, Cherish, Irish Women's Aid,
Irish Countrywomen's Association, Irish Housewives
Associaton, Irishwomen United, Women's Political
Association among those listed.

HOMILIES

2126   A.B. "How the Women of a Country Can Influence Its
    Destiny." Celt 1 (4) (Aug. 22, 1857): 49-51.

    An exhortation to women to use their influence to foster
    National literature and music.

2127   Beattie, (Mary.) My Life Is Mine. What Shall I Make of
It? Talks To Girls on the Threshold of Life. Dublin: M.H.Gill
and Son, Ltd., 1947. 127pp.

    Hortatory manual aimed at adolescent girls deals with
    role model (The Blessed Virgin), etiquette, work,
    courtship and marriage.

2128   Council for Young Women, Especially Those in Domestic
Service. Compiled by a Member of the Ursuline Community.
Sligo, Dublin: Sealy, Dreyers and Walker. Middle Abbey
Street. [   ]

    The first 50-60 pages are like ordinary books of devotion
    but the remainder of part II offers advice for domestic
    servants. The last part is a selection of prayers and
    hymns.

2129   Cusack, Mary Frances. Advice to Irish Girls in
America! by the Nun of Kenamre. (Sister Mary Frances Clare) [
i.e. Mary Frances Cusack] New York: McGee, 1872. 201pp.
front.

    Homily includes practical and spiritual advice for female
    emigrants to the United States — most of whom were at
    least at the beginning employed as servants — aimed at
    reconciling these to their status.

2130   Eithne. "The Saving of Girls." Ir Mon 53 (1925): 127-
132.

2131   - - - "Where Are You Going To My Pretty Maid?" Ir Mon
53 (1925): 404-409; 458-466; 518-526; 580-587; 628-634.

2132   - - - "Can I Come With You My Pretty Maid?" Ir Mon 54
(1926): 718-725.

2133   - - - "What Is Your Father, My Pretty Maid?" Ir Mon 54
(1926): 131-137; 187-194; 238-244.

A series of homilies decrying the situation of young
working girls with the relaxation of religious standards
and appealing to lay apostolate to run evening classes
for these in religious education. Also exhorts women to
live up to Christian ideals of womanhood so men will
respect them.

2134   An Epistle to the Fair Sex on the Subject of Drinking.
Dublin: G.Faulkner, 1744. 55pp.

Details the consequences of indulgence in drink for
ladies of all stations in life - separately considered.

2135   Eymard (S.M.) P.B.V.M. : "This Girl Is You." Dublin:
C.T.S.I., 1964. 20pp.

Advice to young girls on male-female relationships, sex,
work and vocation in life from a Catholic perspective.

2136   Fielding, Sarah. The Governess: or Little Female
Academy. Being the History of Mrs. Teachum and her Nine
Scholars. Dublin: printed by P. Wogan, 1804. 240pp.

A series of fables and morals designed for moral
improvement and education of female readers.

2137   Newcomen, George. "The Beauty of Women." New Ire R 4
(Dec. 1895): 205-210.

Effusive tribute to woman's beauty and a warning to women
not to neglect the care of this, their most valuable
endowment.

2138   O'Brien, Mrs. William. "Dawdling." Cath Bull XXVI
(Dec. 6, 1936): 1020-1021.

Faults of Irish girls, particularly procrastination and
carelessness reproved.

2139   O Colmain Domhnall. Parliament na mBan [A Didactic
Treatise on Public Morality in Seventeenth Century Ireland]
Edited with introduction, notes and vocabulary by Brian O
Cuiv. Baile Atha Cliath: Instituid Ard-Leinn, 1952. 270pp.

(See #2072.)

2140   O Doherty, Thomas, Bishop. Catholics and Citizenship.
And the Influence of Women In Catholic Ireland by The Rev.
J.S.Sheehy. Dublin: Comhlocht na Firinne Catoilice in Eirinn.
[c.1921?] 24pp. front.

An exhortation to the women of Ireland stressing the high
ideal of womanhood which has always prevailed in Ireland,

and their obligation to live up to this heritage.
Specifies their duties as mothers, wives, daughters and
sisters, rejects the ideas of the "New Woman" and argues
that a woman's place is first and foremost in the home.

2141   Pentrill, Mrs. Frank. "On Clever Women." Ir Mon 10
(Dec. 1882): 749-752.

Brief homily on the lives of women of genius who are seen
as less happy than homely women who follow their
instinctive urges to devote themselves to caring for
others.

2142   Pentrill, Mrs. Frank. "On the Choosing of Wives." Ir
Mon 10 (Sept. 1882): 578-581.

Moralistic musings on how pretty girls do not have a
monopoly on virtue and their plain sisters may have more
charming natures.

2143   Poncheville, T. (S.J.) "Woman's Social Activities." Ir
Mon XLV (April 1917): 231-240.

An exhortation to women on what their duties and
responsibilities are to their families and to the
community.

2144   Shaw, George Bernard. My Dear Dorothea. A Practical
System of Moral Education for Females. Embodied in a letter
to a young person of that sex. London: Phoenix House, 1956.
55pp. il.

Some unconventional advice on character and behavior
stresses self-respect, independence, individuality and
tact.

2145   Stockley, William F.P. "To Young Women in Ireland."
Cath Bull IX (Oct.-Nov. 1919): 596-602.

Fulsome, rhetorical address to Irishwomen to model
themselves on the heroines of literature and history.

2146   Walsh, Nicholas (Rev.) Woman. Dublin: M.H.Gill and
Son, Ltd, 1903. 114pp. front.

A consideration of the "proper and special mission of
women in this world" as ordained by God sees the proper
care of her household as paramount and to this end she
must first of all be virtuous and religious. Also
includes advice on education, training of daughters,
religious duties and practices and her married life.

2147   Wilkes (Wetenhall). <u>A Letter of Genteel and Moral</u>
       <u>Advice to a Young Lady</u>. 2nd. Ed. Dublin: Nelson, 1741.
       144pp.

       Covers religion, friendship, education, reading matter
       and marriage.

Doctoral Dissertations

2148   Alldredge, Betty Jean Edwards. "Levels of Consciousness: Women in the Stream of Consciousness Novels of Joyce, Woolf and Faulkner." University of Oregon. 1976. 197pp. DAI 37:6:3610-A.

2149   Allen, Maridee Jane. "A Contradiction Still: Some Eighteenth-Century Characterizations of Women." University of Oregon. 1976. 474pp. DAI 37:09:5798-A.

2150   Anderson, Thayle Kermit. "Concepts of Love in The Novels of Iris Murdoch." Purdue University. 1970. 223pp. DAI 31:10:5385-A.

2151   Bannister, Ivy. "Sirens, Wisewomen, and Sorcerers: A Study of Women in the Plays of Bernard Shaw." Trinity College Dublin. 1978. 395pp.

2152   Barnes, Mary Emma Wadlington. "Mrs. Frances Sheridan, Her Life and Works: Including a Study of Her Influence on Richard Brinsley Sheridan's plays, and an Edition of Her Comedy, 'The Discovery.'" Yale University. 1914. 91pp.

2153   Bell, Carmine Jane. "The Role of Monastic Women in the Life and Letters of Early Medieval England and Ireland." University of Virginia. 1975. 239pp. DAI 36:2835-A.

2154   Berrow, J.H. "Somerville and Ross: Transitional Novelists." University College, Dublin. 1975.

2155   Besant, Lloyd. "Shaw's Women Characters." University of Wisconsin. 1964. 315pp. DAI 25:04:2661-A.

2156   Boyle, Emily Joan. The Irish Linen Industry 1825-1914." Queens University, Belfast. 1979.

2157   Cashdollar, Paula Mauro. "'My Female Friends:' An Examination of Women and Women's Roles in the Writings of Jonathan Swift." University of Rhode Island. 1978. 142pp. DAI 39:2950-A.

2158   Charles, Samuel John. "Irish Women Writers 1800-1835."
Trinity College, Dublin. 1967. 310pp.

2159   Chew, Samuel Peaco, Jr. "The Life and Works of Frances
Sheridan." Harvard. 1936. 576pp. DAI W1937, 87.

2160   Connolly, Sean. "Vita Prima Sanctae Brigitae: A
Critical Edition." Union College, Dublin. 1970. 236pp.

2161   Cotter, Eileen M. "The Deirdre Theme in Anglo-Irish
Literature." University of California, Los Angeles. 1968.
270pp. DAI 28: 1815-A.

2162   Crane, Gladys M. "The Characterization of the Comic
Women Characters of George Bernard Shaw." Indiana University.
1968. 382pp. DAI 29:09:3250-A.

2163   Curtler, Elizabeth Seaver. "'A Woman Young and Old':
Love in Yeats' vision." Duke University. 1977. 232pp. DAI
38:4840-A.

2164   Davenport, Gary Tolleson. "Four Irish Writers in Time
of Civil War: Liam O'Flaherty, Frank O'Conner, Sean O'Faolain
and Elizabeth Bowen." University of South Carolina. 1971.
238pp. DAI 32:10:5780-A.

2165   Eagleson, D. "Employment and Training of Girls Leaving
Belfast Primary, Secondary, Intermediate and Grammar Schools
in Relation to the Educational System and the Employment
Services." Queens University, Belfast. 1958.

2166   Elliott, A.G.P. "Sex and Selection: A Psychological
Study of the Employment Interview." Trinity College, Dublin.
1979.

2167   Epes, Sister Alice Regina, SC. "Her Fertile Fancy and
Her Feeling Heart: The Anatomy of the 18th Century English
Woman Novelist." Fordham University. 1964. 251pp. DAI
25:03:1909-A.

2168   Ewens, E.G. "Maria Edgeworth A Study." Trinity
College, Dublin. 1946. 537pp.

2169   Fine-Davis Margret. "Structure, Determinants and
Correlates of Attitudes Toward the Role and Status of Women
in Ireland, With Particular Reference to Employment Status of
Married Women." Trinity College, Dublin. 1977. 272pp.

2170   Fitzgerald, Mary Margaret. "The Dominant Partnership:
W.B. Yeats and Lady Gregory in the Early Irish Theatre."
Princeton University. 1973. 275pp. DAI 34:04:2066-A.

2171   Ford, Jane M. "The Father/Daughter/Suitor Triangle in
Shakespeare, Dickens, James, Conrad and Joyce." State
University of New York at Buffalo. 1975. 318pp. DAI
36:07:4507-A.

2172   Freeman, Alma Susan. "The Androgynous Ideal: A Study of Selected Novels by D.H. Lawrence, James Joyce and Virginia Woolf." Rutgers University, The State University of New Jersey. 1974. 294pp. DAI 36:02:877-8-A.

2173   Gaudin, Elizabeth. "Les femmes dams l'evolution de la societe contemporaire en Republique d' Irlande: these present." [par Elizabeth Gaudin] Lille: University de Lille. 1983. 330 leaves.

2174   Goshgarian, Gary. "From Fable to Flesh: A Study of The Female Characters in the Novels of Iris Murdoch." University of Wisconsin, 1972. 354pp. DAI 33:07:3583-A.

2175   Goodman, Theodore. "Maria Edgeworth: Novelist of Reason." New York University. 1936. DAI W1936, 85.

2176   Harris, Katherine Sumner. "The New Woman in the Literature of the 1890's: Four Critical Approaches." Columbia University. 1963. 258pp. DAI 24:11:4678-A.

2177   Harrison, S.F.J.C. "Irish Women Writers 1800-1835." University of Dublin, Dublin. 1947. 310pp.

2178   Hayes, Dennis B. (O h Aodha Donncha). "Bethu Brigte: The Old Irish Life of St. Brigid." University College, Galway. 1975.

2179   Herzog, Callie Jeanne. "Nora's Sisters: Female Characters in the Plays of Ibsen, Strindberg, Shaw and O'Neill." University of Illinois at Urbana-Champaign. 1983. 222pp. DAI 43:9:2988-A.

2180   Hoffeld, Laura Diamond. "The Servant Heroine in 18th and 19th Century British Fiction: The Social Reality and Its Image in the Novel." New York University. 1975. 259pp. DAI 36:06:3730-A.

2181   Humphreys, Alexander J. "The New Dubliners: A Study of the Effects of Urbanization Upon the Irish Family." Harvard University. 1953. 336pp. DAI W1953, 246.

2182   Kellogg, Patricia Rossworm. "The Myth of Salome in Sybolist Literature and Art." New York University. 1975. 175pp. DAI 36:11:7410-A.

2183   Kline, Gloria Cornelia. "'That Fierce Virgin' : Mythopoesis of Courtly Love in the Works of W.B. Yeats." Florida State University. 1976. 278pp. DAI 37:07:4368-A.

2184   Knight, Eunice Edna. "The Role of Women in The Don Juan and Faust Literature." Florida State University. 1973. 220pp. DAI 35:02: 1106-A.

2185   Linn, William J. "The Life and Works of the Honorable Emily Lawless, First Novelist of the Irish Literary Revival." New York Uiversity. 1971. 228pp. DAI 32:07:4007-A.

2186   Little, Sherry Burgus. "The Relationship Of the Woman Figure And Views of Reality in Three Works By James Joyce." Arizona State University. 1971. 342pp. DAI 32:03:1518-A.

2187   Longerbeam, Larry Simpson. "Seduction as Symbolic
Action: A Study of the Seduction Motif in Six Victorian
Novels." George Peabody College for Teachers of Vanderbilt
University. 1975. 196pp. DAI 36:04:-2222-A.

2188   McBurney, A. "Sociometric And Sex Status as Factors in
the Development of Children's Moral Concepts." Queens
University, Belfast. 1969.

2189   McCarthy, Eunice B. "Women's Roles and Organizational
Context: A Study of Interactive Effects." University College,
Dublin. 1979. 2 vols.

2190   Messenger, B. "Folklore of the Northern Irish Linen
Industry, 1900-1935." Indiana University. 1975. DAI 36:02:
1018-A.

2191   Mood, Robert G. "Maria Edgeworth's Apprenticeship."
University of Illinois. 1938. DAI W1939, 95.

2192   Moore, Miriam Anne. "Irish Attitudes and Sex Roles."
Trinity College, Dublin. 1976. 275pp.

2193   Mullet, Olive G. "The War With Women and Words: Lady
Gregory's Destructive Celtic Folklore Woman." University of
Wisconsin. 1973. 277pp. DAI 34:06:3351-A.

2194   Murphy, Daniel Joseph. "The Letters of Lady Gregory To
John Quinn." Columbia University. 1961. 244pp. DAI 22:09:
3204-A.

2195   Nardella, Anna Gayle Ryan. "Feminism, Art, and
Aesthetics: A Study of Elizabeth Bowen." State University of
New York at Stony Brook. 1975. 210pp. DAI 36:05:2851-A.

2196   O'Donnell, Beatrice. "Synge and O'Casey's Women: A
Study in Strong Mindedness." Michigan State University. 1976.
228pp. DAI 37:02:699-A.

2197   O'Grady, John. "Sarah Henrietta Purser; Her Life and
Her Work." University College, Dublin. 1974. 2 vols.

2198   O'Higgins, Eleanor Ruth Elman. "Psychological
Functioning and the Menstrual Cycles of Professional and
Managerial Irish Women." Trinity College, Dublin. 1983.
360pp.

2199   O'Reilly, Kevin Richards. "Population Dynamics and
Family Planning in Dublin, Ireland." University of
Connecticut. 1981. 246pp. DAI 42:01:0278-A.

2200   Portner, Ruth Lee. "A Study of Marriage in the English
Novel." City University of New York. 1977. 300pp. DAI 37:
11:7146-A.

2201   Potter, Roseanne Guiditta. "The Rhetoric of Seduction:
The Structure and Meaning of Shaw's 'Major Barbara.'"
University of Texas at Austin. 1975. 259pp. DAI 36:05:
2853-A.

2202   Roark, Bobbie Jean. "Mary Lavin: The Local and the
Universal." University of Colorado. 1968. 205pp. DAI 29:
09:3153-A.

2203   Roberts, Dorothy Hutcherson. "James Joyce's Ulysses: A
Study of the Motifs of Androgyny." University of South
Florida. 1977. 246pp. DAI 38:04:2144-A.

2204   Robinson, Marian Schouler. "Eire and the High Kings of
Ireland." University of California, Berkeley. 1971. 210pp.

2205   Rogers, Katherine Munzer. "Jonathan Swift's Attitude
Toward Women." Columbia University. 1957. 259pp. DAI 17:
08:1767-A.

2206   Rose, R.S. "An Outline of Fertility Control Focusing
on the Element of Abortion in The Republic of Ireland to
1976." University of Stockholm. 1978.

2207   Ross, Judy Joy. "Marriage, Morals and the Muse: The
Vindication of Matrimony on the 18th Century Stage." New York
University. 1962. 548pp. DAI 24:05:2019-A.

2208   Runnels, James Alan. "Mother, Wife and Lover: Symbolic
Women in the Work of W.B. Yeats." Rutgers University, The
State University of New Jersey. 1973. 277pp. DAI 34:01:
0336-A.

2209   Russell, M.F. "A Controlled Study of the Relationship
Between Gynaecological Illness and Marital Problems in a
Belfast General Practice." Queens University, Belfast. 1968.

2210   Scanlon, Leone. "Essays on the Effect of Feminism and
Socialism Upon the Literature of 1880-1914." Brandeis
University. 1973. 187pp. DAI 34:07:4218-A.

2211   Shields, Jean L. "Shaw's Women Characters, An Analysis
and A Survey of Influences from Life." Indiana University.
1958. 350pp. DAI 19:09:2347-A.

2212   Shiltes, John A. "To Him She Would Unveil Her Shy
Soul's Nakedness: A Study of Sexual Imagery in Joyce and
Proust." Penn. State University. 1975. 266pp. DAI 36:11:
7415-A.

2213   Siemens, Reynold G. "One Role of the Woman in the
Artist's Development in Certain British Artist-Hero Novels of
the 19th and early 20th centuries." University of Wisconsin.
1966. 255pp. DAI 28:03:1059-A.

2214   Sinfelt, Frederick William. "The Unconventional
Realism of George Moore: His Unique Concepts of Men and
Women." Penn. State University. 1967. 310pp. DAI 29:03:
913-A.

2215   Spector, Judith Ann. "Sexual Dialectic in Four Novels:
The Mythos of the Masculine Aesthetic." Indiana University.
1977. 235pp. DAI 38:05:2818-A.

2216   Sporn, Paul. "The Transgressed Woman: A Critical
Description of the Heroine in the Works of George Gissing,
Thomas Hardy and George Moore." State University of New York
at Buffalo. 1967. 341pp. DAI 28:02:645-A.

2217   Stephens, Evelyn Delores B. "The Novel of Personal
Relationships: A Study of Three Contemporary British Women
Novelists." Emory University. 1976. 505pp. DAI 38:01:290-A.

2218   Stevenson, Mary Lou Kohfeldt. "Lady Gregory: A
Character Study." University of North Carolina at Chapel
Hill. 1977. 310pp. DAI 38: 06:3490-A.

2219   Tudor, Kathleen Richardson. "The Androgynous Mind in
W.B. Yeats, D.H.Lawrence, Virginia Woolf and Dorothy
Richardson." University of Toronto. 1972. DAI 35:02:1126-A.

2220   Twomey, T.J. "A Study of the Involvement of Farmwives
in Farm, Home and Family Decisions and Tasks." University
College, Dublin. 1976.

2221   Vanderhaar, Margaret Mary. "Yeats' Relationships With
Women and Their Influence on His Poetry." Tulane University.
1966. 156pp. DAI 27:05:1387-A.

2222   Walsh, J.A. "The Law of Marriage In Ireland - A
Comparative Study in Civil and Canon Law." Trinity College,
Dublin. 1968.

2223   Watson, Barbara. "A Shavian Guide To the Intelligent
Woman." Columbia University. 1963. 336pp. DAI 27:08:2549-A.

2224   Wedwick, Catherine Cowen. "The Treatment of Women in
The Plays of William Butler Yeats." Bowling Green State
University. 1975. 152pp. DAI 36:11:7057-A.

Master's Theses

2225   Barry, Bernadette. "Journalists on the Women's Pages of Irish Newspapers: What They Write and What They Say." 2 vols. University College, Dublin. 1976.

2226   Bloomfield, Edna W. "Unmarried Mothers in Northern Ireland... Residential Accomodations." Rupert Stanley College, Belfast. 1968.

2227   Boland, Sr. Leonie. "A Study of the Validity of the Selection Procedures for the Admission of Women Students to Irish Training Colleges for Women Students." University College, Dublin. (n.d.)

2228   Bolster, Ellen. "Mother Mary Francis Bridgeman and the Irish Sisters of Mercy in the Crimean War." University College, Cork. 1959.

2229   Bowman, Eimer Philbin. "The Sexual Behavior and Contraceptive Practice of a Sample of Single Irish Women." Trinity College, Dublin. 1977. 73pp.

2230   Breathnach, Eibhlin. "A History of the Movement for Women's Higher Education in Dublin, 1860-1912. University College, Dublin. 304pp.

2231   Brennan, P. "Inghinidhe na h Eireann and Nationalism in the Irish Dramatic Movement." University College, Dublin. 1974.

2232   Burke, Sr. Katherine. "An Analysis of Open and Closed Belief Systems in a Religious Community." University College, Dublin. 1970.

2233   Burston, W. "A Study of Religious Women Novices With The Bernreuter Personality Inventory." University College, Dublin. 1970.

2234   Clayton, Helen R. "Societies Formed to Educate the Poor in Ireland in the Late 18th and 19th Centuries." Trinity College, Dublin. 1981.

2235   Colbert, Mary. "The First Years at Work - A Study of Young Women Workers in the Clothing Industry." Trinity College, Dublin. 1975. 237pp.

2236   Cole, Sr. Fionnuala. "A Study of Factors Related to Interpersonal Relationships in a Religious Community." University College, Dublin. 1970.

2237   Collins, Finola (Mrs.) "The Ladies Land League." University College, Cork. 1973.

2238   Comer-Bruen, Maire. "Alienation: A Study Of a Possible Allergy to School Among Some One Hundred Younger Teenage School girls in Five Second Level Schools in the Dublin Area." Maynooth College. 1974.

2239   Cooper, N.R. "Attitudes to Shift Working By Female Employees. Queens University, Belfast.

2240   Corbett, J.M. "Women in Management." University College, Dublin. 1978.

2241   Costello, Noel W. "Equal Pay." Trinity College, Dublin. 1981. 87pp.

2242   Creigan, Mary Frances. "Unmarried Mothers: An Analysis and Discussion of Interviews Conducted in an Irish Mother and Baby Home." University College, Dublin. 1967. 179pp.

2243   Cryan, M. P. (I) "The Sisters of Mercy in Connaught, 1840-1870." University College, Galway. 1962.

2244   Curran, Peter A. "Adjustment to Widowhood: An Examination of Sociological Factors." University College, Galway. 1976.

2245   Curtin, C.A. "Kinship in a Middle Class Housing Estate." University College, Galway. 1973.

2246   Curtin, Christopher. "Family and Kinship in a Middle-Class Housing Estate." University College, Galway. 1973.

2247   De Barun, R. "Toruigheacht Shaidhbhe Inghine Eoghain Oig." (The Pursuit of Sadhbh, daughter of Eoghan Og.) University College, Dublin. 1932. 42pp.

2248   Donovan, Daniel C. "Lady Gregory and The Abbey Theatre." University College, Cork. 1951.

2249   Donovan, Hanna. "History of Woman's Higher Education During the 19th Century." University College, Cork. 1919.

2250   Doyle, Eileen Margaret Mary. "An Evaluation of the Effectiveness of the Alternative Religion Programmes in the Development of Values, Moral Judgement, Self-Esteem in a Sample of Adolescent Girls." Trinity College, Dublin. 1979.

2251   Doyle, Sylvia E. "Anyone for Tennis." University College, Dublin. 1983.

2252   Drake, Nuala M. "Younger Widows in Cork City." University College, Cork. 1971.

2253   Duane, Mary. "The Life and Letters of Jane Barlow." University College, Dublin. 1955.

2254   Feeney, Mary. "Alexandra College and the Higher Education of Women, 1866." Trinity College, Dublin. 1977.

2255   Fluger, Katherine M.L. "The Portrayal of Females in Contemporary Literature for Children: Ages 10 to 14." Trinity College, Dublin. 1977. 293pp.

2256   Gahan, Ruarc. "A Survey of Provision for and Attitudes Towards Sex Education in Dublin City and County." Trinity College, Dublin. 1978. 241pp.

2257   Gautz, John R. "Equal Pay: A Job Evaluation Approach." University College, Dublin. 1972 107pp.

2258   Gallagher, Carmel Mary. "A Sociological Analysis of Young Women's Role Preferences." University College, Dublin. 1980.

2259   Geoghegan, Ceara. "Barriers to Women's Progression: A Study in Banking." University College, Dublin. 1985.

2260   Graham, J.E. "Divergent Thinking: An Anlysis of the Relative Performance of Young Men and Women." Queens University, Belfast. 1962.

2261   Hanrahan, Ellen. "A Social Study Among Final Year Student Nurses in Dublin City and Suburbs." University College, Dublin. 1970.

2262   Holland, I.A. "The Relationship of Age, Sex and Social Class to Implicit Verbal Reinforcement For Primary School Children." Queens University, Belfast. 1970.

2263   Hudson, Karen. "A Study of Shyness in a Sample of Irish Teacher Trainees." Trinity College, Dublin. 1985.

2264   Hynes, Seamus O. "Women in the Factory: A Study of Withdrawal Behaviour." University College, Dublin. 1972. 82pp.

2265   Keane, Catherine Mary. "A History of the Foundation of the Presentation Convents in the Diocese of Kerry and Their Contribution to Education During the Nineteeth Century." Trinity College, Dublin. 1976. 231pp.

2266   Keane, Desmond. "Lives of St. Monenna." University College, Cork. 1982.

2267   Kenny, Mary A. "The Writings of Edna O'Brien." University College, Galway. 1976.

2268   Kinnane, Elizabeth. "A Study of Irish Institutional Girls." University College, Cork. 1969.

2269   Kirke, D.M. "A Sociological Study of Unmarried Mothers." University College, Dublin. 1974.

2270   Lal, R.R. "Women In the Novels of Miss Fanny Burney, Mrs. Charlotte Smith, Mrs. Ann Radcliffe and Miss Maria Edgeworth." Royal Holloway College, London. 1964.

2271   Laurie, Hilary M. "The Correspondence of Edith O.E. Somerville and Violet Martin With Their Literary Agent James B. Pinker 1896-1922." Queens University, Belfast. 1969.

2272   Leonard, J.J.D. "A Cross-Sectional Study of Academic Motivation and Reward Preferences in Relation to Differentiation and Polarization in a Girls' Grammar School." Queens University, Belfast. 1972.

2273   Lillis, H.I. "A Survey Of Some Activities of a Girls' Secondary School From Academic, Religious, Cultural and Recreational Points Of View." Maynooth College. 1972.

2274   Long, Helen. "The Creative Evolution of Shaw's Womanly Woman." University of Vermont. 1962.

2275   McAfee, S.L. "An Investigation Into The Effects of Maternal Deprivation." Queens University, Belfast. 1958.

2276   McAllister, M.A. "Cultural and Intellectual Development in Contemporary Society: The Relevance of Matthew Arnold's Educational Ideas With Special Reference to an Empirical Study of Belfast Schoolgirls and Female University Students." Queens University, Belfast. 1972.

2277   MaCarthy, J. "The Contributions of the Sisters of Mercy to West Cork Schooling 1844-1922 in the Context of Irish Elementary Education Development." University College, Cork. 1979.

2278   MacCormack, Bridget Agnes. "Treithe na mBan mar Leititear iad i Litriocht na Gaedilge." University College, Dublin. n.d.

2279   McDonagh, F.M. "Bunus Beathai Bhrighde, Cholmcille, Chiarain, Ghrigoir Agus Mhartain." (The Composition of the Lives of Brigid, Colmcille, Ciaran, Gregory and Martin.) University College, Galway. 1965.

2280   McDonald, A. "A Study of the Influence of Physical Characteristics and Bodily Functions Upon the Physical Education of Girls and Women." Queens University, Belfast. 1958.

2281   McGennis, Brenda. "A Study of the Role Structure and Decision-Making In a Sample of Rural Nuclear and Non-Nuclear Families." University College, Dublin. 1971.

2282   McKenna, A.T. "Attitudes of Irish Mothers to Child-rearing: A Cross-cultural Analysis."   University College, Dublin. 1974.

2283   McLaughlin, Brian Patrick. "Maternal and Fetal Nutrition: A Study of the Possible Biological and Social Determinants." Trinity College, Dublin. 1980. 35pp.

2284   MacNally, M.F. "Marital Expectations and Attitudes of a Group of Women Reared in a Working Class Suburb." Queens University Belfast. 1975.

2285   Maxwell, E.M. "An Investigation of the Development of Moral Judgement in Some Irish Girls. Based on the Theory of Jean Piaget." University College, Dublin. 1969.

2286   Monks, K.M. "Women in Factory Jobs: Absenteeism, Job Satisfaction and Work Commitment of a Sample of Women Workers." Trinity College, Dublin. 1979.

2287   Morley, Rev. Br. Berchmans. "Maria Edgeworth." University College, Dublin. 1940.

2288   Mulholland, A.J. "Adolescent Girls' Perception of Parents and Teachers." Queens University, Belfast. 1971.

2289   Mullarkey, M. "Working Mothers and Stress." University College, Dublin. 1985.

2290   Neeson, W. "The After-School Life of the Adolescent Linen Worker." Queens University, Belfast. 1951.

2291   O'Broin, T. "Toruigheacht Shaidhbhe." (The Pursuit of Sadhbh). National University of Ireland, 1936.

2292   O'Connor, Anne. "Influences Affecting Girls' Secondary Education in Ireland 1860-1910." University College, Dublin. 1981. 548pp.

2293   O'Connor, M. "An Investigation Into Psychological Stress in School-Going Adolescent Girls." Trinity College, Dublin. 1978.

2294   O'Connor, Patricia. "Suburban Married Women's Conception of Attachment to and Identification With Familial Roles." University College, Dublin. 1979.

2295   O'Driscoll, Jeremiah Finbarr. "Dominican Convents in the Diocese of Dublin and their Contribution to the Higher Education of Women, 1882-1924." Trinity College, Dublin. 1984. 496pp.

2296   O'Dwyer, Gerard. "Factors Operative in the Occupational Decision-Making and the Job Choices of a Sample of Urban Leaving Certificate Boys and Girls." University College, Cork. 1978.

2297   O'Floinn, Seosamh. "Caillin Naomhtha Azus Mainistear Fiodhracha." University College, Dublin. n.d.

2298   O'Higgins, Kathleen. "Marital Desertion in Dublin." Trinity College, Dublin. 1974. 189pp.

2299   O'Mahony, H. "The Needs and Problems of Farm Families at the Early Stages of the Family Life Cycle." University College, Dublin. 1982.

2300   Owens, Rosemary. "Votes for Women: Irish Women's Campaign for the Vote (1876-1915)." University College, Dublin. 1977. 202pp.

2301   Regan, Mary J. "Lady Gregory, the Dramatic Artist: A Critical Study." University College, Dublin. 1952.

2302   Scully, Margaret C. "Galway Schooling and the Presentation Sisters: An Account of the Work of a Religious Body in the Practice of Education 1815-1973." University College, Cork. 1973.

2303   Shipman, Mary E. "The Women of Ireland: A Portrait of Women in a Revolutionary Society." California State University, Fullerton. 1980. 43pp.

2304   Slowey, Maria Gorelli. "The Structure and Meaning of Women's Involvement in Adult Education." Trinity College, Dublin. 1980.

2305   Smyth, Leo. "The Motivation of Female Workers in a Piece Rate System." University College, Dublin. n.d.

2306   Tansey, J. "Selected Perspectives on Girls' Secondary School Education in the Republic of Ireland, 1925-1975." Trinity College, Dublin. 1978.

2307   Taylor, A. "Sex Education and its Provision in Northern Ireland Secondary and Grammar Schools." Queens University, Belfast. 1967.

2308   Trant, Una. "The Vision and Ministry of Nano Nagle (Foundress of the Presentation Congregation)." Trinity College, Dublin. 1985.

2309   Turner, E.A. "The Social Adjustment, Attitudes Towards Discipline and School Preference of Boys and Girls from Co-Education and Single-Sex Secondary Modern Schools." Queens University, Belfast. 1970.

2310   Ward, Kathleen. "Grace O'Malley: A 16th Century Heroine of the Province of Connaught." University College, Galway. 1934.

2311   Watson, Helen. "Choice of Contraceptive in Ireland: A Profile of Women Using the Intrauterine Device." Trinity College, Dublin. 1980. 47pp.

2312   Wickham, Claire P. "Haemopoietic Nutrient Status of Young Dublin Women." Trinity College, Dublin. 1983. 99pp.

Author Index

Listed here are the authors, compilers and editors of the bibliographical works. Corporate authors are listed as well. Reference numbers refer to bibliographic item numbers.

Subject Index

Reference numbers refer to bibliographic item numbers.

A. E. see Russell, George
    William
AIM (organization), 1236,
    1575, 2052, 2071
Abban, 695
Abbey Theatre, 16
    see also Gregory, Augusta
        Isabella, Lady
    founding of, 193
    master's thesis, 2248
    Maire Nic Shiubhlaigh and,
        473
    staging of Shaw's The Shew-
        ing-Up of Blanco Posnet,
        190
    Anne Yeats and, 504
Abduction, of women, 1235,
    1606, 1846
Abortion, 1218, 1444, 2206
    Catholics and, 1356, 1418,
        1433, 1455
    characteristics of women who
        seek, 1370
    feminist case against, 1361
    getting one in England, 1473
    in Great Britain, compara-
        tive study, 1443
    history of, 1357
    legislation against, 1329,
        1344, 1586-87, 1605
    as murder, 1600
    in Northern Ireland, 1356
    psychological effects, 1478
    right to, McGee case and,
        1520
    rights of the fetus and,
        1602, 1604
    statutory provisions, 1602
Abortion Act of 1967, 1473
Accountants, 1625, 1807
Adamnan, St., 1528, 1857
Adamnan's law, 1528, 1845
Adapt (voluntary program),
    1224
Adolescent girls
    moral advice for, 2127,
        2135, 2147

Adolescent girls, cont.
    alternative religion pro-
        grammes for, 2250
    career planning and, 1040
    education of, 2292
    linen workers, 2290
    moral judgement in, 2285
    occupational decision-making
        in, 2296
    perception of parents and
        teachers, 2288
    problems of, 1266
    school, alienation and, 2238
    self-image and, 1512
    sex manual for, 1416
    socialization of, 1513, 2309
    stress and, 2293
Adult education, 1044
    women's participation in,
        1063, 2304
    working-class women and,
        1037
Aer Lingus, sex discrimination
    and, 1651, 1787
Agitation and Tithe Wars, 141
Aikenhead, Mary, 541, 543-60
    beatification and canoniza-
        tion, 545
    founding of the Irish Sis-
        ters of Charity and,
        1121-24
    letters of, 546
        excerpts, 559-60
    novel about, 986
    spiritual sayings of, 559
    tribute to, 554
Air hostesses, 1651, 1765,
    1787
Aircraft cleaners, 1627
Alcoholism
    in Dublin, 1475
    fetal alcohol syndrome and,
        1333
    in Larne (No. Ireland),
        1339
    in Republic of Ireland, 1476
    women and, 2134

Cailleach Bheara (hag of
    Beare), 895, 918, 948
Cailleach Geargain, 830
Cain Lanamna, 1582
Calvert, Frances, 108-09
Capitalism, oppression of
    women and, 2084
Cara, Mother of Brendan, the
    Voyager, 537
Carbery, Ethna (Eithne), 110-
    14
  Alice Milligan and, 290-92
Career planning, for
    adolescent girls vs.
    boys, 1040
Careers and career
    development, 1623
  market gardening, 1688
  opportunities for women,
    1676-79, 1689
Carelessness, homily about,
    2138
Carleton, William, female
    characters of, 852
Carlile, Anne Jane, 636
Carlow County, women organiza-
    tions in (1914), 1936
Carmelite nuns, 1090, 1092,
    1097
Carr, Sarah, 138
Carroll, Bridget, 637
Casement, Roger, death of, 778
Casey, Juanita, 115
Cashel, Rock of, carved stone
    effigy on, 868
Cashel (County Donegal), kin-
    ship organization in,
    1194
Castle Rackent (Edgeworth),
    154
Catholic Church
  Irish government poli-
    cy-making and, 1482
  Irish Women's Movement and,
    2089
  marriage law and, 1537
  oppression of women and,
    2101
  role in education of women,
    1051
  status of women and, 2076-
    77, 2079
  Women's Liberation Movement
    and, 1071

Catholic Church, cont.
  women's role in, 1075
Catholic education
  Penal Laws and, 1052
  university-level, 1039
Catholic literature, Irish
    women and, 1073
Catholic Women's League of
    Great Britain, 1077
Catholics for a Free Choice,
    1418
Cavan County, family life in
    Killeshandra, 1198
Cecil, Frances Alexander,
    116-17
Celibacy, 1259
  mental illness and, 1448
  rates in Ireland, 1307
  recent trends, 1464
Celtic poetry, 35
Celtic society, 593
  marriage customs, 1212, 1240
  status and treatment of
    women in, 1850, 1860
Chamber Music (Joyce), 840
Chamberlaine, Frances see
    Sheridan, Frances
Chaucer, Geoffrey, "Merchant
    Tale" of, 974
Chenevix, Helen, 1936
Cherish (self-help group),
    1213, 1217, 1311, 2052
Child abandonment, in Republic
    of Ireland, 1443
Child custody
  divorce and, 1553
  Guardianship of Infants Act
    (1964), 1559, 1567, 1572
Childbirth see Pregnancy and
    childbirth
Child-rearing, 1301
  attitudes of Irish mothers,
    1275, 2282
  education in, 1049
  handicapped children,
    1317
  manuals, 1277, 1338
  state assistance for, 1258
Children
  development of moral con-
    cepts in, 2188
  sex stereotyping in, 1490
Children's Hospital (Temple
    St.), 46

Nuns, cont.
  decline in vocations, 1084
  in early Medieval England
    and Ireland, 2153
  practices and lifestyle of,
    1072
  right to vote and, 1878
  study of novices, 2233
  survey of (1971), 1082
Nursing and nursing education,
    1036, 1764
  status of, 2087
  Catholic teaching in, 1010
  in Dublin City, 2261
  training course, 1015
Nutrition, young Dublin women
    and, 2312

O'Brien, Charlotte Grace,
    786-88
O'Brien, Conor Cruise, 355
O'Brien, Edna, 341-48, 2267
  sexuality in work of, 925
  unhappy endings in work of,
    977
O'Brien, Kate Cruise, 349-55
  female characters of, 950
O'Brien, Nora Connolly, 11,
    789
O'Brien, Sophie, 790
O' Brien, Lady see Strangways,
    Susan Fox, Lady
O'Bryne, Fiach Mac Hugh, 804
Obsession (emotional problem),
    in Irish males/females,
    1507
O'Byrne, Dermot, 923
O'Carrol, Margaret, 19
O'Casey, Eileen, 474
O'Casey, Sean
  depiction of women, 980
  female characters of, 905,
    2196
  Lady Gregory and, 186, 201,
    205
  Ria Mooney and, 472
  mother figures of, 832-33,
    842
O'Connell, Daniel, 802
  women's rights and, 2095
O'Conner, Frank, doctoral
    dissertation about, 2164
O'Connor, Arthur, 745
O'Connor, Margaret, 791

O'Connor Eccles, Charlotte, 40
O Criomhthain, Tomas, 340
O'Dogherty, Rose, 792
O'Doherty, Mary Izod see Kel-
    ly, Mary Eva
O'Donnell, Nuala, 19
O'Donnell, Siobhan and Nuala,
    793-94
O'Donoghue, Power (Mrs.), 31
O'Faolain, Sean, doctoral
    dissertation about, 2164
O'Flaherty, Liam, doctoral
    dissertation about, 2164
Ogilvie, William, 740-41
O'Grady, Geraldine, 476
O'Hagan, Mary see Mary Francis
    of the Blessed Sacrament,
    Sister
O'Hara, Mary, 475
Oldham, Charles (Mrs.), 1885
O'Leary, Ellen, 26, 356, 709
O'Mahony, Nora Tynan, 357
O'Malley, Grainne (Grace), 19,
    24, 27, 795-801
  master's thesis about, 2310
O'Malley family, 801
O'Mullane, Catherine, 802
On the Hill (O'Byrne), 923
O'Neill, Elizabeth, 12, 14,
    477-82
O'Neill, Eugene, female char-
    acters of, 2179
O'Neill, Maire see Allgood,
    Molly
O'Neill, Owen Roe, 792
O'Rahilly, Cecile, 686
Ordination, of women see Woman
    ordination
O'Rourke, Mary Lenihan, 803
O'Shea, Kitty, 1
Ossory, Bishop of see Ledrede,
    Bishop
O'Sullivan, Seamus, 257
O'Toole, Rose, 804
Our Lady of Charity of Refuge
    (order of nuns), 1111
Owenson, Olivia see Clarke,
    Olivia Owenson, Lady
Owenson, Sydney see Morgan,
    Sydney Owenson, Lady
Oxford Movement, 116

Pagan Place, A (E. O'Brien),
    344

About the Author

ANNA BRADY is Assistant Professor and bibliographer for Irish Studies and Women's Studies at Queens College, City University of New York. She is the compiler of *Union List of Film Periodicals* (Greenwood Press, 1984).

DATE DUE

Demco, Inc. 38-293